THEOLOGICAL ETHICS

THEOLOGICAL ETHICS

Volume 2: Politics

THEOLOGICAL ETHICS

Volume 2: Politics

by

Helmut Thielicke

edited by

William H. Lazareth

WILLIAM B. EERDMANS PUBLISHING COMPANY
GRAND RAPIDS, MICHIGAN

This is an abridgment and translation of *Theologische Ethik,
II ' Entfaltung: Ethik des Politischen* (Tübingen: Mohr,
1958), and *Theologische Ethik, II ' Entfaltung: Mensch und
Welt* (2.Auflage; Tübingen: Mohr, 1959).

This edition published 1979 by Wm. B. Eerdmans Publishing
Company through special arrangement with Fortress Press
and J. C. B. Mohr.

Printed in U.S.A.

Library of Congress Cataloging in Publication Data

Thielicke, Helmut, 1908-
  Theological ethics.

  "An abridgement and translation of Theologische Ethik."
  Vol. 1-2 are reprints of the 1966-1969 ed. published
by Fortress Press, Philadelphia; v. 3, of the 1975 ed.
published by Baker Book House Co., Grand Rapids, Mich.,
under title: The ethics of sex.
  Includes bibliographical references and indexes.
  CONTENTS: v. 1. Foundations.—v. 2. Politics.—
v. 3. Sex.
  1. Christian ethics. 2. Sociology, Christian
(Lutheran) 3. Christianity and politics. 4. Social
ethics. 5. Sex (Theology) I. Lazareth, William
Henry, 1928-   II. Title.
BJ1253.T5213 1979   241   78-31858
ISBN 0-8028-1792-0 (v. 2)

EDITOR'S FOREWORD

The present volume is the second in the series planned to comprise the English edition of Helmut Thielicke's massive *Theological Ethics,* the first having appeared already with the subtitle *Foundations* (Philadelphia: Fortress, 1966). Future volumes will contain Thielicke's treatment of such major themes as economics, law, and art. (Another major section on *The Ethics of Sex* was published separately by Harper and Row.)

Our Foreword to the first volume described the method being employed to produce an abridged translation that is both faithful to the original and yet geared to meet the special interests of English-speaking readers. The present volume is based on the 800-page German edition of Professor Thielicke's *Development: The Ethics of Politics (Theologische Ethik* II[2]), with the addition of a relevant 40-page section on the church's witness in the political realm taken from his *Development: Man and World (Theologische Ethik* II[1]). As with the first volume, major reductions have been achieved largely by eliminating those sections addressed to the European technical specialist, and by limiting the (almost exclusively foreign) critical apparatus to a bare minimum.

Although the general reader can understand this book as a self-contained unit, its political judgments are grounded firmly on the biblical and theological foundations laid by the author in the first volume of this series. Consequently, the German edition rightly calls attention to the following themes in *Theological Ethics 1* which are especially crucial as background material for evaluating Thielicke's positions in the study: Law and gospel in Lutheranism and Calvinism (Chapter 7), Luther's doctrine of the "two kingdoms" (Chapter 18), the Roman Catholic view of natural law (Chapters 20-21), compromise as an ethical problem (Chapter 25), the limits of truthfulness (Chapter 27), and the meaning of the "borderline situations" (Chapter 29).

As this page is being written, American Christians are agonizing over such political ethical challenges as conscientious objection to our military involvement in Vietnam, the brutal assassinations of Martin Luther King, Jr. and Robert F. Kennedy, wide-spread white racism, civil disorders, and poor people's protest marches to Washington, D. C. May Helmut Thielicke's soul-searching analyses of political "border-line cases" in Nazi and postwar Germany help us to understand and eradicate our own shameful "signs of the times."

Lutheran Theological Seminary, Philadelphia　　　William H. Lazareth

CONTENTS

PART TWO

THE NATURE OF THE STATE

A. Phenomenology of the State

PART THREE
BORDERLINE SITUATIONS

B. War

PART FOUR

THE THEOLOGICAL DEBATE ON CHURCH AND STATE

PART FIVE

THE MESSAGE OF THE CHURCH TO THE WORLD

xiv

ABBREVIATIONS

BC — *The Book of Concord.* Translated and edited by Theodore G. Tappert (Philadelphia: Fortress, 1959).

LCC — *Library of Christian Classics.* John T. McNeill and Henry P. van Dusen, General Editors (Philadelphia, 1953-   ).

LW — American Edition of *Luther's Works* (Philadelphia and St. Louis, 1955-   ).

PE — *Works of Martin Luther.* Philadelphia Edition (Philadelphia, 1915-1943).

ThE 1 — *Theological Ethics,* Volume 1: *Foundations,* by Helmut Thielicke. Edited by William H. Lazareth (Philadelphia: Fortress, 1966).

WA — *D. Martin Luthers Werke.* Kritische Gesamtausgabe (Weimar, 1883-   ).

WA, Br — *D. Martin Luthers Werke.* Briefwechsel (Weimar, 1912-1921).

WA, TR — *D. Martin Luthers Werke.* Tischreden (Weimar, 1930-   ).

Part One

POLITICAL ETHICS
IN THE MODERN WORLD

1.

Preliminary Questions of Method

One crucial distinction between the thinking of the theologian and that of the philosopher is that the philosopher, for all the weight of tradition, begins fundamentally with himself, whereas the theologian as a matter of principle relates himself to the believing community within which he has his theological existence. In so doing the theologian refers back to the historical realities which determine the path of that community, namely, Scripture and the fathers. From the Reformation point of view these historical realities are of very different rank. Scripture is an original authority (*norma normans*), whereas the fathers are a derived authority (*norma normata*). For our purposes, however, they have this in common: it is to them that theological thinking refers "back." Both chronologically and in terms of substance these are the realities from which theology derives. They stand behind it. Theology's task is to carry on. Hence it is characteristic of theological thinking (even where this may not be structurally apparent) to begin with this backward reference and to make the body of affirmations from Scripture and the fathers relevant to the present.

This fundamental backward reference, however, can be made in quite different ways. It may, e.g., be made directly, by first setting down actual quotations from the Bible and the confessions or other authoritative writings and then interpreting them in such a way as to bring out their continuing relevance for the present situation. On the other hand, the reference may be made indirectly and covertly, the theologian examining straightaway the problems of the present in terms of an approach dictated by all that stands behind him, of which he himself is constantly aware but to which he only later makes explicit reference. These two methods are distinguished by the fact that in the first case the backward reference is explicit and deliberate from the very outset, whereas in the other case it is initially only implicit, becoming explicit as the presentation progresses

A typical example of the first approach is the Barmen Declaration of 1934.[1] Here the concern is a very concrete one: to dissociate the Confessing Church from the totalitarian state. Yet despite the urgency of the situation which called it forth, the Declaration begins not with an analysis of that situation but with the backward reference of which we have been speaking. Each of its six articles "begins with a text of Scripture."[2] Only in the process of expounding these texts does the Synod arrive at a diagnosis of the totalitarian state and a course of action for the believing community. In this instance the backward reference is explicit from the very outset. Such an approach is possible, as we shall see, only because the situation of the totalitarian state has an extraordinary kind of apocalyptic affinity with the biblical situation. A sign of this affinity is to be found in the fact that such books as Daniel and Revelation are seen to contain direct and even startling references to ideological tyranny.[3]

A typical representative of the other approach in this matter of the backward reference is perhaps Paul Tillich, whose systematic theology is so constructed that he first analyses the present situation in terms of a question inherent in the situation itself and then gives the biblical and Christian answer. The formative feature of his theology — and this determines his method — is thus the "correlation" between the question which arises within an ontology of existence and the answer which derives from the kerygma. Tillich, however, is not a mere secular ontologist who occasionally tacks on at the end a Christian postscript. We misinterpret him if we fail to note that for him the reference back to the Christian message is implicitly present and operative already in the very concern with which he

[1] See the text of the "Theological Declaration Concerning the Present Situation of the German Evangelical Church" adopted by the Synod of Barmen, May 29-31, 1934, in Arthur C. Cochrane, *The Church's Confession under Hitler* (Philadelphia: Westminster, 1962), pp. 238-242.

[2] This was specifically noted already in Hans Asmussen's "Address on the Theological Declaration," which the Synod adopted as an expression of its own witness. See Cochrane, *op. cit.*, p. 253.

[3] The following could be named as examples of books characterized by such an interpretation in that period: Walther Lüthi, *Die kommende Kirche. Die Botschaft des Propheten Daniel* (Basel, 1937); Hellmuth Frey, *Weg und Zukunft der Gemeinde Jesu* (Stuttgart, 1939) which deals with Revelation 12-14; Karl Hartenstein, *Der Wiederkommende Herr. Auslegung der Offenbarung Johannes* (Stuttgart, 1940); Hanns Lilje, *Das letzte Buch der Bibel* (Berlin, 1940), translated from the fourth German edition by Olive Wyon as *The Last Book of the Bible* (Philadelphia: Fortress, 1957).

examines and formulates the various questions of the moment. He has the kerygma behind him as he tackles the questions of the present human situation.[4]

The Barmen Declaration and the theology of Tillich both seem to represent extreme types of the theological methods we have been discussing, and this makes them particularly cogent examples. Which of the two methods one ought to use is normally a much-debated question among theologians. One may even argue with some justification that both are right in principle, and that the question is not to be decided on the basis of substantive considerations but by the nature of the particular problem at hand or even by the intellectual disposition of the particular thinker.[5] On the other hand, the present situation could be so very different from that of the past that it would be inadvisable or impossible for the theologian to begin with explicit quotations from the Bible or the fathers. Even though certain chapters of Revelation may seem to have direct relevance in the situation of the totalitarian state,[6] it is doubtful whether the situation in a democracy, e.g., affords any direct access to Paul's understanding of the state (as in Rom. 13) or to Luther's concept of authority. (It should be noted that what we are questioning here is not these concepts themselves, but only their direct application to a modern situation.)

In view of this difficulty it is perhaps best for us to proceed here with an examination of the state as it is today — keeping these concepts of course in mind as we do so — and then go on to a direct comparison between the results of such examination and the corresponding statements of Paul and Luther. The goal of our inquiry will then be to discover and bring to light that understanding of the state which is inherent in the political order of our time, as well as

[4] See, e.g., Paul Tillich, *Systematic Theology* (Chicago: University of Chicago Press, 1951), I, 3-8; *idem, The Courage to Be* (New Haven: Yale University Press, 1952), pp. 160-163; *idem, Love, Power, and Justice* (New York: Oxford University Press, 1954), pp. 18 ff.

[5] This would be my view, even though for my own work I personally incline to the second of the two methods. I think it most unfortunate that the Barth school absolutizes the first method; to make it the trademark of all "legitimate" theology is to draw the lines of demarcation at the wrong point.

[6] See Gerhard Ebeling's account of how on learning of Hitler's death he read Isaiah 14 aloud to his fellow soldiers, and was impressed by the text's direct relevance to their immediate situation. *The Problem of Historicity in the Church and its Proclamation*, trans. Grover Foley (Philadelphia: Fortress, 1967), p. 11.

the view of man and his life and of existence itself which is implicit within that understanding.

By choosing this kind of inquiry as our starting point, and referring back to the biblical statements only on the basis of its results, we also reduce the risk of anachronistically inflating to kerygmatic status the political reality in which Paul and Luther found themselves. The important thing is to recognize that the state of which they spoke can be nothing but a historically conditioned illustration. It may be of assistance to us in our effort to set forth certain theological intentions, but these intentions themselves are actually independent of any such specific examples. By interpreting first the political order of the modern period we are thus prevented from drawing a too hasty analogy between past and present and so failing to do justice to either. The situations of past and present are vastly different, and it is because the question of politics and the state brings this out so well that it constitutes a test case in the matter of method. Indeed, as we pursue the question it will repeatedly force us to return to considerations of methodology.

First, however, the distinction between past and present situations must be pinpointed in greater detail. This will be done as we consider in the following seven chapters three main problem areas in which the change from past to present is dramatically expressed. The first – which ties in directly with what we have just been saying – has to do with the transition from the authoritarian state of antiquity and of the Middle Ages to modern democracy. The second involves the question as to how far modern ideological tyranny allows for political preaching at all in the older – e.g., the Reformation – sense. The third and last involves the question as to how far, in face of the newly discovered – or newly assumed – autonomy of politics, it is still possible to speak of freedom, and hence of genuine ethical opportunity, in the sphere of civil justice.[7] We shall now turn to the first of these three themes.

---

[7] A fourth form of transition might be mentioned: Whereas Luther saw in the state a bulwark against chaos provided by the order of divine patience, the modern state with its attained or attempted perfection of the social order has itself become a theological problem. Less to be feared today than chaos is the rationalized superorder. We shall deal with this particular change later in our discussion of the relation between welfare and the state (see below pp. 289-317).

AUTHORITY AND DEMOCRACY

2.

The Transition from Authoritarian to Democratic Thinking

The Concept of Authority in Luther and in Paul

We can best come to grips with the difference between the situations of past and present by asking whether the concept of authority in the New Testament and the Reformation is still pertinent and applicable in the twentieth century, either in the sphere of the so-called free world or in that of the world controlled by totalitarian ideology. With respect to the so-called free world the question may be asked: In terms of the Western understanding of the democratic state is not "authority" an outmoded idea, a foreign concept alien to modern thought and no longer used except by theologians? Is the term ever found anywhere in the pages of a modern newspaper? Gustaf Wingren has stated the problem excellently: "The concept [of authority] is no longer serviceable, for those who govern [who were formerly referred to as the authority] are today simply agents of the will of the people; they execute the will of the legislature [which itself executes the will of the voters]. Every citizen [insofar as he is a voter] represents a partial authority." [1] The difference between ruler and subject is now one not of status but of function. This means that we no longer have two groups hierarchically — and perpetually — distinct in rank. Instead there is only one group, the

---

[1] The citation — apart from the brackets which are my own — is from Walter Künneth, *Die evangelische Lehre vom Staat* (Bonn, 1954), p. 3. Wingren has pointed out again and again that in every situation we must grasp God's law afresh as it is at work in the orders of the time or the prevailing ethical consciousness (see, e.g., *Theology in Conflict: Nygren, Barth, Bultmann*, trans. Eric Wahlstrom [Philadelphia: Muhlenberg, 1958], pp. 72-76). This is why he attacks certain tendencies in the Luther renaissance, which "insofar as it becomes a substitute for the contemporary task, is pure romanticism born of impotence" (*ibid.*, p. 76). Cf. also Margaret Boveri, *Treason in the Twentieth Century*, trans. Jonathan Steinberg (New York: G. P. Putnam's Sons, 1963), pp. 19-20; and Romano Guardini, *The End of the World: A Search for Orientation*, trans. Joseph Theman and Herbert Burke (London: Sheed and Ward, 1957), p. 118.

people, which both assigns the tasks of representation and receives directives from the representative body it has itself set up.

The very concept of "representation" indicates that it is one and the same group which is in fact both the subject and the object of the governing. Where large numbers are involved there must of course be this distinction between rulers and subjects. For it goes without saying that so-called direct democracy, in which all members of the group order their affairs together and exercise a common will in every detail, is possible only where small and manageable numbers are involved. Beyond a certain number the group as a whole must delegate its affairs to a smaller enclave which is capable of acting, whose action however, will correspond "at least theoretically to the will of the ruled." [2] The very concept of representation in political affairs thus gives clear-cut expression to the fact that the subject of the governing is in effect **the people**, that group which has provided for its being represented.

The question how far such representation is genuine and not just a fiction cannot be discussed here. At this point we would only point out that as far as the representation done by delegates sent to the legislature is concerned there is both a limitation and a disruption involved. The limitation lies in the fact that the delegate is fundamentally responsible only to his own conscience; his task is not simply to implement the will of the people but also to stand over against it, which means that at times he will have to make some rather unpopular decisions. The disruption can come when the delegate's representative capacity is diminished by the interposition between himself and his constituency of parties and special interest groups. It is altogether possible that he may in fact become more the functionary of a particular group than the representative of the people, and take his mandate solely from the interested party or parties. [3] We shall return to this problem when we discuss the matter of the distribution of powers. [4] For the present we shall use the term representation only in the sense of its original intention.

The autonomy of the people which expresses itself and is at least in principle asserted in the fact of representation implies that, in the matter of governing, subject and object are one and the same.

[2] Georg Dahm, *Deutsches Recht. Die geschichtlichen und dogmatischen Grundlagen des geltenden Rechts* (Stuttgart: Kohlhammer, 1951), p. 219.
[3] *Ibid.*, p. 228.   [4] See below pp. 215-222.

Each person does both the commanding and the obeying. In order not to be subjected to the heteronomy of a dictatorship or the autocracy of an absolute monarch, in order "not to be ruled by others, the ruled rule themselves." [5]

This personal union between rulers and ruled, which is characteristic of democracy, and which through the medium of representation is divided into different functional forms, shows with almost unsurpassable clarity how questionable the older concept of authority has become. For "authority" seems actually to imply a distinction of status between rulers and ruled, not just a functional distinction but a distinction of persons and hence the very opposite of a personal union. [6]

Is not a modern political ethics therefore compelled to demythologize, as it were, the concept of authority? But if we demythologize it by taking away the idea of a pre-eminent position bestowed by the grace of God, what is left? Is democracy indeed the end product of such a process of subtraction? Do "authority" and "democracy" really mean the same thing? Are they simply two different historically conditioned ways of referring to the same thing, namely, "statehood"? [7]

If that be the case, it should be possible to transfer to the modern situation the theological substance of the concept of authority. But is that really the case? Do not the two systems of political thought vary so widely that there is no essential connection between the authoritarian state and the democratic state? Is not the difference fully as great as that between heteronomy and autonomy?

The answer to this question will have significant implications.

[5] Dahm, *op. cit.*, p. 217, alluding to Nietzsche's dictum on Governing: "Some people govern because of their passion for governing; others in order that they may not be governed — the latter choose it as the lesser of two evils." Friedrich Nietzsche, *The Dawn of Day* (No. 181), trans. J. M. Kennedy ("The Complete Works of Friedrich Nietzsche," ed. Oscar Levy [New York: Russell & Russell, 1964], IX), 182.

[6] Indeed it was Romanticism which pressed the medieval concept of "authority" to its extreme but logical conclusion when it spoke of the hereditary monarch who is subject to no one else: his rule is absolute and independent of any human legitimation because it is given him solely by the direct and specific action of God. As a typical example we might cite Friedrich Julius Stahl, *Das monarchische Prinzip* (Heidelberg, 1845), and *idem, Rechts- und Staatslehre auf der Grundlage christlicher Weltanschauung* (2nd ed.; Heidelberg, 1847), esp. p. 219.

[7] I take this term *Staatheit* from Leopold Ziegler, *Von Platons Staatheit zum christlichen Staat* (1948).

What is at issue is ultimately the continuity of ethical tradition. The question is whether the modern age is not so clearly outside the framework of previous history that the traditional concepts of the Western world lose their cogency in face of the new phenomena. To put the problem as sharply as possible, we would point out that the new understanding of the state has taken a double turn in relation to the past.

In the first place, the prince was for Luther a member of the church, indeed its "chief member." [8] He stood therefore, at least potentially, under the pulpit. The representative of the state – in other words, the authority – did not only stand over against the church; he was *in* the church. It was this personal union between church membership and governmental authority which allowed Luther, e.g., in writing to the "Christian nobility," [9] to address the aristocratic estates not merely as representatives of government but also as bearers of a *Christian* obligation.

Quite apart from the question whether Luther regarded all the nobles of his day as truly Christian, his purpose was to remind the nobility that on the basis of baptism and the gospel the prince had both the opportunity and the duty to "certify his personal membership in Christ and his free rights as a Christian." [10] This meant in cases of extreme necessity that the prince should indeed intervene in the life of the church, as one of its members, not by virtue of his governmental office but nonetheless with the authority of one who governs.

Even though Luther was always skeptical as to the actual qualifications of the princes – at the very end of his treatise he could remind the nobility that lords and rulers will be "rare birds" in heaven – [11] the fact remains that church and state for him were fused in the person of the prince. Though the concept of a "Christian state"

[8] As rightly noted by Harald Diem in *Luthers Lehre von den zwei Reichen* (Munich, 1938), p. 126, the expression *primum membrum ecclesiae* first occurs in Melanchthon's *Treatise on the Power and Primacy of the Pope* (*BC* 329), though this fact has no significance for the present context.

[9] See Luther's *To the Christian Nobility of the German Nation* (1520) in *LW* 44, 123-217.

[10] See Karl Holl, *Gesammelte Aufsätze zur Kirchengeschichte*, I (Tübingen: Mohr, 1923), 335; cf. Karl Müller, *Kirche, Gemeinde und Obrigkeit nach Luther* (Tübingen, 1910).

[11] *LW* 44, 216.

was perhaps unreal, in a personal sense there was nonetheless such a thing as a Christian representative of the state, one who could be addressed in terms of the church's claim upon him.

One can hardly fail to see how significant this personal union was for political ethics and for the practical application of the doctrine of the two kingdoms. For since the prince was the "chief member of the church," the kingdom on the left hand was not left to itself in a secular sense. On the contrary, both ontically and in terms of the ruler's own awareness it was related to the kingdom on the right hand. It admittedly came within the scope of the church's proclamation. Certain theological implications of this relationship immediately suggest themselves.

First, the state was constantly reminded that it was subject to the sovereign commandments of God. Hence it could not possibly claim to be a law unto itself. Neither could it dare to make purely pragmatic considerations the measure of its conduct, saying, e.g.: "My country, right or wrong." Thus limited, the state could not be autocratic, ordering things as it saw fit. On the contrary, it was always called to order itself. It could never be authoritarian in an absolute sense, for it operated itself within the bounds of an authorization marked off by the divine imperative. If the power of the prince was unlimited downwards in relation to his subjects, it was correspondingly limited upwards in relation to the author of law.

The result was a situation which for modern thought is quite paradoxical. The unlimited authority of the ruler, whose authority could not be questioned from below, carried with it an unquestioned limitation on the authority of the state. Institutionalism, the sheer weight of the governmental apparatus, could not make the state a law unto itself. For since the authority of the state was represented by a sovereign person, there was an accountability before God for the way it was exercised; it was thus safeguarded against the anonymity of the machine. This safeguard obviously applies only to that authority which understands itself to be authorized, as was the case where the ruler was also the "chief member of the church."

Second, such a state was constantly reminded that it was not an end in itself. It had to see itself as an emergency arrangement of God in the fallen world, something which would one day be abolished. The ruler, who at least potentially was also present in the church,

11

was told of course that the things that are Caesar's must be given to Caesar, but also that the things that are God's must be given to God (Matt. 22:21), and that there is thus a limitation on our obligation to Caesar. He was also told that the governing authority must execute justice as the servant of God (Rom. 13:3), i.e., as a *norma normata*, not a *norma normans*. And finally he was told that God would one day abolish all authorities and powers (I Cor. 15:24). Thus did the state learn of its power and authority, but also of the limitation of its power inasmuch as that power was something accorded to it and not inherent in it. The state was reminded of the fact that it was willed by God, but that it was willed to be only temporary and provisional. A safeguard was thus provided against a trend which is plain enough in secularism, namely, the trend toward the totalitarian state which in its ideology posits itself as absolute.

The situation is quite different today. The state is not represented in a single person, as in the case of the medieval prince. Neither is it possible to suppose, even hypothetically, that the various branches or houses of government are made up of Christians. No theologian or churchman today would maintain that a state is illegitimate and unable to act unless it has at least a minimum number of Christians at its head, or professes so-called Christian principles.

No church meeting or body, Roman Catholic or Protestant, can address a "word" to the state today the way Luther did in his *To the Christian Nobility of the German Nation.* For the estate of the ruling nobility no longer exists, not even in the British House of Lords. Neither is the group which has replaced it, whether in party or government, Christian. The one to whom Luther addressed himself in that treatise has moved out, and the house in which he dwelt is now inhabited by someone who would not understand the treatise, or even know that it was meant for him.

In asking about the double turn whereby the understanding of the state today has changed from what it once was we have come upon some difficulties which can perhaps be overcome by going back even further and shifting our attention from Luther to Paul. For while Luther's concept of authority no longer seems applicable today, because there is no longer a personal union between church membership and governmental authority, Paul's concept does hold out greater hope of transferability to the present situation.

To begin with, there is no doubt that the concept of authority is to be found in Paul, particularly in Romans 13. For the "governing authority" (ἐξουσία ὑπερέχουσα, Rom. 13:1) undoubtedly means the ruling power of the state. What makes Paul's concept seem closer to our own situation than Luther's concept is the fact that in Paul the reference is to the non-Christian state of the Roman emperor. The emperor of course is not a member of the church. Indeed he may well be the representative of a paganism which has to be militantly anti-Christian. Directives governing the conduct of Christians vis-à-vis such a state seem to have a much greater relevance to the political situation within secularism than do directives relative to medieval Christendom, even as this was affected by the Reformation.

Nevertheless, there arises even here the question whether the concept of authority in Romans 13 is not now equally outdated and totally lacking in analogy to the modern situation. Paul says of this authority or power that it is instituted by God (ὑπὸ θεοῦ τεταγμένη, Rom. 13:1), and its authority to punish the wicked and to reward the good (13:3-4) is likewise ordained by God. But does not this strengthen Wingren's objection against transferring any ancient concept of authority to the modern situation? Are not the rulers of a democratic state — by virtue of the personal union between rulers and ruled — ordained by men? Are they not delegated from below rather than from above (τεταγμένη ὑπὸ τῶν ἀνθρώπων, or even ὑπὸ τοῦ ὄχλου)?

If this is a correct statement of how the modern democratic state understands itself, then it may be asked in return whether the Roman state did not understand itself in basically the same way, even though the authorizing power in the case of Rome was not the common man but the imperial god-man. The point of comparison at any rate would be the negative circumstance that, according to both the ancient and the modern understanding, God is apparently *not* the one who does the ordaining.[12]

Is not the world really changed, and is not the change seen best in the fact that social and political concepts of former times — such as the

[12] See Ethelbert Stauffer, *Christ and the Caesars* (London: SCM, 1955), p. 66. Stauffer points out that the inscription CAESAR DIVI FILIUS borne upon the Roman ruler's head means Son of God in the sense of "Son of eternal Caesar." To be sure, Stauffer indicates too that the equestrian statues of Augustus can also bear the inscription "By command of the people" or "By resolution of the Senate." So there is also this note of a commissioning by the people. It goes without saying, however, that this involves no true analogy to modern democracy.

concept of authority – cannot be applied to the situation today? Still, the fact that neither the Roman state nor the modern democratic state has, or has to have, a self-understanding in terms of which it derives its power from divine ordination ought to remind us of two things. It should remind us, first, that we are not to dramatize the discontinuity between past and present, or overlook certain constant factors. And second, it should suggest that too great importance is not to be attached to the way a particular state understands itself. For, after all, this self-understanding says nothing about whether that state in fact is or is not ordained by God. It tells us only whether this ordination by God is something men do or do not acknowledge. Theologically, the true nature of the state is not determined by its self-understanding. That self-understanding simply tells us about man and his attitude toward the state; it tells us whether the true nature of the state is apparent to him or concealed from him.

The statement of Paul may therefore still be true even of a state which, like the Communist state, understands itself in purely pragmatic and secular terms: It too is in fact ordained by God, or at least used by him in a special way, and hence permitted. The fact that Pharaoh is obdurate in face of the plagues and does not *perceive* the divine visitation (Exod. 5:2; 7:3; 8:15; 10:1) does not alter in the least the fact of the visitation. If Christ gathers men as a hen gathers her brood (Matt. 23:37) yet men do not understand his call, and if God sends the autumn rain and the spring rain as a sign (Jer. 5:24) yet the people fail to discern the sign (Matt. 11:16-24; 16:1-4, 8-9; Rom. 1:19-20), this does not alter the source and background of that sign. Cognitive failure cannot annul ontic fact.

Similarly, the state does not cease to be ontically an institution of divine grace when men cease to discern its theological background. The theological meaning of the state is not determined by how men understand it. It stands firm and unshakeable while man's understanding of it fluctuates and changes, approximating it only to greater and lesser degrees. Just as faith does not effect – or unbelief nullify – the existence of God, just as faith and unbelief merely signify man's acceptance or rejection of a fact, so the Christian or the atheistic self-understanding of a state cannot at all affect its theological reality.

This is why Paul describes the state of the Caesars as instituted by God, even though it understood itself quite differently. This is also why in Revelation 13 the state of demonic imperial illusion is integrated into a divinely effected event of salvation and judgment of which the state itself has no inkling.

We must probe a little deeper, however, into the self-understanding of the modern democratic state. We granted for a moment that this state seems to think, or could conceivably think, that it is ordained not by God but by the people. Now there can be no doubt that such a self-understanding is possible — there can obviously be atheistic democracies — but the question is whether such a self-understanding is also necessary. Are we really confronted here by an authentic either-or? Only if one assumes that the democratic state seriously believes its commissioning by the people to mean also its creation by the people. If this be the case, the either-or is indeed authentic. For this would mean that a human creator has supplanted the divine creator.

The question may thus be put as follows: Does a democratic understanding of the state *necessarily* lead to this change in the role of creator? In other words, is not a commissioning of the state by the people something radically different from its creation by the people? Indeed, does not the commissioning actually presuppose an existing reality with reference to which the commission is given? Would it not therefore be altogether possible to combine the idea of a divinely instituted state with that of a commissioning by the people?

It is evident from these obviously rhetorical questions that the older authoritarian state and the modern democratic state have — or at least can have — a common root. Even on a philosophical view of the state it is evident that, though it is upheld by the will of its citizens and acts in harmony with their ethical autonomy (their vital interests), the state is not simply a product of their own making. Even the contract idea of Kant and Fichte does not mean that the state derives from or is constituted by such a contract. It simply means that the contract formula effectively describes the primal phenomenon of human life in society with its attendant relationships of superordination and subordination.

What in philosophy is a datum that transcends man — and is not produced by him — is interpreted theologically as an ordinance of the will of God. This theological notion that the state is an ordinance of God, a mode of his rule in the kingdom on the left hand, does not refer only to authoritarian states like those of the Roman Empire or of

15

medieval feudalism. On the contrary, it is immediately transferrable to the modern democracies as well, for what it refers to is statehood as such. The particular historical illustrations which Paul and Luther may have used, i.e., the states known to them, are not to be confused with the matter itself.

How then does this basic concept of statehood as such look when transferred to the situation of the modern democracy? We are now in a position to trace — or, more precisely, to "construct" — this line of transferral. Our task is to establish the ultimate reference and sanction, in Luther's sense, of the democratic state, that state in which authority is exercised by the citizens rather than by a hereditary monarch. To put it in popular, if somewhat misleading terms, the question is: Given his view of authority, what would Luther have to say about modern democracy? Whether or not this "constructive" exercise is legitimate will depend on what comes out of it.

Divine Creation and Human Control in Government

We will first fix the decisive geometric points for the line we are about to draw. The following theses are taken from Luther's theology.

First, it is the fall that leads to man's self-destruction. It makes of men raging beasts. It produces a centrifugal tendency which drives men apart from one another, witness the fratricide of Cain and the dispersion at Babel.

Second, God puts a stop to this self-destruction in order to give man a καιρός, a space in which to repent. He sets over the world after the flood a rainbow of reconciliation, giving it a new constitution in the Noachic covenant.[13]

Third, the institutional form of this preservation is the state. Thus Luther can say in his 1530-1531 Lectures on Ecclesiastes, "Where there is a state, a miracle takes place," and again, "There is nothing greater on the whole earth than a state." [14] If we are to give to this gracious ordinance of God its proper theological locus it is important to note something implied already in the first two points, namely, that for Luther the state is not an order of creation but an emergency order

[13] It is unnecessary to provide specific Luther references here since these are elementary scriptural ideas found not only in his Genesis commentary [LW 1-8] but throughout his entire theology. Pertinent quotations will occasionally be given later.

[14] WA 31^{II}, 590 and 593.

evoked by the fall. Before the fall the state was not needed. As originally created, man was in harmony with God. He allowed himself to be ruled by the "moving of one finger." [15] It was only after he turned from God that he refused to be guided by such easy means. Only then did he have to be brought to heel by force.

Hence the state is simply the institutionalized form of God's call to order. It is a "remedy required by our corrupted nature. For it is necessary that lust be held in check by the bonds of the laws and by penalties lest it riot in freedom." [16] This is why the state by rights must be called "a kingdom of sin," for its theme is nothing but sin and the checking of sin. [17] We may thus say that for Luther the state is a gracious intervention of God which puts a stop to the self-destruction of the fallen world with a view to giving men a καιρός and bringing them to the last day. It is "an awful remedy by which harmful limbs are cut off that the rest may be preserved." [18] Thus the state is to be understood theologically in terms of its function within salvation history, and hence as an ordinance of God.

Fourth, there is yet a further thought in Luther, however, which seems to stand in tension with this inclusion of the state in salvation history; that is his view that the governing of the state is entrusted to human reason. [19] To formulate this point more sharply in relation to our problem: God seems indeed to ordain the state in a highly personal way. Having once done so, however, he decides not to provide further directives on which the state might be dependent in theocratic fashion. Instead he delegates, as it were, all responsibility for its further course to human reason, and therewith to man.

Franz Lau has rightly pointed out that "it is not the orders and their *ratio* but man and his *ratio* which provide the criterion whereby the orders are measured." [20] Thus if Luther speaks of reason as being

---

[15] *Uno moto digito.* LW 1, 104.   [16] *LW* 1, 104.

[17] *Arcere peccatum.* LW 1, 104. Hence it is "the function and the honor of worldly government to make men out of wild beasts and to prevent men from becoming wild beasts." LW 46, 237. Cf. Friedrich Gogarten, *Politische Ethik* (Jena, 1932), pp. 108 ff.

[18] *LW* 1, 104.

[19] "God made the secular government subordinate and subject to reason, because it is to have no jurisdiction over the welfare of souls or things of eternal value but only over physical and temporal goods, which God places under man's dominion, Genesis 2:8 ff." LW 13, 198.

[20] Franz Lau, *"Aeusserliche Ordnung" und "Weltlich Ding" in Luthers Theologie* (Göttingen: Vandenhoeck & Ruprecht, 1933), p. 49.

fully adequate for the state and its affairs, this is not to say that the state has within itself an immanent law from which political affairs may be automatically and autonomously derived and directed. For Luther the state is not a law unto itself but only a form whereby the relations of man to man are regulated. The regulating is entrusted to the reason and rational decisions of man, not to the immanent reason of an order. Because Luther thinks in terms of the person rather than the institution, and accordingly uses a personalistically determined concept of reason, he has no explicit doctrine of the state. His theme is not the institution as such, but man as he relates to his neighbor within the framework of the institution. Hence when Luther speaks in this context of reason what he means is not some law of reason immanent in the institution but the responsibly used reason of persons. Since government is tied not to theocratic directives but to the rational judgment of man, Christians are not the only ones qualified for political office. It is enough for a ruler if he has reason.[21] Indeed, pagans can sometimes be better rulers than Christians.

With these considerations we seem to have arrived at a first crucial point in our attempt to construct a theological line from Luther's concept of authority to the situation of the modern democracy. When Luther speaks about delegating governmental affairs to reason, he is unquestionably thinking — in accordance with his concept of authority — of the reason of the emperor or the prince, or of the magistrates appointed by them. But we surely do no violence to Luther's intentions if we say that the important thing is not so much who the office-holder is who exercises his reason, but the fact that it is the reason of *man* that is being exercised. The accent is not so much on the person ruling as on the assertion that the state is *not* ruled theocratically, by God. The gospel is not a code of statecraft. Statecraft is a matter of reason, and is accordingly delegated to reason. The ruler to whose reason the state is committed represents human reason in general, its dignity and its limits. This, then, suggests a line of connection between the older authoritarian state and the modern democracy: in both cases the business of state is delegated to human reason. In one case, of course, it is delegated to the emperor or prince, in the other

[21] See Luther's 1528 sermon on Matthew 22:15-22 in *WA* 27, 418, and cf. *ThE* 1, 141-142. On the role and limitations of reason in Luther's view see Bernhard Lohse, Ratio *und* Fides. *Eine Untersuchung über die* Ratio *in der Theologie Luthers* (Göttingen: Vandenhoeck & Ruprecht, 1958).

to the citizens. But these are only minor differences within an over-arching unity: in both it is human reason which receives the mandate.

Fifth, reason is given a real mandate. What this means may best be seen in terms of the negative possibility that reason will forget — or even fail to perceive — this mandate. In such a case, according to Luther, reason loses the criterion of its competence. Instead of being a reason which receives, hearing and accepting a mandate (in the sense of the *usus organicus*), it becomes a reason which acts on its own (in the sense of the *usus normativus*).[22]

The arrogance of this self-authorization of reason is that it tries to fix the basis, goal, and meaning of all that is. It gives birth to world views and other ultimate values together with their symbols, instead of carrying through its intellectual acts only on the basis which is allotted to it, in relation to the goal which is set for it, and in the name of the meaning which is proclaimed to it. In the sphere of political ethics this arrogance finds expression in the fact that reason does not receive the miracle of the state from the hand of God and then administer it in terms of a mandate it has received. Instead, reason imagines that it produces the state itself, and that the state therefore rests on the insight and resolve of reason, i.e., on a "contract."

Luther is convinced that of itself reason is blind to the true nature of the state, which consists in its function in salvation history and is therefore not immediately apparent but must be proclaimed and believed. Reason, then, is not competent to fix the meaning of the state or to work out a metaphysics of the state. That could only lead it to pride and idolatry. Its task rather is simply to administer that which it has received as its mandate, and to do so according to its own best judgment, according to equity,[23] by a natural sense of justice,[24] as the times and circumstances demand.[25] So must it go about its task of rewarding the good and punishing the evil, seeking good government and establishing proper order. In the language of Tillich one might say that what is involved here is not ontological reason, but technical reason.[26] Reason thus remains within its limits only when it accepts

---

[22] See *ThE* 1, 143-144.

[23] On the concept of ἐπιείκεια or *Billigkeit* in Luther see Lau, *op. cit.*, pp. 42-44, and *LW* 46, 102.   [24] *Ductu naturae. LW* 36, 98.

[25] *Secundum occasiones et tempora.* Cf. *LW* 7, 219.

[26] Paul Tillich, *Systematic Theology* (Chicago: University of Chicago Press, 1951), I, 53, 77.

its purpose as something assigned to it, and when it knows its autonomy to be purely a technical autonomy in relation to the fulfilling of that purpose.

Luther expresses this clearly in his doctrine of the two kingdoms.[27] The fact that historical and rational considerations are normative in the worldly kingdom does not mean that this sphere on the left hand is emancipated from the will and commandments of God and given over "instead" to reason. On the contrary, reason is understood here too as being altogether a receiving organ, to which the norms and purposes of secular action are committed and which has then to exercise its technical autonomy only in deciding on the means to achieve the goals transmitted to it.

The norms and purposes consist in the fact that the worldly kingdom is linked to the kingdom on the right hand — and thereby integrated into salvation history — in two ways: first, the preservation of the world through the state is not an end in itself but only a means to secure for man a new time of grace;[28] and second, I am obliged to discharge my secular office in the name of love, not with reference to an institution which is an end in itself, but with reference to my neighbor.[29] The secular task is thus committed to us by God, and its accomplishment ultimately serves his ends. It provides us with our physical existence as the necessary presupposition for hearing his word, inheriting his kingdom, and thus fulfilling the real purpose of our lives.

Christians and pagans thus have something in common, but there is also a difference. Common to them is the fact that they have received (on the subjective side) reason and (on the objective-institutional side) the state. The difference is that the pagan does not perceive the efficient and final cause of the state, whereas the Christian does, and because of that knowledge stands under a claim and obligation.

Sixth, if we apply to the theological understanding of democracy all that we have just said about reason receiving a mandate, we reach the following result. Democracy in these terms must mean that the citizens indeed control the state with their will and in virtue of the in-

[27] See ThE 1, 359 ff.
[28] See ThE 1, 374.
[29] See ThE 1, 376-377.

sight of their reason, but only in the sense that the state is *placed* under the control of their will and reason. Reason does not of itself concoct the idea of the state. Neither does it produce the state, e.g., in the form of a rational agreement or contract. On the contrary, it *receives* both. Its task is simply to make the most of what it has received, within the limits of its own judgment to develop it as best it can. This is the decisive point where the line of the older authoritarian state and that of the modern democracy intersect.

Hence it is not necessary that we do away altogether with the statements of Paul and Luther concerning the state, as might at first glance seem to be indicated by the words of Wingren. Our task is rather to de-institutionalize them. The authoritarian state, in terms of which Paul and Luther developed their view, is to be understood simply as a historically conditioned example. The purely illustrative nature of their particular example is shown by the fact that all the theological teachings associated with it can be transferred without difficulty to other kinds of state. Theirs is simply one of a variety of forms which the state has taken and may take. The totalitarian state alone departs from this pattern, and in so doing shows that theologically it is no longer a state but a pseudo church.

3.

Ideological Tyranny

The Totalitarian State in Soviet Doctrine

In considering how political ethics has so changed in the modern period as to make the application of traditional concepts (such as the concept of authority) difficult or even impossible, we touched first on the modern democracy. But it is obvious that its rival, the ideological power state, brings us face to face with the same problem. A moment ago we indicated that the totalitarian state cannot be brought into theological co-ordination with the authoritarian state of former times, for it represents a doctrinaire ideology which claims the whole man. As such, it goes beyond its sphere of competence as an order of secular power, a kingdom on the left hand, and purports to be a dispenser of salvation.

A Communist theoretician reading this book would be shocked by the terms we have just used, not so much because of our reference to ideological tyranny as because we have subsumed the Communist system of government under the rubric "totalitarian state." Since this expression does not occur in Marxist-Leninist doctrine, at least in its description of its ultimate goals, the Communist would accuse us of terminological imprecision, even falsification. For him, "every political expression such as 'the people,' 'democracy,' 'freedom,' 'the nation,' 'socialism,' and so on had a precisely determined meaning . . . any use of these terms which did not correspond to our definition was called 'unscientific.' We assumed it to have been written by people who had not . . . 'the slightest basic political education.' " [1]

Since we will thus be using a term which is not current in Communist doctrine — and we shall do this later with other terms as well inasmuch as we are not bound to do our thinking exclusively within

[1] Wolfgang Leonhard, *Child of the Revolution*, trans. C. M. Woodhouse (Chicago: Regnery, 1958), p. 381.

the categories of our opponents — it is essential that some brief explanation of our usage be made. To begin with we will adhere to a definition of the totalitarian state proposed by O. Stammer who says that totalitarian rule is present "when a mass movement which is centrally oriented, rests on a monopoly of power and government, and is authoritatively led by a political minority develops — with the help of a dictatorially ruled state — a bureaucratically sustained machinery of government which asserts itself in every sphere of society." [2]

Every unbiased reader will see in this precise and perspicacious definition a description of the state constructed along Marxist-Leninist lines, e.g., states such as the Soviet Union and its satellites. But the Communist theoretician would raise certain basic objections against this understanding of his state. He would say that the definition does not apply because Marxism-Leninism does not give such centrality to the state and hence cannot be regarded as a proponent of state totalitarianism.

What can be said in reply to this objection? It is true of course that in an early work entiled *Kritik des Hegelschen Staatsrechtes* (§§261-313) [3] Marx objects to Hegel's thesis that the state exists essentially to provide a rational and just social order. For Marx the state is rather an institution which serves to represent private interests. To maintain this thesis Marx had to attack the foundations of Hegel's philosophy of the state, namely, his doctrine of the "objective spirit." The point of this doctrine, as far as our specific question is concerned, is that the highest form in which morality is objectively realized is the state; family and society are only preliminary steps to this supreme form. Marx calls this notion a "mystification," because he necessarily rejects from the very outset Hegel's idealistic starting point, whereby the objective spirit is accorded ontic priority over such a concrete reality as that of the family. In Marx's view, Hegel has reversed the roles of the conditioning factor (family and society) and that which is conditioned (the state), thus executing that inversion of the order of reality which dialectical materialism seeks to correct. The state accordingly is not to be understood as a "universal," given a priori. It is rather a product, deriving a posteriori from real given factors. That which truly exists,

[2] Wilhelm Bernsdorf and Friedrich Bülow (eds.), *Wörterbuch der Soziologie* (Stuttgart: Enke, 1955), p. 551.

[3] Karl Marx, *Frühe Schriften* (Stuttgart: Cotta, 1962), I, 258-426.

the real given factor, is the particular citizen, the citizen however not in the sense of his being an individual (an individualist derivation of the state is rejected as surely as an idealist derivation) but in the sense of his being that real subject which — as "socialized man" — has raised itself to the level of universality.

It is easy to see how this leads to a relativization of the state. Such relativization, however, does not necessarily mean that the state thus relativized cannot still be totalitarian. For "socialized man" — who is obviously the antithesis of individualized man — will undoubtedly be somewhat more amenable to the embrace of an apparatus which totally encompasses him. This is not to say, of course, that the totalitarian apparatus in question will necessarily be the state. It could be the monopoly party. Which it really is becomes clear only as one comes to understand the actual relation of state and party in Marxism-Leninism. At this point, though, it is important to point out that the initial thesis of the young Marx, that the state is less a means to a just social order than a tool of private interests, established itself in dialectical materialism and then was given a most peculiar twist in the Communist state.

From the assertion that the state is an organization of private interests it is only a step to the further assertion that these interests are class interests, and that the state, being the champion of particular interests, is a "machine" for maintaining the "rule of one class by another."[4] To this degree the state is "the product and the manifestation of the irreconcilability of class antagonisms. The state arises when, where, and to the extent that the class antagonisms cannot be objectively reconciled. And, conversely, the existence of the state proves that the class antagonisms are irreconcilable."[5]

Such a statement implies the provisional nature of the state. For if the goal of history is the overcoming of class antagonisms in the classless society, then the function of the state will in the end be abolished. But only "in the end"! In the preliminary stage prior to the ultimate socialist form of society it has again an all-encompassing significance. For if the state is an "organization of violence for the suppression of some class," then the victorious proletariat can in the first instance use

[4] V. I. Lenin, *The State and Revolution*, translated from the Russian as issued by the Marx-Engels-Lenin Institute in Moscow ("Selected Works" [New York: International Publishers, n. d.]), VII, 16, 9.
[5] *Ibid.*, p. 8.

a state of its own to help suppress "the exploiting class, i.e., the bourgeoisie." [6] Lenin can say that Marxists agree with anarchists concerning the final abolition of the state, only they use a different route to the same goal. For Marxists hold that there must first be a dictatorship of the proletariat sustained by a power state which will oppress the opponents of the working class and so bring in the classless society.

Stalin, who is certainly no deviationist in this respect, also says that the route to the abolition of state power is by way of a temporary intensification of it. The bourgeois "formal logician," being unable to interpret history dialectically, will of course be forced to assume that a state dictatorship involves the indefinite perpetuation of state power. This is why such formal logicians arrive at the foolish conclusion that to do away with the state one must begin by limiting it. In fact, says Stalin, the very opposite is the case. Only the most extreme intensification of the state can lead to its abolition. [7]

Here there are obviously two overriding considerations. There is first the strategic consideration that the presuppositions of a stateless society can be created only by an instrument of force, i.e., the state; they cannot arise without a more or less forceful intervention. The second consideration is that Hegelian dialectic plays its part in this plan, the thesis of state dictatorship calling forth the antithesis of statelessness.

We believe that in the light of these considerations we are justified in identifying ideological tyranny with the totalitarian state. For even according to the self-understanding of Marxism-Leninism there has to be a dictatorial intensification of state power, at least as a transitional stage. Since it is with this stage, however, that we have concretely to do, what we have to do with is in fact the totalitarian state.

Whether the totalitarian apparatus of the state will subsequently be replaced by that of the party or something else, or whether its dissolution will take a completely different form from that prognosticated by Communists, need not concern us here. The point is that we see no

[6] *Ibid.*, p. 24.

[7] See J. V. Stalin, *Questions of Leninism* (1926), esp. Chapter IV on "The Proletarian Revolution and the Dictatorship of the Proletariat" ("Works" [Moscow: Foreign Languages Publishing House, 1954]), VIII, 22-33. See also Stalin's "Report to the 8th Congress of Soviets, November 25, 1936, on the Draft of the Constitution of the USSR," a partial text of which appears in M. R. Werner (ed.), *Stalin's Kampf: Joseph Stalin's Credo, written by himself* (New York: Howell, Soskin, 1940), pp. 209-230.

reason whatever for regarding the relativization of the state in Communist doctrine as a true relativization, or for refusing to equate ideological tyranny with totalitarianism. Perhaps even the dedicated Marxist would grant us, if not the rightness of our polemic, at least the right to regard his supposed transitional stage – the state we see today – as the age of the totalitarian state.

The Concept of Ideology

If we are to grasp theologically the implications of a development whereby the state becomes an ideological tyranny, going beyond its role as a force for order on the left hand and illegitimately presuming to be a dispenser of salvation, we must be clear also as to what we mean by "ideology." To put it very generally and not very precisely we may say at the outset that by ideological tyranny we mean a state having a particular world view. By world view we mean the attempt to subsume all cosmic phenomena under a single theme or formula from which they will derive their ultimate meaning. Thus no matter what sphere of life we are concerned to understand, be it history, nature, science, or art, all are brought under a common denominator. The state that espouses and represents such a world view is actually present in all spheres of life. There are no spheres outside it. Thus a state that has a particular world view is always a totalitarian state.

Now man exists in the zone where these spheres intersect. If, then, they are totally taken over by the state, man in his totality is also claimed by the state. He loses his personal autonomy and becomes a functionary. Should he claim any area of privacy for himself he makes himself an enemy of the state. The totalitarian state, therefore, is not an organism in which persons are related to other persons individually and communally. It is rather a mechanism in which all have been relegated to the status of group functionaries. By thus subjecting man to itself, the totalitarian state actually violates the image of God in man. To this degree it is atheistic in its very nature, even though – as in National Socialism – it may maintain the idea of God as a kind of metaphysical undergirding.

Such a state cannot in principle be brought onto that line which we have seen to be common to the authoritarian state and the modern democracy. For one thing, such a state is not something "entrusted" to man; it is rather the institutional expression of man's claim to be the one who alone gives meaning to his world. Furthermore, the reason which gives shape to such a state is not endeavoring to accomplish a ·task that has been given to it as a "recipient"; instead it insists on determining its own purpose in its effort to become absolute (and in so doing reason of course becomes unreason, i.e., the reason which has abandoned its vocation).

This brief sketch of the essential features of the totalitarian state is hardly enough, of course, to show us why the intellectual constructs which determine it should be referred to as ideologies rather than ideas. It is intrinsically conceivable that they could be called ideas. In other times and contexts men have championed the idea of a "Christian state" or of "Christian civilization." Why should one not speak also of the idea of a Communist state or the idea of a classless society? Why is it that both friend and foe speak here so emphatically of ideologies, the former in the sense of a program, the latter as a term of reproach?

We can answer this question only if we examine the concept "ideology" a little more closely. To do this, we must first discuss the Marxist concept of the superstructure and then, in the next chapter, set forth the pragmatic background of ideologies and their theological character as idolatry.

The Concept of the Ideological Superstructure

Marx's materialistic view of history holds that all historical movement is determined by what is going on in the area of "production," which in turn is determined by the degree to which the "material means of production" have developed and are available. Production as a whole constitutes the economic structure of society, and this in turn gives rise to a "superstructure" or "social consciousness." The life of the spirit, which grows out of this social consciousness, expresses itself initially in the form of legal and political convictions but also in art, morality, and religion. All of these are thus "echoes and reflections" of the social process. They are called ideologies because they reflect this basic material event. They derive from it, and in impelling power of reality are secondary to it. Hence it is the material means of production which determine social consciousness and the life of the spirit. "It is not the consciousness of men that determines their existence, but on the contrary, their social existence determines their consciousness." [8] In a famous definition Stalin expresses well this ontological inferiority of the ideologies: "If nature, being, the material world, is primary, and mind, thought, is secondary, derivative; if the material world represents objective reality existing independently of the mind of men, while the mind is a reflection of the objective reality, it follows that the material life of society, its being, is also primary, and its spiritual life secondary, derivative, and that the material life of society is an objective reality existing independently of the will of men, while the spiritual life of society is a reflection of this objective reality, a reflection of being." [9]

In principle, a similar understanding of man's spirit as being the function of prior realities can be found elsewhere in the modern world, even outside the sphere of the various materialisms. For Nietzsche, e.g., all occurrence — including intellectual processes, judgments, true affirmations, etc. — is "reducible to the intention of increasing power." [10] What spirit does in its own supposed sphere is thus an "echo and reflection" of the true primal reality. Only this reality is now defined not in terms of economics, as in Marx, but anthropologically, as the "will to power."

There is also some reason to interpret Oswald Spengler along these same lines. For him cultures are like plants. They are to be defined according to the method of scientific morphology. They have their regular biological periods of youth and age. In respect at least of their "great events," they follow a course for which they are destined by fate. The life of the spirit follows the same rhythmical pattern as is found in the successive phases of culture. A philosophical statement,

[8] The quotation is from the Preface to Karl Marx's *A Contribution to the Critique of Political Economy* (1859), and appears in the excerpt from the N.I. Stone translation which is reprinted in Lewis S. Feuer (ed.), *Basic Writings on Politics and Philosophy: Karl Marx and Friedrich Engels* (Garden City, New York: Doubleday, 1959), p. 43. The full text of the Preface is given in *Karl Marx: Selected Works in Two Volumes,* prepared by the Marx-Engels-Lenin Institute of Moscow under the editorship of V. Adoratsky, English edition edited by C. P. Dutt (New York: International, n. d.), I, 354-359.

[9] Joseph Stalin, *Dialectical and Historical Materialism* (New York: International, 1940), p. 20. Reprinted by permission of International Publishers Co. Inc. Printed also in *History of the Communist Party of the Soviet Union (Bolsheviks): Short Course,* edited by a commission of the Central Committee of the C.P.S.U. (B.) (New York: International, 1939), p. 115.

[10] Friedrich Nietzsche, *The Will to Power* (Book III, No. 663), trans. Anthony M. Ludovici ("The Complete Works of Friedrich Nietzsche," ed. Oscar Levy [New York: Russell & Russell, 1964], XV), 136.

e.g., so far as specific intellectual and spiritual content is concerned, will accordingly have to be judged, not in terms of its conformity to some non-temporal norm of truth but in terms of its morphological place within this cycle of successive phases. Philosophies are not, as it were, either true or false; they are only early or late. Thought and artistic expression too are thus in effect the ideological reflection of a prior reality, namely, that of the ineluctable process.

Our assertion that there are analogies between Marx and Spengler in the way they interpret the life of the spirit as a secondary reality — though Marx alone speaks of ideologies — is supported by the fact that both claim that the course of history can be plotted in advance. Marx refers to the way history moves with the ineluctability of natural law in the direction of revolution and the classless society. Spengler calls his major work *The Decline of the West* and claims that he can show what "must happen, because it will happen." [11]

Such exact prognosis, however, is possible only within the framework of the necessities of natural law, where the factors and impelling forces are known. It is not possible within the sphere of personal freedom, where living men encounter norms and must decide with respect to them. The very claim that historical events can be accurately foretold implies that history is determined not by man's free spirit (whether in decisions of thought and action or in the spontaneity of artistic creation) but by some underlying natural and material foundations. The spirit can be accounted for only in terms of its being a function of calculable factors, and hence an "ideology."

More recent Communist doctrine tends to regard the relationship between material substructure and ideological superstructure dialectically, involving an influence which is reciprocal rather than unidirectional. Thus Stalin's letters on linguistics, which seem to have survived the dethronement of their author, show that ideologies, once they are evoked, have a power of their own and exert an influence on the substructure. They develop a creative initiative of their own. [12]

---

[11] Oswald Spengler, *The Hour of Decision, Part One: Germany and World-Historical Revolution*, trans. Charles Francis Atkinson (New York: Knopf, 1963), p. xiv.

[12] J. V. Stalin, *Marxism and Problems of Linguistics* (Moscow: State Publishing House for Political Literature, 1955); see also Gustav A. Wetter, *Dialectical Materialism: A Historical and Systematic Survey of Philosophy in the Soviet Union*, trans. Peter Heath (New York: Praeger, 1958), pp. 325-329.

It would be a mistake, though, to see in this new turn a departure from the original principle that ideologies are dependent. It is rather a good example of the "cunning of the idea." [13] For this thesis that the superstructure has a rising power of its own is itself a kind of ideology developing out of, and reflecting, material social progress. This can be shown rather easily.

The material basis of history — that which creatively sustains all other fields — is actually "production." Unequal distribution of the means of production gives rise to antagonistic classes, and the war between these classes determines the face of history. If in Marxist teaching history is "the history of class warfare," then the course of events is determined by social forms which are a manifestation of the various levels of production. It is these social forms which, by virtue of the antagonism between the two classes, contain the creative polar tension which is the source of vitality and progress in history.

But this principle has always been a problem for the theoreticians of Marxism-Leninism. Since their goal is the classless society, this eschatology of theirs confronts them from the outset with the perplexing task of having to conceive of a non-historical state of affairs. For in the final stage of society, as they conceive it, there is no longer present that creative impulse which consists in the antagonism of the classes, and which is taken to be the theme of history! At this point Communist theory has had to look for a way out. Since with the triumph of Communism — i.e., in the eschatological phase of history — there will be neither revolution nor class warfare, and yet an ennervating non-historical state of utter immobility must not arise, new impulses of historical movement have to be found. These new impulses accordingly are sought in a new form of dialectic. The creative antagonism is located elsewhere. Antagonism between the classes is supplanted by an antagonism between substructure and superstructure.

This antithesis, this polar tension between substructure and superstructure which issues in a creative impulse, did not arise at first because the superstructure (according to Marx) was completely dependent and so could not involve any autonomous, tension-producing

---

[13] The phrase is from Georg Wilhelm Friedrich Hegel, *The Philosophy of History;* in *Hegel,* trans. J. Sibree ("Great Books of the Western World," ed. Robert Maynard Hutchins [Chicago: Encyclopedia Britannica Inc., 1952], Vol. 46), pp. 162-170 (hereinafter cited as "Great Books").

opposition. But the more history presses on toward the eschaton of Communist fulfillment, the more autonomy is conceded to the superstructure. Certain of its values (such as the moral and political unity of the people, the friendship of Soviet nations and nationalities, even the newly rediscovered "personality") and certain of its processes (such as criticism and self-criticism) begin creatively to exercise an influence of their own on social conditions, and to attain the rank of a creative opposition, a corrective to imperfect conditions.

Movement in history thus comes to be rooted in a basic tension which is different from what it was before. Whereas the driving historical impulse originally was found in a basic social antagonism whereby the revolutionary masses rose up against the ruling classes — the initiative was thus from below — in the classless Soviet society things are quite different. Here the initiative is from above and is directed downwards. This is true first in the sense that the initiative derives from the Soviet state — or from the party which controls it — as the institutional representative of the classless society: "The masses of the people *actively support* [!] such a revolutionary initiative from above." [14] It is true also in the sense that the initiative derives from the sphere of the superstructure where Communist doctrine, even though it was originally only the reflection of social conditions, now fulfills normative functions in relation to these conditions. This is worked out, e.g., in the matter of the Soviet satellites, for these cannot be subjected to the Soviet Union by way of an ideology that springs up out of the material substructure of their own society. On the contrary, an ideology which has taken shape, at least been well advanced, in the Soviet Union itself is brought in to exercise a missionary influence on the satellites. It bears down on them from above and hence alters the original direction of the history-shaping impulse. Thus does ideology become a relatively independent power capable of shaping history itself.

These two initiatives from above are obviously interrelated. For the Soviet state also occupies the infallible teaching office; indeed it is, as

---

[14] This statement by Georgi Alexandrov (the italics are my own) appears in a report entitled "The Further Development of Dialectical and Historical Materialism in J. V. Stalin's 'Marxism and Problems of Linguistics'" which was delivered at a session of The Academic Council of the Philosophical Institute of the Academy of Sciences of the U.S.S.R., and is quoted in Wetter, *op. cit.*, p. 327.

it were, the institutionalization of doctrine. For this reason the two initiatives from above are ultimately one and the same: the initiator is the Soviet state, which is charged to watch over ideology.

These newer tendencies in the understanding of the superstructure deserve notice because they give evidence of a significant change in the nature of ideologies themselves. Marxism-Leninism does not regard only the intellectual and spiritual spheres in general as ideologies and dependent reflections. Implicitly and almost involuntarily, if not expressly, it regards also its own doctrine as ideology of this kind. For whether it will regard the relation between substructure and superstructure as exclusively one of dependence or as one of reciprocity depends on the stage of social order in which the question arises. When it is taught that the ideologies have a power of their own by which they exert an influence in return, this is not to be understood as evidence of advanced insight. The teaching is only the reflection of an advance in the development of society.

Hence Marxism-Leninism is itself subject to the relativity of all ideology. It cannot live in its own right, but only as the reflection of some other life which is regarded as of prior reality. Communism does not merely have a *doctrine* of the ideologies; it is *itself* an ideology. And, paradoxically, it is nothing but a reflection even though that reflection seems to be full of vitality, even though it seems to have a mind and voice of its own and to be capable of taking the initiative from above. For this notion about the ultimate autonomy of ideology is something Communist doctrine *has* to devise as it moves towards the last stage of society; it is compelled to come up with some new antithesis to replace the antagonism of the classes now disappearing. It is this aspect of compulsion or necessity which certifies that Communist doctrine itself is nothing but a reflection of elemental historical processes.

Once entered, the vicious circle within which the doctrine of substructure and superstructure is embedded affords no avenue of escape. The relativity of all intellectual, moral, and musical processes and values persists. And the ancient rule of all relativism is again demonstrated, namely, that whoever stirs up the whirlpool of relativity by building a doctrine concerning it will himself be drawn into its vortex. The relativizing of man's spirit is avenged by the relativizing of the one who does it.

4.

The Pragmatism and Idolatry of the Ideologies

The Pragmatic Background of Ideologies

The Synthesis between Objectivity and Party Loyalty

Marxism-Leninism seeks to overcome the objection that it relativizes itself — and is basically only one ideology among others — by an argument which one can only describe as an Indian rope trick in the area of thought. If we are not mistaken, the place where this trick is performed is right at the very heart of the system. Authentic debate with Marxist-Leninist theory depends wholly on a correct fixing of this point. To maintain its claim to absolute validity and, as it were, to protect itself against itself, it has to synthesize the following antinomy.

On the one hand, it claims to be objective, based — as Stalin has put it — on "the objective reality of the material world." For the opposite of objective is subjective. If Communism cannot claim objectivity for its statements, then its doctrine degenerates into a subjective expression, a mere confession, even an arbitrary set of ideas which is not at all binding; it is reduced to the lowly status of an ideology. It goes without saying that Communism cannot "voluntarily" accept, much less intend, such a result. It must claim to be objective.

On the other hand, however, it passionately repudiates objectivity, or, better, the objectivist stance which it regards as an expression of the capitalist mentality.[1] For its job is not to understand the world, but to change it. Its doctrine accordingly aims not at the disclosure of objective truth but at the advancement of certain interests. As we shall have to show in greater detail, it is decidedly pragmatic. This forces it to reject objectivity. For the term "objective" is not just the opposite of "subjective." It is also the opposite of "interested." If one is to be objective, he has to renounce self-interest and personal bias.

[1] Objectivist is a term of opprobrium like idealist, deviationist, etc.

33

He must be disinterested and neutral, rising above both himself and the subject-object relation. This is something, however, which Communist doctrine cannot permit. For objectivity in the sense of neutrality would rob it of its active character, its class interest, and its will to achieve. Thus A. A. Zhdanov regards objectivity as "toothless vegetarianism" [2] and criticizes Georgi Alexandrov for having been "insufficiently partisan in his *History of Western European Philosophy*." [3] Objective in this sense means disinterested, and hence non-political.

This, then, is the antinomy which Communist doctrine must overcome. On the one hand, objectivity is demanded: one must discover the objective reality of history and claim absolute validity for the axioms of his exact science. On the other hand, objectivity is to be negated: one must be committed to the party. In other words, one must be objective in the sense of not being subjective, but he must not be objective in the sense of being neutral.

The intellectual trick whereby this antinomy is synthesized is as follows. Political science is not a neutral or uncommitted discipline. It is admittedly and intentionally partisan. Its partisanship robs it of its objectivity, however, only when it is directed toward a *particular* party, that is to say, toward one party among other *competing* parties. So long as this is the case, there can be no such thing as a single, integrated, and universally valid political science. There can only be rival claims, claims which are forever incompatible. Since universal validity, however, is integral to the concept of objectivity, such objectivity cannot be had — in principle — so long as there are different classes, and hence different parties, in society, e.g., the bourgeois middle class, the proletariat, the petty bourgeoisie.

The objectivity which alone can assure universal validity is sociologically possible only when there is a *single* class "whose interests are identical with those of the progressive development of the race." Since the goal of this development is the classless society, or, in other words, the society which is identical with the triumphant proletariat, the goal of history — to put it in Hegelian terms — thinks itself when the triumphant proletariat thinks. Only then is that objectivity attained

[2] A. A. Zhdanov, "On the History of Philosophy," *Political Affairs*, XXVII, 4 (April, 1948), 352.

[3] See J. M. Bocheński, *Soviet Russian Dialectical Materialism [Diamat]*, trans. Nicolas Sollohub, revised by Thomas J. Blakeley (Dordrecht, Holland: Reidel, 1963), p. 102.

which is universally valid and yet partisan, objective and yet "interested." For now there is no conflict of interests, as in the interim stages of history; it is the interest of history's own "purpose" to realize itself.

This "purpose of history" — which is almost mythically personified — is thus "interested," yet without losing its universal validity. It is partisan, yet without forfeiting its objectivity. For the party which champions it is precisely that class which is itself so closely identified with the purpose of history. Present-day (i.e., pre-eschatological) Soviet philosophy shares in this objectivity even now, because it does its thinking — already now — in the name of this goal of history.

The trick of thought involved here is obvious. First, "the" objective basis of history is axiomatically posited and then the postulate of a classless society is deduced from it. Second, this ideology is proclaimed as a battle cry which purports not to interpret the world — i.e., to know it and to be objective in this knowledge — but to change it into the classless society, i.e., to be "interested" and hence not objective. Third, this conception of the classless society is used in turn as a means to make objectivity possible, and thus to validate itself as a product of objective thought.

Here if anywhere it is obvious that the ideology of Communism, above all the other ideologies against which it polemicizes, stands in the half-light between the passive reflection of living processes, the pragmatic invention of ends, and scientific axioms.

Ideology as a Means of Rule

If ideology as thus defined is to be accessible to the grasp of understanding, it cannot be left in this half-light. Its true center and driving force must be known. As we shall discover, this lies in its pragmatic tendency. Ends are invented. This may be seen above all in the fact that wherever an ideology enters normative spheres like science, law, and ethics, it robs the norms of their authoritative position and turns them into mere means for attaining certain ends and serving certain "interests." [4] The pragmatic purpose of ideologies is beyond

[4] For a classical instance of the subtle balance between objectivity and interest see p. 14 of the official *Lehrbuch der Politischen Oekonomie* written under the auspices of the Soviet Academy of Sciences and used in all Eastern universities. [See also I. Lapidus and K. Ostrovityanov, *An Outline of Political Economy* (Martin Lawrence, Limited, 1929), p. 5; and A. Leontiev, *Political Economy: A Beginner's Course* (New York: International, n. d.), pp. 22, 31.— Trans.]

question. Our concern, then, is not so much to assert this fact as to inquire concerning the degree to which this pragmatic tendency works in opposition to such non-material norms as the true, the righteous, or the good, actually swallowing them up.

So far as pragmatism itself is concerned, we may simply note the statement of Marx that "theory itself becomes a material force when it has seized the masses." [5] Stalin takes this to mean that Marx is referring to the tremendous "organizing, mobilizing and transforming role" of such political theories.[6] To this degree ideologies are "the tools of life." "A social idea is considered right not because it corresponds to objective reality but because it is a good tool for the class which has brought it forth." [7]

Hence ideologies are subject, not to the truth, but to the end which they serve. They are variable, not merely in the sense that they change in accordance with the material substructure on which they depend, but also in the sense that they change with changing ends. As means of actualization, ideologies are controlled by men, whereas truth controls men. The consequence is that the statements made in ideologies are not shaped by the truth even if they resemble truth. The form of their statements is wholly an expression of the will to power, in Nietzsche's sense. By *appearing* to pronounce truths, while in fact proclaiming a program, they supply an intellectual alibi for the exercise of a collective will to power.

The norm of the good is similarly swallowed up by the ends sought. In this connection one may draw upon illustrations from quite different sources, such as the sayings: "God is whatever serves my country," or: "My country, right or wrong." Or one may think of the demand of Machiavelli that in practical politics the good not be made the ideal, but that ethical phrases be used only in order to establish the moral credit which will be useful in achieving political ends.

Georges Sorel laid his finger on a real truth when he described

[5] This statement is from the Introduction to Karl Marx's *Contribution to the Critique of Hegel's Philosophy of Right* (1844) which is reprinted in T. B. Bottomore (trans. and ed.), *Karl Marx: Early Writings* (New York: McGraw-Hill, 1964), p. 52.

[6] Joseph Stalin, *Dialectical and Historical Materialism* (New York: International, 1940), pp. 23, 24; reprinted in *History of the Communist Party of the Soviet Union (Bolsheviks): Short Course*, edited by a commission of the Central Committee of the C.P.S.U. (B.) (New York: International, 1939), pp. 116, 117.

[7] Bocheński, *op. cit.*, p. 101.

social ideologies of this sort as myths which are "not descriptions of things" but an "expression of the resolution to act." [8] Hitler says exactly the same thing: "Even the best idea becomes a danger as soon as it pretends to be an end in itself, but in reality only represents a means to an end." [9]

Precisely because Rosenberg's *The Myth of the 20th Century* is so banal (and because his thinking, as distinct from Marxism-Leninism, does not press on to the point where an attempt is made to harmonize truth and end), its trivial simplification brings out the more clearly the true nature of these tendencies. For Rosenberg the myth in question is in the first place the ideological reflection of a racial-biological substance (the substructure-superstructure schema applies exactly). In the second place this myth is simply a tool for exercising non-material power, a tool for which the question of truth is wholly irrelevant. The totalitarian state has need of such an ideological instrument. For if it relies only on terror, it creates opposition for itself, if not in the form of a movement then at least in the form of an inner emigration that may or may not be outwardly apparent. Inner resistance cannot be controlled by terror. It can be overcome only as the inner antagonism — which is inaccessible to force — is conquered, i.e., either by persuasion or by the power of suggestion (propaganda). This can be accomplished only by non-material means, by intellectual and spiritual weapons called ideologies or political myths. Religions can be used for the same purpose, and have been — even Christianity. And where there is no living religion available by which to control the masses, a substitute can be fabricated. Rosenberg's myth is just such a synthetic product of the laboratory.

The common feature of all such attempts is that they claim the whole man and that they endeavor to actualize the claim by means of ideologies. Over and above the surgery of terror, these ideologies supply an internal and psychological therapy which brings man's inner being into subjection, either convincing him through arguments or stirring him to enthusiasm and fanaticism through emotional appeals.

[8] See Walter Theimer, *Der Marxismus* (1950), p. 240.
[9] Adolf Hitler, *Mein Kampf: Complete and Unabridged*, ed. John Chamberlain *et al.* (New York: Reynal & Hitchcock, 1939), p. 288; cited in Alan Bullock, *Hitler: A Study in Tyranny* (London: Odhams, 1952), p. 68. On this whole question see also Jean F. Neurohr, *Der Mythos vom Dritten Reich. Zur Geistesgeschichte des Nationalsozialismus* (Stuttgart: Cotta, 1957).

The Claim to Absoluteness

It is now evident why every ideology must involve, at least implicitly, the claim to absoluteness. If it seeks to master the whole man, it can brook no rivals. Hence it does not discuss with opponents; it does away with them. This points to a dialectical relation between power and ideology. Ideology has to validate the will to power, to buttress it, as it were, with supporting arguments. On the other hand, ideology itself needs power so that it will not have to discuss with — and in so doing recognize — its ideological rivals, but can simply destroy them. Ideology dare not let itself be called in question, for it would thereby lose its force and fall apart. This is why it must crush everything that challenges it. It therefore not only serves power, but also uses power to stamp out opposition. This is why political ideologies by their very nature are linked with terror.

Indeed, this is what distinguishes ideologies from matters of real conviction. For convictions necessarily expose themselves to challenges. They are strengthened when they lift the drawbridge and allow their opponents to enter. The man of conviction gains independence precisely through standing "against" something: through opposition he becomes what he is. This the champion of an ideology never does. He refuses to derive his very being from resistance to a challenge. He cannot let an opponent come near him. Conviction aims at true existence, ideology at mere functioning. Conviction creates persons; ideology depersonalizes. Conviction lets the other be an end in himself; ideology makes him a means and an object. The man of conviction asks: What is truth? The victim of ideology asks: How am I influenced, and how can I influence others? Ideology asserts itself therefore by silencing its opponents, even liquidating them completely. Truth on the other hand asserts itself by persuading others. Ideology will not permit the kind of division which truth allows.

Goebbels' practice of cutting off all discussion at party meetings right after the main speech shows that while ideology may disguise itself as truth, it is in fact only a form of the expression of power. The ideological tyrant must inevitably construe every alternate claim to truth, e.g., the expression of a different view, not as a position to be refuted but as an enemy to be suppressed. If the force of an intellectually or spiritually based claim to truth is to be blunted, it has to be refuted. But a dynamic — and this is how an ideology necessarily regards the opposing claim to truth — can only be destroyed or, once I am exposed to it, suppressed. It is well known, however, that acts of suppression do not overcome the thing to be suppressed. They actually preserve it by forcing it down into deeper levels of the psyche where it hibernates as in a state of incubation until such time as it is convenient to emerge and become active again.

This is perhaps the basic reason — though it is not usually thought out with any clarity — why the ideologist cannot allow his opponent to speak, why he silences or even kills him. The category of the dynamic, under which all claims to truth are subsumed, does not allow for an individual to have any convictions of his own. Consequently an opposing view or claim cannot be overcome by way of existential persuasion, but only by suppression. As the dynamistic ideologist sees it, the appeal to conscience, existence, and conviction can lead only to pathological states of weakness, i.e., to a state of tension whereby a man is involved in conflict with himself instead of mobilizing all his forces for the external conflict.[10]

Science and Ideology

For all these reasons we need not be surprised — indeed we have already suggested — that the pragmatic tendency is the true center and driving force of ideology which affects or swallows up all other norms. It will have to suffice if we give only a few examples of this, examples taken from the spheres of science (which, being exact, might seem to be secure against ideological influence) and of law.

Though the axioms of ideology are used even to take issue with Einstein's theory of relativity, the demand that science provide the arguments to validate ideological interests is most clearly illustrated in the field of biology. The genetics founded by I. V. Michurin and worked out by T. D. Lysenko teaches the inheritance of acquired characteristics. Alteration of the environmental conditions offers man the possibility of effecting a change in the organism which can be passed

---

[10] See, e.g., Josef Goebbels, *Kampf um Berlin* (1936), pp. 188 ff. where he speaks of the newspaper as something designed "not to inform" but to stir up "like a whip." It is an instrument of propaganda and is not intended to give people the factual information for making up their own mind. "Whoever can see a thing from two sides loses his own assurance and uncompromising conviction"; he becomes bogged down in internal conflict.

on by inheritance to its descendants.[11] This thesis necessarily lends support in three ways to the axioms of the presupposed ideology.

First, it presents man as the lord of nature who has to "alter" the world, in the sense of the thesis which Marx maintained against Feuerbach. Here one thinks of the countless abortions performed especially in the early years of the Soviet Union.

Second, it gives biological support to the Marxist theory of environment whereby man is a product of his social milieu and accordingly has socially acquired characteristics. The logical conclusion — that by altering his environment man alters himself — is here carried over into the sphere of biology: plants and animals can be changed by changing their environmental conditions. The characteristics thus derived are determinative of their very nature. That these changes go to the very roots of their nature and thus are "genuine," is proved by the fact that the characteristics thus acquired are actually transmitted. For only that which is of the essence is transmitted hereditarily. One's environment is thus determinative of what one is.

Third, support is given to the axioms of the ideology when nature and history are treated as if they were analogous. This is possibly only because the doctrine of historical materialism already applies to history the methods of physical science (though a very dubious physical science). History is not thought to be played out in the sphere of personal decision where man is a personal subject. It is derived rather from a material base. Accordingly, physical analogies such as the inversion of quantity into quality are constantly adduced, e.g., in explaining the revolution. Similarly, history can be foretold as surely as a lunar eclipse.

Since science has to confirm ideology, science too becomes an instrument of the power conflict in exactly the same pragmatic sense as ideology itself. Hence it is easy to detect in the pertinent Soviet writings not so much joy in the attainment of knowledge as joy in the practical usefulness of this knowledge, i.e., joy in applied science. Whereas Einstein could describe the impulse behind research as "divine curiosity," Lysenko would presumably say that his motive is to serve the Soviet Union and the class it represents.

[11] See Gustav A. Wetter, *Dialectical Materialism: A Historical and Systematic Survey of Philosophy in the Soviet Union,* trans. Peter Heath (New York: Praeger, 1958), pp. 457 ff.

More important therefore than the genetic discovery of Michurin is the fact that it could be used to produce bigger crops, extend arable acreage, and in the future perhaps even propagate a new race of supermen. Hence the scientist is not just one who discovers the processes of nature. He is a "front line fighter for the Soviet Union and its allies." In his own way he aims to breach the front lines of monopolistic bourgeois capitalism.

The primary task with respect to nature — as with respect to history — is therefore not to "understand" it, but to "change" it. Statements concerning nature and history are perfectly interchangeable. The distinction between them fades when man is no longer a free personal subject. Basically, nature and history both represent instances of material change.

These slogans — and the terminological connecting of scientific and political positions — which are all so highly repugnant to a man of the West, are in no sense inarticulate cries. Even on the lips of minor officials they are the distant echoes of a basic doctrine which in its origins, even though already a slogan and a dogma, is nonetheless wrapped up in a sublime intellectuality.

If this pragmatism is to be discerned already in the "green wood" of the physical sciences, one may expect that in the social sciences, humanities, and other disciplines, with their greater immediacy to man and to history, it will be found on an incomparably greater scale. We shall restrict ourselves to a few comments on the relation of ideology and law.

Ideology and Law

In view of what has been said already, there is obviously no need to look for either a norm such as justice or an authority such as natural law in the Communist system of law. They simply are not there. On the Communist view, law cannot derive exclusively from the idea of justice. On the contrary, it involves in principle a tension between three basic values: justice, utility, and security.[12] Right is a highly complex concept inasmuch as it combines both normative and pragmatic considerations.

Although the relationship between the two is highly complex and

[12] See Gustav Radbruch, *Vorschule der Rechtsphilosophie* (Göttingen: Vandenhoeck & Ruprecht, 1947), pp. 23 ff.; and *idem, Einführung in die Rechtswissenschaft,* ed. Konrad Zweigert (10th ed.; Stuttgart: Koehler, 1961), pp. 36 ff.

there are borderline cases in which the supremacy of the normative considerations over the pragmatic is in doubt,[13] there can be no question that in the Western legal tradition justice is regarded as an absolute, of equal standing with such other absolutes as the good, the true, and the beautiful. One might say that law is a cultural phenomenon involving the externals of the social order which "is designed to express and support the idea of what is right." [14] Thus the body of laws always has at its core the idea of justice. The normative outlook prevails as a continuing corrective to all the pragmatisms which also come into play.

Ideological law, however, bears the mark of heresy — of *legal* heresy — because it absolutizes the subsidiary outlook. Pragmatism, no longer significant only as a part of the total organism, is made the organizing center. Law becomes an instrument of the will to power, a political weapon. Just as science exists to justify pragmatic ideology, so law exists to justify legally the interests of the system by making the idea of justice subservient to them.

In the early stages the purely pragmatic ends of the ideology are still manifest without any concealment. But then the inherent urge for expansion which slumbers in them comes to the fore. It finds expression not only in external power conflicts but in its conquest of what we might call the arsenal of norms present in the human consciousness. The ideologists note that this conquest increases their power potential. They invest their use of force with the trappings of legality, thus making it harder for anyone to oppose them in the name of law. This neutralizes some of the opposition and at the same time attains some of the secret goals of the ideological power, which aims not merely at an external consolidation of power by means of terror but at a conquest of the inner spheres of man, including his conscience.

Hence it is in keeping with the way ideological power is exercised that public trials leading to a predetermined result are staged. These are no more than a power play in legal guise. The dominant power interest might well have attained its objective without this juridical interlude. But by using a moral instrument as well, by the investiture

[13] We are thinking of the irony involved in the saying: *Vivat justitia, pereat mundus!*

[14] Gustav Radbruch, *Rechtsphilosophie*, ed. Erik Wolf (4th ed., Stuttgart: Koehler, 1950), pp. 123 ff.

of justice as a handmaiden of politics, it can invade also the inner spheres of man. Even the obvious lack of credibility which attaches to such perversions of justice does not cause those in power to fail completely of their purpose. For the staged trial at least prevents the spectators from bringing the full emotional weight of their sense of justice to bear against the excesses of naked power. Being forced now to wrestle with certain legal considerations, they are thus entangled in a debilitating debate with themselves. They are confronted with a situation which is undoubtedly more complicated than that which would have been posed by an undisguised abuse of power. Since complicated situations are less easily handled — even inwardly — than those which are simple and straightforward, their moral powers of resistance are dissipated.

This precisely is the secret goal of all ideological strategy, something which Trotsky failed to see in the early days of Communism. He proclaimed an open tyranny which was to be established without any concealment, without "transposing the dictatorship of the proletariat into enigmatic legal forms." [15] The moral debilitation which results from this pragmatic combining of interests and law may be seen in its most radical form, not among the people generally who are spectators at the trials, but in the defendants themselves where it leads to those self-incriminations and expressions of remorse which are so puzzling to the West. Since the defendants usually demand their own execution, and hence could not be hoping to gain anything through their self-accusations, their strange conduct is usually explained in terms of psychological pressures (the power of suggestion, etc.), drugs, torture, and brainwashing. While there may be a measure of truth in all this, the real explanation lies in the ideological structure of the law itself.

In this connection the statements made by the old Hungarian Communist Lajos Cseby about the rehabilitation of Laszlo Rajk, Minister of the Interior who had been executed in 1949, are most significant for our analysis, since they contain a personal diagnosis of the man's own history and therefore shed a light from within on these puzzling procedures. When asked why those being rehabilitated in 1956 had confessed their guilt and solemnly expressed remorse seven years before,

[15] The Trotsky quotation is from Bert Dirnecker, *Recht in West und Ost* (1955), p. 51.

Cseby answered: "Do not think that the matter is so simple. When we were in the capitalist prisons we were interrogated by our enemies, but now we were being questioned by representatives of our own Communist party. They claimed to speak in the name of the party, and they demanded that we confess regardless of what might happen to us personally, because such confession was in the interests of the party and of the workers' movement. And even if in the depths of our souls we suspected that this was not so, we nonetheless came gradually to believe the constantly repeated phrases. The ground, the moral support, was cut away from beneath our feet, and then we confessed." [16] Here in Cseby's statement all the pragmatic tendencies of ideological law are present as in summary form.

There is first of all the aim of the trial: The accused represent an opposition which must be robbed of its moral foundations. Their confession accomplishes that. Opposition cannot rally behind leaders and champions who liquidate themselves. Martyrs forcefully done to death are the "seed of the church," or of the group which they represent. But martyrs who "voluntarily" recant discredit their group and blunt its purpose. The purpose of the trials is to provide the technical possibility for this sterilization, this inner liquidation of opposing groups. As this is the task of the law, its pragmatic character is vividly apparent.

In the second place, the pragmatic character of the law is shown in the relation between the court and the accused. For the technique of interrogation is designed to weaken the defendant by entangling him in a twofold conflict, thus making him the agent of the sterilization process.

On the one hand the defendant is entangled in the conflict between party interest and law. The tactical goal of the hearing is to resolve this conflict in such a way that the accused no longer regards the law as an authority standing above both sides in the trial, mediating between the rights of the party and his own rights. The law instead becomes identical with the rights of the party; it is simply an instrument of the party's interests. Thus this first conflict ends – to the detriment of the accused – in a conjoining of law and interest to the point where they completely overlap.

[16] *Die Welt,* 1956, 236, p. 4.

On the other hand the defendant is also entangled in the debilitating conflict of the party within itself, i.e., the conflict between the party as he represents it and the party as his accusers represent it. Since here he is not facing a hostile front, as he would be in relation to capitalism, since he has no quarrel against Communism but represents a quarrel within it, it is not a case of his being one of two opposing factors in a conflict. The conflict is rather a battle of two souls within his own breast. He does not *stand on* a battlefield; he *is* the battlefield! The weakening and neutralizing of the opposition accomplished by this inner conflict ends in full capitulation, because one of those two voices in the same breast is continually strengthened from the outside. The accusing party, whose voice is heard also within the defendant himself, strengthens this voice by the constant action of its prosecutors and court officials. Their monotonous arguments, incessantly repeated by a variety of persons, finally drown out the lonely voice of opposition.

This is all the easier because the duet of voices is engaged in a debate that is essentially about interests, not about law, a debate which solely for the sake of the external effect must finally issue in a legal formulation, i.e., confession and judgment. This debate about interests takes place in such a way that party unity takes priority over everything else. In this, both accusers and accused are in agreement, that party unity must be maintained if the party is to remain in power. Now the moment the struggle for power is decided in such a way that one faction remains in control while the defeated antagonist sits in prison, the obligation of unity — recognized by both groups — can be discharged only by submission on the part of the defeated faction. The unity of the party can be restored only by their moral capitulation, their acknowledgment of guilt and expression of remorse.

This is how the potentially dangerous situation of martyrdom is neutralized. Ideological law is made into a power tool in the hands of the ruling class. In an intraclass dispute it becomes a power tool in the hands of the dominant faction. It is used — and this is the only reason that "law" is necessary at all in ideological tyranny — to resolve certain debilitating and paralyzing conflicts. The best example of this usage is to be seen in these personal confessions and self-incriminations on the part of the accused in public trials.

To sum up, law is "the totality of the rules of human conduct imposed by the state power acting in behalf of the ruling class in society, and of the customs and rules whose usage is sanctioned by that power and enforced by the machinery of state in order to maintain, strengthen, and develop those conditions and circumstances which are acceptable and advantageous to the ruling class." [17] Indeed, we append some typical statements to illustrate, sometimes in the crassest form, the pragmatic character of ideological law.

The significance for law of the social consciousness may be seen in the fact that for Soviet law proof "consists not in the establishing of facts, after the Roman pattern, but in the judging of these facts." [18] Notice that this definition leaves room for a judgment – an ideological evaluation – of facts not yet established; the criterion of *truth* is thus subordinated to the *goal* of the proceedings. This "judging" is particularly prominent "in matters involving social, i.e., class, relationships and where the act in question represents a threat to society . . . from the standpoint of the interests of socialism." [19]

"The courts in our Soviet state are part of the machinery of political guidance, and appropriate measures assure that they are actually instruments of the policy of the Communist Party." [20] "The court exists not to replace terror but to justify it in principle, clearly, openly, and relentlessly." [21] The courts of the state are "instruments for classes to oppress classes. To the hostile classes, the state apparatus is the instrument of oppression. It is violent, and not 'benevolent.'" [22] In *Darkness at Noon* Arthur Koestler has given a notable literary presentation of ideological trial and punishment.

Ideologies as Idolatry

The statement that ideology is in its very nature pragmatic, and that it pragmatizes all the spheres of life which it claims – and it claims

[17] Andrei J. Vyshinsky, *Fragen der Rechts- und Staatstheorie* (Moscow, 1949), p. 84.
[18] Andrei J. Vyshinsky, *Rechtswissenschaftlicher Informationsdienst* (East Berlin, 1952), No. 5.
[19] *Ibid.*
[20] Professor Poliansky, "Parteidirektiven und Strafjustiz," *Mitteilungsblatt der Moskauer Universität*, 1950, 11.
[21] V. I. Lenin at the conclusion of his address of April 29, 1918, to the All-Russian Central Executive Committee; *W. I. Lenin Werke* (Berlin: Dietz, 1960), Vol. 27.
[22] Mao Tze-Tung, *On People's Democratic Dictatorship* (Peiping: English Language Service of the New China News Agency, 1949), pp. 10-11.

them all! — involves a theological judgment. We have intimated this already in our previous analysis. Indeed, the theological judgment constituted the criterion for that analysis. Our task now is to give that judgment final and explicit formulation. We have five main points.

First, the norm for all thought and action is not an *authority* binding upon man but a specific *interest* determined by man himself. Man therefore — in the Communist view man as representative of the class — is the lord of all. Since all life is determined by its environment, and environmental factors can be shaped by man, literally everything falls within man's capacity to create, including those characteristics of man, animals, and plants which are transmitted hereditarily. The dominion of man is thus the rightful successor to the creatorship of God; it is an imitation of the divine *doxa*.

Second, the man thus filled with the passion to create, however, is not only one who makes; he is himself made. He is manipulated as an object. He is not an active participant in the sense of having a personal autonomy of his own. He is simply a functionary having no will of his own, or a passive fellow worker, or even a sacrificial offering. A personal being who resists such depersonalization cannot be tolerated, and that for two reasons.

In the first place, the person who makes independent decisions cannot be fully integrated into the apparatus of the power structure. He cannot be used like a tool because he has his reservations, voices his criticisms, and pursues his own goals. Potentially at least he is always an opponent, and that potential is actualized all too often. The ideologist has control over the category of the dynamic. Thus it follows that for him the "person" can only be a counterforce or obstacle. This is why the "person" cannot be allowed to exist. He must be absorbed in the collective.

Then in the second place, since the concept of the personal does not exist in ideological thinking, man is never anything but the representative of a class or social group. Any appeal to a man's moral or intellectual conscience is merely a cover-up for another appeal, the true appeal, which is to a certain class interest. As the ideologist sees it, there can be no appeal to something which binds men unconditionally; there is only the appeal to the dictates of interest. The ideologist not only understands himself pragmatically, he credits all others with the same motivation.

Third, Christianity therefore is not an allegiance to God as ultimate authority. It is merely another ideological expression of a particular social situation.[23] In two senses, then, ideology is anti-Christian. It is so, first, in relation to the Christian, for it has to regard his allegiance to Christ as a contesting and truncating of its own claim to allegiance, and hence as opposition. It is so, second, in relation to Christianity, not merely because Christianity is something which seeks to bind and enslave the Christian but also because, as an ideology, Christianity represents an outmoded stage of class development. Hence from the standpoint of materialistic thinking Christianity is (1) untrue; from the dynamic standpoint it is (2) a hostile authority; and from the historical standpoint it is (3) reactionary inasmuch as it represents a religious ideological superstructure which is no longer in step with the base, the "contemporary" social situation. From this further theological consequences necessarily follow.

Fourth, within the framework of ideologies the word degenerates. For the word draws its life from the fact that what it expresses is an ultimate reality. The word is the medium of confession, and this fact of its origin lives on in all other forms of utterance, whether it be a word that informs (and so is related to ultimate truth), or a word that gives shape (and so is related to ultimate being), or a word that expresses judgment (and so is related to ultimate righteousness). The word also draws its life from the fact that it establishes and expresses – or ruptures and puts an end to – communication between persons. Its power to maintain and dissolve fellowship extends from the lovers' pledge of faithfulness to the judge's sentence of death. Where the word no longer has anything to say (where it has lost its "ultimate" reference) and where the word is no longer a medium of communication (there being no *persons* left to do the communicating) it necessarily loses its force. When the word has lost its reference to norms and to persons, then in spite of whatever continuing tactical goals and relevance to material facts it might have – as used, e.g., by an engineer – it has become a word without a real purpose, a word which, like the ideology in which it has its origin, can have only dynamic interests.

[20] Cf. Friedrich Engels, *On the History of Early Christianity* (1895) in Lewis S. Feuer (ed.), *Basic Writings on Politics and Philosophy: Karl Marx and Friedrich Engels* (Garden City, New York: Doubleday, 1959), pp. 168-194; also W. I. Lenin, *Sämtliche Werke* (Berlin), VIII, 566: "The importance of the exploited class . . . elicits . . . inevitably faith in a better life after death."

In a basic sense it is simply the expression of power, the stuff with which power operates.

This may be seen particularly in that which is the normal form of the word as the ideologies use it, namely, propaganda. Propaganda is really the decisive instrument whereby an ideology exercises its power, which is why it is used to an extraordinary degree in the totalitarian state,[24] e.g., through broadcasts and banners, appeals to the eye and to the ear which bombard the individual from all sides at all times, smothering him with signals and effecting the omnipresence of the ideology.[25] The word of propaganda is unable to persuade. That is not its purpose. Quite apart from its inherent incapacity, it is simply too shallow and empty to do so.[26] It is intended only to load down the psyche, to make dents and impressions, to exercise the power of suggestion by way of endless and unvaried repetition. Such a word does not persuade; it pummels. It is not meant to convince but to smite. It is a slogan. As we have suggested already, it has a purely dynamic function.

In two ways the slogan is indicative of depersonalization. First, the one who wields it regards the one against whom it is wielded not as a person but as an object, a force to be either captured and integrated into his own power potential or else destroyed as a hostile power, but in either case a force and not a person. Second, the slogan strikes a man not at the personal center, where he makes up his mind, but only at the extremities of his nervous system. It operates with visual and audial stimulants. When fellowship between persons (even personal fellowship within a group) is broken, there no longer exists that stratum of the ego in which convictions can be formed. Indeed, where centers of personal autonomy still exist, the effort is to do away with them because the more there is of personal substance the greater is the immunity to manipulation through external stimuli, and the more there is of independent reflection and inspiration the stronger is the resistance to impression through the senses.

[24] In *The Rains Came* Louis Bromfield shows the degree to which the Western democracies have "come to be the propagandists par excellence" and so taken on ideological features.

[25] George Orwell has unforgettably portrayed the omnipresence of the dictator in his *1984*.

[26] We are thinking of the banners everywhere displayed on buildings, in shop-windows, and along the streets in Communist countries.

This is what leads Simone Weil rightly to observe: "Propaganda is not directed toward creating an inspiration: it closes, seals up all the openings through which an inspiration might pass; it fills the whole spirit with fanaticism." [27]

Developed personal fellowships accordingly are atomized. The collective is not a fellowship at all but a conglomeration of unrelated particles no longer connected to one another by any norms. Paradoxically, the collective is just another form, the collective form, of isolation. The members of the collective, unrelated to one another as persons, have in common only that sphere which is below the level of the ego, namely, the nerves. There is a certain homogeneity only because their nervous systems are all affected by the same influences and permeated by the same stream of propaganda. Unlike personal fellowship, however, this homogeneity does not establish any solid bond. It persists only so long as the nerves are being artificially stimulated from without. The moment the current is turned off, the artificial facade of ostensible fellowship crumbles. The collapse of National Socialist ideology is the great historical example of this. Convictions can usually survive disasters. But when the power of suggestion ceases to operate the result is a disenchantment which plunges the victim into a vacuum and shatteringly reveals the centrifugal tendency which was secretly operative within that ostensible fellowship.

A circus crowd is a good example of the atomized homogeneity of which we have been speaking. A host of people varying in age, education, intelligence, wealth, and persuasion will tense up, breathe, relax, and applaud as one under the stimulus of the high-wire act with its taught drama and rolling drums, only to disband a moment later as isolated individuals bearing never a trace of the artificial fellowship which had so recently bound them together — without ever really binding them together! Such is the sham fellowship produced by ideological tyranny.

Fifth, to sum up: Theologically ideology has the character of idolatry, and that in two respects. First, in ideology it is man who sets himself up as lord and master. He sets his own goals, enunciating them in the axioms of his ideology. He is the one who has the power

[27] Simone Weil, *The Need for Roots: Prelude to a Declaration of Duties Toward Mankind*, trans. Arthur Wills (New York: Putnam's, 1952), p. 187.

THE PRAGMATISM AND IDOLATRY OF THE IDEOLOGIES

both to fix and to realize these goals. At one and the same time he is both the inaugurator and the functionary of the forces of life. He has a will to power, and what he wills he wills not in the name of something above him but only in his own name. This is idolatry. Not only does man contest the existence and authority of the true Lord of all, he even usurps His place.

The idol made by man has no power to judge: it cannot call in question the one who made and worships it. For a reality which is ultimately identical with me cannot of course call me into question. The class or collective in which man objectifies himself, in which he finds himself to be reflected in macrocosmic form, in which he sees himself as lord of all, such a class or collective cannot call man in question because it is bone of his bone and flesh of his flesh. The idol is innocuous.

This is why the false prophets of the Old Testament and all idolaters are always known by the fact that they have innocuous messages. They bring good tidings alone, whereas the true God is proclaimed by his servants to be the Judge of history, who makes himself known as an adversary in messages of judgment.[28] It is for this reason that the gospel is always bound up with the Law and with its challenge. For the gospel is the good news that the divine opposition has been overcome by God himself. It is for this very reason that the gospel forever calls in question Christianity itself. It is its inner disquiet. The gospel is that which prevents Christianity from becoming merely a religious component of this world, an item fully integrated into the cultural inventory, or even an ideology. Dostoevski's "Grand Inquisitor" is the classical example of how the gospel always stands opposed to the perilous attempts made again and again to pragmatize Christianity.[29] The gospel is what keeps Christianity from degenerating into an ideology.

The second mark of the acute idolatry of ideologies consists in the fact that here a creaturely reality is illegitimately elevated to the rank of the creator. In the case presently under discussion the creaturely reality involved is the material base of history, which is

---

[28] I Kings 22:15 ff.; Isa. 23:9 ff; 28:7; Jer. 2:8, 26; 5:31; 6:13-14; 23:8, 16-17, 25; 28:1 ff.; Ezek. 13:1 ff.; Mic. 3:5 ff. Cf. Otto Procksch, *Theologie des Alten Testaments* (Gütersloh: Bertelsmann, 1950), pp. 131 ff.

[29] See Fyodor Dostoevski, *The Brothers Karamazov*, trans. Constance Garnett (New York: Macmillan, 1948), pp. 253-272.

regarded as the ultimate source of everything else and is endowed with pseudodivine qualities. Such a divinization of the creaturely always carries with it the seeds of its own dissolution. For a creaturely entity cannot have binding authority over other creaturely entities; that would carry it quite beyond its appropriate sphere of action. "Matter" is a creaturely entity which cannot envelop such other creaturely entities as "spirit" or "person" anymore than Idealism's divinized "spirit" can embrace – or bind – the material bases of existence.

The course of the various world views over the centuries can be interpreted in terms of a world which at any given time is seen to stand under the aegis of a particular theme. Because this theme has been enunciated by man, it is nothing but a creaturely entity. Though absolutized by man, it is still unable to subordinate to itself the other spheres of creation. The very attempt to do so drives them to revolt. When individuality is deified in terms of personality, the social forces revolt. And when the collectivity is deified, individualism rises up in rebellion. What is often called the law of the pendulum in history, or the polarity of thesis and antithesis, is simply the structure of the rhythms of the historical process as these are set in motion by idolatry, i.e., by false absolutization. The idol, as deified creature, disrupts the organism of the creaturely. The members, which can be directed and integrated only by the head, fall apart and run amok when one of them tries to take over the function of the head. A member may suffer from elephantiasis but that does not make it a head. And members left without direction soon rise up in revolt.

To the degree that history is a history of absolutizations, it is also a history of revolutions, of hostile uprisings against the pseudo absolutes which claim lordship. Creation stands together when it stands over against its creator. It is ruptured when it is compelled to accommodate within itself the distance which can only obtain between creator and creature.[30] The ideologies form part of this history of idolatry. Hence they do not fall outside the sphere of the history of revolt. They are in fact its most flagrant example. For they not only have the form of a confession, they also raise a claim to power – and are armed with an unparalleled machinery to enforce this claim.

[30] I have dealt with this law of rebellion in my book *Der Glaube der Christenheit* (4th ed.; 1958), Chapter 21.

5.

The Relation of Ideological Tyranny
to the Authoritarian State

Revelation 13 as a Model of Ideological Tyranny

We now return to the question with which we began this section, the question as to how the ideological tyranny of today is related to the authoritarian state of older times. We recognize at once that, while there is a clear line between the older authoritarian state and modern democracy, so that Paul's statements in Romans 13 may indeed be applied to the modern democracies, there is no such link with the ideological tyranny of the twentieth century. Applicable to a state thus controlled by totalitarian ideology is not Romans 13 but Revelation 13.

Revelation 13 stands in antithetical correlation to Romans 13. Though it uses mythical materials, the actual historical background is clearly that of imperial Rome, a state which — since it regards itself not merely as a state but also as a religious institution dispensing salvation — displays unmistakable ideological and totalitarian features. The question thus arises as to the degree to which this interpretation of Rome may be applied to the understanding of modern ideological tyranny without doing violence to the historical setting of the particular passage.

A first point in reply is that Revelation does not describe the Roman Empire after the manner of a chronicle. What it offers is a theological interpretation. But to interpret a historical phenomenon theologically is to understand it in such a way as to show its significance as a typical "case" in the history with God.

This history with God is the movement of the divinely created world between the fall and the judgment. It is thus a story of repeated preservation and revolt, a history of the orders and their repeated perversion. Whereas Paul interprets the Empire in such a way as to disclose in it the features of a provisional order of divine preservation, Revelation sees this same Empire from a different angle. Here the state throws off its provisional character, its commission, its relativity, and proclaims itself to be definitive, absolute, lord by its own grace.

Now the state as such is undoubtedly capable of such self-proclaimed emancipation. The particular circumstances which obtain at a given time merely serve as an occasion. That to which they gave rise accordingly has within it tendencies of a supratemporal nature. What is involved therefore is really an original model that presses for repeated manifestation in succeeding periods. It is probably because of this supratemporal character of his particular historical model that the author of Revelation borrows terms and figures from Near Eastern mythology and from the emperor cult.[1]

It is wrong to suppose that a statement must *either* be mythological *or* have reference only to the concrete political situation of the particular period in question. The falsity of such an alternative becomes apparent the moment the particular "case" is regarded as a model that can be continually repeated, and consequently is just one manifestation of a law which obtains in the history with God. The law involved here is not the law in the "members" of the individual (Rom. 7:23); it is the law in institutions.

The mythological language of Revelation is thus a stylistic reflection of a particular understanding which affirms the presence of the supratemporal in the particular temporal phenomenon being analyzed. In this connection we are reminded of the neat definition of myth by Nicolas Berdyaev: "Myth is no fiction, but a reality; it is, however, one of a different order from that of the so-called objective empirical fact. Myth is the story preserved in popular memory of a past event . . . [it] transcends the limits of the external objective world, revealing a subject-object world of facts." [2]

From this standpoint we are justified if in the model depicted by the author of Revelation we look for those characteristic features which we have seen to be the hallmarks of ideological tyranny. Among these may be mentioned the self-absolutization of a creaturely

---

[1] Think, e.g., of the beasts (Rev. 13:2, 11 ff.) and of the mythological significance of the sea as a sea of nations (Rev. 13:1), etc.

[2] Nicolas Berdyaev, *The Meaning of History*, trans. George Reavey (London: Bles, 1949), p. 21. For how this applies to Revelation see Oscar Cullmann, *The State in the New Testament* (New York: Scribner's, 1956), pp. 72-73.

phenomenon and the resultant idolatry; the reduction of the human spirit to a mere instrument for the practical exercise of power (propaganda, slogans); the establishing of the state as the secular antichurch; and the depersonalization which turns anthropology into zoology. These features will clearly appear in the five points here to be considered.

First, that the beast is said to rise up out of the sea (Rev. 13:1) is a mythological way of saying that it has its starting point in the depths of the world and that the direction of its movement is upward from below. There is a demonic kind of contradiction between the beast's origin from below on the one hand, and on the other its speaking with authority as from above, its adornment with the insignia of divine power (horns and diadems), and its ability to make fire rain down from heaven (Rev. 13:13). In this coming up out of the sea there is both a reference to something contemporary and a symbol of something supratemporal. On the one hand, the sea lies to the west, where Rome is. In this sense, there is expressed a specific historical and geographical actualization of the Antichrist. On the other hand, the sea from which the satanic beast rises and on whose shore it stands (12:17) is at one and the same time both a mythological concept for the sea of nations and a symbol for the depths or the bottomless pit (11:7), for the coming which is from below.

That which in this figure purports to be more than mere world, that which dominates men totally — i.e., both politically and religiously — and ascribes to itself divine attributes, thus derives from the depths of the world. What is involved here is a demonic inversion of creator and creature. Right down to the last detail it represents a seductive imitation of God, and hence an "abysmal phenomenon" in the fullest sense of the word.

Because this is a typical event, however, a "case" within the history with God, the power of this totalitarian state does not fall completely when the tyrant or emperor falls (13:3, 12; 17:8). It may receive mortal wounds, but the system recovers because it is merely representative of an original figure, a primal tendency in the history of revolt. Wounds of the system may impair a particular institutional or individual representation of it but they do not affect the root. Seen from the outside, what transpires is a kind of resurrection from the dead.

Actually though it is another instance of the theological imitation of divine reality, an "anti-Christian parody." [3]

Second, the state set up by this beast is bestial as regards the way in which it exercises its power. It can be described only in terms of wild beasts: the leopard, bear, and lion (Rev. 13:2). Moreover the list of animals ties in with the symbolism of Daniel 7, where the four beasts signify four kingdoms. But even as geography is mythically transcended, so also is zoology: the wild beasts are merely vassals of the dragon (Rev. 13:2).

Thus the state has become the representative of a chaotic and inhuman power, the perpetrator of terror and deceit. It is no longer a power commissioned for the sake of order; it is a revolt against all order. It is organized chaos, though it gives the impression of order by the strictness of its organization. By regulating and regimenting all things (13:7, 16-17) and in many other ways it disguises its real nature.

The bestial and inhuman form of this exercise of power degrades those dependent on it to the level of mere objects. They are no longer persons participating in the affairs of state; they have become mere functionaries. They can do nothing on their own initiative, as personal subjects; they cannot even buy or sell (13:17). They operate wholly under orders. They have no individuality. They are defined exclusively in terms of their functions within this state. They are "characterized" by nothing — not even their humanity — but the marks (charagma) they receive from the state (13:17; 14:9).

Here again may be seen a devilish imitation of the manner in which God characterizes his people. For God too "marks" his people. Paul bears on his body "the marks of Jesus" (Gal. 6:17), and the 144,000 have the "Father's name written on their foreheads" (Rev. 14:1). But this marking from above confers freedom and makes men to be persons,[4] whereas the characterization from below plunges into bondage and inhumanity.

Third, the beast demands worship. It claims to be the ultimate power. It pretends to be God and diverts worship from God to it-

[3] The term is from Heinrich Schlier, "Antichrist: On the Thirteenth Chapter of the Apocalypse of St. John," *Principalities and Powers in the New Testament* (New York: Herder and Herder, 1961), p. 78.

[4] Matt. 17:25-26; John 8:36; Rom. 6:18; I Cor. 9:1 ff.; Gal. 4:22 ff.; I Pet. 2:16.

self. As the object of a false belief, it uses the binding power of faith to extend its own power. It has itself venerated in the form of an image (13:14). It utilizes the power of suggestion inherent in symbol and pseudoreligious ceremonial, in order that its rule may not stop with a terror-based domination of the externals of life but extend into the very souls of men. It "ideologizes" everything. There is nothing one can do, not even such ordinary operations as buying and selling, without serving its ideological power (13:17), without taking sides either for or against it.

Thus does the beast achieve a total presence. There are no spheres outside its reach. And here again what is involved is an imitation of God, this time of his omnipresence. Here again it is a case of parody. When those who succumb to its ideology ask: "Who is like the beast, and who can fight against?" (Rev. 13:4) there is the suggestion of a diabolical parallel to the attempts of man to oppose God (Dan. 5:23; 11:36; Ps. 109:3; Acts 5:39) — or to the devout question of the righteous: "Who is like thee, O Lord, among the gods?" (Exod. 15:11), or to the cry of thanksgiving: "O Lord, who is like thee?" (Ps. 35:10).

Cultic and political ceremonial is the mark of a state which seeks more than mere rule by outward terror. They represent the state's takeover of old liturgies under new rubrics. Indeed they become the instrument of its ideological power.

Fourth, this concentrated application of totalitarian power does in fact accomplish incredible things (13:13-14), things which are regarded as miracles, disruptions of the laws of nature. One may see yet another expression of the pathos of this autonomous power in the presumption that the natural laws of genetics can be amended to include the thesis on the inheritance of acquired characteristics. In the field of literature too authors have repeatedly made reference to this passage in describing the capacity of anti-Christian power to accredit itself by miracles, be they social miracles [5] or the miracle of international peace.[6]

The one who wields ideological power thus makes himself to be an

---

[5] Cf. Selma Lagerlöf's novel *The Miracles of Antichrist*.

[6] See, e.g., Vladimir S. Solovyov's *A Short Story of Antichrist*, which is given in a slightly abbreviated version in S. L. Frank (ed.), *A Solovyov Anthology*, trans. Natalie Duddington (London: SCM, 1950), pp. 229-248.

idol: [7] the emperor accepts such titles as *divus Augustus, dominus ac Deus, potens terrarum dominus*. The inscription from Tegea speaks of "the sixty-ninth year of the first parousia of the god Hadrian in Greece." Christians too may have noted and referred to this parallelism between the parousia of Christ and that of the emperor.[8] Indeed, this may have been what caused the seer to speak of the faithfulness and alertness of those who are not guilty of confusing the two (13:9-10; 14:4-5).

Fifth, the parallelism goes further. In Revelation 13:11 we read of the rising of a second beast. This second beast is related to the first in that it exercises the authority of the first (13:12). But it is also distinguished from the first in that it has no power of its own. It is merely an instrument. Its impotence (again in devilish imitation of the figure of Jesus Christ) is expressed in the fact of its similarity to the lamb. Hadorn [9] rightly sees here an allusion to the false prophets criticized in Matthew 7:15, who "come to you in sheep's clothing but inwardly are ravenous wolves." Satan "disguises himself as an angel of light" (II Cor. 11:14); he dons the mask of ancient symbols in order to turn their meaning inside out, transforming it into its very opposite. He knows the power of the image and uses it accordingly, either by cloaking himself in old images — such as that of the lamb — or by creating new ones (13:14). Under the mask of the lamb, however, it is really the dragon which speaks (13:11).

It speaks! This is a reference to the way in which the second beast exercises authority in the name of the first: it speaks in the other's name. Even a scholar like Hadorn, who keeps so closely to the historical background of Revelation without looking for modern applications, takes upon his lips the modern word "propaganda" to describe the function of this second beast.[10]

[7] See Schlier, *op. cit.*, pp. 80 ff.

[8] The parallelism in technical language between the cult of Christ and the cult of Caesar is extensively demonstrated in concrete detail in Adolf Deissmann, *Light from the Ancient East: The New Testament Illustrated by Recently Discovered Texts of the Graeco-Roman World;* 2nd English ed.; trans. Lionel R. M. Strachan from the 4th (1923) German ed. (New York: Doran, 1927), pp. 338-378; see esp. p. 372.

[9] See D. W. Hadorn, *Die Offenbarung des Johannes* ("Theologischer Handkommentar zum Neuen Testament" [Leipzig: Deichert, 1928]), XVIII, 144.

[10] *Ibid.*, p. 143.

It is like the first beast in having a great mouth (13:5-6).[11] At any rate this second beast, which has been called the prophet of Antichrist, and the state priest, has the special task of using the word in the service of the state tyranny. This is what gives it its relationship to spirit, albeit a perverted relationship. It has a task wholly in keeping with the ideological state, namely, the task of imparting spirit to man's spirit, of taking over at the level of imagery the imagination, mind, and will of those dependent upon it (13:14-15). The image involves the power of suggestion and of terrifying constraint. It has spirit. It has the power of speech (13:14-15). It is omnipresent, a matter of fateful necessity (13:16-17).

Its task, then, is to complete the external terror by inner conquests. What would otherwise be only a limited domination by force, exercised apart from spirit, speech, or power of persuasion, is transformed by this second beast into a total domination of the whole man. Here, then, is the prototype of totalitarianism, in which may be seen quite clearly and legitimately the lines of the modern ideological tyranny.

From what has been said on these five points it is no wonder that this New Testament model of ideological tyranny has always stimulated the imagination and been instrumental in shaping various depictions of the totalitarian ruler. This has happened not merely when an actual historical figure such as Hitler or Stalin has been interpreted in terms of this pattern in Revelation, but also in less turbulent periods of history when totalitarian figures have been imaginatively conceived along lines which are simply an extension of the apocalyptic outline. Indeed, such portraits have often come to be regarded as truly prophetic, when situations subsequently arose which were actually comparable to those originally portrayed.

Thus Jung-Stilling has an astonishing description of this kind: "He [the man of sin who will be king] will set himself up in the temple of God and seek to gain dominion over the whole world, partly by force and partly by political means. . . . He will exalt reason above everything, and his own reason will be his god, which all must worship and adore in him. Moreover, he will introduce a public cult

---

[11] Schlier suggests that the haughty (RSV) or great (KJV) things ($\mu\epsilon\gamma\acute{a}\lambda a$) attributed to his mouth, the mighty speeches and elevated words, may again be an allusion to the imitation of the "mighty works" ($\mu\epsilon\gamma a\lambda\epsilon\hat{\iota}a$) of God extolled in Acts 2:11. See Schlier, *op. cit.*, p. 79.

or worship, which will inevitably be military in character. . . . He alone will always be right; he will be a man who opposes both God and men." [12]

We thus maintain that the tyrannical state of Revelation is not really a state at all, because it misses the very point of statehood. So far from regarding itself as a provisional order set up by God to do emergency service, it actually usurps for itself the authority of God himself.[13] Such a state cannot by any stretch of the imagination be coupled with democracy as if they were both in some sense direct relatives of the legitimate authoritarian state.

Because the ideological tyranny is not a state, but an antichurch, Luther's doctrine of the two kingdoms cannot be applied to it. For the heart of this doctrine is the insight that the world and its representatives (e.g., the state) know themselves to be "only" world. This fact is very important as regards the proclamation of the church in the totalitarian state. Those who attempt to find in Luther's theology a parallel to the statements of Revelation, and to align his view of authority with this totalitarian and demonic perversion of authority, invariably come up against his many warnings against confusing the office of emperor with the office of bishop. The former is restricted to the temporal sphere of ruling over bodies, and must under no circumstances claim authority over souls. The emperor's sphere is solely that of the *second* table" of the Law, beginning with the commandment about honoring parents. "He cannot be above it, unless the devil leads him . . . he has no business in the first table . . . for here God alone rules." [14] "The soul is not under the authority of Caesar." [15]

At this point the two kingdoms must be kept distinct. The temporal kingdom is *only* world. It must not take on sacral significance or equip itself with the dynamic — or, as we might say today, the fanaticism — of a religious sense of mission. It must not become an idolatrous imitation of the kingdom of God, a pseudo church.

---

[12] These excerpts from Jung-Stilling, *Erster Nachtrag zur Siegesgeschichte der christlichen Religion* (1805), pp. 95 ff., are taken from a fuller quotation cited in Schlier, *op. cit.*, p. 83, n. 11.

[13] The fusion of the sacral and administrative institutions was a guiding principle in the provincial organization of the imperial period. See Theodor Mommsen, *Römische Geschichte* (1927), VIII, 318.

[14] *LW* 41, 248.

[15] *LW* 45, 111.

The danger in this respect was particularly great during the Turkish wars. For the Turk was not just an enemy of the empire in a political sense. He was also a pagan who would extirpate Christianity if he were victorious. The emperor was thus tempted to regard his war against the Turks both as a normal war of defense and also as a religious crusade. In the name of Christianity, not merely of the beleaguered nation, he would fight and beat back not just the national enemy but the Antichrist!

But this, for Luther, was a dangerous error. For in the first place the church's task is not to maintain itself by force but to undergo the suffering of the cross; hence the kingdom of God can be neither extended nor defended by weapons, except to the detriment of the church in respect of its task and its promise. In the second place, it would mean that the temporal kingdom would be overstepping its bounds; so to overestimate human power, particularly as represented in the emperor, would be to exalt it religiously to the point of idolatry — to the hurt of the state as well.[16]

This is why Luther has a passionate interest in distinguishing between the two kingdoms, and between Law and gospel. Obliteration of the distinction leads to falsification on both sides.[17] If we take what Luther regarded as an overextension and follow it backward as far as Revelation 13 and forward to the modern totalitarian state, we discover what all three forms of perversion have in common. In the first place, the state goes beyond its lawful control of body, goods, and the externals of life to claim the whole man. In the second place, to accomplish this self-absolutization it uses an ideology which is pragmatic and which has as its goal the enhancement and extension of the state's own power. Within its own pragmatic sphere this ideology can assume a variety of forms. It can make use of contemporary myth, as in Revelation 13. It can command what passes for science, as in Communism. It can either make use of existing religious institutions or else synthetically construct spiritual edifices of its own, as in National Socialism. It can even use the gospel itself, as did the crusades ideology in Luther's judgment. Christianity too can

[16] "The state has always been made a hell by man's wanting to make it his heaven." Friedrich Hölderlin, *Hyperion,* trans. Willard R. Trask (New York: New American Library, 1965), p. 44.

[17] See pp. 371 ff. below where in speaking of the crusades we have more to say about how Luther guards against letting the state overstep its limits.

become an ideology, and be used to maneuver men into bondage instead of setting them free in the truth.

The Demonism of Ideologized Christianity

The ideologizing of Christianity itself is perhaps the most exaggerated form of the demonic in history. For in it the demonic law of imitation reaches its climax. Here the abuse of the image of the lamb (Rev. 13:11) is complete. For whereas the secular state tyranny only borrows and adapts to its own use certain religious structures (e.g., symbols and secular liturgical forms) – as a kind of sheep's clothing (Matt. 7:15) – the Christian theocracy takes over for its own purposes the inner substance of these structures, the message itself. Like Satan in the wilderness (Luke 4:1-13) it does not merely speak with religious fervor; it fervently speaks the very word of God, for purposes of thereby promoting its own interests. The ideologizing of Christianity is the most dangerous of all the various perversions of the state, as may be seen by an examination of that which is most alarming about it.

Christian faith by its very nature is possible only within the framework of a decision. The decision not to believe, such as is made in avowed atheism or in the militant anti-Christianity of the ideological state tyranny, is at least a genuine decision! The ideologizing of Christianity, however, is a monstrosity inasmuch as it evades this decision. Actually it obscures the decision character of what is involved so that the decision is made only indirectly, unknowingly, and in a covert manner.

For what the ideologizing does is to make Christianity susceptible of use even by unbelievers. The theologically unguarded but piously intended statement of Kaiser Wilhelm I, that "religion must be kept alive for the sake of the people,"[18] could also be uttered by someone who was not a believer. The Kaiser himself was a Christian, and his reference was only to the political effects of personal faith. It is quite possible, however, for men to assert on a purely pragmatic basis that faith makes men more docile, easier to rule. Faith can indeed be used as an "opium of the people." With its hope of the hereafter it makes the misery of the present more tolerable, thus relieving the

---

[18] The words are inscribed in an altar Bible in the Evangelical church at Altwasser.

62

ruling class of the duty to initiate reforms. It can even induce fanaticism by telling men that what is at issue in their particular social reform or their particular war is actually the cause of God. Thus it is that faith can be exploited, even by those who do not themselves believe.

In his *Pictures of Travel* (1828) Heinrich Heine appropriately castigates such a pragmatic use of religion: "This religion [Christianity] is at bottom utterly and entirely wanting in them [the Berliners]. . . . But as they know that Christianity is necessary in a State, so that the subjects may be nicely obedient, and so that people may not steal and murder too much, they endeavor with great eloquence to at least convert their fellow-beings to Christianity," though to practice it themselves would give them "too much trouble," so they dispense with that.[19]

In such a case there is no overt opposition to the faith, as when an anti-Christian decision is made. Faith is, in fact, affirmed; a Christian standpoint is adopted. But inwardly there is no real faith. The political unity of faith is merely affirmed from without. A relative allegiance is cynically given to that which in terms of its own self-understanding is absolute.

In this sense one may say that the idea of "Christian civilization" has become an ideological slogan, a battle cry. It was not this originally, and still is something more than this. But by and large this is what it actually is today. It is a counterideology to the spirit of the East. The outlook therein expressed might be stated as follows: For want of a militant ideology which can match that of the East, we will hark back to the values of the Christian tradition in order to find a measure of unity in them.

There are two variations of this outlook. There is first the cynical form, which is concerned only that the West should maintain itself politically (along with its standard of living!); it "uses" Christianity as an ideological bedfellow — without actually making true and real use of it — by simply commending it to others as a cohesive factor. Then, there is also the liberal variation. The distinctiveness of the liberal view is that it involves a personal stance — though not un-

---

[19] Heinrich Heine, *Pictures of Travel: Italy*, Part III: *The City of Lucca* (Chapter XII) ("The Prose and Poetical Works of Heinrich Heine," trans. Charles Godfrey Leland [20 vols.; New York: Croscup and Sterling, n. d.], VI), 304.

reservedly – within the sphere of Christian influence; Christianity is not intended exclusively "for others." The thing in question here, though, can be called Christian only in a secondary sense.

By secondary Christianity [20] we mean those ethical and social attitudes which are commonly evoked as by-products of Christian faith, such things as the worth and dignity of the individual, regard for one's neighbor, the fostering of personal contacts in the name of love, respect for the basic orders of being, the sense of authority, as well as such virtues as humility and loyalty, justice and honesty, etc. We call this "secondary Christianity" because the reference is not to Christian faith itself, but to certain derived phenomena of which faith is no doubt the *sine qua non* even though the phenomena themselves can continue on for a time without it, like a mummy which keeps its shape even after the life has gone out of it, or a shell which outlasts the turtle that carried it.

This second or liberal attitude toward Christianity is certainly not cynical like the first. After all, it does not remain aloof but aligns itself with it. However, it is still ideological, for its concern is not that faith should be present for God, as an end in itself, but that faith should exist for men or for society, as a means whereby they may be enabled to exist. Faith is important – and is acknowledged – only to the degree that it creates socially or ethically productive values. It is acknowledged to be a means only because the ends that it serves are acknowledged. Once faith has completed its productive work it can, like the moor who has discharged his obligation, just pass away. Faith is consequently a means which renders itself superfluous the moment the ends have been achieved. Inasmuch as one subscribes to the ends, he need not be cynical or have a bad conscience about using the means. Indeed, this very attitude is conducive to "tolerance"; after all, other forms of faith can also lead to the same ends, like the rings of Lessing's *Nathan the Wise*.[21] It is this very attitude, however, that makes of faith an ideology, an instrument of social and ethical cohesion. The characteristic sign which indicates the presence of ideology in this non-cynical variation is

[20] The term is adapted from Hans Freyer's concept of the "secondary system"; see his *Theorie des gegenwärtigen Zeitalters* (Stuttgart: Deutsche Verlags-Anstalt, 1955), p. 79.

[21] Gotthold Ephraim Lessing, *Nathan the Wise*, Act III, scene 7.

that the entire interest centers not in the truth of faith but only in the end which it can serve. This approach obviously misses the point of faith altogether.

The error becomes dogmatically apparent in the reversal of the relationship between indicative and imperative. In Pauline and Reformation theology the imperative, i.e., that we are to actualize ethical values, is a kind of by-product (the result as in a consecutive clause rather than the purpose as in a final clause) of the indicative stipulation that we have died and risen again with Christ and thus are a new creation.[22] But in the ideological misunderstanding of faith this order is reversed. Here the evoking of the imperative, the setting in motion of the tendency to produce values — these are regarded as the real goal.

To be sure, this brings us up against a difficult question, one that the modern church simply cannot get away from: What is a state to do if it would maintain itself in an age of declining values in which generally accepted standards have all but collapsed? In medieval Christendom the prince, whether Roman Catholic or Protestant, could appeal to a sense of values which was everywhere present among his Christian subjects. The modern state can no longer do this. On the other hand, without such a sense of values it cannot even exist except as an institution of naked power. The state, however, has to be more than this, and it has to seek to be more than this. Even the Communist state in the very darkest periods of its history, has sought to be more than this.

But how to accomplish it? Only such a generally accepted sense of values can provide the framework within which authority can exist. Has the state, then, any other option but to call forth of itself this sense of values? And how can it do so except by actually creating values, and so becoming the creator of ideologies?

This pressing question at least explains why there is a trend in our modern world towards the ideological state. It suggests why the prospects of ideological tyranny seem to go up as values decline in the scope of their validity. Like bacteria, ideologies grow only in specific localities. They thrive in a vacuum and in chaos.

This helps to explain too the stategy involved as the ideologies

---

[22] On the indicative and imperative see *ThE* 1, particularly pp. 74 ff.

pursue their policy of expansion. They have as their fixed base a certain institutional consolidation (e.g., that of the Soviet Union). Working out from here they try first to destroy traditional values and orders elsewhere. The psychological groundwork on which this work of destruction proceeds is that of dissatisfaction. They argue that the situation of the working class, social conditions generally, and hence the concrete historical situation, are no longer compatible with prevailing values; and the argument itself helps to undermine the values of which it speaks.

The torch of "dissatisfaction" is set first to the base of the social structure, its material circumstances, and from there – following the law of all fires – blazes upwards to engulf the sphere of values. The act of destruction creates the desired vacuum and necessary chaos in the sense of values to make possible the influx of ideologies.

The ideologies are thus subject to the law of dialectical movement back and forth. They are evoked by the question how a state can maintain itself when it can no longer count on a generally binding sense of values. This question is answered by the ideological creation of values. To be generally binding, however, these values stand in need of unlimited expansion. And such expansion is possible only where propaganda is used to hasten the process of decay and replacement in the values outside the ideologies themselves. It is important to view realistically what this means for the prospects of ideology within the modern world.

But are these really nothing but prospects? Must we not speak rather of the drift toward ideology as an onrushing tide that cannot be stemmed? Ought not Christianity itself accede to being ideologized – on the ground that it would be better for the world to be controlled by a Christian than by a Communist ideology? Would not the world be better off subject to a reconstructed faith which did once come down from above, rather than to the monster of the abyss which rises up from below?

Human Rights between Ideology and the Minimal Norm

Modern states which seek to protect themselves against ideologizing have answered the question whether ideology is inevitable by pointing to what they regard as the residual minimum of a universal sense of values. They use the term "human rights" to describe what they mean by this minimum. Though the concept derives from rationalistic natural law — and is consequently filled with anthropocentric content — one may say that it is indeed a legacy of the Greco-Christian tradition and thus can provide at least provisionally a kind of emergency basis. To be sure, the attempt to base human rights on natural law — indeed natural law itself — will inevitably be regarded with a measure of skepticism on the part of a Reformation theologian.[23] Nevertheless, it must be admitted that there is here an insight which cannot be surrendered, however dubious the wrapper in which it is contained. There are values which stand authoritatively over us, refusing to be brought under our control or to deliver themselves into our hands as mere means.

On December 10, 1948, e.g., the United Nations adopted a Universal Declaration of Human Rights which, as drafted, envisions a host of national and international agreements concerning the rights of individuals and of members of society (the right to work, just reward, personal freedom, etc.); it seeks thereby to create for all the different peoples and cultures a common base, in the sense of a universally binding sense of values. Again, Pope Pius XII defined the basic rights in the sense of natural law as follows: "Furthermore, individuals — each and every one — and families have certain rights and liberties which the State must always protect; which it must never violate or sacrifice to a pretended common good. We have in mind, to cite a few examples, the right to honor and to a good reputation, the right and freedom to worship the true God, the inherently primary right of parents over their children and their children's education. The fact that some recent constitutions have adopted this conception is a happy omen which we joyfully acclaim as the dawn of a renewal of respect for the true rights of man, such as they have been willed and established by God." [24]

It should not be overlooked, of course, that human rights as abstract quantities, cut off from the soil of faith in which they all had their origin, are in danger of withering away. This can take place in two ways. One possibility is that they will be sucked into the stream of

[23] See *ThE* 1, 400 ff.
[24] See the address of Pope Pius XII delivered at Rome August 5, 1950, to delegates from the fifteen countries attending the eighth International Congress of Administrative Societies at Florence. Vincent A. Yzermans (ed.), *The Major Addresses of Pope Pius XII* (St. Paul: North Central, 1961), I, 141.

ideologizing. That is, instead of continuing to accept them as authorities in their own right, as axioms of humanity, men came to believe only in the contribution they make to society – and so distort them pragmatically just as Christianity has been distorted. Every level of faith, even where it is ultimately diluted to the point of complete abstraction, has its practical value. The second possibility is that the vaunted universality presumed to attach to these fundamental rights will have shrunk to the point where it no longer endows them with any binding authority; then the door will have been opened wide to a rudderless capriciousness of action, which may well take the form of capriciousness of *motive* in respect of good or moral action.

Thus there is no guarantee of the constancy of human rights, even though all men should desire them and even though this common will should find expression in written constitutions. For everything depends on the *way* in which men desire them: as ends or merely as means, because they exist or merely because they are useful. There is never any safeguard against a relapse into the pragmatic form of desire. It steals up unawares. It enters under the guise of the familiar terminology. Indeed, the ideologizing process deliberately takes advantage of this cloak. It makes use of imitation. It acts "as if" it were concerned for values, while in fact it subjects values to other ends.

Grillparzer points this out in his well-known saying that mankind is on the slippery slope leading from divinity by way of humanity to bestiality. What he means is that when humanity is severed from the divine it represents merely an interim stage which cannot last, because it has been stripped of its unconditional character and relativized by the capriciousness of the ends to which it is subject, whose field of force is controlled by bestial instincts.

This statement at the same time articulates a devilish temptation to which the Christian church is exposed, the temptation to extol and offer itself as the good soil in which alone these indispensable minimum values – human rights – can be conserved and promoted. Should the church yield to this temptation and attempt to validate itself in terms of its social utility, it will itself become subject to the very ends against whose ideological dominion it is seeking to offer protection. What is important here is that we take a sober and realistic view of the matter and understand that to stem this course of ideologizing and bestializing by strategic means is an impossible undertaking. Even

Christianity cannot do this. Nor should it try. If it does, it will not only fail to salt and conserve the earth; it will, as salt, lose its own taste (Matt. 5:13). Christian varnish — the ideological cloak — is worse than evil itself in unvarnished form.

The Non-Ideological Efficacy of Faith

Christian faith can be effective only in the name of its substance, the Lord in whom it believes, not in the name of some derived or associated ideas. It can also address itself only to the substance of man, i.e., to his heart.

To state the matter negatively, faith cannot be effective by primarily proclaiming and fostering Christian social orders and the values which sustain them. This would be to put the cart before the horse. The preaching of Christian faith aims at the conversion and transformation of the heart, at having a man seek first the kingdom of God (Matt. 6:33). The changing of the world is promised only to him who himself changes. It can take place only as a by-product, and only for him whose first and real concern is for the kingdom of God.

The renewal of faith proceeds from within. It moves from the indicative of my own history with God to the imperative of my dealings with my neighbor, and finally to the matter of institutions. It goes without saying that the Christian must have in view also this final stage of the process of renewal, a process which begins without his doing and yet is also a task laid upon him. If this were not so, there could be no such undertaking as Christian ethics. In the actualization process, progress or advance (*proficere*) and completion or fulfillment (*perficere*) can rightfully take place only in a perpetually new beginning (*incipere*), an unending return to the substance.[25]

The Christian's action in the world is a sallying forth which proceeds from the inner lines and always returns to the same starting point. Ideologized Christianity, on the other hand, has in view only the strategic purpose which the sortie will serve. It loses the backward connection. Being thus untrue to itself, it becomes untrue also to the very goal for which it sacrifices itself. It becomes a net cast over men from without to bind them, a net from which they will break

---

[25] On these concepts of Luther, see Rudolf Hermann, *Luthers These 'Gerecht und Sünder zugleich'* (Gütersloh, 1930), pp. 234 ff., and *ThE* 1, 97 ff., 120 ff., and 180, n. 3.

free because it is threadbare. The face of the new creature is replaced by a Christian mask which will be put off as soon as the face beneath has outgrown it.

Gregory of Nyssa, in his treatise addressed to Harmonius, "On the meaning of the Christian name and profession," [26] tells a story which satirizes this kind of Christianity which is simply put on like a mask and does not control the heart as a living experiential faith: A traveling showman trained an ape so that it could appear with dancing girls and conceal itself behind a mask in such a way that it appeared to be one of them and could not be recognized as an ape. The act, which was warmly applauded, was rudely ended by the knavish trick of a spectator. He threw nuts on the stage. Immediately the ape's true nature broke through the assumed humanity vouchsafed by the mask. The animal tore off the mask and ate the nuts. The illusion was over.

Gregory points the moral: It is exactly the same with some people to whom Christianity is affixed like an outward mask but who are not apprehended and changed by it in the depths of their person, in their heart. Pressure from without strips off what is only superficially attached and abruptly causes the elemental nature to emerge.

The moral of the story today would be that the mask of ideologized Christianity will be stripped off when crises come. Man will provide himself with new ideologies of his own making which will be more consonant with his elemental nature — and help to vindicate it. With their help man will no longer need to play at the business of being human. He can simply be what he is in his natural state, the state of bestiality, which is the last stage in his emancipation from all norms.

[26] See the text in J. P. Migne, *Patrologiae graece* (Paris, 1844-1866), XLVI, 239-242.

6.

The Concept of Autonomy

Ineluctable Necessity versus Ethical Opportunity

Along with the institutional changes involved in the transition from the older authoritarian state to modern democracy and to the totalitarian state, there is yet another matter which poses a considerable problem for the traditional kind of political ethics. This problem lies on a different plane. It involves a transition, not in the sphere of objective institutions, but in the subjective mode of viewing historical processes.

The way we look at things has changed categorically. We no longer think of history as being controlled simply by decisions of the will (whether on the part of God or of men). Instead we think we discern in history ineluctable forces which are analogous to natural laws. Thus we speak of the autonomics *[Eigengesetzlichkeiten]* of the individual spheres of life, e.g., the autonomy of economics, of politics, of art, and even education. The concept of autonomy implies that within these spheres there are certain immanent principles which so control the processes involved as to make them proceed automatically. As a result, there are within the sphere of these processes no acts of freedom and no ethical opportunities. Thus Carl Schmitt, e.g., argues that the friend-foe relation determines the course of development in politics; the law of supply and demand, of service and reward, determines economics; and the law of the beautiful (art for art's sake) determines art.[1]

Or, instead of understanding the individual spheres as autonomously unfolding entelechies, one may regard the totality of being as standing under a law of necessity. Such a law can of course be viewed in very different ways. It can, e.g., be regarded as the law of the self-development of spirit, which according to Hegel underlies and permeates all

---

[1] See Carl Schmitt, *Der Begriff des Politischen* (Munich, 1932). We shall discuss his views more fully in Chapter 8.

decisions of the will; for Hegel, even the volitional potency of the "world-historical individuals" is simply a function of the "cunning of the idea." [2] It can also be regarded as the law of the self-development of the material foundations of society, as in Marxism; here, as we have seen, the ineluctability of the historical process, which is analogous to natural law, finds expression in the fact that the law of dialectic applies to it and that this law is illustrated in terms of physical images (e.g., the conversion of quantity into quality). Spengler's concept of the inevitability of the processes of the morphology of culture might be mentioned in the same connection.

Now in terms of substance there is, of course, a connection between these two interpretations of autonomy, i.e., between the autonomy which is seen to be at work in a specific sphere and that which is seen to be at work in the totality of life. The connection is that in the latter case, where one inclusive law is assumed to control all of life, a single sphere is lifted high above the rest and declared to be the dominant factor in history. This too is clear in the case of Marxism (and other schools of thought) where the state of production — economic circumstances — constitutes the base of the historical process. Again the autonomous course of all history is derived from the autonomy of one absolutized sphere.

This categorical change in the way we look at historical phenomena simply finds an extreme expression in the several philosophies of history elaborated by the various world views. From the nineteenth century on, however, it has been at work also in the more sober and non-metaphysical views of things. Indeed, it affects everything we think and do as we go about our daily work in the various callings.

Thus the business man, to take only one example, whenever he takes a hard look at his situation, repeatedly says: I simply "have" to do such and such. It is not a question of whether I "want" to or not. The course of my action is determined for me by a law dictated by my competitors. If I follow my scruples and forego certain actions, or if I undertake certain measures economically because ethically they seem to be socially desirable, I will sacrifice my competitive position. Thus in the economic sphere I may exercise an ethical option only to discover the next moment that it was no true option at all but merely

---

[2] See above p. 30, n. 13.

the fleeting appearance of an option. For if I go bankrupt because of my choice, if I am put out of business altogether, then it was no true option *on* the economic level. There I had no real choice — my only choice was to leave that level altogether.

But it is precisely this kind of necessity that seems to suggest that on any given level there may in fact rule an autonomy which, to put it cautiously, restricts the sphere of ethical decision to a minimum. Of what value are the prescriptions of Christian ethics if they cannot be put into practice? Those who view their work from this standpoint recognize at every point that, so far as an ethics of the calling is concerned, this reduction of the areas of freedom is the major problem.

From this we gain an important hint too as to the reason why Luther's doctrine of the two kingdoms has played so devastating a role in the last hundred years.[3] It is not simply a question of its theological content. The doctrine has unquestionably run afoul of this recent categorical change in structure. For the business man, if we may pursue further his inner workings, will probably be forced to conclude that because autonomy rules on the material level of his calling and ethically leaves him no options, he can only migrate to the tranquility of inwardness, his own inner disposition or attitude, and perhaps a very private circle, are the only places left to him where he can still give expression to ethical concerns.

This migration to inwardness seems to have the support of Luther's two kingdoms doctrine. For it is evident that in Luther's eyes love takes on a different form and is differently implemented when it is carried over from the direct I-Thou relation to the spheres of the orders. The judge and the hangman, as Christians, love the delinquent. But they will express that love in different forms (in sentencing and execution) from that whereby a father shows love for his child.

There can be no doubt, then, that Luther had an instinct for the autonomy of the orders even though the concept itself is alien to his thinking. Nevertheless, there can also be no doubt that his teaching is gravely misunderstood if it is used to cloak the migration to inwardness and the simultaneous surrender of the orders to an ethically uncontrolled autonomy. But it is obvious that such a fallacious construction has been attempted. Because theology was too late in unmasking

[3] See *ThE* 1, 359 ff.

this autonomy, and in some cases has not done so even yet, it laid itself wide open to this particular deception — and then tried to place the blame for the fatal error at the wrong doorstep, on the doctrine of the two kingdoms itself.

Because we are here concerned with the vital nerve of all the questions confronting modern political ethics, it is important at this point that we try to work out more precisely this tension between ineluctable necessity and ethical opportunity. We shall do so with the help of three sketches chosen deliberately from widely differing fields. These preliminary sketches, of course, are designed merely to shed light on our main model, political ethics itself. For it is precisely in the political sphere that the problem of autonomy is most sharply crystallized. Indeed, this is why we have decided to include this matter of autonomy among the themes of political ethics.

Preliminary Sketches of Autonomous Processes

The Way to Equality of the Sexes

A certain ineluctability is evident in the course of development leading to equality of the sexes. If for reasons of Socratic method we may play for a moment the role of devil's advocate, we may ask whether there is any point whatever in trying to dig up a Christian answer to the question of equality, by citing, e.g., the statements of the Apostle Paul in Ephesians 5:22 ff. For there seem to be real historical reasons — a kind of causal sequence — leading to the abolition of all the once firmly established hierarchical distinctions between the sexes. The apparent causal processes may be set forth in terms of four stages in the development of society.

The first stage involves the change in the structure of homemaking as a result of industrial development. Luther's Katie still brewed her own beer and spun her own linen. No one would dream of doing this today. The making of essential goods is left to industry, even to the point of mass-produced clothes and precooked foods. Homemaking has thus lost its earlier autarchy. It has been extroverted, as it were, so that women now spend less time at home and have more going on outside.

The second stage involves the resultant concentration of factories in certain places, especially in large cities, which means more time must be spent in getting to and from work. The result is that the husband spends even more time away from home than his wife. He plays a correspondingly smaller role in the upbringing of the children and delegates most of the task to his wife, which again means an extension of her sphere of activity.

The third stage involves the mechanization of production which opens up opportunities for lighter work to unskilled labor. These include jobs that women can do, and frequently want to do — indeed must do when in times of full employment the recruiting of women becomes unavoidable.

The fourth stage which carries forward the emancipation of women is that of the great wars. For one thing, when men are away, women often have to take their places in jobs previously reserved for men, and for understandable psychological reasons, after proving themselves in these jobs, they cannot be drawn back to a life of isolation. Then too, the killing of so many men in war leads to a comparatively large surplus of women. The women who are affected by this, who have no hope of a family life of their own, will obviously seek to escape a meaningless existence as old maids by finding jobs commensurate with their abilities. If the work is not to be limited, or morally degrading, it must obviously carry with it the implication that men and women do have equal opportunity and ought to enjoy the same social privileges as will allow for the exploitation of these opportunities.

While these four are by no means the only factors causally at work in this movement towards equality of the sexes, they are perhaps the most important. The question arises, then, whether this is really a "theological problem" at all, whether it is not rather just a matter of a realignment in society which is mathematically unavoidable and quite unrelated to values. Are not theological postulates in this connection about as meaningless as the attempt to command or forbid lightning in the sky?

In any case one can see already that the problem carries with it a host of theological questions that must be thought through. The question must be asked whether there is room at all for decision in this process and if so at what point. How is involvement in such an autonomy to be assessed ethically? Is it ethically a matter of complete neutrality, in the sense of natural law? Finally, there is the same question we had to ask in respect of democracy: Is it possible to draw a line from Paul's theology of the sexes to the concrete situation in modern society?

Supply and Demand

Our second sketch is like the first in that it too involves an encroachment of sociological viewpoints which strengthen the impression of an automatic process. Sociology – which like psychoanalysis has almost become the vogue in modern scholarship – plays a part not unlike that of historical and literary criticism in the field of theology. Once its problems and questions have been raised, one can no longer engage in the naive pretence that they are not there, irrespective of one's attitude to the specific sociological solutions offered. In all its various forms – and there are naturally many – sociology is characterized by two elements.

First, the individual is not viewed primarily from the standpoint of the scope of his ethical action. He is regarded primarily not as the one who creates and fashions the world but as the object of that world. To be precise, we must emphasize the word "primarily," for sociology certainly does not view society alone as the subject of history, nor the individual as merely its product. It goes without saying that there is a correlation between the individual and society. Within that correlation, however, sociology's main stress is on the latter.

Now this is not necessarily evident in what sociology does and the way it goes about its business. For its first concern is obviously just to inquire into the role of society as such and to investigate the structural connection between society and the individual. It seeks to do that without establishing any a priori scale of values, and without prejudging the significance of social considerations vis-à-vis those of the individual.

Nevertheless, the inquiry can never be wholly neutral. It has to accept, surreptitiously at least, certain normative postulates. Indeed, this points once again to the determinative significance for all that follows of the way one frames his initial question – and hence to the measure of inevitability that also attaches to every scholarly enterprise. The meteorologist has a tendency to explain history in terms of climatic conditions. The biologist does it in terms of his own criteria of observations. And the same is true also of the sociologist.

All heuristic principles have a tendency to become dogmatic. So while it is justifiable to assume that social considerations and sociological criteria provide a key to the understanding of history, there is the danger that in working with this particular key and this particular castle, one will come — perhaps quite unconsciously — to regard it as *the* key.

Thus it sometimes seems that for a sociologist like Helmut Schelsky, for instance, society is determined essentially by sex — though this of course is not said in so many words. He rightly opposes the thesis that masculinity and femininity are fixed quantities, and he rightly points to their social variability, but in so doing he comes awfully close to ascribing thematic rank to the cause of this variability.[4]

The second characteristic of sociology is that the conditions of society under which the individual exists are to a large degree regarded as operating and developing automatically. The extent of the autonomy here assumed may be detected from the almost desperate attempts of such significant sociologists as Schelsky and Arnold Gehlen to find some trace of personal influence, some remaining affinity to ethics.

That there are such attempts is important, for they show that leading sociologists are trying to overcome a one-sided determination by society. This is why we say not that sociology actually makes social conditions the theme of history, but only that it has a tendency in this direction. The sociologists are concerned to make some room for ethics within the sphere of social determinism. This may be seen, e.g., in the statement of Schelsky that the chances for the individual enmeshed in these processes to take a moral decision in his work have been reduced to the point where "only the development of an unbelievably refined moral screen will enable him to meet with high moral sensitivity those minute variables in that tiny part of the total operation still under his control." According to Schelsky we can expect to witness the development of "micromorals," and a "diminution of the possibilities of ethical guidance and direction."[5]

Gehlen too lays bare with an almost merciless precision the auton-

---

[4] See Helmut Schelsky, "Die sozialen Formen der sexuellen Beziehungen," in H. Giese (ed.), *Die Sexualität des Menschen, Handbuch der medizinischen Sexualforschung* (Stuttgart, 1954), pp. 241 ff.; also *idem, Soziologie der Sexualität* (Hamburg, 1955), pp. 23 ff.

[5] Helmut Schelsky, "Zukunftsaspekte der industriellen Gesellschaft." *Merkur,* VIII, 1 (January, 1954), 26-27.

omous structure of social processes. All the more impressively, then, do the remaining ethical possibilities stand out against this background. Every personal relationship, even including that of slavery, can be regulated ethically, but not — as Max Weber has rightly perceived [6] — the rationalized economy which functions mechanically on the basis of established automatic relationships or on the basis of a planned production and consumption. [7]

The autonomy with which developments take place in the economic sphere, as brought to light by the sociologists, may again be presented in terms of stages in a progression. Since the Enlightenment, society has been dominated by the idea that the goal of human development is the greatest possible happiness for the greatest possible number. According to Johan Huizinga, [8] the theme of this development may be described as the "craving for the highest possible and most widely distributed material well-being," for consumer prosperity. Once the initial decision had been taken in favor of pursuing this search — and this is indeed an ethical decision — there arises a circular movement reminiscent of the ineluctability of certain physical forces, which may be described in terms of the following four stages.

First, there arises, in the name of consumer prosperity, the desire for the satisfaction of needs.

Second, the economy charged with producing and distributing the goods which meet these needs inevitably has an interest in seeing to it that the needs are met — but not fully! For if the needs were fully met the market would be flooded [9] and business would slow to a standstill. In a highly industrialized society this could lead to economic disaster. For it would mean that the machinery of production and distribution would be idle; invested capital could not be amortized and hence would become sterile. It would also result in an inability

[6] See Max Weber, *Wirtshaft und Gesellschaft* (3rd ed.; Tübingen: Mohr, 1947), I, 335.

[7] Cf. Arnold Gehlen, *Der Mensch. Seine Natur und Seine Stellung in der Welt* (4th ed.; Bonn: Athenäum, 1950), pp. 338-339.

[8] Johan Huizinga, *In the Shadow of Tomorrow: A Diagnosis of the Spiritual Distemper of Our Time*, trans. J. H. Huizinga (New York: Norton, 1936), p. 207.

[9] The problem has been elaborated at length, particularly as regards the advertising and marketing approaches of the American automobile industry, by Vance Packard in such books as *The Hidden Persuaders* (New York: McKay, 1957); *The Status Seekers* (New York: McKay, 1959); and *The Waste Makers* (New York: McKay, 1960).

to keep pace with technological developments through modernization and investment in new machinery, with the consequent threat of ruin at the hands of one's competitors, e.g., the competition from products imported from abroad.

Third, to open new opportunities of growth and to assure that consumer satisfaction will never be total, business has to awaken new needs and make people want more and more. While insatiable desire may be wrong for an individual, as a collective phenomenon it becomes an economic necessity. Thus it is economically fruitful to arouse a need for social prestige. The man who owns a car accordingly has a higher status than the pedestrian, and the one who owns the newest and biggest model has a higher status than the one who drives a beat-up old jalopy.

It is beyond question that advertising counts on this demand for prestige, and that it seeks to awaken and enhance it. The modern sales approach is psychologically well considered. Its pitch is not that this is the best you can find in terms of your specific need, but that you may not yet have come to a clear awareness of your wishes or systematically measured the full extent of your wants.

Linked with this is the fact, not merely that there is such a thing as sales psychology, but that its approach and procedures increasingly spill over into the sphere of psychoanalysis. Unconscious and submerged desires are brought to the surface of consciousness. Industry fabricates objectifications of the unlimited drive for increasing power, enjoyment, and mastery of life, and what industry thus supplies becomes the consumer's conscious wish, which in turn reciprocally evokes and further enhances the original drive.

In terms of practical economics — which is to say, reduced to the superficial level of symptoms — this means that supply does not merely correspond to a given demand. It also gives rise to the demand. It awakens needs. It is the economic counterpart of sex appeal, and could be called happiness appeal.

Fourth, if happiness consists in the satisfaction of needs — and that was the philosophical starting point — then the more needs one has craving satisfaction, the happier he is. Thus the "logical consequence" — and this in itself represents a truly paradoxical situation for ethics — is a further autonomous development in the ethos of production and distribution, whereby mass consumption is made technically possible through mechanization and automation, which bring down prices, and then as many desires as possible are stimulated to get this mass consumption rolling, which in turn facilitates further mass production. The "ethical" pathos in all of this might be reduced to the formula: In this way we make men as happy as possible while we ourselves do a better business.

If we thus survey the entire process, with all its individual stages and cycles, we see at once that ethical decision enters into it significantly only at the beginning and end. Whereas during the actual course of events — as seen from outside — ethics crops up only in the form of what Schelsky calls "micromorals" and a highly refined "moral screen," at the beginning and the end it is expressly present. It is present at the beginning inasmuch as the Enlightenment concept of happiness involves a decisive ethical judgment concerning the nature of man and how he is to be served. It is present at the end, if we are right, in two forms.

In the first place, it is present in that producer and distributor think they must provide an ex post facto ethical legitimation in terms of the Enlightenment motif for the way they go about satisfying needs and evoking new needs. We serve men, they say, by meeting their needs and by awakening new needs. In order that this may be seen to be a real "service" in the ethical sense, man has first to be understood in a specific way, namely, as the consumer who is made happy by consumption and whose life finds its fulfillment therein.

In the second place, ethics crop up at the end of the process in that the consumer is asked whether he will accept the satisfactions offered and allow for further stimulation of the sense of new need *or* whether he will keep aloof and favor a certain "asceticism." At this point the ethical question is removed to a deeper level. For the choice which the consumer will make here is determined by the prior and more fundamental decision as to what he thinks man is, what he takes to be the meaning and purpose of life, and whether he has adopted for himself the happiness motif of the Enlightenment.

When he sees that he is confronted by this decision — and this is the question posed at every stage of the process — then the beginning and the end of the process coalesce and are present in the "moment" (Kierkegaard) of an ongoing decision. For the question he had to face at the beginning of the process is still there at the end, namely, whether his life is fulfilled by the utmost in consumption — and accordingly depends on the height of his standard of living — or whether the fulfillment of his life is to be sought elsewhere. It is thus that the beginning and end meet at the present moment of a decision which has constantly to be taken.

We maintain that this is an important preliminary finding in our investigation of the place of decision within the autonomous processes of this world. The ethical question thus arises even in respect of the way a man comports himself within these processes, how he comes to terms with them: whether he resists them or lets them take their course, whether he allows them to intensify his own self-seeking or so far as possible turns them to a valid purpose, whether he regards them as a necessity or extols them as a virtue. Even if it is assumed that these processes actually have the ineluctability of natural law, there is still the ethical question whether he hates or loves his fate. In some cases the ethical question is not one of freedom *or* necessity, but of freedom *in* necessity.

The Origins of War

We turn briefly now to the third of the autonomous processes we planned to sketch. This one will also form a transition to the specific form which our problem takes in the political sphere, and which leads finally to the question how far politics as an actual shaping of history — how far man's action on a big scale — is subject to ethics at all. We will illustrate this third process in terms of an ultramodern situation and then in terms of a concept from the political philosophy of antiquity.

The modern illustration is that afforded by the armaments industry. It has been pointed out that in the technological age, and hence in the age of technological warfare, the assembled equipment of war can be protected against obsolescence only by using it, and that the armaments industry itself presses for this use because such use boosts production and profits. In the first instance, it is the state itself which is exposed to this urge as the owner of the equipment. In the second instance, though, industry is exposed to it as the producer of the equipment. The two tendencies are concurrent and thus intensify the pressure.

If we follow the English economist Edwin Cannan in defining man as a munitions-making animal,[10] and thus narrow down to the world of armaments the Marxist thesis that man is a "tool-making" animal,[11] then it would seem indeed that the trend could be regarded as "fate."

But if we eliminate such a prior philosophical determination, then the trend must be regarded primarily as a matter of interests, and its outcome is not a foregone conclusion. (One has only to think of the opposing element of risk, especially in the case of atomic warfare.) Insofar as interests are involved, the ethical question is always posed.

Moreover, it is quite possible to suffer from an optical illusion as regards the armaments industry. Even when war is unleashed because one side presently has the greater war potential, and its weapons might become obsolete – or be too costly to replace, or eventually be surpassed by those of the enemy – the act of war may not at all be due to the autonomous operation of the particular store of armaments. It could be simply a matter of fixing the date for a struggle which is regarded as inevitable anyway or even desirable; only the *date* is determined by the state of the equipment. There could thus be a totally different motivation or impulse behind the war, and the ethical question would be raised by factors other than simply the store of armaments.

In spite of this reservation, however, it must be admitted that the trend which accompanies the armaments industry is rightly to be feared. Our point simply is that this trend seems to fall under the category of temptation rather than that of ineluctable necessity. Complicated though the matter may be in detail, the relevance of the ethical question is thus basically clear.

The second illustration, which belongs directly to the sphere of political ethics, comes from the political philosophy of Plato. In Book II of *The Republic* Plato maintains that the state has an inherent tendency which compels it to go to war.[12] Socrates opens the discussion with Glaucon by asking where the origin of a state is to be sought.

---

[10] Cf. Jakob Schoch, *Der soziologische und tiefenpsychologische Aspekt des Krieges* (Zurich: Orell Füssli, 1955), p. 38.

[11] Karl Marx borrowed the phrase from Benjamin Franklin. See Karl Marx, *Capital;* in *Marx*, trans. Samuel Moore and Edward Aveling ("Great Books," Vol. 50), p. 86.

[12] See Leopold Ziegler, *Von Platons Staatheit zum christlichen Staat* (1948), pp. 56 ff. Augustine refers to this same tendency in *The City of God* iv. 15; cf. Walther von Loewenich, *Augustin und das christliche Geschichtsdenken* (Munich, 1957), p. 23.

Both agree that the state is to be traced back to necessity ($\chi\rho\epsilon\iota\alpha$), the needs of mankind for food, shelter, and clothing. Such needs cannot be met without mutual help and co-operation. The state which arises in this way organizes first only the elemental and precultural needs, and is thus described by Glaucon as a "city of pigs." [13]

But the urge to advance is just as elemental. The most primitive necessities of life "necessarily" came to include sofas, tables, dainties, perfumes, incense, courtesans, and cakes. Thus arises — of itself — the "luxurious state" which far "exceeds the limits of necessity" and hence necessarily leads to war. [14] For "a slice of our neighbours' land will be wanted by us for pasture and tillage, and they will want a slice of ours, if, like ourselves, they exceed the limit of necessity, and give themselves up to the unlimited accumulation of wealth." [15] "And so we shall go to war." [16] Jacob Burckhardt would refer to this as the compulsion to expand without limit in order to "round things off" very nicely. [17]

This autonomous development of society which impels towards war raises again a problem which confronted us already in relation to Gehlen, and which we shall have to discuss more fully later, namely, that the processes involved here are ethically of very different character. As regards both the shaping of these processes and the place one has within them, there is a world of difference between an attitude which approves the trend as "felicity" and one which resists it, seeks to arrest it, and regards it as a "bitter necessity." [18]

At any rate, Plato's contention that the process which leads to war

[13] Plato *The Republic* ii. 372; in *Plato,* trans. Benjamin Jowett ("Great Books," Vol. 7), p. 318. According to U. v. Wilamowitz-Moellendorf, *Platon* (1920), II, 127, the expression is intended to describe the rudimentary character of the primitive state and is not derogatory.

[14] For Plato's teaching on war see Wilhelm Nestle, "Der Friedensgedanke in der antiken Welt," *Philologus,* Supplementband XXXI, 1 (Leipzig: Dietrich, 1938), pp. 28-30.

[15] Plato *The Republic* ii. 373; *loc. cit.*

[16] *Ibid.,* p. 319.

[17] See Jacob Burckhardt, *Force and Freedom: Reflections on History,* ed. James Hastings Nichols (New York: Pantheon, 1943), pp. 115-117.

[18] Augustine notes the ethical issue inherent even in an apparently historical ineluctability: "To carry on war . . . seems to bad men to be felicity, to good men necessity." *The City of God, loc. cit.;* trans. Marcus Dods, *A Select Library of the Nicene and Post-Nicene Fathers of the Christian Church,* First Series ed. Philip Schaff, Second Series ed. Philip Schaff and Henry Wace (Buffalo and New York: Christian Literature Co., 1886-1900), II, 72 (hereinafter cited as *NPF*).

is autonomous does not seem to lift it altogether out of the sphere of values. Indeed, Plato is not trying to pose an alternative between autonomy and ethical affinity at all. For in the *Sophist* he regards the art of war as an "acquisitive art" and derives it from self-interest.[19] Likewise in the *Phaedo* he explains war in terms of the satisfying of human needs.[20] This satisfying of need acquires an ethical dimension from the fact that, while we are impelled to fight the needs of the body, this impulsion arises only because we are already in the service of the body and pledged to care for it. One ethical quality, namely, commitment in service, thus gives rise to another kind of commitment, namely, subservience to ineluctable processes.

[19] Plato *Sophist* 219; in *Plato* ("Great Books," Vol. 7), p. 552. Aristotle too echoes this understanding of war in his *Politics* i. 8; in *Aristotle II* ("Great Books," Vol. 9), p. 450.
[20] Plato *Phaedo* 66; in *Plato* ("Great Books," Vol. 7), p. 224.

7.

The Ethics of Politics in Actual History

Our primary concern in the previous chapter was simply to elucidate the concept of autonomy. Almost involuntarily, however, we repeatedly came up against the limit of the concept where the question
arises whether the autonomies are subject at all to ethics, and whether
they are indeed purely automatic processes, free from all values.[1] We
shall now tarry deliberately at this limit in order to investigate
thoroughly the whole question of whether ethics has any place in the
sphere of autonomous processes. Since our concern is with the problem of autonomy particularly in relation to political processes, and
since we regard politics as an illuminating example, it will be helpful
to be even more specific and to bring out concretely the ethical affinity
of politics by an analysis of two political figures from actual history,
Bismarck and Hitler.[2]

The Case Study Method

We shall begin by sketching the two main methodological considerations which suggest this effort at concreteness. They bring to light the

---

[1] In *Saint Joan of the Stockyards* Bertolt Brecht gives the question an amazing
twist which only serves to underscore the breadth of its scope. In the fifth scene
the packers are decrying the laws of economics which have presumably produced
such widespread unemployment in the packing industry:

> Nothing can be done about crises!
> Unshakeable above our heads
> Stands economic law. . . .

The stock breeders, however, interpret the packers' "hold on our throats" as
"wickedness," at which point Joan breaks in to speak of the ineluctable necessity
of wickedness too. As surely as unemployment deprives of purchasing power so
surely does an egocentric order do away with morals by destroying "moral pur-
chasing-power," and so the ineluctable necessity which springs from injustice goes
merrily on its way ethically untouched. Eric Bentley (ed.), *Seven Plays by Bertolt Brecht* (New York: Grove, 1961), p. 186.

[2] We have already contrasted the two briefly in *ThE* 1, 500-501.

general methodological background of this entire ethics.[3] For at this point our method of speaking in terms of concrete cases will be carried to an extreme and hence put to a critical test.

The first point to be observed is that ethical reflection always runs into its severest difficulties when the problems become concrete. It is at the moment when an ethical norm must be put into practice that it suddenly seems no longer to fit the case. The hypothetical cases which the textbooks take to be typical turn out paradoxically to be rather rare in everyday life.

A textbook case is a practical case – of appendicitis, e.g. – which follows the "classical" course, i.e., proceeds according to its own law. It follows the norms and hence is a "normal" case. But, as we have seen, in medicine as well as ethics the normal case is almost the exception. This is why when one consults the textbooks concerning complications – which are *really* the normal cases – they rarely have anything to say on the very points about which the reader seeks instruction. Their indexes are not inventories of real life but a collection of abstractions wholly incommensurate with life in its manifold fullness.

Thus, in medicine there is no "pure case" if one ailment is accompanied by others. The same is true in ethics. The norm of truth, or of telling the truth, is seldom found as a pure case. Often it is combined with the claims of other norms, and acute conflict can arise. The physician, e.g., in a case of severe illness may either withhold the truth from his patient, or even tell a lie, out of loving pity.[4]

This already suggests why and how the paradoxical fact arises that "normally" there are no textbook cases. In this connection, however, it is not enough simply to say – as many do – that life is more complicated than theory. We must try rather to define precisely wherein the complication consists. It lies in the fact that the spheres of competence of several norms intersect. Thus the two norms of love and truth may both lay claim to the physician, and even at the same time!

This is why the student of ethics, or of medicine or law, has to look beyond the textbook or the book of rules. Two other things are required: first, a hermeneutical concern which can help to establish which norms actually apply in a specific case; and second, an act of decision which ventures to determine the relative weight and merits

[3] See *ThE* 1, 455 ff.
[4] See *ThE* 1, 551 ff., and the whole discussion of compromise in *ThE* 1, 482 ff.

of the various norms and to assume full personal responsibility for whatever aspect of the deed cannot be subsumed directly under a certain norm.

The one who makes a decision, therefore, does not do something customary or routine. He cannot simply take over decisions arrived at earlier in connection with the "pure case." On the contrary, he always stands in the situation of the exception. He is always in some sense alone. He cannot appeal to the textbook. This is one reason why in medicine, law,[5] and ethics there can be no such thing as a recipe book, i.e., a collection of casuistical prefabricated decisions covering all conceivable cases. From ancient times the theme of tragedy has always been that life does not run smoothly, not only in the sense that it calls forth ventures which may sometimes be disastrous, but also in the sense that it knows areas where values are in fundamental conflict.

This would seem to suggest that in certain spheres ethics ought to take the opposite course and proceed, not from norm to case, but from case to norm, indeed to norms! This approach is particularly indicated when one is dealing with areas in which, as in politics, there seems to be both a high degree of autonomy and a host of competing norms.

It is evident that political action contains this complexity to an extraordinary degree. For, in the first place, the larger inclusive order within which political action takes place is so structured that it includes such partial spheres of life as economics, social development, culture, and domestic and foreign affairs. Standing thus a level above them, and representing as it does the whole, the political order is the guiding authority for the several parts. Now the distinction between whole and part, organism and member, is easy to make in theory. But it is by no means easy in actual life. For there is no given hierarchy of parts. Moreover, it is also possible, given a particular world view, that one part may achieve a dominant position and itself become a guiding authority, using the state as its chief executive organ, as in Marxism-Leninism.

[5] This is why in law too there exists the problem of hermeneutics, the task of dealing with a particular case which cannot be subsumed directly under an extant statute. The case must be interpreted according to the "intention" of the framers of the law and in light of the present situation, which is fundamentally different from any they had envisioned. See Konrad Zweigert, "Juristische Interpretation," *Studium generale*, VII, 6 (1954), 380 ff., and Josef Esser, "Die Interpretation im Recht," *ibid.*, pp. 372 ff.

The complexity of political action is to be seen also in the fact that the most varied norms may lay claim to the politician himself. In this dimension the ethical question arises as to how the politician's political responsibility, which must allow for a certain autonomy of politics, can be reconciled with the principles of an ethical outlook. Is ethics confined to the private life of the statesman, or can it determine the business of politics itself? [6]

In view of the complexity posed by this conflict of norms, it is thus advisable to take the opposite approach in our ethical analysis of politics, expounding the concrete case ethically in terms of a specific politician as a model, and thus pursuing the essential, though by no means all the threads in the web of norms. What were the tensions, the conflicts of norms, in the case of a figure like Bismarck, who regarded himself both as a Christian and as a defender of the business of politics?

Here we are confronted at once by a highly complex phenomenon. And when our analysis is done we certainly will not be able to say that as a Christian one must necessarily act thus and so in this or that case. We will see rather that the commission I fulfill is inextricably bound up with the sins I in fact commit. We will see concretely what the doctrine of justification means when it says that our works are in vain even in the best life. We will come to understand that all actions within the estates and callings stand in need of forgiveness.[7] And hav-

[6] We touched upon this question in connection with the white lie in the political sphere, remembering the comment of Frederick the Great: "I hope that posterity will be able to distinguish the philosopher in me from the prince, and the man of honor from the politician." See *ThE* 1, 535.

[7] At this point Luther's doctrine of the estates and callings needs some correction in the light of our better acquaintance with the excesses of secularism. For Luther the estate of, e.g., the politician, judge, or soldier, is a divine commission which one may discharge with a good conscience. The statement, of course, is correct as it stands. The only trouble is that Luther derives these commissions from creation rather than from the emergency measures God has taken in the world after the fall. As a result, conduct within the estates receives too direct and thoroughgoing a justification. In fulfilling my calling within the orders I am simply doing God's will in the secular sphere. Since such action is justified by the divine commission, it does not need forgiveness (cf. *LW* 37, 364). The fact that Luther was thinking primarily in the more personal terms of marriage and parenthood made it difficult for him to see the critical points involved in the more public estates that must operate in a fallen world (cf. *WA* 30 II, 174; *LW* 45, 125; and *LW* 54, 40, No. 289). Implicated in sin according to Luther is not the estate itself (cf. Franz Lau, *"Aeusserliche Ordnung" und "Weltlich Ding" in Luthers Theologie* [Göttingen: Vandenhoeck & Ruprecht, 1933], pp. 107 ff.), but only the misuse of it whereby man seeks to make of it a means of salvation (*LW* 37, 365).

ing seen all this, we will in addition be aware of what a complex structure and conflict of values the politician finds himself in, and in what direction decisions are to be sought in the sphere of politics.

Proper ethical reflection and discussion aims not at providing specific directives for concrete action — which would be to make a man the object of someone else's decisions — but at enabling a man to tackle the decision himself, as a subject, and to act responsibly. To become such a subject, to be able to arrive at his own decision, one must perceive both the substantive and the normative factors which make decision at all possible, and which must be considered in the actual making of a decision.

For this reason, we select at this point a path which begins with the analysis of concrete persons and situations. What is new about such an ethics is not the provision of new and perhaps more modern directives, but the finding of new methods. With this in view we shall analyze Bismarck and Hitler in order to discern the factors which were really at work in their decisions, and hence also the complex web of reality in which they were "caught."

Because this procedure is unusual in theological ethics, it needed the express methodological justification we have attempted to give in Volume 1 on *Foundations*. There the fundamental axiom which pointed us this way was that theological ethics as an academic discipline endeavors to investigate not man's subjective disposition — as in the moral instruction of Kant — but the coincidence of man's subjective disposition (determined by Law and gospel) with the objective structure of reality (determined by creation and the fall).

Our second main methodological consideration at this point concerns the question how a historical figure can be made the subject of ethical discussion. In this regard one has to say that Bismarck is here taken only as a good subject for a case study of ethical problems. This means negatively that he is not the object of a historical investigation in the narrower sense. The individual features to be presented, which may recall the work of the historian, only serve to assist us in following the essential threads in the web of reality to where we can bring out the ethical aspects of vital decisions.

By choosing Bismarck as representative of the "Christian statesman," we are not setting him up as an example to be emulated. In using this particular model we are concerned with factual, not normative, considerations. For while his case may be typical, it cannot be regarded as exemplary, and that for several reasons.

In the first place, the so-called faith of Bismarck, which because of its tension with the autonomy of his political action demands our special attention, is from the human standpoint open to question in many respects, mainly because it is not a constant pole and therefore cannot maintain a steady or equal tension. In addition, it is subject to many theological criticisms. Again, there are many dubious features in the character of Bismarck which make it impossible to idealize him. One need only recall his violence – which inclined him to tolerate only nonentities and tools around him – or his vengefulness in the personal sphere, his thirst for power, or his ambition. These and many other traits seem to rule him out as an example to be imitated in the moral sphere, though they do not permit us to indulge in facile condemnation inasmuch as these negative aspects are also the shadow of his greatness.

The fact that the Bismarck portrait contains dark and dubious features points up another aspect of his excellence as a case study. For when we become aware of these doubtful elements we are protected against a kind of abstraction to which the method of using models might easily lead.

One such abstraction is the much decried idea of the "Christian statesman." We are never merely Christians or merely politicians. We are always also men of a specific time, and a specific social setting, temperament, and heredity. All these things shape and color both our Christianity and our position in politics. Our Christianity, e.g., is fashioned by a churchmanship which is either orthodox or liberal, confessional or influenced by current theological tendencies. My position in politics varies according to whether I come from a conservative or a more radical tradition, whether I live in a liberal or a totalitarian state, and, irrespective of my social standing, according to my own personal character which always affects the way I go about my business.

The historical features of my situation and the given nature of my own being thus belong also to the complex of factors which affect my decisions. The very fact that they are so largely overlooked gives most ethics the pallid aspect of a docetic remoteness from reality.

We certainly do not make our task easier by including these many concrete factors. For we thereby reject the shortcut of simplifying abstraction and refuse to submit our problems to the naive remedies of ethical norms. But it seems to be the true dignity of a theological ethics to be able to renounce such simplification. For the renunciation rests on an eschatological fact, and thus points to a focal sphere of Christian theology. It shows us that even as it is impossible to give concrete directives so it is also impossible to judge.

Why is this the case? All judging is possible only under three conditions: I must know the norms which apply; I must know the character of the reality to be subsumed under the norms; and I must be able to say how far, with respect to this particular reality, justice has been done to these norms. The prohibition against judging in Matthew 7:1 implies a prohibition against maintaining the presuppositions of judgment. Thus I am denied the possibility of being able to fulfill the three conditions on the basis of which the relation of norms to reality may be perceived.

Now it goes without saying that the judge, when he passes sentence, must make an evaluation as to whether the criminal has transgressed the laws and values of society. It is also obvious that the historian must judge which acts of Bismarck were right and which were wrong, and in both cases what traits of character he displayed. But we have to realize that these judgments of the judge and the historian apprehend only a very thin film of reality.

The figure of Bismarck (understood as a model) and the figure of the man who stands accused before the law (again understood as a model) both escape our human judgment and are remitted to God's last judgment. For only here are the spheres of reality in which they find themselves, only here are the presuppositions, talents, and limitations, only here are all the components of their actions really known.

The pictures of the last judgment found in many courtrooms are a reminder of this. They speak of how the earthly courts are superseded, of the relative nature of judicial decisions, and of the fact that at the last judgment both the accused and those who sentence him will stand before the same bench.

A host of methodological considerations thus stand behind our attempt to analyze ethically at this point such figures as Bismarck and Hitler, and in the next chapter Machiavelli and Thomas More. By sharing these considerations with our readers, we may perhaps dispel the notion that what is involved here is simply a collection of illustrations or a literary device to ease the hard work of ethical reflection by the use of anecdotes.

The point of the contrast between Bismarck and Hitler may be stated at once. As a Christian, Bismarck knew of the dubious character of all that he did in his calling as statesman, because he was aware that it was ultimately called in question. Hitler either was not aware of any ultimate accountability or he rejected it; as a result he made the autonomy of politics the criterion of his actions.

This way of stating the problem raises the question whether the two diverse positions represent merely different personal attitudes which belong to the inward and private sphere, or whether these positions are creatively and normatively at work in the political sphere as such. As we shall see, the answer to this question is of decisive importance for the question whether the autonomy of politics is restricted and influenced by ethical positions.

Bismarck the "Christian Statesman"

To work out the problem which here arises in relation to Bismarck, it seems best to consider first the external impression which he made on others, both on his admirers (from whom we have least to learn), and also on his critics, who do not deny that this politician is a Christian.

In adopting this approach, we are not using a mere literary device such as Schiller uses in the opening scenes of, e.g., *Wallenstein's Camp* and *The Piccolomini* where he does not introduce the protagonist of the drama directly but causes him to be seen only in the mirror of his soldiers and surroundings. On the contrary, we have a theological purpose in mind, for this approach leads us at once to the important observation that the external aspect is ambiguous and does not reveal the various levels of motivation, and that there is no such thing as a demonstrably clear portrait of a man in world affairs who is also basically Christian. If there were, ambiguity about, and denials of, his Christianity could not exist from the very outset, almost as a matter of course.

In this respect the criticism of Bismarck's conservative opponents is interesting. Thus Ludwig von Gerlach can write: "We [i.e., we Prussians who are represented by Bismarck's government] exclude the highest ideas from our practical consciousness; this is our most fundamental weakness." [8] Gerlach accuses Bismarck of the "most dreadful error" of not seeing that the sacred commandments of God apply also to the sphere of politics,[9] and admonishes him: "Love for God and man must also be the law of politics even to points of detail." [10] He could not accept "the distinction between private morality and public life," [11] and deeply deplores the fact that the Ten Commandments are intolerable to Bismarck the politician. He can only ask his political friend H. H. von Kleist-Retzow to "preach the catechism" to Bismarck.[12]

The accusation of von Gerlach is that Bismarck is without scruple in politics, that he has no deeper principles, that he is without Christian standards except possibly for his own private life, that he is dominated by an icy opportunism which in its unpredictability is alien to Gerlach and to many other conservatives of the time. In terms of our present study, Bismarck's politics seem, to Gerlach, to present a picture of amoral autonomy. Thus K. v. Bodelschwingh too speaks of Bismarck's "brutal and ungodly power politics." [13]

Having seen something of Bismarck from without, through the eyes of his contemporary Gerlach, we must now try to find out what is concealed behind this rough facade. We shall do so in three steps. We shall first consider Bismarck's personal relation to the Christian faith. Then we shall examine both his considered and his spontaneous utterances on the situation of the Christian in actual history. Finally we shall try to show, not how the two can go together objectively, but how from within, subjectively, in an existing politician, the two may appear to be connected in a personal union.

Bismarck's Personal Relation to the Christian Faith

Bismarck experienced a conscious conversion, of which he often spoke. It came about under the influence of a pietistic Lutheranism

---

[8] Jakob von Gerlach, *Aufzeichnungen aus Ludwigs Leben* (1903), II, 270 (September 8, 1865).

[9] Herman von Petersdorff, *H.H.v. Kleist-Retzow* (1907), p. 371 (Gerlach's letter of May 8, 1866).

[10] Von Gerlach, *op. cit.*, pp. 272-273, 276.

[11] *Ibid.*, p. 278.

[12] Von Petersdorff, *op. cit.*, p. 389.

[13] Gerhard Ritter, "Die preussichen Konservativen und Bismarcks deutsche Politik," *Heidelberger Abhandlungen* (1913), No. 43, p. 146.

and a reawakening among the aristocracy of Pomerania. His inner history we know only from his own reminiscences: "I was already actually quite aged in my twenty-third year — at any rate, far and away more *blasé* than at present; and I regarded myself as quite unhappy, found the world and life in it stale and unprofitable." [14] "I do not know how I managed to keep going in those days; if I had to live now without God, without you, without children, I should not be able to see any reason for not discarding this life like a dirty shirt." [15] "The happy married life and the children God has given me are to me as the rainbow that gives me the pledge of reconciliation after the deluge of degeneracy and want of love which in previous years covered my soul." [16]

Sometimes the almost nihilistic melancholy which darkened his disoriented pre-conversion life, and to which he here refers, can be depicted in almost poetic language: "It is, I think, deeply inherent in human nature — I would say, in the unconscious recognition of suffering and woe on earth, and vague yet mighty longing for better and nobler conditions — that, among people who are not quite easygoing and superficial, the dwelling upon the fragmentariness, the nothingness, the pain, that rule our present life, awakens more response. . . . The thing that in an earthly sense is impressive and affecting, that can ordinarily be represented by human means, is always related to the fallen angel, who is beautiful, but without peace; great in his plans and endeavours, but without success; proud and sad. Such things as there are, outside the province of religion, to stir our emotions, cannot, therefore, be cheerful and happy, but only serve us as a constant finger-post, showing where we may find peace." [17] Thus the basic feeling prior to his conversion was not one of guilt and sin, but of unrest and cleavage which demanded inner satisfaction, which cried out for meaning, purpose, and content in life, and which tried to crowd out the feeling of emptiness by a flight to excess.

[14] From a letter of Bismarck to his fiancée dated February 28, 1847; *The Love Letters of Bismarck*, trans. Charlton T. Lewis (New York: Harper, 1901), pp. 63-64.
[15] From a letter to his wife dated July 3, 1854; H. Rothfels, *Bismarck-Briefe* (Göttingen, 1955), p. 155.
[16] From a letter dated June 19, 1852; *Love Letters*, p. 281.
[17] From a letter to his fiancée dated February 17, 1847; *Love Letters*, p. 42.

The conversion itself, as we learn from the famous letter of entreaty to his future father-in-law and from letters to his fiancée, consisted in the fact that "news of the fatal illness of our late friend . . . tore the first ardent prayer from my heart, without subtle questionings as to its reasonableness. God did not grant my prayer on that occasion; neither did He utterly reject it, for I have never again lost the capacity to bring my requests to Him." [18] From this point on the language of the Bible crops up repeatedly in his letters. Out of this conversion there thus developed a living, personal Christianity, a Christianity which for all its ups and downs — one might say despite all the fluctuations in his consciousness of it — did not ever fail.

In this respect the notes in his daily devotional books are interesting. The remarks and comments increase in times of tension and dwindle in calmer periods.[19] Sometimes these marginal notes establish a direct connection between the word of God and the events of the day, and sometimes — and this limits an overly pious interpretation — they are simply trivial entries in a calendar. E.g., the fact that he records in a daily devotional book the killing of a cat by his dog Tiras, and the confinement of another pet dog Rebekka in order to have a litter of seven puppies, four of them born dead, surely does not mean that these commonplace occurrences are to be given an exaggerated meaning in terms of some eternal significance.[20]

The Situation of the Christian in Actual History

The piety which grew out of this conversion soon displayed all the characteristic features which would eventually come to stand in tension with his life as a politician. These are perhaps most vividly expressed in an admittedly later letter to his brother-in-law Oscar von Arnim: "We are powerless and helpless in God's mighty hand, as far as he will not himself help us, and can do nothing but bow down in humility under his dispensations. He can take from us all that he gave, and make us utterly desolate, and our mourning for it would be all the bitterer the more we allow it to run to excess in

[18] From a letter to Heinrich von Puttkamer dated December 22, 1846; *Love Letters*, pp. 6-7.
[19] Arnold Oskar Meyer, *Bismarcks Glaube* (Munich: Beck, 1933), pp. 28-29.
[20] *Ibid.*, pp. 18-19.

contention and rebellion against his almighty ordinance." [21] In these lines is expressed a Christian awareness of existence which one might provisionally describe as belief in divine guidance.

We must hasten, however, to state the matter more precisely. For one thing, it is not a case of man's ferreting out the will of God, nor of God's will being susceptible to human reckoning, as, e.g., in the arrogance of Hitler when he identifies his own will with providence and declares that his goals are obviously the goals of divine providence, whose purposes can be known. If we are correct, in Bismarck there is repeatedly found instead an act of pronounced trust in the Lord of history, whose immediate intentions are *not* knowable but whose ultimate will may indeed be known. This ultimate will, for Bismarck, is that all things must work out for the best. Since the execution of this will, the concrete historical guidance, remains inscrutable as in Job, one has simply to trust, go forward "as a child into the dark," [22] though occasionally Bismarck can speak boldly of "the footstep of God" which is "echoed by events." [23]

Even such a saying contains less a theologically garnished interpretation of history than a negation of the power of human calculation. For the fuller quotation actually runs: "One cannot produce anything of oneself; one can only wait [!] until one hears the footstep of God echoed by events." In a conversation with Karl Büchsel in 1864, Bismarck states the negation in similar terms: "I wanted it one way, but it turned out quite differently. I'll tell you something: I'm happy if I can just catch a glimpse of which way our Lord God is going, and then hobble along behind." [24] It is not a case, then, of man ferreting out the will of God either in terms of a philosophy of history or by virtue of his own instinctive feelings. It is emphatically a case of trust, a trust which repeatedly shows signs of involving an outright "nevertheless" (Ps. 73:23). That is the first point.

It is to be noted too, in the second place, that this divine guidance does not mean the reception of direct prescriptions for political action,

---

[21] From a letter dated August 16, 1861; Rothfels, *op. cit.*, p. 280; English translation by Fitz^h Maxse in *Prince Bismarck's Letters: to His Wife, His Sister, and Others, From 1844-1870* (London: Chapman and Hall, 1878), pp. 161-162.

[22] From a letter to his wife dated July 20, 1864; *Love Letters*, p. 389.

[23] Meyer, *op. cit.*, pp. 6, 7.

[24] The quotation appears in a note in Otto Schiffers, *Bismarck als Christ* (4th ed.; 1915), p. 97.

as from the divine commandments. Bismarck shares, not only with many others of his own calling but also with many prominent Lutheran theologians of his age, the view that one cannot rule the world with the Sermon on the Mount.[25]

Such direction as he receives always relates, so far as we can see, to his personal relationship to the divine will with which he is seeking agreement. It thus works always to counteract the instincts and attitudes which threaten to arise in the statesman who is active in shaping the course of affairs, and which lead him to think that it is men who make history, and that the politician is a creative subject in political processes. Bismarck states repeatedly, as we have seen, that on the contrary we are "powerless and helpless in God's mighty hand . . . and we can do nothing but bow down in humility [we are not the creators of history!] under his dispensations." The divine direction thus refers not to the political program as such — i.e., to its content, to a supposed "Christian politics" — but rather to the personal existence of the statesman, the "Christian politician."

This, then, is one of the main reasons why Bismarck keeps politics and Christianity strictly apart. For him Christianity does not contain direct and normative guidance for political resolves. Christianity is rather the place of retreat, the chapel, of the *man* who seeks peace with the Lord of history and with himself so that, equipped with this peace and with its power, he may enter again the battlefield of historical conflicts. The dichotomy certainly does not mean that Bismarck merely wanted a free hand. He was not just seeking moral justification for an unfettered and opportunistic use of the autonomy of politics. What he really sought to emphasize was his reservations about the tempting view that the statesman is the executor of the will of providence. Admittedly, he feels that he is "God's soldier," [26] impressed into service, but not in the sense of Hegel's "world-historical individual" who is a transitional point and instrument in the self-development of the spirit.

In face of the Hegelian and Idealist attempt to make a final equation between the world spirit and the shaper of history, two points

---

[25] Cf. at Erlangen, J. C. K. v. Hofmann, *Weissagung und Erfüllung im AT und NT* (1841-44), pp. 292 ff.; Franz Herrman Reinhold von Frank, *System der Christlichen Sittlichkeit* (Erlangen: Deichert, 1884-1887), II, 456.

[26] From a letter to his wife dated May 3, 1851; *Love Letters*, p. 229.

are important. The first is that Bismarck does not claim any metaphysical or religious justification for his political work. It is in repudiation of such seductive possibilities that he stresses the factuality and the intrinsically "necessary." character of political action. This seems to be the real basis for his separation of Christianity and politics. The second point is that Bismarck refused to assume that he was a transitional point of the world spirit, or an envoy of providence. He was always aware of the fact that his action, being finite,[27] guilt-ridden, and imperfect,[28] stood in contradiction to the divine guidance of history. He thus refuses to be the arrogant agent of providence or the equally arrogant political prophet who thinks he can discern the will of God in history.

What is involved in all of this theologically is the question of maintaining the salvation of the *man* in politics while repudiating the question of salvation in respect of the political *order*. Though Bismarck was not aware of it, and though in his case many questions deserve to be raised about the theological background, the influence of Luther and his doctrine of the two kingdoms seems apparent in Bismarck's dichotomy between the man and the order, between Christianity and politics. For the political ethics of Lutheranism has always been shaped by the fact that it contests (as a confusion of the two kingdoms) any theocratizing of the state, any political prophecy, and any confusing of Christianity and politics. The fact that Lutheranism's position is only very brokenly expressed in Bismarck's separation of Christianity and politics does not invalidate the assumption that it is nonetheless present.

We are strengthened in this assumption by the fact that for Adolf Stöcker and especially for Friedrich Naumann the doctrine of the two kingdoms — distorted, to be sure, to the point of caricature —

[27] In a letter to his wife dated July 2, 1859, Bismarck speaks of the fate of the nations being only a question of time, "if only the mercy of God and the deserving of Christ remain to our souls. . . . What are our states and their power and honor before God except as ant-hills and bee-hives which the hoof of an ox tramples down, or fate, in the form of a honey-farmer, overtakes?" *Love Letters*, pp. 343-344.

[28] In a letter to Alexander von Below-Hohendorf dated May 16, 1864, Bismarck writes that his "gratitude for God's help hitherto mounts to the confidence that the Lord knows how to turn even our errors to our advantage," and that he has experienced this "daily to a wholesome humiliation." Rothfels, *op. cit.*, p. 313; English by Maxse, *op. cit.*, p. 222.

echoes in the dualism between the law of politics and the command of the Sermon on the Mount. The resultant separation between Christianity and politics, as Naumann sees it, is so extreme that Christian morality is said to apply only to the personal sphere and not to statecraft and culture. In these areas a different morality is demanded. While the individual may be obligated to a love which bears all things, "the struggle for existence has taught the nations to be armorplated beasts." [29] This leads Naumann to the assumption of a double morality, indeed to the seductive notion — dismissed as quickly as it arises but not very convincingly — that there are two gods: "Following the god of the world produces the morality of the struggle for existence, and serving the Father of Jesus Christ produces the morality of mercy. Yet there are not two gods, but one. Somehow [!] their arms interlock." [30]

Here the separation of the two kingdoms is radical and complete, contrary to the true intentions of Luther, who desired a distinction between them but not an ontic separation. Now it may be that Naumann is simply representative of a temporally conditioned theological situation which affected all Christians of that age who were involved in secular action, including Bismarck and his political-theological understanding of the Christian in government. It may be too that Luther's doctrine of the two kingdoms is here forgotten or distorted. It is nonetheless striking that in this connection the theologian Naumann adopts a theological position which is far less satisfactory than that of the child of this world, Bismarck.

For Bismarck has a concern — justifiable at least in intention — not to misuse Christianity to sacralize politics. He therefore restricts Christianity to the personal sphere: The statesman is to let Christianity order his personal life and guard him against the temptations of his office. Naumann, on the other hand, is not primarily concerned that Christianity might dominate world history; he is more afraid that Christianity might be bad for the world. It might deprive the beast of its scales and thus render it incapable of fighting the battle for existence.

[29] Friedrich Naumann, "Briefe über Religion" (1903), No. 25; in Walter Uhsadel (ed.), *Friedrich Naumann Werke* (5 vols.; Cologne: Westdeutscher Verlag, 1964), I, 623.
[30] Naumann, "Briefe," No. 22; *Werke*, I, 617.

For Bismarck, then, the autonomy of politics – if we may cautiously use that term in this connection – consists simply in a secular action which derives from a Christian disposition but for which there are no immediate Christian directives absolving one from personal responsibility. For Naumann, on the other hand, political autonomy in this sense implies a completely independent sphere in which it is a mistake to ask concerning a Christian disposition, a sphere which operates without distinction as regards Christians and non-Christians.

The idea of dualism or two gods would certainly have been quite inconceivable to Bismarck. His personal piety never relates to an encounter between the soul and its God, but always to an encounter between man in his estate or calling and the God of history. This implies the unity of God. Naumann, on the other hand, seriously raises the question of two gods, though he does not stop short of this conclusion and is forced to state, with resignation, that no mortal knows where or how the arms of the two gods interlock.

The theological question which arises here, and for which Bismarck represents a significant case in point, is whether this norm of Christianity means that the divine commandments apply only to the personal sphere, as in a kind of pietistic subjectivism, or whether they also embrace the objective sphere of politics. Is there such a thing as an indirect influence of the Christian position upon the sphere of actual programs even though the Christian faith provides no immediate and specific directives?

In other words, if we accept this radical distinction between Christianity and politics, if we accept this extended doctrine of the two kingdoms, can the attitudes induced in the statesman by faith, e.g., humility, trust, gratitude, and the freedom of forgiveness, themselves provide specific impulses in the objective sphere of politics? Can the indirect line to which we have referred take more precise and concrete form? Does it refer only to the presuppositions of politics, in the person of the politician, or does it point beyond these to the possibility of interventions in the political process itself?

The Significance of Personal Faith for Concrete Political Action

At first glance it does not appear that ethical motives can actually intervene in the objective political process. For when we turn from

Bismarck's statements about his self-awareness as a Christian to his objective self-awareness as a politician, we seem to be confronted by the proclamation of an almost undisguised autonomy. The great speech of December 3, 1850, contains a classic passage in this regard which declares the egoism and interest of the state to be the sustaining forces of political action: "The only sound basis of a great state . . . is national egoism, not romanticism. It is not worthy of a great state to fight for a cause which is not in its own interest." [31] To represent an interest there are two means available which share the elemental character of this interest and which are thus autonomously subject to it as elemental historical forces. These are the increase of power — without which the interest could not be represented at all — and the principle that every action should serve an end or purpose.

There thus arises a fixed relationship between means and end. The primary means which serves the supreme end of interest is power, and the secondary means is action which secures and consolidates that power. This correlation of means and end has the character of necessity. If a nation's place in the world is dependent upon its power, then everything done in that nation must necessarily serve the end of enhancing that power. These three concepts — power, utility, and necessity — occur in every conceivable variation in Bismarck's utterances. They constitute the autonomy of the political process.

In any case it may be stated negatively that politics as the representative of interests is *not* — at least not primarily — concerned to serve some sort of ideal, such as a particular social order, the progress of the race, or the brotherhood of nations (if we may use modern slogans to illustrate the point). In this sense Bismarck accuses Ludwig v. Gerlach and his conservative fellow Christians of romanticism and idealism, by which he means unrealistic subjection to a system of goals and norms which is constructed in a vacuum, outside the world of means, and hence with no possibility of attainment.

The methods by which the interest or sacred egoism are represented stem from the winning of power, and are thus dictated to a great extent by historical circumstances. They thus allow little or no play for a purely ethical action which is not in any sense condi-

[31] Horst Kohl (ed.), *Die politischen Reden des Fürsten Bismarck* (14 vols.; Stuttgart: Cotta, 1892-1905), I, 264-265.

tioned. On the contrary, political action is conditioned in principle. It is controlled by the conditioning circumstances. Politics, after all, is "the art of the possible." This implies that the only means which will lead to the desired goal are certain specific means available at the moment. But the converse is also true, namely, that one can desire only those goals which are attainable, i.e., those for which the requisite means are available. Thus "the possible," i.e., the sum of available means, autonomously controls not merely the realizing but also the fixing of the goals.

Bismarck says again and again that what is "necessary" must be done, and he has in view this necessity which almost completely excludes any area of freedom. As politicians we can only act as we must, in the sense of sacred egoism and the means to fulfill it. In this light one may venture the formulation that politics involves primarily the interpretation of a situation with a view to seeing where it is necessarily leading and what inherent and intrinsically necessary means are available in it for carrying this tendency through to a conclusion. Only secondarily does politics involve the overt act itself.

Having considered in all its crassness Bismarck's view of the autonomy of political occurrence, we must now return to the initial question as to how there can be anything in the nature of ethical intervention within this process. First, we must note and interpret the remarkable fact that Bismarck's acknowledgment of an almost Machiavellian necessity about concrete historical action does not really have a cynical ring. In his case, there is a quite different tone about it. We must ask, then, whether the difference is related to the background of his faith.

In Bismarck's *Gedanken und Erinnerungen* the statement is made: "Ours is not to discharge a judicial office, but to pursue German politics." [32] Taken together with similar references, this means that the statesman does not have to fulfill the office of a world judge. The primary requirement is not that he be just, but that he represent interests. In the world court – if world history is to be understood as world judgment – he has to fulfill the office, not of a judge but of an advocate.

One might obviously understand such a thesis in the sense of a

---

[32] *Gedanken und Erinnerungen von Otto v. Bismarck* (3 vols.; Stuttgart: Cotta, 1898), II, 46.

pragmatic egoism, as though it denoted only what we have called the autonomy of interest. But the question arises whether it is meant in this way, or whether it does not have another nuance.

In relation to the statements which we have already quoted concerning the humility to which one is driven by one's own shortsightedness and by the inscrutable will of the Lord of history, another interpretation is very probable, namely, that it would be arrogance to try to be more than a mere partner in the actual play of historical forces, to arrogate to oneself the office of conductor of the orchestra instead of being content to be one of the players (be it even the first violin), to claim to know and "be playing" the whole score as the Lord of history wrote it. Such arrogance would be surpassed only by that of Hitler, who was not content just to be the conductor, but who wrote the score himself, and then tried to impress himself as well as others even more by maintaining that he received it as a gift entrusted to him by providence.

Bismarck, as is well known, was astonishingly direct and realistic in the way in which he spoke of political plans. But it would be wrong to try to explain this purely in terms of his psychology or character, as though he were by nature inclined to openness and directness. It is more probably related to what may be called the "theological" background. The moral or ideal concealment of political ends, which Bismarck despised, is distasteful to us not merely because it contains an element of the hypocritical but also because there is usually associated with such concealment the arrogant claim to be a partner of providence and to exercise a judicial office. Bismarck rejected any such claim.

It would be a mistake, therefore, to interpret in purely pragmatic terms his concentration on the interests of his own state. In Bismarck's view such concentration certainly carries with it a denial of the arrogant claim to be anything more than merely a representative of interests. Inherent in this limitation is an element of political ethics which is not adequately captured or described merely by the catchword "pragmatism."

It is not so much this intention — which is hard to see from the outside — as the resultant political realism which distinguishes Bismarck from the Liberals on the one hand, who represent philosophical ideas of history, and from his friends of the revival movement on the other, who incline to a religious direction of history and therewith to a claiming of the judicial office. One may thus say that the objections raised from these two sides are not strictly relevant. It is the Christian element in Bismarck which makes him content simply to represent interests as a partner. His supposed lack of principle, for which he was blamed by representatives of the revival movement, consists essentially in his rejection of lofty goals and philosophies of history which involve more than mere partnership.

With that we have now finally arrived at our real question as to how faith relates to concrete political action. We have gained one insight into this relation already. By bowing beneath the divine providence, by accepting duties, and by trusting the guidance of the Lord of history in spite of one's own fallibility, faith manages to provide a certain freedom to political realism, and to protect it against moral self-justification, moralizing, and idealizing. This is one influence of faith on political action.

It is just because Bismarck receives this freedom from his faith, and hence takes up his allotted historical function under forgiveness, that he polemicizes against a Christianity which evades this test and is afraid of "dirty hands" (Sartre), which would rather leave this business to the children of the world, and which therewith isolates faith from politics. It is interesting that in this polemic Bismarck's point is not that such people fail to perceive their political duties but that they do not take their faith seriously enough. For they do not respect the freedom which their faith gives them. "Most of you [Pomeranian relatives and friends of the awakening] have so little confidence in your faith, and wrap it carefully in the cotton-wool of your isolation, lest it take cold from any draught of the world; while others are vexed with you, and proclaim that you are people who esteem yourselves too holy to come into contact with publicans, etc." [33]

Bismarck insists that faith has an affinity to political action. He objects in principle to any pious retreat into inwardness. "Faith that allows the believer to segregate himself from his brothers on this earth, so that he contents himself with a putative isolated relation to the Lord alone, in mere contemplation, is a dead faith, that I char-

---

[33] From a letter to Johanna dated February 7, 1847, quoted by Meyer, *op. cit.*, p. 12; English translation in *The Love-Letters of Prince Bismarck*, ed. Prince Herbert Bismarck (London: Heinemann, 1901), I, 18.

acterized . . . in an earlier letter as quietism . . . an erroneous way, in my opinion, into which pietism easily and often leads, especially with women. By this I mean with the isolation — surely not the spiritual arrogance that esteems itself holier than others — but, I might say, the quiet waiting for the Lord's day, in faith and hope, but without what seems to me true love. Where that is, there the need exists, I believe, to unite one's self in friendship or through other ties more closely to some visible being than through the bonds of the universal Christian love. Jesus himself had a disciple whom he 'loved,' that is, loved more deeply and differently from what the saying means, 'Love one another.' " [34]

Bismarck is alluding to what is often called today the secularity of Christian existence (Bonhoeffer). In modern theological terms, he is protesting against the dehistoricizing of love in the name of eschatology.[35] He undoubtedly has in mind the political affinity of the gospel. For with his criticism of Pietism he thinks that one should move away from a generalized and abstract love to a differentiated love whose character is determined by degrees of nearness and therewith also by the friend-foe relationship encountered in politics. Clearly Bismarck, in spite of his own very different distinction between Christianity and politics, will not accept the accusations of the Pietists. He does not want Christians to retreat from the political front nor to call others to order in a Pharisaic and doctrinaire manner from a post of their own selection. Thus he writes: "As a statesman I am not ruthless *enough*, but according to my own feeling fainthearted, because it is not easy, in the questions which occupy me, always to attain to the clarity on whose soil confidence in God grows. Those who chide me for being a politician without a conscience do me an injustice, and should first test their own consciences on this battlefield." [36]

Having established this connection between faith and politics, however, we have not yet finished our examination of Bismarck. For thus far we have simply shown that Bismarck, in his own view, had been given a freedom to act in as Machiavellian a way as anyone else, yet

[34] From a letter to his fiancée dated February 28, 1849; *Love Letters*, pp. 65-66.
[35] Cf. Wilhelm Kamlah, *Christentum und Sebstbehauptung* (Frankfurt, 1940), pp. 9 ff.; 2nd ed., *Christentum und Geschichtlichkeit* (1951), pp. 24 ff.
[36] From a letter to Alexander Andrae-Roman, dated December 26, 1865; Rothfels, *op. cit.*, pp. 323-324.

still be honest and relaxed about it. Realizing the dubious nature of his actions, he could act with less hypocrisy. What he thus receives from his faith is in the first place a purely inward gift. It is a psychological state with respect to a political act which, so far as the laws of its development are concerned, is and remains the same as the act of the non-Christian. This inwardness which empowers him for political action is what distinguishes him from his pietistic friends, who clung to an unrealistic absolute and thus became politically sterile.

The question which now concerns us is as follows: Does faith also intervene actively in such a way as to affect not merely the understanding of the action but the action itself? This active concretizing of faith in the sphere of politics seems to us to find expression primarily in various forms of restraint. Such restraint is the more astounding in Bismarck because it contradicts the natural bent of his own character.

Bismarck's expressed reasons for this restraint bear constant reference to theological considerations: "Every great power which endeavors outside its own sphere of interests to bring influence and pressure to bear on other lands and to direct affairs, runs a risk in going beyond the sphere which God has allotted to it. It pursues a politics of power rather than the politics of interest, and makes a bid for prestige. We shall not do this." [37] It seems to be important that interest here is not, as one might expect, a blank check for unrestricted expansion, but a limiting concept which guards against both the development of mere power or prestige and the assumption of a judicial role.

Bismarck's idea that he must not be a judge finds direct political expression in his opposition to punitive wars and the exacting of tribute. "Vengeance is God's," he writes to his son Herbert in 1870.[38] The fact that this insistence on the divine judgment, this refusal to claim all judgment for himself, is also tactically very clever,[39] does not invalidate the genuineness of the appeal to the Lord and Judge of history. On the contrary, the piety of Bismarck is constantly con-

---

[37] Speech in the Reichstag, February 6, 1888; Kohl, *op. cit.*, XII, 447.

[38] September 23, 1870; Rothfels, *op. cit.*, p. 361; English translation by Armin Handler in *Bismarck's Letters to His Wife: From the Seat of War 1870-1871* (New York: Appleton, 1903), p. 60.

[39] "A well-treated Napoleon, however, will be more *useful* to us, and that is the only and most important thing to me." *Ibid.* [italics by H. T.].

trolled by the thought that harmony with the divine will, and consequently with the judicial will of God, makes historical action possible and easier, and to this degree is also clever. The idea that political cleverness might be in contradiction with the will of God is one which seems hardly to have occurred to him.

His well-known rejection of preventive wars is along the same lines. This rejection certainly cannot be deduced from what he says about sacred egoism. For why should he not be forced from that standpoint into what seems to be a politically favorable war of aggression? The reason is a theological one which is linked with his renunciation of the role of shaping history. One must "accept" the situation as God "makes" it. Man cannot create or direct the stream of time. Preventive wars are a presumptuous attempt to "create" situations for oneself, and to this extent to "make" history. There is seen here, moreover, not merely the arrogance of the man of action but also the arrogance of the seer who claims insight into the divine planning of history. One can never know the ways of divine providence in advance with sufficient certainty.[40] At this point too it is evident that the humility of being content and of "accepting the situation" is also clever. It maintains a realistic sobriety and is a safeguard against reckless adventuring.

Theological Results of the Analysis

Now that we have examined the model of the "Christian statesman" from all essential angles, we are in a position to draw certain theological conclusions from our observations. We may begin with the point just advanced, namely, that faith mediates the freedom both of objective insight (into historical processes) and of objective action. Four main conclusions suggest themselves, after which we will again return to the contrast between Bismarck and Hitler.

In the first place, it may of course be argued that the restraint which we noted in Bismarck is based on the arguments of reason. But to say this is to raise the further question as to the foundation on which reason itself rests. More precisely, one would have to ask on what the possibility of rational *existence* rests. For even though faith cannot alter the facts established by reason, it can and does

---

[40] Cf. the speech delivered at Jena on July 30, 1892; Kohl, *op. cit.*, XIII, 129-134.

affect a man's relationship *to* reason. Faith has something to say about whether a man can or cannot have a rational *existence*.

Objectivity, the attitude that accords with reason and with the things that fall within its purview, is itself a human stance. It is something man does, and hence the product of those formative powers which fashion all human behavior. Since faith is one of these powers, we can only conclude that objectivity does indeed have something to do with the emancipation in which faith believes. It is quite possible both to believe and to be objective. Indeed, faith and objectivity, so far from being distinct dimensions of human behavior, actually come together at the point where the "believer" is freed to be "objective."

That this is in fact the case becomes clear the moment we consider wherein this emancipation for rationality consists. It consists in the fact that reason is protected from above and from below, as it were, and helped to stand on its own two feet.

First, it is protected from above. Once we understand the dialectic of Law and gospel — and this understanding is for Luther the alpha and omega of all theology — we learn to distinguish the two kingdoms, and to use reason in the kingdom on the left hand. If we make the gospel a kind of constitution for the secular kingdom, and consequently for politics too, we make reason heteronomous and pervert the gospel into Law. This is why there can never be a theocracy, but only an order which is fashioned in the name of the maturity of man [41] and according to the law of the reason which God has given man.

A pseudo theocracy in which reason is made heteronomous can occur even in ideological tyranny or in the dominion of all kinds of political and social utopias. For here the world is not mature and standing on its own. It is instead the agent of pragmatic ideas which it has to accredit by its stock of arguments.

The redemption of man, therefore, aims at his maturity, at the liberation of reason to be itself. We may also say that it liberates man from servitude and brings him into sonship.

---

[41] That this maturity does not imply an emancipation of reason, but is the maturity of the son bound to his father, has been perspicaciously noted by Friedrich Gogarten in "Theologie und Geshichte," *Zeitschrift für Theologie und Kirche,* L (1953), 339-394, esp. 349 ff.; cf. also Dietrich Bonhoeffer, *Letters and Papers from Prison* (New York: Macmillan, 1962), pp. 194 ff., 208 ff., 224.

When we speak of protection "from above," we are thinking of reason's subjection to authoritatively given laws, of its dependence on divine directives, a dependence which ignores reason's coming of age, turns gospel into Law, and gives rise to all kinds of theocratic fanaticism.[42]

Reason is also protected, however, "from below." Without this protection reason is always in danger of being ruled by the emotions, by hope and by fear. "Thy wish was father, Harry, to that thought."[43] Thus does Shakespeare express one of the perils to which reason is exposed. The opposite peril is that posed by fear: whatever I fear "just cannot be."[44]

This is why my objectivity, my respect for the facts, is not to be trusted — precisely because I am *not* disinterested. On the contrary, I am very much interested, and always on the lookout for rational grounds on which to justify my assertion (positively) that what I hope for really is, and (negatively) that what I am afraid of really is not. Luther must have had this in mind when he spoke of reason as "the devil's whore":[45] it can be bought for a price! To state the case somewhat more exactly, reason is something man buys *back*, after first having sold it out!

Objectivity results, then, only as man is emancipated from fear and from hope. I.e., he must first be released from what he fears into the custody of him who saves from the anxieties of this world (John 16:33). He must first be released from what he hopes into the custody of him who insists on being the sole object of man's hope. Only release from

---

[42] We are in fact inevitably reminded here of radicals such as Thomas Münzer, who tried to make of the Sermon on the Mount a constitution for the world.

[43] William Shakespeare, *King Henry the Fourth, Part II*, Act IV, scene 5.

[44] Cf. the suppression of God, Rom. 1:18 ff.

[45] See LW 40, 174-175; 51, 374-379; and Bernhard Lohse, Ratio *und* Fides. *Eine Untersuchung über die ratio in der Theologie Luthers* (Göttingen: Vandenhoeck & Ruprecht, 1958), pp. 70-72. According to Lohse, Luther sees a close connection between reason and existence (hence also between reason and *fallen* existence) inasmuch as he conjoins both "reason" and "will" in the concept of the "free will" (see Martin Luther, *The Bondage of the Will*, trans. J. I. Packer and O. R. Johnston [Westwood, New Jersey: Revell, 1958], pp. 303, 309, 310, 312). Because "reason is fond of itself" (*LW* 4, 375) the act of knowing is itself no longer free, bent solely on its object; on the contrary, it is itself influenced by the knowing subject. On the implications of man's fallen existence for reason cf. also Jacques Maritain, *An Essay on Christian Philosophy*, trans. Edward H. Flannery (New York: Philosophical Library, 1955), e.g., p. 28.

such constraints and bondage can make man truly unconstrained and unfettered, i.e., truly objective.

A second conclusion grows out of the fact that the restraint proposed by the reason which is redeemed, brought to itself and called to order once again, is connected in still another way with faith. It relates to the faith in forgiveness. The question then is: How are forgiveness and action connected?

Theoretically one might easily suppose that forgiveness involves a complete autonomy of action. One might take forgiveness to mean that the believing ego which claims forgiveness is no longer threatened in its Christian existence by any dubiety of action, however severe, and that it may thus give itself to such action without restraint. In connection with the thought that redemption restores maturity and a corresponding autonomy of reason, forgiveness might be taken to imply that reason has free rein, that as political reason it may thus be as pragmatic and Machiavellian as it pleases, that no check is placed on its function as an advocate of interests.

Now we have already pointed out that the maturity of reason is always linked with the one who declares me to be mature, that it stands always within the context of sonship rather than servitude (cf. John 15:15; Gal. 4:7; Heb. 2:15; etc.). Maturity is inside and not outside the relationship to the father. When we here describe it as independence, the selfhood we have in view is that of the child, his coming to himself. Autonomy, accordingly, is not the self-determination of one who has been emancipated, but the self-determination of one who has been called.[46]

In Romans 6:1 ff. and 6:15 ff. Paul discusses the problem of the freedom opened up by forgiveness: "Are we to continue in sin (in virtue of forgiveness and the freedom therein contained) that grace may abound? . . . Are we to sin because we are not under law but under grace?" To both questions Paul gives the answer: "By no means!" For in the first place, liberation consists in the fact that sin, the claim of licence and egoistic caprice, has lost its power over us. We have "died to" it (6:2). We no longer react to it. The loudest command is hollow for a dead man. In the second place, it must be remembered that we are liberated "to" something. Commitment to

[46] Cf. my analysis of autonomy in the Introduction to *Glaube und Handeln*, ed. Heinz Horst Schrey (Bremen: Schünemann, 1956).

sinister forces has been replaced by commitment to the One who has overcome them (John 8:36). Demonic fellowship is crowded out by fellowship with God. To false commitment there corresponds not the freedom of caprice — which would simply plunge us into new bondage (Luke 15:12-24) — but security. Paul certainly speaks of a new servitude (Rom. 6:16), but this is not the old slavery under the Law. He is using a paradoxical expression to denote the freedom which can be achieved only in commitment.

Forgiveness thus implies the call to discipleship, to obedience. A grace which gives free rein to uncontested libertinism is not the grace of the Lord which is operative within history and summons to commitment. It is instead a timeless principle of indifference. It is not the costly grace which demands expenditure, but a "cheap grace" which costs nothing. Misunderstood in this way, forgiveness is no longer the justification of the sinner. It is the justification of sin, the legalizing of caprice, of interest, and therewith of opportunism.[47]

Forgiveness, then, is not a validation of laissez faire, of an unrestricted play of political autonomy. It represents rather a permanent active intervention in the sense that it appeals for the responsibility of discipleship. It urges moderation, i.e., a halt to the movement of passion and of the autonomous processes. It demands (1) that there should be respect for the divine rule in history, that we should not make ourselves the subjects of historical action, e.g., in preventive wars; (2) that we should not yield to the pressure of the quest for power and prestige but limit ourselves to representing our own interests; and (3) that we should keep in view not merely the machinery of power but responsibility for men.

In the third place, the problem of restraint becomes acute in yet another theological connection. Even if one cannot rule the world by the laws of the Sermon on the Mount, the question still arises whether they can influence this rule in some another way.

There can be no such influence if the Sermon on the Mount — as in Naumann, Troeltsch, or Schweitzer — is either restricted to the personal sphere of saints and holy persons or limited to the span of the apocalyptic end of history as an interim ethics. But it is a question whether the Sermon on the Mount should be esoterically limited in

---

[47] On the concept of "cheap grace" see Dietrich Bonhoeffer, *The Cost of Discipleship,* trans. Reginald H. Fuller (New York: Macmillan, 1959), pp. 35 ff.

this way, or whether it does not rather contain a message precisely for our "being-in-the-world." And on this score there can really be no question at all!

By radically claiming me, not within the orders but above them, the Sermon on the Mount calls the orders as such into question. It shows that they are structural orders of "this aeon." They are laws which apply because of the hardness of our hearts. They are not orders of creation with an absolute claim but emergency orders with only a relative claim.

Their ambivalence is thus clear. They represent not merely the will of God in creation and preservation, but also the fallenness of the creature. They are an objectification of this fallenness. Hence the laws which are native and proper [Eigengesetze] in this world, e.g., the laws of jurisprudence and politics, are really strange and alien laws [Fremdgesetze] so far as the kingdom of God is concerned.

From this two conclusions may be drawn. The first is that I cannot absolutize the orders of this world, e.g., I cannot possibly make the state an end it itself, I cannot exalt it ideologically. And the second conclusion is that the need for compromise which arises in face of the absolute demand and its actual unattainability cannot be understood in the sense that compromise is the resultant in a parallelogram of forces, something in which we can acquiesce, so that we can legitimately live on the middle line between the absolute claim and the necessity posed by the autonomies. Ultimate validity is not geometrically calculable in this way. The Sermon on the Mount is instead a disturbing fire which does not allow me to settle down but keeps me constantly on the move. It causes me to be totally called in question, and points me — precisely where I am compelled to act and to act on the basis of sheer necessity — to my attendant need of forgiveness.

All of this again acts to break the laissez faire instinct and the compulsion to give in to unguarded action. To this degree it also works itself out on the level of practical politics.

It seems, then, that we are not unjustified in seeing in Bismarck's hesitation and skepticism with respect to responsible and far-reaching resolves, as well as in his awareness of fallibility and guilt, not merely an insight into the limited nature of man's own foresight and resources but also an indication of the dubious and broken nature of every action within the orders of this world, no matter how great the fidelity to duty therein displayed.

One certainly cannot be charged with an undue straining of interpretation if one sees in this radical questioning the fruit of a Christian understanding which derives from the challenge of the Sermon on the Mount and which keeps every secular action, including political action, from being surrendered wholly — "fanatically" — to the movement of passion and of the autonomy of the earthly orders. Here too what is involved is faith's active though indirect intervention in political processes and political action.

Fourth, and finally, it is true that in all these respects faith seems to function more as a brake than a motor. That this is so is probably due to the fact that the sphere of politics seems to call forth the strongest driving passions, so that interventions from outside the political sphere naturally tend to take the form of restraint rather than incitement.

But we must certainly steer clear of the prejudice that such checks are detrimental to the creative forces of history or that what is checked is inferior to the unbroken impulsion of what is not checked. It is obviously an insight not merely of Christianity but also of Platonism that lack of moderation is destructive. It leads to what Augustine called "perverse love." [48] It also distorts the hierarchy of norms and thus blinds to reality. Hitler is the historical figure who best illustrates such a lack.

The converse is also true, namely, that restraint, resistance to the temptation to "relate oneself absolutely to the relative" (Kierkegaard), is a sign of realism both in the diagnosis of historical processes and in action.

At a later point we shall have to consider the question whether in respect of the goals and impulses of action faith acts as a motor as well as a brake. A theme we will emphasize later — the safeguarding of humanity in the midst of organizational machinery — will continually bring us up against this problem. (It will be recalled that the negative intervention of Law and gospel as a protest, a call to order, has its own specific theological place, and that this was why we spoke earlier not of a positive setting of goals by natural law but of the negativity of natural "lawlessness.") [49]

[48] Augustine *The City of God* xii. 8.
[49] See *ThE* 1, 440-447.

Hitler and Dynamic Amorality

The counterpart to this binding of the Christian statesman, and to the theological conclusions to be drawn therefrom, may be depicted with the help of our second model, Hitler, the representative of National Socialism. We have already discussed the essential features of National Socialism – the features relevant to our present purpose – in our treatment of ideologies.[50] We may thus restrict ourselves here to a few theses on the contrast between Hitler and Bismarck.

Hitler is unaware of the fact that the world is radically called in question. He is also unaware of the challenge to his own particular view of the world.[51] Both points are significant.

The fact that he raises to doctrinaire absoluteness a specific view of the world, namely, his own, is linked with the ideological character of political philosophy as such. A politically determined world view, since it claims the whole man, cannot itself be questioned. It is not open to discussion. For if it were, its monolithic character would immediately be jeopardized and man would be enmeshed in a wasteful battle with himself instead of a clear and straightforward struggle against external enemies.[52] Since man exists only as the agent of a militant dynamic applied instrumentally, no such challenge can arise. On the contrary, the absolutizing of ideological dogma is specifically designed to unleash fanaticism and to nourish the spirit of grim infallibility which will cause men, in the name of the dogma, to sacrifice themselves for the goals of those in power.

The real basis of the world itself, of which the world view is the ideological superstructure, is also secured against all challenge. If it were not, if it too could be called in question, then the constructing of such pragmatic absolutizations as the ideologies would be ruled out from the very first. Only in a world which is unconditionally affirmed, which is not affected by the fall, can there be unconditional commitment.

These two sides of the world – the objective structure and the subjective orientation to this structure – are linked together in National Socialist ideology by the biological principle. On the one side, the

[50] See above pp. 22-70.
[51] See Hitler, *Mein Kampf: Complete and unabridged,* ed. John Chamberlain *et al.* (New York: Reynal & Hitchcock, 1939), pp. 675 ff., 877.
[52] Cf. our reference above at p. 38 to Goebbels' silencing of all discussion.

world is regarded as created nature just as it is, including the laws of conflict, the right of the strong, and the methods of cunning and brute force which seem to prevail in the battle for existence. On the other side, there develops in relation to the world a kind of animal-like activity devoid of all ethical values, an action which finds its model in the amorality of the beast, maintaining the law of nature intact and accepting no ethical restraint whatsoever. As Hitler sees it, "In the end, only the urge for self-preservation will eternally succeed. Under its pressure so-called 'humanity,' as the expression of a mixture of stupidity, cowardice, and an imaginary superior intelligence, will melt like snow under the March sun. Mankind has grown strong in eternal struggles and it will only perish through eternal peace." [53] Amorality is the result. Hitler can boast that he "is prepared to commit perjury half-a-dozen times a day," that he "will make an agreement in good faith today and unhesitatingly break it up tomorrow." [54]

It has been shown repeatedly and quite correctly that in this thesis of dynamic amorality Hitler has adopted ideas of Machiavelli and carried them to their logical extreme.[55] The parallel between Hitler and Machiavelli does in fact shed light on what Hitler really was and on the decisive theological point of difference between him and Bismarck. To be specific, it would be a mistake to compare Hitler and Bismarck merely from the standpoint of an unscrupulous use of power and on that basis conclude simply that Hitler was an utter scoundrel but that Bismarck too was no angel. The real point at issue is the understanding of power, not the use of power, except insofar as the use is seen in terms of the understanding. What unites Machiavelli and Hitler as distinct from Bismarck is not simply that they represent the unscrupulous power politics of common usage, but that they do so consciously, making a philosophy of it, and that in addition they legalize such unscrupulousness, even exalting it to the rank of a political virtue.

Tyrants prior to Machiavelli might still have a guilty conscience in respect of their worst excesses of brutality; at least they had still to

[53] *Mein Kampf,* p. 175.

[54] Hermann Rauschning, *The Voice of Destruction* (New York: Putnam's, 1940), pp. 103, 110.

[55] See Jacques Maritain, "Das Ende des Macchiavellismus," *Frankfurter Hefte,* I, 5 (August, 1946), 15 ff.

repress their conscience. But Machiavelli and his pupil Hitler had a fundamentally different view of political action. "According to Machiavelli not merely the princes and conquerors of the sixteenth century, but the great leaders and creators of modern states and modern history, have a good conscience; indeed, they are convinced that they do their duty when, to create order, they act unjustly, or when they make use of every kind of evil that may help them satisfy their will for power." [56]

This brings out the essential distinction between the Christian statesman and the Machiavellianism of Hitler. Bismarck could never have called politics an amoral expression of the animal nature of man. He could never have advanced without qualification the thesis of its autonomy, which in the circle of Machiavellian zoology takes on the rank of a natural law. As a politician Bismarck was continually brought into conflict with his conscience. By way of conscience his faith exercised a restraining and disturbing influence on what he did in politics. It held him to a course of moderation. All of this shows that in the politics of Bismarck the dominant force is the human element rather than animal self-assertion. This is true even where what is involved is essentially a matter of self-assertion within the human sphere. For such self-assertion falls under a different rubric. It is not an amoral virtue but a "bitter," a morally bitter, necessity.

Bismarck has been accused, whether justly or unjustly, of a *de facto* Machiavellianism. But even if the charge were true this is not a *deliberate* Machiavellianism. Even a conscience caught in the net of autonomy, indeed almost swallowed up in it, is still a conscience; it still holds sacred that which bears the sign of humanity. For in the last resort the unscrupulousness involved is not proclaimed as a matter of principle, as in the case of Hitler.

The critical point of Hitler's thesis is as follows: Might before right is the perennial trademark of human history. The strongest power determines right and therewith nullifies the opposing right of those who are weaker. This has been called the "necessity" of history. But Hitler makes of the necessity a virtue. "Perverse love" is triumphant. His battle cry is: "The forest of the world is full of wolves, therefore let us howl with the wolves." But if the law of the jungle thus prevails, then humanity is simply a humanistic illusion.

[56] *Ibid.,* p. 15; cf. also p. 16.

Thus for Hitler the structure of the world no longer stands under a law which calls it in question; it is its own law. The autonomy of the structure hence becomes the only law. Norms are simply attachments to goals designed to guarantee the structure. Hence ideas become ideologies.

This is why it is only logical for Hitler to boast that he will break a dozen oaths each day. In the context of his thinking an oath cannot invoke the authority of truth, because truth is no longer an authority. Ideology has degraded truth to where it is nothing more than a name for the arguments used by ends and interests to provide for themselves an intellectual justification.

The Third Reich certainly made dramatic use of the custom of taking oaths. But the custom had simply a pragmatic aim. It was intended not to bind the conscience — the ethical presuppositions for this were totally lacking — but to create allegiance by the power of suggestion through the mass experience and the psychic impression of ceremonial. Only from this standpoint can one understand the tendency to repeat oaths so often and also to multiply their number within the various political associations.[57]

In the same light one can see why Hitler said contemptuously that he was ready to sign any treaty at will and then immediately annul it. The ethical norm of loyalty to a treaty has no force within the basic amoral conception. It is a humanitarian illusion. A treaty too serves only a pragmatic purpose. It can provide a momentary respite, only to be broken without warning when the time is opportune. Indeed the treaty is not even seriously intended, for it does not bind both parties — as its ethical nature would demand — it binds only the other party. It is a tool of interest.

The Absolutizing of Autonomy in Ideological Tyranny

These deliberations now put us in a position to establish an ultimate theological affinity between Communism and National Socialism (and indeed any other ideological tyranny). Neither sets over against the trend of history any normative imperatives which would be unaffected by empirical conditions, i.e., would retain their normative character even though they could never be empirically realized. Instead they

---

[57] See Chapter 21 below.

both make the existing trend itself the imperative. And they have common reasons for thus absolutizing the trend of history.

In the first place, they seek to intensify the force of political action by developing uninterruptedly its outward thrust, rather than letting it be dissipated in conflicts of conscience or similar discussions and debates between the I and itself. Conscience as the retention of an unconditional awareness of norms is a power-consuming luxury which one cannot afford within the bestiality of a history ruled by the laws of the jungle. Hence instead of the discord of ethical disputes what is sought is unbroken uniformity. History is thus transformed into nature, and anthropology into zoology.

In the second place, one's own political power is enhanced by not fighting against the trend of history but by making this trend an imperative instead. In this way one trims his sails to the winds of history. Instead of resisting it, instead of swimming against the tide, one uses the wind and the current as forces of propulsion in one's own journey. All cleavage in human existence is thus excluded on this score too and changed into uniformity. It is not that the discord which arises between the ethical I on the one hand, and the laws of the jungle and the trend of history on the other, is now set aside. On the contrary, the trend and the current are exploited. Indeed, they are affirmed to be the original order of being. They are made a source of power. In this way it is hoped geometrically to increase one's own historical dynamic.

In the case of National Socialism this is seen at the point where the trend of history which sets might before right is made the principle of one's own action. A necessity of history (i.e., that this is inevitably so) is thus declared to be a virtue.

This same element typifies all radical dictatorships and is to be seen also in Communism. Communism perceives that the trend of history in an industrial age is towards collectivization and depersonalization. Even where it believes this to be an ineluctable development of the time, as in early Marxism and the original humanitarian intention of Marx himself, its own theory of historical dynamic demands that it make no effort to fight it, but rather accept it, and thus again make a virtue of a necessity. For there is presumably no point in resisting anything which history decrees. To do so would be to suffer an ir-retrievable loss of power. Bound by tradition, the West may make such an effort, but the result will be its demise before the dynamic of the East. Moreover, the person who stands on his own two feet is like sand in the political machinery. He causes friction. He cannot be functionally integrated. He is too broadly developed in his own life to become a mere cog in the machinery of power.

Ideological tyranny regards its attitude to history as consistent realism. To acknowledge norms that call the historical trend in question is regarded as unrealistic idealism, humanistic illusion. At the same time, though, it is itself guilty of a highly unrealistic attitude toward history. For it overlooks one of the basic realities of all historical life, namely, the power of confidence and trust. The man who is not conscious of being bound to an authoritative standard which stands above his own interests and is binding upon both himself and the other party is quite unpredictable, and unqualified for true partnership. When the ethical axiom *pacta sunt servanda* [agreements are to be kept] is set aside, the possibility of fellowship is destroyed.

Since the establishment of partnerships is a vital aspect of politics, ideological tyranny in effect makes politics impossible. This means that powers condemned to play politics with ideological tyranny must endeavor to end an unpredictable and dangerous coexistence with it by eliminating it as far as they are able from the sphere of political interplay, in other words by creating the facts which will correspond to its disqualification as a partner. This is what happened historically in the events leading up to the Second World War. For this war broke out not merely as the result of a specific crisis, such as that of Czechoslovakia or Poland. It was due basically to the fact that Hitler had disqualified himself as a partner to any understanding. He could not be the member of an order because he was the enemy of all order and therefore had to be destroyed.[58]

While the peculiar situation of the atomic age may prevent a direct expression of these crass consequences and produce instead other symptoms of conflict, such as the cold war, this does not alter the basic fact that within the structure of historical situations any power that has become unpredictable is no longer capable of partnership.

---

[58] See, e.g., Winston S. Churchill, *The Second World War*, Vol. I: *The Gathering Storm* (Boston: Houghton Mifflin, 1948), pp. 325-326. According to Hans Windisch, *Führer und Verführte* (Seebruch: Heering, 1946), p. 64, Hitler broke 69 pacts and treaties from 1933-1939.

Those who disregard the ethical reality in history – which means here the power of confidence and trust – those who seek to eliminate the discord caused by this reality in order to enhance their power of action, may enjoy initial successes but only until their approach is generally known. In the long run they weaken themselves. For to regard material being or the trend of history as the true realities is to think and act unrealistically. At an ultimate level of being, therefore, obedience to the norm of the good is thus congruent with both cleverness and realism of action. The biblical statements that the godless are fools (Ps. 14:1) and that sin brings destruction (cf. Prov. 14:34) have their basis here.

Autonomy and Ethical Decision

We can sum up the result of this examination – and throw light on the problem of autonomies – in four main points. The first is this: Far more important than the fact that there are autonomies, which is obvious, is the question of what rank is to be conceded to them.

Our second point – as became clear from our consideration of both Bismarck and Hitler – is that they may be accorded different ranks. Autonomies can enjoy, e.g., an absolute rank. This occurs when a principle valid in one sphere of life – such as bios, or spirit, or the economic factor, or the aesthetic law of form – is invested with metaphysical significance and hence absolutized. The linguistic sign of this type of thinking is the use of words ending with "ism" (biologism, idealism, aestheticism, etc.). In cases of such absolute rank the autonomy becomes a natural compulsion, a law of nature, and man becomes a natural, non-human factor which functions according to patterns from the realm of biology or physics. Even if this functioning is set in motion with a great expenditure of planning energy, and therefore of will, such a will is not to be interpreted as expressing an ethical decision carried through in opposition to the trend of impulse and inclination. "Will" in this context is simply an expression for the impelling dynamism which wills what, according to natural law, it must will. The congruence of fatalism and voluntarism is integral to such a doctrine of autonomy. Here is the one instance where fatalism does not have a crippling effect (because destiny forces the impotent will) but incites to action (because destiny causes itself to be fulfilled by the will).

Autonomies, however, can also enjoy a relative rank. They can be directed by regulative rather than constitutive principles. There can be no doubt that every sphere of life has some immanent order which is relevant only to itself, which prescribes, as it were, the laws of action within that sphere. It would be quite irrational, e.g., if in manufacturing (think of automobile production) technical requirements did not take precedence over purely aesthetic considerations, if technical utility were subordinated to the tastes of the purchaser, even as it would be quite irrational if business enterprises were directed primarily not by the economic consideration of profit but by humanitarian and social motives. There can also be no doubt that immanent in these factual requirements of the various spheres of life there is a tendency which impels them to demand that they be given not merely primary but exclusive consideration — in technical or economic matters, e.g., only technical or economic aspects are to be taken into account — and which impels them also to invade and take over the other spheres of life and to become the total theme in the sense of a world view. In Marxism-Leninism, e.g., the economic principle is no longer restricted to the economic sphere but determines the theme of all history. Thus does the autonomy of an individual sphere tend to become an autocracy.

Our third point by way of summarizing is the important observation that the trend at work in autonomies, whether they be regarded as absolute or as relative, appears not merely on the objective side in terms of operative factual requirements but also on the subjective side in terms of passion or orientation of the will. Thus hand in hand with the autonomy of power and its use there is on the subjective side the "will to power." Hand in hand with the autonomy of aesthetics there is the inclination toward aestheticism.[59] From this standpoint, and with the subjective trend in view, the laissez faire suggested by autonomy implies more than just letting things take their course. It implies going along with them.

It is the conjunction of this subjective factor which gives rise to the ethical question, and that in two ways. In the first place, man lives at the point of intersection of the individual spheres and their autonomies. He is therefore exposed to the conflict of values and must make

[59] We are thinking, e.g., of Kierkegaard's *Either/Or*, Part I. Cf. also my book *Das Verhältnis zwischen dem Ethischen und dem Aesthetischen* (Leipzig, 1932).

decisions. Even the attempt to avoid the conflict by absolutizing one autonomy as a world view involves a covert but nonetheless fundamental ethical decision. It involves the self-surrender – indeed the suicide – of the person, his transformation into a functional element. It is a flight into some sphere beyond good and evil. In the second place, the subjective trend poses the ethical question in virtue of the fact that man is set in the antinomy between indicative and imperative, between the indicative posited by the trend and the imperative demanded by conscience, which forbids man to be subject to any trend, be it that of impulse or that of factual requirements. In this antinomy there is a twofold battle, on the one hand with the impulse of what Kant calls the "sensible ego," and on the other with the impulse of the world itself. We have already shown the significance which this presence of the ethical question has for the problem of "moderation."

Our fourth summary point is simply this: The rank I accord to the autonomies, and the degree to which I thus recognize or contest the presence of the ethical question, is dependent on a basic decision. Either I regard the autonomies as a fateful necessity which exercises a natural kind of compulsion (which is simply a brute fact not subject to ethical evaluation), or I say that the autonomously determined structure of history is: I myself, my objectified ego reflected in the macrocosm (the Babylonian world bears traces of the Babylonian heart; it is "my" world).

In the latter case, even though I adapt myself to certain necessities, I do not regard them as a law which compels – and consequently absolves – me. Instead I see in them only a transsubjective symbol for that wherein I am subject to a trend immanent in myself. E.g., if sacred egoism causes me to make war, or to fight in a war, this is not just destiny or fate. Neither is it merely a case of the divine calling in my particular estate. On the contrary, I have to regard this sacred egoism – which in this case is oriented to a historical order, to my state or nation – as a sign of myself, my own egoism, indeed of "my" world. For this reason, as a soldier I am never justified outright by the fact that I live in an order [Ordnung] which forces me to fight and to kill. This order is for me the emergency order of a fallen world, in whose fall I am implicated. To be sure, I may be "ordered" to fight and to kill by this emergency order of a world which is both harried and preserved by the law of sacred egoism. But this can happen only in the name of the *emergency* order, only in the sphere of the *fallen* world, only to one who stands in need of *forgiveness*. This too leads to restraint, whereas the "god of iron" causes the unchecked fighting instinct to triumph.

Two further decisions also affect the rank accorded to the autonomies. First, I may say that the objective and subjective movements established in the autonomies are a necessity, or I may say that they are a virtue. Second, I may believe that I am under the imperative to resist, or I may love my fate and accept the nature, structure, and trend of the world as it is.

8.

The Autonomy of Politics in Theory

Having examined the ethical affinity of the autonomies in the light of two historical models, we must now test our findings by demonstrating this affinity, not in the life of a politician actually wrestling with the autonomies, but in the strictest theoretical assertion of the autonomies known to modern times. A classical example in this respect — a modern counterpart to Machiavelli — is provided by Carl Schmitt and his concept of politics.[1]

Carl Schmitt and the "Friend-Foe Relationship"

Schmitt defines politics as the actualization of a "friend-foe relationship." Indeed this, for him, is the basis of its autonomous teleology. What he means is that in virtue of the ends pursued all politics leads to alienation from the men or groups who reject these ends or whose own ends stand in *de facto* opposition to them. Thus divisions and conflicts arise between those who are agreed as to the ends and the way to achieve them, and those who have competing intentions. The resultant cleavage between friend and foe is the fundamental rule which applies in all actualizations of power and which has autonomous features.

Purely phenomenologically, this is in fact a unique rule which must be distinguished from all other rules of human intercourse. To be sure, it happens repeatedly in the political sphere that value concepts of another provenance are taken into account in characterizing friends and foes. Thus the friend is said to be good, pious, handsome, industrious, biologically sound, and useful to society, whereas the opposite is said to be true of the foe. But these are falsifications of the autonomy of politics, which is an independent category quite unaffected by evaluations of this kind, and which can cause friend-foe relationships to cut right across them.

[1] See Carl Schmitt, *Der Begriff des Politischen* (Munich, 1932).

Indeed, we must go further. For Schmitt regards these evaluations ultimately as secondary predicates; they stand in service of the primary reality which is the friend-foe relationship. Thus, I do not choose the other as a friend because he has certain estimable qualities. On the contrary, he is, as it were, tossed to my side by the play of historical forces, and I then deck him out with these positive qualities in order to cement my alliance with him.

The more qualities I detect which make him appear not merely useful in his momentary historical role but actually congenial,[2] the more I can embellish the reasonableness of the alliance with emotional values which bring it closer to the masses, make it popular, strengthen it, and which in so doing make it politically the more potent. Conversely, the fight against an enemy can be intensified by defaming him and by attributing to him all kinds of despicable traits, for in this way passion and hatred against him can be increased and the sense of one's own historical importance enhanced.[3]

The friend-foe relationship is thus a primal phenomenon. It cannot be derived from ethical, religious, aesthetic, or economic values. On the contrary, it impresses these values into its own service,[4] and thus has the rank of a "category" with whose help historical connections can in the first place be understood. Accordingly, it is a mistake to regard ethical, religious, or any other evaluations or expressions of value as the true driving powers of history. It is rather the polar and dynamic tensions arising from the elemental friend-foe relationships which fill this role. The values invoked are merely the ideological superstructure erected on this elemental basis. They are ex post facto attempts to justify and intensify the elemental relationships which already exist.

This schema of substructure and superstructure recurs in every form of ideological tyranny. Carl Schmitt has performed the dubious service of working out a final, purely formal, and highly abstract formula which fits the whole range of such tyrannies, namely, the formula of

[2] Think, e.g., of Hitler's glorifying of the Japanese and their "Prussian" Samurai-spirit.

[3] National Socialist propaganda inveighed against "drunken Churchill," "degenerate France," and "perfidious England." It depicted churchmen as traitors, reactionaries, capitalist agents, obscurantists, opium peddlers, etc.

[4] When both Nazi and Communist propaganda speak of "degenerate art," e.g., it is clear that even aesthetics has been impressed into the service of the political friend-foe relationship.

"the friend-foe relationship." This formula is the result of an analysis of the structure of politics, whose autonomy in the case of such state tyrannies is posited absolutely and hence presented in a kind of "pure" form. Greater precision is needed, of course, to distinguish politics from other kinds of friend-foe relationships. In this respect six points are normative for Schmitt's conception.

First, politics does not embrace every kind of hostility. A sports contest or an academic discussion does not have a political character, since what is at stake in such a battle is something less than the very existence of an individual or group. Politics is not concerned with maintaining or upholding some "thing," e.g., a position in a game or a thesis in a debate, but with maintaining and upholding one's "self." Where the possibility of self-destruction is involved it thus becomes a critical matter. For this reason politics always implies a friend-foe relationship of fateful significance.

Second, related to this fateful character is the fact that the concept of politics implies not private or personal struggles but a public conflict which takes place in the arena of actual history. The outcome of these hostilities changes the course of history and thus affects human destiny.

Third, these hostilities must owe their origin too to destiny. I.e., they achieve political rank only if they do not spring from personal emotions — e.g., hatred or the thirst for revenge — but are brought on ineluctably, quite independently of favorable or unfavorable feelings, by the objective course of events, by objective constellations of interests, or by ideological conflicts. Since this kind of conflict is "objective," it cannot be evaded by subjective arguments, by appeals, e.g., to the fact that one desires peace and is thus against war. Since it is also a fateful matter entailing the question of one's own being or non-being, there is no possibility of escape into neutrality. The political character of the friend-foe relationship thus finds expression in the fact that everybody is forced to take a position, to be either a friend or a foe.

Fourth, the fateful character of politics is ultimately grounded in the nature of history itself. History receives the impulses for its movement from the polar tension between friend and foe. The element of destiny lies not merely in the fact that the concrete stuff of conflict is present at any given time, but rather in the fact that history is always actualized in conflicts. The subjects of conflict change; conflict itself remains. Man becomes "political man," subject to the friend-foe relationship, not simply because he is projected into a specific present with its current antithesis but because he is projected into history as such, and hence is "historical." To exist historically is to be subject to political existence.

Fifth, since we are thus projected *into* history, and cannot assume a position outside it, neutrality is impossible. We cannot stand above the friend-foe relationship and claim for ourselves the objective standards of a judge. On the contrary, we are in principle parties to what is going on. We are either friends or foes. Any third option we might seek is not to be had by way of impartial binding arbitration, but only as the object fought for. It can be attained only by the successful venturing of oneself. When conflicts of interests take the form of war, there can be no binding arbitration, not simply because there is no higher authority above the sovereign disputants, but also because their claims cannot be validated except by the trial of strength. Even an international authority, e.g., a council of nations, cannot arbitrate the matter since the criteria for such a judgment would have to be taken from past historical situations and the resultant rights, claims, and limitations to which they gave rise. But these criteria will always be contested, since fundamental changes in power potential have probably taken place quite unobserved and these cannot be comprehended in legal form but must be revealed through trials of strength. It is thus the trials of strength which first lay down the criteria for historical law by bringing to light what could not previously be known objectively. If the friend-foe relationship is the ultimate reality of history — and our main quarrel with Schmitt is that he takes this view — then the supreme trial of strength, i.e., war, is indeed the only legitimate judge. War is in truth "the father of all things," for it is the impulse which begets all historical movement. But this also means that the instrument of war is not a necessity but a virtue, for war brings us close to the primal laws of history.

Sixth, one final consequence arises out of the absolutizing of the friend-foe relationship: All values are impressed into the service of the parties which constitute the relationship and there are thus no norms left which transcend the parties and which both might recognize as authoritative. All norms are determined by the parties, and — since the parties exist only in historically concrete forms — this means that norms are always determined by the particular situation. At any given time, then, the supreme value is highly variable. In addition, since the norms and values help to shape a world view, world views too are extremely variable. This means that the world view is not a definitive view of the world but one that changes with the situations and parties for which it exists.

The same might perhaps be said by the historian of philosophy who writes a history of world views and who is impressed by their fluctuations according to changing situations. But Schmitt gives a particular nuance to this thesis. For him, a world view, even though it may be mistaken as to its *de facto* relation to time, cannot really intend to have supratemporal validity. It means to be time-bound for it aims to end up not with norms which parties and situations will have to serve, but with norms which will serve the various parties and situations.

Hence too the distinction between necessity and virtue may be adduced in interpretation. The historian of philosophy mentioned above will notice that the world views which intend to be absolute are in fact related to their time and hence relative. But he will regard this link with the situation as a necessity of human knowledge and consequently as a tragic limitation. For Schmitt, however, it is a virtue when thought desires no more than to validate intellectually a supreme value which is actually determined by the particular party and situation involved in a given friend-foe relationship.

It is at once apparent how far Schmitt with his concept of political autonomy lays down the ultimate formal laws of the structure of the ideological state and its use of power. For to absolutize the friend-foe relationship is to understand all values, norms, and ideas pragmatically, and to set up a system of categories within which the concept of ideology necessarily arises. The way is thus paved for the National Socialist and Marxist-Leninist thesis that there can be no science free from all presuppositions, but only party science, and that this is equally true of law, art, ethics, etc.; all are conditioned by the party. Schmitt is thus the theoretician of totalitarian doctrines. By reason of his concept of absolute political autonomy, they owe homage to him.

There is only a methodological distinction between Schmitt's thinking and that of totalitarian doctrine. Totalitarian doctrine begins by absolutizing a value of the moment as determined by the situation, and ends by stating that all other values must serve this one. All other values thus have a rank which is only instrumental, not authoritative and normative. Thus Marxism absolutizes the economic value which was supreme at the beginning of the Industrial Age, when the working classes were economically threatened. On this basis it develops its thesis of the ideologies, i.e., of the significance of spiritual values merely as reflections, and of their pragmatic function. It ends up with the thesis that history is a history of class conflicts, of socially determined friend-foe relationships. These conflicts autonomously determine all political action. What serves one's own class is good and what harms it is bad, in every sphere of life. The very same thought processes were also operative in National Socialism.

Carl Schmitt, on the other hand, takes the opposite path. He begins with a pure elevation of the political autonomy of the friend-foe relationship, and then works his way back logically to the axioms with which totalitarian doctrine starts, namely, the absolutizing of the values of the moment. Because Schmitt is a theoretician and does not himself stand in a political situation which forces him to absolutize a specific value, he is able to lay down the ultimate formal structural laws of all conceivable doctrines which are either constructed on the dogma of autonomy or move irresistibly toward it.

In our presentation of Schmitt's view we have not merely given an exposition of the essential features of his conception but also indicated the conclusions to which his premises lead. We have suggested some points of criticism, which we shall now summarize and weigh theologically in terms of three main points.

First, Schmitt's attempt to liberate politics from any teleological reference and to present it as a mere means leads to a revolt of this means. A means which in its function is not limited and checked by an end necessarily becomes unchecked and unlimited. In other words, it becomes its own end, an end in itself. Instead of having its place within a more comprehensive anthropology, it constitutes itself an anthropology, the first principle of which is that man is by nature a political animal. Man is characterized not by the fact that he is seeking ends but by the fact that he is on a road with no destination, an endless street which involves him in conflict and delivers him up to the friend-foe relationship. This street is characterized not by its destination but by what takes place on it, by the movement of traffic and by the pedestrians who disrupt it.

In this statement about man is implicit a further statement about history (we must remember that politics is not defined as one element in history, but as an isolated phenomenon of means which itself defines history): History, as the sphere in which friend-foe relationships are worked out, becomes a play of forces, as noted earlier in Machiavelli.[5] The stronger is the enemy of the weaker; he profits at his expense. The essential impulse of the unbridled and autonomous friend-foe relationship is the equally unbridled "will to power," i.e., the quest of power for its own sake, that power which enables him who has it to live and thrive at the expense of everybody else, undeterred by any authority which could serve as a norm for the use of power. Thus the "master race" of National Socialism as the biological subject of this will to power is presumably justified in expanding to the limits of its capacity.

This revolt of means (whether the means be called politics or power) thus leads necessarily to distinguishing between men in terms of whether they are stronger or weaker, healthy or degenerate. When consistently worked out, the autonomy of politics thus leads to the assumption of processes, or isolated acts of self-assertion, which have no goals, but simply arise out of the constellations of the moment, and which are thus similar to those with which we are familiar from the animal kingdom. But it also leads to the conclusion that autonomy is itself the absolute law of the world: Life *is* conflict.

Second, the character of politics as a "mere" means can be secured – in opposition to Schmitt – only by defining it in the light of its goal, e.g., the goal of establishing a just social and international order, or of balancing interests and so keeping peace.[6] If this goal is kept in view, there arises a different concept of politics and of the friend-foe relationship, one which is not defined in terms of autonomy. We are untrue to reality if we do not see that division is an element of history. Such division, however, is to be interpreted as division with respect to

---

[5] See *ThE* 1, 536-539.

[6] If the reader thinks this contradicts what we said concerning Bismarck, who denied the utopian character of politics and insisted on doing what seemed called for at the moment, in the particular situation, then we must remind him that it is necessary to distinguish between the proximate tactical goals of politics and its ultimate strategic meaning. The utopian fails to make this distinction; he – e.g., the pacifist – insists on having absolute means for attaining absolute goals. Bismarck's critique of utopian idealism is directed only against such an unrealistic approach, not against the idea of ultimate goals.

this goal. The meaning of history does not lie, as the doctrine of absolute political autonomy would have it, in division and union in and for themselves. It lies in the purpose with respect to which the division first arises. This purpose may be defined in two ways, and there are two corresponding forms of division.

In the first place, the division may consist in what we have called proximate or partial goals. A statesman may, like Bismarck, regard the unification of his people as an immediate goal which can be attained. Or he may plan to make a colony independent. Or a great power may aim to protect itself by means of a ring of allies or bases. These proximate and partial tactical goals cause differences with those who represent other interests. They thus give rise to friend-foe relationships. These relationships, though, are just as relative as the goals sought. Once the goals are reached, or compromises effected in the form of treaties, there is an understanding; hostilities are neutralized and enmity may even give way to friendship.

But the purpose with respect to which divisions arise may consist, in the second place, in an ultimate end, indeed, in the meaning and goal of history itself. The divisions and unions which arise with respect to *this* goal are unbridgeable. Even if they do not precipitate open warfare, they do lead to permanent disputes and crises, to cold wars, or at the very best to thaws and coexistence.

Once it is realized that the friend-foe relationship arises as the result of division or union with respect to different forms of purpose, it is evident that this relationship can be qualitatively very different. There can be both ultimate and penultimate divisions, and amongst the latter there can be constant shifts and even neutralizations of the friend-foe relationships. Since these relationships are structurally determined by a transcendent factor, by a purpose, it is impossible to speak of them in terms of their immanent teleology. Neither can one say that their autonomy is the controlling norm of the historical process.

This is the point where Schmitt's conception goes wrong. If the friend-foe relationship is basically a means to an end, then it must be understood in the light of this end and not in terms of itself. To view it in isolation as a structural characteristic of history is to elevate it to the rank of a norm, an end in itself. When this is done the structure of history — whether it be understood in terms of National Socialism or

Communism, of biological materialism or economic materialism — itself becomes the law of action. Its necessities and doubtful aspects become virtues.

Third and finally, Schmitt overlooks a further relativization of the political means. This relativization, which has a directly theological character, arises from the fact that the means of the friend-foe relationship finds its actualization in the world after the fall, in a disrupted and divided world. If the friend-foe relationship is something that the world has "incurred" then we cannot ascribe to it any independent dignity. And this is precisely the case. To begin with, there is in this world no longer any ultimately binding norm. Such a norm could be found only in the will and commandments of God, but these man has rejected. And it is because man is no longer under the will of God that there can arise the tragedy of Babel: dispersion, division, and centrifugal forces, including the friend-foe relationship (Gen. 11:1-9). Then in addition, egoism, fear, and hope prevent individuals and nations from being objective with themselves and ready to restrain themselves for the sake of others. Egoism allows a man to be nothing but an advocate of his own interests — and for this very reason a party within the friend-foe relationship.

It is a fact that after the fall man must see to his own interests. For these are threatened by the interests of others; the organizing center is lost. It is also true that there are different ethical interests, the individual and collective, usually described as lower and higher. These too may be in conflict with one another. These differences are not the differences in "kind" of which we read in Genesis 1, which derive from creation and which are related to one another in creation's peaceful hierarchy. These differences express rather the diffusion which occurs in the tragedy of Babel.

If nevertheless there is in this world, in the sense of the Noachic covenant, a balancing of interests by conflict such that the world is thereby preserved, then the interests involved are neither sacred nor derived from creation. For the Noachic order is an emergency order.[7] This brings us back to the distinction we have repeatedly made: The world of interests, and consequently of political means, must not idealize its structure or make of it a law, for this structure is a necessity, not a virtue, and must be so regarded.

[7] See *ThE* 1, 147-148, 439-440.

Theologically the cardinal error of Schmitt is this: He gives an exact phenomenological description of the fallen world as it is driven by the impulses of interest, but fails to see the background of this state of the world and hence ascribes to the phenomena a false rank. He thinks that one can establish the nature of this present world as one knows natural phenomena and analyzes them in their ordered interconnections. In reality, however, the world with which we are dealing is a world called in question, a world which has forfeited the value it possessed at creation. By failing to note this devaluation, Schmitt inevitably elevates the known data, i.e., the structure of the world, to normative rank, and makes the prevailing autonomy of means into an ultimate law — with all the serious consequences which follow.

In conclusion, we may say that politics has at its disposal no general rational criteria which can serve as norms to or from which appeal can be made. On the contrary, the politician is always an involved party, not a judge. He is the advocate of an interest, not an umpire between interests. Only the Lord of history knows what is the legitimate or illegitimate interest of each player in the game of history. This knowledge can be attained neither by the attainable degree of human objectivity — for all are committed and involved, all feel that they are either threatened or commissioned — nor by the attainable degree of information. There simply is no ultimate court of appeal. There are only interested parties scattered throughout the dispersion of Babel. This unfortunately is a necessary fact. The decisive question is whether men will attempt to make a virtue of this necessity.

If this is done, councils of nations and similar organizations can be regarded only with cynicism, since they seem to claim that they are established in a neutral zone above the differences of interest. In this sense Hitler quite logically made mockery of them. If, however, one does not thus confuse virtue with necessity, one will certainly not overestimate an institution like the League of Nations or the United Nations, unless utterly blinded by utopianism and unreality. One will even reckon with the possibility of its degenerating to the point where it involves nothing but longwinded discussion, disagreeable horse trading, and veritable orgies of hypocrisy. But one will at the same time recognize what it signifies. For such an institution, by its very existence, reminds us that the criterion of interest, if laid down absolutely, is a very poor goddess of history, that this criterion is in fact a necessity, not a virtue, and that it needs to be relativized as much as is humanly possible by such institutions. Turning historical necessity into a virtue leads to demonic perversion.[8]

The View of Man in Machiavelli and Thomas More

We have asserted repeatedly that to absolutize autonomies is to change history into nature and man into a non-human, depersonalized functionary. But this happens only theoretically. In reality it is impossible for man to migrate into a zone devoid of values, a sphere beyond good and evil. Even the attempt at such a migration is a decidedly ethical act freighted with values. The man who turns anthropology into zoology or into a doctrine of economic functions is not making a neutral assertion; he is making an ethical decision. He is deciding against man, against his own nature. Paradoxically, migration into a sphere beyond good and evil is itself evil. Whoever insists on speaking of non-man, or sub-man, or super-man thereby reveals what kind of man he is himself.

The same is true of those who would insist on a non-human form of the autonomies; they reveal thereby a specific form of humanity. As distinct from the scientist, man here is not just the subject who knows and establishes certain data. He is not just one who fulfills functions of understanding or purpose. On the contrary, he is the "existing" man who makes decisions.

What emerges from every political conception, even from one which engages in a non-human absolutizing of the autonomies, is in like manner an understanding of man, a particular self-understanding. This can be illustrated from the different conceptions of man to be seen in Machiavelli, the representative of purely autonomous politics, and in Thomas More, the representative of a utopia which transcends autonomy.

We recall that for Machiavelli man is a fixed bearer of powers. He cannot transcend himself. He must be treated as a natural phenomenon who acts in keeping with the developmental processes inherent in his own nature. When Machiavelli on occasion speaks of man as one who nonetheless takes ethical decisions, this is purely an ironic trick: Man as natural force is repeatedly driven by ethical illusions. One might

[8] See above p. 61, n. 16.

say that man, in the view of Machiavelli, is moved not by genuine imperatives, but by ethical sentimentalities, by loyalty complexes, etc., which the prince intentionally takes into account in his use of power.

History is a mere play of forces, completely free from ethical values. But this freedom is purchased only at the cost of a contempt for man which may everywhere be detected as a mood. This contempt for man is a decision against man. It condemns him to be a mere force, and so robs him of his dignity as a person. Thus anthropology becomes zoology, as in much modern teaching on sex.[9] Machiavellianism is the Kinsey Report on political behavior in the human male. The thesis which Machiavelli champions, i.e., that these forces proceed autonomously as a law unto themselves, thus derives from a personal decision. The existential background of this political conception contains an unmistakable judgment on zoological autonomy as represented by Machiavelli.

The antithesis to Machiavelli, and therewith to his anthropology, is Thomas More. While Machiavelli describes the real course and direction of the play of forces impelled by the human power centers, Thomas More — as the title of his main work *Utopia* already indicates — concerns himself with a goal which is sought, and which transcends the autonomous course of these forces. A genuine difference of starting point may be seen here.

The difference does not rest, as a first glance might suggest, on the fact that Machiavelli takes a realistic and pessimistic view of man whereas Thomas More takes an idealistic and optimistic view. The latter too is aware of the ambiguity of man, of his impulsion by blind passions and fierce interests. He too is aware of the possibility that man might become the function of undirected forces which acknowledge no norm. But More's approach to this known ambiguity of man is different from that of Machiavelli. He does not accept a psychology which renounces all values and is contemptuous of man. He is not content to maintain that man is by nature the function of his elemental forces and has no will of his own.

Thomas More is a genuine utopian in the sense that he sees man divided between what he is essentially meant to be and what he actu-

[9] Cf. P. H. Biederich and Leo Dembicki, *Die Sexualität des Mannes, Darstellung und Kritik des Kinsey-Reports* (1951).

ally is. In Aristotelian terms, More distinguishes between man's essence and existence, between his nature and his condition. It would be incorrect, therefore, to say that utopias are unrealistic dreams. On the contrary, what utopians depict is a world order or social structure in which what is objectified is the essence of man, not his empirical state. In utopias man may see his true self, a self which in existing reality is present to be sure, but concealed under distortions. In More's *Utopia*, therefore, there lies a distinct anthropology which in at least five respects is significant for the ethical problem at issue, as we shall presently seek to indicate.

In the first place, man is here most emphatically not a mere natural force which can be noted and taken into account as such. On the contrary, man is seen as a being which transcends himself and is oriented toward something beyond himself. Indeed, if one were to try to say what man is, it would be wrong to describe him merely in his actual state and to say that he is a murderer, thief, and adulterer, self-centered and power-hungry. That this description does to a great extent apply to man's actual condition More would allow. But he would reject the idea that this is a definition of man's essence. Similarly, a Christian, however realistic his view of the world, is bound to object if someone describes fallen man as essential man, or fallen history as a process in which might essentially takes precedence of right (even though it might claim such precedence *de facto*). To the essence of man belongs rather what man was before the fall, and what he will be in the eschaton.

Herein lies the decisive distinction from Machiavelli's anthropology. Machiavelli identifies essential man with his actual state. He regards man as one who is driven by passions. He consequently holds that the only person who can exercise political rule is one who knows and controls these forces, and combines them in a symphony of corporate action. In contrast, More regards man as one in whom what should be is in conflict with what is. Man is man in contradiction.

This has important consequences for what man does politically, which is our second main point. The essential dimension of man belongs to his reality as surely as does the factual dimension. Consequently, the essential dimension too is a power which can be mobilized and which has political actuality. The longing of man to find his way through to himself and to his essential nature is at least as strong a political force as his powerful drives and instincts.

This can be seen from the political significance which attaches to utopias. Ideas of a kingdom of peace, a state of justice, or social equality, unleash fanaticisms and are high-powered engines of historical progress.

Utopias are falsely interpreted if they are regarded as mere fairy tales. Fairy tales always deal with what is outside. They have an effect only on children who cannot distinguish between inside and outside. Adults, though, can make this distinction. For them fairy tales are mere dreams which lead to higher or lower forms of indolence and perhaps seduce into sentimentality. The political impact of utopias cannot be understood along these lines. It can be understood only if one sees that the eschatological depictions of utopias bear a correlation to the essence and potentiality of man himself, and that in them man sees himself in terms of what he should be. Utopias are filled with the pathos of the potentiality and destiny of man. The kingdom of peace and the classless society are never a mere antithesis to present conditions. They are the mature, fruit-bearing tree which is already contained — or still contained — as a seed in what man presently is.

In the third place, this side of man's potentiality cannot be released by statistical data after the manner of Machiavelli. It can be released only by imperatives which appeal to what man can be and to what he is ordained to be. Machiavelli, who regards politics as an autonomous natural force, necessarily despises imperatives. He finds a place only for physical pressure (terror) and for commands (proclamations of the right of the strong). But More, who distinguishes between essence and existence, must appeal to essence. That is, he works with imperatives, with ought factors, to awaken the real man. The utopias constitute this appeal. They are a summons in the form of eschatological symbols.

Fourth, as an active politician More has a realistic view of historical processes. He thus allows for an autonomous sphere in history. He takes arrogance and egoism into account. He realizes that political action is bound to specific laws which are dictated by these qualities. But for him the essence of man is also an operative factor. Hence history does not move only in natural processes, in self-evolutions of these impulses. On the contrary, the imperative which stems from man's essence, and which finds expression in utopias, is also present. This intervenes and makes the history of man a dialectic of necessity (autonomy) and ethical opportunity.[10]

Finally, in the fifth place, Machiavelli stands for the indicative aspect of the state, whereas More stands for the imperative aspect. Machiavelli arrives at his view on the basis of a one-sided anthropology which regards man as a moving and moved force that operates according to its own laws and is to be dealt with accordingly. Thomas More, on the other hand, arrives at his view of the state on the basis of an anthropology which affirms a dialectical two-sidedness of man in the polarity of nature and condition, essence and present state.

The very fact that both conceptions presuppose a specific anthropology is enough to show that there can be no question of purely autonomous processes. Zones of decision are left, whether voluntarily as in the case of More or involuntarily as in the case of Machiavelli. The author of political conceptions stands in relation to man. He decides for man or against him. He constructs a latent anthropology. He stands himself, therefore, in the zones of decision, even though in his theory he may dispute their very existence.

Thomas More, who in spite of his awareness of autonomous spheres expressly recognizes these zones of decision, makes it quite clear that man cannot simply "go along" in the political world, as Machiavelli supposes. Man is directed instead to tread specific paths. The vision of utopia is a constant appeal to the true nature of man. It has the effect of a disturbing intervention, indeed, of a judgment.

Man's historicity is thus protected. He is kept from plunging into a nature which would necessarily make him not animal but non-human. He may never reach his utopia. His guiding stars may shine in Platonic unreality and remoteness above him. But awareness of what is demanded keeps the cleavage open and protects him against the blind dynamic of a play of forces. As we saw in Bismarck, this can have a political effect, namely, in the form of restraint.

We have now considered all aspects of the problem of autonomy

---

[10] Among modern interpreters of world history Arnold Toynbee expresses best the dialectic of autonomy and ethical opportunity. Within the laws which determine the rise and development of cultures there arises the mythical-suprahistorical necessity that man respond to the challenge posed by situations which are naturally or historically given, i.e., that he relate to them in a way that involves decision. Toynbee's view contrasts with that of Spengler who in his *Decline of the West* understands history one-sidedly in terms of autonomous processes.

using politics as our model. We have seen that the question is not whether we are to accept or deny this autonomy, but what rank is to be accorded to it. Are we to absolutize it, and thereby turn history into (a distorted) nature? Or are we to relativize it, and thereby respect the zones of decision upon which man's existence as a person is dependent? We have contended that these zones of decision have an indelible character and will always be in force even if they are not respected in political theory, e.g., in Machiavelli or Carl Schmitt. In this case they exist behind the author's back while his vision embraces only processes which seem to operate irrespective of values. It is evident from the antithesis between More and Machiavelli, between the different anthropological backgrounds of their conceptions, that there exists this twofold possibility of consciously respecting the zones of decision on the one hand or of unconsciously living in them on the other.[11]

---

[11] We have already touched on the related question of the relation between freedom and necessity in *ThE* 1, 290-297, and will do so again in a subsequent volume where we treat of law.

Part Two

THE NATURE OF THE STATE

9.

The State and the Individual

Retrospect and Prospect

We have already discussed [1] the problem of the state, e.g., in connection with our treatment of the two kingdoms, natural law, and ideological tyranny. In addition, the state has constantly served as a paradigm for the Noachic covenant. The theses we have developed to this point, not only in the *Politics* but also in the *Foundations*, may be briefly summarized.

First, the state is ordained by God as a necessary remedy for corrupt nature. In man's primal state God ruled by the "moving of one finger." [2] For before the fall man paid heed to such movements. Now that man no longer pays heed, God uses an order equipped with power. [3]

Second, the state contains an element both of judgment and of grace. It involves judgment to the degree that, in its restraint of evil, it calls fallen man in question. It is an order of grace to the degree that God's gracious preservation is in many ways displayed in it. E.g., one can see from the instance of the state that God does not desire chaos and human self-destruction, but gives to man a *kairos*, an "acceptable time" for repentance, which implies the continuing possibility of physical life. [4] Again, one can see from the existence of the state that God in the Noachic covenant does not turn against man the impulses of the fallen world, e.g., the principles of force and retribution, but brings out of them possibilities of order which are designed to preserve man by setting over against blind and egoistical force the legitimate force of government and law. The state is thus a sign of God's goodness. "After the Gospel or the

[1] See the topical entries in the Index of Names and Subjects in *ThE* 1.
[2] *Uno moto digito. LW* 1, 104.
[3] See *ThE* 1, 361, 373-376.
[4] See *ThE* 1, 273-274, 277-278.

ministry, there is on earth no better jewel." [5] "It is a glorious ordinance of God and splendid gift of God." [6]

It follows that the state is an emergency order of the fallen world, not an order of creation. This understanding of the state protects us against either idealizing it or making it totalitarian. Ideological tyranny regards the state not as an emergency order to be seen always against the background of the fall but simply as an order per se. On this view the state is not restricted to the kingdom on the left hand but becomes a pseudo church.

We shall pause now for a moment here at the beginning of this new Part to get our bearings once again in respect of methodology. We discussed this already in Chapter 1 and would apply it as we proceed now to a theological analysis of the state. We said that we would deliberately start not with the New Testament but with a phenomenology of the state — e.g., with an extensive investigation of autonomy — and only then proceed to the New Testament doctrine of the state. This does not mean that we are attempting first to lay a secular or natural foundation and then use what is said in the New Testament merely as a supplementary or subsequent theological commentary upon it. On the contrary, from the very outset we have viewed the phenomenology — e.g., the nature of power and the relation between necessity and ethical opportunity — in the light of the New Testament message.

We have thus considered the phenomena in the light of biblical questions. E.g., we inquired concerning the empirical forms in which the deification of the state depicted in Revelation 13 is realized. Again, we treated the question of autonomies from the standpoint of whether and how far they set a limit to the possibility of ethical action, and therewith to the applicability of the divine commandments. Again, in the next several chapters we shall be considering the problem of power, which as God's power is unambiguous but as man's power is plunged into the shadowy half-light between creation and sin.

Even the "worldliness" of a phenomenology of the state is a theological concept, since worldliness cannot be known on the basis of what the world knows of itself but only on the basis of what is

[5] LW 13, 54.
[6] LW 46, 237.

known of the world by someone who encounters it in the name of him who has overcome it (John 16:33; I John 5:4), someone who has it as though he had it not (I Cor. 7:29-31). The world never sees itself merely as world, but usually as heaven or hell. True world-liness comes to light only when we see things "as if there were no God," but such a view is possible only when we stand "before" God (Bonhoeffer).

The world so viewed, from the standpoint of Law and gospel, has some questions of its own to put to Law and gospel. This is not a case, however, of "the world" putting questions to the gospel. It is a case of the world, being called in question by the gospel, putting questions in return.

By our method we preserve this dialectic between world and gospel. Because what is involved is a dialectic, the question of which member should be the starting point of our consideration is purely a matter of judgment, not of radical decision. We have given already in Chapter 1 the reasons for our own choice of priority.

To get at the nature of the state in this manner, we do best to treat it in terms of the various relations involved in it. E.g., one may ask — as we shall in this chapter and those immediately follow-ing — whether the individual exists for the state or the state exists for the individual, whether the state is a legal society or a moral so-ciety, and whether the state is an authority that stands over against its citizens or is merely a function of their own self-governing. As we are forced to recognize that none of these relations fully covers the case and that the state cannot be subsumed under any of these alternatives, we shall learn to view the state as a unique entity, and thus be prepared to listen to what the New Testament has to say concerning it.

For in the statements of the New Testament the uniqueness of the state, which is at first only negatively suggested by our phenom-enological considerations, i.e., its refusal to be subsumed under a master concept, is explained by the fact that the state is a special institution of God in the history of man's salvation and judgment. Since this history is an object of faith and cannot be demonstrated empirically, there will always remain, after all man's natural attempts to explain the state, a residual factor which ultimately cannot be known.

The State as a Goal and as a Means of Individual Existence

The eighteenth and nineteenth centuries produced two extremely different theories on the relation of the individual to the state. On the one hand, the goal of all historical processes was declared to be the moral personality. Think, e.g., of Schiller's guiding concept of the "beautiful soul," [7] or of Goethe's idea of personality in *Wilhelm Meister's Travels* (which relates not to suprapersonal works of culture but to the "simple demands of the day," and in the light of these to the development of one's own entelechy), or of Wilhelm von Humboldt's ideal of personal humanistic education. Connected with this goal of personality, at least implicitly, is a concept of the state in which the state is held to serve the self-development of the individual.

On the other hand, for Hegel — and this is the second type, produced by the nineteenth century — the state is the "moral idea actualized." To this extent the state is the "real God," "the divine which exists of and for itself, and is of absolute authority and majesty." Hence the state does not exist for the people (and consequently for the individual); the people exists for the state. Hegel thus stands at the head of a long line of doctrines of the state which from Heinrich von Treitschke to theoreticians of the totalitarian state proclaim state and nation to be the foremost task of history, the purpose of all individual and cultural life.

As we see it, a much more dialectical view — in which the greater stress, however, still falls on either the individual or society — is to be found already in antiquity, with Plato and Aristotle on the one side and Socrates on the other. Since this antithesis illumines in a most instructive way the theme of the present chapter, we may give here a brief description of it.

The chief task of the state, according to Plato, is to effect justice (δικαιοσύνη) in its citizens, i.e., to bring them under that law which is the foundation of the political society. This justice is regarded as a kind of basic virtue which is superior to all other virtues.

---

[7] The concept is developed in Schiller's essay "On Loveliness and Dignity" (1793), which appears in Charles J. Hempel (ed.), *Schiller's Complete Works* (Philadelphia: Kohler, 1861), II, 459-478; see esp. p. 471. See also Helmut Thielicke, *Das Verhältnis zwischen dem Ethischen und dem Aesthetischen* (Leipzig, 1932), pp. 208 ff.

From it derive such virtues as wisdom, the fear of God, manliness, moderation, and justice in the narrower sense of "to each his own."

Plato entrusts the formal representation and inculcation of this basic virtue to the state as a kind of moral institution. Of course, this particular virtue ($\dot{\alpha}\rho\epsilon\tau\dot{\eta}$) does not have in Plato the same features it had in the middle-class morality of eighteenth-century humanism. It has instead the political character of classical Greece. The state characterized by these virtues does not have the function of ministering to the perfecting or to the self-development of the individuals within it. On the contrary, individuals, as well as the three main classes into which they are grouped,[8] are in their very essence related to and dependent upon the state. The state, however, exists for its own sake, since it is the state itself — not the individuals within it — which is the representative actualization of the good and the beautiful.

The state is thus a more direct reflection of being than is the individual. Individual life is for its part essentially a reflection of the life of the state, for in it the hierarchy of classes or estates crops up again as a hierarchy of spiritual powers.[9]

To be sure, this is not to be understood in the sense of a modern impersonal collectivism. That the individual is not swallowed up by the state is clear from the very proximity in which the philosopher, as pure man, stands to the ideas. Hence the state can never be the guiding concept, for in relation to the primal or original ideas it is itself a derived reality. Nevertheless, this safeguard against absolute absorption does not alter the fact that it is the state, not the individual, which is *the* representative actualization of the good and the beautiful.

Still Plato clearly links with his special emphasis on the state a certain independence of the individual. Socrates, for his part, gives special emphasis to the independence of the individual, and in this

[8] The state in Plato's *Republic* includes three main classes or estates: rulers, guardians, and artisans.

[9] The soul is divided into three main principles. The rational principle of the soul, involving love of wisdom and learning, is related to the wisdom and knowledge of the ruling class. Passion or spirit, involving love of victory and honor, is related to the courage and valor of the guardians. Concupiscence or desire, involving the love of money, is related to the temperance of the third estate. This threefold division preserves the dominion of reason over impulse. See Plato *The Republic* iv. 435-444; in *Plato* ("Great Books," Vol. 7), pp. 350-355.

he differs from Plato. The difference, however, is not one of antithesis, as a first glance might suggest, but of nuance.

In Socrates it is the individual, not the state, which is the main theme of philosophical reflection, or, in this case, of philosophical action. This is clear already from the maieutic form of philosophical address. For Socrates, the state enters the picture only through the political "consequences" which ensue as a result of this maieutic concern for the individual, and which subsequently issue in his trial.

The Socratic method is a kind of midwifery. It involves dialogue aimed at bringing to himself the person addressed, leading him to the virtue of being able to exist in his own right. Ordinarily this individual independence is concealed by the fact that men tend naively to take over the opinions or actions of others while imagining them to be their own. Thus countless things are familiar to us only in the form of conventional views or agreed actions ($\theta\acute{\epsilon}\sigma\epsilon\iota$), not according to their true essence and nature ($\phi\acute{\upsilon}\sigma\epsilon\iota$). Now a man does not stand alone when he accepts these conventions, the self-evident patterns of his day. On the contrary, he is the slave of others. He is the victim of illusions, not merely about things, but also about himself.

It is this diagnosis of the human condition which makes it impossible for Socrates simply to foist off his own views, i.e., a specific philosophical system, on the young men of Athens. For if he were to do that he would simply be plunging them the more deeply into a childlike bondage to something that is merely accepted, swallowed as alien material, and hence without substance. They ought rather to be freed from precisely such an entanglement. His art of dialectical discussion is designed to achieve this liberation. It makes the other person a partner in dialogue rather than the listener to an address. Step by step it leads him to his own convictions, which are pedagogically drawn forth by questions. The goal is to make the other not a disciple but a partner who thinks for himself. The point is not that something alien is imparted to him but that something of his own is brought forth from him. It is in this sense that Socrates is a midwife.

The midwifery therefore is not merely a question of method, a matter of instructional technique. On the contrary, it rests on a material axiom, namely, that knowledge of the truth is already concealed in the other party to the discussion; it is something which he has on his own, something which is already present at least potentially (as ἀνάμνησις). The method of Socratic dialogue is simply a precise factual expression of this philosophical theory of knowledge. In any case, the virtue (ἀρετή) to which Socrates seeks to bring the other is not something which can be taught by the impartation of knowledge. It can be only the goal of instruction. For the goal of instruction is to make the instructor superfluous, to lead the pupil to independence through an awakening of his own powers.

The Socratic dialectic thus involves a leading over, whereby the prior judgments of an existence in untruth are broken down, and a leading into, whereby self-assurance and individual conviction are built up. Establishing the contrast between the original views which were not my own and the knowledge which is truly my own is of the very essence of Socratic irony.

This Socratic purpose of bringing a man to himself, so that he is no longer just the function of some universal, exposes Socrates to the suspicion of being an enemy of the state. For the philosophical clarification which he seeks does not allow a man to remain merely a functioning member of the state. It awakens him to an existence of his own which gives him an independence even over against the state.

In this connection Socrates believes he must show that such independence has a positive significance for the state, that the state is not a collective of impersonal elements — to put it in modern terms — but that it can endure only if it embraces the diversity and tension of having independent citizens, people who have come to themselves. To this degree Socrates actually serves the state by liberating its members from a politically innocuous functioning which is enslaved to mere appearance.

Thus he says in his defense at the trial that his task was to spend his life making inquiry for wisdom and searching into himself and other men. This is how he dealt with young and old, with aliens and citizens, but especially with the Athenians themselves "inasmuch as they are my brethren. For know that this is the command of the God; and I believe that no greater good has ever been rendered to the state than this my service to the God." [10]

[10] Plato *Apology* xxiii, xxviii, xxx; in *Plato* ("Great Books," Vol. 7), pp. 203, 206.

Here too, then, we find the same dialectic between state and individual as in Plato, though with a different accent. For, even though for Plato the state is the primary reflection, he thinks that it should be directed by philosophers because they above all are individuals in the Socratic sense: they have come to themselves and are no longer guided by appearances and shadows, but have found their way to the vision of ideas as the true realities and guiding concepts. Because for Plato the state is the institutional reflection of the essential, of the basic order of being, it can be responsibly guided only by those who themselves have access to the original or primal ideas, by those who thus have come to themselves. Here is the point at which Plato's connection between state and individual intersects with that of Socrates.

The sharp question whether the individual exists for the state or the state for the individual is thus wrongly put, as the example of Plato and Socrates plainly shows. For state and individual stand in a reciprocal relationship to one another even where one of them may loom larger than the other, as the state does in Plato and the individual does in Socrates. Neither is comprehensible apart from the other. Each contains a secret, however, which is not solved even by reference to the other. For there is always the question as to how the individual comes to that independence which makes it possible for him to stand over against the state and prevents his being swallowed up by it. And there is always the further question as to how the state comes so to limit itself as to respect the independence of the individual – a self-limitation which in the trial of Socrates the Athenian state did not achieve.

Now obviously both kinds of self-assurance can be lost: The individual can become a non-political personal entelechy, and the state can become God and Moloch. As we have seen, both these extremes were explicitly advocated in the nineteenth century. The more pressing, then, is the question as to how the false antithesis can be avoided. Obviously this is possible only when state and individual attain to self-assurance not simply in the light of their reciprocal relation but because both are referred to a third thing which spans the polarity, something without which they would be inexplicable and unmanageable forms of being. In Socrates and Plato this third thing is the true being from which all that is, whether state or individual, derives its being. Where are we to find this third thing which is so important in determining whether or not the two sides drift completely apart?

The Overarching Third Factor

That we are on the right track in this search for a third factor is indicated by a brief consideration of Paul's doctrine of the state. In Paul's view of the matter, only he who has come to see the true nature of the state really understands it and knows how to be a good subject or ruler. But to see this one has to realize that ultimately it is God who rules and sustains through the state. The state is thus provisional. It is outlived by and dissolved in the rule of God (I Cor. 15:24), and consequently carries within itself the possibility of demonic perversion. For the state can forget that it is commissioned by God. It can make a bid for emancipation. It can reject its God-given purpose and try to usurp the place of God. The vision of the demonic power state in Revelation 13 is implicitly present in Paul too.[11]

From this arises awareness both of the power and authority of the state and also of its limitation: the state can be honored as the "mask" of God, but it must not be taken for God himself. This understanding of the nature of the state is open, however, only to him who sees the state in the context of the plan of salvation which is normative for it. It is precisely this plan of salvation which is the third factor of which we spoke; it stands above both state and individual, causing both to refer to something beyond themselves.

The individual, to take him as an example, learns to know the nature of the state not from a so-called Christian idea of the state or from a sociology with a Christian slant, but only as he stands in personal fellowship with the Lord of the state, only as this Lord is also his Lord. Only thus does he have the independence which does not degrade him to a functional dependence in relation to the state, but permits him to see both his own power and limits and also those of the state — and hence enables him to "render to Caesar the things [and only those things!] that are Caesar's" (Matt. 22:21) and to "obey God rather than men" (Acts 5:29).

Only he who is himself brought to the truth (John 18:37) — and

[11] See Chapter 14 below.

151

thus brought to himself — only he who is no longer a mere appendix of contemporary movements or institutions or other given factors (θέσεις) can use the state aright. The man who has not found himself, who has not come into relationship to this third transcendent factor, corrupts the state. For he constitutes the raw material out of which ideological dictatorships and collectivisms of all kinds are made. He is only too ready to take direction. He succumbs to whoever shouts the loudest. He has no will of his own, and is an easy prey for propagandistic powers of suggestion.

We have noted the same situation in Luther's doctrine of the two kingdoms. Only he who knows the kingdom on the right hand knows also the worldly kingdom. Only he sees how it is protected both below (against the demonic influences of a blind "will to power" and against the excesses of human self-glorification) and above (against a theocratic misuse of the gospel as Law). The world which does not see itself thus limited cannot be "world" in the strict sense but becomes the kingdom of the devil, a pseudo kingdom of God. It undergoes either demonic or sacral perversion. The kingdom on the left hand must take its orientation from the kingdom on the right hand if it is to find itself, if it is to know that it too is *God's* kingdom. Only thus can it find its own true worldliness, and within the framework of sonship truly come of age.[12] As "right" and "left" are interchangeable terms which reciprocally define one another, so the kingdoms on the right hand and on the left stand in a correlation which can never be dissolved unilaterally.

The Pauline ideas which theologically define the relation of state and individual along these lines are at least in form analogous to those of Socrates and Plato. Plato and Paul, of course, define very differently that third factor which overarches both state and individual. For Plato it is original being; for Paul, the Father of Jesus Christ. Still, there is one feature which at least formally is common to both: neither state nor individual is wholly absorbed in the relation with the other, and consequently neither can deduce the essence of the other from itself, in terms of its own essence.

If the individual, his nature, task, and destiny, are described ex-

---

[12] Gogarten alludes to this distinction where he differentiates between "secularization" (as the world come of age) and "secularism" (as worldly emancipation carried to excess) in his *Die Kirche in der Welt* (Heidelberg, 1948), pp. 133 ff.

clusively in terms of the state, then the individual becomes no more than the bearer of political functions. (This is the key point in Socrates' defense.) If, on the other hand, the state is defined exclusively in terms of what it must be for the individual, then the state loses its character as a divinely instituted order and becomes instead a voluntary association directed to a specific purpose and having no magisterial dignity.[13]

Thus the question whether the state exists for the individual or the individual for the state is wrongly put. What is involved is rather a reciprocal relationship of two historical elements, to which both are appointed by yet a third factor.

The state exists for the individual to the degree that it makes social existence possible at all in the post-Babel world. The individual[14] exists for the state to the degree that by existing as a person, as a unique being, he makes true society possible in the first place — and therewith also makes himself possible.

To depersonalize the individual, to assume that man exists only for the state, is not only to degrade man — evidences of this may be seen in collectivism — but also to destroy the state, something which Socrates sought to forestall. The perfect state is surely the state of perfect citizens, and the perfection implied here is not just that of functioning, but of unperverted selfhood. We may even say that the political service of the individual is service only when it is rendered in freedom, only when individual freedom is *not* delegated to a supra-individual entity like the state or the group.

The totalitarian state always tries to justify its encroachments on personal freedom in terms of just such a delegation of freedom. The state, it is said, or the classless society, will lose its needed capacity for historical action, its efficacy, if the machinery of state must have regard for the sum of individual wills; hence individual freedom must be delegated to collective freedom, for the freedom of the state or group is possible — this is the decisive thesis — only when the freedom of the individual is sacrificed.

[13] The latter conception may be seen in Rousseau, who begins with the individual in a situation of primal freedom. The most consistent recent exponents of the notion that the state exists simply to fulfill certain purposes, quite apart from any metaphysical quality, are the American pragmatists William James and John Dewey.

[14] "The individual" is here taken as an artificial abstraction, in the manner of Kierkegaard.

The dedication to freedom thus becomes something very different. The totalitarian state too marches under the banner of freedom. But the subject of that freedom has been changed. Here then is a fresh confirmation of our thesis that the totalitarian state has heretical features in that it absolutizes a partial truth. The partial truth in this instance is that all human society involves the limitation of one freedom by another. If men are to live together there must be some sacrifice of freedom, even in the most liberal of democracies. This sacrifice of freedom, however, is offered to freedom itself, i.e., to the circumstance that one's own freedom cannot be construed absolutely. My freedom must not make another unfree or degrade him to a mere object. On the contrary, it must serve also to guarantee his freedom, making it possible for him to enter into common relationships as a person in his own right. This sacrifice of freedom for the sake of freedom is heretically absolutized when it is elevated to the point of self-sacrifice for the sake of the freedom of the state, the group, the class, or the institution.

10.

The State and Moral Society

Now that we have seen that the state is not dissolved in the relation of state and individual, but conceals within it a content which transcends this relation, we turn to the relation of state and moral society. Here too we give due regard to the transcendent element.

At the outset, for heuristic purposes, we shall champion for a moment the thesis that the state is in fact a moral society. The thesis, of course, is not without some validity. For the state certainly binds the individual to society. Under certain circumstances it is even justified in demanding the sacrifice of an individual's life. It exacts oaths of loyalty.

Then too from the standpoint of the categorical imperative as the representative ethical norm there seems also to be a connection between state and ethos, for here it is a question of individual maxims taking their orientation from universal law. And even if what is involved here is thus the principle of universal legislation — which is not identical with state legislation — there is nonetheless a connection with state legislation if we concede to the state an affinity to the moral sphere.

The Meta-Ethical Exercise of State Power

There is, to be sure, only one conclusive sign that the state cannot be fully comprehended in the concept of a moral society, that as a unique entity — and this is the fact to which we must attend — it defies identification with any other normative schema. This one conclusive sign is the fact that the state is by nature equipped with power. Within its constitutional limits it has the possibility of enforcing its rules and regulations.

Now when citizens are forced to keep the laws this is not a matter of ethics in the narrower sense. Only voluntary obedience on one's own autonomous resolve is ethical. From the ethical standpoint enforced obedience is a matter of heteronomy.

Is power then in this sense only a matter of being able to compel the obstinate? Is power justified by the motive of checking evil [coercere malum]? Is it provoked by human wickedness and hence to be deduced theologically from the fall? Theology likes to jump to the conclusion that the answer is Yes. In this chapter and the two that follow, however, we shall necessarily come to see that the background of power is essentially far more complicated. For the moment, it is important to see that the state's authority to pass laws and enforce them is only in part a matter of ethics, and hence related to the fall. In another respect it is wholly meta-ethical. We shall consider the meta-ethical aspect first.

In one sense, laws are purely a matter of convention. To take a simple illustration, traffic laws simply express certain arbitrary agreements. The demand to "keep right except when passing" is unquestionably meta-ethical. In Great Britain the rule is just the reverse, but countries which drive on the right and pass on the left do not conclude that the traffic laws in Britain are therefore immoral. If, however, instead of punishing such things as murder and theft a country were to permit or even command them, the charge of immoral legislation would be appropriate. The fact that such a charge would be absurd in the case of divergent traffic laws shows how different the relations between state law and morality can be.

Thus there exist a host of decisions and arrangements which have no ethical intention whatever, and in respect of which power is by no means used simply to contain the rebellious impulses of the human will, though traffic laws, at least some of them, do in a measure intend the restraint of evil [arcere malum]. Posted speed limits, e.g., are not just neutral and factual prohibitions. They embody an opposition (an arcere) to recklessness, inhumanity, and the speed kick. Speed limits would be superfluous if these impulses did not exist. They thus bring into the sphere of law and define as punishable conduct forms of behavior which would not even exist if caution and care instead of egoistic impulse were the rule of the road. "If we had no rule of the road a nasty side of human nature would make its appearance amongst motorists more often than it does at the moment."[1]

[1] Herbert Butterfield, *Christianity and History* (New York: Scribner's, 1950), p. 34.

Again, there is another category of state law which is without reference to the wickedness of man, and hence ethically neutral, not deploying power to restrain evil. This involves those laws which represent a general standpoint such as can be established only within the framework of a structure like that of the state, a standpoint which is not immediately accessible to the will and insight of the individual. It is very possible, and also quite justifiable, that opinions may vary widely on some question that is simply a "matter of opinion" yet must be resolved in common and cannot be left to the judgment of the individual if there is to be any kind of ordered life together.

To return to our previous example, it was not long ago that Sweden held a referendum on whether to drive on the right or on the left side of the road. Good arguments were passionately presented on both sides of the question, and the very fact that a referendum was held demonstrates that more than one view of the matter may well be justified. But in a case like this the practice of private judgment would lead to chaos. Some common resolution of the question is needed. Even if the government were to flaunt the expressed will of the majority by ignoring the outcome of the balloting, all drivers would nonetheless welcome whatever decision it made. They would unanimously prefer any kind of uniformity to such respecting of minority or majority rights as would allow some drivers to pick and choose whichever side of the road they happened to prefer.

We thus maintain that, while the state has the authority to pass laws and the power to enforce them, this does not always mean that it is necessarily practicing a forcible restraint of evil. There are meta-ethical spheres in which arbitrary agreements and conventions are given legal sanction. Nevertheless, the very fact that even in such instances the state is equipped with power and uses it shows that the state is qualitatively different from a moral society. To put it cautiously — as we did a moment ago — the state cannot be fully comprehended in the concept of a moral society; even in the form of a heteronomy it can assert its will and punish violations of this will.

The Difference between Law and Morality

We must now reflect further on the difference between coercive state law and the moral law which is grounded in freedom. Gustav Radbruch illustrates the difference in terms of the radicalizing of the

Mosaic Law by the Sermon on the Mount (Matt. 5:21-22, 27-28): whereas Moses establishes a "legal statute," the Sermon on the Mount is concerned with the inner "disposition," and thus moves from the juridical to the ethical plane.[2]

Now we have already seen,[3] and will come to speak of this again later, that Moses too is not concerned at all with statute law. Nevertheless, we may provisionally accept Radbruch's distinction and assume that the law which is backed by the power of the state manifests itself primarily in the legal order. Our task, then, will be to show the differences between legal order and ethical order.

Law is supposed to refer to what is outward, morality to what is inward. But if the moral sphere is restricted to disposition and the level of motives, then the sphere of law would seem to be merely that of outward acts. On such a view, law and morality are almost completely antithetical; their spheres in no wise overlap.

Now it is true that law and morality have to be distinguished.[4] Nevertheless, a radical separation, a severing of all relation between them, is a fateful heresy (in the sense in which we used the term earlier[5]). Since we are using law as a model in terms of which to study the state as a legal society and a moral society, we must consider in greater detail this distinction and separation between legality and morality.

To a certain extent it may in fact be appropriate to distinguish legality and morality along the lines that law has to do with the outward side of man, the stratum of action, whereas morality has to do with the inward side, the sphere of motives and disposition. The best proof of this is that it is the so-called "facts of the case" which constitute the legal criterion of culpability in a court action. It is not "the thief" but the theft which must be punished. The law is concerned to characterize not the person and his essential features but those acts which can be clearly defined in a legal sense. When the law says that if anyone takes something belonging to another with a view to its illegal appropriation he will be imprisoned for stealing, it is referring to the

[2] See Gustav Radbruch, *Einführung in die Rechtswissenschaft*, ed. Konrad Zweigert (10th ed.; Stuttgart: Koehler, 1961), p. 16.

[3] Cf. *ThE* 1, 348-358, 440-447.

[4] Kant expressed the opposition between legality and morality in terms of the distinction between heteronomy and autonomy.

[5] See above p. 42.

facts, the theft, not the thief. Law is concerned with the "externals." As the proverb says, no one can be hanged for thinking, i.e., for what goes on inside a person.

This is why relationships which have their center not in a specific act but in the disposition behind the act can hardly be the subject of regulation, or at best only in a very limited way.[6] The intimate sphere of my relationships to God, to loved ones, or to friends is beyond the scope of law. How severely law overreaches itself — and is consequently perverted — when men try to apply it to the inner sector is clearly illustrated in the case of totalitarian states and their inner snooping. Once this road is taken, torture becomes a legal instrument for probing the disposition.

The Common Root

Although the law is outward and takes the "facts of the case" as its criterion, law and morality are nonetheless not complete opposites. There are also zones of overlapping. Three aspects of this positive relation demand attention.

First, even though the purpose of law is defined very differently from that of morality, law must still be understood, not as the expression of morality, but as the ground of its possibility. For the state, as the majestic organ of law, makes ordered existence possible, and this means that it makes ethical existence possible by creating its physical presuppositions.

Second, law for its part is grounded in basic moral convictions which even in pragmatically or positivistically perverted law still attest their latent or distorted presence under the rubric of utility or historical inevitability. For — to pursue the thought of the preceding paragraph — law takes under its protection moral values and institutions like the state, marriage, and property. Where law is still aware of the reason for punishment, it seeks through punishment to sustain in people a sense of guilt and retribution, and therewith an awareness of ethical values. And even if this awareness refers only to good and evil acts, and does not reach down to the deeper levels of ethical inwardness, still there are instances enough in which the outward and the inward can hardly be separated. Thus the concept of loyalty, though it be-

[6] See Radbruch, *op. cit.*, p. 17.

longs to the level of motives within the sphere of ethics, has an external side which is capable of legal objectification, e.g., as loyalty to a legally recognized firm or corporation, or loyalty to a pact, treaty, or nation.

Third, while it is true that the spheres of law and morality are very different, and while it is also true that the difference becomes apparent in the evaluation of specific acts – as we shall presently see in the next section – nevertheless law as such, in its totality, is grounded in a sense of moral values which affirms an ordering of the common life and hence also the rules for such an order. Where a legal order overlooks or contests this relation to basic moral norms law has degenerated to the mere art of exercising power. Such a pragmatic pseudo law is always characterized by two essential features.

First, it displays a tendency to become a mere political function, providing those in power with a legal means of exterminating their opponents; ironically, the apparent need for such a legal instrument indirectly bespeaks the validity of a moral concern. Second, lacking any moral basis, law can no longer appeal to a sense of ethical values; it must therefore use naked force and terror to establish compliance.

Tolstoi, in a typically radical train of thought, alludes to this when he sees a connection not merely between law and moral righteousness, but also between law and love: It is the original sin of those in power, and the special sin of lawyers and judges, to believe that there are circumstances in which one can deal with a man without love. For Tolstoi there are in fact no such circumstances.[7] With Socratic irony, he expresses this basic danger in the form of a complete negation of law. As an impersonal machinery of order, law is in danger of denying that love is the force which sustains personal life in society.

Hence it is true that the legal and the ethical evaluation may diverge widely in respect of individual acts. It is true too that obedience to the law may sometimes be a matter of ethical indifference for the person who renders it, if he does so merely out of fear of punishment. It is also true that an offender may not understand why he is punished. Nevertheless, there can be no doubt that law as such (irrespective of individual cases) is affirmed by a sense of moral values. It is sus-

---

[7] Luther had an analogous concern to check the autonomous growth of the orders and to understand them as personal relations in which love is to be practiced. See *ThE* 1, Chapter 18, esp. p. 377.

tained by the ethical distinction between good and evil. While any particular legal order may be open to question, and any concrete application of law may be very dubious, there is nonetheless an ethical principle inherent in the postulate that "there must be order."

This connection between law and morality brings us to a reconsideration of Radbruch's assumed radicalizing of the Mosaic Law in the Sermon on the Mount. What he had in view is that the Sermon on the Mount claims even the thoughts of the heart, and in so doing represents the moral claim, in distinction from the Mosaic statutes which demand only the obedience of act and hence represent only legal claims. It is a question, however, whether we have here a true distinction between law and morality, or whether we are not referred instead to the ultimate common root of both spheres.

The Mosaic Law too had a moral background, in the sense that it laid claim to the whole person, his heart and not just his actions. It was a norm based on the covenant of God, i.e., on the fact that the people Israel, with all its members, belonged to God. What the Mosaic Law demanded is that this membership in the covenant be actualized in obedience, in a confession involving the whole of life. Hence the Sermon on the Mount "radicalizes" this Law only in the literal sense that it understands the norm in terms of its *radix* or root. It reminds man that the Law has to do not just with his outward conduct but with him, the one who stands before God. He is summoned to realize that in his totality he belongs to God, and hence must dedicate himself to God both body and soul, inwardly and outwardly, in heart and action.

To this degree both the Mosaic Law and the Sermon on the Mount go back ultimately to the same authorization; only in the penultimate sphere of function are they distinguished from one another. The theological and ethical reference of the covenant is to the whole man, even to the depths of the heart, whereas the legal reference is simply to that which is socially demonstrable (one cannot be stoned for unchaste glances). For the Lord of the covenant who looks on the heart (I Sam. 16:7), evil is significant even in its first stages; for the earthly ruler, however, evil is of concern only when it becomes an active threat to society.

We are hereby pointed, however, to the common origin of both law and ethics. For disorder in the vertical dimension, the emancipating of the person from the relation to God, works itself out on the horizontal plane of historical life in society, either as lovelessness and Pharisaic pride under the cover of external order (Matt. 6:1, 5; 23:23-27), or as the disintegration of external order (Rom. 1:24-32).

The Dialectical Relationship

In spite of their common root, however, law and ethics are still different in the penultimate sphere. This difference finds expression in the fact that law is coercive, whereas the ethical imperative appeals to the freedom of the will. The coerciveness of law has an objective and a subjective side. The objective side consists in its equipment with coercive power. The subjective side consists in its appeal to the fear of punishment.

The tension with ethics which is involved on both sides necessarily carries with it the possibility of an open contradiction between law and ethics. This contradiction can take either of two representative forms. On the one hand, what is immoral can be legally right; e.g., a man may pursue a debtor at law out of personal resentment, or he may initiate a suit in order to take revenge or to remove a rival or business competitor. On the other hand, what is morally right can be illegal; for examples we may cite the plot of July 20, 1944, against Hitler's life, or the instances during the Nazi period in which Roman Catholic priests had to sanction ecclesiastically domestic cohabitation on the part of people who would not or dared not comply with state marriage laws, or, in some countries, conscientious objection to military service.

Yet instances of conflict between law and ethics should not blind us to the fact that such conflict is acute only in certain cases. It is usually restricted to borderline situations. These do not justify us in assuming that there is a fundamental conflict between legality as such and morality as such. The two are related in many ways despite the differences in function.

Hence the well-known definition of Georg Jellinek that law is "the ethical minimum," [8] that law reduces the total demands of ethics to the partial demands presented by the *modus convivendi,* is a very dubious definition. To reduce the problem thus to a mere exercise in subtraction is to miss the dialectical relationship between the two levels.

[8] Georg Jellinek, *Allgemeine Staatslehre* (5th ed.; Berlin, 1929).

For one thing, the authority of law, as we have shown, rests on unconditional ethical norms. In respect of the Old Testament Law this is expressed by the fact that the Mosaic statutes concerning deeds and the prophetic commands relating to disposition [9] are both grounded in the First Commandment. Both are authorized by God's authority.

For another thing, all law is grounded in a specific anthropology, in an ethical determination as to what man intends to be and what he regards as the purpose of his existence. All law is thus grounded in a non-legal — indeed an ethical — predetermination concerning the purpose of man's existence, whether he is simply a functionary or has personal dignity, whether marriage is founded on loyalty and a sharing of life or is an instrument of population policy, etc. Law is thus compelled again and again to reflect on its foundations, and to ascertain whether it is in keeping with the accepted end of man and his existence in society, i.e., whether it is good law.

This question can be put in very different forms and under very different signs. It can have reference to the will of God, natural law, universal human rights, or the common sense of traditional values at any given time.

Even if law has a utilitarian aspect, e.g., to regulate common life in society, and even if from this standpoint there always arises a tension with the ethical, there can be no doubt that even this pragmatic element can never banish ethics from the sphere of law. For the social structure itself, as an institutional expression of fellowship, is of ethical significance inasmuch as the members who make it up are persons, and as such moral beings. Utilitarian purpose is not a purely pragmatic concept but a moral concept, when the question involved is one of ascertaining means to make possible an ordered common life for moral beings — so long as these moral beings are acknowledged to be such, and hence enjoy the ethical dignity of being ends in themselves and are not swallowed up in the end of the common life and its orders.

The supremely dialectical relation of legal and ethical problems is displayed finally in the fact that the state, whose normative will we find represented by law, may not oppose egoism, as ethics does, or even call it in question, but must use it and even desire it.

---

[9] See, e.g., Isa. 1:10-17; Amos 5:14 ff.; 5:21 ff.; Mic. 6:6-9. Cf. Ludwig Koehler, *Old Testament Theology* (Philadelphia: Westminster, 1958), pp. 107-110.

Thus in Thomas More's *Utopia* Raphael Hythloday demands that private property be abolished as a nest of greed and avarice, but More answers that it nurtures industry. Without it there would be only "laziness and corruption." To deny property, social distinctions, and all the rights of egoism would lead to "murder and revolutions," for, since these are elemental impulses, men would secure what is theirs independently, and hence illegally.[10]

As Herbert Butterfield says, "Society caters for human cupidity in all of us and secures its ends by making a skilful use of this side of human nature; so that when all things are nicely balanced men may be doing their duty without realizing that their self-interest has come into the matter at all — they may hardly be conscious of the neat dovetailing of public service and private interests."[11]

The state, then, must create opportunities of advancement and appeal to the ambition to excel others. It must accept competition to encourage the zealous will to assert and surpass itself. In totalitarian states, where it is hindered by a planned economy from developing initiative and enterprise, it must arouse and utilize egoism by means of artificial competitions, awards, premiums, public recognition, etc. The state must also 'appeal to other instincts. Even if decorations and medals do have a better side, it must not be overlooked that by mobilizing vanity they bind vital forces to the state and make them fruitful in its service.

In respect of individual and collective egoism the state consequently represents basic principles which, even if extremes are avoided, do not tally with ethical principles in the narrower sense.[12] The dialectical relation between political or legal principles on the one side and ethical principles on the other is expressed here in the fact that in individual cases the tension between the two spheres can become an open antithesis, but that the state as such, and law as such, is itself again an ethical phenomenon. For the state has the task of establishing the coexistence of men which alone makes an ordered ethical life possible. And because of its instrumental significance it is continually

[10] See Gerhard Ritter, *The Corrupting Influence of Power*, trans. F. W. Pick (Hadleigh, Essex: Tower Bridge, 1952), p. 65.

[11] Butterfield, *op. cit.*, p. 35.

[12] See our discussion of Frederick the Great and diplomatic cunning in *ThE* 1, 533-545.

forced to examine its ethical presuppositions, and in its constitutions to make pronouncements on ethical matters such as the concept of man, freedom, righteousness, etc.

Law and the Noachic Covenant

Now that we have examined the significance of the state as a moral society, and concluded — as expected — that the state cannot be fully comprehended in the concept of a moral society but stands as an entity *sui generis* in a wholly dialectical relationship with it, we can try to tackle the theological question raised by the inquiry.

First, the distinction between law and morality points to the fact that the ultimate norms sought in ethics cannot be represented in absolute purity in the world of orders with its relative autonomy. Indeed, when we consider this outside world, it is clear that its claims to be universally binding have to be reduced. Herein lies the element of truth in the otherwise dubious statement of Jellinek that law is an "ethical minimum." We discovered in our examination of the Sermon on the Mount,[13] that its demands cannot be realized directly in this aeon, and this is true to some degree of every ethics: it suffers a reduction when put into practice in the orders. This is an indication of the fact that the present world is not the pure world of creation but is subject to the emergency order of the Noachic covenant.

Second, the coerciveness of law, which is of the very essence of the state, points to the fact that the human will no longer aims at "the principle of universal legislation." It is no longer oriented to this but conceals within itself destructive tendencies which the state must partly resist and partly claim and utilize. This ambivalence of the human will has been noted in philosophical ethics too, which is built on the radical cleavage of our existence. Ethics rests on the imperative, the "ought," a negation of other strivings which seek to dominate man. But life in society cannot count on the acceptance of this imperative at any given time. Hence a minimum of coercion must be added to guarantee its functioning. This is a further indication of the loss of the world of creation.

Third, the fact that egoism is taken into account, is not set aside but limited, controlled, and used so that its force may be directed into

---

[13] See *ThE* 1, Chapter 17.

positive channels, is a sign that the community of law — the state — no longer counts on man's remaining in the order of creation and being directed by the eye of God. On the contrary, it must use the forces unleashed at the fall — forces which it cannot destroy — as beneficially and purposefully as possible. (This was perceived with relative correctness by Machiavelli.)

It would, of course, be a mistake to see here only the negative aspect. Law does not merely turn against the sinner; it also turns to the creature. It ties in with man's perverted but nonetheless persistent primal orientation to ultimate origins and goals. This is why the First Commandment is significant also as the basis of *law*. This is also why all law is nourished by constant reference back to its ethical and anthropological foundations, whether in terms of religion, natural law, or general humanism.

Nevertheless, the distinction between egoism in the state and egoism in the individual, and the corresponding distinction between the ethics of the state and the ethics of the individual, is a reminder of the loss of the order of creation. It is distressing to note that a secular historian like Jacob Burckhardt has seen this with greater clarity than many theologians. In his own way, without even knowing it, he proclaims the idea of the emergency Noachic covenant: "The forum of morality lies quite outside the State, and we may even wonder that it can do as much as to uphold conventional justice. The State will be most likely to remain healthy when it is aware of its own nature (and maybe of its essential origin) as an *expedient*." [14]

[14] Jacob Burckhardt, *Force and Freedom: Reflections on History*, ed. James Hastings Nichols (New York: Pantheon, 1943), p. 118 [italics by H.T.].

11.

The Nature of Power

In considering the question of the relation between the state and moral society we came up against the problem of the fall. We shall encounter the same problem when we try to specify the lines of connection (already suggested) between the state and power. The question of the state and power really involves a huge and complicated complex of problems, within which the only thing that is certain is that there is no state without power, just as there is no law without the power to establish itself. But it is hard to define the nature of power, not just because there are many different forms of power in the many different spheres of life (state, society, family, culture, etc.), but also because the term itself has many nuances.

It is important that we should face this difficulty at the outset. We will see how great it is as we consider the many definitions of power which have been attempted. Power is a difficult thing to pin down because, as we shall see, it is rooted in a theological mystery: it stands between creation on the one side and sin on the other. Our preliminary philosophical consideration of the question is thus designed to prepare the way for the theological mystery and to show that in its very nature power obviously involves something which philosophy cannot fathom.

The General Concept of Power

In attempting to elucidate the concept of power as such we are immediately confronted by the prior question whether to define power psychologically in respect of its origin, teleologically in respect of its end, or phenomenologically in respect of how it is exercised. We may briefly consider these three aspects.

The Psychological Aspect

Plato speaks already of the pathological drive for the extension of power which dwells in all of us from the very outset. He illustrates it in terms of the soul of the tyrant, which is characterized by the fact that it is goaded by the drive for power, and that as its power is extended it is — like tyranny itself — increasingly enslaved rather than liberated.[1]

In the modern period it is pre-eminently Nietzsche who explains the nature of power in terms of the psychical structure of man: Desire is what determines man's quest for power, and his possession of it too. Accordingly Nietzsche attempts to prescribe how this lust for power is to be achieved,[2] for "the love of power is the demon of mankind"[3] which drives man to a "maximum feeling of power."[4] The will to power is so elemental an impulse that it subordinates all other norms — the good, the true, the beautiful — and makes all events subservient to itself.

The Teleological Aspect

The teleological view considers power as a means to specific ends. We came upon this view already where we said that law needs the help of power in order to establish itself. The instrumental significance of power is obvious at this point. If we have till now considered power primarily in this legitimate aspect, this is due to the fact that what we had in view at the time was the particular "ends," the law or the state, so that the significance of power as a means was self-evident. But the aspect changes completely when we try, so far as possible, to consider power in and for itself, and when we try to establish whether in power itself — or, more precisely, in the will to power — there may be seen a self-affirmation of this instrumental character, and, if so, to what end or ends it is directed.

This is a hard question to answer. For even the man who has a blind and impulsive will to power — who in Nietzsche's sense enjoys power — and for whom power is an end in itself will always pretend that the power he seeks or wields is dedicated to a particular end. The fact that the naked power impulse is always disguised in this way, that it always takes the form of a will which is controlled by ends, is

[1] See Plato *The Republic* ix. 577 ff.; in *Plato* ("Great Books," Vol. 7), pp. 419 ff.
[2] Friedrich Nietzsche, *The Dawn of Day* (No. 56), trans. J. M. Kennedy ("The Complete Works of Friedrich Nietzsche," ed. Oscar Levy [New York: Russell & Russell, 1964], ix), 58-59.
[3] *Ibid.*, No. 262, p. 248.
[4] *Ibid.*, Vol. 15: *The Will to Power*, No. 689, p. 164.

grounded in the very nature of the exercise of power. A ruler's un-
concealed proclamation of his pure thirst for power would at once
arouse in his subjects both opposition and an assertion of their own
will to power. Instead of overcoming restrictions, such a proclamation
would actually impose restrictions upon the expression of the pure impulse. Hence to confess one's will to power would be a tactical error,
a self-contradiction. It is for this reason that even the most unadulter-
ated will to power, which regards power as altogether an end in itself,
must proclaim convincing goals in order to deceive its subjects into
thinking that their own interests are being championed and that they
can therefore adopt the goals of the ruler without question, even regarding him as an advocate and exponent of their own position. This
is why Machiavelli recommended moral facades — and totalitarian
states use ideologies.

May it not be that, under the veil of ends which it is supposed to
serve, power is really an end in itself? In other words, may it not be
that the values which power pretends to actualize are themselves — in
the ideologies — only the means whereby power actualizes itself? In
our analysis of ideological tyranny and its pragmatism we have seen
that this is indeed possible.

The fact that power can thus be an end in itself shows how important for any inquiry is the way of stating the question concerning it.
If the question with which we approach the subject has to do with
normative institutions like the state or law, then power will be seen
largely in terms of its instrumental significance. If our initial concern,
however, is with power as such, if we purpose as fully as possible to
isolate power and to consider it in and for itself, then the end which
transcends and controls power becomes hazy and nebulous, and in its
stead the one who exercises the power, or desires to do so, takes the
center of the stage. Then our concern shifts from the goal to the
(psychical) origin of power. It focuses on the drive for power, with
the result that power as an end it itself unavoidably becomes the
major theme. Thus the way of putting the question itself rests on a
prior decision.

By pointing out in this way the danger inherent in making direct
inquiry concerning the nature of power, we wish to draw attention to
the significance of our earlier question concerning the goal of power,
and hence our earlier discussion of the state and of law. In other

words, we would show what prior decision we have ourselves taken in this theological ethics.

Our reference to the way of stating the question is also meant to suggest that the true order of things can be disclosed only on the basis of a theological approach, which always begins with the question of the ultimate end. Any attempt to begin with a penultimate or proximate end, with a means, will necessarily result in absolutizations and idolatry. Only God can be absolute as the ultimate end. This fact must work itself out in our way of putting the question — if we are not to end up with pseudo absolutes autonomously imposed by the frame of reference from which we proceed.

This is the only reason, but a cogent reason, why theology must begin with prior decisions. The presupposition of its objectivity is that theology cannot be a science without presuppositions. For a supposed freedom from presuppositions, which is ostensibly concerned only with phenomena, will become subject to these very phenomena; it will ascribe to them absolute significance and thus create philosophical presuppositions. This insight from the sphere of theological prolegomena finds impressive illustration in this very matter of how best to approach the question of power.

The Phenomenological Aspect

The phenomenological approach is concerned with the way power is in fact exercised, and it raises again the theological question we have just been discussing. For such an approach threatens to become more than merely an attempt to describe the exercise of power and the techniques of using it. There is the danger that it will instead fall victim to the autonomy of this technique in the way that always happens (at least in the sphere of human history) when attention focuses exclusively on the course of an event. Then the structure of the course of the event, or the technique by which it is controlled, becomes a philosophical law and is thus invested with the dignity of being an end in itself.

We have seen already how an exclusive consideration of the phenomenon of politics leads to the philosophical idea of political man (Schmitt), and how an exclusive consideration of the course of events in history leads to the idea of politics without values (Machiavelli) or to the thesis of might before right (Hitler). It will suffice if we simply recall here the implied theological problematic and limit ourselves to describing the forms in which the phenomenological aspect of power finds expression.

The phenomenology of power is usually viewed from one of three angles: that of those who exercise it, that of the means employed, or that of its extreme forms.

If power is viewed from the standpoint of those who exercise it, two radically different groups must be distinguished. First, there are those in power who rely on social prestige, physical or intellectual superiority, native or inherited authority, or the power of suggestion which Max Weber calls the charisma of power.[5] Second, there are ruling institutions (institutionalized power) which can establish themselves in the form of priestly and religious, princely and monarchical, or military and economic power.

If power is viewed phenomenologically in terms of the means employed, then a distinction must be made between those means which involve physical force and the use of terror, and those which involve superior powers of persuasion based on the moral, religious, or intellectual authority of the man in power. Power can in addition employ means which are justified by the end — e.g., by power itself — and which thus defy ethical censure. Finally, power can utilize means which are regulated and restricted by the same end which power itself serves, and in face of which it has itself only the ministering function of a means. (A democratic government uses power in this sense; it serves the same constitution and constitutional principles as the citizens over whom the power is exercised.)

If power is viewed, finally, in terms of its extreme forms, two such extremes must be considered. One is naked power; its influence lasts only as long as its threat is acute. The other is the ability to awaken convictions and to exercise a moral influence quite apart from any external pressures whatsoever.

This schematic outline will suffice for our present purposes. If we see clearly how different are the systems in which the definition of power emerges, and how they can disclose only specific aspects of the nature of power; and if we also see clearly that these partial aspects

---

[5] Max Weber distinguishes three forms of authority: the legal, the traditional, and the charismatic in *The Theory of Social and Economic Organization*, trans. A. M. Henderson and Talcott Parsons (New York: Oxford, 1947), pp. 328 ff.

are prone to be taken for the whole and hence absolutized, then we may say of power what Augustine said of time, namely, that everyone knows what time is, but when he has to say what it is he no longer knows.[6]

Power has also an instrumental significance inasmuch as it cannot itself be a thematic object of knowledge in the strict sense, but always serves the knowledge of the man who uses it or strives for it. The one thing which remains constant in all the bewildering vicissitudes of the phenomenon of power is that the way man seeks, exercises, suffers, and understands power actually reveals his own nature and interests.

In order that we may proceed on a conceptual basis, we shall choose as general and formal a definition as possible, one which belongs to the phenomenological rather than the psychological or teleological approach and in its empty generality neither claims nor denies any theological reference: " 'Power' is the probability that one actor within a social relationship will be in a position to carry out his own will despite resistance, regardless of the basis on which this probability rests." [7] In this definition there is — intentionally — no reference to whether the origin of the power is legitimate. Whence it arises is not specified. Neither is it stipulated whether the power has defensible aims, or indeed any aims at all. The definition is concerned not with the *nature* of what is to be done, or whether it is right or wrong, but only with the *possibility* of its being done, its capacity for actualization.

The Ambiguity of Power

We have pointed out that there are different ways of achieving and using power: legitimate and illegitimate, under the control of norms and as an uncontrolled end in itself. In view of this, it is no wonder that power has always been seen in terms of its dangerous and ambivalent character, and regarded as a temptation.[8]

More surprising, and not so self-evident, is the view of Jacob Burckhardt that "power is in itself evil." [9] To understand how Burckhardt

---

[6] Augustine *The Confessions* xi. 14.

[7] Weber, *op. cit.*, p. 132.

[8] Think, e.g., of the last temptation in the wilderness (Matt. 4:8-10), the Grand Inquisitor in Dostoevski's *Crime and Punishment,* and the "theology of glory" concept in Luther's *Heidelberg Disputation* (*LW* 31, 53).

[9] Jacob Burckhardt, *Force and Freedom: Reflections on History,* ed. James Hastings Nichols (New York: Pantheon, 1943), p. 115.

arrives at this pessimistic interpretation we must recall once again the concept of autonomy. For Burckhardt begins by supposing that power has an immanent teleology which finds expression in the fact that any seizure of power automatically involves a drive to safeguard and extend that power. He thus sees in power a tendency similar to that which Thomas More ascribed to property, and Marx to economic influence with its trend towards the concentration of the means of production.

According to Burckhardt this autonomy works itself out in four steps or stages: (1) The state arrogates to itself "the privilege of egoism which is denied to the individual" and subjects or annexes weaker neighbors "to prevent another taking them and turning them to his own political ends." (2) Next "such things are done in advance, without any real motive" until "a permanent appetite for territorial 'rounding off' is created" and "the lure of joining up small territories becomes irresistible." (3) Power is then interpreted in such a way as to justify the ill deeds, or they are "committed naively" in order to do away with attendant moral objections and shame. (4) Finally, "there is a great, indirect vindication of the evil-doer, namely that, without his foreknowledge, great historical purposes lying in the remote future were furthered by his deeds." [10] One might add as a fifth stage the tendency of our century for power to become "totalitarian," reaching even to the subjection of men's souls; as Lord Acton, the English historian, has put it, "Power tends to corrupt, and absolute power corrupts absolutely." [11]

For Burckhardt, then, power is autonomously evil. But this example makes it clearer than ever that we cannot be content just to stop here, for the concept of autonomy transcends itself. It points beyond itself to what we have called the "anthropological background," the view of man.[12]

Is it not inherent in the constitution of man — not of power but of *man* — that there should be this urge toward an inevitable expansion of power? Burckhardt has a kind of "myth" of power which leads him to invest it with demonic personal qualities. But if this is so, then this mythical being is to be understood simply as an objectification of man himself. And this means that we must still interpret it existentially.

---

[10] Burckhardt, *op. cit.*, pp. 115-117.
[11] Letter to M. Creighton (1887); John Emerich Edward Dalberg-Acton, *Historical Essays & Studies* (London: Macmillan, 1907), p. 504.
[12] See above pp. 134-139.

In fact, all that is said about power can be put in anthropological categories. The power which acts as if it were a being of great cunning possessing a will of its own, as if it were an acting subject, reflects only too clearly the essential features of the one who *really* wills and acts here, namely, man. (1) Man is the one who has the drive to extend his power and to intensify his enjoyment of it. (2) Man is the one who is harried by anxiety and who, seeing in himself the need for future security, resorts to a preventive drive for power. (3) Man is the one whose desire for self-justification leads to ideological embellishments. (4) Man, finally, is the one whose inclination to arrogance leads him to view himself as the subject of history, or at least as the instrument of the self-actualization of spirit and the tool of providence. Such is the existential interpretation of Burckhardt's myth with its four stages.

The impression of autonomy and of inevitability is not altered by this reference to the anthropological background. But the impelling force is seen to reside elsewhere, not in the dialectic of power itself — which would lead to the type of mythologizing we have seen in Burckhardt — but in man's very nature. To see this, though, a real demythologizing is needed. Man "cannot" do otherwise than to use power in the sense we have just described. He cannot because he is under the dominion of the four motives to which we have alluded: desire, anxiety, self-justification, and arrogance.

To say this is to argue that the demonism of power does not encroach upon man from the outside but grows entirely out of his own ethical decisions. But, even though we allow that such decisions are in fact taken, we do not thereby weaken the element of inevitability and autonomy which still remains. We thus come up against one of the ultimate theological problems which loom on the horizon of human existence, namely, that of the relation between freedom and necessity, responsibility and fate — two dimensions of human reality which are not mutually exclusive but interconnected.[13]

In sum, power as such is neither good nor evil, no more divine or demonic than the sex drive or technology. It is just that man when he no longer sees his own horizon — the horizon determined by judgment and grace, the fall and redemption — simply makes the mistake of con-

---

[13] We have treated of this dialectic in our discussion of original sin and responsibility in *ThE* 1, 290-299, where we would refer the reader particularly to p. 297.

struing goodness or evil as properties of things, of factual requirements and spheres of life, all of which lie completely outside himself. Man speaks of the tragic necessity of events when he ought to speak instead of the error of his own ways and the evil of his own choices.[14]

This is not to deny that there are processes involving tragic necessity. But it is to point to their specific origin. They were not tragic "from the beginning" (Matt. 19:8). It is man who has given them this character of tragic inevitability. It was the fall which initiated these tragic processes and set them autonomously in motion. A terrible necessity lies over the events which lead from the seizure of the forbidden fruit (Gen. 3:6) to fratricide (Gen. 4:8), blatant apostasy (Gen. 6:3-5), the tower of Babel (Gen. 11:4), and the destruction of Sodom (Gen. 19:24-25). Once the process begins there is no stopping it.

The story of the fall as it depicts this initiatory event is the primal pattern of what constantly recurs. What it sets forth is an interpretation of history in terms of a particular figure,[15] similar to that in Goethe's story of the sorcerer's apprentice who unleashes powers which he can no longer control and hence becomes subject to the spirits he has himself conjured up.[16] We can, as it were, take the first step. We can open a door which, because it has no handle on the other side, prevents our turning back and compels us to go on. What is past cannot be reversed and therefore acts in effect as a switch or turning point which determines the way ahead and subjects it to a certain inevitability.

The concept of original sin tells us in this sense that we always have behind us just such turning points, such traversed thresholds and

[14] Jawaharlal Nehru, a non-Christian, has seen this more than many spokesmen of the Christian West. He speaks of technology's tendency to foster the concentration and monopolization of power, but goes on to fix the roots of this process essentially in anthropology: "Nobody can say how, ultimately, human nature will develop. Because in the final analysis it is the human being that counts." Tibor Mende, *Nehru: Conversations on India and World Affairs* (New York: Braziller, 1956), p. 47.

[15] This kind of interpretation is skillfully presented with reference to the sacrifice of Isaac (Gen. 22:1-13), as well as the scar of Odysseus, in Erich Auerbach, *Mimesis: The Representation of Reality in Western Literature*, trans. Willard Trask (Garden City, New York: Doubleday Anchor, 1957), Chapter 1.

[16] See Goethe's ballad, "The Magician's Apprentice," which appears among other places in *Select Minor Poems of Goethe and Schiller*, trans. John S. Dwight ("Specimens of Foreign Standard Literature," ed. George Ripley [Boston: Hilliard, Gray, 1839]), III, 82-85.

initiatory events, whether the determinative factor be something we have ourselves brought to pass or whether it be something that precedes us and of which we are simply the heirs,[17] we who find ourselves in a historical milieu which has been formed already in advance.[18] This process, from the freedom of its commencement to the necessity of its continuation, bears witness to the Christian understanding of time as following a single irreversible course from the fall to the judgment.[19] Where the fall is not taken into account, the processes themselves may still be seen but not the inaugurator.

We may thus record here in passing the important theological insight that apart from knowledge of the fall there is nothing but myth, in this case the mythologizing of powers and processes. By "mythologizing" we mean that "things" are taken to be divine or demonic powers; they are endowed with souls and made into living creatures. Theologically viewed, myth is a process of repression and an act of evasion: man regards himself as innocent, held in the hands of seducing powers, because it is in his interest to conceal or look away from his own hand and culpability.

With this observation we have actually moved from the phenomenology of power to the problems of theology. But before we take up the theological question we must pause to ask how man seeks to restrain and check this power of his, which he himself (with his mythological categories) acknowledges to be dangerous. To be pre-

---

[17] Cf. Johann Wolfgang von Goethe, *Faust*, Part I, scene 4 in the study, where Mephistopheles addresses the student: "Woe unto thee, that thou art a grandson born!"; trans. Anna Swanwick (n. p.: A. L. Burt, n.d.), p. 63.

[18] Schleiermacher and Ritschl both recognize the pre-forming of society by sin as a sign of original sin. However, they go on to confuse the sign with the thing signified. Schleiermacher speaks of the "sinfulness that is present in an individual prior to any action of his own, and has its ground outside his own being" (Friedrich Schleiermacher, *The Christian Faith*, ed. H. R. Mackintosh and J. S. Stewart [Edinburgh: T. & T. Clark, 1928], p. 282). In elaborating his doctrine of the "kingdom of sin" Ritschl speaks of the "illimitable interaction" of sinful acts which leads to an avalanche of common sin in society and — in connection with my evil "habit" or "inclination" to be sure — draws me into it (Albrecht Ritschl, *The Christian Doctrine of Justification and Reconciliation*, ed. H. R. Mackintosh and A. B. Macaulay [New York: Scribner's, 1900], pp. 334-338).

[19] Karl Heim has repeatedly spoken of the irreversibility of time. See, e.g., his *Christian Faith and Natural Science* (New York: Harper Torchbooks, 1957), pp. 58 ff., 102 ff.; cf. also Oscar Cullmann, *Christ and Time*, trans. Floyd V. Filson (Philadelphia: Westminster, 1950), pp. 51 ff.

cise, we must inquire as to how man, imperiled as he is by power, seeks to limit and restrain himself. As we consider this aspect of the matter in the next two chapters we may cherish the hope that, though coming at it from another angle, we shall still arrive at the same point of theological concern.

12.

Power and Authority

The demand for a limitation of power is twofold. There is first the demand in terms of principle, and second the institutional requirement. The demand in terms of principle is that power must be distinguished by authority. The institutional requirement is that power must be distributed. We shall speak in this chapter, then, about the nature of authority, and in the next chapter about the matter of distribution.

Force versus the Power of Persuasion

Power as authority is quite a different thing from power as mere force. As force, power depends simply on superior strength. Typically, it takes the form of terror, seeking not to win men over by persuasion but to compel them by sheer might. The mark of a power which regards itself as mere force is that it conceives of those dependent on it exclusively in terms of strength. The man in power is the man of superior strength. Those ruled by him, whether individuals, groups, or whole nations, are men of lesser strength.

Understood thus in terms of strength, man is degraded to being a mere object. External forces play upon him, and he is himself a force that can be exploited, e.g., to the point where his strength to work has been completely sapped. Man can be a subject in a personal sense only when he is not compelled to be a functionary but is won over to participation as a partner. But to win a man over means to persuade him. And this implies in turn a respect for the other as a person, one who makes and implements his own decisions, and is not merely the object of an alien will.

The ruler who rules by force foregoes all such attempts to persuade and win to partnership. He does so for two main reasons. First, it takes a lot of time and trouble to win someone over; the task of explaining and justifying has to be accepted on a permanent basis. It is much more rational and economical simply to issue commands. Even though military service is not a sphere of blind force but a sphere of authority, it can still serve well to illustrate what this means.

In time of war or other danger everything has to be done quickly. There is no time to win over subordinates, to give a moral vindication of the authority of officers, or to secure consent to a hazardous mission. To attempt that would be to abandon the initiative to the enemy. Orders simply have to be given. This is why in the military there is a particular danger that force will predominate and that subordinates will be degraded to mere objects.[1] Second, to treat others as persons capable of making their own decisions involves a risk. They may say No. They may refuse to function, to hew to the desired line.

The ruler who uses his superior power in a cynical way need not subject himself to such extra effort and extra risk. His superior power enables him to play the role of a puppeteer who pulls the strings that cause human puppets to dance.

By contrast, the ruler who thinks of his power in terms of authority takes a very different position. This may be seen from Lessing's *The Education of the Human Race.* Here God is understood in the strict sense as the one in authority.[2] In relation to the human race still in its childhood, God claims full authority for himself. He issues commands and works miracles to demonstrate that authority. But in thus enforcing his will he does not act blindly and capriciously. He simply acts in the name of a reason which is not yet accessible to the race yet in its childhood, a reason towards which it is still maturing. God consequently uses his authority to bring to the race disclosures of reason which at its given stage of development it could not attain for itself. But by the very means of these disclosures he hastens the development of the race toward that point in history where it will itself be able to exercise control over the "external pure gospel of reason" and thus become independent.

The authoritarian power of God is marked accordingly by two essential features. First, this authority does not exercise its power

---

[1] On this problem see Pierre Boissier, *Völkerrecht und Militärbefehl,* trans. Dirk Forster (Stuttgart, 1953), esp. pp. 30 ff.

[2] See Helmut Thielicke, *Offenbarung, Vernunft und Existenz. Studien zur Religionsphilosophie Lessings* (1957).

capriciously. On the contrary, it accepts authorization itself. It sets itself into the service of that reason to which both God and man are subject.[3] Second, the authority of God leads to autonomy and thus seeks to make itself superfluous. In true Enlightenment fashion, it is understood as the authority of a teacher who pursues the same aims as that to which the educational development of the pupil is also directed. Hence a pupil does his teacher no credit if he always remains a pupil, for the teacher was trying to lead him to independence.

Authority and Autonomy

This brings us up against a connection between authority and autonomy which we probably did not at first expect. We usually associate the concept of authority with the idea that those who are subject to it will have to surrender at least a part of their sovereignty. But the connection of which we speak does not involve such an antithesis. It may be formulated in terms of two principles which we shall have to elucidate: first, that authority can be acknowledged or conferred only where there is autonomy; and second, that authority always insists upon autonomy.

As regards the first principle, authority — as distinct from sheer force — is present only when the person who has it stands on what is in the last analysis the same level as the one over whom he exercises it. This can be seen, e.g., from the authority of the trial judge in a judicial proceeding. The judge represents authority inasmuch as it is he who conducts the trial and acts at the behest of the larger community of law. But this does not set the accused into a position of pure dependence on the will of the judge. On the contrary, it makes him a partner within that community of law. Both parties stand under a common law, the judge as its champion and the accused as its real or supposed violator.

This partnership in the name of some third thing which embraces and transcends both judge and accused has always been a matter of basic legal principle. Indeed it is because of this principle that the judge must give reasons for his verdict. He does so not merely in order to explain to the community at large the technical process

---

[3] In the history of dogma it was this very problem of whether God establishes the ultimate norms — the good and the true — or is himself subject to them that stood at the heart of the controversy between the Scotists and the Thomists.

on which his decision rests, i.e., to show how the deed in question is subsumed under existing laws. There is the further purpose of addressing the accused himself to persuade him that the verdict is just, and to that extent to integrate him into that community of law which is empowered to exact retribution.

The question whether the judge actually succeeds in convincing the accused is unimportant. What is important is the fundamental position he takes towards him. He appeals to him for agreement, thereby addressing him as potentially the judge of his own action. Thus does the court respect the autonomy of the criminal. His autonomy is placed on the same level as the judge's authority. Both have fundamentally the same rank under the authorizing law. The correlation of authority and autonomy here is evident.

The same phenomenon may be discerned in other persons and institutions which represent an acknowledged authority. If Luther, e.g., is recognized as an authority in the Evangelical church, it is not because of any personal attributes he may possess but because he speaks in the name of Holy Scripture as the court which authorizes him. To the degree that this authorization is taken seriously, to the degree that Luther's authority is acknowledged only insofar as he stands with all other Evangelical Christians under the common court of Holy Scripture, to that degree this authority can be controlled. Luther must be tested by Holy Scripture even as the verdict of the judge must be tested — and in certain cases can be reversed!

This brings out a further essential characteristic of authority. Because it stands in correlation with the autonomy or mature independence of those who are subject to it, it can never be a permanent authority. It is always authority for the present, valid only for the time being, so long as it is positively vindicated before the higher court.

This is how Luther understood his own authority.[4] Similarly

---

[4] See Karl Holl, *Gesammelte Aufsätze zur Kirchengeschichte*, I (2nd ed.; Tübingen: Mohr, 1923), 381-419, esp. 398. In a letter to Melanchthon Luther vigorously rejects any use of the term "authority" in relation to himself (*WA*, Br 5, 406, lines 43-45), and in a letter to Hartmuth von Cronberg he repudiates those who "believe on my account" rather than "for the sake of the Word itself" (Preserved Smith and Charles M. Jacobs [trans.], *Luther's Correspondence* [Philadelphia: Lutheran Publication Society, 1918], II, 108). To Spalatin he writes, "It is nothing to me if my authority declines" (*Luther's Correspondence*, I, 344).

both the Lutheran [5] and the Reformed [6] confessions claim to be no more than *normae normatae* which must themselves be tested by the *norma normans* of Holy Scripture. Indeed, even Holy Scripture does not claim to be an authority in the sense of positively declaring itself to be the ultimate court of appeal. According to the Reformation — and especially the Lutheran — understanding of Scripture, we do not believe in Christ because of Scripture, we believe in Scripture because of Christ. It is on this basis that Luther arrives at his well-known hermeneutical principle that Scripture, especially the Old Testament, is to be regarded as God's Word only insofar as it "inculcates Christ." [7] His relativizing of Esther, James, and Revelation rests on the same principle, as does the Lutheran view that in principle the canon is open and subject to revision or augmentation. A closed canon necessarily results when Scripture is regarded as a definitive book of law. [8]

Even Schleiermacher seems to have understood this critical christological principle. [9] On the other hand, Helmut Echternach, in what can only be described as an odd piece of work — Ebeling calls it "tomfoolery" — completely misunderstands it when he regards Luther's translation as the literally inerrant text, and argues that even the doctrine of verbal inspiration represents a compromising departure. [10] Echternach's work, although it belongs among the curiosities of church

[5] See Edmund Schlink, *Theology of the Lutheran Confessions*, trans. Paul F. Koehneke and Herbert J. A. Bouman (Philadelphia: Muhlenberg, 1961), pp. 5 ff.

[6] See Otto Weber, *Grundlagen der Dogmatik* (Neukirchen: Erziehungsverein, 1955), I, 296 ff.

[7] *Christum treibet.* See LW 35, 396 and 236.

[8] The Council of Trent defined its closed canon in 1546 (see *The Church Teaches: Documents of the Church in English Translation* [St. Louis: Herder, 1955], pp. 44-45) and its definition was reaffirmed by the First Vatican Council in 1870 (see *ibid.*, p. 47). Reformed confessions too, unlike the Lutheran, stipulate the contents of the canon, e.g., the 1559 Gallican Confession (Art. III), the 1561 Belgic Confession (Art. IV), and the 1648 Westminster Confession (Chapter 1).

[9] "The authority of Holy Scripture cannot be the foundation of faith in Christ; rather must the latter be presupposed before a peculiar authority can be granted to Holy Scripture." Friedrich Schleiermacher, *The Christian Faith*, ed. H. R. Mackintosh and J. S. Stewart (Edinburgh: T. & T. Clark, 1928), p. 591.

[10] Helmut Echternach, *Es stehet geschrieben . . . Eine Untersuchung über die Grenzen der Theologie und der Autorität des Wortes* (Berlin, 1937), pp. 9, 13, 64. Cf. the famous reply of Gerhard Ebeling, "The Significance of the Critical Historical Method for Church and Theology in Protestantism," in *Word and Faith* (Philadelphia: Fortress, 1963), pp. 19-20.

history, is mentioned here because — as a caricature — it represents a position diametrically opposed to the Reformation concept of authority.

We have now established the correlation, or partnership, between authority and autonomy on the basis of a third thing which is above both. But this seems to raise a new problem. The correlation seems to imply an equality between the one who has the authority and the one who is subject to it. Yet the essence of authority undoubtedly consists in a relation of superiority. How can the two be harmonized? The apparent contradiction is to be explained by the fact that two dimensions of human reality intersect here: first, the dimension of principle with its a priori validations, and second, the dimension of experience with its a posteriori validations.

The postulate which derives from the dimension of principle is as follows: Autonomy and personhood must never be destroyed. Men and groups must never be made mere objects of mere force. Hence there must be an ultimate equality between the one who has authority and the one who is subject to it.

The thesis which derives from the dimension of experience takes a different course: Till now it has always been true that the one in authority is right, that he stands in a more immediate and familiar relationship to the common court than I do. Hence I must in the first instance accept the validity of what he proclaims and commands; I must recognize his superiority over me.

Authority is consequently a phenomenon which occurs within experience, within the confines of temporality. This is why we have to speak of it in temporal terms — "in the first instance." What this means is that I trust the authority until the contrary is proved, i.e., until my independent and autonomous relation to the authorizing court may compel me to be critical of it. The superiority of authority does not rest, then, on the reduction of its subjects to immature dependence, on a violation of their autonomy. It rests rather on an advance credit willingly granted to it by the mature and independent person because of the way it has proved itself heretofore in his experience.

It is thus false in principle to speak of the authority of parents in relation to very small children, or of the authority of masters in relation to animals. For here there is no background of experience out of which credit can be advanced, nor is there the kind of maturity which would be in a position to confer or grant authority. In these instances what is involved is simply the power of influence, the radiant strength of love, parental force, and the ability of the trainer to train.

The advance credit of experience can be granted to tradition [11] as well as to authority. The two terms are in fact related, for tradition contains the collective experience of the generations. Hence the advance which one's own experience grants to collective experience is always credited until the collective treasury has been adequately corroborated, or contradicted or qualified, in one's own experience with life — though there is an element which in principle cannot be transcended, as in the dogmatic tradition of the church. [12]

There is thus in all historical existence a conservative element, since history is always integrated into transmitted experiences. On the other hand, a conservatism which absolutizes tradition denies its own maturity. It parallels exactly the case in which authority is absolutized, reduced to mere force, and man is degraded to the point where he is nothing but a function of force.

Only from this twofold standpoint — that authority is both equal in principle and superior in experience — does it make sense for authority to be invested with power. The power is then one that is open to testing, and hence limited by that which tests it. Power is then "entrusted" to authority in order to give it the possibility of developing itself freely through proving itself with a view to further establishing its credit.

Jawaharlal Nehru is an impressive example of the role of experience in the emergence of authority. He says of Mahatma Gandhi: "Repeatedly I was astonished at his appraisal of the situation, of what should be done. First, most of us reacted against it. 'What's the good of that?' we asked and, a little later, we found that it was the right policy. So, step by step, we came to rely on his judgment, apart from his basic principles." [13] But Nehru is also an excellent

---

[11] Here we mean tradition in the general sense, not in the special ecclesiastical or Roman Catholic sense.

[12] I am thinking here of Werner Elert's well-known definition of dogma as the statement of what the kerygma ought to contain. *Der christliche Glaube* (3rd ed.; Hamburg: Furche, 1956), p. 39.

[13] Tibor Mende, *Nehru: Conversations on India and World Affairs* (New York: Braziller, 1956), p. 23.

example of how authority counts on mature independence and contributes to its growth, for Nehru pursued a path which was independent of Gandhi.

Mature independence in respect of authority is particularly well-illustrated in a borderline case which may be clearly seen in Luther. When confronted by texts of Scripture which seem to be unintelligible or even offensive we should, says Luther, doff our hats and pass on.[14] Mature independence is shown in the decision to pass on. The continuing unimpaired authority of Scripture is acknowledged at the same time by the doffing of the hat. This shows an awareness that Scripture's knowledge of God is always greater than our own, and that we shall perhaps have to return later to the text which we have left for the moment. The object of faith is always greater than faith itself. In principle, then, the advance credit granted to Holy Scripture is inexhaustible. This gives it a unique authority. For Holy Scripture could never be exhausted by the individual, "even though he were to rule the church with the prophets for a hundred years." [15]

We thus conclude that, since authority can be conferred only by autonomy, precedence — a temporal *prae* — is conceded to it on the basis of independent insight into the authorizing entity plus the independent diagnosis of experience. Authority thus enjoys superiority as long as it proves itself.

This means, first, that authority is in principle open to criticism; its pronouncements or measures are subject to ex post facto control. It means too that in principle authority is subject to change or replacement; it may be approved or rejected, or part of its claims denied or suspended.

This distinction also throws light on the two forms of authority known as "outward" and "inward." There is an authority of office which is ideally identical with inward or personal authority. In accordance with our findings, both forms are to be defined in terms of principle as well as experience. In principle, the man in authority, whether that authority be official or personal, stands under the same binding norm as those who are subject to him. Empirically, the power of office confers an advance credit on the one who holds it, and this applies not only officially but also personally, i.e., to his

---

[14] *WA* 20, 571.
[15] *LW* 54, 476, No. 5677; Holl, *op. cit.*, I, 577.

inward authority. In general, judges and teachers are responsible people, and the social order is based on the subordination of pupils to teachers, apprentices to masters, and children to parents. The commandment about honoring one's parents does not constitute this relationship; it simply confirms ontic relations which are known already to experience. It connects to them the authorizing word of God, even as this word is "connected" with the water of baptism.[16] Thus a credit is conferred on the person of the one who holds power, a credit which lasts until he proves quite unworthy of having authority. For the judge can be brought under discipline, the teacher can be dismissed, and the father can lose his parental rights to a legally assigned guardian. Thus it is apparent that "outward" and "inward" authority are only two different forms of the general concept of authority, and that both are embraced in the characterization of authority which we have just given.

Having elucidated the first of our two main principles as regards the relation between authority and autonomy, we turn now to the second, namely, that authority always insists upon autonomy. Authority is distinguished from tyranny by the fact that its correlate is the free partner, whereas the correlate of tyranny is the slave. From what we have said about authority being in principle subject to criticism and revision, it follows that there can be only a relative dependence upon it. He who is relatively dependent owes it not only to himself but also to the authority that he should maintain his freedom. In this sense Socrates is the prototype of authority for he brought his pupils up to think for themselves and be independent.

This maintaining of freedom in dependence presupposes a self-limitation of authority. When we, therefore, consider that on the one hand the man in power is caught up in a movement involving the expansion of power, and that on the other hand authority is a specific mode of power, we seem to be confronted here by a genuine problem. How can there possibly be any self-limitation of power if it runs counter to the inherent autonomy of power? How is it possible in the midst of the inevitabilities of power to seize upon the ethical opportunity of being an authority?

The answer certainly cannot be that this self-limitation is possible

---

[16] Cf. Luther's Small Catechism in *BC* 349.

through the subjective virtue of modesty. The inevitability inherent in the expansion of power is an objective thing; it can be checked only by another form of objectivity, only if authority itself is embedded in some higher ontic context and does not stand on its own, or root in a mere disposition or readiness for asceticism. In fact, it is the true nature and essence of authority to be thus embedded, to know that it is thus transcended.

We learn what it is that thus transcends authority when we formulate our question more precisely: How can the desire of authority to maintain the freedom of its subjects possibly be realized? The partnership thus desired is possible only under one condition — if the authority and its partner are both subject to a third entity superior to either of them. In other words, an authority can maintain the freedom of his subject only when he is himself regulated and validated by a criterion to which the subject too is directly related.

We touched on this matter of the third entity a moment ago when we were discussing the question of equality between authority and subject. We must now consider it more closely. To help us, we shall use some models of authority provided us in the writings of the Apostle Paul.

Paul alludes constantly to the limitation of his apostolic authority. He feels he has to do so. The members of the congregations must be mature (autonomous) enough to be independent of his authority by virtue of their direct relation to that third entity in the total picture, namely, the gospel. It is precisely where he finds such maturity to be lacking that Paul speaks up on behalf of this understanding of his authority.

Thus it is for Paul an obvious discrediting of his apostolic authority that the Corinthians should be so unstable as blindly and uncritically to approve and follow every new teacher and message. For this simply proves that they are not mature. Hence he takes no satisfaction from the fact that they cleave for a time to him and to his message: "For if some one comes and preaches another Jesus than the one we preached, or if you receive a different spirit from the one you received, or if you accept a different gospel from the one you accepted, you submit to it readily enough" (II Cor. 11:4).

In this complaint one can plainly detect a note of disappointment not merely that the Corinthians are immature but that they are thereby compromising his apostolic authority. They become merely the instruments and objects of whatever influences happen to be working upon them at the moment. Authority presupposes mature independence or autonomy; otherwise it ceases – indeed does not even begin – to be authority.

Paradoxically, then, Paul bears strongest witness to his apostolic authority precisely when he insists upon this mature independence in his hearers and accepts the possibility of being called in question himself. The more he refers to the court which authorizes him – and which opens up the possibility of his being called in question – the stronger is his claim to authority. For he is certain that he can stand before this court, and that he has the gospel on his side.

Similarly, he demands that the Galatians should not depend on his authority, lest he, or a greater than he, i.e., "an angel from heaven," should preach to them another gospel (Gal. 1:8). By cursing himself or that angel in respect of this possibility, he in effect requires the Galatians to cleave, not to persons in authority, but to the authorizing entity, the gospel. His own authority consists quite simply in the fact that he can thus be called in question by those who are mature.

Paul brings to light the same structure of authority in I Corinthians 7 when he delivers his own authoritative opinion on the relation of the sexes but clearly refuses to give it the rank of a dominical saying ("I say, not the Lord . . ."), thus opening up the possibility that the authority of his opinion may be disputed in the name of a better knowledge of the Lord's teaching (I Cor. 7:6, 12, 25). These words contain the whole dialectic of authority, its claim and its self-limitation, its superiority and its equality with others.

Paul gives us an important hint in the same direction when he affirms his credentials as an apostle, and accordingly "as a fool" recounts what he has suffered and done for the sake of the gospel. For in this way he shows that he is a servant who does not aspire to dominion and who would rather boast of his weakness than of his power and greatness (II Cor. 11:30; Gal. 2:17). I am accredited only when I live in accord with the teaching which I represent, when I am of the truth and exist in it (John 18:37), when my life does not bear witness to itself in order thereby to establish its authority, but when it proves its attachment to that third thing, and thereby persuades those who are addressed through both life and teaching. This is why the Apostle "pommels" and "subdues" his body, lest while preaching to others he should himself be disqualified (I Cor. 9:27) and in this way forfeit his authority in the eyes of those who ask for validation.

In relation to the problem of authority this means that there are two senses in which the authority can lose contact with the one who authorizes it. It can displace the truth which authorizes it from the center of its teaching (Gal. 1:8 ff.), and it can cease to live in this truth, thus discrediting itself (I Cor. 9:27) by so living in its own strength as to bear witness only to itself.

It is thus of the very essence of authority, as distinct from tyranny, that it regards itself only as a *norma normata*. To put it even more precisely, we should have to say that it must also regard itself as a *norma normanda* in the sense that its authorization is never complete. It never takes on an indelible character. For all the confidence in its past attestation *(normata)*, it has to be confirmed again and again by those who are mature. Authority can never get beyond the point where it must forever be constituted anew *(normanda)*. Thus it is that authority accords to its subjects the freedom to criticize or accept on the basis of their own direct relation to the *norma normans*.

Authority and Loyalty

One cannot conclude, of course, that this structure of authority, this being "forever constituted anew," implies necessarily a series of points in time. The advance credit, the criticism, the revision, and the new acceptance need not be divided into distinct and independent stages. It is enough that the subjects be potentially ready to criticize and to revise, that their dependence on the authority never be blind. It is also enough that the authority for its part be potentially ready to allow criticism and revision, that it never be a blind force which is an end in itself. At any rate, the attitudes involved in advancing credit, criticizing, revising, and accepting anew cannot be fixed psychologically. They may merge into one another. They need not reach the level of reflection but can be quite unconscious. They can remain in the sphere of pure potentiality and never come to expression.

It is quite possible that the principles on which an authority acts — especially if they are simple and elementary — will be so convincing, and that the persons or institutions which implement them will be so worthy of trust, that the mind "will be able to grasp them once and for all, and not find itself brought up against them every time a decision has to be made." [17]

Indeed, it is very likely in practice that criticism will never gain an entry, precisely because genuine authority has become what it is by virtue of its power of persuasion, because in contrast to tyranny genuine authority is consonant with the autonomy of its subjects. Hence it is "not looked upon as strange or hostile, but loved as something belonging to those placed under its direction." [18]

Strictly speaking, then, authority is vested, not in the institution, but in the person or persons who represent it. For only persons can be loved. Because love here enters the picture, authority cannot be regarded as "punctual," existing only at isolated moments in time. For love — which relates not to things or processes or things about the person but to the persons themselves — is oriented to loyalty. And loyalty is in turn a personal attitude; it refers to persons, not to the regularity of functioning things, e.g., the reliability of a machine.

The personal element in loyalty finds expression in the fact that loyalty withstands the assaults of doubt, and that it is thus emphatically more than merely "punctual." The loyal man, even though he does not understand the measures, conduct, or arguments of authority, even though he disapproves of them, does not for that reason reject authority. He will rather take to himself the psalmist's expression of loyalty (which has, of course, a theological sense): "Nevertheless,. I am continually with thee" (Ps. 73:23). He will regard the insight of authority as greater than his own. He will not accept blindly everything the authority does and says, but he will be concerned to view what to him is unclear in the light of that which is clear, that which once persuaded him and won him over to recognition of the authority. It is even conceivable that despite the darkness he will yet remain loyal. Even though there is no light, he will believe that the authority he acknowledges is great enough to stand up to these difficult tests.

The main objection to the idea that authority is "punctual" in character and must seek constant reaffirmation — and thus is necessarily the object of permanently repeated creations out of nothing — consists in the fact that authority is vested in the person, not in his several words

[17] Simone Weil, *The Need for Roots: Prelude to a Declaration of Duties Toward Mankind,* trans. Arthur Wills (New York: Putnam's, 1952), p. 12.
[18] *Ibid.*

and deeds. His words and deeds may be contested. They have validity only from moment to moment. But the authority of the person rests on love and loyalty, attitudes whose constancy involves more than merely the sum of isolated points of agreement.

On the other hand, the very fact that authority is open to revision means that points of rejection can add up to the overthrow of authority, when the cup of criticism overflows. Indeed, a single criticism can do this if it is sufficiently basic.

The fact that authority attaches to the person, and thus leads to the constant attitudes of love and loyalty, means that authority forms traditions and that it has a long-range effect (once again a temporal aspect is involved!). This may be seen particularly in the doctrinal tradition of the church. Characteristic here is the fact that doctrine is never handed down merely in terms of its substance alone. It is always linked with the persons or groups who taught and bore witness to the specific truths. The authority of doctrine is bound up with that of the teachers who are regarded as fathers of the faith. It is these two dimensions of authority which together go to make up tradition.

This is why our relation to tradition is analogous to our relation to authority. All that we have said about the temporal precedence of authority, the credit advanced to it, its openness to revision, and the fact that it is more than a series of points, applies equally well to tradition.

We can now see why the autonomy which is addressed, sustained, and even awakened by authority, for all of its potential criticism does not make of authority a flimsy and transitory structure which exists only at isolated moments in time.

The element of constancy within authority is not antithetical to the autonomy of those who are guided by it. On the contrary, it is this very autonomy which effects the constancy. It is precisely because authority insists upon autonomy that it constitutes itself by the power of persuasion. Persuasion begets confidence or trust. And trust is mistrust overcome. Confidence is a constant attitude which is demonstrated in loyalty. Authority is itself constant because the counterpart of authority is one who trusts, not one who mistrusts. Potentially, the advance credit given to authority can be revoked at any time. In fact, however, it is preserved from fluctuations of the moment by the loyalty of persons.

The question arises in this connection whether authority in this sense can truly be claimed by the teaching office of Roman Catholicism. This is hardly possible in our definition, for the claim that the teaching office is infallible means that its promulgations are not subject to control. Even if we do not take the oversimple view that this teaching office will define dogmas capriciously; even if we recognize that it appeals to the assistance of the Holy Spirit, and thus to an inner authorization, there is still lacking any third entity, any norm (e.g., the Holy Scripture understood in this sense) which is above both those who teach and those who are taught and which alone constitutes a valid criterion by which to judge the pronouncements of the office.

To this extent our concept does not apply here. For the inner authorization of the office by the testimony of the Holy Spirit, while it corresponds to the postulate of a third entity inasmuch as the Holy Spirit is authoritative both for those who teach and those who are taught, nevertheless fails to meet the postulate of controllability, since the Holy Spirit understood in this sense is not linked to a demonstrable norm, a word, in such a way that he may be had only through this vehicle. It is because they dissociate word and Spirit that Luther in the final analysis classifies both "papists" and "fanatics" together.

Nor can the Roman Catholic concept of tradition function as a norm to control authorization. For the concept of "active tradition" means that the church does not simply inherit tradition as a fixed entity ("passive tradition") which it can then apply, but that the church also forms tradition, again on the basis of the ongoing work of the Holy Spirit, the validation of which is entrusted to the teaching office.[19]

For the same reason, we as Protestants must say that, while Holy Scripture can be said to be a final authority, Christ himself is not to be described in terms of authority. (It is worth noting that the church, or its teaching office, on the Roman Catholic side is here in the same position as Christ on the Protestant side.) Scripture derives its authority from Christ. It is to be tested by him. It is to be interpreted in the light of Christ and with reference to him. Since Christ always does the authorizing and is never himself authorized — unless we think of

[19] On "active tradition" see Karl Adam, *The Spirit of Catholicism*, trans. Justin McCann (New York: Macmillan, 1944), pp. 60 ff., and esp. pp. 155, 173-174; on tradition and infallibility, see F. Diekamp, *Katholische Dogmatik* (1949), I, 58 ff., 63 ff., and also H. Strathmann, "Heilige Schrift, Tradition, und die Einheit der Kirche," *Theologische Blätter*, 2/3 (1942), 33 ff.

his authorization in Trinitarian terms, which is another question — he does not come under the concept of authority. He is the "Lord," which is quite another matter, involving more than authority.

The Lord is validated by the Spirit. But the Spirit is not above the Lord; the Spirit is from him and with him, and identical with him: the Spirit will only "take what is mine" (John 16:15).

Authority and Freedom

We must now consider an even deeper aspect of the relation between authority and autonomy. Authority not only appeals to freedom and upholds it; it actually creates freedom. This may be briefly established as follows.

By nature authority is that which is superordinate to man. Man credits it in advance with being authorized by the norm which for him is the superior and authoritative standard. To this extent authority represents that which is "above," namely, that norm which determines man and therewith the order by which man comes to himself. In the terminology of Anselm, man comes to himself, to his *rectitudo*, only through the rectitude of the relations in which he is set.

He reaches this self-rectitude, not merely by the development of his entelechy, but also — this is the true *sine qua non* — by being in conformity with the *ordo* of his existence. More precisely, man's entelechy, his true humanity, consists in this conformity to the order.

In respect of this conformity we need not think exclusively in terms of Anselm's ontology of existence. We may conceive of it much more generally. One might say that to stand in the order means above all to be able to distinguish between the higher and the lower, to be controlled by normative entities rather than by impulses, or — in Kierkegaard's terms — to be related only in a relative way to what is relative, and in an absolute way only to what is absolute.

On an Anselmian understanding, this conformity then implies that only the authority authorized by God — for Anselm only the church — orients man aright with respect to what is higher and lower. Hence it orders man within himself, in such a way that reason is accorded the higher place and the impulses a lower place.

These statements of Anselm also apply independently of the ontological framework in which he presents them. Man comes to himself only when he is in a right relation to what is higher and lower, only when he knows the difference between heaven and earth and what is appropriate to each. To this degree authority, as the representative of what is higher, is an ordering factor which helps man to be himself.

The alternative to this *rectitudo* is the disorder of man which delivers him up to what is lower. A case in point is the prodigal son (Luke 15:11 ff.). He renounces allegiance to the authority of the father and after his emancipation is enslaved by impulse, vainglory, and homesickness.

We may thus say that I become free only through an authority which, as the representative of what is higher, binds me to the final *norma normans*, namely, to God. Since God reveals himself to man not directly but indirectly through the Word, there is required a mediating, commissioned authority.

Freedom, then, is not the antithesis of commitment but a specific form of commitment, as we have already noted.[20] He whom the Son makes free is free indeed (John 8:36). He is free precisely because he is caught up in a commitment which expresses his nature. For, since man's nature is simply his relation to God, he finds himself only in the measure that he finds God. He becomes free in himself only when the Son of God sets him in relation to Himself. Because man is himself only in the measure that he is related to God, the authority authorized by God sets him on the way to being himself.

This is what we were trying to express when we said that authority does not merely appeal to freedom, but creates it. We could say the same thing in terms of a well-known saying of Luther that man is free insofar as he is "lord of all, subject to none." [21] He is that, however, not in virtue of autonomous positing or by self-creation, but only as one who is himself authorized, ordained to lordship, i.e., only as one who himself has a Lord, and who by commitment to authority is integrated into a structure in which the relation of higher and lower finds expression.

For the same reason that commitment and freedom are not antitheses, theonomy and autonomy too are not mutually exclusive. On the contrary each requires the other. Since this brings us up against a basic problem of theological ethics, we shall need to examine further the relationship between them.

[20] See, e.g., pp. 107 ff. above, esp. p. 110.
[21] Martin Luther, *The Freedom of a Christian* (1520); LW 31, 344.

Theonomy and Autonomy

Ever since the time of Kant, Christian ethics has been exposed to the charge of involving an inner contradiction: an authority which orders man from without — as the Ten Commandments are said to do — ignores the autonomy of man and "heteronomizes" the moral consciousness. To state the objection more precisely, such an external authority makes man the object of a law instead of granting him freedom to choose his law, and hence to be a moral subject. It thus attacks the personal dignity of man. Theonomy is said to be heteronomy. Accordingly, theology is incapable in principle of fashioning an ethical discipline, or even of finding a place for it within its domain. In claiming nonetheless that it can, theology is turning back the clock and frantically trying to preserve a pre-Kantian framework of ethics.

Now it must be conceded at once that the question raised by the Enlightenment — and especially by Kant — as to how to bring the divine Law into relation to our autonomy, the divine command into relation to our conscience, is a question that cannot be ignored or suppressed. In the Middle Ages, even in Luther, conscience was grounded in the authority of the church or the Word of God. It always had a norm and a content, and accordingly was not reflective. But modern man is confronted by the fact that conscience still exists and functions even when released from all authorities and emptied of all content. "The movement . . . towards the autonomy of man . . . has in our time reached a certain completion. Man has learned to cope with all questions of importance without recourse to God as a working hypothesis. . . . it is becoming evident that everything gets along without 'God', and just as well as before." [22]

I have experienced that I have within me a conscience, or, more generally, a functioning moral criterion, which is active and remains active even in the circumstance of an extreme autarchy (or freedom from authority) on the part of the world, and this is an experience which cannot be undone or invalidated. Kant demanded that I render responsible obedience to the commands of God. I am not simply to accept them as heteronomous commands but must first subject them to the control of my own conscience, giving my own assent to them.

---

[22] Dietrich Bonhoeffer, *Letters and Papers from Prison* (New York: Macmillan, 1962), pp. 194-195.

This demand of Kant cannot be reversed. But if this is true, i.e., if we cannot go back behind the postulate of autonomy, and if, on the other hand, Christian ethics cannot surrender the axiom of theonomy, we seem to be forced into the impossible position of trying to bring into synthesis that which is basically irreconcilable. If it is impossible even to conceive of wooden iron or a four-cornered circle, is not the idea of a theonomous autonomy just as paradoxical?

If this elementary objection is to be overcome we would be well-advised to examine the idea of autonomy more closely, and in so doing to concentrate less on the *nomos* part of the concept and more on the *autos*. What is meant by this "self"? For Kant the self is the isolated person who shares in the intelligible world by perceiving within himself the practical *logos*. Man as a moral person is thus fundamentally autarchical. Indeed, to look outward for the determinants of action in the world apart from myself, e.g., to look for a commanding authority or to let myself be controlled eudaemonistically by objects of fear and hope, simply destroys the moral structure of the ego. Hence the moral self is the lonely ego which listens to itself and is shut off from the world outside.

The way to the outside opens up only in the second phase of the moral process, namely, when I am ready to act and I seek things in the external world which can serve as objects for the outworking of the disposition I have already formed within. Love of neighbor may be taken as a case in point. For Kant, the impression made on me by the neighbor whom I encounter is not what provokes my love or readiness to help, i.e., my disposition. On the contrary, I first form the disposition of a non-eudaemonistic readiness to help, whose ethical character is measured by the criterion of whether it may be made "the principle of universal legislation," and only then do I seek neighbors toward whom the disposition may be implemented. This is why we were justified in saying that for Kant the self is the lonely autarchical I. Behind his developed concept of autonomy there lies a prior decision concerning man.

We thus come up against the important insight that in the antithesis between autonomy and theonomy what matters is not so much the existing view of the *nomos* and where it comes from as the prior anthropological decision, i.e., the view of the *autos*. Theologically, the *autos* is something quite different from the *autos* of Kant. It can be understood only in terms of its relation to God. In Christian thinking the self is the ego which is created by God, which has fallen from him, and is then visited and called to redemption by him. There is no theological statement about God which does not take this relation into account. If one were to attempt a statement about God apart from this relation, one would be venturing into the inscrutable and inaccessible spheres of a "God in himself," a *Deus absconditus*. My knowledge of God can have as its object only Emmanuel, i.e., the God who discloses himself in a history which has to do with me. To know God is to know him in his history with us, in his "for me" *(pro me)* to adapt a well-known saying of Melanchthon.[23]

But the converse is equally true. There is no theological statement about man which does not take account of his relation to God. If one were to venture a statement about man apart from God, one would only come up with something about physical or psychical functions or about the agents of such functioning, or at best with metaphysical assumptions and explanations. If man is seen apart from his relation to God, the point of his existence will certainly be missed.

This implies — to take up again an earlier thought — that I can only *believe* in man, since the God who determines man's nature is for me also an object of faith. The infinite worth of man, and hence also his inviolability, cannot be established empirically. Empiricism only devaluates man. On the basis of empiricism I may, like Nietzsche, view man as vermin on the surface of the earth. I can also arrive at less harsh diagnoses, to be sure. But even then the true and proper nature of man will still be beyond my grasp.

If, however, I take seriously the fact that man can be defined only in terms of his relation to God, then even that self which autonomy has in view takes on a distinctive quality. Man comes to himself only when he comes to God. Apart from God he misses his true self.

This is again evident in the parable of the prodigal son, which we must once more briefly expound. When the son asks his father for the portion of the inheritance due him in order that he may go away into a far country, he is in effect hoping to come into his own. He is seek-

---

[23] Cf. Philip Melanchthon's Preface to the *Loci Communes* of 1521, in Henricus Ernestus Bindseil (ed.), *Corpus Reformatorum* (Brunsvigae: Schwetschke, 1854), XXI, 85: "To know Christ is to know his benefits"; English translation in Charles Leander Hill (trans.), *The Loci Communes of Philip Melanchthon* (Boston: Meador, 1944), p. 68.

ing himself. He is afraid that in his father's house he will not find himself. For at home he stands under an authority which commands, in a system of values determined by his parents, and in a tradition which lays down what one may do and not do. These all seem to be heteronomous influences which make him an object of leading strings and do not permit him to be an autonomous subject who can decide things for himself. Only in the far country, he thinks, can he enjoy self-determination. So it is that he seeks himself.

But it is apparent that he does not find himself. Breaking free from the higher authority of his father, he falls under the dictatorship of what is lower. He comes into the sphere of impulse, vainglory, and anxiety. When he ends up at the pigs' trough, he knows that freedom is not the opposite of commitment but simply a form of commitment. With the father he is free, a son of the house. Outside, i.e., outside the relation with the father, he is a servant of what is lower. Hence he finds his true self only with his father; outside he loses it. For his self is not, as he imagined, a self-contained entelechy. On the contrary, his self exists only in the lived-out relation of sonship.

His existence becomes one of freedom, not by his throwing off sonship (for the alternative to sonship is slavery) but by his coming to mature sonship (Gal. 4:1-7). This is why the assurance of freedom given us in the words: "All things are yours," is coupled with the statement: "And you are Christ's" (I Cor. 3:21-23).

It is thus plain that theonomy and autonomy are not antitheses on this level. For God is not a *heteros nomos* to man. It is only when man is with God that he is also himself; when he is not with God, he misses what is properly his for he is not himself.

Some distinction, of course, is needed here. For there is always the possibility that God may indeed be a *heteros nomos* for man. This is the case when I do not exist in the truth, and consequently am not in the fellowship to which he has called me. I am still related to God, but in a negative way, as it were. In this case God is for me merely opposition, enmity, and challenge. It is to this situation that the teaching of the Law draws attention. As Luther says, to the God who commands me in the Law I can react only with ill will, servile obedience, or even hatred. I am then not on the side of the divine Law. On the contrary, I oppose it, as least on a certain level of the ego (Rom. 7:17 ff.). To this degree the Law of God, if it is the exclusive mark of my relation to God, confronts me as a *heteros nomos*. On the human side the servant corresponds to the Law — the servant in all his various guises, from the one who obeys grudgingly and in fear, to the consistent saboteur, and even to the runaway who suppresses the concept of the fearful God and replaces it by mythical or intellectual constructs of his own wishful thinking.

One may thus say that by nature, i.e., in virtue of my own quality as natural man, God is in fact heteronomous. To this extent the objection with which we started is right, but in a way different from that intended. Salvation consists not simply in the fact that I learn to understand my own self afresh, but in the fact that I receive a new self; my "old man" passes away and I become a "new creature."

It is in keeping with the character of this new self that it is necessarily autonomous. For, being called to exist in the truth, I actually desire such existence. I will to be what I now am. God's call is now no longer the call of a stranger, against whom I must defend my autonomy. On the contrary, God calls me as the Father in whom I find my true nature as a child, and in whom I thus for the first time attain to autonomy. What previously appeared to be autonomy is now revealed to be nothing but a sublime form of self-alienation, an act with whose help I evaded the ultimate challenge.

Only in this light is it clear why Paul calls love "the fulfilling of the Law" (Rom. 13:10). To love God is to will what he wills, to be at one with his will in the sense of conformity. For this will has come upon me as the will of one who loves me and who discloses himself to me in the establishing of the father-child relationship. The demand that I love the Lord my God with all my heart and soul and mind (Matt. 22:37) no longer comes upon me like an alien law. It does not have the distinguishing mark of such a law, for it does not provoke opposition or divide the ego.

For him to whom God has revealed himself as the loving God this demand to love is simply the release of a new spontaneity of the total ego. In the act of returning that love I am totally engaged. My will — for love is a total movement — is taken up into this spontaneity. For he who truly loves, even as between men, does not choose love as one possibility among others, the one which he willingly affirms while consciously repressing the other possibilities which crowd in upon him. On the contrary, he has no choice but to love. His will is caught up in loving. Indeed, it has become a factor within love, an element of it.

This is why Jesus can select a very remarkable expression and say that the command to love our neighbor is "like" the command to love God (Matt. 22:39). He can say this only because God and neighbor are not different realities. Indeed, it is God who makes the neighbor what he is for me, because God has bought him with a price and taken him up into the same history of love.

Hence the act of love is indivisible. It cannot be divided between God and the neighbor in respect of object (Jas. 2:14 ff.; I John 4:19-21), nor can it be divided in its fulfillment in the sense that half of the ego indwells it while the other half stands outside. This twofold indivisibility is inconceivable unless God "wins" love from me and, by calling me to fellowship, posits a new self, a new creature. When this happens, I cannot in the strict sense say that I have become another person, but I must confess that now for the first time I have come to my true self. In the eyes of God I have become what he intended me to be.

By thus becoming theonomous — not as one who resists under the Law but as one who has become conformed to God under the gospel — I win autonomy in the true sense. And thus is resolved the original contradiction between the ethical concept of autonomy and an assumed theological heteronomy, and therewith the contradiction between authority and autonomy.

To be sure, the principle we asserted at the beginning of this section on theonomy and autonomy still stands fast. There can be no going back behind the discovery of the autonomy of the moral consciousness. It is and will always be impossible for us to characterize servile obedience to the divine commandments as an ethical stance. Indeed, we can go further and say with Kant that, because of the dignity of the moral person, the supposed claims of supposed commandments, even though they insist on having had a lofty origin at Sinai, can be accepted only if they pass the control point of the ethical consciousness and receive its endorsement, demonstrating to the ethical consciousness that they are simply an objectification of the imperative heard within it. The claim of statements which allege that they are divine commandments and hence represent authority is subject to the condition of all authority, namely, that it must be in harmony with autonomy and must satisfy certain criteria.

Our only difference with Kant — and it is a fundamental one — is that the concern of the Christian is with the ethical consciousness of the *new* ego, the ego of the son come of age. On this altered level all the formal marks of autonomy remain the same. Indeed, the discovery of these structural marks by Kant, and their varied definition since Kant (e.g., in existential philosophy), can be very helpful to theological ethics. For they help to illumine from the side of philosophy the distinction between servile obedience and filial love.

This observation is of basic importance, for it teaches us not to regard secularism as purely negative from a theological standpoint. Theologically, secularism is a mammoth experiment which throws new light both on specific structures of humanity and on the contents of traditional Christian teaching. Thus one may see how the doctrine of Law and gospel, judgment and grace, obedience and love, authority and freedom, has received from the debate with the modern concept of autonomy a meaning and content which were certainly there from the outset (e.g., in Luther) but which have undergone a development and refinement that would hardly have been possible without this experiment. In any case, theology and Christian ethics would certainly be ill advised to see in secularism only the element of anti-Christianity and negative opposition. As surely as the Christian message is proclaimed in the midst of the world and its ideologies, so surely does the world also have something to say to those who do the proclaiming. Perhaps what it says will be in the nature of a protest. In Kant's concept of autonomy at any rate there can be no mistaking the note of protest, or at least of correction and reservation. But those who listen to such protest learn to know themselves and their cause better. They are thus equipped to repeat their summons with new authority. Indeed, precisely through Kant's concept of autonomy they are enabled the better to understand the mystery of authority.

We pause here for a moment to consider the point which we have now reached in our analysis of authority. We have been concerned with the question of how power can be held in check, and have seen that it cannot be restrained by mere reflection on its instrumental character, on the fact that it is a means to specific ends. For it may be that the ends are ethically negative; and if good ends do not justify the means, bad ends certainly cannot do so. Again, the ends may be deceptive; they may be simply the sheep's clothing which covers the wolf of power-determined ends. This became plain in the case of the ideologies, which in the pragmatic sense are "end"-ideas by which the will to power seeks to create for itself a moral alibi.

The mere fact that power presses on towards ends or goals is consequently not enough to restrain it. Restraint is possible only if power looks backwards to that which authorizes it, so that it claims to be "only" an authority and limits itself by respecting the sovereign sphere of freedom (autonomy) in its subjects.

The tendency of power to become an end in itself cannot be halted merely by having power reflect on its instrumental character. Far more crucial is the question by whom or by what is this instrument of power appointed and authorized, and in whose service does it therefore stand? Its tendency to become an end in itself is checked not by the fact that power is directed toward ends but by the fact that power has the status of a servant. Only when power is referred back to that which authorizes it does it become authority, i.e., a commissioned and validated power which is bound to its commission, and hence restrained.

Authority and Confidence

In this connection power which thus regards itself as authority is also limited by the fact that it is grounded in trust or confidence. Our clarification of this matter will simply be an extension of what we have already been saying about the problem of authority.

The link between power and the confidence of those dependent on that power brings out once again the contrast between authority and tyranny. Tyranny has no need of confidence. It relies on the superiority of physical force. It exerts pressure and compels co-operation without troubling to earn confidence and without exposing itself to the risk of a no confidence vote.

More precisely, one might say that tyranny speculates on confidence. For the machinery of power runs more smoothly if there are no outbreaks of opposition but only a consensus, a certain trusting readiness to co-operate on the part of the subjects. This statement seems at first glance to contradict the thesis that tyranny does not need confidence. But the apparent contradiction fades when we consider the nature of the confidence which tyranny seeks.

In our discussion of ideologies we saw that their task is simply to secure a bridgehead for power in the souls of the subjects, i.e., to weaken any potential resistance morally from within. This is why ideologies use the benumbing power of suggestion (propaganda, slogans) and specious arguments. In this way an artificial basis of confidence is created. It is artificial because it rests not on the sober maturity and independence of the ruled but on psychological tricks designed to foster the impression that confidence exists. Like the confidence itself, the authority involved is more apparent than real.

That we have here two radically different forms of confidence, the one genuine and the other false, may be seen from the difference in practice between a democratic and a totalitarian regime. Confidence is the very life of democracy. If a government in power loses the confidence of parliament, that government is dissolved, or if confidence is withdrawn from elected officials and representatives in a general election their tour of duty ends. This shows that in a democracy confidence is not a means by which power is exercised. It is a superordinate criterion for judging who may exercise the power and what means he may use to do so. The concept of confidence in this case has genuine authority. Abuse of confidence and the false gaining of confidence are of course possible in a democracy, but only as empirical perversions of something which both in principle and in the constitutional expression given to it is seriously intended.

The rulers of a totalitarian state, on the other hand, do not depend at all on the confidence of the subjects. There is no possibility of forcing their resignation by the withdrawal of public confidence. This shows that confidence here is something subordinate, not superordinate. It is merely a means by which power is exercised. But a mere means has no authority over me; indeed, I am the authority over whatever means I employ. Hence the unauthoritative character of confidence is simply a logical consequence of the ideological axiom of tyranny. (This clarification of the concept of confidence and its various nuances may also help to clear up some of the much lamented linguistic confusion of our day, in which East and West use the same terms but in radically different senses.)

True authority, then, is linked with confidence and is destroyed by legitimate lack of confidence. The reason for this is that confidence arises only when the bearer of authoritarian power and the person subject to him are both related to a third factor common to both.

The classic biblical model of this concept of confidence is to be found in the story of the building of the tower of Babel [Gal. 11:1-9]. Some of the most important points in the story may be mentioned here. The human race was originally united under God. But man's emancipation produces a wish to be independent. Hence man no longer acknowledges God's authority. He then sets out to build a tower with its top in the heavens. The effort is in many ways a sign of man's desire for self-glory. On the one hand, he desires to be his own lord and thus to take possession of heaven, the dwelling place of God; indeed, he must put himself in the place of God. But in addition, in this incredible role of superman, he must prove himself; he must objectify himself in supradimensional architecture if he is to believe that he really possesses this supernatural greatness.

There is undoubtedly a touch of humor when the biblical account says that God has to stoop down [Gen. 11:5] to survey more closely these titanic projects of man. The irony is that the true God and the real heaven are obviously so high above these towers meant to reach to heaven that from his place in heaven God cannot even see them.

God scatters the men who rebel against him and confuses their speech. We have already noted earlier that the story is more than the demonstration of a supernatural miracle of wrath. For to the contingent act of the wrath of God there corresponds the necessity of a process whose inner law must be discerned. The question of this law leads us directly to the problem of confidence, as will appear in the discussion which follows.

True fellowship, e.g., the original fellowship of the race, which is the thing here in question, is possible only in virtue of the confidence of the members. This bond of confidence is the alternative to the force of circumstances whereby men are simply thrown together at random, and to the compulsion which is exercised by tyranny.

But confidence can arise – this is the first condition – only when the other is not wholly unpredictable, only when I know what to expect of him. The alternative to this aspect of confidence is dread in the face of his unpredictability, i.e., not knowing what to expect of him. As Wilhelm Herrmann has shown in his magnificent analysis of confidence,[24] the predictability of the other arises only under two con-

---

[24] See Wilhelm Herrmann, *Ethik* (2nd ed.; Tübingen-Leipzig, 1901), pp. 27 ff

ditions. The first is that I know the normative authority which directs him. I must have knowledge of the route which he is following. Only then do I have a key to his conduct. Only then is his conduct predictable.

The second condition which must be fulfilled if there is to be confidence is that I must myself be under the same normative authority, i.e., following the same route. If I am not bound myself, I cannot expect it of others. Only if I am myself predictable and worthy of confidence is it possible to presume the same of others. The man who instead acts capriciously, i.e., on an opportunistic or pragmatic basis, can never be in a position to perceive in others an act of genuine ethical commitment. He is forever condemned to suspect that others are simply pretending to be motivated by such commitments whereas in reality they too are acting purely out of self-interest or selfishness. Joseph's brothers assumed his unpredictability until they heard his call to confidence ("Fear not") buttressed by a declaration of the ultimate commitment under which he stood ("Am I in the place of God?"); only after he had admitted the ultimate obligation under which he stood could they count on his forgiveness (Gen. 50:19).

Only when these two conditions are met, then, is confidence possible. Only then can the organism of a society grow from within. An order which is not the objectification of this relation of confidence can be nothing but a compulsory schema which chains together — but cannot unite — the conglomeration of unrelated individuals thrown together within it.

We have had to interpose this discussion on the nature of confidence in order to show the inner processes at work behind the blow that befalls in the Babel dispersion. What is involved here is a centrifugal tendency which results from a "loss of the center." [25] A humanity loosed from all higher commitment becomes an agglomeration of unpredictable individuals devoid of confidence and consequently filled with dread. What takes place here is a judgment immanent in the offense. It is a prototype of what always happens when fellowship is broken.

[25] This phrase derives from the title of H. Sedlmayr's *Verlust der Mitte. Die bildende Kunst des 19. und 20. Jahrhunderts als Symbol der Zeit* (Salzburg: Müller, 1948), translated by Brian Battershaw as *Art in Crisis: The Lost Center* (Chicago: Regnery, 1958).

We must still protect the concept of predictability against certain misunderstandings. In this connection three considerations deserve mention.

First, with reference to our exposition of the story of the tower of Babel the suspicion might arise that we regard trustworthiness and predictability as possible only when there is allegiance to God, i.e., only in the case of Christians. This is simply not true. We have no desire whatever to defame in this way those who are not bound in the Christian sense. Trustworthiness arises wherever there is a common allegiance to an authority which has normative significance for the sphere of ethical principles and maxims. This implies two essential delimitations.

In the first place, authority in any particular sphere of reality – e.g., the social, economic, or political – is not able to produce a society built on confidence. For this authority is not binding except within the situation controlled by it, and even here the sphere of human motives cannot be controlled.

Then too, as regards the second delimitation, there is no possibility of confidence if the authoritarian norm is understood in a purely pragmatic sense, e.g., if the rights of man or the concept of man as such are regarded simply as moral means of regimentation, so that rulers do not take them seriously but simply use them as a humanitarian smoke screen. Confidence can be created only by allegiance to an authoritative norm which is indeed taken seriously, which indeed is binding but cannot itself be exploited.

This raises the further question, which constantly recurs in ethics, whether and how far norms which are severed from the ultimate *norma normans* can finally resist being sucked into the stream of pragmatic degeneration, in other words, whether and how far they can continue to be legitimate authority. Is it not a primal law that when life severs itself from the creator it forgets its creaturely rank, posits itself absolutely, and is thus forced to relativize all other phenomena, including the sphere of norms? Where life seeks its own glory does not everything become a means of self-aggrandizement and so take on a purely pragmatic aspect? Apart from faith, even the so-called norms of Christianity are drawn into this pragmatic stream. They are ideologized and degraded to the point of being nothing more than the "spiritual foundations of the West."

At this point the tendency toward a loss of confidence is plain to see. One can never know how the adherents of these false ideological authorities and norms will conduct themselves if there is a shift in power relationships. For all ideologies, including that of the "Christian West," are always prepared for ideological inversions, shifts, regroupings, and reconstructions. They are always ready to trim their sails to any breeze (cf. Eph. 4:14; Heb. 13:9). One never knows what to expect of them. This is why only a genuine, non-pragmatic authority has the ability to awaken confidence. While this form of authority may be possible outside the Christian faith, still there always arises the question whether it can maintain itself, and hence the question of the *norma normans*.

This brings us, then, to the second consideration we proposed to advance in relation to the concept of predictability. The question arises whether there may not be something like a negative predictability. The answer is unquestionably Yes. I can predict how a consistent opportunist, or even a criminal, will act in a given situation. Indeed Kant contended that, as one can work out with certainty the date of a lunar eclipse, so one can predict how a kleptomaniac will act when he comes across some silver spoons and observes that no one is watching him. In this case there seems to be no correlation between confidence and predictability, for even though I can predict the conduct of a sinister character I still do not trust him.

There seems to be a similiar breakdown of the correlation — and this is our third point — when I have confidence in someone and yet cannot predict what he will do. Thus a child trusts his father even though he cannot guess how his father will respond to his request, and even though he has no understanding of many of the measures taken in his upbringing. This child-father relation has even become a parable of the man-God relation. Assaults of doubt have always arisen at the point where believers are unable to predict what God will do, and are nonetheless — indeed for that very reason — called upon to trust him.

We thus learn from our second and third points that there can obviously be a confidence devoid of any corresponding predictability, and a predictability devoid of any corresponding confidence. This observation forces us to define more precisely the correlation between the two concepts. Such a definition must show the range of the correlation.

207

It will also make clear that the correlation established in our exposition of the Babel story is correct.

The purpose of establishing the correlation in the present context is simply to characterize the unpredictable *tyche*, the accidental and contingent, as the epitome of lack of confidence on the negative side. On the positive side – and herein lies the truth of our third point – while I cannot always predict the actions of the one in whom I have confidence, I can at least count on his moral maxims. I can rely on his loyalty and unselfishness. I know that in his case disloyalty and selfishness are ruled out. It thus follows that in respect of his actions, as distinct from his principles, it is only hypothetically possible to predict them. Such prediction would be a real possibility only if I had access to his concrete perspectives on the facts and an insight into the goals he was seeking to realize within the framework of his moral maxims. In other words, the thing which really produces confidence is the predictability not of actions but of maxims.

On the other hand – and herein lies the truth of our second point – there may indeed be a negative kind of predictability. But it cannot be equated with confidence because it involves no constancy of maxims. In this case I cannot assume that the other party will respect the dignity of one's person, one's humanity. His predictability, accordingly, is like that of a natural process, such as the instinctive reactions of a beast of prey. This amoral form of predictability finds an exact, if paradoxical, diagnosis in the statement that the only thing I can rely on is the fact that this man is not to be relied on. The first part of the statement expresses the predictability of instinctive reactions, the second the unpredictability of his relation to ethical maxims.

We can now define precisely the correlation between confidence and predictability. Confidence is the predictability of positive dispositions in changing situations. Confidence counts on the continuity of maxims and on an abiding allegiance to authoritative norms.

From different angles we are thus brought back to the theological background of power even though we set out to analyze it only phenomenologically. We have also unavoidably and repeatedly come up against the mystery of man's nature which objectifies itself in power, and we have had to speak of the limitation of power, of its quality as the bearer of authority, and therewith of the authorizing court which stands behind it. The fact that even within the framework of a phenomenological analysis the theological question is inescapable ought to show us that the two cannot be separated, and that the wall between these two problem areas is very flimsy. Because power is a human phenomenon the same problems arise here as in the discussion of man himself. Man too is an entity which constantly transcends itself. Man too cannot be treated as a mere phenomenon, severed from the ultimate relations within which he exists.

13.

The Distribution of Powers

Authority and confidence, as means of limiting power, are by nature moral entities. As such, they cannot be forced. For this reason one has to allow for the possibility that they may not exist. There can be government without them, e.g., in the form of terror, an uncontrollable power which has taken on a monopolistic character. Granted the possibility, then, that authority and confidence may not be present to assure the control of power, and the acknowledged fact that power is dangerous and men very tempted to misuse it, it becomes necessary to consider institutional safeguards to prevent such misuse. The device which political theorists and constitutions use to limit power and prevent its abuse is usually called the distribution of powers.

From a theological standpoint one might say that the distribution of powers is an institutional expression of an abiding mistrust of power, or rather of the people in power. The call for a distribution of powers is a partly conscious and partly unconscious recognition of the reality of the fall and the unreliability of fallen man.

The Basic Problem of Dividing the Indivisible

Because the state is sovereign there has to be some unified exercise of supreme power if the state is not to degenerate into a mere umbrella organization embracing diverse and often conflicting individual forces — which would be contrary to its very nature. Yet even then the operation of this supreme power would need to be regulated in such a way as to provide a harmonious balance among the partial forces: they would have to be mutually checked and controlled on the one hand but also integrated into purposeful co-operation on the other. The centuries-old British policy of endeavoring to maintain a balance among the leading powers on the continent affords a good example, though on an international scale, of this form of controlling power by distribution and counterbalance.

Whenever we think of this matter of the distribution of governmental powers, however, the example which comes first to mind is that of Montesquieu, the French constitutionalist and politician.[1] As he sees it, there should be a threefold division into legislative power, executive power, and judicial power. While the separation of the first two raises no immediate problems, the relation to them of the third is more difficult to define.

As concerns the first two, it is obvious that the executive branch must receive its norms from the legislative, and that the legislative must therefore be furnished with the necessary power effectively to restrain the executive. The common historical experience that, e.g., the army or the police will press for independence and try to evade normative control means that the legislative branch has to have corresponding constitutional safeguards. The attempt of the executive to break loose is simply an institutional expression of the capriciousness of actual rulers, i.e., of terror. On the other hand, the legislative branch too has to remember its limits. If by passing laws it actually engages in administrative procedures, this is an illegal invasion of the executive sphere.

The place and the limits of the judiciary power are in principle not hard to fix, but they are particularly exposed to the complications of borderline cases. In principle, the frontier of the judiciary in relation to the legislative and executive powers may be defined as follows. When the judge pronounces a verdict, he does so within the laws, and consequently — in principle — in subordination to the legislative power. It is equally clear that the administration of justice is not the task of the executive, and that the judiciary must never be permitted — as in ideologized law — merely to give legal sanction to executive measures of the state or of a particular group, and thus become a mere instrument of the executive. Nevertheless, there are borderline cases, of which two types may be mentioned. We shall discuss them in the form of two questions which are difficult if not impossible to answer within the framework of the basic distinctions just made.

The first question is this: Has the judge the right and duty in certain cases to go beyond simple obedience to existing laws and to inquire into the justice of the laws themselves? The point at issue here

[1] See Charles De Montesquieu, *The Spirit of Laws* (1748), in "Great Books," Vol. 38.

goes beyond that of simply determining the constitutionality of laws. Constitutional courts and superior courts are customarily set up for this purpose. The question is rather whether the laws, and perhaps the constitution itself, may be tested in respect of their agreement with justice — e.g., with natural law — or with the postulates of humanity, and whether this can be done casuistically, i.e., within the context of concrete judgments arrived at in specific cases.[2]

While this first question concerns the relation of the judiciary to the legislative branch, the second, to which we must now devote a brief discussion, concerns the distinction between the judiciary and the executive. This second question becomes acute when it is a matter of defining the limits of competence of justices in a constitutional or supreme court. We can best illustrate the problem in terms of circumstances which arose as a result of certain radical shifts in the German situation since the Second World War. The fact is that situations can arise which were not foreseen either by the constitution or by prevailing law (including treaties), with the result that wholly new decisions are demanded. An example of how this happens in any land where drastic changes have taken place is provided by the constitutionally guaranteed demilitarization of Germany and the subsequent remilitarization under the pressure of political necessity.

Involved in the problem of **remilitarization** were very complicated questions of political judgment. It was not solely a question of demilitarization or remilitarization. In view of the division of Germany, and the resultant possibility of "civil" war, there had to be detailed discussion and decision as to the method of rearming (e.g., whether to have a volunteer army, a professional army, or conscription).

In view of the newness of various situations and their demand for new political decisions, it can be very difficult, even impossible, to

---

[2] The question arises with particular urgency in respect of the administration of justice under totalitarian tyranny, and was dealt with in connection with the determinations of the war crimes trials at Nuremberg (See *ThE* 1, 384 ff.). Jacques Ellul sees it as the duty of the church to "judge the legal system . . . in terms of the greater or lesser respect accorded by this system to human rights and to the divinely created institutions," to remind jurists of the importance of this criterion, and to "openly fight against . . . [an] erroneous system." The church is thus construed to be a guardian of law precisely in the area of the borderline cases, for its task is to awaken the juridical conscience and call it to criticize the law in the name of a higher *norma normans* (see Jacques Ellul, *The Theological Foundation of Law*, trans. Marguerite Wieser [Garden City, New York: Doubleday, 1960], p. 136).

clarify such situations by subsuming them legally under constitutional norms. The need may arise — and this has never been contested in theory — for the broadening and even the correcting of constitutional provisions. In practice, though, it can happen that existing constitutions are inadmissibly strained in order to wrest from them criteria for decisions which they had not envisioned.

This may happen when there is neither the courage nor the power to make independent and pioneering decisions, or to implement such decisions legally, e.g., by parliamentary changes of the law or the constitution. It may also happen when one faction in the political arena cherishes the hope of tactically putting across its political platform by appealing to existent constitutional provisions, hoping thereby — in spite of the admitted outdatedness of these provisions — to find in the letter of the law a prop for its position. Even an antiquated provision can be exploited tactically for specific ends.

In such cases this is where the rub arises as regards the administration of justice, for the constitutional court may be compelled in two ways to intervene — and thus to transgress the true limits of its jurisdiction. It can do this in the first place by giving judicial sanction to a political reality, thus breaking down the separation between the two spheres and producing real heteronomy — and in this sense arriving at inauthentic decisions. Or it can do it in the second place by a *de facto* exploitation both of itself and of its *norma normans* — the constitution — as a mere instrument of the political executive, whereby it calmly helps either to implement or to block political decisions by means of legal pronouncements.

Where no basic safeguards are provided against such a misuse of constitutional or supreme courts, constitutional states can furnish an exact and frightening analogy to the status of law under an ideological tyranny. What in ideological tyranny is consciously exalted to the level of an explicit theory of law — or, better, lawlessness — may also take place within the so-called free world in a way that may be more latent but nonetheless real, at least in certain spheres of law such as that of constitutional law. Even if it happens only in isolated cases, and despite the opposition of the legal conscience, law can in fact become a function of political factions and therewith of specific forms of the executive.

In Germany this danger of giving judicial sanction to that which does not really belong in the sphere of the judiciary is enhanced psychologically by the German father complex. For, quite apart from tactical considerations and maneuvers, this father complex is inclined to seek authoritative — in this case legally sanctioned — decisions of the kind which in autocratic days would have been taken by a king or *Führer*. For these deep psychological reasons constitutional courts may be exposed to the danger of trying to represent the image of a supreme sovereign.

The distribution of powers between the judiciary and the executive is thus threatened at this point of least resistance for a whole host of reasons. The only means to ensure distribution here is to see to it that justices in the constitutional or supreme court are not compelled to render a verdict in every single case but may disqualify themselves in terms of competence and declare a typically political case to be political, and hence not subject to judicial decision. Such a provision is indispensable to the status of the highest courts if the distribution of powers is to be taken seriously and law is to enjoy independent dignity.

We thus come to the following conclusion. The power of the state as such is indivisible, but it must be divided into different branches on two grounds. First, there must be no concentration of power at a single point, whether in an individual, an institution, or the nation itself. Safeguards are needed against a power monopoly. Power must be limited because man is invariably tempted to misuse it. Fallen man is simply unable to overcome the temptation posed by power. The second point is related to the first. Those who hold power — the government and the parliament, the ruling party and the opposition, office holders and unofficial bodies like the press and radio — all need to be brought into a system of reciprocal controls which will guard against its misuse and limit the drive for power.

This distribution should not lead, however, to the idea that the state is simply an umbrella organization embracing various sovereign and independent powers which derive their commission from another source and have simply to be brought into a measure of political coordination. On the contrary, it is decisive that the power of the state as such is indivisible. This one indivisible power is simply delegated to different organs which work together in its name and at its commission. The power of the state is not the end product of a co-ordination of independent powers; it is the starting point of delegations. The state is the original delegator, not the final co-ordinator.

The state acquires this significance on the same grounds as those which led us, at the very beginning of our whole discussion of politics,[3] to retain the term authority for that which is divinely ordained. It is this authorization by God which gives the state its special pre-eminence vis-à-vis all other secular powers and authorities.

One indication of this pre-eminence — one among others — is the fact that the state can demand oaths of loyalty and in some cases even the sacrifice of life, whereas the partial spheres to which the state delegates its authority do not have this ultimate power. Other indications of the special position of the state as the initial indivisible power will come to light in the next chapter when we investigate the biblical concept of the state.

What we have, then, is really a dialectic: On the one hand the authority of the state is unified and indivisible. On the other hand it is expressed in a multiplicity of forms. This sounds highly abstract and theoretical. But we see its concrete significance the moment we consider its consequences. We shall deal with these under two heads. First, we shall consider the undermining of state authority which occurs when the state loses its delegating authority and there develop within it independent structures which in effect constitute a state within the state. Involuntarily the modern democracy provides dangerously fertile soil for such a development. Independent constructs, which usually establish themselves as groups characterized by a totalitarian tendency, come to undermine the distribution of powers insidiously from below. We shall speak of this here, and then in the section that follows we shall consider, in the light of the principles thus far worked out, the concrete steps necessary to ensure the distribution of powers.

Individual Freedom and the "Totalitarian Group"

Our contention is that the distribution of powers is necessary because fallen man is not able to handle uncontrolled, monopolized power. Such power becomes an instrument of egoistic expansion and thus poses a threat to the freedom of others. By guarding against the mis-

---

[3] Cf. pp. 7 ff. above.

use of power, the distribution of powers thus has the positive task of safeguarding freedom, of making freedom possible in the political sphere where a variety of power constructs necessarily arise.

For reasons which we shall show there can in fact arise within a democracy groups which are prone to become totalitarian. These represent tendencies which necessarily run counter to the principle of the distribution of power. They tend toward a monopolization of power, and thus undermine the democracy within which alone they are possible.

This is paradoxical. Democracy provides for a distribution of powers precisely because it knows the danger of power. It delegates power, and thus confers the rights of freedom. But in so doing it also creates the possibility that some will use the freedom of action thus afforded them in a way different from that intended. This risk is essentially inherent in democracy.

In discussing this problem of the latent monopoly of power we shall use the labor union as a model. It must be stated emphatically that we use it only as a model. Unions are not in any sense a peculiarly dangerous example of monopoly. They simply represent processes which might equally well occur in other groups, e.g., associations of manufacturers or retailers, political parties, etc. We choose unions as our model only because the power or pressure they exert — in the form of strikes — is dramatically evident.

To avoid oversimplification, and especially to avoid the implication that there is some kind of planned attack or conspiracy at the outset which leads — or, to put it more guardedly, might involuntarily lead — to the power of the totalitarian group, it should be noted that the beginnings of union organization can claim to be justified on the grounds of historical necessity, even of ethical obligation. When faced by a more or less absolutist state representing a particular social order, the underprivileged class can protect itself only by concerted measures, e.g., by organizing unions. There are no other forms of protection against social injustices. The only form of self-protection is collective. Since this is not a question simply of self-seeking, of protecting selfish interests, but of protecting wives and children and of guarding against physical, intellectual, and moral degradation, there can be no doubting the ethical legitimacy of this self-protecton.

Not least as a result of this initial class struggle, though later by reason of more general economic considerations, the state engages in social renewal. But as it does so, certain programs of the unions become superfluous. The danger thus arises that an existent union machinery, which is less and less needed to fulfill its original tasks, will be applied in a different direction. E.g., there arises a tendency to struggle for positions of political power. Even where there are no conscious and explicit revolutionary intentions whatever, nor any subjective craving for power, there can still be this growing quest for political power.

Possessing the structure of institutional autonomy, this drive is always in one basic direction even though it may take very different forms. Three main factors seem to be at work. First, machinery outlives the intentions which led to its creation. It is a common experience of life that bureaucracy is most tenacious. When its original ends are attained, it continues to run around in meaningless circles, and finally — even when it is dissolved — it still spends a long time in the business of self-dismantling and self-liquidation. Second, existing machinery, as already indicated, constantly absorbs new raw material for processing. And third, the union machinery, even when it is not completely superfluous but continues to sustain major portions of its original program, can still engage in the quest for political power, not merely because it is too big for the work which engages it but also because the gaining of political influence may be of no small consequence for the attainment of its primarily economic objectives. Political influence creates more favorable points of departure and gives greater leverage than can accrue when social struggles are confined within the economic sphere.

It must be honestly admitted that this obvious tendency towards the expansion of power does bear some relation to the goal sought by the unions. But it is also an expression of the general law of the concentration of power. (Indeed, the antidote — the distribution of powers — exists only because there is this law.)

In a democratic state this drive for political power can only mean that the unions may be exposed to the temptation of assuming what is usually regarded as a party function, that of representing a particular program or platform in a way that is usually left to the parties as organizations for fashioning the political will. This party function can be distinguished from that of the political parties themselves only by the fact that it is a hidden function which cannot be defined democratically, and which is thus largely exempt from parliamentary representation and control. Because it is not subject to control, and because it has at its disposal a tremendous concentration of economic power, including the deadly weapon of the general strike, this pseudo party will naturally tend in the last analysis to become a state within the state. There may thus arise in this way largely impersonal monopolies which are difficult to control. Potentially at least they set over against the legitimate state — in which powers are distributed — an illegitimate totalitarianism. Above all, they limit that freedom of the individual which the self-limitation of the state was designed to protect.

We must now give specific attention to this second point, namely, the restriction of individual freedom. This can sometimes go so far as to involve economic and social ruin. If a union contract specifies that a firm must employ only union members, this might mean — depending on the degree of monopolistic power — not only the hindering of a career but sometimes its complete destruction. The personal politics even of an avowedly Christian group can pose a danger in this respect.

It is highly important to recognize the way these latent exertions of power actually work. Typically they seem to employ anonymity as an instrument in the restriction of individual freedom by the group. At the same time, wherever they are at work — whether in union organization or management collaboration, whether in the practical programs of Christian bodies or of fraternal organizations — they expressly prefer the way of personal politics. Personal politics is the classical field of action for all forms of the latent and impersonal exercise of power; it can be carried on by telephone, or the top man can indicate acceptance or rejection of a name by a mere frown or gesture.

When power comes to be exercised anonymously by groups, this leads of itself to bureaucratic structures whose existence and activity are hard to pinpoint, at least in any official way. For their various functions are not out in the open. They take place backstage, and those who really pull the wires are never even seen.

What we have here are democratic processes in which there is inherent an element of tragedy. The democratization of life leads necessarily to a host of measures which are designed to safeguard the freedom of the individual against the state, and thus to check the totalitarianism of the state. The achievement of these human rights, or of these constitutionally guaranteed fundamental rights, is meant to be served by the technique of distributing powers. Yet observation of certain processes set in motion by this democratic principle of fundamental rights and distribution of powers leads to the conclusion that the desired increase of freedom for the individual is latently threatened by the possibility that groups will fill the vacuum left by the state, so that the deprivation of freedom which was feared from an uncontrolled concentration of power in the state will become an acute problem from a very different angle. The problem now is that the rights of freedom conceded by the state will not reach those for whom they are intended, namely, individuals, but will surreptitiously be changed into the freedoms of corporate groups, so that they can only be claimed collectively.

In fact it is difficult to prevent this changeover. For the self-limitation of the state effected by the distribution of powers is predominantly negative in orientation. A sphere is proclaimed in which the state will not intrude. If, then, the state is not indirectly to become totalitarian again, it must refrain from any attempt to divide up this state-free zone. The latent totalitarianism implicit in such intervention would involve an intolerable self-contradiction. But if the state genuinely releases this zone, the possibility is almost unavoidable that the right of the stronger will prevail among such non-state constructs, and that the state-free zone will be divided up accordingly.

The stronger in such a case will always be a collective, not an individual. Unparalleled opportunities are thus given to the group. Its privileged position as a state-free, or relatively state-free, entity makes possible that anonymity in the exercise of power to which we have referred. Moreover these groups, by attaining a degree of power, can proportionately influence the activity of the state. They have at their disposal not only the possibility of personal subversion but also a weapon of frontal assault in the form of a strike, even a general strike. Hence the state may well be forced into counteraction (e.g., the declaration of a state of emergency or the adoption of emergency measures) which as a democracy it has expressly repudiated.

It is thus incumbent on the state to use every constitutional means at its disposal to bring under control this subversion of its fundamental rights and democratic ethos by groups. It has to be admitted, of course, that there are few direct possibilities along these lines, and that reliance will have to be placed on long-term processes like that of education or the gradual formation of a civic ethos. Here is one of the points where government cannot resort merely to legislation and techniques of power but has to use indirect influence on individuals. This involves the state in a task directly akin to that which devolves upon the preaching and social action of the church, namely, to awaken citizens to a sense of responsibility with respect to the divinely willed order of the state and with respect to the humanity of man.

In addition, this latent shift of power shows afresh how dangerous power is. It brings to light its indelible character. Wherever man attacks it frontally, power adopts evasive tactics and counterattacks from the rear.

Concrete Measures to Ensure Distribution

We have already stated that the self-limitation of the state through the distribution of powers can take many different forms. We shall now consider some forms which have actually arisen in the course of democratization and of general social and technological development.

Representation and Delegation

The first point, so far as the distribution of powers is concerned, is that in a democracy "the people" as such does not usually have undivided power. Theoretically this might be conceivable if the people as a whole passed laws (legislative power), determined direct acts of government (executive power), and even invaded the judicial sphere, e.g., by taking the law into their own hands as in a lynching.

This system of direct as distinct from representative democracy is possible only in very small communities where the scope of political participation is very limited, as in the cities of ancient Greece and the Swiss cantons, e.g. Even here, however, we do not have a pure form, for society's standard of what constitutes maturity allows only a limited circle to make decisions; the Greek cities, e.g., exclude slaves, women, and children. Here too, then, what we have is really an early form of representative democracy, since the composite will is determined by a smaller group of persons qualified to make decisions.

In practice there never has been an instance of "all" power residing in (and not just deriving from) the people. Generally, power is divided in this respect too. The direct power of the people is limited to the election of representative persons or groups to whom the concrete tasks of decision are delegated.

This involves a certain distribution of power. For the persons so delegated make their decisions in the light of their own conscience and their insight into the facts, though naturally within the guide-lines laid down at their election. At any rate, the people gives over to its representatives the power to execute its will as laid down in the guide-lines, the party platform, etc.

This division of power between the people and its representatives is of great significance because it expresses serious distrust of such blind power as has no insight, or very little insight, and is directed by stupid instincts (of the masses). Quite apart from the fact that in certain larger states the direct participation of the whole people would be technically impossible, the decisions to be reached are also too complicated for any but professional politicians or persons of special competence to tackle.

Again, the whole people is hardly qualified, since many decisions demand a degree of disciplined objectivity and therefore an ethical quality which cannot reasonably be expected of the general public but only of a circle of persons who measure up to the more stringent technical and ethical demands. It is thus the wisdom of all the great modern democracies that, while allowing some matters to be decided by the people, they radically exclude from this kind of decision two spheres, namely, that of taxation and that of declaring and conducting war. Because these matters touch the roots of existence and can thus arouse egoistic instincts to a special degree, the power to decide them cannot be ascribed to the masses, but only to a responsible circle. The public has an indirect, but not a direct share in these decisions by virtue of its electing the members of this circle. The principle that the participation of the people is generally restricted to the election of individuals and does not include the making of actual decisions is an illustration of the theory of the distribution of powers.

On the other hand, democracies have fashioned various correctives to prevent parliament from assuming the kind of power that would be — even if only in the legislative field — unlimited. Thus one finds such provisions as a presidency, or a second legislative chamber, or constitutional rules for dissolution of the legislative assembly, etc.

221

The way in which power is divided between people and parliament can be quite varied. Many states leave specified issues to be decided directly by the people. Thus Switzerland provides for a constitutional referendum which makes it obligatory, or at least possible, to consult the people if any changes are planned in the constitution. Again, e.g., in the constitution of the Weimar Republic, the people may be summoned to act as arbitrators in cases of conflict between the supreme constitutional organs.

If the West German Republic in its constitution does not allow public decisions of this kind, even in exceptional cases, this is perhaps because experience has shown that to ask the people as a whole to make such decisions, even occasionally, is to ask too much. For a man is qualified to make a real decision only when he can grasp and formulate the point at issue. But this is not possible for the general public. If a question is proposed for decision, people can certainly give an answer one way or the other. But the answer given is essentially dependent on the way the question is put and the vigor with which it is presented. Hence what is given is not an authentic answer but only an elicited reaction. This is the problem inherent in a constitutional referendum, and it applies to a great extent also to ordinary individual and parliamentary voting.

The Political Party

A second factor affecting the distribution of powers in a democracy is that of the political party. In a modern democracy parties do not serve simply to make possible a legal acquisition of governmental power. They also guarantee that the power thus acquired can be only a divided power. If they strive after the unlimited power of a totalitarian state, they are untrue not only to the state (the goal of their struggle) but also to themselves (their nature as instruments) and become a political superstructure.

A party is a group which serves to shape the political will. Its basis is voluntary participation. Within the framework of the constitution the party seeks to win such influence as will enable it to attain its ends through legislative and executive participation.

Now a party may represent only or primarily special interests, e.g., those of the middle class. Yet it is distinguished in principle from a mere union of interests by the fact that it is oriented not just toward an individual end but toward the shaping of the total will of the state. Potentially, then, it serves the larger whole and accordingly must also have an inclusive program embracing all spheres and segments of the national life.

The party thus has an affinity to the totality of the state, though it cannot represent this totality in any exclusive or monopolistic fashion. It is by nature only a "part" of the whole, and its influence is and should be limited.

This limitation is provided in part by the fact that each party competes with other parties, or makes coalitions with them, or is confronted by an opposition even when it enjoys an absolute majority. (These factors need not be mutually exclusive; they can be present and operative in various combinations.) It is also limited by the legislative term set, for when its term expires the party in power may be succeeded by the opposition party. Most of the features of a party here adduced tend to foster the division of power. Four such features may be considered.

1) As distinct from the state, the party is not something into which one is born. Entry is by choice. There must be an act of decision. And this decision implies a dissociation, for to choose in favor of a particular party necessarily means to choose between parties. Hence the existence of a single party with monopolistic rights falsifies the act of choice. It turns decision into mere acclamation. The party thus ceases to be an instrument for fashioning the national will and becomes instead an end in itself which precedes all such shaping of the national will. One might even say that it merely sees to the shaping of that will from above. The party thus comes to represent absolute and undivided power. It is no longer the product of decisions. On the contrary, it makes the decisions itself for those who — according to the democratic conception — should be the decision makers.

2) The fact that a party is different from a mere interest group also suggests the inherent tendency towards the distribution of power. Interest groups such as labor unions, employers' federations, taxpayers' associations, etc. have a built-in tendency to expand their interests, a tendency which can be checked only as they run up against external opposition, i.e., opposing interests. Since their function is simply to foster and advocate particular interests, they are one-sided.

But a party, because it is potentially the governing authority, must represent the whole of the state. It must be prepared to take power and exercise power in the state as such. Hence it is forced not merely to advocate its own interests but also to be judge in its own cause. It has to seek the larger good, and thus to relativize itself. While it represents a specific interest, namely, its own, it must also perceive and keep in view the interests of the whole.

This is not just a matter of ethical obligation. Paradoxically, it is also in its own interests. For if the party represents only a special interest, e.g., that of a class or a religious persuasion, the range of its operations is so limited that it cannot appeal to all voters. And even if it came to power in spite of this handicap, its one-sided government would have such disastrous consequences for the state as a whole that it would hardly be able to live out its full term or hope for another.

Things are thus the reverse of what one might expect. At first glance a group which served its own exclusive interests might seem to be limited, whereas a party, which seeks power in the state as a whole, is comparatively unlimited. In reality, however, striving for the key position in national government leads to self-limitation.

A political party by its very nature has to struggle not only with competing factions on the outside but also with itself. There is a struggle between the party as advocate of its own interests and the party as potential representative of the whole state and guardian of the interests of all. The party must stimulate itself dynamically and at the same time relativize itself politically.

There is no question but that this polarity inherent in the very nature of the party is exceedingly fruitful. Indeed, this is why there can be in the party what Carlo Schmid has called a kind of "spirit." This is also why parties should not be viewed merely as a necessary evil. For the only alternative would be pure interest groups. But interest groups merely advocate, they do not also judge. In their hands, therefore, the state would become the football of heterogeneous interests.

Now it is not as though this danger were wholly obviated in states where parties exist. There are dramatic examples of its having been actualized. Nevertheless, the fact that the party by its very nature has reference to the state as a whole means that in such a state there are, with varying degrees of effectiveness, correctives which the interest groups simply do not have at their command.

3) The relation to the state as a whole also implies self-limitation insofar as the party can work politically only by way of parliament, and has thus to accept the fact of parliamentary control. In contrast, there is in the mere interest groups, as we have seen, the immanent danger that because they are not subject to parliamentary control they will, on attaining some measure of power, become a state within the state, and even subvert the legal organs of government. The legitimation of government by parliament — which in practice is based on control by others who also bear power and hence on the distribution of power — is thus essentially a form of the limitation of power.

4) To this context belong also the other limiting factors touched on in our definition, namely, opposition, coalition, and the set term of office. One might thus say that parties aim, not at power, but at divided power, when they understand themselves in terms of the axioms of democracy. In spite of this, the dangers of a concentration of power are still present, even though they run counter to the axioms as such.

The Separation between Party and Government

A third and particularly important aspect of the distribution of powers in a democracy, one whose significance is often overlooked, is that involving parties on the one hand and the legislative and executive organs of the government on the other. Just as the people delegates its political will to the party elected by it, so the party delegates the functions of state to the persons who are to discharge them. In a democracy these persons are selected either directly (e.g., the members of parliament) or indirectly (e.g., the officers of government) by the party, which itself, however, is not involved in the machinery of state.

It would countervene this limitation of party power if, e.g., party chiefs were to participate in cabinet meetings of the government or if party members in the government were to be bound or coerced by the directives of party leaders. The independence of deputies in relation to party instructions — or more precisely the freedom of deputies in their parliamentary work to make their own decisions according to facts and conscience — and the freedom of members of the executive branch are equally threatened if parties thrust their own high officials into these spheres of government. The official is dependent not just morally but also materially on the one who commissions him. If he does not follow the party line, he can expect not only that he will not be proposed again as the candidate of his party but also that his career and calling will come to an end. Thus, in a concealed and indirect way, he is put under pressure and made to become merely an extension of the arm of his party, unable to fulfill his task of making decisions on his own responsibility.

This is perhaps the most dangerous, and yet also the most deeply concealed, threat to the integrity of a democracy. It is concealed in the sense that it is largely, if not wholly, beyond control by way of constitutional stipulation. And it is a threat to the integrity of a democracy in the sense that it is in basic conflict with the principle of the distribution of powers which is democracy's chief antidote to the excessive growth of privileged power.

The only answer to this threat too is the awakening in men of a sense of responsibility, i.e., an ethical appeal. As addressed to responsible party leaders, this appeal can only mean that they should resist the temptation to pack the offices of state with their own party officials. If this is not to involve an unfair renunciation of power and afford an intolerable advantage to competing parties, it will have to be accomplished by agreements among the parties. (We are not referring, by the way, to a radical exclusion of all party officials. Since the top officials of the parties are often their most influential political leaders, parties cannot refrain from giving them national posts, nor can the state dispense with those who have gifts of political leadership. Our purpose is simply to stress the need of restraint in this respect.)

It is very difficult, however, to develop a negative initiative, i.e., to foster restraint. Again, the agreements among the parties, to which we referred, are very hard to reach. Hence the ethical appeal can be made only in the sense of summoning independent persons from all walks of life to active political responsibility. But a whole series of measures will then be needed to prevent the possible one-sided selection of independents, e.g., in the sense of a predominance of civil servants.

Two Borderline Cases

Having discussed three measures to ensure the distribution of powers, we must mention now only two further cases, both borderline cases. Strictly speaking, the first is not a matter of political "power" and the second concerns a regulation of the distribution which does not involve "political" power. Since both of these cases merely border on our present theme, we will restrict ourselves to dealing with them only in very brief compass.

The first borderline case is that of the welfare state. The social perfection of the welfare state — which is the direction in which society seems to be moving — threatens to overload the state with an excess of social tasks and responsibilities, especially in caring for its citizens. This means a concurrent concentration of power. For one thing, the state is forced increasingly to take the initiative in the social sphere, whereas the people become increasingly passive, content to play the role of the recipient and possessor of duly-acquired rights. Again, when it is overburdened with welfare tasks, the state needs higher revenues to offset its increased expenditures, and through the resulting legislation it inevitably comes to exercise a kind of financial dictatorship which restricts the free play of economic forces. In addition it begins to require a swollen bureaucracy.

Quite apart from the threat to more direct person-to-person care of a fellow human being posed by a consistent welfare state — of which we shall have to speak later [4] — what is important in terms of our present theme is that the state should refuse to accept all the social initiative men would require of it and should instead seek a sensible distribution of initiative between itself and the various private agencies and institutions. In other words, the state should aim at a "social" distribution of powers so as to guard against a national monopolizing of social tasks.

This obviously does not mean that the state should avoid as many social tasks as possible. On the contrary, it will have to accept many such tasks. Our concern here is not with the number of tasks but with the principle of distribution.

The second borderline case which we would briefly mention is that posed by developments in technology. Here many questions will have to remain unanswered. Our primary task is simply to put the question.

Atomic science and automation seem to have inaugurated an

[4] See Chapter 16.

intrinsically antithetical development. On the one hand, there is a tendency towards huge and complicated machinery and the consequent concentration of power. Since big machines are so enormously expensive, the state is one of their privileged possessors, and there has rightly been seen in the tendency towards mechanized centralization a drift towards the totalitarian power of the state which comes to command a decisive technical monopoly. Possession of electronic brains makes possible political and strategic calculations of probability against which "all opposition is irrational." [5] But such technological centralization amounts to an attack on one form of the distribution of power.

On the other hand, though, there is also a tendency towards decentralization, not merely in the sense that big machines benefit wide areas, as electric power stations have done for some time, but also in the sense that it may well be possible to transport atomic power stations quite easily and thus put them to work on the periphery of the present civilized world, i.e., in some of the so-called developing countries.[6]

It must be noted, however, that the contradiction between centralization and decentralization is only apparent. It is due to the optical illusion that both are on the same plane. In fact, however, the centralization is institutional and has to do with the state, whereas the decentralization is geographical and has to do with the exploitation of electronic and atomic machines on behalf of wide areas. In any case, if this interpretation is correct, the decentralization does not constitute a corrective. It does not amount to a distribution of powers in face of the concentration of technological power in the state. It is rather an expression of this very concentration, indeed, a possible means of increasing it. A theological ethics can do little more than point out that forms of totalitarian power may even now be crystallizing at new points, and that the principle of the limitation of power and the distribution of powers will have to take new forms as yet hardly discernable.

[5] Helmut Schelsky, "Zukunftsaspekte der industriellen Gesellschaft," *Merkur*, VIII, 1 (January, 1954), 25. See also "The Electronic Oracle" in Robert Jungk, *Tomorrow is Already Here*, trans. Marguerite Waldman (New York: Simon and Schuster, 1954), pp. 227-235.
[6] Tibor Mende, *Nehru: Conversations on India and World Affairs* (New York: Braziller, 1956), pp. 47, 69-72.

The Theological Locus of the Problem

We have now discussed the problem of power and its limitation from many different angles. In considering the many different forms of limitation, however, we have not forgotten the decisive point. What is primarily at issue is the limitation, not of power, but of the persons in power, those who in the fallen state of man are not equipped either individually or corporately to handle power of a certain quantity, and more especially of a certain quality, namely, monopolized power.

Since the real problem is not power itself as a mythical entity, but the man in power, the forms by which power is limited — e.g., the distribution of powers — cannot really cure. They can only help to check the symptoms. These forms are the emergency orders of the fallen world, as prefigured already in the prototype of the Noachic covenant.

We certainly could not venture to say that the redeemed are immune to the temptation of power and that the problem of those in power would therefore no longer arise in a world comprised wholly of Christians. But then this is not the question. In the theological sense such a question would be highly unrealistic, for we live in an aeon in which the world and the kingdom of God are intertwined, and Christians and non-Christians intermingle and live together. Hence the task is that of checking evil. It is not the task of reducing man's susceptibility to temptation, which would be impossible. It is rather the task of diminishing the things which tempt. Only when we see the problem in this way do we correctly perceive the theological locus of this matter of the distribution of powers.

In conclusion, the theological arc within which the problem of the distribution of powers and the limitation of power arises may be described as follows. The seizure of the forbidden fruit and the declaration of man's self-glory unleashes the blind power which finds expression in self-assertion, undiscerning expansion, and the extirpation of the neighbor. This wild force is restrained by legitimate power, whose normative institutional representative is the state.

But legitimate power for its part is also involved in rebellion. For if it bears the marks of a preservation graciously granted by God, it bears also the marks of the fallen world whose instruments it uses.

As the representative of divinely willed order, it uses the egoism of the group and of the institution to fight against the egoism of the individual. In this sense the state is not just a remedy against the fallen world. It is at the same time an exponent or expression of the fallen world. This explains its ambivalence. Because legitimate power is thus imperiled by its very nature, it too needs to be limited in some way. The distribution of powers provides that limitation.

What is involved in these different uprisings or rebellions, however, is not some mythical power working autonomously; it is men in positions of power acting responsibly. It would thus be an error to think that the checking of power can be guaranteed by institutional measures. Just as the legitimate power inherent in the state can revolt, so too can distributed power. Even where the distribution of powers is constitutionally guaranteed, there are other concentrations of power which it is very hard to control, e.g., in the economic or the social sphere.

These latent upsurges of power are a sign that the problem of power does not have its roots in the institutional sphere and consequently cannot be solved by institutional means. The problem is man himself. It is man who undermines and overthrows all his institutions. Institutions are merely the "arms of flesh" on which no reliance can be placed (II Chron. 32:8; Jer. 17:5). To trust in them notwithstanding is arrogantly to attempt some kind of self-redemption. Institutions progress, to be sure. They may even attain to the refined perfection of the welfare state. But man himself is always the same. Thus the problem of power leads us into the area of redemption and eschatology.

Human Rights and the Limitation of Power

In the light of these findings one may say that the various attempts to distribute power and to safeguard this distribution all express an awareness, however concealed, of the true nature of man. Even where power is construed as a mythical entity and statements are made about its corrupting influence there is still an awareness that man is unable to handle too much of it and that he must be protected especially from a monopoly of power. The principle that power must be divided can be stated anthropologically: man must be protected against himself.

The so-called basic rights, or human rights, have been formulated in the light of this insight. From the dawn of their first realization they contain a protest against the trend of the state towards omnipotence. They rest on the tension between the individual need for freedom and the state's claim to dominion. In this sense John Locke sees a close connection between the right of the individual — deriving from his freedom in the natural state — and the need to divide the power of the state lest it encroach on individual rights to freedom.

Hence the assertion of the fundamental rights of man always implies the protection of man against himself. More precisely, it implies the protection of man as individual against man as controller of the machinery of state.

Yet we do not fully grasp the significance of human rights if we see in them only an awareness of man and of the threat he poses to himself. In these basic rights man does not merely declare his awareness of the threat. He also establishes effective means to protect himself in actual history against the threat of power. Hence the assertion of human rights does not have the purpose — certainly not the sole purpose — of philosophical proclamation. It is also intended as political action. Human rights do more than simply proclaim the need to limit power; they actually effect that limitation. That this is indeed their significance may be seen from two angles.

1) When a state in its constitution — or a league of states in its covenant — accepts human rights as a binding criterion for the legislative and executive branches, it is in effect limiting its own power by guaranteeing the rights of the individual to freedom. This is true, of course, only when the rights of man are taken seriously, i.e., when the state regards them as having the authority of unchangeable norms. It is not true when they are regarded in the ideological sense as merely a humanitarian symbol which subserves psychological strategy and is hence a means of exercising power rather than of controlling it.

It should not be overlooked that the rights of man do not easily attain this authoritative position. They are constantly in danger of becoming nothing but an ornamental or ideological flourish, the mere mention of which brings a knowing smile to the student of public affairs. The reason for this threat to the normative character of human rights is easy to perceive. Such rights have necessarily to be formulated in quite general terms. For they have to apply to men of the most varied intellectual, philosophical, religious, and historical backgrounds. Thus they refer to man's right to voice his opinion and to freedom of worship, e.g., without being able to specify what is meant by opinion, religion, or indeed freedom itself. One has to realize that this is the point at which the most varied norms and anthropologies will always obtain. To satisfy all these graphic differences which arise within a nation — and especially between the parties to a covenant on human rights, i.e., between different nations, races, continents, and religions — declarations of this kind can contain only a minimal anthropology. Hence, however important and inescapable may be this binding reminder of the things men ultimately have in common, it is inevitable that the necessarily broad base of such joint statements should make them attenuated and unsubstantial. To see this, one has only to compare these watered-down generalizations with the firm, comprehensive, yet very specific complex of norms which is to be found in a developed and as yet unaffected ethics of class. This will show how attenuated the anthropology of human rights really is.

The minimal character of this anthropology means that it cannot be used legally and politically in any direct sense, but stands in need of interpretation, regulation, and above all specification by the legislator. A passionate concern is needed for the validation, formulation, and acknowledgment of basic rights, but this fact should not blind us to the truth that such rights can hardly constitute fully developed ideals. They are necessarily too general and vague.

In fact, they are an emergency measure, and that in a twofold sense. First, they express the need to protect man against his own susceptibility to the temptation of power. Second, they protect man against the excessive variation and confusion of values in the post-Babel world. It is a sign of this protective function that the problem of human rights always arises in times of an emergency when at least one of these two threats is present, if not both. It is important to recognize this emergency character of human rights if we are to free them from the inadmissible pathos which so often attaches to them.

2) If human rights are to be of use, they must be effective rights and not just Platonic images. Hence they must be asserted not just as a part of the state's voluntary self-limitation but also in opposition to the state. In fact, ever since the rise of the constitutional state

the rights of man have increasingly assumed this effective role. They have done so in two respects.

First, since they were declared in 1789 the rights of man have increasingly come to be the rights of citizens. I.e., they have been guaranteed constitutionally, and have thus acquired political force. (One need only think of the right of the ballot.) Second, in the European Convention on Human Rights signed at Rome in 1950 a first attempt was made — and it is typical that this came after and concurrently with two most serious threats to human rights on the part of ideological power states — to anchor these rights in international law by setting up courts before which any of the signatory states could be arraigned if it did violence to them. The political force thereby given to basic rights can hardly be overestimated even though it is mainly of an indirect and prophylactic nature, and even though it may lead to a great deal of hypocrisy and to mass attempts at tactical evasion.

We need not speak here of the content of the several freedoms thus guaranteed. More important for theological ethics is the fact that even the international and constitutional acknowledgments of human rights do not constitute an institutional guarantee against the abuse of power. What we said earlier applies here as well: Man cannot get away from what he is. He always undermines and overthrows the very institutions he has himself set up as guarantees. In the present context this may be seen in two respects.

In the first place the concern is not merely to protect the individual against the trend towards state omnipotence but also to see to it that the freedoms thus protected should not for their part give rise to concentrations of power in a particular individual or group. A destructive concentration of this kind could easily arise if freedom of speech, e.g., were to be granted without any restrictions whatever. Even the freest state must set some limits to the freedom of speech. E.g., it will not allow the axioms of its constitution to be attacked. It will not tolerate the use of freedom by totalitarian or ideological propaganda aimed at the overthrow of freedom. It will accept the fact that the moral law imposes some restraints, e.g., in respect of pornography. It will also respect the principle that every fundamental right is limited by the rights of others. Protection against a concentration of power on the one side — that of the state — can lead to a concentration of power on the other side. For it is the same man who encounters himself in these various relations, and who is subject to the threat of power in constantly changing guises.

In the second place protection against the power of the state can lead to a new concentration of power if the space secured against the state by human rights is occupied, not by the individuals for whom it was earmarked, but by social, economic, or philosophical groups. We have already dealt with this problem in relation to the undermining of the state by groups, and a bare reference must suffice in the present context.

In the problem of fundamental human rights there may thus be seen again all the questions posed by the threat of power, the distribution of powers, and above all the indelible character of the persons who control the exercise of power.

14.

The Biblical Concept of the State

The phenomenology of power has shown us repeatedly the appropriateness of the theological categories we have used in our study of the state. It has demonstrated the ambivalence of power. Power, as we have seen, is by nature a means of actualization, but a means which is itself in constant revolt inasmuch as it is wielded by the hand of rebellious man. In the secular sphere this leads to the variously expressed but ever unabated tendency towards a limitation of power. It leads to the moral postulate of a limitation by confidence and authority, and to the institutional postulate of a limitation by way of the distribution of powers. Thus it is impossible to study the phenomenology of power without constantly running up against theological perspectives. The notions of creation and the fall are continually encountered. We may sum up these theological considerations as follows.

The Theological Background of Power

First, the endowment with power is implied already in the command at creation that man should "subdue the earth" (Gen. 1:28). Here, however, power is still ordered. It is integrated into the hierarchy of creation. It is power used "under God" and in his name. It is the means whereby power is exercised from above downwards, by God over man, and by man over plants and animals. In the fall, however, man breaks out of this hierarchy, and throws this power into disorder. It still exists for the sake of certain ends, but these ends are now chosen by man himself and hence do not fit into the original all-embracing order.

Second, in the Noachic covenant there is a new emergency order for the fallen world. Here power means no longer merely a symbol and restitution of the hierarchy of creation but a powerful restraint of evil. It is the power of might, which uses the fallen world's own structure of laws to enforce order within it (Gen. 9:2, 6). One might characterize power under the Noachic covenant by saying that the divinely given power of order which preserves creation is here used to check the rebellious power, that the judicial power of the judge (*potestas*), e.g., is thus set against the "disorderly power" of the murderer.

How completely power is here integrated into the fallen world and its system of co-ordinates may be seen from Luke 22:24 ff. where the disciples ask which of them is to be the greatest, and the answer is given that in the kingdom of God there will be no lordship after the manner of earthly kings and rulers. What this says is that the true counterthrust to the fallen world is not the possibility of self-limitation through the immanent means of power, but the kingdom of God with its very different law of love, a law whose origin is not of this world. For the word "serve" in Jesus' answer is simply a synonym for the word "love." The kingdom of God, then, leaves no place for the state. With its coming, all rule, authority, and power will be ended (I Cor. 15:24; cf. Dan. 2:44).

Third, within the world of the Noachic covenant the fall can be operative once again, and precisely in connection with legally instituted power (*potestas*). The power of the order [*potestas ordinans*] committed to kings, states, and rulers can become disorderly power [*potentia inordinata*], a tool of the lust for power, of rebellion, and of pride.

In the Bible this may be seen, e.g., in the hardening of Pharaoh (Exod. 4:21; 7:13; 8:15; 9:7, 35; 10:20; 11:10; 14:4, 8), and also in the pagan kings and peoples whom the prophets condemn and threaten with punishment for arrogantly overextending their judgmental authority and their role as rods of correction (cf. Isa. 10:5 ff.; 17:12 ff.; 37:33 ff.; Ezek. 29:9 ff.; Wisd. of Sol. 6:1-11). The prophets too can abuse their spiritual authority, especially if for opportunistic reasons they become false prophets of salvation and fail to announce judgment. The legitimate prophecy of true men of God is directed against this disorderly power of the false prophets (cf. I Kings 22:22 ff.; Isa. 28: 7 ff.; Mic. 3:5-8; Jer. 6:13-14; 23:9-10; 28:1 ff.; Ezek. 13:1 ff.).

In any case, when it is the power of order rather than disorderly power, the power of the fallen world is an unbroken reflection of the original significance of power, namely, to carry forward, if only in a broken way, the hierarchy of creation. If we would know the true purpose of power, then, we must inquire concerning the nature of God's power and the powerlessness of Jesus. The point of this inquiry will be to see the link between power and love in God, and to ask what this link implies for a Christian understanding of the state.

The Power of God

To try to set down all the biblical statements about God's power would be to copy the whole Bible. All that we can do is to note the thematic accents which generally determine the concept of power when it is used with any kind of emphasis. The concept occurs chiefly in contexts which focus on God's power in nature or in history. The nature psalms[1] and many passages in Job[2] speak of God's dominion in nature. It is primarily the prophets who refer to God's acts of guidance and judgment in history, including that of the nations and the whole earth.

One feature is common to all these very different statements concerning God's sovereignty over the world, at least insofar as they refer to the sphere of history. God's power is always understood as in some sense a qualified power; it is regarded either as the power of the divine wrath — God's power to visit, judge, and punish — or as the power of his sustaining patience and saving grace. Omnipotence in the sense of a neutral and purely dynamic overall power free of all values is an artificial abstraction which does not occur in the Bible. Within the framework of personalistic thinking, then, the power of God never appears as a purely formal dynamism. It is the instrument of personal attitudes such as we find in the two poles of judgment and grace, or in solicitude, providence, patience, and pity. This fact that it is determined by the personal background is what we meant when we spoke of it as being qualified.

God's power never appears as power in itself, or, better, God himself can never be understood as power in itself, as "the Almighty." He is always either the gracious God or the wrathful God — and in either case the One who subjects himself to his own "higher thoughts" and will (Isa. 55:8-9). What this means is that almighty God[3] submits to

[1] See, e.g., Ps. 104; 19; 74:12 ff.
[2] See, e.g., Job 38:4 ff.
[3] It seems to be characteristic that we can use the term almighty as an adjective — while its use as a substantive is questionable — because then it is qualified by the noun it modifies: God.

a self-limitation of his power. His power is subservient to his purposes as Creator, Redeemer, and Perfecter. These purposes in fact constitute the limits of his power. Both the exercise and the limitation of this power derive from the same motive: love. We must consider three main forms of this self-limitation.

1) The creative power of God limits itself. It does this in the sense intended by dogmatics when it speaks of "secondary causes." This means that the preservation of the world does not consist in an infinite series of new creations (out of nothing), after the manner of the many pictures of a film which are projected one after the other on the screen. On the contrary, God has given the created world a continuity of its own, a continuity though that rests on his own unceasing collaboration. Thus God works along "with" natural laws. He causes our lives to be conditioned by the biological law of birth and death, by the polarity of the sexes, by the law of historical processes, and by many other structures established or permitted in the world. For the troubles of nature he also provides natural remedies. The physician, e.g., can work with nature because God allows him to cure by means of healing which are taken from nature or developed from its materials. Indeed, the practice of medicine shows clearly that the context of the world is not to be bypassed. It is not God's manner to preserve the world — as the prayer healers might wish — by way of a continuing series of direct interventions. God gives the world a power of its own. To be sure, this independent power is possible only in concurrence *[concursus]* with God, only as he incessantly authorizes it. But this life which it has from him is derived not directly and moment by moment, but indirectly and continuously.[4] Indeed, it was this same use of factors immanent in the world, even in the fallen world, which we had in mind when interpreting the Noachic covenant we said that God uses that which exists within the world after the fall (e.g., power and the principle of retribution) as a means to preserve the world and to serve the goals of his love.[5]

---

[4] According to David Hollazius, "Preservation is the act of Divine Providence whereby God sustains all things created by him, so that they continue in being with the properties implanted in their nature and the powers received in creation." Quoted in Heinrich Schmid, *The Doctrinal Theology of the Evangelical Lutheran Church*, trans. Charles A. Hay and Henry E. Jacobs (Philadelphia: Lutheran Publication Society, 1889), p. 179.

[5] See *ThE* 1, 567-577.

2) God also limits his own power by causing man to stand over against him as a person, by allotting to man a sphere of decision which carries with it the fact of responsibility.[6] Man is the only creature whom God addresses in the second person, as standing over against himself (Gen. 1:28; 1:29-30; 2:16-17; 3:9, 11, 13, 16-19). The rest of creation is simply the object of God's creative word: "Let there be" (Gen. 1:3 ff.). Even though man's sphere of decision is bracketed by that other dimension in which decision is made concerning him, and even though this complicates the relation between predestination and responsibility,[7] in Christian theology — even a strictly predestinarian theology — man is never regarded as a mere puppet in the hand of God. God limits his control of man by causing man to be a person. One might say that in love God takes upon himself the risk of creating man.

3) There is yet another limitation which God puts on his power, however, and this is theologically the most significant of all: The ultimate mystery of God's nature consists in the fact not that he.is the author of the Law, but that he is the author of the gospel. What does this mean?

The Law always appeals to fear and hope, the fear of punishment and the hope of reward. The author of the Law exercises power — within the limits of man's personhood just mentioned — as the Lord of reward and punishment, i.e., as judge. The result is the cleavage into which man is plunged by the Law: He can be obedient out of fear and hope, and so live an orderly life outwardly while inwardly his heart is not in it (Matt. 23:25-28).

Now this, of course, is not the real intent of the Law. As the First Commandment shows, the Law claims the whole man for God; it claims his heart. But the very fact that we must be forever reminded of this commandment,[8] and the further fact that this reminder can take the form of a protestation: "But I say to you . . ." (Matt. 5:22, 28, 32, 34, 39, 44), shows the degree to which this original intent can be perverted.

While the Law exercises its power by appealing to fear and to

---

[6] See *ThE* 1, 281 ff.

[7] See *ThE* 1, 297.

[8] Cf., e.g., Luther's repeated references to it in his explanations of the Ten Commandments in The Small Catechism.

hope, the heart of God when it speaks, appeals to love. As Melanchthon says, by making himself "an object that can be loved," [9] God evokes love in man. God gives his heart in order to win the heart of man. As author of the gospel God wills to win our love. He refuses to command it by force or bring it into being omnipotently. Instead, he gives himself to us by giving us his Son. He causes his mercy to triumph over his wrath. He seeks his people "as a hen seeks her brood" (Matt. 23:37). He makes covenants. He sets up signs of grace and grants seasons of grace. He has us "bought with a price" (I Cor. 6:20; 7:23). He gives his Son (John 3:16). In short, he serves us in order to win us. This is the extreme renunciation of power as laid down in the *Magna Carta* of the law of the kingdom of God (Luke 22:25-26).

Love too is power, unquestionably. But — it must be stated paradoxically — God's love is the power of service which vanquishes the heart. He is a servant and I a lord — what an exchange! Thus it is that the limitation of the power of God, of which we have been speaking, is seen to be the framework within which we must now consider the powerlessness of Jesus Christ.

The Powerlessness of Jesus Christ

This mystery of the love of God is radicalized to the utmost in the existence of Jesus Christ and his complete renunciation of power. This renunciation has been formulated most expressively in Kierkegaard's notion that Jesus rejected any "direct recognizableness." [10] The main idea here is that in love God became one of us in Jesus Christ.

But if God accepts this solidarity and becomes one of us, he has to subject himself to the possibility of mistaken identity. I.e., he must

---

[9] *Objectum amabile.* Apology of the Augsburg Confession, IV, 129; *BC* 125.

[10] "The true God cannot become directly recognizable; but direct recognizableness is what the merely human, what the men to whom He came, would pray and implore of Him as the greatest alleviation. And it was out of love He became man! He is love; and yet every instant He exists He must crucify as it were all human compassion and solicitude — for He can only be the object of faith. But everything that goes by the name of human sympathy has to do with direct recognizableness. Yet in such a way He does not become the object of 'faith', He is not very God; and if He is not very God, He does not save men. So by that step which He took for love's sake He precipitated the individual, the whole human race, once for all, into the most dreadful strife of decision." Soren Kierkegaard, *Training in Christianity,* trans. Walter Lowrie (Princeton: Princeton University Press, 1944), p. 137.

of necessity lose his direct recognizableness as God. For the things whereby he may be directly known are all things which distinguish him from us and exalt him above us. Direct recognizableness would thus make any real solidarity with us impossible.

As "knowing" on our part corresponds to God's recognizableness, so believing or trusting corresponds to unrecognizableness. Faith alone is commensurate with the God who humbles himself.[11] The self-abasement of Christ to powerlessness, to the renunciation of all divine marks of distinction, is thus intended to render a service. It is designed to evoke faith and to incite to what Kierkegaard calls "passionate" decision. It consequently radicalizes what God does already in creation when he sets man over against himself as a person and thrusts on him the responsibility of decision.

The self-limitation of power for reasons of love is developed in the New Testament in the story of Jesus' temptation. This temptation arises out of the efforts of the devil to have Christ declare himself by performing miracles and claiming demonstrable power (Luke 4: 1-14; Matt. 4:1-11). To do this, however, would be to abandon his task of loving service to his brother-men. For by demonstrating his divine power to do miracles Jesus would be making men objects of suggestive compulsion rather than subjects of decision. He would thus contradict his mission by evading the risk of having to suffer under sin, i.e., by allowing men to decide against him. In the conflict between love and power he would side with power and choose in favor of self-preservation.

The Relation between Power and Love

We are thus set before the decisive ethical problem. Can this law of love which comes from the "wholly other" sphere of God's kingdom, can this eschatological and transcendent law take on any significance in terms of actualization in this aeon? Is it not wholly without analogy?

Now it is true that in this aeon outright renunciation of power for the sake of love is quite impossible. For the fallen world, the world

---

[11] Cf. also Kierkegaard's notion that God cloaks himself in the guise of humanity as an incognito in order to shake man's security and assurance, and thereby provoke "the infinite passion of inwardness," i.e., make the matter of decision a total affair in which the whole person is fully engaged. See *ibid.*, pp. 140-143; and *idem, Concluding Unscientific Postscript* (Princeton: Princeton University Press, 1941), p. 182.

of the Noachic covenant, has need of a power-equipped order. It is also true, however, that in this aeon there is love, and that the command of love applies. Nor are any limits set to this command in the sense that the spheres of power are fenced off from its claim. Accordingly, love and power cannot possibly be mutually exclusive, any more than this aeon and the coming aeon can exclude one another; for the coming aeon has already invaded this age, and is "in the midst of us" (Luke 17:21). Power and love are no more mutually exclusive than the divine and human natures of Jesus Christ, which are both present in the one person without either confusion or separation. Love and power, then, are not simple alternatives.

But neither can they be regarded in terms of a synthesis between them. The Sermon on the Mount, as the law of the coming aeon and the representative of the radical command of love, simply cannot be brought into synthesis with the laws of this aeon, whether by regarding normal moral laws as "precepts" and the demands of the Sermon on the Mount as "counsels," or by dividing up their spheres of validity — either spatially in the sense that the Sermon on the Mount applies only to an esoteric circle of disciples or temporally in the sense that it is an exceptional law for the last times.[12]

The history of Christology shows that the two natures of Christ cannot be brought into synthesis. It does so in three ways. First, all its statements necessarily take the form of paradox. Second, there is a constant need to resort to categories other than that of "nature" (e.g., historical categories as in the doctrine of the offices) in discussing the christological mystery, and this is an indirect admission that harmony is not to be attained in terms of the "nature" concept. Third, the history of dogma constantly alternates between an overemphasis first on the one nature and then on the other.

But if power and love are not mutually exclusive alternatives and cannot be understood in terms of synthesis either, how are we to define the relationship between them? One can only conclude that love is the fundamental motive on the basis of which and in the name of which power is both exercised and limited; indeed, love is the motive which validates the rule of power of the Noachic covenant.

It was in this way that Luther defined the relationship. For him

---

[12] These several views are dealt with more fully in *ThE* 1, 332 ff.

power derives from paternal authority and is thus always integrated into a relationship of love.[13] In the fallen world, which admittedly needs power in order to restrain evil, this restraint of evil is understood wholly in terms of the motive of paternal and sustaining love. For in an uncontrolled play of mere forces it would be the weak and miserable who would get crushed. It is in order to defend *them* against injustice, to extend paternal love to *them,* that God provides the protection of force.[14] Thus in equipping the state with punitive power, e.g., God is actually expressing love, for in so doing he takes the weak, oppressed, and persecuted under his wing.[15]

The distinction we have made between God's love as expressed without refraction in the original estate and the refracted form love takes in the sphere of the Noachic covenant is also stated by Luther in another way, in terms of the distinction between the "proper work" and the "alien work" of love. The more direct the I-Thou relation, the clearer is the proper work of love and the original intention of creation. In the relation between man and wife or between parents and children, e.g., are to be found the spheres of gentleness, mercy, pity, and true understanding. The more public and institutional the spheres, however, where the "orders" of this aeon are involved, the more the "manner" of love changes, and the more evident is its alien work of judging, killing, and repressing evil. What Luther means could be expressed in the words of Paul Tillich, that "it is the alien work of love to destroy what is against love. . . . Love, in order to exercise its proper works, namely charity and forgiveness, must provide for a place in which this can be done, through its strange work of judging and punishing. In order to destroy what is against love, love must be united with power, and not only with power, but also with compulsory power." [16]

We must not be misled, of course, into thinking that the proper and alien forms of love are to be understood only in terms of different

---

[13] See Luther's explanation of the Fourth Commandment in The Large Catechism, I, 141 and 150; BC 384, 385. See also Franz Lau, *"Aeusserliche Ordnung" und "Weltlich Ding" in Luthers Theologie* (Göttingen: Vandenhoeck & Ruprecht, 1933), pp. 129-131.

[14] *LW* 21, 24; 45, 89.

[15] *PE* 4, 267; *WA* 41, 325. See Karl Holl, *Gesammelte Aufsätze zur Kirchengeschichte,* I (3rd ed.; Tübingen: Mohr, 1923), 255-256.

[16] Paul Tillich, *Love, Power, and Justice* (New York: Oxford University Press, 1954), pp. 49-50.

spheres of validity. Pushed to the extreme, this view would mean that in the spheres of public order there would obtain a kind of political, economic, or other autonomy which would soon repress the original motive of love.[17] On the contrary, it is simply a case of love being expressed in two different forms. Love cannot operate as directly, e.g., in the case of a judge as in that of a father dealing with his child. For the judge judges and punishes for love of neighbor, whom he must protect. Even his relation to the defendant whom he must sentence is not just an objective or juridical relation, a relation of mere distance. The judge is summoned to love him too. In all spheres of life, then, love is the same. It is simply expressed in different forms. This is why we intentionally speak here of the differing "manner" of love.

Now that we have pointed out the different aspects of the relation between power and love on God's side, we must undertake to show how this relation may be re-enacted on the human side, the extent to which it can take on ethical form. Some indication of how we ought to proceed has already been provided by the fact that God performs both the proper work and the alien work of his love in such a way as to utilize the partnership of man. He does the proper work of love by evoking our love through his love, our mercy through his mercy, our forgiveness through his forgiveness (I John 4:10, 19; Matt. 18:23-35). And he does the alien work of love by causing human individuals and institutions forcefully to restrain evil. Whether he loves or chides, forgives or judges, creates or destroys, God is always in relation to man, all tied up with man. He makes man his instrument, and never does he work without this instrument (Acts 9:15; Rom. 9:22-23).

Hence when it comes to the ethical application of the relationship between love and power in God it is not necessary that there be some kind of "transformation" of divine reality into human reality. No "trans" whatever is involved, for God has already entered into human "formations." He is accessible to us men only because he has initiated a history between himself and man, and has himself become man.

[17] Luther's doctrine of the two kingdoms has often been misunderstood in this way — e.g., by Ernst Troeltsch, and following him Georg Wünsch — in terms of a strict distinction between private and official morality, the latter being a wholly impersonal affair. See *ThE* 1, 364-367.

It would thus be wrong to look for some kind of analogy between divine and human action and then to arrive at ethical direction by way of drawing conclusions from this analogy, for what God does in love he always does to man and with man. God has set himself in analogy. The only question, then, is that of our entering into this ongoing history of God with us and of our re-enacting it according to his intention.

What this re-enactment can imply becomes clear when we consider its opposite. In the parable of the wicked servant (Matt. 18:21-35) the history of forgiveness, which begins with God and moves on by way of the man who receives grace all the way to his neighbor, is broken by the folly of the servant. It is only partially correct to interpret this by saying that man ought to act like God, for this "like" — which posits an analogy — threatens to treat God and man as two static and separated entities. It would be more accurate to say that when man enters into a history (of forgiveness) with God he must allow this history to proceed on its way. He is not to regard himself as its terminal point, as if God's grace were simply a matter of satisfying his own opportunism. He must instead integrate himself into the ongoing history of grace as a member and an instrument. One might even say: he must will what God wills.[18] Only then can he attain to "conformity" with God.

This concept of conformity, which is occasionally used by Luther, is better adapted than that of analogy to express what we called the "re-enactment" [Nachvollzug] of the divine action. For conformity connotes a history which transpires, whereas analogy is a more static and ontological concept. If God's history with us entails his use of power in love, and also his limitation of power in love — even to the point where Jesus is divested of all power — what then is involved in man's re-enactment of this relation between power and love? We can only indicate its main features. Political ethics in all its parts is nothing but the working out of this re-enactment. The decisive thing is this: The power of authority entrusted, e.g., to a statesman or judge, will be used in keeping with the motive of responsive and re-enacting

---

[18] In Luke 15:25-32 the faithful elder brother sabotages the action of the father by not willing what the father wills, i.e., to treat the prodigal with kindness. See Helmut Thielicke, *The Waiting Father: Sermons on the Parables of Jesus*, trans. John W. Doberstein (New York: Harper, 1959), pp. 30-40.

love only if the human officebearer knows that he is caught up in a history with God, and only if – as a result of this "situation" in which he stands – he understands and takes his bearings from the theological background of power.

This understanding of power embraces a twofold perception and acknowledgment. There is first the perception and acknowledgment of the purpose of power, namely, that as ordered and ordering power *[potestas ordinata et ordinans]* it protects the fallen world from chaos, creating order and bringing this threatened aeon to the last day. And second, there is the perception and acknowledgment that power is always something assigned or delegated, so that it has the character of authorized authority.

Implicit in this is the postulate of a twofold limitation of power. In the first place, it does not permit any institutionalism of power. By institutionalism we mean the tendency for the orders equipped with power to consolidate themselves as independent constructs and to be construed exclusively in terms of their immanent functional autonomy. At the end of this road stands the myth of a fixed, factually determined autonomy. But if instead of such institutionalism what is involved is rather the re-enactment of that which takes place in the divine conjoining of power and love, then political, social, and economic forms of organization will be sought which do not make it impossible – in the interests of caution we prefer to express the matter negatively – for human motivations to be discerned.

It is obvious that the great size of certain economic organizations (e.g., large corporations) and certain aspects of their organizational structure (e.g., the non-personal character of their shareholders and the complicated collective administration) make it much harder to perceive personal features in them than in constructs of a more manageable size in which there are clearly defined personages and individual responsibilities. Confidence, in the sense of a personal commitment and attachment, is always easier in relation to organizations which are made up of persons than in relation to non-personal functioning things.

Even in the present age of democracies and republics there is a human longing, often undirected and of uncertain origin, to hear news reports about royalty. There can be little doubt that at root this longing is not unconnected with the fact that government which is nothing but a machine with more or less anonymous rulers is not constitutive of personal relationships, and that men consequently desire to see personal representatives of the governmental apparatus in order to realize through them the kind of personal relationships for which they yearn. The inclination in our day to violate without mercy the personal and intimate lives of prominent people, to invade their privacy, is perhaps only another — a perverted — form of this primitive urge to have not just material contacts with things but human communication with persons in the world around us.

Even ideological tyranny has to come to terms with this basic urge. It has to face the fact that men want the ideology to be represented by persons. It thus allows fantasy to build up myths around the chief leaders. Stalin did not invent the personality cult, as was claimed after his death. He simply exploited the longing of collectivized society for personal images of leadership. Indeed, this is why all leading statesmen, even bloody tyrants, like to be photographed with small children and pet dogs. However extreme the caricature and however hypocritical the disguise, what we have here is a play upon this primal fact about power, namely, that it is supposed to be integrated into personal motivations, into love and kindness, into the heart's field of force. Such distorted pictures have to be understood in terms of the original image which unwittingly and unconsciously comes to expression in them.

To this context belongs also the effort of impersonal organizations to provide a personal coloration under the rubric "human relations." Human relations in this sense can admittedly be a cynical exploitation of the personal impulse. But it can also be a genuine and meaningful attempt to show, through a concern for persons, that a commercial enterprise has more than a purely economic character, that it also bears human features in that it provides men with work and sustenance, cares for men, and indeed may even be trying to give to work itself a more than inanimate character by bringing to light its purpose and meaning. In any case the original relation between love and power, dynamism and person, is here making a very determined, however distorted, attempt to come to expression at this point. Thus there can be no doubt that all institutionalism and all organizational apparatus is confronted by the task of bringing human motives and personal features to light.

The notion that man re-enacts the divine conjoining of love and power implies in the second place a concern lest rulership be understood as an end in itself, and the exercise of power as the satisfaction of an impulse. In this way power could become an instrument of egoism rather than of service, and thus lose its authorization. The concern lest power should lose its connection with love will find expression not only subjectively, in an appeal to the motives behind the exercise of power, but also and primarily in institutional safeguards designed to ensure against its abuse. One such safeguard is the distribution of powers.

But this distribution is a weighty reminder that the original intention — that power should be combined with the motive of love — cannot be fulfilled by institutional means alone. For the distribution of powers can neither effect nor help to effect this intention by binding power to love. Such distribution has the purely negative function of preventing the worst excesses where the link of power with love is broken. Institutional means can do no more than that.

The greater the framework within which it is exercised, and the more impersonally and mechanically it is exercised, the more seriously are the personal connections of power threatened. This is why it is imperative that there be a distribution of powers in political associations of any great size, e.g., the state, and in correspondingly large social and economic organizations.

The Provisional Character of the State between the Fall and the Judgment

Even in the kingdom on the left hand there is thus a use of power in the name of love. But the nature of this combination is determined by the state of things between the fall and the last judgment, even as the distinction between the two kingdoms is a characteristic feature of this interim. Hence the combination of power and love is a broken epilogue to the inwardly composed and tranquil (and hence powerless) hierarchy of creation, and an equally broken prologue to the invading kingdom of God in which there will be no more rule or power (I Cor. 15:24).

In the New Testament, accordingly, the state insofar as it is equipped with power has a provisional character. Oscar Cullmann speaks pointedly of the fact that the state, even though in many ways it runs counter to the kingdom of God, can nevertheless demand obedience of us.[19] What is the significance of this "nevertheless"?

It is certainly wrong to take Paul's injunction to be subject to the governing authorities (Rom. 13:1 ff.) absolutely and without the reservation of this "nevertheless," as though it applied to every specific state and justified an unbroken ethos of subjection, even within the framework of ideological tyranny. As Cullmann has impressively shown, the context here and the sayings of Paul in I Corinthians 6:1 ff. and 2:8 — not to speak of the contrapuntal relation of Romans 13 and Revelation 13 — provide an essential corrective to this misinterpretation. In particular, there are two elements in Romans 13 and I Corinthians 6:1 ff. which point to a relativizing of the state: first, the eschatological aspect, which shows the state to be provisional; and second, the tension in which the order of the state stands to the commandment of love.

As regards the eschatological aspect, the last part of the same chapter (Rom. 13:12) contains a reference to the night which is far gone and the day which is at hand, and demands that we cast off the works of darkness and put on the armor of light in view of the approaching end which will terminate all rule, including the order of the state (cf. I Cor. 15:24). To use the terminology of Luther, statements concerning the state as the normative representative of the kingdom on the left hand finally issue in statements concerning the kingdom on the right hand, i.e., statements on the immediacy of the Christian to the returning Christ.

The passage on the state is also linked retrospectively to statements about the kingdom on the right hand, since just prior to the eschatological references Paul speaks about immediacy to the neighbor in love. This, then, is the context into which Paul inserts what is said about the mediacy of the state order. The kingdom on the left hand is linked, as it were, both behind and before to the kingdom on the right hand. It is thus protected against a false assumption of autonomy in the sense of a false doctrine of "orders in themselves."

---

[19] See Oscar Cullmann, *The State in the New Testament* (New York: Scribner's, 1956), pp. 57 ff. I am indebted to him for much of the exegetical discussion which follows. His exegesis confirms in large measure the theological interpretation set forth in my *Geschichte und Existenz* (1935), particularly his insistence that the state is not a direct divine order but an explicitly postlapsarian and hence provisional order.

The eschatological aspect is brought in again in I Corinthians 6:1 ff., where Christians are forbidden to bring their disputes before pagan courts. The argument with which Paul supports the prohibition is expressly eschatological: The saints are to judge the world (6:2). How, then, can they let themselves be judged by it? They will even judge angels. How, then, can they yield to the trivialities of this age (6:3)? This line of argument is of vital significance for a theological evaluation of the state. Since judging is one of the state's main functions, aloofness from the courts means aloofness also from the state itself.

Both the state and its courts have certain clearly defined tasks, tasks whose theological validation we investigated in the context of the Noachic covenant. The state and its courts are ordained for this age as measures of preservation undertaken by the divine patience. This is why within the sphere of their validity they demand obedience, respect, and gratitude. But we misunderstand and blaspheme the giver of this good gift if we overlook the context, i.e., the salvation history, within which he gave it. The gift is rightly honored only when we see it in terms of its relativization by salvation history, i.e., in terms of its limitation, its character as ministry. Otherwise we absolutize it, deify the orders, and embrace the idolatry of institutionalism.

Eschatological relativization of the state implies a certain aloofness. In his discussion of the demand to shun the state courts, Cullmann expresses this tendency to aloofness very well: "Wherever the Christian can dispense with the state without threatening its existence, he should do so." [20] This principle is of far-reaching importance in theological ethics. For awareness of this eschatological relativization leads necessarily to the postulate of the minimal state. A provisional emergency order does not apply to spheres which can be handled by other means on a non-emergency basis.

This means concretely that social responsibilities which can be handled apart from the state (by families, neighbors, business enterprises, etc.) should not be sloughed off onto the state. The welfare state does not appear in this light to be ideal. In mass society, where communication between persons has largely broken down, it may be a necessary evil to be accepted with reservations, but in no case is it to be exalted as a social ideal.

[20] Cullmann, op. cit., p. 61.

We are also led at this point to the postulate that so far as possible education and family life must remain independent of the state. Since the state has a legitimate interest in the training of its own citizens, it must of course be granted no small voice in education. But because man is more than merely a citizen, normative control of education is to be vested in parents, who are responsible for the total life of the younger generation. Care must also be taken to limit the role the state must play in regulating affairs within the family, e.g., by casting the deciding vote in matters where husband and wife may disagree. With equality of the sexes legally assured, it is an important question what course to take when parents cannot agree, e.g., on the education of their children. Should the state itself in such a case act as guardian and make the decision? Our contention — for which we shall give reasons in the next two chapters — is that such intervention by the state is to be avoided if at all possible, even if this can be done only by formally declaring the decisions of the mother to be final at one stage of the child's life, and those of the father to be final at another.[21]

The demand for a minimal state is the opposite of the totalitarian desire for a maximal state. The eschatological relativization of the state is thus an essential antidote to all totalitarian tendencies. It is easy to see the ethical implications of this understanding of the state as a provisional order. Each affirmation of the state, including that of Romans 13:1 ff., must be accompanied by a "nevertheless." The state is not a definitive order. It is a temporary institution.

Besides the eschatological aspect there is a second factor which points to the provisional character of the state: Paul's statements about the state grow out of what he says about the immediate I-Thou relationship (the command of love and forgiveness). This factor is equally significant, for it too shows that the state is provisional and conditional.

The contrast between the indirect form of the I-Thou relationship in the state, and its direct form in love, is patent. The immediacy of love requires that the Christian not repay evil for evil (Rom. 12:17), but leave vengeance to God (Rom. 12:19). The mediacy of the state requires that evil be punished and avenged in the name of God (Rom.

[21] See "Die Gleichberechtigung der Frau und ihre Grenzen im Familienrecht," *Herder Korrespondenz*, V, 2 (1950-1951), 89 ff., esp. p. 91.

13:4). The sword is entrusted to the state. It has to resist evil (cf. Matt. 5:39). In the kingdom on the left hand evil is forcibly resisted, though out of the very same love — indirect in this case — which finds expression in the direct relationship between God and man, and man and man. The state is equipped with authority and power in order to discharge this very function in the service of God and at his commission.

Here again the dignity and the limitation of the state are apparent: its dignity inasmuch as it acts by divine commission; its limitation inasmuch as it has a mission which is limited both in time (i.e., to the age between the fall and the judgment) and in substance. The substantive limitation becomes clear when one realizes that if the state is to reward the good and punish evildoers (Rom. 13:3), it has to be conceded the right to distinguish between good and evil. But the state can be conceded only a limited knowledge in this respect. For the evil which it is ordained to resist cannot be for it, as state, that evil before God which we call sin. If it were, the state would be the opponent of all selfishness, which it cannot be. For the state needs selfishness. In the form of ambition and the desire for power selfishness is a normative impulse of historical life.[22] Indeed, in its sacred egoism the state itself is an exponent or expression of collective selfishness.[23] We thus maintain that the state, when it restrains evil, is not aiming at sin itself — in whose representation it has a share — but simply contesting the excesses of selfishness. It resists the selfishness which is inimical to order.

This substantive limitation of the state also has as its counterpart aloofness on the part of the Christian. For the Christian cannot regard the state simply as God's representative against the power of the enemy. He sees that the state is on both sides in this conflict. It is not simply the representative of good. Why not? Because it does not know the true power of evil for one thing, but also because it opposes only a specific form of evil. Hence the state cannot be the ultimate measure. On the contrary, it must itself be measured. For this reason too it cannot be the Christian's true home, as the ideological state seeks to be. Our citizenship is in heaven (Phil. 3:20). This is why

[22] See Helmut Thielicke, *Geschichte und Existenz*, p. 175.
[23] *Ibid.*, pp. 168 ff.

aloofness is indicated in respect of the earthly state. In it we are resident aliens (Eph. 2:19).

The upshot of all this is once again the demand for a minimal state. A further plain implication is that to the degree that the true function of the state is overlooked there will be a corresponding intensifying of the temptation to exalt the state as the epitome of all values and hence to make it totalitarian.

Nevertheless, even a society which is no longer Christian, which is not aware of the state's true function, nor of its consequent limitation, will not unconditionally resist and reject the demand for a minimal state. For even if it does not see or accept the theological basis of the demand, its remaining awareness of humanity will enable it to see the threat implied in an overestimation of the state. It will not be completely blind to the concentration of institutional and moral power which arises with a maximal state, or to the tendency towards dehumanization which goes with totalitarianism.

If the statements and demands of theological ethics, at least in this sphere, apply not merely to the Christian community but to all men everywhere, this is because the theological thesis concerning the provisional and emergency character of the state touches upon a reality of life whose symptoms are to be detected even where there is no faith. Faith contains — as it were incidentally and in addition — the most profound interpretation of life as a whole. Only because this is so, only because faith is realistic, can Christians and non-Christians coexist in the same order — provided that order derives from, or at least is not blatantly inimical to, the controlling insights of Christianity.

The totalitarian state is thus institutionally the borderline case in which the situation becomes truly critical as regards the coexistence of Christians and non-Christians, at least so far as the latter are ideologically committed and hence are functionaries of the state. The state which regards itself as definitive and absolute demands at every point a confession of loyalty. It demands marks (Rev. 13:17; 14:9). By loyalty it understands the unreserved and unconditional acceptance of its ideological bases, which for Christians is tantamount to denial of their Lord. And it demands this confession, not merely in the form of explicit ideological agreement, but also implicitly in the form of active co-operation in its orders (education, law, social action, etc.). For these orders are no longer just factually and functionally determined. Right down to their minutest details they are permeated by ideology.

It would doubtless be false, however, to describe the possibility of the totalitarian state and its self-absolutization as simply a demonic possibility inherent in the state as such. We must be on guard here against false mythologizing of the state, even as in our discussion of power we had to reject Jakob Burckhardt's theory which exalts power mythically and ascribes to it demonic potencies,[24] and even as we repudiate the notion that there is a demonism of technology. When we speak of the demonism of the state or of power or of technology, this is simply a convenient kind of shorthand, just as it is a convenient simplification to say that the sun rises even though we know that in fact it is the earth which encircles the sun. The important thing is to recognize the parabolic character of such routine abbreviations. In reality the things themselves do not turn and twist demonically; it is rather we men who turn and are twisted.

As the problem of power is in reality the problem of the people in power, so the dubious absolutizing of the state is not the action of the state itself, but something which is done to the state by men. Only because man posits himself absolutely does he posit absolutely the objectification of himself and of his favorite values in the state. Only because he tries to produce and grasp his own salvation does he reject the salvation history which relativizes him and his posited salvation and values.

If the state itself were entangled in demonism, it would have to be summoned as an institution to repent, and ultimately it would be able to do so. But this is so nonsensical as to need no demonstration. It is only the men who establish and operate the institutions — not the institutions themselves — that can be summoned to repent and be converted. Thus if it is necessary on rhetorical grounds to use such shorthand and to speak of the demonic perversion of the state, of its forgetting its proper function and limits, and if — even in these pages — the state seems to be the subject in these figures of speech, let it now be expressly stated that we are here employing the same stock mythology of everyday usage as in allusions to the sunrise. No theological dignity is to be allotted to what is simply a manner of speaking.

[24] See above pp. 172-177.

We may now summarize the basic theses which have been decisive for all we have been saying. From the standpoint of salvation history the state is an emergency measure for the interim between the fall and the last judgment. Hence it is not to be absolutized but subordinated to the relativization by the divine purpose. As regards the danger that the state will become dissociated from its primal basis, be driven to emancipation and made totalitarian, the ethical consequence of this is the postulate that there should be no more than a minimal state. This means concretely that we should commit to the state, not everything we can, but only what we must. In other words, of all the tasks involved in the distribution of powers the most important is that the machinery of state leave some of its powers to the responsibility and initiative of free citizens and of relatively free institutions, i.e., those which have large powers of self-direction.

CONCRETE ILLUSTRATIONS OF THE ETHICAL CONSEQUENCES

15.

The Minimal State in Education

The thesis of the minimal state has already pointed the way for the concrete consequences now to be deduced. Indeed, we have already indicated some of these consequences — e.g., when we made reference to the equality of the sexes — and we will do so again in other connections. At this point, however, we would simply select two models which are particularly appropriate for illuminating the thesis. We shall deal in this chapter with the first of these, namely, the role of the state in education, and in the next chapter with the second, the role of the state in welfare.

The sphere of education is usually a field of lively and often bitter controversy between several partners who claim a share in the responsibility for it and whose specific zones of competence cannot be demarcated with precision. The three main partners in this controversy are the state, the church, and the parents. It goes without saying that each of the three could be further differentiated. Political parties, e.g., influence state decisions, sectarian approaches affect the church's role, and parental rights are frequently nothing but a propagandistic slogan employed by particular pressure groups. For our purposes, however, the threefold division will suffice.

Since one of the three competitors is the state, the problem of education can be treated as a model in terms of which to study the minimal state. We shall have to anticipate here things which belong to the ethics of education. But we shall do so only insofar as may be necessary to establish our essentially negative thesis, namely, that the state does not have an educational monopoly.

To give the model the clearest possible contours, and to avoid getting involved too deeply in the problem of church and state, to which we shall return on pages 541-614, we may simplify the inquiry by reducing from three to two the number of rivals competing in the sphere of education. By church we shall understand, not the ecclesiastical institution but, if the expression may be allowed, the particular group known as "Christian parents." Thus the state and Christian parents confront one another with their claims, and our problem is reduced to that of the tension between the claims of the state and parental rights.

Christian parents are representative in a double sense, and thus serve as a good example or model. Being Christians, they represent the church's claim to a voice in education. Being parents, they represent parental rights in general. For within a secular democratic state, a state based on freedom of opinion and hence dedicated to tolerance, the Christianity of the parents cannot confer any special privileges. On the contrary, the rights claimed for the Christian point of view apply equally well to parents of different religious and philosophical persuasion, and consequently to all parents.

This, then, is the basic systematic conception within which we shall now study the confrontation between the state and Christian parents in the matter of education. Within this framework it will be our purpose to strengthen the thesis of the minimal state by contesting the educational monopoly of the state.

The Interests of the State

It is to be noted at the very outset that the state, of course, does have a legitimate interest in education, and for this reason must also have a voice in it. Indeed, the state is interested in the problem of education from at least three standpoints.

First, if the state is to function effectively some instruction for its citizens is necessary. To put it very simply, they must be able to read, write, and do simple arithmetic. Without these skills the cultural and intellectual demands of the state could not be met. Indeed, there could be no democratic state, for democracy presupposes in its citizens a certain maturity which is not possible without the rudiments of education.

Second, the state also has an interest in engendering a sense of national identity and responsible political life. This can hardly be attained without (among other things) some instruction in history and geography.

Third, to produce echelons of leadership higher levels of education are also needed such as high schools, colleges, and universities. But in the present context we can ignore this field, since the claim of parental rights is less of a factor here.

There can be no contesting the fact that the state must have a responsible voice in the educational field, even to the point of drawing up courses of instruction and training teachers in both the subjects they are to teach and the pedagogic skills with which to teach them. There can also be no doubt that the state has a right to supervise the institutions it provides for such purposes.

But the moment this is granted, the question immediately arises as to the limits of such state control. For even elementary instruction goes beyond the technical ABC skills and involves matters of world view which are outside the competence of a philosophically neutral state. Certain texts, e.g., are prescribed for reading, and certain songs for singing, and both can cause friction in respect of their contents. Can Roman Catholic children be forced to practice their reading on texts from Martin Luther, or Protestant children to develop tonal accuracy by practicing Roman Catholic chorales? This is obviously a rather artificial example, for there is little need to fear that crude instances such as this will arise. But the caricature draws attention to problems which may very well arise in subtler forms, and which will serve to indicate that the sphere of pure objectivity is very narrow indeed. In fact, it hardly goes much beyond arithmetic and general mathematics.

The test case in this field is the teaching of history. There can be no such thing as a supraconfessional or objectively neutral history of the Reformation, e.g. This being so, it goes without saying that the competence of the philosophically neutral state in this field is clearly called in question, and the problem arises whether and how far there is not already in this elementary sphere an encroachment on the competence of other authorities, e.g., the parents (or in this instance the church as an institution).

In specific cases, at any rate, it is very difficult to mark off the several spheres of competence. Should it be the state alone that determines the types of schools, and hence also the forms of instruction? Should parents be limited merely to choosing between available forms and not have the privilege of determining those forms for themselves, even if only by way of establishing private or experimental schools? Obviously the type of school has something to do not only with the specific goals of education (e.g., vocational schools) but also with specific anthropological ideas, as is evident, e.g., in the debate over denominational schools. Particular views of man correspond to particular types of schools.

But if this is so, is it not also beyond the competence of the state to attempt to determine the types of schools, inasmuch as the state — if it is not to be an ideological and totalitarian state — dare not have a specific view of man? This is obviously a rhetorical question. The very fact that it is raised supports the thesis that the state can actually violate the limits of its competence if it claims a monopoly in determining the types of schools.

But caution is needed when we say this. The demand for a minimal state — in this case the demand that the state not claim exclusive rights to determination of the types of schools and the materials of instruction — must not be allowed surreptitiously and unjustly to distort our view of the state. Can philosophical neutrality mean that the state is to be no more than a mere night watchman performing insignificant marginal functions? This is obviously a perversion which does not do justice to the theological dignity of the state and hence can only bring discredit on the postulate of a minimal state. Two points need to be made in this regard.

First, the democratic state is not without its guiding views of man, or at least the rudiments of such views. These are usually laid down in its constitution, and are broad enough to allow for the holding of a variety of specific views, among which common basic elements may be discerned. Among these anthropological axioms — with respect to which the democratic state is not neutral but committed — there is, e.g., the thesis of different freedoms, of the dignity of humanity, and of regard for the maturity, especially the political independence of citizens. Even the tolerant democratic state is impatient with and dogmatically opposed to all attitudes which would deny freedom and toleration. The thesis of freedom does not permit attacks on freedom. To this degree there are limits to the philosophical neutrality of the state. And the postulate of the minimal state will always mean in addition that the state guards and stands up for its acknowledged right to a minimum, including a minimum of dogmatic rights and philosophical substance. Now this does not rule out but actually presupposes the continuing question whether and how far the state may transgress this minimum, and thereby encroach upon the competence of other authorities which represent specific views of man, e.g., the church, and Christian parents, or parents of any other persuasion for that matter.

A second point needs also to be made. The demand that the state exercise restraint in fixing the types of schools, and avoid using indirect institutional ways of championing particular views of man which are beyond its sphere of competence, does not mean that decision as to the types of schools should be left to the inexhaustible imagination of educational reformers or to the pedagogic preferences of parents or groups of parents. For this would lead to chaos and to uncontrolled sectarianism in education. Here too the state has a function of order which must be acknowledged. It must prevent excessive individualism in this matter of the types of schools which can be allowed. For certain general goals have to be reached, and there have to be some general standards in the granting of diplomas, e.g., as regards qualifications for a vocation or for entering a university.[1] It must also be possible to transfer from one type of school to another. Finally, individualism cannot be allowed if it tends to establish or perpetuate social cleavages or a caste system.

Our demand, therefore, that the state show restraint in fixing the types of schools can only mean that the state, within limits which guarantee a minimum of uniformity, and under its own state supervision, should give free play to the will of the parents in the form of additional schools owned and operated by private persons or groups, and in so doing provide opportunities for experiments in education. So far as education is concerned, it is along these lines that the desired minimal state will have to be sought.

The corresponding maximum would be a consistently applied state monopoly whereby education would be made exclusively the servant of the state and its needs. In respect of content such a monopoly would mean that teachers would be steeped in state ideology. Institutionally, it would mean total control of youth. Indeed, the tendency

---

[1] The situation will differ in different countries. Thus in the United States there is greater freedom in the granting of diplomas than in Europe. The only point is that there is little meaning in a diploma or degree unless it conforms to certain general standards.

toward totalization would not stop with seizure of the schools alone. There would also be pressure in the direction of a state youth organization. In fact, such organizations are characteristic of all forms of totalitarianism. This opposite extreme — the maximal state — shows how necessary it is that in the educational field too the state be as little normative, regulative, and dominating as possible, and that room be left for initiatives other than those of the state.

Beyond the several concerns already mentioned, the state has yet another legitimate interest in education, of which we take note here because it contains a warning that we for our part should not overstress this postulate of the minimal state. The interest to which we refer arises out of the fact that the state functions within a pluralistic society. This alone accounts in large measure for the fact that the state must assume the task of ordering affairs in the field of education. It is important to take cognizance of this interest if we are to have any understanding of the many encroachments modern democracies have made in the educational field, for they are largely the outgrowth of school conflicts, parental disputes, and ecclesiastical protests.

Once secularization has advanced to a certain point, it is not easy even for a democratic state to be content with a minimal role and to accept only the essentially negative task of restraining evil and preserving external order. The state is more inclined to press on to positive ideas which will sustain life and provide an intellectual undergirding for society. Nor is it easy to say whether these are legitimate duties or dangerous temptations, or both.

The state has to advance in this direction because at this stage of secularism it is dealing with two types of men. First, there are those who are guided by divergent world views, e.g., Communism, Fascism, Roman Catholic theocracy, liberalism, etc. And second, there are the masses who have lost all capacity for personal communication and are not guided by any norms.

As regards the antithetical world views, the state must try to achieve a balance by finding a common basis which will serve as a norm, even in the case of Christians and non-Christians. To appreciate the scope of this task it is necessary to set aside the traditional concept of "Christian nations" and to realize that the citizenry of the so-called Christian countries are made up in large measure of non-Christians. In general this attempt at compromise on the basis of views common to all, views which can thus unite even the extremes, will take as its starting point prevailing ideas of natural law, and especially the concept of human rights. For in the last resort what can the state in its difficult situation do but seize such a crutch,[2] such inflated ideas? [3] The human rights to which appeal is made are, as it were, a minimal norm which still stands at the disposal of the secular state.

As regards the depersonalized masses, the problem is that even the basic notion of human rights has been shoved so far from the center of their consciousness that appeal to it hardly moves them at all. Hence the temptation to appeal to those parts of man which remain intact even in the advanced stages of depersonalization, and which offer an entry, a back door, for the insinuation of impulses of will — and thereby for some kind of leadership — namely, the instincts and the nerves. The appropriate form of address to them is propaganda: working (visually and acoustically) on the emotions, using slogans and especially ideologies.

If the state is not to rely merely on external regimentation and on its power to enforce compliance — and in the interests of its own self-regard it cannot desire this — then it has to try to form some common will in its citizens. Only when there is a measure of agreement between the will of the people and the will of the state (or its constitution or government) is it possible to have a state without the compulsion of tyranny.

But this axiom of state life gives rise to the typically modern problem of how such a common will is to be achieved if in a great segment of the people personal identity has been largely submerged in a muffling collective, if the normative consciousness, by appeal to which something like a directed but authentic orientation of the will might emerge, has very largely vanished. In these circumstances, is it not tempting to take the path of propaganda, demagogy, and other devices for leading the masses?

To answer this question affirmatively is to admit that there is a trend toward totalitarian rule in this age of the mass society. It is also

[2] Cf. Karl Barth's essay on "The Christian Community and the Civil Community," in *Community, State, and Church: Three Essays* (Garden City, New York: Doubleday, 1960), p. 164. The full text of the pertinent citation is given in *ThE* 1, 430.

[3] Cf. Helmut Schelsky, "Zukunftsaspekte der industriellen Gesellschaft," *Merkur*, VIII, 1 (January, 1954), 24-28.

to note the existence of an immanent threat to democracy.[4] The first stage of this trend is the attempt to make of democracy itself a kind of pseudo religion. It must be realized that this democratic ideology will then necessarily incline to establish itself precisely in the educational field. Paradoxically its aim here will be a state monopoly whereby it can engender, protect, and organically nourish democratic ideas in the oncoming generations.

Now it would seem to us to be a dangerous error to try to counter the assertion that there is such a trend with some kind of statistical evidence that in modern democracies such a monopoly cannot be demonstrated inasmuch as those who pursue education apart from the state are allowed a wide measure of freedom. It is true enough that the manifold variations which are native and proper to a democracy make it difficult to discern the forms of a persistent trend. But when it comes to diagnosing such ultimate matters the statistical approach can lead to all kinds of dangerous errors.

More reliable for an analysis of the real situation at any rate is the fundamental truth that democracy depends in principle upon having mature and independent citizens, and that it can be in for serious trouble in an age when citizens have lost such independence, i.e., in the age of the mass society. Ideological tyranny is always an immanent threat to democracy. By nature, ideological tyranny establishes itself particularly in the field of education. This is why education is particularly endangered by the totalitarian trend in a democracy.

In both instances, then, namely, in that of the antithetical world views and in that of the depersonalized masses, there is little point in the church and Christian parents merely protesting, negating, and drawing limits in respect of public spheres which are a matter of common concern to them and to the state. They cannot just charge that the concept of human rights on which the democratic state is based is tenuous and inflated. For democracies are not Christian states and do not purport to be. They are inhabited by pagans and

---

[4] This threat has been perceptively noted by Reinhold Niebuhr in his *The Children of Light and The Children of Darkness: A Vindication of Democracy and a Critique of its Traditional Defence* (New York: Scribner's, 1945). The pertinent statements from his various writings have been assembled by Hans Hoffmann in *The Theology of Reinhold Niebuhr*, trans. Louise Pettibone Smith (New York: Scribner's, 1956), pp. 16 ff., 68 ff., and 198 ff. Cf. also Werner Kaegi, "Die Absolutheit des modernen Staates," *Universitas*, 1954, 2, pp. 135 ff.

semi-Christians. Neither can Christian parents merely protest against the totalitarian trend. For that would be only to protest the depersonalization of the age, and its symptomatic expressions in the state.

They cannot simply demand Christian preambles to the constitution, or Christian schools, and repudiate the wicked omnipotence of the state which continually refuses both, at least to the extent demanded. It is not enough, whether on the basis of Romans 13 or of Luther's social ethics, to postulate the state as it *ought* to be according to the will of God. (This leads only to abstract declamation, to which no one listens anyway.) For we are obviously dealing with men, with nihilisms and world views which are not in accordance with the will of God, and which therefore cannot possibly find expression in a state order which for its part is designed to be conformable to God's will.

The Role of the Church

The church's battle for a kind of education that is not incompatible with Christianity must not take the form of mere protests against signs of the growing danger of omnipotence on the part of the state, or of trying to win from the state a Christian coloration or as many Christian safeguards as possible. The effort cannot be, e.g., to inflate denominational statistics and then demand a corresponding increase in the number of denominational schools – which would in fact be as much of a sham as the statistics themselves ultimately are, however correct they may be in the formal sense.

The real task of the church is to make its presence known in the state in the form of a living reality which derives its life from the Word. In respect of the problem of education, e.g., this would mean that the church should be present as a living community of parents. Only in this way is it a legitimate entity which can play its part as a mature and independent subject in the democratic state. And only in this way can it be a true bulwark against the trend towards state omnipotence with its implied threat of educational monopoly. For even the degenerate state of complete and cruel omnipotence is such that it will be impressed only by other powers with which it must actually reckon. We could cite many instances of this from the experiences of the Third Reich, which was an extreme form of the omnipotent state.

This kind of approach to the state, whereby the church confronts the state with the living power of the believing community — in this case the community of parents — is appropriate both to the church and to the democratic state. It is appropriate to the church because the church is then present as a living reality, not just as a legal entity, a corporation of public law. And it is appropriate to the state because, as a democracy, the state is dependent on there being mature and independent partners and a true interplay of forces, i.e., of powers, within it.

This method of dealing with the state by way of a living community of Christian parents is incomparably more authentic, and in the long run far more effective, than for the church to try to win privileges — perhaps Christian or denominational schools — through intervention and negotiation on the part of ecclesiastical officials. In saying this we do not mean to discredit in principle official negotiations for arrangements or concordats with the state. The point is simply that, if these actions are to be legitimate, they can only express in contractual or legal form what has already, through the play of living forces, become indisputable fact. Or, in extreme cases, they can only prepare the ground contractually and legally for making effective forces which are already present and discernible.

Contractual or legal measures, however, which bear no relation to an existing or developing situation lead only to the building of facades with nothing behind them. They also cause the church to overburden itself with rights achieved in this way. E.g., the church might win the right to denominational schools and yet not have the contributing parents and available teachers which alone can make these schools meaningful, and hence legitimate. Such schools could be inauthentic, mere facades, crumbling party-walls which contain neither the recollection nor the promise of life.

Much would be gained if this negative side were clearly seen. We would at least know one way in which the church is *not* to fulfill its office of watchman. Later in the chapter we shall return to this matter of the watchman's office and how it is to be positively discharged, but first we must try to see clearly the precise nature of the rivalry between the state and the church (Christian parents) in the field of education. Then we shall endeavor to determine the rights of parents as one of the competing groups, and to ask the practical

— and theological — question as to how these rights are to be implemented.

The tension between the tasks of the state and those of the church is particularly pressing in the sphere of education. For the concern here is with the upbringing and nurture of man, and man is related to both state and church. The sphere of the state embraces the public ordering of man's life in society here on earth. That of the church embraces a claim which relates to the totality of his existence both temporal and eternal, to his existence before God. That sector of man's life which relates to the state is integrated into this larger whole and receives its meaning from it, even as Paul's theology of the state in Romans 13:1-17 is integrated into his total view of Christian existence as set forth in the larger context of the entire letter and of his writings as a whole.[5]

If it were possible, which it is not, to distinguish clearly between the natural and the supernatural goals of education, there would be a speedy end to all basic problems. For the natural sector could be assigned to the state, the supernatural to the church. This would be the kind of division which was sought in the ideology of the Third Reich, which proclaimed the state to be the lord of this world and generously left the world beyond (heaven and the sparrows) to the church.

The real problem arises precisely because, as we have stated, the sector of human life which relates to the state is interwoven into the totality of man's existence before God. For this means that even the so-called natural sphere, the relation of man to his fellow men, to his neighbor, to the orders, to the true and the beautiful, etc., depends decisively on the so-called supernatural goal, namely, man's destiny, what is said concerning him in Law and gospel. Decisive for my relation to the neighbor, e.g., is the question where I acquire my concept of man (and hence also of the fellow man), whether I regard man simply as a functionary in human society and hence see in him only the citizen, the business partner, the employee, the boss, or whether he is instead defined for me by the fact that — apart from all his functions — he has an existence under God, by the fact that he possesses a dignity not his own, and is "bought with a price" (I Cor.

[5] We touched on this above at pp. 248 ff.

6:20; 7:23). In like manner it is utterly decisive for my relation to the orders whether, e.g., I absolutize the state or regard it as altogether relative, an emergency order which receives its meaning from God's salvation history.

The church must consequently view the men entrusted to it in this total aspect. It cannot be content with a so-called supernatural destiny. It has to be concerned also with the natural or secular sphere.

This integration of the secular into the church's perspective is much more clearly perceived when we regard Christian parents, or better, the community of Christian parents, as the church's chief representative in the sphere of education. For what is entrusted to the parents as integral to their Christian responsibility is education in its totality, not just instruction in such rudiments of life as learning to eat and drink and to conduct oneself in society, but "training in Christianity," actual leading up to and into that existence before God. The task of Christian parenthood reveals in particularly clear contours the totality of the Christian claim.

Now obviously the state for its part has a specific standpoint from which it views the men entrusted to it, and from which they in turn are to view the state. We shall best express this as follows: The state regards its young citizens from the standpoint of equipping them for life, so that they will not become a burden to the state but play an active role in the political, cultural, and moral spheres. The state also regards them from the standpoint of bringing them up in such a way that they will get along well with all the other citizens under its aegis. At both these points it has a legitimate interest. There can be no denying that the state has here a duty at least to supervise, if not to initiate, appropriate measures to these ends.

Its interest, then, is not strictly in the philosophical or religious backgrounds which lead to the ends it seeks in education. To the state it makes no difference whether youthful capacities are developed, and an inner orientation attained, in consequence of an anthroposophical, a Marxist, or a (so-called) Christian world view. To this extent education might readily be delegated to these groups if the state could be sure that they would in fact attain the goals in which it is interested.

But there are drawbacks to this solution. For the state must reckon with the possibility that these groups, if allowed to be too independent, will press on to full emancipation and tend to become a state within a state, thus menacing the homogeneity of the body corporate. This would involve at once a jeopardizing of the ordering function of the state. For the state must hold together in one not only Roman Catholics, Protestants, and anthroposophists, but also Christians, neopagans, and atheists. Here then are the first seeds of conflict: Who is to guarantee to the state that the freedom of the church, e.g., will not lead to autocracy in a sphere where the state too is concerned, as in the sphere of education?

One might wonder whether in respect of this difficulty there could not be worked out an orderly division of roles between the forces which play a part in education, namely, the state, the parents, and the church. Could not religious instruction, e.g., be entrusted to the church, personal upbringing to parents, and academic learning to the state? Such a division of roles in fact affords no solution because, as we have seen, the spheres of competence of the three authorities overlap.

This is why it is impossible to see any clear solution. Indeed, our findings show that there cannot be any such solution. The zones of overlapping of the three authorities are charged with explosive material which is repeatedly set off in actual conflicts. And it is only within such conflicts, which cannot be headed off by drawing a priori lines of demarcation, that compromise solutions arise.

The theological background of compromise is evident again at this point. Compromise is the *modus vivendi* of a world which does not run smoothly. Because this world is composed of emergency orders, and because it reflects the divine likeness only in refracted form, there have to be such things as pragmatic arrangements and agreements.[6]

Nevertheless, even in this dark night of the world all cats are not gray. Even within the circle of compromise there are constant factors which provide direction. The chief of these, as regards the present case, grows out of the fact that the function of the state is to serve and not to rule. It receives its purpose and meaning not from itself but from the salvation history within which it has to exercise its interim functions. Hence it is neither authorized nor able

[6] On compromise see *ThE* 1, Chapters 25-28.

to assume responsibility for the whole man, as is required in education. Indeed this wholeness of man is brought to light only in the same salvation history from which the state unwittingly derives its own task. This is why responsibility for the whole man is allotted to those authorities which are aware of their integration into this salvation history, and which see both the wholeness of man and the function of the state in its light. These authorities are the community under the Word, and, in the sphere of education, the community of Christian parents. The thesis of the minimal state is thus enunciated in the sphere of education too.

Luther pointed out again and again that the state must not concern itself with man's salvation. There must be no theocratic tendencies. The state must limit itself to matters of secular order, to life and property, and leave the soul alone. To use the terms of our present discussion, the whole man is *not* entrusted to it. Wherever the state attempts to do more than this, it must be resisted.[7] It must not try to become "a shepherd instead of a hangman."[8] In making this distinction Luther did not have in view the typical modern instances of the ideological state or the pseudotheocratic welfare state which claims the whole man. He was thinking rather of the state which claims to advance the Christian cause, e.g., by representing the Turkish wars as crusades: "The emperor, poor, mortal maggot-fodder that he is . . . has the gall to speak of himself as the foremost defender of the Christian faith."[9]

If the state claims the whole man and seeks to have saving significance for him, it is guilty of two fatal confusions. First, it confuses Law and gospel by transferring itself from the side of the former where it belongs to the side of the latter where it claims the soul and pretends to be its savior. Second, it confuses the two kingdoms by not being content with its allotted kingdom on the left hand but interfering in the affairs of the kingdom on the right hand. Both lead to revolt

[7] See Luther's *Temporal Authority: To What Extent it Should be Obeyed; LW* 45, 111-112.

[8] *LW* 45, 113; cf. also *LW* 45, 83-84, 105 and the Luther passages cited in Johannes Heckel, *Lex charitatis. Eine Juristische Untersuchung über das Recht in der Theologie Martin Luthers* (Munich: Bayrische Akademie der Wissenschaften, 1953), p. 151.

[9] *WA* 15, 278. Cf. Helmut Lamparter, *Luthers Stellung zum Türkenkrieg* (Munich: Lempp, 1940), pp. 80 ff.

against the proper order of the state and are to be resisted. Only in terms of the doctrines of Law and gospel and of the two kingdoms is it possible to see and establish the limits of the state and its restricted functions within salvation history.

But we have not yet come to the fundamental arguments in support of our thesis of the minimal role of the state in educational matters. We come up against these only when we establish from another angle the primacy of the educational claims of parents over those of the state, or, more precisely, when we examine the question as to who is here delegating his claims to whom. Does the state perhaps delegate its educational rights at some points, e.g., in personal instruction and training for life, to the parents? [10] Or is it rather that the parents delegate their educational rights in some points, e.g., academic instruction, to the state? From what has been said thus far about the state as an emergency order we can already guess where the answer to this question must lie. Yet we must consider the matter afresh. We shall do so at this point by undertaking to examine the matter of parental rights in education.

The Rights of Parents

There is no doubt that for Luther (and for Lutheran social ethics generally) all education derives ultimately from parental authority alone, irrespective of the particular orders in which it is practiced. The main proof of this is to be found in Luther's exposition of the Fourth Commandment in the Large Catechism, in which parents are taken to be authorized by God, indeed to stand towards me in the place of God. "Young people must be taught to revere their parents as God's representatives." [11] As God is above man, so by way of analogy parents are representatives of the "proper distinction" — and consequently of the "inequality" — between superiors and subordinates. [12] They thus represent a basic law of the whole social structure, which in all its aspects — even in its form as the state, involving

[10] The question is legitimate, for the state does take over the care and rearing of children in cases of parental neglect. In such instances, though, is the state taking back a function once delegated to the parents or is it simply performing the function of a guardian?

[11] Martin Luther, The Large Catechism, I, 4, 108; trans. Robert H. Fischer in BC 379.

[12] Ibid., p. 380.

the relation between ruler and subject or state and citizen — derives from this primal relation between parents and children.

Luther writes: "Out of the authority of parents all other authority is derived and developed. Where a father is unable by himself to bring up his child, he calls upon a schoolmaster to teach him; if he is too weak, he enlists the help of his friends and neighbors; if he passes away, he confers and delegates his authority and responsibility to others appointed for the purpose. Likewise he must have domestics (man-servants and maid-servants) under him to manage the household. Thus all who are called masters stand in the place of parents and derive from them their power and authority to govern. In the Scriptures they are all called fathers because in their responsibility they act in the capacity of fathers and ought to have fatherly hearts toward their people." [13]

Here the parent-child relation is regarded as a truly "primal" relation, inasmuch as parents actually represent God himself. Whether this thesis is right or not we shall have to consider later. For the moment we shall treat it simply as a thesis, and restrict ourselves to indicating *how* this representation of God takes place.

Parents represent God on the one hand in respect of the Law, for they represent the will of God, the will of him who is over us.[14] But they also represent God in respect of the gospel and of grace. For watchful care and protection is shown us through our parents from the first day of our lives. Without them we should have "perished a hundred times in our own filth." [15] They thus represent the mercy of God.

Naturally the question still remains by what right this primal authority is given to parents, an authority which makes all other authority, including that of office and of orders and of the state, a delegated authority. By what right is the structure of authority so conceived that God himself stands at the head of the hierarchy, and the first delegated authority is vested in a person (the earthly father) while the authority of office is derivative from these two?

[13] Large Catechism, I, 4, 141-142; *BC* 384. Luther distinguishes between fatherhood by blood and fatherhood by office, between the father at home and the fathers of the nation (*ibid.*, I, 4, 158; *BC* 387). His derivation of the latter from the former has been traced by Heckel, *op. cit.*, pp. 107-108.

[14] See Luther's Large Catechism, I, 4, 149 and 151; *BC* 385 and 386.

[15] *Ibid.*, I, 4, 129; *BC* 383.

Such a ranking of earthly authorities is not something self-evident. For the other side of the coin is that persons, i.e., father and mother, are subject to the governing authorities, i.e., to an authority of office. How are we to explain the singular fact that the structure of authority as it actually exists is just the opposite of what it ought to be in principle, that office is in fact above person whereas person is in principle above office? How is it that father is in fact subject to the very authority of which in principle he is the source?

So far as we can see, this important and basic question has not received the attention it should have in Lutheran theology.[16] But where it is ignored, there easily arise those authoritarian-sounding statements so dear to the heart of some kinds of confessionalism. Confessionalists are sometimes satisfied with the simple affirmation: "Lutheranism says . . ." Or they regard a thesis such as this as the product of its age and setting, reference being made to the patriarchal tendencies by which Lutheranism was conditioned.

If, dissatisfied with such unsatisfying explanations, we would examine the theological basis of this thesis of the father's primal authority, we would do best to begin with the prior question whether in Luther and Lutheranism there are not, in addition to a mere assertion of the hierarchical structure, other elements which distinguish the office of father from that of governing authority.[17] The fact is that there are such elements. It is said consistently concerning the order of marriage — which underlies and alone makes possible the office of father — that it is a holy estate which is well-pleasing to God, was instituted by him, and is confirmed by his Word.[18]

Of no other order would it be conceivable that the relation of the participants involved should be seen in direct analogy to the relation of Christ to his church or to the Father. Yet this is how Ephesians 5:21-33 and I Corinthians 11:3 ff. view the relation of husband and wife.[19] The other orders, however, e.g., the state, are postlapsarian

[16] Werner Elert barely touches on the problem in his *Morphologie des Luthertums* (Munich: Beck, 1932), II, 93.

[17] The sharp distinction we have been making between the authority of office and that of the person ought not to obscure the fact that in Lutheran theology paternal authority also bears the mark of an "office" entrusted by God.

[18] Apology of the Augsburg Confession, XXIII, 28 ff., to cite only one of many examples.

[19] See, to cite just one example, Luther's "Order for Marriage for Common Pastors" which he incorporated into his Small Catechism in 1529; *LW* 53, 114.

emergency orders. They belong to the kingdom on the left hand, and what takes place in them is part of God's "alien work." [20]

Marriage, however, does not have this broken relation to God. Nowhere do we read of marriage — or of offices such as the paternal office which arise within it — that it is an emergency order, assimilating itself to the laws of the fallen world after the manner of the state with its power of the sword. In the Noachic covenant such assimilation is basic to the order of the fallen world. But in the Noachic covenant marriage is *not* one of the entities thus modified by the fall. On the contrary, Luther can speak of marriage in terms of a loving and serving I-Thou relationship, terms which otherwise occur only where he is speaking of the "proper work" of God, and of immediacy to the neighbor in the kingdom on the right hand. Indeed, when Luther sees the state itself in the light of the paternal office he seems to forget for a moment that it belongs to the kingdom on the left hand, for the idea of love and service then becomes central.[21]

This pre-eminence of marriage vis-à-vis all other orders admits of only one theological explanation, namely, that marriage has the dignity of a true order of creation whereas the other orders do not. They have a purely interim and provisional function whereas marriage goes back to a direct divine command in a world still innocent and is the only order not evoked later by the fact of a broken and fallen world.[22]

It is no contradiction of this original dignity of marriage as an order of creation if the purposes it serves (though not marriage itself) can be changed by the fall, and if — somewhat analogously to the state — it can be regarded as a remedy against sexual chaos. "Because of the temptation to immorality each man should have his own wife" (I Cor. 7:2, 9). This function of marriage is also mentioned in the Confessions, where it is appended without a break to the original purpose at creation.[23] Such close association is possible only on the ground that the order of marriage as such is not established because of sin. It derives from creation and survives the fall intact, but then takes on

---

[20] Recall how Luther derives the state from the fall in his *Lectures on Genesis* (2:16-17); *LW* 1, 104. See also WA 52, 26.

[21] See WA 10$^{\text{I},1}$, 656; 15, 625, lines 8-9; 8, 328, lines 15 ff.; and 623, lines 4ff.

[22] Cf. Gen. 1:27 ff. See the Apology of the Augsburg Confession, XXIII, 7, 12, 29-30, and (in the German version) 67. See also Luther's "Order for Marriage for Common Pastors"; *LW* 53, 114.

[23] See the Apology of the Augsburg Confession, XXIII, 7-22.

additional healing functions, so that it is not merely oriented positively towards the goal of creation but is also directed negatively against that which imperils this goal in the interim.

After these necessary deliberations on the rank of the paternal office and its primal authority, we may now return to our original line of thought. We recall that the point at issue is whether the state delegates educational authority to the parents, or vice versa. Only when this question is cleared up can we attain to a perspicuous doctrine of parental rights in the Reformation sense.

The mere assertion that Lutheranism proclaims the paternal office to be the source of state authority could not be regarded as adequate, for we had still to ask on what grounds Lutheranism could legitimately make such an assertion. We have now seen that the assertion is based on the original character of marriage, which is what distinguishes it from all other orders.

To say that marriage is an order of creation is to say that paternal authority too is an order of creation, in which there is an implicit relation of superordination and subordination which constitutes the basis of the educational process. This is the only adequate reason for regarding the parental office as the true agent of education, and for regarding all other agents (e.g., the school, and indirectly the state) as delegates of parental authority.

There is involved here, however, a complex web of relations between parents and the state. For the fact that educational authority is delegated by the parents does not mean that the state is merely an object of parental will. To put it rather crudely, the state is not simply an agency for providing teachers and instruction as may be required. For parents are themselves citizens, and hence "subject to the governing authorities." In their quality as agents of creation parents outrank the state and are a model of its authority. In their quality as persons, however, the state outranks them, for the state is always a prior reality in which they have their being. Nevertheless, paternal authority is the center and source of all educational authority.[24] And it is evident that this principle is not without significance for the thesis of a minimal state.

[24] On the question of how far primacy belongs to the father as over against the mother within the family see Helmut Thielicke, *The Ethics of Sex,* trans. John W. Doberstein (New York: Harper & Row, 1964), esp. pp. 3-13 and 145-162.

The Personal Element in the Orders

It is here, in the cell of life constituted by parents and children, that the order of the world has its basis. This order is thus built up from below, from personal elements. It is not deduced and constructed impersonally from above, e.g., out of principles. This personal element, which is an integral part of the orders by derivation from the parental office, has already been presented in its essential features. We shall simply add here a few thoughts to underscore the point.

1) Obedience to those above us does not have the character of servility or compulsion. If obedience is genuine, it is rendered gladly and cheerfully, in love and freedom. "Therefore man-servants and maid-servants [who here represent subordinates generally in all kinds of orders] should take care not only to obey their masters and mistresses, but also to honor them as their own parents and do everything that they know is expected of them, not from compulsion and reluctantly but gladly and cheerfully." [25]

What is ultimately at stake is not the prestige of orders but the respecting of persons. To go back to the results of our investigation of the concept of authority, we may put it thus: When authority is legitimate and is based on confidence, it does not involve compulsion but is an overpowering authority which induces obedience by persuasion and which addresses itself to freedom. This is possible, however, only if its basis is personal rather than institutional.

For an order cannot be the object of love and confidence but only of judgment (e.g., as to its utility or inutility, its legitimacy or illegitimacy) and of either a readiness to submit to it or a resolve to resist it. Only a person, or an entity personally defined and expressed, can be the object of love and confidence. This is why the paternal basis of all order — and the fact that the various representatives of the various orders are only acting on behalf of the paternal office — is of such incomparable importance.

For the same reason, what is of crucial importance in the huge organizations of modern mass society is that they should establish possibilities for the expression and recognition of human motives — with a view to the maintenance and kindling of human qualities (e.g., love, confidence, readiness for sacrifice) and to preventing social and

[25] Luther's Large Catechism, I, 4, 143; *BC* 385.

economic structures from becoming no more than inhuman pragmatic machinery. (Awareness of this is the positive element in the idea of "human relations." Where it is construed as merely a psychological trick, however, it cynically abuses the human element.)

Lutheran social ethics consequently is safeguarded against the abstract dominion of the institutional, and especially against all forms of statism, because it is oriented, one might say, to the institutional minimum. It carries within it, as we have seen, an appeal to gladness and cheerfulness, to immediate readiness [promptitudo] and spontaneity, to freedom and initiative, which logically demands that law and regimentation be kept to a minimum.

The influence of the Reformation doctrine of justification may be seen here. One of its axioms is that wherever the gospel predominates, wherever it kindles our love toward him who first loved us (I John 4:19), the Law recedes. Where spontaneity arises, commands become superfluous.[26] Now the orders are institutional forms of the Law. Thus, to the degree that there is success in achieving within them truly personal relations – and the resultant spontaneity – regimentation is unnecessary.

Naturally, one must recall at this point our earlier distinction between orders of compulsion and orders of direction.[27] It goes without saying, e.g., that the regulation of traffic is very largely – though not wholly – independent of our spontaneous readiness to comply. Yet even here the stock argument against the endless multiplication of traffic signs and signals is that more initiative, responsibility, and discretion should be left to the drivers. The more successfully orders are personalized and their human background – motives, intentions, concern, readiness for service, etc. – brought to light, the more the orders lose, as they should, the quality of regimentation. And, in addition, the more the way is prepared for a diminution of the purely institutional aspect.

This is true even where Christians and non-Christians coexist and countless multitudes fail to discern the paternal background of the world, and hence the ultimate validation of such processes. The spon-

---

[26] See *ThE* 1, 56 ff., and Wilfried Joest, *Gesetz und Freiheit. Das Problem des Tertius usus legis bei Luther und die neutestamentliche Paränese* (2nd ed.; Göttingen: Vandenhoeck & Ruprecht, 1956), pp. 21 ff.

[27] See above pp. 155 ff.

taneity involved in our relation to God the Father, as posited in the doctrine of justification, has both brought to light and itself made use of certain structures of the mystery of personhood in general, structures which continue to have significance and play a role in the order of the world even where men are no longer aware of the person of God, who is the basis of all personhood. Even then there remain, as it were, ethical echoes of a Christian awareness.

2) Parents must realize that they are themselves authorized, that theirs is a derived authority. They must "consider that they owe obedience to God." [28] Thus do parents always come up against their limit. In contrast, the suprapersonal order, the order which emancipates itself from the person, has a tendency to absolutize itself and to become an abstract system.

On the political level this tendency reaches its extreme in the totalitarian state. On the intellectual level it manifests itself as a tendency to construct metaphysical systems and thereby to absolutize the spirit. On both levels, however, it is obvious that ultimately even God himself is absorbed in the all-embracing system. On the political level he becomes an expression of the power of religion: "Religion must be maintained for the sake of the people." On the intellectual level he becomes a religious symbol for the absolute spirit (e.g., in Hegel).

For this reason too it is important that the order not become impersonal, lest there arise a kind of impersonal autonomy. Only persons — persons under God — can be and remain authorized. If persons violate their dependence, they "sin," and can be called to account for it. Systems, orders, and institutions, however, are material spheres which cannot sin. At most, they can only be called bad in respect of functional efficiency, but this is not yet to put the finger on the real reason for their failure. If one may speak in terms of this kind of value category at all, then the reason for their failure lies in the sin of the persons involved in them.

Because the reference is to persons, and because institutions cannot be summoned to repent, it is important to note that Luther refuses to speak of "Christian" institutions (states or guilds) and reserves the attribute "Christian" for persons (princes, etc.). He who claims to be

---

[28] Luther, Large Catechism, I, 4, 168; *BC* 388.

Christian must be subject to judgment and grace, repentance and forgiveness. This cannot be true of an institution.[29]

The more impersonal an order becomes – one has only to think of the anonymity of the great corporations – the less can persons be called to account for their sin. This is why the most strenuous efforts must be made to preserve or to restore the personal character of institutions, to give prominence to persons (even in the external sense of representation) and to bring to light human motives. Only thus can institutions be kept from sinking into the abstract world of things and machines, and from being viewed exclusively in terms of the factual requirements which obtain. But such personal awareness is possible only if awareness of the paternal basis of the orders is preserved.

3) In Lutheran social ethics the personal element in the orders may be seen in two other essential respects.

It may be seen first in the fact that the dualism of state and church is in some degree transcended in the office of father. At the point where authority first arises this dualism does not yet obtain, for the father is both in one. He is the lord who rules his family – here is the basis of state authority. And he is also the priest and pastor of his household – here at least in part is the basis of the authority of the preaching office. In this twofold function the earthly fatherhood derives from the heavenly, for it is God who both sustains the orders in the kingdom on the left hand and also calls individuals by his word into his kingdom on the right hand.

This union of secular government and spiritual pastorate in the person of the father, where the orders have their origin, should not mislead us into thinking that there can be the same positive and tension-free relation at points other than this source, i.e., in world processes. This, e.g., is the contention of Karl Barth when he tries to depict the two kingdoms geometrically as two concentric circles.[30] Barth can think in this way because of his doctrine of gospel and Law. The Lutheran distinction of the two kingdoms makes such a view impossible.[31]

[29] Cf. Karl Holl, *Gesammelte Aufsätze zur Kirchengeschichte,* I (Tübingen: Mohr, 1923), 347 ff.

[30] See Karl Barth, "The Christian Community and the Civil Community," *op. cit.*

[31] See *ThE* 1, Chapter 7, and the discussion of Reformed teaching pp. 565 ff. below.

The personal element in the Lutheran doctrine of the orders may also be seen in the fact that these orders all represent the one sphere in which love is active.[32] It is not true of Luther in any case, as it may be of Melanchthon, that the orders (political, economic, etc.) are there first, and that men are then embraced within them only as functionaries. Indeed, the reverse is true. Men are there first, the I and the Thou, men who are summoned to love, and their personal relations are now regulated by the various orders.

This means that my relation to another is never defined or limited by a mere order. The other person is for me never the representative of a purely material function. He is not just a politician, boss, subordinate, colleague, or competitor. And my relation to him can never be restricted to this material connection. Even within the framework of the orders the other is for me always a man, an object of love, a personal Thou. For the presiding judge the offender is not just an object to be sentenced. He is also a neighbor. The personal relation transcends the material sphere of the legal order.

This express consideration of the relation between the material and personal aspects in the doctrine of the orders was necessary in order that we might set forth the theological presuppositions underlying the relation between state and parents in the sphere of education.

The Primacy of Parental Rights

When in debates on educational policy and similar matters the slogan "parental rights" is used by Evangelicals, it is usually in naive appropriation of the Roman Catholic concept of parental rights, which is based on natural law. This is why we had to blaze a new trail to the concept which would be more in keeping with Reformation theology. We have now reached the point where we can deduce from our present findings the consequences for the relation between state and parents in education, and therewith also for parental rights in the Reformation sense.

1) In respect of education the state has no right or competence — in the light of the primal authority of the paternal office — to allocate to parents their place in the educational process, as if the state were in substance the superior authority and could allow itself to be repre-

---

[32] Cf. the distinction between Luther and Melanchthon set forth in Elert, *op. cit.*, II, 23 ff.

sented by parents in such limited way as it might itself deem appropriate.[33] Indeed, the case is the very opposite: The state has to derive its educational task from that of the parents. Accordingly it has to respect its limits vis-à-vis the competence of the parents. Lutheran ethics thinks in terms of persons, not systems. By its very nature the state is only an instrument for getting the job done; it does not itself assign the task, much less determine its scope or meaning.

2) As ultimate authority over education does not reside in the state, neither does it reside in the educational system, despite the thesis that education is autonomous. For education must always proceed on the basis of the goal envisioned. What a man is to become, however, can be determined only in the light of God, and of the fact that man himself is an object of faith. For every doctrine of man rests on a particular faith, whether that faith be true or false. And education can proceed only within the framework of a particular view of man, whatever that may be. Accordingly, education must give thought to the ways and means but it cannot determine the ends. These it must accept from a source outside itself. The presumed autonomy of education really rests on the illusion of an assumed autarchy.

From this angle too we thus arrive at the central principle of Lutheran ethics, namely, that teachers and educators are only the representatives of parents, deputized to execute their will. For it is the parents who are responsible for the goal of education until their children are sufficiently mature to assume responsibility for themselves. The oath which parents customarily take when they bring their children for baptism expressly imposes this responsibility upon them. Nor does the responsibility relate only to instruction in faith, in the narrower sense. It relates rather to being a Christian in the world, and hence also to a corresponding understanding of all the secular spheres dealt with in the school curriculum. Granted the Reformation understanding of faith, this breadth of responsibility is beyond question.

3) One of the fundamental requirements of every educational enterprise is that those responsible for it, i.e., the school and the parents, should be agreed in their basic orientation, in their view of what is the goal of education, or — to put it more modestly and cautiously — that in respect of this goal they should at least not be in open disagree-

[33] This was the position of National Socialism.

ment, pulling in different directions. Otherwise the result will be that pathological phenomenon of modern life, especially of modern youth, which we call schizophrenia of consciousness.

This pathological phenomenon is inevitable if in different classes different teachers operate on the basis of different philosophies, history being presented, e.g., from the standpoint of pragmatic or historical relativism, English from the standpoint of humanism, and biology from the standpoint of a vitalistic understanding of the world and of man. The younger the pupil, the more defenseless he is against authoritarian positions, and the more he will be overpowered and torn and confused by what for older students would be merely a Socratic provocation forcing them to adopt a position of their own.

In the light of what has been said, true philosophical homogeneity, or — again to put it more cautiously — the avoidance of a destructive philosophical antithesis, can be achieved only if the primacy of the rights of parents in education is asserted and established. This means concretely that it is the parents who should decide on the kind of school which seems best to them. To give a new twist to our thesis about the minimal state, one might say that parents should be granted "maximal" authority in the sphere of education.

The Implementation of Parental Rights

The fundamental principles of the Lutheran doctrine of education as we have just expounded them are empty declamation so long as parents in fact are not what in Lutheran ethics they are taken to be, i.e., so long as they are not Christians, and so long as they are ignorant of the relationship between their Christian faith and the problems of school and education. The state can ignore, or at least fail to take seriously, the rights of parents — and is indeed led to do so — only because parents do not seem to espouse a faith or pursue a purpose with respect to education. Indeed, from the perspective of the state parents seem to be what in fact they very largely are, namely, a segment of the population which is unable to make up its mind, which is without direction and open to suggestion from clerics and others, a sum of isolated individuals. The fact that they happen to be parents does not constitute them a purposeful unit any more than the fact that they are of medium build, collect stamps, are blond or brunette, or male or female. None of these things is conducive to the solidarity of a social group. Parents are in fact an amorphous body with no true contours, and groups of parents who really know what they want are rare.

This is as true of non-Christian as of Christian parents, at least insofar as they too stand for definite principles or positions and are necessarily interested in implementing their will in the area of education. We shall discuss the problem, however, only in relation to Christian parents, leaving it to the reader to make appropriate application of the ethical conclusions to the responsibility which devolves upon non-Christian parents.

Who then are these so-called Christian parents? In large measure they are people who are essentially unchurched. In the state churches of Europe particularly the situation is such that large masses of the people are only nominally Christian. They have been baptized and they want their children to be baptized. But apart from that they do not consider themselves active members of the church. This situation makes it difficult, of course, to speak of the rights of Christian parents and thereby to conjure up the picture of a group of parents having a particular mind or will. Even to mention such a thing can evoke knowing smiles and disrespect among knowledgable legislators.

This means that the church is guilty of a lie if it uses statistics relating to its extensive membership as the basis for its claims in the field of education, e.g., its right to establish denominational schools. "Today, in the age of advanced secularism, the demand for Christian or denominational schools on the ground of parental rights can only smack of power politics. It is in keeping with neither the dignity nor the integrity of the Church to support such a demand by appeal to the membership statistics of the folk church. . . . The highest freedom of all, that of believing in Christ, should never be made a matter of compulsion" [34] — as would be the case if the children of all those who for sloth, or for other irrelevant or only semi-relevant reasons, have failed to take their names off the church rolls, were to be placed in Christian schools. We might even go so far as to say that the church ought to protect the conscience of unbelievers against all such clerical and theocratic strivings. In so doing it will protect the faith committed to it from degenerating into a Christian ideology and becoming the shibboleth of hypocracy.

In the first place, then, the rights of parents are illusory so long as

[34] O. Hammelsbeck.

the parents themselves do not know why they have them, so long as in their own lives they are not themselves oriented to the goal toward which they are presumably to educate their children. But in the second place, parental rights are illusory so long as they are something which can be farmed out, so long as it is possible for them to be handed over to the church or the school, so long as parents are not capable of accepting and exercising them themselves because they lack any true relationship of their own to these rights.

This farming out is different in principle from the delegating of which we have spoken. A man can delegate only when he himself has full power to act and then exercises this power through a representative. To delegate is to transfer power which the one who delegates could himself accept and exercise. But in educational matters many parents simply are not capable of accepting the power which is properly theirs. Hence they do not carry through a true act of delegation to state, church, or school. This is why we have chosen to describe their action in terms of the apparently more appropriate concept of farming out. They hand over a right which they themselves are incapable of using. But such a right is a forfeited right. This is why it cannot be legitimately subsumed under the rubric of parental rights.

To say this is to bring to light the difficulty to which any modern debate on parental rights is exposed. Parental rights are necessarily inherent in parenthood as it ought to be. The empirical state of parenthood, however, is such that it threatens to discredit parental rights.

It is because of this type of man, this nominal Christian, that the state continually threatens to become omnipotent, and is led and even forced to claim a monopoly in education. Where the masses have no will or goal of their own, the strongest voice of command is always likely to have its way. At this point totalitarian trends can arise even in democratic forms of government. Immaturity is the torch which kindles the fires of totalitarianism.

In the light of this, certain tasks are set for the church, both negative and positive. (These naturally apply also to people of other philosophical persuasion, and the Christian statesman or legislator will have to consider this fact when he is called upon to decide what rights are to be granted to specific philosophically or religiously oriented groups within the population, e.g., groups of parents.) Negatively, the rights of Christian parents, as we have said, are not to be championed along legal lines in the sense of demanding Christian or denominational schools for that portion of the population which can be called Christian on statistical grounds. This could only lead to an educational policy for the church which would be rampant with hypocrisy and conflicts of conscience, and dedicated to the building of a mere facade of Christianity. Positively, the church in its preaching must pay particular attention to young parents. It must lead them to an awareness and acceptance of their powers, as well as to purposeful and legitimate acts of delegation.

First, as regards the negative task, no order should ever be established, whether in school or church (e.g., a liturgical reform) which is simply handed down from above by way of contract and official negotiation. Only those orders should be set up which develop from below, even though their development may be stimulated and fostered from above. In practice this means that the emergence and acceptance of parental rights has to come from communities of parents which are fashioned by the Word of God. Only these can do more than merely farm out forfeited rights (an attempt which is intrinsically nonsensical). Only they can delegate, in the true sense of the word, and only thus can action in this sphere be spiritually legitimate.

This may mean that for the moment the church will fight only for the right to establish experimental and model schools. It will not renounce its claim to denominational schools, but neither will it claim more in this respect than what is rightfully its due and what it can actually handle. Concretely this means that the church will never — not even when things take a Christian turn or at other tactically favorable moments — the church will never anticipate developments by staking out advance claims to an expanded educational province, claiming areas which for the moment it can neither occupy nor cultivate because it has neither the necessary teachers nor enough children of Christian parents. The church's claims must never outstrip the background and source of supply provided by Christian parents.

At this point there is need of warning against a certain misunderstanding. We are not suggesting that a certain degree of "Christianity" has to be attained before there can be a right to set up denominational schools. How could such a thing be ascertained anyway? Would we not first have to set up and practice a specific phenomenology of the religious consciousness? More urgent than this question concerning the distinguishing marks of Christianity, however, is the need of warning against inauthentic and exaggerated claims on the part of the church. The church must guard against making excessive claims — claims which lack validity because they are merely formal and statistical — in a sphere where for lack of personnel and resources it simply cannot do the job.

By the way, we concede that it is perfectly legitimate theologically to ask whether Christian schools should not be demanded irrespective of the will and capacity of the parents. Such a demand might rest on the desire to set up mission schools in areas which are particularly secularized and alienated from the church. In this case one would have to give serious consideration to the idea of a kind of emergency right in the sphere of education whereby the organized church would be obliged to speak up for and act on behalf of parents who are no longer competent in faith. Thus proclamation would proceed not by way of first evangelizing the parents and then bringing into being a Christian school, but by way of first establishing the Christian school in order thereby to influence the parents.

The following argument might be used to support this idea. Like the press, the school is dialectically related to its environment. Rightly understood, both must be not only an expression of their milieu but also a normative authority for it. Both have to shape the world in which they are set. Hence the school does not always have to arise out of the faith of a believing community; it can also serve to induce this faith.

Nevertheless, it would be quite false to make of this — i.e., the promise of such faith — a constructive principle of educational policy from which to deduce a corresponding educational strategy. For even from the standpoint of the mission school idea the question necessarily arises how far the believing community already undergirds the school, and hence is already in existence. Even if there be no community of believing parents, even if such a community is expected to arise only by way of the witness of a Christian school, one must surely assume the existence of a community of believing teachers. A denominational school is impossible without at least this minimal presupposition. Even if it is conceived as a mission school, one has to think first in terms of constituting this much of a church, i.e., this community of believing teachers, and the training of teachers would have to be a prior order of business. Even in connection with the mission school idea there thus arises again the problem of the facade, of hypocrisy, and of illegitimate claims which we discussed in relation to the community of believing parents. The problem is the same. It simply crops up at a different point.

Second, as regards what we called the positive task of the church, the demand that teaching and preaching should concern itself particularly with young parents cannot mean only that the church should invite these people to the worship services. It must also gather them into communities in which they can be taught what the command and gracious gift of God implies for the education of their children, as regards both goals and methods, or – as one might say – what the baptism of their children implies. Only in this way can there be an organic growth and expansion of the educational province of the Christian community. Each strip of new land must be won in order that it can be truly occupied. It cannot simply be passed down by legal inheritance or taken over on the basis of denominational statistics. Only the vitality of the community can validate its extension.

This is the only way in which parents can represent a true will in the political sphere, and thus counter as a power in their own right the state's tendency towards omnipotence. In the educational sphere church politics – and the church has to deal politically with political authorities – can only be a matter of securing by law and contract the opportunity to set up Christian schools and to establish Christian influence in other schools. It can only be a matter of ensuring that the legal presuppositions will be there when the time is deemed right to move ahead with concrete action in ways that are authentic.

Concretely this might mean that the right to denominational schools is guaranteed in principle, perhaps even in some relation to denominational statistics, but that no attempt is made to build facades on these lands which are guaranteed in principle. Only those portions are claimed which can actually be occupied.

The same would hold true of hours granted by the state for religious instruction. It would be foolish, unrealistic, and inauthentic for the church to insist that these hours all be used regardless of whether there are enough qualified teachers, and regardless of what the non-qualified teachers actually do in these hours. It can be part of the church's obedience and faithfulness to forego religious instruction, leaving part of the ground allotted to it lie fallow, but to work the more intensively at the preparations which must precede actual cultivation.

The educational policy of the church must not be swayed, then, by the externally favorable opportunities of the moment, opportunities which could be anything but spiritual! Opportunities of this kind may arise where the people in power incline toward a certain denomination, or where denominational statistics are democratically applied, or both. Ecclesiastical officials who try to capitalize on such opportunities would be like officers without a crew. They would be representing and promulgating not the verities of their faith, but its vacuity.

Here too the best, and above all the most realistic, policy for the church is simply obedience, obediently to proclaim the message of Jesus Christ, to whom children too belong. Here, and here alone, is the starting point of the battle for education. In other words, the battle must begin in the church. Only as the church seeks first the kingdom of God will all other things — including the Christian school — be its "as well" (Matt. 6:33). But if it makes that which can only be added in passing the main object of its striving, it will become a church of power politics and clericalism, a pseudo church. More important than any results it might achieve, therefore, is the insight that the church itself is confronted by the decision between obedience and disobedience, between truth and falsehood. Both judgment and renewal always begin with the household of God itself (I Pet. 4:17; Jer. 25:29; Ezek. 9:6).

In conclusion we repeat that the thesis of the minimal state, which we have been trying to defend, is connected in principle with the fact that the state is a secondary order as compared with the paternal office. It is secondary because its authority is derived from that of the paternal office and because — unlike the latter — it is an emergency order and not an order of creation. Whether in fact such a minimum can be attained depends on whether there is a mature and legitimate counterpart that can stand over against the state, or whether in the field of education, e.g., the state is the only power involved or is faced with a mature and authentic competitor in the church, particularly the community of believing parents.

Whether the needle points towards the minimal state or the maximal state, then, does not depend primarily on what the constitution of the state in question may say on the subject. Neither can the self-understanding of a democracy preserve it from involuntary tendencies towards the maximal, the totalitarian state. Whether the movement is towards the minimal or the maximal state depends rather on the partners involved. In effect the pointer tells more about the partners than about the state itself. The fate of a democracy is thus decided, not by the actions one demands of the democratic state, but by one's own actions. Democracy stands or falls with the participation of its citizens.

This fact simply underscores once again the personal structure of the orders, which is one of the axioms of Lutheran social ethics. Action in the orders is based ultimately not on institutional constructions but on personal decisions. The institutional is related to the personal as the secondary is to the primary, as superstructure is to substructure. Where the personal presuppositions are lacking, institutions are left hanging in the air. They become an institutional lie. Thus, the negative postulate that the state be minimal is identical with the positive postulate that the personalization of life be maximal.

We have spoken of the play of forces involved in a democracy, and we have examined one basic form of it in terms of a concrete model, namely, the competition between the state and parents — in this case specifically Christian parents — in the field of education. In so doing we have accomplished two things. We have investigated a basic political question. We have also gained insight into an ethical question which could not be clarified without raising some very fundamental issues, namely, the question of parental rights and their implementation in the sphere of education.

16.

The Minimal State in Welfare

The Problem of Institutionalizing Love

The question whether a maximal or a minimal state is desirable takes concrete shape today — and in any foreseeable future — in the general movement towards social perfection and its political expression in the welfare state. This movement is an alarming phenomenon even from a purely political standpoint inasmuch as the totalitarian state and the democratic state are both caught up in it, each in its own way: the totalitarian state because it necessarily seeks to penetrate every sphere of life and hence to take over the care of children, the chronically ill, the sick, and the aged; the democratic state because it hopes to validate itself from a humanitarian standpoint as the representative of social concern.

Indeed, they have yet another feature in common, for both of them in the process either express or develop ideologies. The totalitarian state plays the role of the "universal father";[1] attending men with its claims and services from the cradle to the grave, it forces on them the same kind of dependence as is evident in all other spheres of life. The democratic state in this connection champions the ideology of the democratic ideal. This seems at a first glance to be somewhat of a paradox. The statement is justified, however, because the pragmatic element in ideology comes to expression where the democratic state for the most part or at least incidentally adopts a propagandistic approach in championing its humanitarian goals. This is particularly evident during election campaigns, when talk about the welfare state

---

[1] The term *Allvater* is borrowed from an address by Eivind Berggrav on "State and Church Today: The Lutheran View." The modern welfare state, says Berggrav, "wants to be omnipotent. There will be no actual demands to worship the state, in the traditional sense; rather it will be said that the state is sufficient; that the state is all we need; that we need no Providence beyond the state." *The Proceedings of the Second Assembly of the Lutheran World Federation; Hannover, Germany, July 25-August 3, 1952*, p. 83.

and social perfection usually goes over big. In the case of the democratic state the tendency toward a social ideology arises primarily out of the groups which run it and only secondarily out of the state itself.

In both cases one may see in the ideological tint of the movement a kind of perversion of the Christian concept of *diaconia*. Care for the neighbor, according to the basic thinking of the gospel, cannot consist merely in the supply of material needs. It must be accompanied by a message which will give meaning to what is done (Matt. 25:34-40; I Cor. 10:31; Col. 3:17). The question immediately arises, then, whether this message is not falsified, whether it is not inevitably perverted into an ideological by-product, if the meaning proclaimed is something other than the God who declares himself in the message, i.e., if it is a human ideal or institution.

We have already drawn attention to the fact that totalitarian tendencies pose an immanent threat to the democratic state.[2] This thesis is now considerably strengthened. For it is obvious that the trend toward the comprehensive welfare state, whether nurtured by directly totalitarian or by democratic-humanitarian motives, is a movement towards the omnipotent state. It makes no decisive difference whether the movement is planned as in the totalitarian state, or is an unintentional by-product as in the democratic state. Either way there may be seen here a latent or patent, a potential or actual trend towards the maximal state. This is why a close examination is needed at this point. For we are here confronted by a fundamental question of political ethics.

The threat of a maximal state is always a threat to the very foundations of the doctrine of the two kingdoms. The state as universal father, the state which intervenes in all things, exploiting even the inner powers of man (his dispositions and convictions) and registering everything and laying claim to everything, transgresses its allotted sphere on the left hand and — whether latently or deliberately — assumes the role of a pseudo church.

Berggrav has rightly pointed out that Lutheranism in particular must be on guard at this point. For it is here confronted by an inversion of its original approach to an ethics of the state. Luther's doctrine of the state was elaborated in answer to the threat of chaos. For Luther the state was a divinely instituted force of order set up to

---

[2] See above pp. 262-264.

counter centrifugal and destructive egoisms. Today the reverse could be true. It is conceivable that the modern threat to human society, to put it bluntly, arises less from chaos than from an overabundance of state order, a political superorganization which acts as an institutional buffer to isolate men from one another, depersonalize them, forestall direct I-Thou relationships, and turn love of neighbor into a welfare machine.

The problem can perhaps be clarified in terms of the parable of the Good Samaritan (Luke 10:30-37). Does not the Samaritan's ministry of mercy become inconceivable, is it not altered in its very substance, the moment it is institutionalized, put into the hands of a "Good Samaritans' League," e.g., or even into the hands of the state itself? Is it not thereby robbed of its very point?

For the theological point of the parable — and it is twofold — is surely this: that the personal relation of love for God is here actualized in the equally personal relation of love for one's neighbor, and that in this personal love for one's neighbor there is an element of improvisation. The good Samaritan finds the man who had fallen among thieves lying right there at his feet. He just comes on the fellow unexpectedly. This man in need is suddenly there, confronting him, devolving upon him as it were, obtruding without advance notice upon a course which had been set with something quite different in mind.

There is a tension between love and advance planning, between love and purposeful intent. At its core the living claim of the Thou resists institutionalizing. It cuts right across all order. It always arises as an interruption, a summons to forego all planned order. Just as the Spirit moves where he wills (John 3:8), refusing to be bottled up or encapsuled in orders, so the neighbor is an event, something that happens, a challenge, and hence something which cannot be normalized as part of an orderly scheme.

This is why love by its very nature is linked with improvisation. Even within a planned ministry, e.g., that of the pastor making his routine calls or giving set hours to sermon preparation or pastoral counseling, the direct call of the neighbor, the summons to an actual case of need, is always regarded as an interruption and may even precipitate a serious conflict of duties.

Love is direct and immediate, order indirect. When the judge serves his neighbor by pronouncing sentence on him, this service sets him in an indirect relation to his neighbor. But if the judge is a Christian, he does not see the defendant merely as a party in a judicial proceeding. He sees him also as one involved in fateful encounter with God, one who is "bought with a price" (I Cor. 6:20; 7:23), for whom far more is at stake than mere earthly retribution for an earthly misdemeanor. And it is possible that the judge may have to cut right through the orderly arrangements which isolate and separate him from the accused in order to disclose the solidarity in which he stands with the condemned man or his immediate neighbor.

The question raised by the parable is thus the question whether directness and improvisation can survive when in the perfect institutionalizing of welfare all I-Thou relations are planned and delegated to machinery. Can the good Samaritan be envisaged as a welfare officer?

There are two logical consequences of this which bring out the destructive tendency of this movement towards a maximal state. The first is that someone is always on hand for every case of need. It has been planned that way. No one is ever summoned personally any more. No one need feel any personal responsibility. The apparatus is available to care for everything. The second consequence is that those who because of their faith, or because of some particular ethics, would champion personal directness in love of neighbor (as do Christians with their *diaconia*) no longer have any opportunity to live out their love and bring it to men, because the planned machinery of the institution is there before their improvisation can even get under way. And because the planning and organization are so complete that there are no holes left for the seed of *diaconia* to slip through.

We grant that this picture of the perfect welfare state is overdrawn. But it represents the same kind of fruitful exaggeration as is found in modern negative utopias, such as George Orwell's *1984*. The concern is not to state the actual outcome of historical processes, but only to use such imaginary outcomes to depict the trend of the processes. In this sense our portrait has real substance to it. Even if, as we have said, it is exaggerated to imagine that the condition will ever arise in which there is no longer any opportunity for love of neighbor, there can be no doubt that such opportunities are seriously reduced by the processes mentioned, at least for the individual and his ministry to neighbors, colleagues, and others whom he happens to encounter —

though even in this field the mesh of the organizational apparatus is still comparatively wide and many opportunities do in fact occur. For life is too rich and varied to be brought wholly under a priori regulations, and in any case there are whole spheres of ministry to others, e.g., the rendering of inner help, which in principle cannot be organized.

In addition to the effect on the individual, however, there is also, and more particularly, the effect on Christian *diaconia*. *Diaconia* itself has to have some organization — though organization is not an end in itself but an aid to the establishment of loving I-Thou relationships in the personal sense. Because of its own need for organization, Christian *diaconia* is seriously hampered by the privileged machinery of the state or society. Indeed, it is driven into the spiritually dangerous situation of rivalry where it must confront the paradoxical question whether love may assert itself and stand up for its own alleged rights.[3]

This consideration and question show the difficulty of the problem. They also show, however, that while the radical welfare state may possibly be a mistake, the church's opposition to it may also be mistaken. It is a mistake for the church to compete with the state for a monopoly of service and welfare.[4]

Any inquiry which asks only concerning the conflict between state and church in this area threatens always to remain unfruitful because it is simply an institutional inquiry and is thus ill adapted to bring to light the personal nature of love, which is the decisive thing in this context. Questions of competence are never ultimate questions. The inquiry must rather be such that we ask concerning the structure of the state itself and the possibilities which it leaves for personal opportunity and direct love of neighbor.

The Development of the Welfare State

If we are to think further along these lines, we must first engage in a close analysis of the rise and form of the welfare state. Only in a

---

[3] This question shows that it is possible for Christian *diaconia* not only to oppose the machinery in the name of direct personal relations but also to conceal within itself the demonic possibility of itself becoming mere machinery.

[4] "Should the church go to war for the sake of maintaining a monopoly in this area? Jesus' words to his over-zealous monopoly-minded disciples provide the answer, clear and unambiguous: 'Forbid him not; for he that is not against us, is for us' (Mark 9:40)." Berggrav, *loc. cit.*

realistic encounter with the phenomenon, and with the complicated web of historical necessity and deliberate intent involved in it, can we hope to do justice to the welfare state rather than just condemning it out of hand as demonic.

There is certainly no sense in trying to undo historical processes and given situations in the name of the gospel. The task for Christians is rather that of proclaiming within the sphere of apparent autonomy the efficacious word of freedom, which is a positive word.

We may begin with a definition: The welfare state is the collective attempt, for which the state provides the theoretical and practical base and support, to deal with human misery by means of rationalized care. If we are to understand and elaborate upon this statement, it will be necessary for us first to investigate the causes, forms, and results of this development. Then we will also consider the problem of how to check it.

Reasons for the Development

We have already touched on the theoretical or ideological reasons for the welfare state as regards both its totalitarian and democratic forms. The historical occasion which gave force to these reasons may be found at two points.

First there was the growth of technology which ushered in the age of industry and the mass society. In its early capitalist stage it brought with it sharp class distinctions and, mainly under the Marxist banner, led to the attempt of the oppressed proletariat to help itself. Mass suffering as a social phenomenon – as distinct from the individual poverty of earlier days, which was of many varieties and could hardly be construed as a homogeneous phenomenon – necessarily impelled in the direction of collective and organized self-help which, once its effectiveness was realized, took on the nature of social help. This type of collective help necessarily sought out as its agent the most comprehensive collective entity available, namely, the state.

The historical occasion may also be found in the fact that as technology came to pervade and control all of life there necessarily arose a kind of faith in the manageability of all things. Technology, which initially had reference primarily to the mechanical sphere, became a sign of the total control of life. Even spheres which once were regarded as the proper sphere of intuition, instinct, the irrational, or

personal freedom, have been increasingly invaded by a rationally refined "technicizing" which tries to see and treat life and its inner
essence after the analogy of mechanical processes. We thus have now
such a thing as sexual technique (not just the earlier art of love), and
we find psycho-technicians, social engineers, human relations mechan-
ics, and many other indications of how technology has been extending
its influence.

Since there can be no doubting some of the successes of this technical control of life, the thesis of the manageability of all things prevails — until in certain moments of catastrophe, in personal crises,
strikes, and other deadlocks, some elemental factor rises up in revolt.
Refusing to be subject to technical control, it suddenly emerges as a
great challenge and disruption, just as the news of the Lisbon earth-
quake came like a dark shadow over the bright rational world of the
Enlightenment. Thus a strike in industries which have perfected their
social techniques can show that the elementary bond of human confidence cannot be woven in this way, and that perfect social machinery
is no substitute for certain human qualities. Similarly, within the
technically perfect welfare state, which applies the principle of the
manageability of all things to the removal of want, there can be a revolt of uncontrolled life, of satiety, tedium, and anxiety. Apart from
these borderline situations, however, the machinery functions smoothly.

We regard it as important, in any case, to consider this historical
background of the trend towards the welfare state. For if the welfare
state is seen to be only a special instance of the general tendency
towards a collective control of life and toward the thesis of the
manageability of all things, this can safeguard us from the very outset
against merely making negative protests against the welfare state, and
by our protests demanding too much of it. We thus arrive already at
this early stage in the analysis, at the same conclusion to which every
theological investigation of any suprapersonal nexus must lead, namely,
that in the complex of historical developments and trends there may
be discerned human attitudes which have yielded to the dictatorship
of false principles (e.g., that of manageability), which rest on false
decisions and hence, for all the appearance of necessity, still involve
responsibility. Indeed, it is our task always to press on to this core of
the matter. The Christian message is addressed, not to processes and
institutions, but to their personal center, to the men who, while im-

pelled and carried along by these processes and institutions, in the final analysis impel and carry them. We need constantly to reassert this decisive starting point of theological ethics.

Now, although we cannot pretend to give even a brief sketch of social history, it will help to clarify the situation if we draw attention to a decisive change in the concept of poverty. We may begin with a bald statement of the change. Originally, i.e., before the modern age, poverty, though interpreted in a variety of ways, was regarded essentially as an individual phenomenon, whereas in the modern age it is usually regarded as a defect in the social structure. It is this basic difference in understanding which has led to the radically different way of dealing with the misery which poverty causes.

The original view, at least in the Christian sphere, bears an individual accent inasmuch as poverty is regarded as a meaningful condition in personal life, in life under God. On this view, poverty as a form of life under God can be regarded in two ways.

First, it can be regarded as a gift and an opportunity. For the poor man, as many New Testament passages show, is stripped of all the false securities which the rich fool (Luke 12:16-21) and the rich young ruler (Matt. 19:16-30) thought they had. Like the beggar Lazarus, the poor man puts his hope — at least this is a possibility — in God alone (Luke 16:20). It is only in this sense that we can understand the blessedness which Jesus ascribes to the poor (Matt. 5:3; Luke 6:20), or his statement that he preaches the gospel to the poor, and that it seems to apply particularly to them (Matt. 11:5; Luke 4:18; 7:22). The Old Testament too regards the poor man as one who has a special opportunity to fix his hope on God alone and to claim God as his "stronghold in distress" (Isa. 25:4; Job 5:16; Ps. 9:9; 10:14; 12:5; Jer. 22:16).

Poverty is also significant in relation to man's dealings with God because it offers us who are not poor an opportunity to take up the poor man's cause, to take pity on him as God takes pity on us, to show him that love which is not just a matter of reciprocity.[5] Caring for the poor is thus a part of the ordered life of the primitive church (Acts 4:32 ff.; 6:3 ff.). This is how we are to understand the legendary saying of St.

[5] Matt. 18:32-33; Luke 18:1-8; Matt. 19:21; 25:35 ff.; Luke 19:8; cf. also Deut. 15:4; Ps. 112:9; 82:3; Prov. 19:17; Isa. 58:7.

Lawrence that the poor are "the treasures of the Church." [6] This is also the only thing which makes sense of poverty voluntarily assumed, as in connection with monastic vows. Modern literature, too, occasionally refers to this meaning of poverty, which is disclosed either to the poor themselves or to those who encounter them. Think, e.g., of Georges Bernanos' suggestion in his *Diary of a Country Priest* that a society which no longer tolerates the poor has impoverished itself and forfeited the opportunity for direct person-to-person care of a fellow human being.

Now poverty so construed undoubtedly has a secular as well as a spiritual aspect. The poor man might be regarded as incompetent, perhaps as lazy or too fond of sleep, and hence deserving of his poverty (cf. Prov. 6:10-11; 20:13; 24:33-34). But here too the concept of poverty is markedly individualistic, and understandably does not provide much of an incentive to combat poverty in an organized way.

This attitude undergoes a radical change, however, once poverty is interpreted sociologically and regarded as the product of a particular social or economic system. For one can tackle the defect in a system only by altering the system itself. But this again has to be done systematically, i.e., by altering the relations of all the components of the system in a comprehensive, sweeping, and well-planned way. Marxism accords with this law of "systematic" action. Whether Marxism in fact defines the relation of the several components of the system correctly is quite another question. It has in any case tackled the problem of poverty and welfare in a logical and systematic manner. In revolutionary fashion it has overthrown the individualistic view of poverty.

We shall note briefly the decisive processes at work here, using Marxism as a model by which to perceive in representative fashion this radical change in the understanding of poverty and welfare. Marxism defines the stratum which underlies and sustains every social structure as the means of production and the economic situation to which they initially give rise. It also defines the social structure as it presently exists, and the way which leads from that initial situation to the present structure. And finally, it defines the state of intellectual life which results from this combination of initial factors, i.e., the function of learning, morality, art, and ultimately of religion. It thus sets

---

[6] The story is told by St. Ambrose in *On the Duties of the Clergy* ii. 28; *NPF*, X, 65.

forth a plan or sketch of all phenomena which makes it possible to see each individual phenomenon in its relation to the whole, and indeed to deduce it from the whole.

Logically, then, there follows not just an empirical assertion concerning the presence of poverty and suffering, but also a corresponding theory (as it is expressly called) concerning its origin. The rise of poverty is defined as an automatic process. Now the subsumption of one phenomenon under higher systematic factors always leads to the assertion of necessary processes. In Kantian terms, it leads to synthetic a priori judgments as distinct from empirical a posteriori judgments which stress individual areas of experience, as in the case of Solomon's principle that the man who sleeps too much instead of working will generally, though not inevitably, become poor (Prov. 6:10-11; 20:13; 24:33-34).

In the particular case under review the law concerning the rise of poverty is stated as follows: The possession of certain technical means of production, specifically heavy machinery, leads to a concentration of economic power in the hands of a small stratum of capitalists. It confers upon them privileges of all kinds, and affords them the possibility of unlimited exploitation of the have-nots, the proletariat. Poverty is the "necessary" result. Since the basic premises of this condition, namely, the means of production placed at our disposal by technology, cannot be altered, the "necessary" trend can be redirected only if there is a different distribution of the means of production, so that they are not concentrated in one sector of society.

This implies, however, the necessity of resisting a certain autonomy inherent in technology. Heavy machinery has a tendency, simply by virtue of its productive capacity, to make possible the acquisition of more heavy machinery, and thus steadily to increase the concentration of economic power in a particular sector. Autonomous processes can be altered, however, only by changing the combination of initial factors. In the case under consideration this means that the trend toward concentration must be contested as soon as it appears. This can be done only by force, for laissez faire immediately sets in motion the natural movement towards concentration. Diffusion rather than concentration in the ownership of the means of production has thus to be attained by force.

This has two results which clearly show that new and crucial tasks at once arise for the state. First, it is the state alone which — once the revolutionary birthpangs are past and conditions are normal — can introduce and guarantee by legislative and executive means this radical diffusion of control. Second, it is the state alone which can assume this dispersed control. There has to be a concentration; but if this concentration takes place at a point which embraces the whole of society, it is — from the standpoint of the parts which make up the whole — diffusion as well. Only in this way can the rise of poverty be stemmed. The first step is to ensure the distribution of want, so that poverty ceases to be an exception. Only after that can poverty be overcome. This is done by means of further measures which in terms of our present discussion are not now at issue.

From the standpoint of our present fundamental discussion, it does not matter whether this experiment in control follows the intended course or whether it involves radical errors which doom it to failure. What is decisive, and significant so far as our model is concerned, is that poverty is here regarded not as an individual phenomenon, an exception, but as a phenomenon which occurs automatically within a given social system and can thus be overcome only by altering the system.

Even though other social and economic systems explain the rise of poverty quite differently, there can be little doubt that since the rise of Marxism, if I may put it thus, the "hermeneutical principle" which underlies the understanding of poverty is everywhere the same. This principle consists in the application of the sociological category.

That the sociological category has emerged and become almost a dominant category is due not least of all to the fact that in the age of technology and the mass society all phenomena take on larger proportions and all antitheses are sharpened. This enlargement and intensification suggest the necessity of looking beyond individual phenomena to the state of affairs in society at large, beyond particular storms to the larger weather patterns, and even to such distant phenomena as sunspots.

Even where these wider analyses are neglected and free rein is given to the practical man's aversion for theories, in one respect the movement is still in this sociological direction which is typical of the new situation: The man who will not analyze but prefers to act finds that there are instances in which he cannot cope with the vast phenomena of modern mass society on an individual basis. He can hope to bring them under control only by a collective and systematic effort. The fact that action has to be taken and social misery met within the framework of a larger order gives rise to a movement which runs counter to that which we have described as characteristic of the Christian love of neighbor. For it does not allow of personal improvisation. Instead it requires a grand impersonal plan, a system. This brings us up against the problem of the form of this development.

The Form of the Development

The systematic and collective nature of the action to which we are impelled by the process just described may be defined by saying that whereas love of neighbor rests on an improvisation called forth by direct encounter with the neighbor and his need, systematic welfare presses in the direction of rationalization. In fact the concept of rationalization affords an exact description of the structure of the new processes.

Rationalization in an industrial process means organizing the effort in such a way that a maximum of production is achieved with a minimum of expenditure.[7] This can be done only if the several productive processes are broken down into their component parts and then so far as possible brought together again in a single mechanical process which moves along without individual intervention on the part of man, to a large degree even without human direction, as in the case of full automation.

The same principle applies in the rationalizing of welfare machinery. For here the machinery is planned and set up in such a way that so far as possible it achieves the goal of establishing security against poverty, sickness, and other crises without the need for any human interventions or improvisations. The size of the "volume" attained when the state enters this field makes it possible, in this form of rationalization as well, to attain a maximum of care with a relative minimum of means. This high rate of return could never be attained by a non-mechanized kind of individual love of neighbor.

There is another parallel between the two, namely, the impersonality which necessarily goes with such processes. In order to make sure

[7] See Helmut Thielicke and K. Pentzlin, *Mensch und Arbeit im technischen Zeitalter* (1954).

that the mechanical process does not have to be "interrupted" by men, rationalization in industry has to split up the work procedures into very small parts which can be handled and controlled by the machines. The worker on the assembly line oversees and has a hand in only that very small part of the total process which is allotted to him. Hence he constantly makes the same movements and, apart from corrections, has no direct part in the finished product, let alone in the overall economic or other nexus of which the finished product is itself a part. This gives his work the mark of impersonality which distinguishes it from that of the craftsman.

The same impersonality arises when welfare is rationalized. It is only at the end of the process, when the recipient is finally reached through the last link in the chain, that there are opportunities for personal contacts, and even then the final stage will often be a welfare office desk or the home mailbox. For the rest, the work procedures are again split up into parts which themselves do not have in view the final product. These parts consist in the printing and filling out of forms, the use of adding machines and computers, and institutional contacts.

The process of rationalization and depersonalization in welfare is expedited — this aspect is to be kept firmly in view — by the sheer numbers of those requiring care, the high total of "cases." No individual can keep track of them all. This factor does not merely work against personal and improvised handling, as we have already seen. It also works against assessment of the situation by direct means. Rationalization involving the use of questionnaires and statistics is needed even to assess the need and to establish the potential or actual number of "cases."

The difficulty of even ascertaining and then supplying the need, and the resulting necessity for a high degree of rationalization in welfare, reaches a climax in times of disaster when the number of "cases" becomes almost incalculable. Think, for instance, of the postwar period in Germany with its mountainous tasks of caring for the victims of war, making compensation, and equalizing the burdens.

How far all this can get from any direct person-to-person care of a fellow human being finally becomes clear in the fact that the burden of the material requirements of state welfare must be borne by general taxation.

The Consequences of the Development

The reference to taxes points to the first consequence of the welfare state, a consequence which has both an external and an internal aspect. As the social burden of the state increases there is necessarily a corresponding increase in the tax burden which is bound to have economic consequences. In a free economy it can make investment difficult, e.g., long-term investment in the means of production, and hence impose an excessive strain on credit. It can thus reduce a country's ability to compete with foreign economies. Finally – because men always try to avoid economic pressures – it can lead to dishonesty in the paying of taxes and thus bring to a head the processes of inner disintegration.

A second external consequence is that as the outlays for welfare increase they can reach the point where the benefits paid in case of sickness, disability, or even wilful unemployment threaten to become the equivalent of a normal wage. But even in those instances where pensions and benefits do not add up to a normal wage it is still a temptation – because of the inevitable competition between wages and benefits – for people to quit their job, justify their action on other grounds, and make up the loss in income by doing part-time work on the side. All this leads to chaotic tendencies in the labor market. It leads too to a rise in both wages and benefits, and hence to yet another vicious circle alongside that of the wage-price spiral. And finally, the competition between wages and benefits also contains within itself the impulses of moral corruption, since it destroys the ethos of labor.

Besides these external consequences there are two main internal consequences of the development toward the welfare state. In the first place, once the state establishes a monopoly in the field of welfare, once it is forced to render "complete care for its citizens in body and soul," [3] it not only reduces individual initiative but also kindles suspicion of the welfare work of other groups, especially when, as in the case of the church, special meaning, indeed a particular message, is attached to this work. The modern state usually demands that all activities which impinge upon its monopoly must first receive official authorization.

Hence if it wishes, or if those who control it (e.g., specific parties) desire, the state can take legislative action to forbid Christian instruc-

[3] Berggrav, *loc. cit.*

tion for those who do welfare work, e.g., in the schools, or it can put a stop to the activity of professional workers who have a Christian background by excluding them from the field of public welfare altogether. It can also achieve much the same result by limiting or withholding grants to private welfare institutions such as denominational hospitals, nurses training schools, etc.

We cannot attempt to say whether authors like Berggrav are right when they claim that experience indicates the existence of "a universal tendency toward the eradication of the diaconate and its activities." [9] To gather statistics on this point is less important anyway than to call attention to the basic and ineluctable character of the movement itself. For hand in hand with a state monopoly of welfare goes a movement toward the maximal state.

The monopoly itself, however, is not the product of man's deliberate intention or contriving, a calculated step toward the long-range goal of the totalitarian state. It is simply the end of a movement. The rationalization of welfare demanded by the character of modern society is what produces the tendency toward total planning, total direction, and consolidation in a single hand.

The result is a process involving two phases. The first phase is the development of the state monopoly. The second is the exclusion of all independent outside actions which seem to dissipate the centrally directed effort and introduce "ideologies" of their own.

For three reasons it is important that we regard this twofold trend as a fundamental fact: Only thus can we decide whether we should reject it or accept it. Only thus — in case of rejection — can we hit upon measures to counteract it. And only thus can we avoid misjudging the concrete situation at any given moment, whether by being lulled into a false sense of security because the situation at the moment — perhaps due to the present makeup of the government — is still innocuous, or by tracing back the empirical symptoms of the movement to such contingent historical factors as the particular individuals or groups presently in the ascendancy.

A second inner consequence of the welfare state consists in the fact that welfare becomes the object of a "claim": In time of need, when I cannot care for myself, I claim to have a right to be cared for; the

---

[9] *Ibid.*

state is obliged to assist me whether or not I act or am capable of acting to help myself. The resultant situation is so complex that it is difficult to assess from an ethical standpoint. This may be seen from the fact that, while the claim is obviously very dubious ethically, it is generally given a decidedly moral accent. It is pointed out, e.g., that welfare which is state controlled, and which to this degree acknowledges a claim, rests on a legal partnership between the state and the beneficiary which entails an obligation. Welfare of this kind is said to be independent of the free initiative and implied ethical resolve of the individual; it is part and parcel of a legislatively enacted system of law. To put it very precisely, welfare is thus transferred from the ethical to the legal plane.

At the same time, it is held, this approach does particular justice to the ethical dignity of the person, for he stands within a community of law as an independent partner having rights of his own. It is these rights, the rights that make him a partner, which are expressed in his claims. It is also pointed out how degrading it was, in the days before the welfare state, for an individual to be dependent upon private benevolence. Quite apart from its unplanned improvisation and its consequent technical inadequacy, such benevolence made the sick, the poor, and the helpless dependent on the good will of the benefactor. It granted them no claims. They were thus put in the undignified position of being the recipients of alms. To be the mere object of another's will is said to be a violation of personal dignity. To be a partner, on the other hand, and to have claims is more commensurate with personal dignity, and hence has ethical dignity.

This line of argument is meretricious. It deceives by seeming to do justice to the Christian understanding of the person. It brings the proponent of Christian *diaconia* into the paradoxical situation of seeing a Christian concern articulated by an agency which may even contest the diaconic form of his own love of neighbor, or at least has within it the propensity to do so. While there doubtless are elements of truth in this argument — and we shall have occasion to refer to them later — it must be stated that the argument makes a false distinction between welfare as a legal act regulated by the state and welfare as the function of private, improvising love. As a result it blocks the way to an ethical discussion of the machinery of state welfare.

Even the expression "private benevolence," which corresponds to the term "recipients of alms," is a linguistic corruption of something which was once called love. Love as *caritas* and *agape* does not degrade the other person. It honors him and puts him on the same level as the one doing the loving. The giver knows that he is one who, in relation to God, receives without merit, and who must therefore act towards his neighbor as God has acted toward him (Matt. 6:12, 14, 15; 18:21-35). The giver is united with his neighbor in a solidarity of receiving. Furthermore, the one to whom he gives is no mere "object" of benevolence. On the contrary, he is the hidden Christ, the one "bought with a price" (I Cor. 6:20; 7:23), the image of God (Gen. 1:26-27) possessing an "alien dignity."

The dominant factor in such giving, then, is not the much lamented subject-object relation between giver and recipient but a partnership in the ultimate dimension. Giver and recipient are both subject and object in one. The giver is subject as the one who gives. But the recipient is also subject because he brings a blessing to the one who has mercy on him (Ps. 41:1-3; Prov. 11:24; 19:17; II Cor. 9:2-11). Because he bears this blessing he is "the treasure of the Church." This is what gives him that creative function which is so prominent in Bernanos. The recipient, however, is also object because he is the target of the love which encounters him and seeks him. And the giver too is object because he is the target of the generous goodness of God and of the blessing which he receives from the one in need.

It seems to us important that Christian love of neighbor and the Christian understanding of giving and receiving should be set forth in terms such as are used by proponents of the welfare state who champion a legal partnership between the state and the recipients of welfare over against the alleged Christian degrading of the poor to the level of an object and against the alleged degradation of giving to the level of a capricious act. For then we can see that the terms subject and object do not really apply here, that in fact Christian love unites giver and recipient in a partnership under God which gives to both, recipient as well as giver, a very different dignity from that which is purely legal.

Indeed, one must go further. Because the recipient is not just an object, because the giver honors the fact that he is meant to be a person in the sight of God, it is quite impossible that he be left in the passive role of a mere recipient. The giver cannot regard the recipient's poverty as something to which he is fated, and then within this fate use alms as a means to secure for him a mere survival, a minimal level of subsistence. If he does, then there is indeed a real danger of turning the poor man into a mere object. There is a real temptation to misapply the paradoxical saying that "the poor are the treasure of the Church" by caring not just for the poor but for poverty as well, to assure that such treasures may never be lacking.

The theological mystery of poverty, however, is that while God accepts the poor he rejects poverty (Deut. 15:4). In this sense Jesus' beatitude has reference not to poverty, but to the poor. We are told to take care of the poor, not to take care that they will always be with us. It is a dreadful and grotesque idea to think that Christianity must inevitably countenance and accept poverty in order that Christians may always have occasion for exercising a ministry of love and service. This would be the cynical position of salvation egoism. It would really degrade the poor to the level of an object.

But if, in contradiction to this idea, the poor man is indeed a subject, and is to be regarded and sustained as such, then it is not enough that we simply give to him while leaving him totally passive. He must also be helped to work his way out of poverty, and even be prevented from falling into it in the first place. This means that he must be restored to economic independence. But once poverty occurs escape is possible only in exceptional cases. What is more urgently needed is preventive action. Prevention of this kind will require first of all a social order in which the right to gainful employment is assured and in which possibilities are created for the attainment of economic independence by way of education, financial credits, and the like.

There was a classic example of this kind of approach in poverty-stricken postwar Germany when the state and other agencies made grants available to refugees and expellees to help them get started. The aim was not to make these people who had lost all their possessions, including their working capital, mere passive recipients of aid. It was rather to activate their working potential, whatever it might be, by putting at their disposal the means to establish an independent life. Hence it was not really an act of welfare, treating the refugees as objects. It was the setting up of a genuine partnership, or, one might almost say, a commercial agreement which, when put into effect, would also benefit the state by creating productive citizens.

Hilfswerk, the gigantic relief program established by Eugen Gersten-maier after the Second World War was constructed on the same principle. He did not ask foreign donors to send finished products to relieve poverty directly by way of providing basic consumer goods. He asked them instead to send raw materials which could be processed in domestic factories, thus giving a boost to lagging production and enabling people to help themselves. In the terminology used above this means that aid was designed, not to make defeated Germany a mere object of welfare and hence a recipient of alms, but to afford it the possibility of once again becoming an economic subject, and thus an independent partner.

This preventive approach enables Christian *agape* to enter upon a path toward that kind of social and political order which will both prevent poverty and afford opportunity to overcome existing poverty. It thus has a point of entry to this side of the welfare state — if one may still wish to call it that.

Here too the problem of impersonal machinery will arise again, obviously. But in two respects the situation is different from that which arises in the consistent and total welfare state. First, the state is now in principle regarded critically. In the kingdom on the left hand the relation to the Thou is mediated essentially through supra-individual orders, and hence is indirect, which is one of the factors which lead us to speak of an "alien" work of God. Second, state welfare is here restricted to the areas of prevention and rehabilitation. This has from the very outset two results.

First, a relation of genuine partnership is hereby set up between the state and its citizens (including the welfare recipients). For the goal of the state's action is the economic independence of its citizens, either in the sense of protecting it from the very outset, or in the sense of restoring it once it has been lost. The kind of "partnership" which means only that for every form of poverty or need there are corresponding "claims" does not create this relation of true partnership, appearances to the contrary notwithstanding. The idea that it does is, as we have said, purely meretricious. For whatever action the state takes by way of fulfilling a claim, if it does not have the character of payment for something the citizen has done or of credit for what he will be doing, simply forces the recipient into a relation with the state which is that of a passive object, and this not only violates the dignity of the person but is also destructive of the dignity of the state and of the relation between state and citizen. For the democratic ethos is nourished, as we have said, by the maturity and co-operation of the citizens. The citizen *is* the state inasmuch as he — at least by way of the ballot box — exercises control and bears responsibility in it.

The total welfare state, on the other hand, in which the assertion of "claims" dominates the consciousness, is remote from its citizens. Psychologically they no longer identify with it but speak of it as a distinct and distant institution, an entity which stands over against them. The Americans, who have thus far been preserved from this degeneration in state consciousness, when they speak of aid to be given either in disaster areas in their own country, or to under-developed or war-ravaged countries abroad, still say, "We" must help. Regardless of whether the aid is given through private initiative, or is undertaken by organizations, or is rendered by the state itself, in all three forms the active agent is the same "we."

The stronger the tendency toward the total welfare state, however, the more the terminology used in this connection alters. It is now "the state" which must help. I have claims on "the state." The state has become an "it." It is no longer spoken of in the first person plural. This corruption of state consciousness can be arrested, and the possibility of genuine partnership between state and citizen restored, only if the state limits itself essentially to the task of preventing poverty and rehabilitating the economically helpless.

But there is also a second result. In contradistinction to the consistent welfare state, a self-limited state, by its very self-restriction, erects a wall against latent totalitarian tendencies. As a result it does not merely allow for selfless service to those who are completely helpless and can no longer be economically reactivated; it actually encourages and fosters such service. For this service can be rendered only in a way which the state as such does not have at its command. There are inner aspects to such complete helplessness which require the kind of aid which the state, with its impersonal machinery and its lack of message, is simply unable to give. The state is thus well advised to place material resources at the disposal of other welfare organizations of many kinds which are able to render this twofold ministry of care.

Nor is this service to be associated only with those who are completely helpless and past rehabilitating, the elderly, incurables, the mentally ill, those who are hard to educate or totally ineducable, the antisocial, etc. There are also other emergency situations — e.g., sickness — which involve special ministries of inner aid, so that the state is prevented from claiming a monopoly in welfare. For the state to claim such a monopoly would be to claim too much. It must at least concede the possibility of these other ministries alongside its own institutions. Christian hospitals, of course, are a prime example.

In short, here in the sphere of welfare, as in everything else, the state must put forth only a minimal claim. Apart from the two crucial aspects of prevention and rehabilitation, it should delegate as many tasks as possible, leaving as much initiative as possible to independent agencies and institutions, and providing as little direct aid as possible. There will still remain plenty of instances in which the state will have no choice but to provide aid directly. But it is important that it not make a virtue of this necessity.

Perhaps one might formulate the principle involved here as follows: The state ought not to be the primary agent of welfare, delegating its function only in exceptional cases, but vice versa. At least this would best correspond to the thesis of the minimal state. In this way, too, personal I-Thou relations would be provided as a corrective to the necessary impersonality of the state and its machinery. In place of the one big sphere of the state there would be several comparatively manageable little spheres.

Checking the Trend

In what we have just been saying we have already touched on this matter of checking the trend toward the welfare state. We will sum up what was said under points 1 and 2 of the four points which follow. But before we do that we must first issue a warning against overestimating what theological ethics can accomplish here.

It cannot be the task of theological ethics to commend particular means, or even the use of means, to avoid the total welfare state. In reference to this theme theological ethics can only have three tasks. First, it must espouse the theological thesis that the state ought to be minimal, and give the relevant reasons. Second, it should set forth its theological understanding of the relation between autonomy and decision, trend and ethical opportunity, by pointing out specific tendencies toward the total welfare state; it should do so with a view to keeping the necessity of historical movement from being made into a virtue, and also with a view to mobilizing ethical correctives through the process of drawing attention to the movement. Third, and related to this, it has to fix the directions in which these correctives are to be sought, particularly that of keeping free from the state certain spheres wherein welfare may be and remain independent, even though it may be subsidized and supervised by the state. Our remaining task is simply to indicate these directions, which we will do even now as we sum up and round out our findings and establish the main points to be considered in any bucking of the indicated trend.

1) Christianity endorses the "relative" welfare state because Christianity's own ministry to the poor, and the promises attendant upon it, cannot mean that poverty as such is to be cultivated. The task of giving medical help, e.g., cannot mean that sickness as such has to be perpetuated in order to provide opportunity for the fulfilling of the task.

On the other hand, Christianity has to warn against the illusion that in principle poverty and helplessness can be abolished and in their stead a state of perfection attained in which human need will be completely overcome (Deut. 15:11; Prov. 22:2; 29:13; Matt. 26:11). For in the first place it is only the relation between poverty and affluence which is altered; the antithesis between them is made less flagrant to be sure, but the distinction remains even in a system of higher and more refined social values.[10] Furthermore, as nations and continents come into ever closer proximity responsibility for the poor of other nations (e.g., in the underdeveloped countries) takes on an increasing degree of urgency. Finally, and above all, with increasing social perfection the form of human suffering changes. As the progressive refinement of antibiotic drugs does not banish infection from the world altogether but instead evokes resistance on the part of the bacteria, and thus creates new forms of sickness, so radical welfare therapy provokes new forms of social pathology and new forms of poverty. Thus, e.g., the contrast between external perfection and inner deterioration becomes the more painful, as may be noted already in the radical welfare states of our own times. External affluence unaccompanied by inner equivalents leads to tedium, anxiety, and a helpless surrender to the external direction of life.

[10] Thus social need means quite different things in, e.g., India and Sweden.

In thus warning against the utopia of a humanly inaugurated perfect state of affairs at the end of history, Christianity has to draw attention to three points. The first is that external perfection unaccompanied by the buttressing of inner substance gives rise to new forms of sickness in society. The second is that if the state would be true to itself, avoid totalitarian perversion, and remain in the kingdom on the left hand, it cannot create these inner equivalents. And the third is that for this reason the state cannot claim a monopoly in welfare, but so far as possible must delegate the tasks of welfare to agencies which have a message and can devote themselves to more than merely external welfare. At any rate, the state must in principle not exclude but allow for such institutions.

Here we may recall a point made in our discussion of the problem of the state and education.[11] As the church ought not to claim a fixed number of Christian schools but only as many as its living communities of parents and teachers can handle, so it ought not to take over a fixed number of welfare tasks on the mere ground that every kind of welfare ought to include care for the inner man as well. If the church were to do that, particularly in the state church, it could only lead to bargaining for offices and to dissembling on a grand scale. Just as teachers would be compelled to be hypocrites if there were openings for them only in denominational schools, so social workers of all kinds would be driven to hypocrisy, and to serious conflicts of conscience, if they could find service opportunities only within the framework of Christian organizations. Such tasks can be entrusted to the church only to the degree that it has the needed personnel and the capacity to train them. The extent to which that is the case, only the church can judge.

This means that, along with the danger that the state will make itself the direct agent of welfare in the total sense, there is also the danger that it will delegate the tasks of welfare blindly. All that the state can do is to provide by law the opportunity for other agencies — e.g., the church with its *diaconia* — to take up welfare tasks, pursue initiatives, and have the possibility of equipping themselves for these tasks, e.g., by being permitted to train welfare workers who will then be regarded as fully qualified. Thus it may well be that in the first instance the state will itself function as the direct agent of the main

[11] See pp. 265, 281-288 above.

tasks of welfare, while always standing ready to give up these tasks as other non-state agents become available. In this way, and only in this way, can there be organic development. The state ought to make legislative provision for such development.

Negatively, this means that the state should oppose the trend toward a total and direct assumption of all welfare tasks, and recognize that in this area too it ought ideally to be a minimal state. Obviously, this ideal arrangement has to be fought for, and the church ought to take the lead in fighting for it. The battle, however, should not take the form merely of demands made in principle. There must in addition and above all be the actual development of initiatives, i.e., visible diaconal activity.

In this sense Bishop Otto Dibelius made a contribution which was exemplary both in substance and in tactics when he offered church help to the state in dealing with the problem of pregnancies resulting from the rape of German girls by colored soldiers during the occupation. Into the discussion of whether or not to legalize abortion in such cases, he injected the church's offer to provide homes for the unwanted children. Here the church acted rightly. In a case in which it was capable of helping both personally and institutionally, it offered its diaconal aid, volunteering to take over a task for which the state had only a very questionable solution. The case serves as a good example because it shows that in the diaconal field the "demand" of the state for a certain service (and therewith its self-limitation) can be evoked only by the church's "supply" of that service. Only thus can the two above-mentioned dangers be avoided.

If modern secularization does not allow the denominations for their part to obtain a monopoly in welfare, they must at least have a part in welfare tasks. A place must be left for the free competition of love. In this case, to avoid a dispersion of effort, the state should accept the task of selecting, co-ordinating, supervising, and subsidizing the welfare organizations. Part of its work of supervision would be to prevent encroachments by welfare agencies which might try to violate freedom of conscience and subject the recipients of aid to inner pressures. Such negative effects can be generally avoided only if the welfare recipients have a free choice among the agencies in question, just as patients must have the right to choose the doctor in whom they have confidence.

2) There will also be welfare tasks, of course, in which the state is the direct agent, tasks which cannot be delegated. But these too must be limited. The question obviously is where to draw the line. That can be debated. But whether the limits are drawn more widely or more narrowly is not nearly as important as the fact that the question concerning them be raised, and that the state not proceed blindly and in utopian illusion assume all the tasks of welfare. If we were to define very broadly the sphere of direct state activity which inevitably belongs to the minimal state we would have to say approximately what we said earlier about measures for the prevention of poverty and about the economic rehabilitation of social rejects.

Among the preventive tasks we may mention by way of example the subsidizing of imperiled elements of the economy, protecting workers against dismissal without cause, extending credit with a view to the establishment of economic independence, providing job retraining in cases of personal or general economic crisis, etc. (We have discussed already the tasks of economic rehabilitation.)

The payment of pensions and benefits is another direct task of the state, but even here, where general oversight and formal regulation is unavoidable, there are still possibilities of delegation. In case of sickness, old age, or disability, e.g., where the family — upon which the moral obligation falls in the first instance — is financially strong enough, it should be legally compelled to provide the necessary support. Even if this practice complicates office procedures and produces only negligible savings to the state, it should nonetheless be maintained in principle, for only thus can there be any direct person-to-person care of a fellow human being, only thus can personal relationships be maintained in face of the impersonal machine.

Now it might be objected, in the name of this same human and personal relationship, that it is humanly more burdensome for an aged father to have to be supported by children who are forced to do so against their will than for him to be supported by a neutral organization upon which he has claims. But this objection does not stand up under examination so far as its long-range validity is concerned.

A social order which provides in principle for every kind of disability and the helplessness of old age will in the long run alter fundamentally and fatefully the relationship between the generations. It will rob parenthood of its human authority, and take from it the protection of human qualities such as love and loyalty. It will make parenthood a temporary function: When the function is fulfilled, parents simply step down and enter another sphere of existence.

But in such a case could parents, even within the span allowed for their functioning, truly nurture and educate? Could they themselves bring love and loyalty to their office if they are nothing but biological functionaries? In contrast, would they not be reminded far more forcefully of the human and ethical side of their task if they are allowed to discharge their office within a union which only death can part?

Furthermore, does not this degenerate understanding of parenthood have as its counterpart a particular view of marriage, namely, as a temporary thing functioning to serve the purposes of eroticism and the procreation of children? And does not this dispense marriage from the bond of faithfulness? Does not this do away with the principle: "Till death us do part"? Are not the marriage partners degraded to the position of mere sexual functionaries?

The question to be asked is where are we heading? The isolated case in which it is more pleasant and dignified for an aged father to be independent of his children is of little account compared with the consequences of a blind system of uniform support payments by the total welfare state. The basic and far-reaching results of the maximal state may be seen clearly at this point.

3) To avoid the passivity involved in being merely a welfare recipient, who is regarded more as an object than as a person, it seems important that opportunity should be provided for paying in advance for later pensions and other benefits (medical expenses, etc.). If premiums, e.g., are calculated actuarially, and if the subsequent benefits differ accordingly, a sense of coresponsibility and personal achievement can be maintained, and the impression of automatic welfare avoided. The borderline cases of total need which cannot be brought under such an arrangement constitute a sphere in which care can be provided by non-state welfare agencies. (We have referred to this already.)

In contrast to this postulate of advance payments (in the form of premiums, etc.), which is the customary and, in principle, proper procedure in democracies, the radical welfare state aims at state pensions for all citizens without distinction, irrespective of need or achievement.[12] The head of state receives exactly as much as the cleaning lady. Here is where the welfare state becomes the total provider. It is no longer even the universal father. It has become instead the welfare robot, devoid of any personal features at all.

4) The role of state welfare in education is deserving of special attention. A glance at the totalitarian systems which devote huge sums to welfare of this kind — grants and stipends for students plus social provision for school children — leaves a divided impression on the citizen of a democratic state. He feels compelled to agree that many democracies do too little in this area, and that their expenditures here compare unfavorably with those of the totalitarian states. But he also feels that totalitarian states are not to be taken as models in this field. Perhaps this ambivalent reaction may best be summed up as follows: The democratic state ought to spend as much, but spend it differently.

The totalitarian state is here a maximal state in the sense that it uses its expenditures to bind the younger generation to itself. It thus pursues ideological goals. The directness with which the state provides welfare has its counterpart in the directness with which it also seeks to bind the young people to itself. This relation between the state and its young people finds institutional expression in the so-called state youth, which can take on concrete form in different sectors of life such as the school or the youth organization. But in the strict sense these are only sectors — in a circle whose center and common point of reference is the state. Thus the titles of the relevant functions and institutions all have the prefix "state." Students are given "state scholarships." Books and equipment are "state property."

Now it must be conceded that this material support on the part of the state does more than merely serve ideology. It is not meant to do only that. In addition it raises the level of education and brings it to a larger number of people. This is why democracies may legitimately be concerned lest their more modest expenditures on education and research diminish by comparison the ranks of trained personnel and specialists, so that one day they will no longer be able to compete with the totalitarian powers. It is the scientific and technical schools particularly which provide a basis of comparison here, because they are especially important for the elemental struggle for survival going

[12] Sweden already has such state pensions.

on between two great spheres of influence. Along the lines of our ethical concern, the demand would be that the democracies should spend at least as much as the totalitarian states, but that they should combine the maximum desirable expenditure with the minimum of state control. This means concretely that the use of the funds and equipment provided by the state should again be delegated so far as is humanly possible.

In conclusion we would repeat that the principle of the minimal state derives ultimately from the theological character of the state as an emergency order. This concept contains within itself the postulate that we should commit to the state, not everything we can, but only what we must. It is in keeping with the provisional and interim character of the state that its claims are possible only with the caveat of an ultimate Nevertheless. Where this caveat is omitted, there arises the totalitarian tendency which we have discussed in detail in terms of the concrete models of education and welfare. This tendency is accompanied by a similar tendency to level down all distinctions, to ignore personal maturity and dignity and to degrade persons to the position of mere objects, and to establish the dominion of the perfected machinery.

It was against this background that we insisted that the state should give up as many tasks as possible and commit them to other agencies. Only thus can such spheres as education and welfare be permeated by the personal. The state should be very largely content with an indirect role, providing subsidies, exercising the right of supervision, etc. To accomplish this arrangements must be made for the "interception" of such relinquished functions. This means that the movement towards totalitarianism will be stemmed only to the degree that non-state agencies actively assume responsibility. The movement will be arrested not by the insight — even the theological insight — of responsible men and groups in government but only by the power of these non-state interceptors, only by men who are prepared to act.

The theological reasons for resisting the total welfare state may be indicated in closing by two biblical texts. The first is the saying of Jesus: "For what will it profit a man if he gains the whole world and forfeits his life?" (Matt. 16:26). What will it profit if he gains the world socially, if he replaces the corruption of unjust and technically inefficient orders with perfect rationality and standardized justice, and in so doing loses the ability to live meaningfully and in accordance with his destiny?

The second is Paul's saying: "If I give away all I have . . . but have not love, I gain nothing" (I Cor. 13:3; cf. Matt. 6:2-4). Not to have love means not to be involved in what happens to others, not to feel it as something that is happening to me. When I farm out to the machinery of state all care of the needy and the whole task of preventing need, I am in effect refusing to be human toward a fellow human being. In the final analysis I am delegating this personal responsibility to a robot; after all, the authorities merely channel a corresponding portion of the tax revenues to welfare purposes. This is the sum and substance of what we have called our non-involvement in what happens to others. Love, on the contrary, is very much involved, and hence cannot be delegated. No substitute is possible. The responsibility of love cannot be transferred. Love that is hidden away in some mechanical apparatus "gains me nothing." And when I am without love I myself "am nothing" (I Cor. 13:2). The perfection of the machinery can actually deliver up the person to nothingness.

It is true that modern society requires some rationalizing of welfare, and the machinery to go with it. Indeed, the motive behind this may well be love acting responsibly. Nevertheless, every conceivable means must be used to find and preserve spheres in which men may deal with and care for their fellow human beings directly. This is the point of the thesis that the state must be kept to a minimum.

Part Three

BORDERLINE SITUATIONS

17.

The Applicability of Scripture and Tradition in the Question of Resistance

In an earlier analysis of the conflict or borderline situation we have already discussed a number of ethical questions arising out of the friction between citizens and the state or its officials.[1] We must now tackle the whole question of resistance in general. This is the more urgent because in our earlier discussions we dealt mainly with the totalitarian state, indeed only some of its more specific manifestations. The right to resist must now be set against a wider background.

In a field which has been so much discussed and so hotly debated, it is essential that we begin with some basic safeguards and preliminary observations concerning method. These will relate to two main areas of concern: the citing of Scripture, and conceding or refusing to concede to ethical tradition a normative significance in respect of the right to resist.

The Authority of Scriptural Citations

Particular care is needed so far as the first of these two areas is concerned, the citing of Scripture. For one thing, a distinction must be made between the state as such — to which the Christian owes obedience — and the form any particular state may take. We have seen from Romans 13 that the particular form accords with the original intention only where the state "rewards the good and punishes evildoers," and that if it does the reverse — and thus becomes an unjust state — a wholly new situation arises. This is why we referred to the tension between Romans 13 and Revelation 13.

Again, it must be noted that the authoritarian state of Romans 13, Titus 3:1, and I Peter 2:13 ff. — and of the Reformation period — no longer exists today. It has essentially been replaced by other forms which in part raise completely different problems.

[1] See *ThE* 1, 529 ff.

Yet another distinction must also be made if we are to apply biblical sayings to our own situation. We have to ask whether occasional resistance to particular organs of the state is directed in a revolutionary sense against the whole state or only against certain of its measures.[2]

Finally, the thrust of the whole thirteenth chapter of Romans must not be overlooked. Because Christians can and should live in the name of the commandment of love and in the name of the eschaton – in which all magisterial power will be abolished – they might easily be tempted to think that on the basis of their election and faith they owe direct obedience only to God and Christ, but not to provisional secular authority as well. For this reason, in face of the threat of eschatological fanaticism, they are here called to order and shown that the state is equipped with the dignity of a divine mandate.

The state certainly stands, as we have seen,[3] under the *reservation* of a Nevertheless. At the same time, though, it is also furnished with the divine *pre-eminence* of a Nevertheless; it has the dignity of the "penultimate."[4] The nuances in the term "Nevertheless" make it clear that the demand of Romans 13 that the state be respected is not to be treated in isolation but must be seen in terms of the state's background in salvation history.

This means, as we have seen earlier, that the command to "be subject" (Rom. 13:1) is not an absolute imperative. It stands under the same reservation as the state itself. The reservation – and hence also the limit of obedience – is suggested in the saying of Jesus: "Render therefore to Caesar the things that are Caesar's; and to God the things that are God's" (Matt. 22:21). Not everything is Caesar's. What he is to be given, or denied, bears a relationship to what we owe God. "We must obey God rather than men" (Acts 5:29; cf. Dan. 3:18). The saying in Matthew 5:39: "Resist not evil!" (cf. Rom. 12:17; I Cor. 13:5; I Thess. 5:15; I Pet. 3:9, 11) can be subjected to a similar isolation, with fateful results for political ethics.[5] The theological import of such sayings is rightly perceived only against the background of salvation history, i.e., along the lines fundamentally laid down in the doctrine of the two kingdoms.

---

[2] In Acts 4:20; 5:29; John 18:23 (cf. Luke 6:29!) the latter is surely the case.
[3] See above pp. 248 ff.
[4] The term is from Dietrich Bonhoeffer's *Ethics*, ed. Eberhard Bethge, trans. Neville Horton Smith (New York: Macmillan, 1955), pp. 84 ff.
[5] See our discussion of Tolstoi and the fanatics in *ThE* 1, 351 ff.

This means in the first place that for Christians the commandment of love has replaced the law of retribution (cf. Lev. 24:19, 20; Matt. 5:38-39; 26:51-52; also Exod. 23:4-5; Rom. 12:14, 20). He who sees in the other a brother will also see in the one who goes astray, yes, even in the oppressor, tormentor, and enemy of the faith, an erring child of the Father. He will be able to distinguish between the man whom the Father bewails and the demonic power which has him in his grip. On the basis of this distinction — and only on this basis — will he be able to love an enemy (Matt. 5:44) and ask God to forgive his sin (Luke 23:24; Acts 3:17, 19, 20; 7:60; cf. Isa. 53:12).

In the second place, however, my direct relationship to this enemy who is at the same time neighbor must be distinguished from the indirect relationship I bear to him in the world of the orders. Satisfaction must be done to the legal order — even to the order of the believing community — by punishing evil instead of tolerating it (I Cor. 5:1-7, 13; Phil. 3:2; Rev. 2:2). In the orders it is not primarily a matter of the evil man, but of the evil deed which must be resisted and done away.

Hence the devil (Matt. 15:22; Luke 13:32; John 8:44; 13:2) or the evil one ($\pi o\nu\eta\rho\delta s$, Matt. 6:13) is distinguished from the man who stands under his power. Evil, whether in the personal sense of the evil one or merely in the neutral sense, must be resisted (Rom. 12:9; I Pet. 5:9; Jas. 4:7). Here it is precisely the order which must keep the contours clear and the lines of demarcation sharply drawn. This is why Jesus at his trial, i.e., within the context of one of the orders, characteristically does not allow himself to be struck without offering resistance (John 18:23). To keep silent here would be to attack the order itself.

The doctrine of the two kingdoms as Lutheranism has developed it within the framework of its doctrine of the orders may be questionable in many points of detail, but at least it is sound in posing the theme of the distinction between the right hand and the left hand of God, between a direct relationship to the neighbor and the indirect relationship afforded within the order, between the neighbor himself and the dubious power to which he is subjected. The handling of this theme may be called in question. It could perhaps be done differently, even better. But the theme itself cannot be dismissed or ignored. If it is, the door is opened to fanaticism — to a fanaticism against which the

323

New Testament itself offers numerous theological safeguards. In theme and intention at least, the doctrine of the two kingdoms is simply a conceptual schema whereby various key statements of the Bible are brought into systematic relationship, not just equilibrium. Without such integration these statements would necessarily remain a chaotic conglomeration of contradictions.

Once it is recognized that within the framework of that schema these biblical sayings about resisting and not resisting are brought together in a meaningful way, then at the very least it will no longer be impossible to take Jesus' statement that we are not to resist evil (Matt. 5:39) as justification for all kinds of passive endurance. Its implicit abrogation of the law of retribution can apply only to direct personal encounters between me and my neighbor. It cannot mean that the Noachic law of legal order and of order generally is to be set aside. On the contrary, within the orders of this aeon the law of retribution is here given a new and clearly delimited kind of authority (Gen. 9:6; Rom. 13:2, 4).

Indeed, we may go further and say that since we always stand within the orders, and since even the relation between husband and wife and between parents and children is integrated into the orders, direct and indirect I-Thou relationships are not two ontically separate spheres of existence but simply two different aspects of one and the same relationship between me and my neighbor. The same man who for me is child of the Father in heaven and brother of Jesus Christ, who is bought with a price and to be distinguished from the power to which he is subject, is also the representative of a hostile order or force against which I must contend as I punish him or put him away.

This means, however, that a problem logically arises in respect of my relation to the hostile and perverted orders and their representatives. The saying of Jesus that we are not to resist evil cannot possibly be construed as a moral excuse for passively enduring the evil and illegal acts of a dubious authority. Indeed, by such an attitude of submission I can actually incur guilt, not only insofar as I abdicate responsibility for things which have been entrusted to my care and allow, e.g., my faith, my wife, or my child to be violated, but also insofar as my very passivity implies an attack on the order of the state and a disrespect for its divine commission.

For there is a kind of respect which is realized only in resistance and the call for redress, whereas passive endurance can on the contrary become a demonic power of temptation. To suffer evil without resisting it is to push it to the recklessness of even greater aggression, and to furnish it with the illusion of supposed validity. The Stuttgart Declaration of guilt of 1945 correctly acknowledges that the totalitarian state would not have reached this extreme of demonic corruption had Christians taken more seriously their duty of resistance and obeyed unconditionally the imperative to resist injustice in its first beginnings [*Principiis obsta!*].

The Relevance of the Church's Tradition

Having dealt with the question of Scripture, we come now to the question of the relevance of ethical tradition in any discussion of the right to resist. Here again it is recommended that we not simply take the statements of the Reformers, or the highly differentiated formulations of Thomas or other traditional witnesses, and set them down at the outset as timeless theses which have then to be applied to modern situations.

The classic revolutions, those in which "resistance" took the extreme form of violent overthrow, have always been directed against an autocratic form of government.[6] In relation to them the ethical problem of revolution and resistance is basically altered because they involve the establishment of wholly new forms of government.

The change which the rise of modern democracies has introduced in this respect is obvious. But even the ideological power state of our day can hardly be compared with the earlier autocracies, and certainly not with the tyrannies of antiquity.

In both cases new questions have arisen which make it advisable that we think the matter through afresh from the very beginning, even though in doing so we admittedly and unavoidably always have the classical position of Christianity in mind in the background. We have already posed this question of method in Chapter 1. In the discussion of war and revolution here in Part Three, the discussion simply takes on added urgency, because of the changed times in which we live. That the situation has changed, and with it the whole question of

---

[6] Think, e.g., of the French revolution of 1789, the Russian revolution of 1917, and the Spanish revolution of 1935.

political resistance, becomes apparent from the fact that the schema of the two kingdoms is no longer even applicable in respect of the totalitarian state.

18.

The Situations of Resistance

The Legality and Legitimacy of Resistance

The first main distinction to be made here at the outset is that between legal and illegal resistance. Already at this point we find that we must part company with the Reformation tradition; even though it too makes similar distinctions.

Luther, e.g., differentiates between admissible and inadmissible kinds of resistance. Resistance is allowed whenever the authority demands of me actions which would contravene the commandments concerning God, his name, and his day;[1] such resistance, of course, is limited to a denial of active obedience.[2] Disallowed is the resistance which contests the authority as such, or openly rebels against it. In the authoritarian state of the Reformation period it is self-evident that even the first type of resistance is "illegal," for it contests certain actions of the authority even though it has no legal ground for so doing. Such resistance may well be "legitimate" in the sense of Acts 5:29,[3] but it could hardly be "legal." In the strict sense, resistance is possible for Luther only within the framework of either a legitimate illegality or an illegitimate illegality.

This distinction between legitimate and illegitimate illegality, however, is very different from the distinction between legal and illegal in the free states of the modern world. Many attempts have been made by theologians to transfer Luther's doctrine of authority into the modern situation, whether democratic or totalitarian. But such attempts all suffer from the fatal flaw that the transfer is made directly and without regard to the basic change which has taken place between

---

[1] *LW* 44, 81, 89.

[2] Franz Lau, *"Aeusserliche Ordnung" und "Weltlich Ding" in Luthers Theologie* (Göttingen: Vandenhoeck & Ruprecht, 1933), pp. 77-78.

[3] Luther frequently cited this passage, "We must obey God rather than men," e.g., at WA 30^{II}, 197; 30^{III}, 411; 47, 267, 564.

Luther's situation and ours. The result is a caricature of Luther's doctrine of the state and of resistance.

The Legality of Opposition in Democracy

Resistance is legal today only in a democracy. Here legality and legitimacy do not follow separate paths. Resistance is so legal in fact that it is an accepted fact of the political routine. The "opposition" is an integral part of every democratic structure. The legality of opposition is provided for and protected by the constitution.[4]

How deeply opposition is rooted in the basic rules of democracy may be seen from the fact that it derives its legality directly from the principle of the distribution of powers. Opposition is a factor in the control of power. Indeed it is more than that. The "opposition" is potentially the successor government. It may one day unseat the present government.

Indeed, the possibility of opposition goes even further. While the constitution secures its legality and is the legal and legalizing framework for the interplay between government and opposition, the constitution itself is subject to attack. It is not an unassailable framework immune from all opposition. Its several articles or indeed the constitution as a whole may be called in question. Still it is the constitution itself which makes provision for legal change, and not only by way of the amending process. A democratic constitution may even be legally suspended or perhaps dissolved.

A classic example is the "legal" parliamentary undermining of the Weimar Republic by National Socialism, though in this case the legal framework of the revolution embraced a whole mosaic of flagrant individual illegalities. Certainly a democracy can provide better constitutional safeguards against suicide than were available in the Weimar Constitution. But in no case can the safeguard be absolute, because such a safeguard would itself involve the surrender of democratic axioms, and a consequent dictatorship. In principle there must always be this borderline possibility of self-destruction, a possibility of which Hitler took skilful advantage. For this is the only way to ensure that democracy will sustain itself not by fixed formulae, but by the living validation of its actual appeal, by real inner strength and an actual

---

[4] In Britain the leader of the opposition is even paid by the state. He renders the state the "service" of opposition.

capacity to survive politically. Democracy must always validate itself anew. This is why it can make use of only limited institutional safeguards. In this sense the Weimar state by its very downfall passed judgment upon itself, even if the judgment was executed by irresponsible bailiffs.

The Illegality of Opposition in Totalitarianism

Legality can be predicated of opposition only where the constitution within which it occurs is itself legitimate. The constitution itself must represent convincing values and norms, and stand in the light of the statement in Romans 13:1 that all authority is from God. Such legitimacy cannot be ascribed to the constitution of an ideological tyranny. Whether it be written (as in most totalitarian states) or unwritten and only a synonym for the will of the leader (as in National Socialism) the constitution of the totalitarian state lacks this legitimacy, and that for two reasons.

The first reason is that it is not constructed, either in terms of substance or of origin, on the basis of the citizens' agreement with its system of values and norms. It simply forces its system upon them, whether by violence or by propaganda and the power of suggestion.

The second reason, though less frequently noted, is of even greater significance. Since the provisions of the totalitarian constitution are not based on authoritative norms (human rights, etc.) but are ideologically conditioned, they do not bespeak or contain a definitive or permanently reliable system of values, but are simply a reflection of the moment. Their statements are strategically and tactically conceived. They therefore change with changing circumstances. They belong, as it were, to the superstructure, and thus find themselves in the status of functional dependence.

A classic case in point is that of the constitutional safeguards of freedom of religion provided in Marxist-Leninist societies. These are clearly only tactical in nature, of and for the moment, until such time as the socio-economic substructure advances to the point where the people no longer need religion and religious consciousness just disappears. Obviously there is no intention of admitting the independent dignity and value of religion, and the inviolability of personal conviction.

Since totalitarian constitutions have this pragmatic and tactical

329

character, there can be no such thing as a legal opposition in the totalitarian state. That possibility is ruled out from the very beginning, and for three reasons.

In the first place, if the theses and guarantees of the constitution are only tactical, if they do not apply in principle but only for the time being, the citizen can never base his resistance to state aggression on constitutionally guaranteed rights. If, e.g., in face of the suppression of religion he appeals to the constitutional guarantee of freedom of belief, it will be replied that the development towards atheism originally envisaged by the fathers of the constitution has now advanced so far that the tactical interim has come to an end, and that he, the citizen, has no right to exploit on his own behalf the constitution's cultural lag behind the new *de facto* situation. Or it will be replied — and this argument was particularly emphasized by Lenin — that the constitutional principle of toleration applies only to the people as a whole, not to the revolutionary elite, and that if he, the citizen, numbers himself among this elite, i.e., if he is a party member or hopes to win promotion and get ahead in life, he has already forfeited his right to appeal to such a constitutional provision. Thus the provision applies not only for a delimited time, but also in a restricted sphere. This is one reason why the constitution of ideological tyranny can never afford a framework for the establishment of a legal opposition.

In the second place, the pragmatic and tactical character of the totalitarian constitution is expressed primarily, as we have seen, in the fact of the existence of "ideology," which is supposed to make possible the claiming of the whole man and the breaking of inner resistance. Even where opposition which is deprived of the possibility of external development and expression migrates into the inner sphere, it will be brought to light by inner snooping, by accusation and self-accusation, and thus nipped in the bud. Opposition even in thought is forbidden.

In the third place, the total claim of the totalitarian power finds expression in the way that power is exercised. A one-party system is imposed which logically leaves no place for opposition but sees every objector as an enemy of the state.

From all this it follows that in a totalitarian state every form of resistance is necessarily illegal, since the constitution does not recognize any legal opposition. To organize opposition is mutiny. To strike is sabotage. Even to think in ways that are contrary to the system is heresy.

Summary Sketch of the Possibilities

To summarize, the democratic state provides for legal and constitutional forms of resistance, whereas the totalitarian power state makes the constitution merely a weapon to support the regime, condemning all resistance as illegal. Now in both cases, whether legal or not, resistance may indeed be legitimate. Its legitimacy will be shown by the fact that it is not anarchical or marked by group egoism, but is exercised in the name of the successor government which is to be. In a democratic state this intention may be seen in the fact that the resistance accepts the constitution as a symbol of the state and attempts to set up a regime which will accord with the nature of the true state. (Herein lies the condemnation of the legal struggle for power waged by National Socialism, for there can be no doubt that the totalitarian regime it envisioned had nothing whatever to do with this true state, however construed.) In the ideological power state resistance shows itself to be legitimate by trying to make the perverted state into a true state.

But further distinctions must yet be made. It is essential, e.g., to differentiate between resistance which fundamentally affirms the state and that which fundamentally denies it and hence is anarchistic. Once the function of the state in salvation history is recognized — and our purpose has been to foster that recognition — there is no need to engage in further theological debate with the kind of anarchistic resistance which would do away with the state in principle, whether it be based historically on religious fanaticism or on a theory of secular social revolution. As regards the resistance which fundamentally affirms the state, two radically different kinds have again to be distinguished.

On the one hand there is the resistance which is directed against the ruling system, and which thus has within it the tendency towards revolution, towards a coup d'état; on the other hand there is the resistance which is directed only against particular measures or structural elements of the state. The former of these, as we shall soon see, is illegal (whether in democracy or totalitarianism), and may also be illegitimate. The latter, while legal in democracy and illegal in ideological tyranny, is certainly legitimate in both.

Before we go on to elaborate these matters in fuller detail we would pause to sketch the several possibilities as follows: Resistance may or may not be anarchic in principle. Resistance which is anarchic in principle is both illegal and illegitimate whether in democracy or totalitarianism. Resistance which, even though it aims at the overthrow of the particular state by revolution, is not anarchic in principle, is illegal in both democracy and totalitarianism; and though illegitimate in a democracy it may conceivably be legitimate in a totalitarian situation. Resistance which, whether active or passive, is not anarchic in principle and aims only at specific limited reforms, is both legal and legitimate in a democracy; and though illegal in a totalitarian situation it is nonetheless legitimate.

19.

Revolution

Our task now is to differentiate between the two forms of resistance which are not anarchic but fundamentally affirm the state. We shall deal first — in this chapter — with the revolutionary attack on the prevailing system as such. Then in the next chapter we shall deal with the critique of individual measures, which in turn may take the form of either active or passive resistance.

The Dubious Character of All Revolutionary Acts

At this point, then, we take up the problem of legitimate and illegitimate revolution within both democratic and totalitarian systems, with special attention to the dubious character of all revolutionary acts. We shall begin by listing three of the main reasons for the dubiety of revolution.

The Residue of "Authority" Even in the Questionable Regime

A first reason why revolutionary tendencies and acts are so dubious is that "authority" unquestionably inheres even in regimes which are far from perfect. In fact, no state is ever perfect. This statement may seem exceedingly simple, indeed even trite, but once we grasp it we will forever be skeptical about all radical opposition to any particular *system.* Luther speaks of the "peculiar lord" who must nonetheless be obeyed. We might well speak in similar terms about peculiar systems. The peculiarity here referred to includes much more than merely individual defects. It has to do with the utterly questionable character of particular persons (e.g., the medieval prince) and systems. Now if in principle these peculiarities cannot call in question magisterial authority as such, one wonders immediately what degree or extreme of peculiarity will have to be reached before a radical and possibly even violent change in rule becomes inevitable.

Luther believed that such a situation is at hand whenever a ruler goes out of his mind. At that point a subject's duty to obey lapses.[1] It is true that Luther does not go so far as to say that a mentally deranged prince must be forcibly replaced. But persistent passive resistance on the part of the subjects, and the development of initiatives which contravene official pronouncements amounts in effect to the same thing, except that at most it could be called only a kind of "quiet revolution." It goes without saying that under conditions such as we know today one is tempted to speak in the same way of the madness of a particular system, and draw analogous conclusions.

The first argument for the dubiety of revolution is thus the difficulty of distinguishing between tolerable and intolerable peculiarity. Except in unusual and extreme cases [2] it is difficult to be sure in one's own mind, and to reach clear and generally approved judgments on the critical degree of peculiarity.

In a doubtful system such as that of ideological tyranny it is also difficult, at least for the majority (individuals sometimes seem to have the gift of distinguishing between spirits, I Cor. 12:10), to say whether certain criminal and foolish acts or policy errors are merely isolated defects in an otherwise fairly acceptable regime, defects which may derive from human imperfection, or whether they belong rather to the very nature of the regime itself and represent its logical consequences. Two examples come to mind. The shortage of consumer goods in a developing Marxist-Leninist society is construed by critics at home as well as abroad as the logical consequence of the planned economy, but the planners themselves explain it as accidental or inadvertent, signs of their economy's infancy, a transitional stage. Again, under Hitler the debate went on incessantly as to whether the crimes against the Jews were the logical consequence of the racial ideology or merely represented vengeful fanaticism on the part of subordinate officials of which the *Führer* knew nothing (and the system accordingly was innocent).

The two contrary views of course lead to very different answers to the question whether a revolutionary change is indicated. If the questionable degree of peculiarity is traced back to the structure of the regime itself, one will be inclined to answer the question in the affirm-

[1] *WA*, TR 1, No. 627.
[2] The obvious madness of Hitler in the later stages of World War II is a case in point.

ative. If on the other hand it is thought to arise in spite of the system rather than because of it, one will be more inclined to reject the revolutionary approach and to work for attainable improvements within the existent framework.

Thus the first reason why revolutionary acts are questionable is really twofold. There is the lack of a clear and generally accepted criterion by which to judge whether the critical degree of peculiarity has been reached. And if it has, there is the question whether it is due to the system itself or to men's defective use of it.

The Ethical Complexity of Revolution and Tyrannicide

A second reason why revolutionary acts are always questionable arises from the fact that the preparation of a coup d'état demands a readiness to enter into borderline situations which ethically are extremely complex. It requires massive duplicity and deception involving the necessity of a gigantic web of lies and all kinds of questionable compromises.[3] Indeed, one may say that the worse the system the greater the need for such questionable conduct, for the worst system is that which exercises the most rigorous control, is most totalitarian in form, and consequently requires extreme forms of deception. The tightness of the system, and the way its supporters and agents infiltrate all groups in society, may even make it necessary to choose tyrannicide as the only way to accomplish the coup. We shall consider this extreme case first.

In defining a tyrant one should remember the important distinction made by Bartolus of Sasso Ferrato between the tyranny which exists in default of any office or official legitimation (*tyrannus quoad titulum,* i.e., *ex defecto tituli*) and the tyranny which involves the abuse of an intrinsically legal office (*ex parte exercitii; tyrannus quoad executionem*).[4] Hitler's case probably falls somewhere between the two. The attempt of July 20, 1944, upon his life affords an important model for any discussion of tyrannicide, for here we have a concrete instance of the extreme case, and here too we have men who were well aware of the ethical problem and yet went on with the preparations for the coup. Tyrannicide was a subject of lively debate among them.

---

[3] See our discussion of the borderline situation in *ThE* 1, 578 ff.

[4] See Friedrich Schoenstedt, *Der Tyrranenmord im Spätmittelalter* (1938), pp. 50 ff.

Helmuth Graf von Moltke was against doing away with Hitler. He was particularly opposed to the planned assassination. In one of his last letters from Tegel prison he describes it as an act of God's providence that his premature arrest prevented his becoming implicated in the conspiracy.[5] Similarly, Carl Goerdeler and Ludwig Beck took very seriously the problem of conscience involved. They only gradually came to accept the plan, when all other possibilities of overthrowing the regime had proved illusory.[6]

Ultimately the conspirators fell back upon two main reasons why the assassination had to be attempted. The first was that the structure of police rule did not permit an uprising from below, by way of a mass movement. In the interest of safety the circle of conspirators had to be kept very small, and logically they could therefore operate only in an equally restricted sphere: they had to concentrate their efforts against the inner circle of the ruling elite, or indeed against the leader himself. The second reason was decidedly paradoxical in that even in connection with an assassination attempt ethical considerations were not suspended but rigorously taken into account. The soldier's oath of loyalty at the time was not to the constitution (there was no constitution) but to the person of the tyrant. It was therefore argued that legitimate release from this oath could be attained only if the tyrant died. If he were merely imprisoned the army, it was believed, would feel bound by its oath and would refuse to overthrow the regime.

These essential aspects of the problem merit consideration in our ethical assessment of tyrannicide, particularly because they are presented not from the comfortable aloofness of the theoretician who is not existentially involved, but precisely from within the situation of action and accountability. The attitude adopted in this particular instance is of importance ethically because it does not rest on either emotion or blind idealism. Emotion is ruled out because the resolve was made only after long and sober discussions by men who, so far as the leaders were concerned, had a strong sense of Christian responsibility. Blind idealism is also ruled out because the planners of the coup did not idealize the proposed assassination and thus pretend that it was

[5] See Alan Bullock, *Hitler: A Study in Tyranny* (London: Odhams, 1952), Chapter 13.

[6] See Gerhard Ritter, *The German Resistance: Carl Goerdeler's Struggle Against Tyranny*, trans. R. T. Clark (London: Allen & Unwin, 1958), pp. 269-287.

ethically beyond question. On the contrary, they were well aware of the dubiety of all kinds of killing. Indeed, this awareness constituted a kind of ultimate barrier which could not be removed except with great difficulty. They finally arrived at the decision that only a very small group should take upon themselves this evil. Out of a sense of responsibility for the *whole* nation they should take upon themselves, vicariously as it were, the guilt involved in this breaking of the oath of loyalty. The ethical character of the coup is thus apparent in the fact that a conflict situation was consciously evaluated and accepted, with full knowledge that it could not be resolved without guilt.

One episode in the story clarifies well this acceptance of guilt. A group of the conspirators, concerned to dispel the doubts of Ludwig Beck, tried to secure the endorsement and Christian justification of the coup by a ranking churchman, Theophil Wurm, the bishop of Württemberg. The plan was to have him convince Beck that no guilt was involved. But the group's emissary, a well-known theologian who subsequently became an important political figure, could not agree to set the proposal before the bishop in the desired form. He had to add a statement of his own position: He, the emissary, agreed with the coup, but he had to justify it in his own conscience before God, and to do so in his capacity as an individual Christian, not as one who held spiritual office or as an "arm of the Church." The bishop, however, represented the church and hence ought not to have anything to do with it. He ought not to provide a cover or justification for something which ultimately involved the acceptance of guilt. As a representative of the spiritual office, he ought to proclaim only the justification of sinners.

This, then, gives considerable theological precision to the matter of one's attitude toward tyrannicide, which is the borderline case in respect of revolution. The question whether tyrannicide is "permitted" is seen to be wrongly put. For even killing "in office" (e.g., capital punishment or killing in war) is not simply "permitted," at least if by "permission" we mean "justification." Killing in office, in the name of that authority which "bears the sword" (Rom. 13:4), is indeed legalized by the Noachic covenant (Gen. 9:6), but only because of man's "hardness of heart." It is a sign of the fallen world, for "from the beginning it was not so" (Matt. 19:8). In this sense tyrannicide too is not "justified." However, it can become an emergency measure in which guilt is responsibly accepted, with the realization that it is not entered into lightly or out of personal egoism or blind caprice, that a guilt thus assumed for the sake of others cannot separate from the love of God, and that there thus may even be hope of forgiveness.

For this guilt is undertaken within the context of a conflict which poses the alternative of either handing over a whole nation to physical destruction and moral ruin, because it is in the hands of a maniac, or of accepting the guilt of attempting to assassinate him. On the horns of this dilemma the guilt is simply a part of the total guilt involved in the fact that — through a whole series of omissions, errors, and shameful deeds of every sort — things have indeed come to such a sorry pass.

Vicarious acceptance of this crystallized form of the total guilt does not release from responsibility, at least if one rejects the category of the tragic. But it is a guilt which is accepted under the protection of forgiveness. This is why we hesitate to speak of it in terms of something we "do" or "commit" and prefer to speak of it instead as something we "accept."

It is obvious, then, that such acceptance is possible only by way of the daring resolve of the individual conscience. We miss the point of the situation if we think it possible that the church should legalize or even sanction the guilt of such an assassination attempt. Whoever in principle cannot himself do such a thing — and this is true of the church for it is not to revolt but to suffer — cannot incite others to do so either, or give his justifying approval. The church can only take the troubled conscience of the conspirator into its pastoral care, and declare forgiveness to him who is conscious of his guilt before God.

There will also be an element of remorse involved. Theologically, of course, remorse is a more complex concept than in common terminology. Remorse is commonly thought to include a resolve to "never do that again." In this sense the conspirators might well have no remorse whatever, since in a similar situation they probably would do the same thing all over again. But remorse, theologically, can also imply sorrow at the fallen state of the world, and at the fact that with it I too have fallen, necessarily so (in Luther's sense of necessity [necessitas], through wilful complicity, not compulsion [coactio]).[7]

The ethical problem involved in the situation of revolution and tyrannicide, however, becomes apparent not merely in this matter of

[7] See Martin Luther, *The Bondage of the Will*, trans. J. I. Packer and O. R. Johnston (Westwood, New Jersey: Revell, 1957), pp. 102-103, and *ThE* 1, 297.

the necessity of accepting guilt but also at another point. In the July 20 attempt on Hitler's life, as we have been discussing it, it was a case of mature Christians striding open-eyed through the situation of guilt. It is precisely because they were aware of forgiveness that they were able realistically to maintain, and not to conceal, the guilt involved. But what if the same actions are demanded of those who are not thus anchored in an awareness of forgiveness? If they are to sustain their ethical existence at all, will they not have to go on and idealize the act, justifying it outright, and thus move in the direction of a progressive loss of all ethical standards? [8]

And how about participants who are immature, mere rebels, those who do not grasp the ethical issues of the conflict situation, and for whom assassination is simply a matter of revenge, or of adventure, or of a clean sweep with a new broom? Even if a brand new world were thereby to be established, would not the deed do spiritual damage to the individual in a way that the guilt "accepted" under the sign of forgiveness cannot possibly do?

In any case one must certainly ask the question — and a consideration of the revolutions that have taken place during the course of human history shows how unavoidable the question is — whether the loss of inner substance, the inner damage, may not offset the gains sought by the violent overthrow of a corrupt system. Unless appearances deceive, one can only say that modern revolutions have been to the detriment of authority as such, and that the freedom they envisaged has been attained only in a more or less perverted form.

This question of course is indisputably linked with the further question whether this undermining of authority and this degeneration of freedom are not attributable already to the systems which the revolutions were designed to supplant. If so, revolutions themselves must be regarded as symptoms of the decline rather than as the motive forces behind it. But however that may be, there can be no doubt that every revolution has its dubious and destructive aspects, and so the question must be asked whether it is worth the cost. The question cannot be answered a priori in the negative. But it does suggest that revolution is appropriate, if at all, only in cases of extreme emergency. This leads us to our third point.

---

[8] We analyzed this law of progressive ethical decline in *ThE* 1, 598 ff.

The Anarchical Results of Revolution

Revolutions are usually preceded by a more or less pronounced and protracted climate of anarchy. This is because they are usually linked with a special psychosis which hardly allows the greater part of those smitten by it to distinguish between their conflict against the particular system and conflict against the state as such. There are two infallible signs of this anarchical mentality.

The first is the fact that practically every revolution, once its goal is reached, has great difficulty in consolidating a new order and ending what almost amounts to a condition of permanent revolution. Revolutions go through such phases, and this law of revolution can only be explained by the fact that the warped, peculiar, or corrupt regime which is the target of the revolution is no longer an authentic representative of state authority. This is what leads to revolt against the remnant of authority which may still be there, and ultimately to a total loss of all sense of authority. This is why it is so hard to achieve stability after the revolutionary phase. In many cases dictatorial power is required, but at best that can only deal with externals.

The second sign of the anarchical climate of revolution is closely linked to the first. The execution of a coup d'état is hardly possible without more or less significant participation by the "revolutionary type," the passionate rebel. It would be against all the ordinary rules of life if, when the carcass of political and social decay is exposed, we did not find a horde of vultures whose native impulse leads them to the spot, and — to change the metaphor — to unbounded freedom and reckless adventuring in the no man's land between systems.

Psychological considerations alone, however, cannot explain this phenomenon. Certain technical requirements also play a role. If revolution necessarily involves what in terms of ethics must be called borderline situations, if it can hardly proceed without duplicity, stratagems, brutalities, and lies, then a revolutionary movement too can hardly dispense with a certain type of person, at least for the lesser roles where the plan is actually carried out. It requires a person who is less restrained and can therefore get on with the job, a person who is almost constitutionally prone to disorderly acts, who likes to live dangerously, beyond the pale of order. (The state itself needs persons of this type for espionage.) The fact is that borderline situations require, as it were, a borderline type.

People of this type are not easily changed. This is why it seems to be part of the law of revolutions that a second revolution, initiated from above, must follow in order to get rid of the original leaders of the coup. For the borderline type, the revolutionary, naturally tends to foster permanent instability, and hence to stand as an obstacle between the act of revolution and its goal.[9]

All these phenomenological marks and accompaniments of revolution pose urgently once again the question whether the liabilities which inevitably attend every revolution can ever be justified. They certainly show that revolution is out of the question except as a last resort, and that any consideration of it must normally begin with the question whether and why this particular case, with its probable ambiguities, is indeed the extreme case.

These concrete marks of revolution as they actually appear in history are part of Luther's argument against the legitimacy of revolution, along with his argument in principle from the doctrine of the orders. As he sees it, revolution is always avenged. Even when it succeeds, it has to pay and pay dearly. This in itself shows that revolution is not in accordance with God's will.[10] Historical experience shows that, while revolutions *change* the world, they do not *improve* it, though they all set out with the claim to do so. There is a world of difference between changing and improving. "It is easy to change a government, but it is difficult to get one that is better, and the danger is that you will not. Why? Because it is not in our will or power, but only in the will and the hand of God." [11]

Revolution as a Last Resort

We must now define more precisely this "extreme case" in which revolution is no longer out of the question. The first thing to be said, by way of limiting the field, is that a high degree of "peculiarity" — whether it be a matter of folly, ideological tyranny, or criminal principles and activities [12] — does not in itself indicate that the extremity has been reached. In such cases resistance to individual measures is

---

[9] Hitler's suppression of the Röhm revolt on June 30, 1934, and some Communist purges may be illustrative of this law.
[10] *LW* 46, 106-107.
[11] *LW* 46, 112; cf. 13, 217.
[12] We are thinking, e.g., of Jewish pogroms, elimination of the mentally ill, secret police, etc.

certainly legitimate, indeed may even be demanded, but this does not mean that violent overthrow is indicated. For even in extreme perversity the state is not wholly destitute of the element of authority. It still stands broadly under the protection of its authorization in Romans 13, even though it may already have entered the zone between this authorization and the proscription of Revelation 13, or even though it may have moved over completely into the zone of proscription. For even perverted authority still preserves a remnant of order, even if only in the area of traffic and monetary regulation (and even if here only partially), and even though in its perverted law right has all but disappeared, except as it continues to be shadowed forth as a principle.[13]

This remnant of order is always better than the utterly chaotic war of all against all, against which the preserving order of the state is instituted. So long as the state displays even a trace of the ordering function assigned it in salvation history, it is always to be supported — if chaos is the only alternative. The question arises, of course, whether there are not situations in which this alternative does not exist because the state itself is already on the side of chaos. (This is the question we shall presently be examining.)

Connected with this residue of authority is the fact that even in that crucial passage on the demonic power state, Revelation 12-13, there is no demand for its violent overthrow. For this state too derives from divine ordination, albeit as an "alien work." Its origin is to be sought in the fact that it is a higher hand which tosses the dragon down onto the earth to rule (12:9, 13). The things he does here are merely the death-throes of his perishing dominion. They are the more incredible and destructive precisely because he knows his end is at hand and he wants to make the most of the short time remaining to him ($\epsilon\iota\delta\grave{\omega}\varsigma$ ὅτι ὀλίγον καιρὸν ἔχει, 12:12). Indeed, this is why he persecutes and makes war on those who "keep God's commandments" (12:17). They, however, are not summoned to violent resistance, for violence would merely bring about their own defeat and judgment (13:10). They are simply commissioned to withhold from the beast their worship (13:8; 14:9), and by honoring God refuse honor to him (14:7). They are to respond not with active rebellion, but with the "endurance of the

___
[13] On ideological law see above pp. 41 ff.

saints" (ὑπομονὴ τῶν ἁγίων, 14:12). To be sure, this will mean in fact unending resistance to all sorts of demands, and even a readiness for martyrdom (cf. 14:13). But it will not mean revolution.

Luther's attitude to tyranny (to which we shall return) is along the same lines, and affords theological ethics two main principles of orientation. In the first place, it has not been given to the communion of saints to overthrow governments, however perverted. The church has rather to suffer, resisting such demands as are contrary to God's commandments. If the church were actively to rebel, it would itself have to become in some sense the successor of the deposed authority. This would put it on the road to theocracy, for which it was not intended, and make of it an entity of "this aeon."

In the second place, perversion of the institution of government is not in itself sufficient cause for active rebellion on the secular and political level. For here the question as to what is to replace the toppled system does not yet arise, and apart from this question there can be no positive authorization of revolution. The purely negative premise that the state is corrupt does not in and of itself imply such authorization on the political level.

At the time of the book of Revelation, and of Luther, the historical situation was such that the question of what precisely should follow in the wake of a revolution did not necessarily arise. In our time, however, with its longer and wider perspective on so many changes of system, and its wider range of historical options, this question can and must play a part.

Premises for an Ethically Legitimate Revolution

Along with the negative presupposition of an unworthy government, certain other premises must also be realized if the possibility of revolution is to be taken seriously. Two presuppositions in particular deserve notice, both of which derive from the same postulate that there must be no lapse of government.

The Availability of a Successor Government

The first premise is that the makings of a new government should already be present, one that plainly possesses the marks of authority. Revolution can be legitimate only if it is something more than just the conflict of undirected rebellious force against the residue of authoritarian order. It must rather involve, as it were, the conflict between two authorities. One of these is, of course, the "peculiar" and impotent authority. The other, though not officially authorized and hence illegal, has moral validation and is prepared to take over as the successor government. A coup initiated without such a potential government at hand necessarily lacks inner authorization because it is wholly negative. It represents hostility to the state but not improvement of it, and so calls forth anarchical chaos.

At the same time, it becomes plain once again that revolution can be carried through only in the secular and political sphere. It cannot be something the church undertakes, for only secular institutions can constitute the essentially secular state and thus provide a succession in government. Because the church cannot do this without being either theocratic or fanatical, it is also forbidden to oppose the prevailing system as such. In principle, the church is not itself a potential government. It consequently has no authority to offer revolutionary resistance. To do so would be not only to offend against its own true nature, but also to violate the nature of authority as such. For, where resistance is not offered in the name of something positive, i.e., a potential successor government, it can only be negatively destructive.

Under ideological tyranny the temptation to revolutionary resistance is very great for the church and its leaders. For one thing, these men are also citizens of the state, and when passions run high it is hard to keep the two things apart. But more importantly, ideological tyranny confronts the church less as a state, a kingdom on the left hand, and more as a counterchurch or pseudo church on the right hand. Since the counterconfession which the church directs against the ideological confession of the state is also a political act (for the ideological state makes no distinction, and the doctrine of the two kingdoms cannot be applied to it), the church is strongly tempted for its part to obliterate the distinction between the disobedience required by faith and political resistance in general, allowing itself to be driven into a radical kind of opposition. But such opposition will either be purely negative and thus destructive, or it will be offered in the name of a potential theocracy. Either way it is a mistake.

Furthermore, such opposition would undercut the church's witness over against the ideological state, for it would involuntarily confirm the interpretation which the ideological functionaries give of the church. They hold that the church is itself an ideological power aiming at self-aggrandizement, and hence on the same plan as the ideological state itself. Radical opposition on the part of the church would only confirm this assumption.

The thrust of the church's witness vis-à-vis the totalitarian state must consist rather in its willingness to suffer. The church must show itself to be something other than the champion of a Christian ideology. It must make its confession by naming and condemning what is corrupt, and by then being willing to suffer in all weakness, content simply to bear its Father's name written on its forehead (Rev. 14:1).

The clear distinction between the counterwitness of the church and all political and revolutionary resistance is vividly seen in the following incident: In connection with the July 20 attempt on Hitler's life a theologian who had taken part in the plot, not as an official of the church, but consciously and openly as a citizen of the state quite apart from his office, was twice led out to execution and each time recalled at the last moment for a new hearing. On both occasions, at the foot of the gallows, he uttered as his last words, "I die as a traitor, not as a pastor." He wanted to distinguish between his spiritual witness and his political resistance. It goes without saying that this did not rule out but actually implied the fact that the resistance he offered at the political level was also offered out of his sense of responsibility as a Christian. It was not offered, however, in fulfillment of his spiritual office. Berggrav makes the same distinction when he says, "According to Augustana XVI there is a distinction between the church and Christian citizens. What the church as such may be forbidden to do [i.e., support or initiate political resistance] is laid upon the citizens as a duty." [14]

The proper form of activity for the church is not resistance but prayer. Only as it calls the Lord of history into its insoluble dilemma does it bear witness that it is not setting its own autonomous Christian ideology over against another ideology, but that it stands on the side of God against the anti-God, letting "the right Man" do its fighting for it. [15]

---

[14] Eivind Berggrav, *The Proceedings of the Second Assembly of the Lutheran World Federation; Hannover, Germany, July 25-August 3, 1952*, p. 80.

[15] See the excellent section on prayer in Gustaf Wingren, *Luther on Vocation* (Philadelphia: Muhlenberg, 1957), pp. 184-199.

The Ripeness of the Situation

The second premise for a legitimate revolution — and it is related to the first — is that the situation must be ripe for it: The existing but tottering government must be outwardly so shaken that only an additional push is needed to bring about its fall. (Obviously the preparation for revolution assumes that this condition will be brought about. Whether this is accomplished legitimately depends on whether the first premise is also present concurrently with the debilitating attacks on the system.)

The ripeness of the situation will find expression pre-eminently in the fact that the existing regime no longer has unrestricted control of the actual power of state, but that this power has passed *de facto* to the opposing group (or is in process of doing so), or has been divided among several competing resistance groups.[16] In the latter case the revolutionary initiative may even need special activation.

The more nearly this state of ripeness is attained, the more organic will be the transition. The shorter too will be the interim period without authoritative control, and the more fully will the postulate of a revolutionary minimum be met.

Legitimation by the People as a Whole

A third premise for a legitimate revolution, if it be directed against the totality of a system, is that it be supported by the totality of the people, i.e., by the clearly discernible will of the whole nation and not just by one group with its special interests. Strictly speaking, "the people as a whole," as Fichte contends, "never can be a rebel," for on our modern understanding of it the people is the true sovereign. "The expression *rebellion*, applied to the people at large, is the greatest absurdity ever uttered. . . . No people have ever uprisen nor ever will uprise as one man, until injustice has become too intolerable." [17]

While the people's sovereignty must indeed be recognized, one might say in objection to Fichte that an uprising of the whole people can be legitimate only in connection with the two premises already mentioned, for, in isolation, it does not carry with it the implication of

---

[16] See Walter Künneth, *Politik zwischen Dämon und Gott. Eine christliche Ethik des Politischen* (Berlin: Lutherisches Verlagshaus, 1954), p. 287.

[17] Johann Gottlieb Fichte, *The Science of Rights*, trans. A. E. Kroeger (Philadelphia: Lippincott, 1869), p. 272. The quotation is cited by Richard Rothe, *Theologische Ethik* (2nd ed.; Wittenberg: Koelling, 1869-1871), V, 373, n. °°.

a successor government and hence could as easily produce chaos as a new political order.

Although Luther's negative attitude toward the Peasants' Revolt and toward revolution in general is surely controlled in the main by his concepts of authority, ruler, and subject, and although the modern concept of national sovereignty and its corollary of a changed view of the state are alien to him,[18] his opposition is unquestionably based also on the view that robber gangs and fanatics deny the state in principle. Quite apart from the question of their right to do so, they are simply in no position to constitute a government.

The Hungarian uprising of 1956 is a good example from modern times of the fact that the clear will of the people as a whole cannot of itself make revolution a legitimate possibility. With all due respect for the oppressed people's readiness to sacrifice themselves, we must also say that this particular uprising was a matter of improvisation and emotion, and that it did not meet the first two premises, namely, the presence at hand of a potential successor government and the ripeness for collapse of the old regime. Hence it was bound to fail, not merely through the massive intervention of the Soviet Union, but also through its tendency to be simply a negative protest movement with no positive constructive program. The case exemplifies well our theory.[19]

A similar objection to that brought against Fichte must also be urged against Richard Rothe's theses on revolution. Rothe distinguishes between rebellion [Aufruhr] and revolution. The former is "against law," the latter "against caprice." The former is carried on by a party, the latter by the whole people, for "the people never rebels" (this is the context in which Rothe cites Fichte). "The former is free and open to blame, the latter is unavoidable and free from blame, for under the pressure of circumstances it is the only means to deliver a nation from imminent destruction."[20]

Here too our criticism would be that even the clear revolt against caprice, if it stands alone as the only premise, does not validate revolu-

---

[18] Cf., however, Luther's statements: "In the absence or failure of those in authority the people is the authority and a man may call upon his neighbors for help" (WA, TR 4, 237, No. 4342); "Where there is no government the people act" (WA 39II, 59, line 30).

[19] See George Mikes, The Hungarian Revolution (London: Deutsch, 1957); also the Report of the United Nations General Assembly Special Committee on the Problem of Hungary (New York, 1957).

[20] See Rothe, op. cit., V, 372, n. **.

tion. For such a revolt against caprice might itself be made in the name of caprice. Revolt against lawlessness does not necessarily take place in the name of law. It might instead rest on the passion of a tormented people. To revolt in the name of law, on the other hand, i.e., in the name of a constructive program of government, would come very close to what we formulated above as our first premise. All the same, we hold that it is a further presupposition of a legitimate revolution that to the totality of the system attacked there must correspond a totality of opposition on the part of the people as a whole.

The Problem of Revolution in Democracy

It must have struck the reader that most of the examples we have adduced to characterize the revolutionary situation are drawn from the sphere of ideological tyranny. This is no accident, for in a democracy that is really functioning revolution cannot possibly be legitimate.

This is not because democracy is so perfect in principle that there can be no reason for overthrowing it as a concrete system. History records so many systems that it would be unrealistic to regard democracy as a sort of eschatological and unsurpassable fulfillment of constitutional history. Obviously history never stands still, and we do not know what forms of state the future might hold which could be appropriate to their own times.

The real reason why revolution can never be legitimate in a functioning democracy arises from our previous deliberations. If a group is legitimately to dissolve a democracy, or basically to change its structure, that group must have the quality of a potential government. This means that it must be dynamically and quantitatively able to come to power by way of the regularly established channels of opposition, i.e., by using the parliamentary means provided for taking over the reins of government. Where a group cannot do this, it may be due to one of two reasons. It may fail to qualify as an opposing group, in which case it has no right to take over, or the state may be a democracy in name only and not in fact, in which case a violent change — under the previously stated conditions of course — is no longer out of the question.

The second alternative, namely, that the state is democratic in name only, can arise when either of the two pillars of the state — power or law — is threatened or has already collapsed. If law is attacked, there is no legal possibility of constituting a new government within the prevailing constitutional rules; this is tantamount to a transformation of democracy into a totalitarian state, and other criteria accordingly come into play by which to judge the legitimacy or illegitimacy of a revolution. If on the other hand the power of a state is threatened, if the army, police, and civil services have fallen into the hands of other (internal or external) power groups or are at their mercy, such loss of sovereignty entails also the loss of title: it is no longer a true state, possessing corresponding qualities of government, much less a regular democracy. In this case too a revolutionary seizure of power comes under other laws. But our thesis remains that there can be no revolution in a democracy that really functions as such.

In all this it is to be noted that as regards the "normal" democratic situation, the two exceptions just mentioned, and the situation under ideological tyranny, all are distinctly modern situations which differ radically from those faced by the Reformers in the political sphere. This observation confirms once again the thesis that we advanced in respect of methodology at the close of Chapter 17, namely, that in dealing with revolution it is impossible to apply the teaching of the Reformers directly to the present situation. Instead, we must bring different theological arguments to bear in the fundamentally different circumstances of our day.

The constant element which persists through every change in situation, and which thus belongs inalienably to the tradition of political ethics, is twofold. First, the state, in whatever form, functions in salvation history as an order of preservation and thus to this extent has a divine mandate. Second, while modern democracy is no longer an authoritarian state in the medieval sense (inasmuch as the citizen — formerly the "subject" — is now potentially the ruler), the state in this altered form nonetheless deserves the title of "authority."

20.

Opposition to Individual Measures

We have now dealt with revolution as the violent overthrow of an existing system by an opposition which nonetheless fundamentally affirms the state (the anarchical opposition which denies the state can here be left out of account), and we have seen how differently the problem appears from the standpoint of the two forms of state which are normative today. In Chapter 18 we sketched briefly the basic differences between the two systems so far as their understanding of opposition is concerned. But we must now pursue the ramifications in detail. Systematic treatment requires that along with the violent and revolutionary overthrow of the systems as such we should now consider also the various forms resistance may take *within* the systems. More precisely, our concern will be with the criticism of specific measures taken by the state, a criticism which is not directed against the state as such and does not aim at violent change.

Opposition in a Democracy

Normal Opposition

So far as democracy is concerned, we may begin with a list of the normal forms of opposition. Opposition in a democracy may be offered in the first place by institutions such as the political parties, the trade unions with their strike weapon, and the mass media with their ability to express and to form public opinion; these and similar institutions have a sphere of action which is guaranteed to them, even laid upon them. But legal opposition can be offered too by the individual, on the basis of his freedom of opinion and of conscience. The limits within which this opposition must function are determined by the constitution and are binding on both sides, i.e., on the organs of the state on the one hand, and on the institutions and citizens on the other.

In this connection the question may become acute whether certain totalitarian tendencies, such as are plainly evident in Communist circles, are inimical to the constitution and hence represent an illegal form of opposition. In the main, however, an open misuse of the freedom of opposition, so long as it is not hostile to the constitution or contrary to the law, will be widely allowed in a democracy, since the very possibility of misuse contributes to the establishment of genuine freedom and is thus the price which must be paid for such freedom.

For if freedom means only the liberty to do what the other side wants, this leads to the kind of thing which is so familiar in totalitarian states, and which with justifiable irony is described as "voluntary compulsion." In this case — and this is also a definition of the totalitarian state — the state alone is free. At best the freedom of the individual and of institutions is then derived from that of the state, and is granted only so far as it serves the will of the state.

Democracy tolerates the freedom of individuals and institutions because it distrusts the concentration of freedom in one place (the state or anywhere else), lest such concentration become identical with an uncontrollable concentration of power. This is the ethical background of democracy's constitutional protection of the opposition and of its granting of corresponding freedoms. Both of these are based on the distinctly democratic principle of the distribution of powers.

Two Borderline Cases

The forms in which opposition can be offered in a democracy are as varied as the institutions and individuals who offer it, as varied too as the situations within which it arises. They range from passive resistance such as staying away from the polls or refusing to hold office, to active resistance such as is mounted in the attack on specific measures by labor unions, leagues of taxpayers, and groups of conscientious objectors.[1]

In this connection two borderline cases should be noted. The first is a form of opposition which surreptitiously undermines the state structure and hence cannot fall under democracy's "edict of toleration." The second has to do with a limitation of opposition in virtue of one's vocation.

The first case, then, involves the undermining of the majesty of the

---

[1] An account of the active resistance I once had to offer myself to particular governmental measures during the postwar denazification of Germany is given in Helmut Thielicke and Harald Diem, *Die Schuld der Anderen* (Göttingen, 1947).

state by groups. It can happen, e.g., that the freedoms granted in the name of the state's self-limitation are claimed not by individuals — for whom they were intended — but by organized groups, e.g., associations representing social, economic, or other interests, with the result that uncontrollable concentrations of power arise within the state. Thus trade unions can hold the state in the palm of their hand by threatening a general strike. Even if they use such power responsibly, it involves potentially the presence of a state within a state.

Democracy's ethos of the distribution of powers, and the freedom of opposition granted under this banner, can thus in certain circumstances have a deadly recoil. Politically this is indeed "deadly" because by nature an association representing social interests can never be a potential government, and hence cannot legitimately carry through a revolution. This means that behind an irresponsible use of such a latent possibility of power there stands, not a new order of state, but chaos. The state must be on guard against the threat to the democratic ethos which is thus inherent in its own principles. It must accordingly be prepared to limit its democratic tolerance.

The second of our two borderline cases involves the freedom of the man in office. We are thinking here particularly of people in government, for their activity poses a special problem in the present context, though the problem is similar in the case of other officials (e.g., those of public corporations, churches, etc.).

The term itself suggests that an "official" is bound to an "office." Office is something which demands not merely technical competence but above all — and this is the important point in the present context — an ethos of vocation. The very history of officialdom shows that the ethos of vocation has always been shaped by obligations of loyalty and obedience, and that "office . . . is not considered as a personal right to be enjoyed, a source of personal advantage," but as selfless service to a commission or cause.[2] Officialdom is of particular importance in a modern state precisely because, in virtue of the objective neutrality of its service, it constitutes a "natural counterbalance to egoistic interests and individual forces,"[3] and also a constant element amidst the fluctuations of political power.

[2] Georg Dahm, *Deutsches Recht. Die geschichtlichen und dogmatischen Grundlagen des geltenden Rechts* (Stuttgart: Kohlhammer, 1951), p. 272.
[3] *Ibid.*, p. 372.

Because his service is objective, and because he stands in this relation of public and legally established loyalty which "begins and ends with the sovereign act of appointment and dismissal," the official is bound by the instructions given him. It is this prescription of duties which can give rise to conflict. For if the official remains a responsible subject, if he does not regard his service merely as that of a functionary, then his own views and their responsible implementation may lead him into conflict with the obedience laid upon him by the instructions of his government. In this case it is incompatible with his obligation of loyalty that he should in his office exercise radical resistance against the directives to which he is bound, and thus in effect be guilty of surreptitiously sabotaging them.

By using here the word "radical" we would guard against stretching the principle too far. For it goes without saying that directives can usually be interpreted and executed in a variety of ways, all of which are still compatible with the obligation of loyalty, especially since the authority which issued the directives is not in as good a position to supervise the details of any particular department as is the official himself. Thus there is always room for some variation at the point of execution. Practical elasticity is one thing, however, and radical opposition to the general tenor of the instructions or to the one who issues them is quite another. The official can legitimately offer such radical opposition only by resigning or by asking to be removed.

At this point we can refer only briefly to the borderline cases which occur here, as everywhere. It must suffice to mention the most important term by which such cases might be defined. To be specific, the case may conceivably arise in which the directing authority can no longer be believed, and an official in a particularly important post is plunged into an apparently insoluble conflict between loyalty to the one charged to issue directives on the one hand, and loyalty to his own department, which is so vital to the state as a whole, on the other. In such a conflict he then opts in favor of the latter loyalty, and therewith decides to offer resistance in office.

There is an example of this from the Nuremberg trials in the case of Ernst von Weizsäcker, State Secretary of the German Foreign Office. Although diametrically opposed to the goal and methods of the National Socialist Foreign Minister, Joachim von Ribbentrop, he chose to stay on in order that he might use the possibilities afforded

by his office to oppose the fatal course leading to war.[4] The Weizsäcker case, which has gained considerable fame as a case in point,
belongs in terms of its historical setting to the sphere of resistance
against the totalitarian state. But there are good reasons for discussing
it already here, because on this matter the situation in the totalitarian
state is simply an extreme form of that which can arise in any state
structure or even in a public institution. The issues which arise include some we have already discussed in principle in our treatment of
the conflict situation.[5]

If it is the task of politics to secure the existence and independent
development of a society both internally and externally, then certain
rules of the game appropriate to that goal are indicated from the very
outset. E.g., one primary rule is that power must be won and used
since goals cannot be attained without it, and even the good cannot
survive in a fallen world except as it is protected.

This undoubtedly applies also with respect to those who hold secondary offices (e.g., important officials at the cabinet or subcabinet
level) insofar as they still in some sense initiate and determine political action. In their case, however, it might be better to speak, not of
their actual power, but only of the influence they exert and of how
they enter the picture. Theologically, the problem was complicated
particularly by the fact that von Weizsäcker knew he was not merely
caught up in the play of forces which goes to make up a political
order – such as that intended in Luther's "kingdom on the left hand"
– but was actually incorporated through his office into a perverted
order. It is this unjust order which is the determinative factor.

If it is true that "even the best of us cannot live in peace unless the
bad neighbor allows it," then it must also be said that even the best
of us cannot remain blameless if he lives in a culpable and unjust
order. Nor need one think only of ideological tyranny in this connection, for the principle holds also – with necessary variations in nuance
of course – for situations which can conceivably arise also in other

---

[4] See Ernst von Weizsäcker, *Memoirs,* trans. John Andrews (London: Gallancz,
1951). See also *Trials of War Criminals before the Nuernberg Military Tribunals
under Control Council Law No. 10;* Volumes XII, XIII, and XIV deal with the
trial "United States of America vs. Ernst von Weizsäcker, et al," otherwise known
as the "Ministries case" (case 11), which lasted from October 1946-April 1949;
see esp. XII, 234-246, and the magnificent closing statement by defense counsel
Hellmut Becker at XIV, 92-126.

[5] See *ThE* 1, 585-594, 643-647, 663-667.

national structures. This determinative significance of the unjust situation becomes clear in the case of the two types of behavior which are theoretically possible at this point.

The first possible response is for the official to lay down his office and go into exile or private life in order both to keep aloof from the unjust order and also do justice to the ethos of office, which calls for either loyalty to those issuing the directives or resignation where the antitheses are unbridgeable. The satisfaction of washing one's hands of the matter privately is greatly diminished, however, by the consideration that in certain crucial situations the one who retreats in this way abandons his sphere of responsibility (in the case of state officials the country too, and the neighbor who has been placed in his trust) to a destructive laissez faire. Indeed he who in principle would evade the sphere of guilt by innocently withdrawing may in some circumstances be merely moving from a personal and direct guilt to a suprapersonal and indirect guilt. But personal guilt too will usually attach to him in virtue of the resultant Pharisaism. In addition, he who thus withdraws overlooks the fact that everyone (himself included) bears some guilt for the development of the unjust situation. Hence withdrawal at a specific point may easily mean that I am trying to evade the consequences of my own action and leave others to clean up the mess I helped to make.

On the other hand, and this is the second possible response, the mandate of political action — to secure the existence of a society both internally and externally — may prompt the official in a dubious order to explore at least the minimal possibilities for saving the situation, namely, to stay at his post and exercise what influence he can. This is possible, however, only if he is willing to practice deception, i.e., take over to some extent the methods of his opponents. And such deception is possible only if he is prepared to accept guilt.[6] "The nature of the situation is such that whoever decides to take upon himself the task of co-operating, even though he is fundamentally opposed to what is going on, can, because of his ultimate intention, be justified in the sight of God, his own conscience, and the fair appraisal of his fellowmen — and still be obliged to bear the odium and in some way pay the

---

[6] Cf. the analysis of the French resistance set forth in these terms by Alexander Miller in his article "Is Everything Permitted?" *The Student World*, XXXVIII, No. 4 (1945), which is quoted in *ThE* 1, 586-587.

consequences of what he has taken upon himself, again before God, his conscience, and the judgment of his fellowmen. The evangelical insight that in faith man may be righteous even though he is a sinner has as its necessary complement that man must recognize and confess he is a sinner even though in faith he knows he is righteous." [7] What is involved here is really resistance by means of – or even "in spite of" [8] – collaboration.

These two possible responses (resistance through retreat or withdrawal and resistance by feigned co-operation) are not of equal worth, i.e., the choice between them is not a matter of indifference; they cannot be counted among the *adiaphora*. On the other hand, neither response is a priori better than the other. Ethics has constantly to weigh things, i.e., to analyze critically the degrees of wrong which attach to each alternative. This means concretely, on the one hand, that feigned co-operation may impose upon me such a measure of guilt (e.g., through preparation for war, doing away with people, persecution) that the straightforward and non-pragmatic resolve to withdraw on conscientious grounds may be the only thing to do; such withdrawal would be less a retreat from the situation of guilt than a confession, a public sign which by causing others to take notice is itself of political significance at least in its effects. On the other hand, continuing co-operation, even when so high a degree of direct guilt is not involved, always carries with it – especially in the case of well-known public figures – the risk that in the eyes of many it will help to validate a disreputable system.

The decision between these two alternatives is not something that can be made on casuistical and a priori grounds. It must be left to the individual conscience. There must be the venture of personal decision. Here too the rule applies that when two men do the same thing it is not the same, and two who act very differently may be doing the very same thing. Indeed, at times it may make sense for two men working side by side to respond differently, the one making the outward demonstration and the other seeking to save the situation from within. This obviously cannot mean that there is a conscious distribution of roles. It can only mean that the impossibility of prior decision, of

---

[7] Karl Barth in a theological opinion concerning the Weizsäcker trial, August 17, 1948.

[8] This is how Barth puts it.

arriving at a general answer valid for all, may also have — as a by-product — its political significance. The main thing, at any rate, is that there should be a recognition of the alternatives open to decision, and that this recognition should entail fruitful ethical disquiet.

Opposition in the Totalitarian State

Christian Resistance

The character of Christian resistance in a totalitarian state has been discussed already in our investigation of the totalitarian state as a model of the borderline situation.[9] Hence we need only allude to it in this context. We shall systematically review only the decisive points.

To begin with, the totalitarian state confronts us with the question whether and in what way we are ready to make public confession of our faith in face of the direct attacks upon it which necessarily arise from the state's ideology. But it also confronts us with the question what attitude we shall take toward its indirect encroachments in terms of world view. These indirect encroachments arise where the state permeates ideologically the whole of life (education, science, the social structure, law, etc.), so that there are no longer any objective and secular spheres, and a Christian stand is demanded at every point. The state becomes a kind of negative theocracy or pseudo church instead of a "kingdom on the left hand."

From a purely logical standpoint, a consistent Christian stance is possible only if the citizen either goes into exile — the only form of radical non-participation — or lives in a state of thoroughgoing and unremittent protest. The first possibility obtains only for a small and dwindling minority; it cannot be regarded as a genuine option fundamentally open to all who would resist. The second is completely impossible, and that for two reasons.

First, the laws and measures of a totalitarian state, even though they inevitably involve abuses, accomplish tasks which serve the preservation of state and people. It is these positive functions which make such a state preferable to chaos. A radical resistance which engages in consistent sabotage would consequently do more than attack the demonic aspects of these abusive measures in detail; it would also adversely affect the positive elements in the actual functioning of the

[9] See *ThE* 1, 578-667.

state itself. Second, total resistance — which would have to extend all the way from a refusal to pay taxes to a disclaimer on the use of the streets — would call forth such reprisals on the part of the totalitarian state as would not merely destroy myself but also be harmful to others; my family and relatives could also be made to suffer.

Hence life in a totalitarian state implies a situation of incessant and fundamentally insoluble conflict. Indeed, such conflict is part of the totalitarian strategy for the use of power, inasmuch as it weakens men's capacity for action and thus limits their possibilities of opposition. The possibility of a confessional stance is effectively circumvented by such tactics. Pyres of witness do not often burn on this political landscape because the state regards martyrdom as tactically inopportune; it tries to eliminate it from the struggle. In bypassing the situations which would make Christians take a stand the ideological system is simply applying the economic principle of seeking the largest possible results for the smallest possible expenditure. To arouse the conscience of the whole church and thus create conscious antagonism would not be economical. Hence the attack focuses not on the center but on the periphery, almost in the fashion of the military tacticians. To strike at America they do not attack New York but undertake actions in the Near East or in Southeast Asia. To strike at the church they do not depose bishops but unknown out-of-the-way pastors, and they do not proscribe Bible or Catechism but only church papers and periodicals. The citizen is thus confronted by a host of smaller matters which make the situation one of incessant conflict.

On the other hand, the impossibility of radical forms of resistance does not mean that there can be nothing but the complete passivity of laissez faire. On the contrary, the specific structure of the totalitarian state calls forth two distinct kinds of resistance.

The first proceeds from the conviction that the tactical goal of the totalitarian state, namely, the radical elimination and extirpation of its opponents, must be sabotaged by staying in the game in order to maintain the possibility of doing something about it. This possibility inevitably involves deception, i.e., a dubious co-operation which is entered into knowingly. We have dealt with this kind of resistance in connection with the problem of the Weizsäcker case.

The second form of resistance involves protest in the name of faith against individual measures taken by the state. There are theological reasons for not engaging in wholesale protest against the total ideology of the state, for such a comprehensive protest would in all probability itself be understood ideologically.[10] The protest of faith against individual measures of the state will take on the character of witness if it does not proceed in the name of some general moral law but instead condemns the particular measure involved as being a logical consequence of the basic choice of world view. (Thus in the Third Reich the specific measure involving the elimination of the unfit could be attacked as the product of the mythical and anti-Christian doctrine of blood and soil.) One might say, then, that the resistance of Christians to the totalitarian regime is not deductively determined, as a protest against the ideology, but proceeds inductively, as opposition to specific measures construed to be symptomatic of an underlying philosophy.

In connection with this form of resistance the church must be careful lest the Christian view emerge as simply a counterideology, with one ideological power pitted against another. The church dare not do that which is demanded of the secular champions of political resistance or revolution: it dare not put up resistance in the name of its own theory of state and of society, based, e.g., on natural law. For the same reason, it must make a precise distinction between spiritual and pastoral questions on the one hand, and questions of objective judgment on the other. As regards the latter, even within Christianity different answers are possible; hence they cannot, without rending the body of Christ, be made the theme of a confession or a synodical resolution regarded as binding on the Christian conscience. In addressing men from the pastoral standpoint rather than in terms of objective goals, the church avoids assuming the role of counterweight to the false state. Instead it allows "the law of infiltration and subversion" to come into play. By this we mean the kind of indirect but nonetheless real influence that is exerted through persons as distinct from formal programs, as, e.g., in Christianity's non-frontal attack on the institution of slavery in the ancient world and on polygamy in the mission field.[11] Indeed

---

[10] The free West should be warned against a too facile radicalism by the fact that almost none of the churches under Communism has engaged in such wholesale protest. It would be unwise to understand this in terms of weakness when it is really the result of theological deliberation.

[11] See below pp. 642 ff.

the law of infiltration and subversion becomes operative to the degree that the church's proclamation is blessed with a harvest of living Christians.

The Agents of Resistance

Following this abbreviated and systematic review of resistance in the totalitarian state, as we had already handled it from a variety of standpoints, we turn now to a special question posed by Walter Künneth which has since become the theme of a lively debate. We ourselves part company at this point with Künneth's otherwise laudable work.[12]

The question he raises, which might be appended as yet another point in the review we have just undertaken, is as follows: Who is actually qualified within a totalitarian situation to be legitimately the agent of resistance? Here one sees with particular clarity how fatal it may be to make tradition the starting point in all questions of political ethics, and to restrict oneself essentially to the exposition of tradition instead of taking as one's point of departure the changed form of the modern state. The approach in terms of tradition immediately involves one in intolerable tension with the changed phenomena.

Until now the question of the agent of resistance has been acute at only one point in our analyses: We have seen that the church itself has no right to be an agent of revolution, because it is not equipped to be a potential government. Apart from this one aspect, the question has not been of any urgency thus far. This is no accident. For in the new political situation of the modern state, marked as it is by the thesis of that mature independence of the citizen which finds institutional expression in democracy, the privilege of opposition and resistance is not reserved in principle for any select group. Before the law and in political matters, all are in principle equal, and potentially of equal maturity.

To avoid misunderstanding, we should like to state our conviction that maturity, if understood as a given fact, is sheer superstition, as the very existence of the modern "masses" dramatically attests. One can properly speak only of a *potential* maturity. A true democracy addresses man (e.g., through the franchise) in terms of his maturity. To put it very bluntly, it treats him "as if" he were mature, precisely in order thereby to bring him to maturity. Democracy is not so much an

---

[12] Walter Künneth, *Politik zwischen Dämon und Gott. Eine christliche Ethik des Politischen* (Berlin: Lutherisches Verlagshaus, 1954).

institution founded upon a statistically demonstrable existent maturity as it is an institution oriented toward this maturity teleologically. And even this is so only within limits. The fact that the levying of taxes and the declaration of war are usually not matters for popular decision shows an awareness of the limits of man's maturity. It is this awareness which exposes the risk involved in treating the masses as potentially mature, or of trying to bring them to maturity, in matters such as these which impinge so specifically on human egoism.

Understood thus, the mature independence of the individual citizen was not a factor in the hierarchically structured society of the Middle Ages. This is why the thesis of the Reformers that only those of high estate can be agents of resistance makes sense only within the sociological framework of their day.

The problem is discussed by Luther in relation to the question how a Christian should act when a lawful regime is intolerant in religious matters and persecutes the Evangelical Christian because of his faith.[13] Because government has no right to apply its secular authority in matters of faith, its demands must be resisted.[14] This can be done without "disobedience." The Christian must offer no active physical resistance to the punishments for resistance which are administered by the government.[15] On the contrary, he must suffer patiently. "The more radical view of the jurists" is not applauded by Luther.[16] They plead the equality of Christians before God and the common duty to serve the Creator with all our powers, and from this they deduce legal conclusions. This (for Luther) amounts to a confusing of the two kingdoms inasmuch as a basic spiritual right is carried over into political life." [17] Thus the average subject, the ordinary citizen has no right to be the agent of active resistance. In reference to such resistance Luther speaks of the task of suffering.[18]

On the other hand, Luther subsequently allowed himself to be convinced by legal arguments that the princes were more than merely

---

[13] On what follows cf. Johannes Heckel, *Lex charitatis. Eine Juristische Untersuchung über das Recht in der Theologie Martin Luthers* (Munich: Bayrische Akadamie der Wissenschaften, 1953), pp. 188 ff., and Werner Elert, *Morphologie des Luthertums* (Munich: Beck, 1932), II, 375-376.

[14] WA 47, 564.

[15] WA 39^{II}, 41, No. 42.

[16] WA 39^{II}, 78, line 23, and 79, line 24.

[17] Heckel, *op. cit.*, p. 189.

[18] See, e.g., LW 46, 130, 112-113; PE 2, 51; and LW 45, 124-125.

subjects of the emperor, and that they were therefore not bound by the same limitations as ordinary citizens. He accepted the jurists' thesis that by his election and by his coronation oath the emperor was bound to the estates by a treaty in which the parties were basically equal and could thus exercise a reciprocal control. The emperor's pre-eminence does not mean that the princes cannot be regarded as equal partners in government.[19] This means logically that princes are justified in resisting by force the encroachments of the emperor, especially in religious questions. Thus in 1539 Luther corrects his earlier view of 1526 that princes are subjects of the emperor, bound to obedience.[20]

Things are much the same in Calvin, though there is a not very clearly supported inclination to believe that the Reformed tradition advocates more incisive political intervention even to the point of tyrannicide.[21] In fact, Calvin is also of the view that high estate alone confers the privilege of offering active physical resistance to state authority. Thus the only legitimate agents of such resistance are the estates, the "magistrates of the people, appointed to restrain the wilfulness of kings," whom Calvin compares to the ephors among the Spartans and the tribunes of the people among the Romans.[22]

To be sure, both Luther and Calvin leave open the borderline possibility that in default of such authorities, competent to resist, God may raise up for himself an avenger.[23] But in both cases this possibility is so vague and indefinite that it cannot be the object of a concrete summons; it has about it more the air of unreality than of potentiality. For "who today would presume to feel himself, like Samson, to be called of God?"[24]

In the case of both Reformers, then, the possible agent of resistance is definitely not the individual citizen or subject but the estates as corporate bodies for these are not subordinate to the "highest" author-

---

[19] WA 39^II, 78, lines 3 ff.

[20] LW 46, 125-126.

[21] The view probably rests at least in part on terminology of the Scots Confession of 1560 where a rather incidental and indefinite formulation in article 14 includes among the works reputed good before God: "to save the lyves of Innocentis, to represse tyrannie, to defende the oppressed."

[22] John Calvin Institutes of the Christian Religion 4. 20. 31; LCC 21, 1519.

[23] On Calvin see the Institutes 4. 20. 30 in LCC 21, 1517; and on Luther see LW 46, 110.

[24] Karl Holl, The Cultural Significance of the Reformation, trans. Karl and Barbara Hertz and John H. Lichtblau (New York: Meridian, 1959), p. 66.

ity but are ranked alongside it on the principle of collegiality. Luther sees here an analogy to the relation between cardinals and the pope. According to conciliar theory they rule the church together as ministers of the hierarchy who by divine right are of equal rank, even though this rule is under the leadership of the papacy.[25]

We can now see what a fatal step it is to apply this Lutheran and Reformed tradition more or less directly to the present. How is such an application attempted? At this point we may listen to Künneth. He asserts that the individual citizen today — like the Reformation "subject" — is in principle under no obligation whatever "to intervene in national affairs, or in exceptional circumstances to engineer a violent coup." [26]

Künneth's statement of the matter is acceptable if what he means is that no private citizen, whether fanatic, pseudo prophet, or chronic complainer, can arbitrarily claim the right to arrogate to himself a sense of universal mission and thus give way to wild revolutionary fervor, for obviously some qualification of character and of factual knowledge is needed before there can be any open and active criticism of measures taken by the state, or any uprising against the existing system. It is to be feared, however, that this is not what Künneth has in mind. For he refers basically not to the *unqualified* citizen, but to the *subordinate* citizen, the "subject" in the Reformation understanding of the matter. This is the one who in principle is not authorized to criticize or to revolt. For it is "historically nonsensical and morally reprehensible to ascribe to him (the individual citizen) this alleged responsibility." [27]

But who, then, is authorized to carry through measures of resistance or rebellion? In respect of this question Künneth goes on to make the kind of direct application of the Reformation tradition which we have viewed with apprehension. His answer to the question points necessarily to that limited circle which corresponds to the earlier estates, the persons of rank. In our changed society this is no longer the princes or the nobility in general. It is rather "those in responsible governmental positions, i.e., duly invested officeholders, or at least those who

---

[25] See Luther's Smalcald Articles, Part II, Art. IV on the papacy; *BC* 298-300.
[26] Künneth, *op. cit.*, p. 308.
[27] *Ibid.*

at one time may have been in government service." [28] This includes "civil servants of high rank, particularly those in responsible position," [29] "the leading generals, statesmen, and jurists." [30] "Only in the light of their unique knowledge and understanding of the situation . . . can the recognition of an emergency one day ripen into the resolve to take the extraordinary and ultimate emergency measure of offering violent resistance." [31]

It is a pity that Künneth's book, which is otherwise helpful in so many ways, should by its attempt at repristination finally lead into a blind alley in respect of this question of resistance. To be sure, the impossibility of transferring to our situation the hierarchical thinking of the Middle Ages, even with the help of minor sociological adjustments, is not yet brought to light with all the clarity one might desire when we think only in terms of an ordinary Western democracy. In this setting the inconsequential character of Künneth's solution becomes apparent. For our analysis has shown that in the strict sense revolution cannot become an urgent problem in a democracy, and the possibility of legal opposition to individual measures taken by the legislative and executive branches of the government is constitutionally provided. Here, then, Künneth's discussion has an air of utter unreality. If he still takes it seriously, it is perhaps because under the pressure of his way of putting the question he is constantly tempted to take the authoritarian state of the Middle Ages as his latent model.

In fact, the question of revolution and of detailed opposition actually becomes urgent only in face of the totalitarian systems. This consideration has indeed determined our very method. We have not spoken of the problem of revolution as such — this would involve an illegitimate absolutizing and generalizing — but have always included in our definition the object against which revolution is unleashed. This means concretely that in the modern situation we are dealing either with revolution in a democracy or with revolution in a totalitarian system. But the problem is altogether different in the two cases. Hence there can be no comprehensive definition of revolution. Neither can the concept of the Reformers, elaborated within the context of a

[28] Ibid.
[29] Ibid., p. 375.
[30] Ibid., p. 309.
[31] Ibid.

single well-defined system, be simply and directly transferred to the present.

Proof of this impossibility is easily seen when we try to apply Künneth's principle of the "estates" to the sphere of the totalitarian and ideological power state. For here the principle implies that only the functionaries of higher standing are authorized to be "agents of a legitimate revolution." [32] One has only to state the idea to see what nonsense it is. (And it is a pity that Künneth is so wrapped up in his medieval models that he does not allow his imagination to move into this area.) For obviously the functionaries of ideological tyranny, whether they be generals, officials, party leaders, or government bigwigs, are fanatical adherents of the system. It is thus quite absurd to say that theirs alone is the prerogative of offering resistance. The Third Reich, of course, does not afford a precise analogy because its short duration still left — especially in army circles — a remnant of persons who had held responsible positions in the pretotalitarian period and who were thus capable of independent judgment. But how could this be the case in older totalitarian states such as the Soviet Union? It is obviously *possible* that even in such states there might be fountainheads of opposition. But one can hardly ground an exclusive privilege of resistance on this vague and remote possibility.

Here the Norwegian bishop Eivind Berggrav undoubtedly represents a more realistic, less inhibited, and theologically more illuminating encounter between Lutheranism and the modern situation. He says, "If the Christian citizen is expected to exercise his political and civic responsibilities, it must be assumed that he has the right and the duty [sic] to make decisions for himself and that he is in duty bound to pass judgment upon the lawfulness of the orders which his government issues [in other words he is treated as being mature]. . . . The Christian cannot evade this function on the pretext that he is not responsible for secular affairs. . . . The hour *may* come when a Christian must ask himself . . . whether he should not offer active resistance." [33]

The mature conscience of the Christian — every Christian, not just those of exceptional knowledge and standing — according to Berggrav

[32] *Ibid.*, p. 308.
[33] Eivind Berggrav, *The Proceedings of the Second Assembly of the Lutheran World Federation; Hannover, Germany, July 25-August 3, 1952*, p. 80.

possesses clear criteria by which to judge the duty of resistance and even of rebellion, though Berggrav does not list the three premises we have adduced nor state with sufficient precision the specific preconditions of revolution: "When a government becomes lawless and acts with arbitrary despotism, the result is a demonic condition, that is to say, the government is god-less. . . . In circumstances of this kind, we have, as a matter of principle, the right to rebel, in one form or another. Otherwise Lutheranism would be forced to concede that it has not found an answer for these problems and that it has to leave the Christian in a state of tension between Romans 13 and Acts 5:29." [34]

In these statements Berggrav manages to provide a vindication of sorts for the political theology of Lutheranism. For many earlier statements of Lutheran theology on the question of revolution, which seek on the one hand to maintain the conservative authoritarian concept of Luther and on the other hand to come to terms with the fact of the coups, wars of independence, and other convulsive movements of mankind today, are guilty of an amazing ambivalence when they attempt to explain theologically both their conservatism and their opportunism. Perhaps the worthy Franz Herrman Reinhold von Frank of Erlangen takes the prize in this respect: However tyrannical the government, the Christian in case of revolution or conflict "must always be found on the side of authority, never on the side of those who try to overthrow or to reform it by force." [35] But then he accepts the coup once it is successful! He says, "The Christian does not engineer revolutions, but he knows that as the eruptions and counterstrokes of sin they are historically necessary." [36] If one wanted to be nasty about it, one might state the case thus: The Christian refuses to be involved in certain necessities of history, but is glad to have other people bring them about in his stead; he then rewards them after the fact by using his clean hands to consecrate as lawful authority the government imposed by "dirty hands." For the *fait accompli* for him is always a fact accomplished by *God;* in retrospect even successful rebels are the instruments of God. But set before a venture involving the future the Christian refuses to be an instrument of this kind. He delegates to

---

[34] *Ibid.,* pp. 77-78.

[35] Franz Herrman Reinhold von Frank, *System der christlichen Sittlichkeit* (Erlangen: Deichert, 1884-1887), II, 437.

[36] *Ibid.,* II, 439.

others the questionable roles in the divine governance of the world, the "alien works" of God.

One can only ask with a measure of astonishment what is left of the Lutheran doctrine of justification if we can thus distinguish between the frontline and the sanctuaries of sanctification. It is in keeping with such massive theological illusion that this pseudo-Lutheran quietism, this assumed holiness of aloofness, is advocated even vis-à-vis patently evil revolutions. "Once it has come to power we cannot arbitrarily deny the dignity of a divine institution to the new regime" even if it be nothing but an outright power grab designed to wrest control from a lawful government.[37] "For all *de facto* government exists in principle by the grace of God." [38]

In this Frank is closer to Kant than to the Reformers. For, having first denied the possibility of a popular revolution, Kant goes on to say that "if a revolution has succeeded . . . the illegitimacy of its beginning and of its success cannot free the subjects from being bound to accept the new order of things as good citizens, and they cannot refuse to honor and obey the suzerain [Obrigkeit] who now possesses the authority." [39]

If we want an incomparably clearer voice among those who accept the authoritarianism of older Lutheran theology, a voice more in touch with historical realities, far more subtle and far less doctrinaire, we might turn to a theologian like Harless,[40] or even to a man like Stahl who plainly states the principle of legality in all its ramifications but does not want it to be taken in such doctrinaire fashion that "there can never be any exception from the principle," or that "resistance can never be legitimate under any possible or conceivable circumstances." [41]

In respect of this possibility that Christians may have a revolutionary responsibility which they cannot delegate to officials or to men of higher rank but must themselves bear directly in the sight of God as those who share responsibility for the kingdom on the left hand, one

---

[37] *Ibid.,* II, 433.

[38] *Ibid.,* II, 436.

[39] Immanuel Kant, *The Metaphysical Elements of Justice: Part I of the Metaphysics of Morals,* trans. John Ladd ("Library of Liberal Arts" [New York: Bobbs-Merrill, 1965]), p. 89.

[40] See Gottlieb Christoph Adolph von Harless, *Christliche Ethik* (7th ed.; Gütersloh: Bertelsmann, 1875), pp. 525 ff.

[41] Friedrich Julius Stahl, *Die gegenwärtigen Parteien in Staat und Kirche* (Berlin: Hertz, 1863), p. 288.

may see once again how profitable it is to use the borderline situation of the totalitarian state as a corrective to traditional political theology, and, conversely, without abdicating responsibility to tradition, to embark upon new and daring ways of theological thinking.

Lutheranism in particular is not free — and herein comes to realize that it is not free — from the social models of its time of origin, from specific concepts of office and estate. The attempt to think the matter through reveals what is time-bound. Yet it also shows that revision of this time-bound element does not affect the basic structure of Reformation theology. Indeed, it brings it out with new clarity and force.

The Relevance of Luther's Theology of Politics

The question remains, nonetheless, as to how such a revision is to be made and how great or small will be the core which is left. The conclusions which emerged from our debate with Künneth seem to suggest that all statements in political ethics are so closely bound up with the contemporary social situation that radically new statements are needed whenever there is a radical change in the situation. That such far-reaching operations can take place, and have taken place, not in opposition to faith but within the context of faith and under its banner, is incidentally a comforting sign that Christian faith is not a world view, a religious spirit-of-the-age, or some other phenomenon of this constantly changing aeon, but has to do with that to which, as Ranke says, all ages are "immediate."

We have already discovered some points at which the basic intentions, not just of Luther's central doctrine of justification, but also of his political ethics are clearly susceptible of being interpreted in the light of altered circumstances, and hence are seen to be of permanent validity. Among these things seen to be of permanent validity is, e.g., the character of the state as an authority, notwithstanding the replacement of the so-called authoritarian state of the Middle Ages by the modern democracy.[42] Democracy presents the idea of authority in another form, but it does not do away with the concept altogether.

Nevertheless, there are obvious limits to the application of Luther's theology of politics. Some modern forms of state seem in a profound sense to be impervious to it. We have already had occasion to assert, e.g., that the doctrine of the two kingdoms cannot easily be applied to

[42] See Chapter 2 above.

the schema of ideological tyranny.[43] A closer look, of course, shows that non-applicability does not have to mean irrelevance, for this very doctrine of the two kingdoms is well adapted to unmask the perversion of the totalitarian state whereby it refuses to be a kingdom on the left hand and instead establishes itself as a pseudo church, blasphemously installing itself at the right hand of God.[44] Luther's doctrine thus remains an effective criterion of judgment, precisely because the totalitarian state makes it impossible for its Christian citizens to regard and treat it along the lines of this doctrine.

Luther's political-theological statements, however, also have an affinity to the situation of the modern totalitarian state which is not simply indirect, or disclosed only by way of hermeneutical considerations. He occasionally refers to specific situations of his own time which are so closely analogous to modern totalitarianism that he seems to be speaking directly to our time, almost in the manner of Revelation 13.[45] Thus Heckel, without specifying ideological tyranny, has assembled essential and — so far as we can see — new material from Luther which can be very fruitful in this area, and better understood in the light of the matters we have been discussing.[46]

For Luther, a construct comparable to modern ideological tyranny can arise when, e.g., the state becomes a "shepherd" instead of a "hangman,"[47] when it goes beyond its assigned sphere of men's bodies and tries to rule their souls as well, in short, when it seeks to exercise *total* dominion. In pursuit of this desire it must inevitably come into conflict with the Christian faith. Then comes the moment when we must obey God rather than men.[48] This moment calls for resistance on the part of Christians against demands which would violate the first table of the Law. However, it does not permit revolutionary acts to overthrow the regime, commending instead a patient bearing of the consequences of the indicated resistance.[49]

[43] See above p. 344.

[44] See above p. 357.

[45] See above pp. 53 ff.

[46] Our discussion here is based on the section entitled "The Christian as a Subject in the Political Sphere" in Heckel, *op. cit.*, pp. 148 ff.

[47] *LW* 45, 113.

[48] "What if a prince is in the wrong? Are his people bound to follow him then too? Answer: No, for it is no one's duty to do wrong; we must obey God (who desires the right) rather than men [Acts 5:29]." *LW* 45, 125.

[49] Heckel, *op. cit.*, p. 153. Cf. WA 40^III, 171, lines 22 ff.; WA 20, 135, lines 25 ff.; and esp. *LW* 45, 124-125 and 46, 106.

How close Luther comes to the totalitarian state with these depictions may be seen from the fact that he sees the clash with the Christian faith taking place not only in the religious sphere, i.e., in the sphere of the first table, but also in that of individual commandments. The totalitarian state conflicts with the faith also in the material sphere of life, e.g., in respect of marriage [50] or education. For the minus sign it places before the brackets of life applies to every integer within those brackets. It calls insistently for a Christian stand at every point in life.

Nevertheless, Luther does not seem in the first instance to draw a line from here to what we have called the legitimacy of revolution against a totalitarian regime. For close though his picture of tyranny is in essentials to our own image of modern tyranny, his concept of authority seems to prevent him from breaking through to the thesis of revolutionary resistance.[51] For him, such a thing is possible, but only in dire emergency. Indeed, the possibility obtains only where there exists an extreme form of that which we have here called the borderline situation.

His analysis of this situation, however, comes surprisingly near to our own investigation of ideological tyranny. For all that we have said thus far about Luther's depiction of tyranny applies only to the relatively harmless figure of an evil ruler who in ruling is guilty of the aforementioned transgressions. To describe such a ruler Heckel coins the felicitous expression a "particular tyrant." [52] This petty tyrant represents that limited form of tyranny which crops up within forms of state otherwise regarded as normal for that area. In connection with the Turkish threat, however, Luther formed the idea of a "universal tyrant." This big tyrant is different from the particular tyrant not merely in the extent of his influence or the intensity of his tyranny, but above all in his nature, i.e., theologically. For while the petty tyrant says, "Might before right," and thus inadvertently still presupposes the validity of right, the big tyrant says, "My will *is* right," thus abolishing the very concept of right.[53] Thus does Luther in effect depict the state which we described in relation to the pragmatizing of law within the

[50] *LW* 45, 28.

[51] Except by the ranking estates, as we have indicated.

[52] Heckel, *op. cit.*, p. 157.

[53] *WA* 39[II], 85, line 10. Heckel correctly takes Luther's remark here to be directed against the thesis that "the will of man is law"; Heckel, *op. cit.*, p. 158.

ideologies:[54] Right does not embrace authoritative norms but is a tactical weapon by which a man advances himself and his systems.

The universal tyrant then — in Luther's view the Turk — does not recognize either divine or human law. He thus stands outside all law, and has himself no legal status. He becomes a child of hell, interpreted in terms of the eschatological figure of the ἄνομος (the "lawless one") of II Thessalonians 2:8.[55] To this malefactor, who bears the sign of God's condemnation on his forehead, an end must be put immediately, as to a raging beast.[56] He is to be treated like a robber or an invader, like a Turk.[57]

Such situations give rise to emergency law which does not allow us to await or to follow judicial decisions or governmental directives.[58] On the contrary, a government which makes itself the prey of the universal tyrant — in modern terms a satellite government — deprives itself of authority, of magisterial status, and is (temporarily) replaced by the people. The people takes over and functions in place of the government which is lacking.[59]

Now it would have been better if, along with these exceedingly vehement statements on active resistance to the universal tyrant from Luther's 1539 *Zirkulardisputation über das Recht des Widerstandes gegen den Kaiser (Matt. 19:21)*, Heckel had introduced at least some safeguards from other areas of Luther's theology of politics. These are provided especially by the thesis that the agent of this radical resistance must not be the church but only individual Christians, who are political beings in the secular sense and, as such, bear political responsibility, whether this be normal responsibility under some kind of government or emergency responsibility in a borderline situation characterized by the absense of government. (We have alluded to this distinction between the church and Christian citizens, which is emphasized particularly by Berggrav.)

In Luther's writings on the Turkish wars the distinction is strongly

[54] See above pp. 41 ff.
[55] See Rudolf Hermann, "Luther's Zirkulardisputation über Matt. 19:21," *Luther-Jahrbuch*, XXIII (1941), 86.
[56] WA 39ᴵᴵ, 42, lines 15-16.
[57] *Ibid.*, line 39; WA, Br 8, 367, line 52.
[58] WA 39ᴵᴵ, 42, lines 22-23.
[59] WA, TR 4, 237, No. 4342; WA 39ᴵᴵ, 59, line 30 (both quoted above at p. 347, n. 18).

maintained.[60] Although he says with sharpest precision and almost shocking bluntness that the Christian should feel he is "the hangman or executioner of God, the supreme Lord, against His great and condemned enemy,"[61] Luther is nonetheless against any crusading emotion in connection with these wars. The idea of a crusade arises when war is made in the name of the church, as a matter of self-preservation, whereas the true calling of the church is to suffer and to see to the salvation of souls, even the souls of enemies. This is why Luther repeatedly points out that we are to fight against the Turk not "because of false belief or evil life, but because of the murder and destruction which he does." [62] In matters of faith, i.e., against heresy or Antichrist, God's Word alone must do the fighting.[63] Any government which would protect the faith by force transgresses its own limits. For how can the emperor, "poor maggot fodder that he is," enter the jaws of hell and protect God! [64]

But the converse is also true: "If I were a soldier and saw a priest's banner in the field, or a banner of the cross, even though it was a crucifix, I should run as though the devil were chasing me." [65] It was not least this religious banner, the claim to be a "Christian army," which turned Luther against the Peasants' Revolt and caused him to make corresponding pronouncements on the theme of revolution. For fanatically to sacralize a political or social act of this kind is to claim to act as the church. But in the church — and in this respect the peasants and Thomas Münzer contradict themselves — there can be no resistance or revolution, for "Suffering! suffering! Cross! cross! This and nothing else is the Christian law!" [66]

Luther can concede rights of resistance, even physical resistance, to Christians insofar as they are Christian citizens. He does so within certain limits, e.g., in opposition to the universal tyrant. When in his statements on the Peasants' War he forbids the "Christian" to revolt

---

[60] See Helmut Lamparter, *Luthers Stellung zum Türkenkrieg* (Munich: Lempp, 1940); and Gustaf Wingren, *Luther on Vocation*, trans. Carl C. Rasmussen (Philadelphia: Muhlenberg, 1957), p. 80.
[61] *WA* 30^{II}, 174, lines 21-22; *LW* 54, 40, No. 289.
[62] *LW* 46, 198.
[63] *LW* 45, 114.
[64] *LW* 46, 185-186.
[65] *LW* 46, 168; cf. p. 169.
[66] *LW* 46, 29.

and demands instead endurance and prayer,[67] he is primarily attacking the peasants' claim to be the church and to be fighting on behalf of their faith. This is the point of his admonition: "Leave the name Christian out of it . . . and do not use it to cover up your impatient, disorderly, un-Christian undertaking."[68] Such revolts — according to Luther's theology of politics — stand not merely under the verdict of being disobedience to divinely instituted authority, but also under the much stronger verdict of having been rendered supposedly in the name of God. They thus plunge us into the deepest self-contradictions of the fanatics, and in addition burden themselves with the ambivalence of a crusade.

It is characteristic of the way in which Luther fulfills the church's duty to act as a watchman that he also turns at the same time to the princes and explains that the peasant uprisings — which he condemns — are surely a matter of God's judgment: "It is not the peasants, dear lords, who are resisting you; it is God himself, to visit your raging upon you."[69]

This possibility of speaking in two different directions from two different angles is certainly one of the reasons why physical resistance is normally out of the question within the context of the social structure which for Luther was normative. The prince as "chief member of the church"[70] sat under the same preaching as his "subjects," even if these were robber bands. The existence of the church established a bond within which both sides — rulers and ruled — could be authoritatively addressed in terms of judgment and admonition. This made it difficult for hard and fast lines to develop between them such as commonly are seen to develop between the numerous divergent power factions and competing interest groups which commonly characterize twentieth-century society.

To sum up, a crusade illegitimately makes the church a government, and the government a church, thus exchanging one kingdom for the other. The battle against the Turks, who to Luther frequently look like the universal tyrant, is a purely secular affair, and thus belongs to the kingdom on the left hand. Wife and child, and hence also the frontiers of the empire, have to be protected against their raging and

[67] *LW* 46, 33-36.
[68] *LW* 46, 31-32.
[69] *LW* 46, 20; cf. p. 41.
[70] See above p. 10, n. 8.

373

snorting.[71] Whenever the spiritual and secular are thus confused in matters of this sort, Luther lifts a warning voice. His dislike for the Schmalkaldic League is of the same provenance.[72] To this distinction of the two kingdoms there obviously corresponds also a distinction of the subjects who may conceivably be the agents of resistance and revolution. Luther allows this only for the "Christian citizen" as one who bears a secular political responsibility; the church can never play such a role. This is something that needs explicitly to be stated by way of supplementing Heckel.

A theology oriented to the Reformation needs to work in responsibility to Luther. If it does it will neither diverge prematurely from his political ethics nor fall victim to inadmissible repristination. From such work a very complex structure results, involving both indirect and direct transferral.

There is needed first a hermeneutical effort to distinguish between the sixteenth-century framework of Luther's statements and the statements themselves, and to see clearly that the political structure to which the statements applied has undergone a radical change. The task is simply to perceive certain basic intentions behind and in the institutional media of that time, and to make these intentions authoritative and fruitful for our own situation by a more or less complicated act of transferral.

We have now attempted this transferral at various points and with some measure of success, e.g., in connection with the idea of the state – whether democratic or totalitarian – as authority; also in connection with the doctrine of the two kingdoms, which runs through the whole of our theological ethics and influences it in important ways at many points; and finally now in connection with the question of resistance.

It is important thus to emphasize hermeneutics and to tackle this question of transferral also in the matter of Luther's theology. For while the need for hermeneutics in the field of biblical exegesis is obvious to all of us, apart from a few fundamentalists, it still seems to require distinct and explicit emphasis in relation to Luther and the Reformers. Luther is only too often quoted "directly" as though he were still among us and no transferral process were necessary. He can

---

[71] See Georg Merz, *Glaube und Politik im Handeln Luthers* (1933), pp. 32-33.
[72] Karl Müller, *Kirche, Geimeinde und Obrigkeit nach Luther* (Tübingen, 1910), pp. 83-84.

hardly be more misunderstood, however, than by quoting him literally, unguardedly, and without hermeneutical effort.[73]

Although with the attempt at indirect transfer there is then in the second place the possibility of receiving Luther's theology of politics as directly relevant without any hermeneutical extrapolation. It is striking that this exceptional possibility arises precisely in respect of exceptional situations. We dealt with a typical case of this kind when we touched on the theme of the universal tyrant.

Where disordered man, the ἄνομος, and hence also the *system* of lawlessness rules, distinctions of historical background suddenly disappear. Change of order is not apparent where no order exists. The intervening periods of history become transparent. In the borderline situation I meet my fellow human being, my fellow Christian of yesteryear, as it were, without any interpreter to introduce me. The man of a previous age becomes my *alter ego*. Historical barriers fall and history seems to stand still in the demonic moments of chaos. This may be why the last book of the Bible, which in normal times seems to be the most remote and strange, in the tragic periods of history manifests the power of direct comfort to the believing community. For it is the book of the woes of history, of the revolt of the abyss against order.

[73] It is intended, of course, as a help to understanding when we put questions to Luther, when we ask, e.g., concerning the relevance of his views of resistance and of authority to modern political structures. We fear that a Luther philosophy which merely examines in detail all the immanent connections in his terminology does not take seriously the theological claim of Luther and his continuing authority for the present. This is a criticism which, despite their considerable scholarly achievements, may be brought against some of the Swedish Luther scholars (among others!). Cf. the penetrating criticism in Gustaf Wingren, *Theology in Conflict: Nygren, Barth, Bultmann,* trans. Eric Wahlstrom (Philadelphia: Muhlenberg, 1958), pp. 153-155.

21.

The Oath of Loyalty and the
Resistance Situation

If we handle the matter of the oath, not in a doctrine of general duties, but in connection with the crisis situation where the oath reaches its limits, this is due to the noetic fruitfulness of the border-line situation, a factor which we have repeatedly had occasion to emphasize. The borderline case discloses, in a situation where I am directly and deeply involved, the extent to which I am bound by my oath. Since the degree of obligation, however, is actually determined by what an oath is, the borderline situation affords the most fruitful approach and perspective for discovering the real nature of the oath.

The Concept of the Oath

We shall first expound the concept of the oath as set forth in almost all the theological definitions of the various Christian confessions.[1] This we shall do in three stages.

The Appeal to a Higher Authority

The oath is an assurance given to the supreme earthly authority — the state and its organs — with an appeal to God as witness. (The oaths taken by soldiers and officeholders are the best known examples.) The oath is thus distinguished by two things, the degree of obligation entailed and the nature of the authority to whom allegiance is pledged.

A pledge of allegiance cannot be accepted by every person, authority, or group (e.g., a business corporation), but only by a supreme earthly authority which is specially sanctioned by God and which I can be obliged to serve with life and limb. Hence the oath has reference not to my own everyday affairs but only to matters having public

---

[1] Special groups such as the Mennonites are, of course, excepted. See the article on "Oath" by Christian Neff and William Klassen in *The Mennonite Encyclopedia* (Scottdale, Pennsylvania: Mennonite Publishing House, 1959), IV, 2-8.

significance. Roman Catholic moral theology refers to this requirement under the rubric "grave cause," i.e., where the common good is at stake.[2]

The oath also entails a particularly high degree of obligation because it is sworn in responsibility before God and involves a solemn confession of this responsibility. The oath thus transcends the partnership between the one who swears it and the one toward whom it is sworn. It appeals to a third entity before which the resultant relationship as such is itself responsible. It is thus impossible to regard the sworn relationship as something ultimate, an end in itself.

This character of the oath is important because it implies already certain limits of obligation. These limits are imposed by the fact that the partnership itself can never be the criterion for determining the measure of obligation.[3] For the partnership itself can conceivably be called in question by that third party to whom appeal is made. It appears paradoxical — though only at first glance — but it is perfectly true that the appeal to God, which is what gives the oath the highest conceivable degree of assurance, should also contain the very elements which at the same time relativize it, elements which can become operative the moment the sworn partnership is in contradiction with him under whose appeal and witness the oath was taken.[4]

Now if this appeal to a higher authority transcending the partnership itself is of the very essence of an oath, then the oath loses its true quality wherever it is devoid of such an appeal. At best it is then only a protestation, a promise, or a vow. Sometimes the oath is temporarily simplified in a kind of therapeutic abstinence. Quite different, however, is the oath which is "castrated" in principle, and thus deprived of its true essence. The oath which is deliberately atheistic characteristically crops up in state systems whose ideology demands the full surrender of the person and therewith an unlimited kind of obligation, systems which make themselves the ultimate end.

We thus maintain that the so-called religious formula is constitutive

---

[2] See Thomas Aquinas, *Summa Theologica,* part 2^{II}, ques. 89, art. 2; cf. Augustine *Sermon on the Mount* i. 18. 51.

[3] Followers are never "committed without reservation" to the leader, as National Socialism literally declared.

[4] This actually happened in the case of many officeholders and military men who took oaths of allegiance at the commencement of the Third Reich when its anti-Christian tendencies were not yet apparent, at least not manifestly apparent.

of the oath. Where it is omitted, the oath is a mere assurance which — technically and officially at least — does not contain within it those elements which relativize both the oath and the ensuing partnership. Without the religious formula the oath is qualitatively changed. It is simply a quantitatively enhanced form of assurance.[5]

Two Kinds of Oath

Two significant aspects of the oath, which to this point in our definition have unavoidably been intermingled, must now be explicitly differentiated. Oaths can be related either to the attestation of a truth — especially of a factual situation by a witness to it — or to the seriousness of a promise. Apart from highly unusual exceptions, the limits of an oath are a question only in respect of the second of these two possibilities, i.e., the promise relating to the future. (We shall return to this later.) The two kinds of oath are distinguished terminologically whenever this is necessary — and we shall observe this distinction from now on — by speaking of the oath of "truth" in the first case and the oath of "loyalty" in the second. The legal distinction is in terms of assertion and promise.

Three Functions of the Oath of Loyalty

The nature of the oath as thus defined is closely related to its function. This function may be said to be threefold. The oath of loyalty has in the first place the function of binding a man to an office. This office can be represented by a person, as in a constitutional monarchy, in which case the oath is made to him not as an individual but as an official person. This distinction between individual and office carries with it the safeguard that when the one to whom allegiance is pledged loses his quality as an official person, e.g., because he resigns or obviously misuses his office, then the oath no longer applies. But since the oath for its part is designed to guarantee a commitment which transcends caprice and personal concerns and establishes continuity of sworn service — the continuity of loyalty! — then this continuity

---

[5] This is not to impugn the seriousness of the atheist who abstains from use of the religious formula in connection with his solemn assurances and promises. We are not trying to draw moral distinctions here. Even the secular man can have reservations in mind when he accepts an obligation, reservations which, e.g., might preclude his offending against human rights. Our point is simply that the atheist is in no position to take an *oath* in the strict sense.

must be seen to refer to *both* persons, i.e., to the one who swears the oath and also the one toward whom it is sworn.

As far as the one who swears the oath is concerned, this means that he cannot allow any vacillation in his own opinions or convictions to affect the oath. Since it is with his whole *self* that he is bound to his office — the concept of loyalty makes any other interpretation impossible — the criterion by which to decide both the obligation and the limits of the oath is not whether he can go along with this or that particular measure but whether he himself, as a *person,* can go along at all rather than resigning his office *for his oath's sake* because of the intolerable demands imposed upon his conscience. These considerations — that it is the *person* and not the detailed facts of the case which is decisive in relation to the obligation of the oath, and that the person is an indivisible whole confronted at all points by the choice between loyalty or resignation from the sworn office — constitute a powerful safeguard against caprice on the part of him who swears the oath, and help to assure the constancy of commitment implied in an oath.

There is a safeguard here too, however, as regards the one toward whom the oath is sworn, inasmuch as not every measure which may seem — from the standpoint of the one who swears the oath — to be a violation of office, an arbitrary or capricious act, will constitute a situation in which he ceases in the strict sense to be an official person to whom allegiance is still due. To vouch for the presence of such a situation more is required than merely a subjective and individual opinion. Two other things are needed as well.

There is needed, first, emphatic reassurance from those concerning whose factual judgment and moral integrity there is no question. (An impressive historical illustration is provided by the men of the German resistance movement who wrestled long and conscientiously with the question whether Hitler had ceased to be an authentic governmental official, a legitimate partner in the sworn relationship.)

Second, it is needful that the incriminating deeds of the one toward whom the oath is sworn be interpreted, after responsible analysis, not merely as isolated mistakes — and hence subject to criticism — but as part and parcel of his very nature and program, that proscribed area which is beyond all criticism.

The second of the three functions of the oath of loyalty is to preclude men's being enslaved by men.[6] We touched on this already when we said that the appeal to God as witness is an appeal to a court which transcends the sworn partnership and reveals its limits. In the name of this court the one who swears the oath is protected from complete subjection to the partnership. He is also enabled to stand over against the partnership – i.e., genuinely to "stand," and not to be swallowed up in it – because of the reservation involved in his obligation to God.

Finally, the third function of the oath arises out of the consideration that many offices which carry with them an oath of loyalty – among them that of the soldier – may demand all that we have and are, and all can demand the expenditure of our energies and strength and other personal sacrifices in their service. Herein may be seen the significance of the fact that the oath claims the whole person – with the limitation just mentioned in the previous paragraph. Thus, the oath demands not merely that I *do* something but that I *be* something, namely, a loyal person.

The Oath in the Bible

In the Old Testament oaths are sworn in the name of Yahweh.[7] It goes without saying that other gods, who "have no real existence," [8] are incapable of serving as witnesses. Hence to swear by them is idolatry (Jer. 5:7; Amos 8:14; Hos. 4:15), just as swearing by Yahweh is not merely a confession of the truth attested but also and supremely a confession of praise to him (Isa. 45:23; Jer. 12:16). In such confession God is appealed to not just as a witness but also as an avenger if the oath is broken.[9]

Sometimes oaths are also sworn by the life of the king, or of the one to whom allegiance is pledged.[10] This is not in contradiction to the oath sworn by Yahweh. For there is at least one point of comparison between swearing by God and swearing by man, namely, that in both I appeal to an independent witness and consign myself to him for

[6] E. Osterloh, "Der Fahneneid in theologischer Sicht," *Evangelische Verantwortung*, 1955, 7/8, p. 11.

[7] Deut. 6:13; 10:20; see Johannes Sehneider, "ὅρκος," in Gerhard Kittel, *Theological Dictionary of the New Testament*, edited and translated by Geoffrey W. Bromiley (Grand Rapids, Michigan: Eerdmans, 1964), V, 457 ff.

[8] Isa. 44:6-20; Ps. 106:19-20; Jer. 16:19-20; I Chron. 16:26; cf. I Cor. 8:4.

[9] Cf. the formulae in Ruth 1:17; I Sam. 20:13; Jer. 29:22; Job 31:8, 10, 40.

[10] Cf. the formula in I Sam. 17:55; II Sam. 11:11.

vengeance in the event that I should break my oath. That there is indeed this point of comparison is clear from the fact that the Israelite does not swear by himself or his own life; for no man can be a witness independent of himself, nor consign himself to himself for vengeance.[11]

Yahweh also swears, and differently from man in that He does swear by Himself (e.g., Gen. 22:16; cf. Heb. 6:13). This shows that Yahweh "is dependent on none other." [12] In thus swearing by himself he glorifies himself and bears witness to his own sovereignty. It is also apparent from this unique form of oath that the covenant which Yahweh has sworn with Israel differs from all other covenants. First, the covenant does not express a partnership between equals who conclude a treaty and confirm it by oath as equals (συνθήκη); it is instead an institution, διαθήκη being the consistent Septuagint rendering for the Hebrew term *berith* (covenant).[13] Second, the covenant instituted by this God who swears by himself is unique in the sense that God is both the witness and also one of those who swear.[14]

So far as the New Testament is concerned, the prohibition of swearing is of particular significance for our present discussion.[15] E.g., it is typical of the Sermon on the Mount that it condemns not just false swearing but all swearing.[16] The only permissible form of assurance is the simply Yes or No. The question whether or how far this is a general prohibition which must apply even in the practice of law and government can be answered only in terms of our approach to the Sermon on the Mount as a whole.[17]

---

[11] Johannes Schneider (*op. cit.*, p. 460) advances as a reason that no man has control over his own life; but this is not very convincing inasmuch as no man has control over that of the king either, or the one to whom he pledges allegiance.

[12] J. Pedersen, *Der Eid bei den Semiten* (1914); cited by Johannes Schneider, *loc. cit.*

[13] Otto Procksch, *Theologie des Alten Testaments* (Gütersloh: Bertelsmann, 1950), p. 92.

[14] *Ibid.*, p. 91. This is why all figures of the covenant (e.g., that of marriage in Hos. 1-3) break down and are only very limited analogies.

[15] Matt. 5:33-37; 23:16-22; cf. II Cor. 1:18; Jas. 5:12; though Heb. 6:13-16 and 7:20-22 presuppose the legitimacy of oaths.

[16] Julius Schniewind points out that Jesus' criticism of the oath was not new, but could appeal to a specific tradition. The oath was avoided altogether, or at least as far as possible, by contemporary Judaism, Sirach (23:9 ff.), Philo, and the Essenes. *Das Evangelium nach Matthäus* ("Das Neue Testament Deutsch," II [5th ed.; Göttingen: Vandenhoeck & Ruprecht, 1950]), 65.

[17] On the different interpretations of the Sermon on the Mount see *ThE* 1, 332-358.

If the Sermon is interpreted eschatologically, in the sense that it commands us as though we were still in a state of innocence or as though the kingdom of God had already replaced "this aeon," we cannot answer this question with a simple affirmative. For the eschatological orientation of the Sermon on the Mount cannot mean that with the radicalizing of the Mosaic *nomos* this aeon collapses. It means rather that the provisional nature of this aeon is disclosed with a view to our learning to live within relativized orders, to have as though we had not (I Cor. 7:29-31), and to quit making of our world an ultimate, a utopia, an idol, indeed a pretended kingdom of God. This is why one cannot derive from Matthew 5:38-42 the constitution of a pacifist world order.

But what is the specific eschatological meaning of Jesus' prohibition of the oath? One can only answer that the need to strengthen my pledged word by an oath implies that the word alone is too weak and carries too little weight, that it needs to be covered with armor and freighted with significance. This surprising phenomenon is due to the fact that falsehood rules in this aeon (John 8:44). Swearing thus points to the prevalence of lying. In this aeon truth is the extraordinary thing. Indeed, it is the exception. This is why unusual forms of assurance are felt to be necessary. This is why we are put on our honor. And this is why the oath is necessary in areas of such great importance that the binding character of the word is particularly threatened due to the human temptation to get out of things by lying. Thus he who swears by God appeals to God not merely to attest that he is now speaking the truth or declaring a serious resolve, but also to attest that ours is an aeon of falsehood and that the particular truth now being uttered is an exception to the rule. Jesus is thus pointing out that the oath is a scandal, and that it is highly questionable because it connects the name of God with undertakings which are very much compromised and compromising.

Thus the essential elements in criticism of the oath are as follows. First, the enhanced form of assurance provided in the oath is a sure sign that we normally live in a world of untruth. The right thing would be not to let truth become an exception like this — much less continually confirm its exceptional character by the use of oaths — but to raise the value of the ordinary word to where it is again an authentic Yes or No.

Second, it is an illusion to think that in a world of lies the oath itself — the exceptional situation — can be protected from the attack of untruth. So long as there is no fundamental renewal of the word itself, untruth will eat away the oath too. This may happen in the first place by way of my mental reservations, whereby I evade the obligation entailed in the oath, e.g., through using a non-obligatory formula whose force is apparent only to the expert. This theological trick was actually performed by means of such solemn circumlocutions for the divine name as "heaven," "temple," "Jerusalem," etc. (Matt. 5: 34-35), terms which only the rabbinically trained would recognize as non-obligatory.[18] It may happen too when I no longer take God seriously in his sovereignty as witness, judge, and avenger, but treat him instead as a mere pledge or pawn. This little trick of swearing by something less majestic, e.g., by one's own head (Matt. 5:36), while intended to turn the Holy One into something expendable, and so to do away with him altogether, could not actually succeed; for the pawn after all is not something independent but something wholly at my disposal, and my own head clearly does not fall into that category (Matt. 5:36; 10:30). There are modern parallels in the attempts to make God merely a device for adding a touch of pious solemnity and enhancing the psychological impact of the situation.

Thus the mere practice of requiring oaths, indeed, the impossibility of dispensing with such a practice in this aeon, contains within itself a judgment. Here — as in the case of divorce — one might say, "From the beginning it was not so" (Matt. 19:8); creation originally set into the world a different word from that which is now so disintegrated by falsehood that it has to be shored up by an oath.

In keeping with our general interpretation of the Sermon on the Mount we can thus say that even if divorces and oaths occur in this aeon because of men's "hardness of heart" (Mark 10:5), the fact that they are declared to be necessary must be heard as the Sermon's *judgment* on the whole situation in this present aeon. If we hear this judgment we will be prevented from regarding the legal orders of this world as definitive and perfect institutions to which we can have an absolute and unbroken relation. Compared with what was intended at creation they are rather to be understood as emergency orders,

[18] See Otto Bauernfeind, *Eid und Frieden. Fragen zur Anwendung und zum Wesen des Eides* (Stuttgart, 1956), p. 94.

provisional and temporary institutions of the Noachic covenant designed to preserve the world despite its faulty condition. The world's secret wound, which is here disclosed, must be kept open. Hence, every word of Jesus in the Sermon on the Mount, is as we have put it,[19] a piece of "gauze in the wound" to keep it from premature, unhealthy healing.

This is also how we are to understand the judgment on oaths. If we view the oath from this standpoint, we shall regard it at best as only an emergency measure in the world after the fall. We shall thus be on guard against construing it, because of the appeal made therein to God, as a good and pious work. It will be accepted only as a necessary evil. We shall see in the oath a reminder of the culpable degeneration of the word generally, and hence an appeal to consider this word and God's continual presence in it (Ps. 139:4; Matt. 12:36), the peril in which it stands (Matt. 15:11, 18, 19; 12:36-37), and the healing for which it is intended (Ps. 145:10; 148:14; 149:1).

The word made whole needs no confirmation. But where in this world is such a healed word to be found? And what state, what law can therefore dispense with such confirmation? Nevertheless, part of the healing may consist in an open and public diagnosis, i.e., in a demonstrative refusal of the oath in certain situations.

That Jesus' prohibition of the oath is intended to call our present aeon in question — to pronounce judgment upon it — and is not to be construed as part of a new world constitution (anymore than the statement that we are not to resist evil, Matt. 5:39), may be seen indirectly from the fact that Jesus himself can make use of oaths.[20] This may be seen particularly in his frequent use of the word Amen or Truly (e.g., Mark 8:12), which is to be regarded as a solemn oath and "probably implies that Jesus responds with a solemn Amen to God's voice speaking to him, and goes on to proclaim this voice of God to his hearers." [21] If this be the case, then Jesus' Amen is "practically the equivalent of the oath of God (as at Isa. 45:23 and Ps. 95:11)." [22] Furthermore, when the high priest at Jesus' trial in Jerusalem puts the question concerning his messianic claim in the form

---

[19] See ThE 1, 95, 147, 315, et al.
[20] Paul too uses oathlike assurances in II Cor. 1:15-23; Rom. 1:9; 9:1 ff.
[21] Schniewind, op. cit., p. 66.
[22] Ibid.

of an oath: "I adjure you by the living God, . . ." (Matt. 26:63) the direct answer which Jesus gives undoubtedly means that he puts himself under oath and thus meets the demand of the high priest for an oath.

But if Jesus thus uses the oath, which he has himself so radically called in question, this can be understood only in terms of his solidarity with sinners and his bearing of the burden of this aeon.[23] For what word is so little in need of confirmation as *his* word? Even though in him — and in his disciples through him — the kingdom of God is already present and the dominion of this aeon broken, he nonetheless carries his condescension to the point of placing himself under the emergency orders of the current age, willing to give that confirmation of the truth required in a world lying in wickedness (I John 5:19).

The assurances given by Jesus himself are thus completely misunderstood if we crassly regard them as inconsistent with what he says in the Sermon on the Mount, and hence as a direct confirmation of the oath. What they confirm is something quite different. They show in the first place that there is an area where the two aeons intersect, a period in which the age that is coming to an end is granted a provisional and temporary extension. And they show in the second place that Jesus Christ condescends not only to eat and drink with sinners, but also to take oaths with them, that he may bear with them the burden involved in the loss of truth and the pressure for assurances.

The Oath in Reformation Teaching

Regarding the traditional view of the oath in Reformation theology, the following points may be noted. The Reformers themselves allow the taking of oaths. Nor, so far as I can see, do they voice any reservation of the sort we have suggested. They see the oath, not so much in light of the Sermon on the Mount as in light of the commandments concerning God's name and God's day.

Although Luther does not seem in this area to have made explicit application of his doctrine of the two kingdoms, it did in fact contribute to the confidence with which he speaks of the permissibility of the oath within the sphere of law and government.[24]

---

[23] The situation would thus be similar to that of his baptism, Mark 1:9-11.

[24] Cf. Karl Holl, *Gesammelte Aufsätze zur Kirchengeschichte,* III (Tübingen: Mohr, 1928), 152.

His opposition to the fanatics probably helped to solidify his attitude on this point. Thus in his exposition of the commandments in the Large Catechism Luther says that even as a wrong use of God's name is forbidden a right use is enjoined. The general rule for this right use is that the name of God should be used only to support truth, not falsehood, and that it should be invoked not in the service of wickedness but of "all that is good." If this rule is observed, the question of the oath is "easily solved," and the difficulties which have "tormented so many teachers" are done away.[25]

Luther gets around the stricture of the Sermon on the Mount simply by arguing that Jesus, Paul, "and other saints" often took oaths. For him the criterion of right so far as an oath is concerned is not *whether* I should swear or in what circumstances, but the substance or content of the oath. This criterion is identical with the rule that we should swear "in support of the good and for the advantage of our neighbor." An oath of this kind is "a truly good work by which God is praised, truth and justice are established."[26] Luther's doctrine of justification may be detected here inasmuch as it is our attitude toward God (faith) and neighbor (love)—as implemented in our deeds—which is the criterion for whether a work is commanded or permitted.[27]

Calvin likewise deals with the oath in his exposition of the commandment concerning God's name.[28] He regards the stricture of the Sermon on the Mount as only a minor problem,[29] whereas the case in favor of the oath begins with the argument that the appeal to God as a witness is "a sort of divine worship." For by appealing to him thus, we honor him not merely as witness to the truth but also as its guardian, "the only affirmer of it, who is able to bring hidden

---

[25] Luther, The Large Catechism, I, 2, 64-65; BC 373. Luther is probably thinking of Augustine and Jerome, whose comments on the subject are gathered in *Decretum Magistri Gratiani*, Secunda Pars, Causa XXII, Questio 1, c. 2-8; and perhaps also of Augustine's letter to Publicola, *Letters of St. Augustine* xlvii. 2 in *NPF*, I, 292.

[26] Luther, The Large Catechism, I, 2, 66; BC 373.

[27] Cf. Luther's understanding of Rom. 14:23 in his Theses of 1520 on whether works contribute to justification; WA 7, 231-232; and our systematic treatment of the matter in *ThE* 1, 250-278. On the admissibility of the oath in the Lutheran Confessions see The Augsburg Confession, XVI, 2; Apology of the Augsburg Confession, XVI, 1; Formula of Concord, Epitome XII, 15; Formula of Concord, Solid Declaration, XII, 20 (in BC 37, 222, 499, 634).

[28] John Calvin *Institutes of the Christian Religion* 2. 8. 22-27; LCC 20, 388-394.

[29] "Some difficulty." *Ibid.* 2. 8. 26; LCC 20, 391.

things to light." [30] Only in two cases can the oath lack this cultic significance and hence involve a desecration of God's name, in the case of perjury, and in the case of the idle or unnecessary oath.[31] Hence, "needless oaths" are to be avoided, and "moderation in swearing" cultivated.[32]

The reservations of the Sermon on the Mount are to be understood along these lines. It cannot have been the purpose of Jesus' stricture "either to slacken or tighten the law, but to bring back . . . a true and genuine understanding." [33] This means that Jesus cannot have intended the total abolition of the oath, but only to restore it to its proper use. This is why there is need for careful avoidance not only of perjury, which "the people then commonly avoided," but also of "empty and superfluous oaths." [34] In exceptional cases extrajudicial oaths may well be admissible.[35]

The Heidelberg Catechism and the Genevan Catechism of 1542 similarly recognize the right of the authorities to administer oaths. In the main, Protestant ethicists have followed the lead of the Reformers in this matter. In particular, so far as we can ascertain, the statement of the Sermon on the Mount is never regarded as a prohibition of swearing in general, but only as a protest against idle or unnecessary oaths.

There is a great difference of opinion as to precisely what kind of swearing this includes. It has been taken to mean private oaths, or excessive swearing, or swearing on the assumption that truth is required of us only when we are standing before a judge. The state has also been thought to be capable of producing idle untruthfulness by imposing the oath as "a religious act." [36]

Never in the older literature, and only once in that which is recent,[37] have we met the view that the stricture against the oath in the Sermon on the Mount is to be understood eschatologically, and that for this reason a conditional acceptance of the oath is indicated. Søe is content

[30] *Ibid.* 2. 8. 23; *LCC* 20, 389.
[31] *Ibid.* 2. 8. 24-25; *LCC* 20, 390.
[32] *Ibid.* 2. 8. 25, 26; *LCC* 20, 390, 391.
[33] *Ibid.* 2. 8. 26; *LCC* 20, 392.
[34] *Ibid.* 2. 8. 26; *LCC* 20, 392.
[35] *Ibid.* 2. 8. 27; *LCC* 20, 393-394.
[36] See Adolf Schlatter, *Die christliche Ethik* (Stuttgart, 1929), pp. 147-148.
[37] See Schniewind, *op. cit.*, pp. 65-66.

with the inadequate observation that "the attitude of the main Christian churches is different" from that of, e.g., the Quakers, who in the name of the Sermon on the Mount radically reject the oath; he devotes only fourteen lines to a brief enumeration of the reasons for this "attitude." [38] In many modern works on ethics the word "oath" does not even appear in the index. Paul Althaus says simply that Jesus' prohibition of swearing "does not apply to the oath required by the state in its administration of justice in a world of sin." [39] The brevity of this treatment may derive from the thetic character of the Althaus "outline" [Grundriss]. At least it does open the way for a consideration of the real problem of the oath such as we have indicated above. Perhaps it takes an age like the present, in which the totalitarian state confronts us in elemental fashion with the problems of the oath – its use and abuse, and hence also its general dubiety and limits – to make us hear the question posed in Matthew 5:33-37 and come to terms with it.

The Limits of the Oath

If we are thus forced to the position that the political and legal emergency order of this world cannot survive without enhanced signs of the binding nature of the word, the question immediately arises as to the scope of the commitment made in an oath. If the oath is to take the place, as it were, of the simple but corrupted Yes and No, if it is to be a kind of emergency protection against the dominion of falsehood, then it must be unconditionally binding. But is the obligation which is effected unconditional in the strict sense?

If we have truly understood the challenge brought against the oath by Jesus' saying, then we will no longer be able to assume that secularism is halted when it reaches the sphere of the oath. If we were to assume that the oath stood somehow outside this aeon, then we should be contradicting the total message of the New Testament, which tells us of no such privileged circles immune from sin. Nor are such circles conceivable on the basis of the Reformation doctrine of justification.

In the fallen world what is radically called in question is not just whether the oath should be sworn but – even assuming the need for

[38] See Niels Hanson Søe, Kristelig Etik (2nd ed.; Copenhagen: Gads, 1946), p. 313.

[39] Paul Althaus, Grundriss der Ethik (2nd ed.; Gütersloh: Bertelsmann, 1953), p. 138.

it — whether the oath can be kept. We alluded to this aspect of the problem when we said that the appeal to God as witness implies also a relativizing of the obligation. This relativizing may become urgent when the partnership contracted in the oath is in contradiction with the witness to whom appeal is thus made.

This aspect of the problem, as one might easily suppose, comes out less clearly in relation to the oath of truth than in relation to the oath of loyalty. It is of this, then, that we would now speak.

In the oath of truth one swears to facts which took place in the past. In the oath of loyalty the oath involves a personal relationship in the future, something that obviously is not a closed case but leaves open all kinds of unforeseeable possibilities. Situations may possibly arise which will not correspond to the presuppositions under which the vow or promise or oath of loyalty is given, and may even call the oath in question.

Since the oath of loyalty involves, not some *thing* that I do but some *person* to whom I am bound, it is decisively called in question whenever confidence or trust is shaken. To see what this means, we must first of all understand what confidence is.[40]

Now I can, to be sure, "trust" a constitution or a monetary system. But here the term is already used in a derived sense, for what is implied is trust in its effective operation, something I can count on. Similarly, the term is used in a derived sense and has lost some facets of its original meaning when in politics (whether as a voter, a head of state, or a leader in government) I express "no-confidence" in someone. This does not mean that I have ceased to trust him personally, or to regard him as a man of responsibility and character. It means rather that I no longer think he can do the particular job in the particular situation.

The original meaning of the term comes to the fore only when I trust someone as a person. Such trust is possible only under certain conditions.[41] First, confidence arises only when I can presuppose in him an inner integrity and independence. If he is simply impelled arbitrarily and at random by unpredictable forces, whether by his own caprice and impulses or by external influences, then I do not know

[40] The classic analysis of confidence is given in Wilhelm Herrmann, *Ethik* (2nd ed.; Tübingen-Leipzig, 1901), pp. 27 ff.
[41] We spoke of these conditions earlier on pp. 202-205.

what he is or is not capable of. But this I must know if I am to be able to trust him. The first condition of confidence, then, is the other person's constancy. I must be able to count on his remaining the man he is. Second, I can trust him only if I know what is the basis of this constancy, i.e., to what he is committed. For me he is unpredictable unless I know the norms which direct him, and am convinced that he will be guided by them. Third, I must myself be bound to these same norms. For only then can I rightly estimate the degree to which they are binding, and hence accord confidence under their auspices. Unless I am myself committed in this way, I cannot count on the other man's being committed either. For it is a basic law of the I-Thou relationship that I can ascribe to the other person only such motives as would have moved me to do what he did. If I am moved by arbitrariness and a reluctance to commit myself, I attribute the same to him, and confidence is thus undermined.

If confidence thus defined is the presupposition of the oath of loyalty, this has two main implications. First, the person or institution to whom I pledge allegiance must be worthy of confidence in the sense that I can see how they are themselves committed and hence can count on their constancy. In relation to the authorities – *and* to the persons in government – this means that I can trust that they are in conscience bound to a legal-political order.

For only so long as I can perceive their self-commitment can I in principle be one with them. And only thus far do they offer me – within the framework of keeping my oath – the legal possibility of being able to revise my factual assessment of the situation, and therefore to withdraw from my oath if the facts are such that to perform the detailed duties it imposes would be to violate its essential purpose.

Second, if I am to be capable of taking an oath, I too must be worthy of confidence. That is, I must realize that I myself am committed to the same legal-political obligation which I demand of the state as the condition for my trusting it.

Whether the one to whom I pledge allegiance is trustworthy is something I must decide at the moment I take the oath. For if I am to swear responsibly I cannot entrust myself to all and sundry. Hence, when I take the oath, I must decide concerning my relationship to the one to whom I thus entrust myself. (This is the difficulty, e.g., in the case of a pact with the devil.)

Nevertheless, the confidence I bring to the occasion does not rule out the possibility of my making a mistake. In far greater measure than in personal life, this possibility exists with respect to my relationship to men in government. For, quite apart from the fallibility of all things human, which can always involve surprises, I usually know government people only at a distance, i.e., only indirectly and by hearsay. Moreover, an official, or even a whole system, can wilfully practice deceit and self-misrepresentation in order to win public confidence.[42] Hence a situation can arise in which I would refuse to take the oath if I had it to do over again. If an oath is to remain intact, the situation in which it was originally sworn must obviously also remain intact.

This needs to be stated even more precisely. This initial situation, which if it changes can affect the inviolability of the oath, cannot be identified merely with the external circumstances. For I knew when I took the oath that these were likely to change. The reference is rather to the inner situation: The other party, whether it be the state, the constitution, or the persons responsible for them, has not maintained its trustworthiness; it has changed in substance, or else its true nature — which was not apparent to me at the time — has now come to light. We may put it very simply as follows: For me to be able to remain faithful, the other must also remain faithful to himself, i.e., he must remain the one he was when I gave him my oath of loyalty.

This problem is particularly acute when the other party is a person rather than an organization or system. Inevitably the very concept of confidence as we have been discussing it brings personal categories to the fore, although in respect of the state this may not be altogether desirable (we shall return to this later). It is thus appropriate to consider further at this point in our discussion these personal categories and implications.

In the marriage vow, which might be adduced here as an analogy, things are relatively simple. It may be admitted, of course, that the pledge of faithfulness, and the implied confidence, carry with them a certain risk, for after all the other party is "only" a human being, and

---

[42] We need only think, e.g., of how when Hitler began the wolf was deliberately adorned with Christian sheep's clothing, or of the tactical accommodations which Communism usually makes when it first takes over a country.

as such has an open future. There are some degrees of confidence which are damaged by the very idea of there being an element of unpredictability. And perhaps we can see from the example of such a "whole" fellowship the extent of commitment involved in a pledge of faithfulness to a person. To what degree, we must ask, does the initial situation which was originally constitutive for the oath or pledge still remain intact?

In the case of the marriage vow in particular we are confronted by continual changes which seem to alter that initial situation. For each person has his history. Love and lovers have their history as well. The beautiful moment in which eros awakens does not last. And even if eros lasts, it creates moments which are more or less different from that first moment. Love can grow cold. Attraction can change into repulsion. The contact involving soul and body can decrease, at least so far as the physical components are concerned. Age can also alter the proportions of a certain quality so that what was frugality becomes avarice, or what was strength becomes hardness. Thus the question arises whether the initial situation which gave rise to the marital relation, and thus determined the pledge of loyalty, has not altered to such a degree as to affect the implied commitment. Experience teaches that this question is not an artificial construction, for an affirmative answer provides the moral excuse for innumerable divorces.

Nevertheless, what we have here is only an *apparent* change in the initial situation. For the vow of loyalty "till death us do part" implies a realization that I am accepting the *history* of the other as well. The changes indicated are thus included in principle in the vow of faithfulness. Indeed, the vow explicitly states that I desire the other person, not only as he is at this present moment, but in his totality, in the whole of his life with all its changes. I want him in his history. I am not trying to make the moment last forever. I am basically ready to go beyond the moment, e.g., the immediate moment of passion. At any rate this kind of will and desire is characteristic of a distinctively human fellowship, a fellowship which is based on communication between persons rather than on co-operative endeavor toward a certain end, as in a business partnership. Loyalty here means clinging to a person through changing destinies. The binding nature of the vow derives from this concept of loyalty.

Hence the question of divorce cannot even arise on the basis of the "history" of a person where this history is viewed from the perspective of confidence or trust. In terms of ethics divorce becomes a question only in borderline cases, e.g., where one of the partners is unfaithful — to himself as much as to his partner — as in certain cases of adultery (Matt. 5:32), or where mental illness radically alters personality and makes one incapable of communication (though even here membership in the church of Jesus Christ sheds a different light on the situation inasmuch as, for the Christian, personhood depends not on one's standing before men but on one's standing before God, on an "alien dignity").[43]

The problem of the oath or vow is thus comparatively simple in the I-Thou relation based on personal confidence. It is much more complicated when the sworn commitment is to a governmental official, as in the case of the civil and military oaths taken to Hitler. (We have already made reference to this, but mention it again here for the sake of completeness.) It is part of the wisdom of tradition in respect of oaths that they are sworn either to a constitution or to individuals — e.g., kings or military commanders — who are themselves sworn to a constitution. The concept of loyalty is at least very strongly protected if the one to whom allegiance is sworn is a personal partner in this sense. For we have tried to show that loyalty presupposes the personal act of confidence, and that strictly speaking it can be given only to a person, whereas in respect of an institution all that we can do is trust that it will function effectively.

The fact is that even when my oath is to a constitution, what I have in view is always the men who drew it up — the "fathers" or "framers" of the constitution — or those who validly administer and execute it. For it is a truism that even the best institution is not protected against misuse, so that even when my oath is to a constitution I cannot leave out of account those who use or misuse it.

That this is so is again shown by the borderline case. For the oath of loyalty to a particular constitution is no less binding because of the possibility that I may later decide that that constitution is ineffective or bad. I already make a responsible decision on this score when I take the oath. My obligation to it can be called in question only when the institution I have acknowledged, the particular constitution, falls into the hands of men who misuse or ignore it, and I for my part am

[43] See *ThE* 1, 21, 151, 170, 242.

in no position to combat this misuse in the name of the constitution itself.

If the binding character of my oath is called in question not by the institution, but by the persons involved, then the positive side of the oath is also illumined by this borderline case, namely, that the oath of loyalty includes a commitment to the persons who represent the institution, and that this commitment is limited by the loyalty of these persons themselves to the constitution. By loyalty to the constitution we mean more than mere legality. Legality refers to purely formal observance, whereas loyalty refers to the intentions expressed in the constitution. Hitler, e.g., acted legally in respect of the Weimar constitution, but by no means out of loyalty to it. This personalistic background of the oath of loyalty undoubtedly finds fullest expression when allegiance is pledged to a personal representative of the state. For in this case the personal character of the oath, which is always implicit, even when the pledge is to a constitution, is made explicit.

Only when this personal character is noted does a further essential aspect of the oath come into view, namely, that the commitment to loyalty is always reciprocal.[44] In religious oaths this finds expression in the fact that appeal is made to an authority which embraces both the one who swears allegiance and the one to whom allegiance is sworn, in such a way that both are committed, and within this obligation each exists for the other. But the secular authority too – in this case the constitution – contains this rule of mutual obligation; this is why the rule was regarded as a serious argument for the nullity of civil and military oaths of loyalty to Hitler if it could be maintained that Hitler for his part had broken his pledge and become an unscrupulous adventurer or criminal.

Thus in a memorandum on the overthrow of Hitler drawn up by his opponents on the German General Staff already in 1939— between the Polish and French campaigns — we read concerning the nullity of the military oath: "Finally let it not be said: The soldier must stand by his oath. The oath was sworn to Herr Hitler as the responsible leader of Germany, i.e., under a reciprocal obligation. This oath has lost its validity, since Hitler, forgetting his duties, has set about sacrificing Germany to his mad goals. Hence the soldier is no longer under

⁴⁴ See Walter Künneth, *Politik zwischen Dämon und Gott. Eine christliche Ethik des Politischen* (Berlin: Lutherisches Verlagshaus, 1954), p. 371.

obligation to his oath. But he still has the supreme national duty of keeping faith with the German fatherland against this destroyer." [45]

This principle of reciprocity inherent in the oath of loyalty can be used as a criterion for the limits of the oath only when there are clear rules as to the mutual obligations. For the civil servant these are laid down in the constitution,[46] for the military services in the articles of war. But they are also defined by the divine commandments, by the basic principles of ethics, and, for Roman Catholics, by natural law.

To sum up, and in some points to carry the discussion further, we may define in several decisive points the limits of obligation involved in the oath of loyalty. The oath is no longer binding when the one to whom allegiance is pledged forsakes the base on which the oath was sworn. This he does when he poses demands which run counter to that higher authority to which both parties to the oath are committed in virtue of its religious character (e.g., massacring the Jews, eliminating the unfit, persecuting the faith, etc.); or when he ignores in blatant fashion, i.e., systematically and not just in individual measures, the principle of reciprocal obligation implied in the oath of loyalty; or when he renounces the secular authority (the constitution, etc.) which is invoked in the oath and which again binds both parties.

In all three cases, which are simply different aspects of the same situation and which thus in principle constitute but one case, there is a radical alteration of the initial situation which was constitutive for the obligation involved in the oath. Those who take seriously both the ultimate personal commitment made in the oath and the presence of the God who is invoked as a witness, are the very ones who find it quite impossible to prostitute the oath to ends which the committed person himself cannot countenance and which are an abomination in the eyes of the divine witness. It is precisely this seriousness of the oath which causes the obligation to be limited and restricted, not unrestricted and limitless. For loyalty is possible only when the subject of loyalty, i.e., the one who swears, remains true to himself, to man in his relation to God. It is this self which makes it impossible for him to accept unconditionally and unreservedly any earthly relation. It

[45] Erich Kordt, *Nicht aus den Akten . . . Die Wilhelmstrasse in Frieden und Krieg: Erlebnisse, Begegnungen und Eindrücke (1928-1945)* (Stuttgart: Union Deutsche Verlagsgesellschaft, 1950), pp. 364-365.

[46] The specific defect of the Third Reich was that it had no constitution, but was grounded in the will of the *Führer*.

makes him a son and not a slave (Gal. 3:24 ff.), independent and subject to no man (Acts 5:29; Matt. 22:21).

In Shakespeare's *King John*, Cardinal Pandulph says:

> For that which thou has sworn to do amiss
> Is not amiss when it is truly done, . . .
> It is religion that doth make vows kept;
> But thou hast sworn against religion,
> By what thou swear'st against the thing thou swear'st,
> And makest an oath the surety for thy truth
> Against an oath: the truth thou art unsure
> To swear, swears only not to be forsworn.[47]

The paradoxical formulation of the last lines expresses precisely what we have sought to say, namely, that the oath swears to the seriousness of the oath, so that it cannot be brought into contradiction to itself. But this happens when I swear "against" that "by which" I swear. It is this contradiction between an oath and its own presupposition that makes it null and void.

But we have to differentiate between two radically different forms of this nullity. We might describe them as the authentic and the inauthentic nullity. Authentic nullity occurs where because of a subsequent alteration in the initial situation the sworn oath is brought into intolerable self-contradiction. The inauthentic nullity occurs where the oath is such as cannot be kept even from the moment it is sworn, whether because the one to whom allegiance is pledged has already forsaken the basis of the oath, or because he is unmistakably and unequivocally on the point of doing so. In relation to this latter situation the Cardinal legate says:

> But thou dost swear only to be forsworn;
> And most forsworn, to keep what thou dost swear.[48]

This is a precise characterization of inauthentic nullity. The one who swears enters culpably into a situation which gives rise to an oath which is null. For the oath here stands in such sharp contrast with its very nature that it invalidates itself. Yet, though the oath is thus null in its effect, it is not null for the one who dares to swear it.

---

[47] William Shakespeare, *The Life and Death of King John*, Act III, scene 1.
[48] *Ibid.*

The nullity is not just nothing, at least not for the one who uses it, and thus treats it as if it were something.[49]

The something thus wrenched out of the nullity is — perjury. The element of perjury can manifest itself here in two ways. First, I may see clearly from the outset that the oath cannot be kept, and I may clearly purpose to treat it accordingly, paradoxically swearing "to be forsworn." Or, second, I may be true to the content of the oath, and thus keep the sworn but impossible loyalty; in this case I allow the oath to come into contradiction with its presupposition, and I fail to keep it, thus becoming a perjurer in this sense.

What really happens when the limit of obligation is reached is not that I break the oath but that the oath becomes null and void. Just as I cannot break a marriage which has been declared null, so I cannot break an oath which has become null — unless it was obviously null already at the moment when it was taken. It is along these lines that Roman Catholic canon law speaks of the possibility that the obligation incurred in a sworn promise may lapse.[50]

Annulment of the Oath and the Church as Watchman

The situation of nullity and lapse has to be considered, of course, from another angle as well. The modern situation with respect to the oath and its limits, distinguished as it is by the workings of ideological tyranny in the twentieth century, is so different that in this, as in many other matters, we cannot simply rely on established ethical tradition, but are forced to supplement it. As we have seen, the oath of loyalty, like any other oath, involves a twofold confession. First, there is confession of God as witness, and then, derived from this, there is confession of the earthly authority to whom allegiance is pledged. In keeping with its confessional structure, the oath therefore can also be broken only if its nullity too is an object of confession. This means that there has to be an annulment or "declaration" of nullity. It is inconceivable, and incommensurate with the dignity of the oath, that the swearing should be a solemn act of confession while the an-

---

[49] The classical New Testament passages on this question of nullity are I Cor. 8:4, 8-13; 10:19-21, 28-30; Rom. 1:23; Gal. 4:8; I Thess. 1:9 where Paul discusses the eating of meat sacrificed to idols. The idol is nothing until it is treated as something by the unbeliever or the weak Christian brother. See ThE 1, 306-308.

[50] Codex Iuris Canonici, III, iii, 19, 2; Canon 1319, 2.

nulment should take place quietly, as it were, without any declaration or confession, without any avowal, merely by a *de facto* failure to keep it. To act thus is not to declare a particular oath null, but to treat the whole matter of the oath as a nullity. This is perjury on a more profound level.

The point is borne out by the following argument. What the oath of loyalty demands of me is not primarily a thing but me myself, as a person. That is what loyalty involves. Hence it is out of the question that I should simply pass over the invalidation of the oath in silence and act accordingly, ignoring duties imposed on me by the one to whom I pledged allegiance. If I simply treat the oath as null, by doing or omitting to do certain things, I miss the very point of the sworn obligation, which is the commitment of the person, not just the commitment to certain things or acts. It thus follows that a sworn obligation cannot lapse unless I dissociate myself from it as a person, i.e., totally, and not just in respect of specific functions. But this can be done only if I confess what I am doing, only if I state that it is my very self that is being released from the obligation.

Yet this is not all that is to be said about the situation of nullity and lapse. For in this situation it is not enough to react with individual confessions. The emergency in respect of the oath is by nature a public emergency, and that in two senses. First, the allegiance involved in the oath has been pledged to a public institution, one that affects everybody, and everybody has a responsibility for its integrity or lack of integrity. And second, the emergency occasioned by that public institution's failure to be true to itself concerns not only certain individuals, but all people who have pledged it their allegiance. The public form of renunciation thus accords with the public nature of the emergency.

Now it frequently happens that in the very places where such emergencies arise — i.e., under ideological tyranny — common actions and declarations on the part of those who have taken the oath are all but impossible. Yet it is precisely here that the confession of annulment must be common and public. Hence, in this as in similar matters pertaining to the limits of the oath and the emergency in respect of it, the church enters the picture in its office as watchman. We believe that three claims in particular are made on it.

As watchman the church must first teach men to recognize the emergency situation. For usually the situation is such that men are tempted, because of the very perversity of the authority, either to cover up their wrong deeds by pleading that as a result of their sworn obligation they have to comply with the demands imposed on them, or else to sabotage their oath by quietly evading the demands.

Second, the overcoming of the emergency through a public declaration that the oath has become null and void is usually beyond the outward resources and inward strength of the one who swore allegiance. It is beyond his outward resources because for such a renunciation the individual cannot usually command the needed public platform; dictatorial states particularly, which is where the situation usually arises, exercise strict control of the public media. It is also beyond his inward strength because the character of the one to whom allegiance is pledged, as it has come to be known in the emergency situation, is such that reprisals can be expected, and not just against the person immediately concerned but against his family as well. Then too there is the peculiar problem faced by those upon whom the borderline situation of resistance, or the preparation of revolution, imposes the duty of deception and therewith the burden of perjuring themselves by breaking their oath.

This leads us to a new aspect of the situation of resistance which we discussed earlier. The necessity of deception implied in it, at least so far as resistance to ideological tyranny is concerned, makes a confessional annulment impossible. For this kind of annulment would involve self-incrimination, and hence the self-extirpation of every resistance group. Yet without such a declaration the nullity of the oath does not take effect. (To say that "a nullity takes effect" is to speak paradoxically, but we believe we have given adequate reasons for the use of such an expression.) Thus a resistance group, insofar as it includes people who have sworn allegiance to the particular system, is forced to commit perjury by breaking the oath even though *de facto* the oath is already null and void.

If we showed earlier that this kind of resistance leads to an insoluble conflict of duties and hence demands acceptance of guilt — Roman Catholic moral theology to the contrary notwithstanding — we must now add that this guilt includes also the inescapable necessity of committing perjury by breaking one's oath. To be sure, the guilt involved here not only stands in need of forgiveness, but may also go hand in hand with a certainty of forgiveness. For it is not entered into lightly but with a sense of responsibility, and under the burden of a total guilt which cannot be done away — at least in the kingdom on the left hand — without new guilt, the vicariously accepted new guilt which is entailed in any revolution, however legitimate. Besides, the perjury is mitigated somewhat by the fact that the sworn commitment is *de facto* no longer valid, though its nullity has not yet taken affect because it has not yet been declared.

We have attempted an exact analysis of this situation because there is a great danger involved in it: To overlook the guilt because of the mitigating factors leads to justification of the sin rather than of the sinner, and consequently to a tragic self-justification.[51]

In this situation of excessive demands and insoluble conflicts of conscience it is the task of the church as watchman vicariously to define by solemn and public declaration the limits of sworn obligation, and on occasion even to issue confessional declarations of annulment. In connection with the first of these two points, namely, defining the limits of obligation, the Confessing Church in Germany once made a statement in connection with Karl Barth's refusal of the oath in 1934. Barth would take the oath to Hitler only with the supplementary proviso: "to the extent that my Christianity will allow" — unless the church itself would make an official declaration to the effect that this supplement is implied in any oath taken by a Christian, and thus applies also to the specific situation at hand. Once the church made this declaration, Barth declared that he was ready to take the oath to Hitler without the addition of this personal proviso.[52]

The church, as distinct from a political resistance group, has no right to evade this kind of vicarious action in the emergency situation. It cannot excuse itself simply by speaking of the need for deception and other tactical means of survival. For the church is called, not to resistance in the sense of self-preservation, but to obedience — and to confidence in the promise that the powers of death shall not prevail against it (Matt. 16:18).

But there is yet a third and supreme claim upon the church as

[51] This is the point Barth was trying to make in his theological opinion concerning the Weizsäcker case, to which we referred at p. 356, n. 7.
[52] *Junge Kirche,* 1934, 23, p. 1002; 1935, 1, p. 61; 3, p. 147.

watchman. It must at all times, and not just in acute emergencies, prophylactically address the government on the duty which devolves upon it. As the body to which allegiance is pledged the state must fulfill its own obligations, for the sake of its own institutional dignity and also in order to spare individuals the conflict of conscience which is otherwise theirs. This admonitory task does not fall to the church only as elemental emergencies of the kind we have been discussing may arise. It is to be discharged with respect to every kind of corruption that may exist in the matter of oaths.

One such corruption is the multiplication of oaths, whether in respect of telling the truth or of promising loyalty. In the third decade of the present century some 2000 perjury convictions were obtained annually in Germany, and it is estimated that there may well have been 36,000 more cases which went undetected.[53] These figures point to a devaluation of the sworn oath which is of concern to the church as watchman. The same is true in relation to promissory oaths, which were renewed each time an official was transferred from one jurisdiction to another, and which were discredited anyway by historical changes in system. Here the church as watchman should not only call for a more restricted use of oaths but also plead for the right of individuals to refuse to swear an oath on grounds of conscientious objection (even as in respect of conscientious objection to military service).

Corruption in the swearing of oaths reached a climax under National Socialism because the ceremonial of the oath was regarded primarily from the standpoint of its propagandistic power of suggestion. It was merely an exercise whose value consisted in the degree of its repetition. Thus there were not only civil and military oaths, but also party oaths; indeed, special political groups even had their own special oaths.

Accepting its office of watchman in exemplary fashion, the Confessing Church voiced its opposition to this practice (even though in a situation of unparalleled difficulty at the end of the Third Reich it did not see its way clear to declaring the oath of loyalty annulled, in the sense in which we have been speaking of it). The statements which are most important theologically are as follows: "The Evan-

[53] A. Hegler, *Die Eidesreform* ("Tübinger Abhandlungen zum öffentlichen Recht," XXIII [1930]), 9, 38.

gelical church must bewail it as a victory of the anti-Christian spirit that the oath as a pledge of allegiance and a commitment has undergone such a shocking increase, and therewith such a shocking devaluation. If every oath — even when the name of God is not expressly mentioned — is a declaration or assurance made in the sight of God, then the fact that many men are made to swear oaths at frequent intervals necessarily robs the oath of its dignity and leads to a profaning and misusing of the name of God. Evangelical parents regard it as particularly intolerable that oathlike pledges are exacted from their children at a very early age. . . . In pastoral counseling cases multiply in which men declare that they do not feel bound by an oath which they felt they had to take at peril of their very life. The Evangelical church could better combat this attitude if the Christian were allowed to interpret the oath to mean — what to him is self-evident — that no oath can cover over actions which are contrary to God's command." [54] Obviously this was not allowed, because the oath was alleged to imply an unconditional commitment.

The attitude of Roman Catholic moral theology on the limits of the oath is fundamentally the same. The main points are formulated in the *Codex Iuris Canonici:* "The obligation incurred by a promissory oath lapses . . . when the substance of what is sworn is changed, or becomes intrinsically bad or completely worthless by reason of a change in the immediate surroundings, or hinders a greater good . . . or when the final cause no longer exists, or the condition under which the oath was taken disappears." [55] The German bishops took a similar position in 1935. Confronted by the July 12 edict of the Minister of Culture that the oath should be taken "without reservations or restriction," they spoke as follows: "For the Catholic Christian there is no need of such reservations or restriction. For it is and always has been Catholic teaching that an oath . . . cannot contain that which is in contradiction with the

---

[54] The statement is from section 5 on "Morality and Law" in a memorial of May, 1936, prepared by the new temporary leadership of the Evangelical church. See the text in Heinrich Schmid, *Apokalyptisches Wetterleuchten. Ein Beitrag der Evangelischen Kirche zum Kampf im "Dritten Reich"* (Munich: Verlag der Evangelisch-Lutherischen Kirche in Bayern, 1947), pp. 141-142.

[55] *Codex Iuris Canonici,* III, iii, 19, 2; Canon 1319, 2 and 3. Cf. the similar statements of T. V. Gerster, *Katholische Sittenlehre,* II (1912), 115; and O. Schilling, *Lehrbuch der Moraltheologie,* II (1928), 340.

duty of divine worship and loyalty to the truth. An obligation to something which . . . contradicts the law of God cannot, then, be the subject of an oath." [56]

What we have said about the necessity of declaring the nullity of a lapsed oath is no more to be found in Roman Catholic canon law than in the tradition of Reformation ethics. Yet there are echoes of this thought, for it is said of the pledge to tell the truth that, if it is extracted "by force or excessive fear," it can be lifted by the ecclesiastical authorities. [57] The same is true — again under special circumstances — of the lifting of a vow or oath of loyalty, whether by annulment or dispensation. [58]

The most public and demonstrative form of such ecclesiastical release from oaths and vows is to be seen in the medieval practice of excommunication. As the Cardinal legate Pandulph says in his discussion with King John, all pledges of allegiance to a prince are cancelled when that prince is excommunicated:

> Then, by the lawful power that I have,
> Thou shalt stand cursed and excommunicate:
> And blessed shall he be that doth revolt
> From his allegiance to an heretic;
> And meritorious shall that hand be call'd,
> Canonized, and worshipp'd as a saint,
> That takes away by any secret course
> Thy hateful life. [59]

If we understand correctly, in spite of similarities between the two positions there is a difference: In Roman Catholic canon law there is, as it were, a transubstantiation of the existent oath into non-existence; what takes place is an ontic annulment performed in the power of the ecclesiastical office. In our view, however, confessional annulment is simply the declaration of a nullity which ontically already exists. If he is sufficiently assured, the one who swore the oath may make this declaration himself. The task of the church — as we have shown in our discussion of the three claims upon the church

[56] C. Gröber, *Handbuch der religiösen Gegenwartsfragen* (1937), p. 150.

[57] A. Retzbach and F. Vetter, *Das Recht der katholischen Kirche nach dem Codex juris canonici* (1947), p. 318.

[58] *Ibid.*, pp. 316-318.

[59] Shakespeare, *loc. cit.*

as watchman — is to help him to such responsible assurance concerning the existent emergency, and, because the emergency is a public one and he himself may be under the pressure of threats, vicariously to make in this instance the declaration which strictly speaking is his to make.

For the rest, it would be unfair to leave the impression that the authoritative annulment of vows and oaths in Roman Catholicism is an arbitrary act left to the whim of the church. On the contrary, the criteria for such annulment are precisely stipulated in the canons cited: change in the substance of what is sworn, lapse of the purpose of the oath, absence of the given condition, etc. All these criteria show that ecclesiastical annulment is possible only in those cases which involve the situation we have described as nullity.

This is an interesting observation because it again shows that even with their different theological backgrounds, e.g., even with different concepts of church and ministry (as in the present case), the two churches can still adopt similar positions and measures in concrete political life. From what has been said, it may be seen that they both recognize in the same way the emergency situation in respect of the oath, and that, in terms of political effect, they both pronounce a release from sworn duty in the same sense. One might almost say that the two churches can pray together and in large measure act together, though only to a certain degree do they share the same theology. On the other hand, the theological difference will appear negligible only to those who do not see the fundamental connection between faith and thought.

This chapter on the oath, like the other chapters in this ethics but with enhanced clarity and intensity, has drawn our attention repeatedly to the problem of the totalitarian state, and therewith to the borderline situation in politics. This is not due solely to the burning historical reality of the problem in our day. It is not just a sign of the times. It is due primarily to the fact that in the very nature of the matter itself the borderline situation provides the classic model for all questions concerning the obligation and limits of the oath. If we have been successful in gaining some insights — and above all in posing some new questions — not previously found in the traditional theology of the oath, this is due not least of all to the circumstance that we have this particular model available for analysis.

For the border or boundary [*Grenze*] is, as Paul Tillich says, "the best place for acquiring knowledge." [60]

[60] See Paul Tillich, *On the Boundary: An Autobiographical Sketch* (New York: Scribner's, 1966), p. 13.

22.

Military Obedience

Our deliberations in this chapter represent a continuation of our discussion of the problem of resistance, specifically in respect of its military variation. They also form a transition to the next section of Part Three, in which we shall be discussing the topic of war; for they have to do with the problem of military service in general, and within this framework, with a special question which can become particularly acute in time of war. Nevertheless, the question of military obedience belongs to the complex of questions relating to the problem of resistance and the oath of loyalty. For in all the armies of the world the promise of obedience is an integral part of the military oath and of other forms of military commitment.

Obedience in the Military and in Civilian Life

To begin with, it is important to note a symptom which points to the fundamental difference between the military and the civilian world in respect of the understanding of obedience. The military has its own law, a law which in exceptional situations (e.g., during a state of siege) may be extended to cover the civilian sphere as well. The special right therewith conceded is particularly enhanced in case of war because to the exceptional character of the military there is added the exceptional character of war (martial law, etc.). What then is the basis of this difference between the military and the civilian world in respect of law? Any ethical discussion which does not begin with this question will necessarily be unrealistic. Five points may be mentioned.

First, the supposed analogy between the serviceman's duty of obedience and that of a public official breaks down for the simple reason that the civilian official can resign if he receives instructions he cannot conscientiously fulfill. Indeed, we have pointed out that he can break his sworn obligation only in this way, and not by secret *de facto* sabotage. But this path of direct or indirect withdrawal is not open to soldiers (except possibly high ranking officers). The soldier may resist an order only by actual disobedience, but in the normative situation — i.e., in war — he cannot claim the legally conceded possibility of resignation. What a fantastic thing that would be!

Second, at stake in war is the life or death not just of the nation involved, but also of the serviceman himself. In face of this elemental threat the normal deterrents of law are too slight an evil to compete with the mortal "evil" of the battlefront situation. If the deterrent with respect to this situation is to be the greater evil, it must be incomparably more severe than in normal circumstances. Applied to the problem before us, this means that military law must give to the military command or order an incomparably higher authority than is ever accorded to a law or directive in civil life. This enhanced strictness is motivated by two things: the war emergency which poses a threat to all, and the weakness of human nature, to whose servile fear appeal must be made. With the enhanced strictness of the order the possibility of resistance is essentially diminished, both as regards its legal presuppositions and as regards the moral demand for it.

Third, acts have to be committed in time of war (the use of force, killing, the application of pressure by taking innocent hostages, etc.) which, though they are limited by rules (such as the Geneva and Hague conventions), still involve within these "allowed" limits deeds which would be considered criminal in normal civilian life. This problem is accentuated if the combatants, e.g., in underground warfare, do not abide by the rules. The bitterness of the struggle can then become so great that the elemental demands of self-preservation lead to wholly illegal acts like the shooting of hostages, etc.

In relation to the question before us, this means that the military command or order must be strict enough to prevail not only over such lower impulses as anxiety and the instinct of self-preservation, but also over certain moral reservations, which have to be set aside in favor of the higher moral good which a "just war" is fought to preserve. To put it more sharply, the military order in time of war claims to legalize and validate certain actions about which there are moral reservations, so that within the framework of military law these moral considerations cannot prevail over the order itself, and be recognized as grounds for refusing obedience.

In constitutional states this does not usually mean that in principle there can be such a thing as a moral objection to military orders. It means only that the boundary between disputable and indisputable moral objections is not the same as in normal life. Things are permitted, even commanded, in war which could not be allowed in civilian life. Hence one might say that those who issue military commands are themselves responsible for where they draw the line. Incidentally, this plunges us smack into the middle of the whole problem of war. Those who are not pacifists in principle, but accept the necessity in the fallen world for defense by force, therewith accept in principle the fact that the law which obtains in war is exceptional. This is true even for those who regard war as absurd in an atomic age but cannot draw from this the inference that all defensive preparations must be abandoned. We shall return to this in the next chapter.

Fourth, it is inconsistent with the nature of military force and the discipline which it demands that in a moment of acute danger arguments should be allowed concerning the reasons for an order. But even in times of peace the soldier practices the kind of conduct which will be required in such a moment of danger. Hence the prohibition applies to peacetime military service as well. This leads many armies to adopt the rule that complaints against an order can be made only *post factum*, i.e., after it has been carried out. The strictness of a superior's legal command, and the consequent restriction of the possibility of legal disobedience, is based on a twofold argument. There is the pragmatic argument which appeals to the need for discipline, and the moral argument which ascribes to the one who issues an order the moral responsibility for it, and which thus presupposes authority, an authority which has to be based on confidence or trust.

Neither argument avails for obedience in civilian life. In the first place discipline is not so critically important here as for the soldier in a moment of acute danger. Then too a democratic state, which is built on the principle of the equal rights of all its citizens, does not permit a superior to bear such one-sided responsibility. Democracy presupposes an equal maturity in the subordinate.

This leads us to our fifth and final consideration. The military command or order can achieve the needed expansion of its authority only by correspondingly restricting the maturity of those subject to it. This curtailment of maturity may be seen in detail at two points.

Restriction of the Soldier's Maturity

The Necessity for Unquestioning Obedience

What Clausewitz calls the "friction" (in the widest sense) of military encounter [1] makes it impossible to "persuade" the broad mass of those on the receiving end of orders, so that they will want to obey because of their own insight into and acceptance of the necessity for the order. The effort to persuade might fail. It would at the very least necessitate the kind of extensive discussion which would severely curtail the capacity to act. Indeed, it would give the cartoonists a field day! But to forego such an effort at individual persuasion is to extend greatly the purported authority of the order or command, and hence to radicalize the demand for obedience. This does not mean that all attempts to persuade the recipient of an order are abandoned, but only that they focus on other points.

The soldier must be made to understand and accept the total meaning of a war, e.g., the fact that it is defensive in character, that it is necessary, and how much hangs on the outcome. The effort thus to persuade him is ethically required. Otherwise the soldier simply becomes a means to an end, a mere mercenary, and this is immoral. [2] Such persuasion, however, is also indicated by the tactical considerations of leadership, for only the man who is thus persuaded is capable of making sacrifices and committing himself totally.

The attempt to persuade also focuses on winning the soldier's confidence in his commanding officers and on thus convincing him of the professional competence and ethical integrity of those who issue the orders. This latter purpose implies that the soldier must delegate to his superiors the task of vindicating the validity of the order. He must agree to suspend his own independent judgment.

In addition to the delay that would be entailed, the risk, and the impaired capacity to act, there are other reasons for not trying to reconcile all orders with the insight and conviction of the subordinates. Two such reasons may be mentioned.

---

[1] See Carl von Clausewitz, *On War*, trans. J. J. Graham (London: Kegan Paul, Trench, Trübner, 1911), I, 77-81.

[2] Kant, *Critique of Practical Reason;* in *Kant* ("Great Books," Vol. 42), p. 304.

First, secrecy is one of the rules of military action. If every order were to be explained in detail, this would mean theoretically that the action of every reconnaissance patrol would have to be related to the objective of the entire battalion, and that of the battalion to the overall strategy of the high command, etc. By its very nature, however, strategic planning must be concealed from the enemy, because surprise plays an integral part in every strategic and tactical action. Hence it is an elementary rule of military command in all armies that, except for top-ranking officers, each soldier should receive only such information as is absolutely indispensable for the performance of his assigned task. This cannot be done, however, without considerably restricting the maturity of the subordinates. It is to be noted, of course, that there is also some restriction of this kind in civilian politics. All states and governments have their secrets and their secret emissaries. Hence only a limited degree of mature judgment can be conceded to the ordinary voter. He too sits beyond the curtain and does not see what goes on backstage. The analogy, of course, is very limited inasmuch as the situation is incomparably more acute in the military sphere.

Second, it is of the very nature of armed forces that to a very large degree they are only "instruments." If they seek to be more, they begin to make policy rather than simply implement it. But for the military to take over the responsibility of making political decisions can be very damaging. Gerhard Ritter is surely right when he says, "By all historical experience . . . the political soldier is more harmful than useful." [3] It is easy to see why this assuming of political competence by the military is necessarily so fateful a step, for war then becomes the criterion of politics, instead of politics being the criterion for the necessity or impossibility of war. This leads to an acute sense of what we have usually called the "revolt of means," and of what is here the rule of the "instrument." Like every other sphere of life, the military too has a tendency to become a law unto itself, a tendency which if not directed can lead from factual autonomy to autocracy. This autocracy then finds expression in the fact that the laws

[3] Gerhard Ritter, *The German Resistance: Carl Goerdeler's Struggle Against Tyranny*, trans. R. T. Clark (London: Allen & Unwin, 1958), p. 69; cf. *idem, Staatskunst und Kriegshandwerk. Das Problem des "Militarismus" in Deutschland* (Munich: Oldenbourg, 1954), I, 97 ff.

of war become general laws. War itself becomes a total thing, embracing all of life; "total war" then leads to "total politics," and total politics for its part is subject to a military concept conditioned by total war.

We may sum up our findings thus far as follows. The first point is that the maturity of those on the receiving end of an order is restricted to the degree that the authority they attach to such order cannot be based on their private conviction that it is right and necessary. For, quite apart from the cumbersome nature of the persuasion process, it violates in principle the rule of secrecy. And it concedes to the soldier a right of decision which goes beyond his role as merely an instrument of policy. As a result it breeds the soldier-politician, and turns politics into an instrument of war.

Of course, the basic structural arrangement within which the subordinate trusts the command of his superior even though he does not understand the reasons for it, and those who wield the instrument of war similarly trust the politician, is based on the assumption that the arrangement itself is sound, i.e., that to trust is justifiable. Already in this regard it is evident that the responsibility of ethical decision inherent in the correlation of command and obedience contains within it a problem which for the individual is almost insoluble. For already at this point in our phenomenology of military life it may be seen that the decision to obey or not to obey is not based exclusively or even primarily on the questionable character of the individual command (e.g., to kill Jews or shoot hostages) but on what is perhaps the questionable nature of the whole system. This problem is almost insoluble not merely because a solution would require an overview of the whole situation such as no individual can attain but also because, even if one attained it and in consequence assessed the situation negatively, there would be no possibility of contracting out anyway, particularly with the enemy closing in.

Discipline and Drill

A further restriction of the maturity of subordinates results from the following observation, which is confirmed by the practice of all modern armies. In situations of elemental danger, such as are common in the "friction" of war, military commanders can expect only a limited degree of dispassionate reflection on the part of those immediately concerned. Psychology is aware that panic leads to rationally uncontrollable reflex actions. Since not every man is a hero, the conduct of the average man in time of danger cannot be based on reflection. It has to be directed by the control of reflexes. It is thus militarily desirable to call forth certain modes of conduct by way of reflex action, in almost mechanical fashion, by pressing the right buttons to produce certain reactions such as stopping, hitting the dirt, getting up, keeping silent, shouting, etc. But this can be achieved only by forms of practice not unlike those used in the training of animals. The justifiable purpose behind all more or less questionable forms of drill and polish is this conditioning of reflexes and training in hardness.

Thus the objection is in a sense valid that drill dehumanizes. For in teaching men how to behave in time of danger it does not appeal to the human character of man (the readiness for self-sacrifice which causes him to think not of himself but only of his duty, or the dispassionate reflection which heroically overcomes the rebellion of the nerves). Drill teaches men how to behave in time of danger by training the nervous reflexes. It is a kind of zoological method.

If there is here an element of dehumanization, it is only a reflection of the dehumanizing of war itself. But merely to assert that war dehumanizes is not to do away with war. It is simply to diagnose a condition in which the plight of the fallen world is seen in all its starkness. This diagnosis tells us that we live and move within the sphere of the Noachic covenant, and that it is mere fantasy to repudiate the laws of this world — which man has produced — as though they could thereby be done away. The point of the Noachic covenant is that it gives us directions for life in a fallen creation, and enables us to trust that the rainbow of reconciliation will even span apocalyptic landscapes (Gen. 9:13 ff.).

Be that as it may, the fact that man lives in a world which is beneath the dignity of his divine creation — because he has made it so! — colors the laws by which he must live and act in this world. If, then, the necessity of defense is one such law, it is unrealistic to reject the elemental means of such defense. That the control of reflexes is among these means is the common view of all military experts.

In the training of reflexes by drill there is thus a restriction of maturity. This training amounts to a no-confidence vote against maturity. For it implies that, apart from a few exceptions, in time of dire peril man is just a complex of nerves to be stimulated and controlled.

What this means, of course, is that the ethical possibility of refusing drill is sharply curtailed. For if we do not rule out the military situation as such, i.e., the necessity of defense, and thus become pacifists, we can hardly object to drill as a logical outcome of this situation.

Even if with some justification I regard drill as an attack on my human dignity, because I think I am a mature human who has no need of such nerve conditioning, I cannot for that reason claim special privilege. For if I did, I should be introducing into this sphere a type of individualized treatment and classification of values which in their very concept carry their own obvious refutation.

Except for those who are pacifists in principle — ethically pacifism is a question unto itself — a fundamental ethical protest against drill is thus unrealistic and inadmissibly abstract, because an ethical decision has always to be made in the situation as it actually is, i.e., concretely, in recognition of the fallen world, and hence realistically. (To make this clear is essentially the only task of this present volume.)

Servile Fear

But we must push our inquiry into even more painful and difficult spheres. A further restriction of maturity comes to light when we consider the following consequence of the "friction" of war: If military leaders cannot trust the deeper insight and individual reflections of those who receive orders, neither can they rely on the presence of such virtues as a sense of responsibility, a readiness for sacrifice, and a regard for duty. (This obviously does not mean that the training they give will not aim to inculcate a soldierly ethos, or that these virtues will not be the goal of instruction. What is meant is simply that the usual results of such training do not permit them to count on these virtues actually being present. It will always be risky to take them for granted.) The realistic factor which they can invariably count on is the instinct of self-preservation. This instinct is so sure and elemental that the other virtues may well be challenged by it in the moment of danger.

Commanders who would reduce risk to the bare minimum and would rely only on sure and certain factors, must consequently try to control the instinct of self-preservation. They can do this, however, only if they so enhance the stringency and severity of the order by making the punishment for breaking it a greater threat to self-preservation than the threat posed by the enemy. To put it in a way which is undoubtedly exaggerated, one-sided, and arguable, one might say that it is of the very nature of military discipline (certainly it is one of its elements) to make fear of one's own superiors several degrees more intense than fear of the enemy. This reflects a skeptical but highly realistic awareness of the human plight, namely, that man is but a "miserable bag of maggot-fodder" — as Luther could occasionally call even the higher specimens of humanity [4] — who in some situations must be coerced into blind obedience by servile fear.

In normal civilian society democracies can afford to appeal to maturity, and thereby perhaps even kindle latent virtues. But the military commander in the borderline situation cannot be content with this appeal to the individual. He has to use a component of terror — though obviously this is only a component and as such must not be allowed to discredit the soldierly ethos.

What in a military order is only a component, however, becomes in a dictatorship the whole package. The parallel between dictatorship and the armed forces is thus limited. But it is obviously there. Hence it is typical that no army on earth is run by democratic rules. Elements of dictatorship appear in all of them.

Nevertheless, this has to be accepted by those who accept the necessity of defense in the fallen world. In war and the military situation the greatness and the misery of man are seen in concentrated form, as in a bright mirror.[5] For the war situation is the perfect crystallization of this aeon.

The decisive thesis, then, which we have been trying to think through and develop in the most varied directions, is that the military command or order can achieve the needed expansion of its authority only by a corresponding restriction of the maturity of those subject to it. From this angle the primary ethical decision a mature indi-

[4] *Madensack;* see, e.g., LW 45, 144, n. 11, and 70, n. 38.
[5] Blaise Pascal correlates the two, suggesting that it is the very misery of fallen man which reflects his greatness. See *ThE* 1, 167.

vidual must make is a decision about this whole complex with its relative restriction of his maturity. His decision will involve a responsible attitude on the whole question of defense as such. This is indeed one of the basic decisions the mature man must make.

If he accepts the right of defense within the framework of the Noachic covenant — which, like · Romans 13, legalizes an official use of force in our broken creation — then a further ethical decision also confronts him. Within the framework of defense the mature individual must willingly renounce some of his rights to independence. We speak of a willing renunciation because only my own deliberate Yes is a free act and hence a matter of ethics. Where I act out of sheer necessity my act has no ethical quality. Indeed, to the extent that it involves mere acquiescence in something which runs counter to my own conviction, it is ethically dubious.

Obviously the question remains open whether these are the *only* areas of ethical decision.

Responsibility in the Military

A word has still to be added concerning responsibility in the military. Within the correlation of command and obedience the first responsibility belongs to those who issue the orders. This question concerning responsibility is falsely put if it is understood merely as a question of obedience and the limits of obedience in an abstract and general sense. The question of responsibility has to be put within a frame of reference which embraces those who command as well as those who obey. Responsibility is thus divided. Whether it is right to obey or to refuse obedience depends on whether the commands themselves are right.

The Responsibility of Commanders

In the military sphere, the necessity for a particular command can be appreciated only to a limited degree from below, i.e., by those who must obey it. For in the first place it is in keeping with the military need for secrecy that the reasons for a certain command are very largely concealed. Furthermore, the justification for a command is also bound up with the irrational and usually obscure factor of the trustworthiness of those in charge.

This means, as we have said, that within the framework of command and obedience responsibility belongs first of all to those who command. It is necessary that they be and represent "authority." But this means — as we have seen in our earlier discussion of the concept of authority [6] — that they themselves must be authorized. They cannot issue orders on the basis of an arbitrary and unpredictable autonomy. They are themselves responsible to a higher court to which those who receive the orders are also obligated. Ultimately, this court can only be identical with the divine commandments. Penultimately, such normative ideas as the nation, freedom, or cultural values, things which are to be defended with all that we have and are, may also represent this transcendent authority. Within the correlation of command and obedience the primary responsibility is accordingly that of the supreme commander. He is the top-ranking officer in the military hierarchy.

If we accept the thesis of Ludwig Beck that, despite all the objections to the idea of the soldier-politician, the supreme commander is to be apprised of all basic decisions reached concerning a war that is either in being or in prospect, then a very high degree of responsibility surely attaches to this head of the hierarchy. If a refusal to obey is ethically indicated, such refusal must begin here. For here there is an overview of the factors which must enter into any such decision.

Thus it was that Beck ascribed the decisive portion of historical responsibility to the topmost military commanders under National Socialism. He charged them with obeying blindly like subordinates, when they had no right to do so and should never have commanded and obeyed contrary to their better judgment: "History will charge these leaders with bloodguiltiness if they do not act according to their professional and political insight and judgment. Their soldierly obedience must end where their insight, judgment, and conscience forbid the carrying out of a command. If their advice and warnings are not heeded, they have the right and the duty, before the nation and before history, to resign their offices." The fact that top-ranking officers can resign where ordinary soldiers cannot increases the measure of their responsibility. Beck continues: "If they act in concert with resolute will, the prosecution of a war is impossible. . . .

[6] See above pp. 178 ff.

It betokens a lack of stature and of understanding of his task if a soldier in high position in such times sees his duties exclusively in terms of the limited sphere of his military task without any awareness of his supreme responsibility to the nation as a whole. Extraordinary times demand extraordinary acts." [7]

The Responsibility of Subordinates

Within the correlation of command and obedience responsibility rests finally, but only finally, with the subordinates who receive the orders. And here responsibility is most difficult to fix in any concrete way. This is partly because, of necessity, very little information is provided to these lower ranks. It is also connected with the fact that the soldier's situation, particularly in time of war, is an exceptional one in which the limits of what is commanded and permitted are not the same as in normal situations. Again, it is linked with the fact that, from below, the trustworthiness of supreme commanders and therewith the justification of a specific war is difficult if not impossible to assess. For included among the modern techniques of waging war is propaganda and concealment of the facts. But the true state of affairs has to be known if there is to be any real judgment as to whether the war is a just war of defense, or a preventive war of aggression and naked imperialism. [8]

Nevertheless, here too there will be situations in which an order clearly requires a breach even of the altered emergency provisions of the Noachic covenant, indeed even of the exceptional rules of war. Cases can arise in which a refusal of obedience is ethically indicated. To be sure, such a case does not always arise in an unmistakeable form which is easy to diagnose, e.g., the mass executions of the Jews, or the torture and other criminal procedures used against prisoners. It often crops up in exceptional circumstances where there is only a hazy line between what is permitted and what is not, between what is necessary and what is avoidable. The pressure of discipline, together with the awareness of the consequences of disobedience, will often enough limit the freedom of vision and the factuality of judgment to such a degree that the case simply does not arise, or is not

[7] In a letter to von Brauchitsch dated July 16, 1938, in Wolfgang Foerster, *Generaloberst Ludwig Beck. Sein Kampf gegen den Krieg* (1953), p. 122.

[8] We dealt more fully with this matter of how concealment of the facts can complicate the problem of decision in *ThE* 1, 413-414.

allowed to arise. Yet this does not rule out but actually implies the fact that such a case is fundamentally possible and must be so acknowledged.

We have said that war is a crystallization of the situation of the world in general. We may also say that it affords certain crystallizations of the problem of ethics. This may be seen in the fact that there is less place here than elsewhere for casuistical directives. For the situational factors which must underlie them simply cannot be discovered in advance, and even in the moment of decision are hardly discernible. Here above all the task of ethics is to analyze the situation in its basic structure in order to create the presuppositions for individual decision, which here more than anywhere else will always be a venture for the one who makes it. Here more than anywhere else the man who ventures a decision will have to look to that forgiveness which does not pass him by because of his mistakes or because of the crystallization of the total guilt of the aeon here involved, but which can sanctify even the military task and duty. This is why there is more to it than merely a technique of ecclesiastical administration, indeed it is a genuinely symbolic act, when the armed forces demand special pastoral care geared particularly to their needs.

23.

Traditional Ethics and
the Atomic Age

As we turn now to a presentation of the theological problem of war, we will simply be carrying forward and rounding out systematically what we have already said on the subject, especially in the last several chapters. It is no accident that we have already had occasion to speak of war rather frequently in other contexts.[1] It repeatedly served as a model in instances where the ethical question as such is particularly acute or complicated. For war represents the situation of "this aeon" in a kind of crystallized form. Hence, even when it is not dealt with specifically, war necessarily forms the background of many exemplifications of the borderline situation, which we have regarded as typical of life in this aeon.

As we proceed to sketch the theological problem of war systematically, we are again confronted by the same question which concerned us when we tackled the problem of resistance, though here we encounter it in an even more intense form: Can we simply follow ethical tradition — Roman Catholic, Evangelical, or any other — or has tradition been radically superseded in this area? In the matter of resisting state authority we noted that tradition is clearly superseded. Ideological tyranny and the totalitarian state constitute forms of authority to which previous theological arguments concerning resistance no longer apply. We could adopt neither the traditional questions nor the traditional answers, but had to seek wholly new approaches.

The Nature of War

The situation is similar in relation to war. For the form of war has changed radically in the modern period. While wars of chivalry in the Middle Ages were still personal in character and fostered the

[1] See, e.g., Chapter 22, also pp. 371-373 and *ThE* 1, 412-414.

development of active virtues, the battles of modern war have become a quite impersonal matter of material and equipment, and the only virtue they foster is that of passive endurance. Even the wars of the eighteenth century were restricted mainly to the combatants; military action was delegated to the armies. But the technology of modern weapons is such that the distinction between the home front and the battle front has virtually been eliminated. War has become an all-out affair which makes women, children, and old people alike both its victims and its agents.

These changes, for which with certain modifications the traditional Christian teaching on war could still allow, are all brought to a qualitatively different stage with the advent of nuclear weapons.[2] The nuclear age confronts us with a change, not merely in the form, but in the very nature of war. If the power of atomic weapons is so great that any defense by nuclear means can conceivably destroy not just the enemy but also that which is presumably being defended — if modern war has become "a weapon far more dangerous than any of the evils from which it is supposed to defend us," [3] — then this is a *reductio ad absurdum* which must have a bearing on how theology assesses war.

In respect of method, this means that the term "war" in the strict sense is no longer serviceable, since it is unable to embrace both pre-nuclear and nuclear war. Tradition, however, uses the term as is, without qualification. This means that in face of the change in the very nature of modern warfare we for our part are no longer able to adopt without qualification the traditional statements about war.

Now obviously this does not mean that tradition is completely antiquated in this area. On the contrary, all that tradition has said — with reference to war as a case in point — concerning the nature of man, human history subsequent to the fall, and the criteria of ethical decision in the kingdom on the left hand, is still significant. The only question is whether these statements can be applied to war itself. Since we cannot live without tradition, and since this question

[2] We use the term atomic weapons or nuclear weapons as a convenient abbreviation for the whole range of modern A.B.C. weapons — atomic, biological, and chemical — together with their numerous delivery systems, both conventional and those involving rockets and missiles.

[3] George Hogarth Carnaby Macgregor, *The New Testament Basis of Pacifism* (New York: Fellowship of Reconciliation, 1936), p. 7.

accordingly cannot be summarily laid to rest but must be seriously considered in detail, we need to make perfectly clear one thing which previous ethics have hardly been able to clarify: What is needed here is not just a modification of the traditional ethics of war, its adaptation to new situations, but a complicated hermeneutical endeavor which will enable us to take over tradition, not so much in terms of its specific statements on war as in terms of the anthropological and cosmological presuppositions which underlie those statements.

Nor can we simply abandon the term war. We need it first of all on heuristic grounds in order, by way of comparison, to gain an impression of the uniqueness of atomic war and of how it transcends the ordinary meaning of the word. Yet the fact should be underscored that this is only a provisional usage of the term, for the dawning of the atomic age marks a qualitative break in the history of the concept of war.

Our first concern is to arrive at a formal definition of war which will embrace both wars of aggression and wars of defense. We find such a definition in the classic work of Carl von Clausewitz, On War. According to von Clausewitz, war is "an act of violence intended to compel our opponent to fulfill our will." [4] The end, formally, is the disarming of the enemy, since this alone can subject him to my will. The means to this end is physical force, "for there is no formal force without the conception of States and Law." [5]

Now there are limitations in a formal definition of this kind, for war does not merely involve a correlation of means and end but is itself embraced within a higher schema of means and end. War must be seen, not as an isolated act, but within the framework of historical processes. [6] This higher schema is politics, which uses war as an extreme means to attain its ends.

---

[4] Carl von Clausewitz, On War, trans. J. J. Graham (London: Kegan Paul, Trench, Trübner, 1911), I, 2. We have some misgivings about citing von Clausewitz because of what was done with his work by National Socialism, which twisted it beyond recognition. Nonetheless, we feel constrained to disregard a tabu that has its origin in an abuse and that might deprive us of the opportunity to learn from this soldier-philosopher who writes of war as one who knows it from the inside.

[5] Von Clausewitz, loc. cit.

[6] Ibid., pp. 6-7, 10 ff.

War and the State

If the task of politics ultimately is to help the state preserve itself both internally and externally, and hence to function effectively, if politics thus serves the orders of preservation in this world, then according to the traditional — and Christian — view war is the final means at the disposal of politics when all other means have failed. Thus, according to von Clausewitz, war is "only a continuation of State policy by other means." [7] The decisive point here is that war is regarded as an interim means, an accident, a mere interjection "of other means." War is something which, in the view of von Clausewitz, has its origin in politics, is a continuation of politics in another medium, and finally leads back to politics. [8]

This traditional understanding of war as a "means" in the employ of politics forces us to consider the question whether in this sphere too there might not be such a thing as a revolt of means. The question has arisen in every age. For there is always the temptation not just to use war but to make it an end. This is what happens when we regard war as the father of all things after the manner of Heroditus, or as a vital law of history and thus, in the manner of classical antiquity, as the normal situation in historical life. It happens too when a conqueror views war as the culmination of his mission, or when the theoretician reverses the relation between politics and war, making politics simply the continuation of war by other means.

The most elemental revolt of this particular means seems to have occurred, however, only in the atomic age, for now every potential end may be destroyed by the particular means or instrument, and the mushroom cloud could well be the last warning sign of a world that has come to its end — "last" even in the sense that there may be no one left to behold and heed the warning. But before studying the revolt of war against politics in its modern forms, let us first consider briefly the way in which war and politics, or war and the state, have customarily been related in theological tradition, particularly in the thought of Luther.

There can be no doubt that Luther found the presupposition of war in the givenness of the state, and hence ultimately in the fact of sin,

[7] *Ibid.*, p. xxiii.
[8] *Ibid.*, pp. 11-13.

which it is the divinely given task of the state to restrain.[9] As the state internally uses law to ward off the chaos which always threatens because of the eruption of sin, so externally it uses war to ward off the threat to peace and order posed by foreign enemies. This is also why the office of the sword is "not the least part of the divine mercy," for it serves that other office of mercy which God has entrusted to governmental authority. If God has instituted the state, and in it an order which is entrusted with the sword for its own protection, then this, for Luther, is a justification of war. If we are correct, his argument at this point is twofold.

First — and this argument is not only of greater importance in our special context but has subsequently received the greater attention and development in Protestant theology — Luther sees a kind of logical connection between the existence of the state and the necessity of war. This may be seen at the very outset of his work on *Whether Soldiers, Too, Can Be Saved,* where he refers to his earlier work on *Temporal Authority,* in which he made this connection, and then continues: "For the very fact that the sword has been instituted by God to punish the evil, protect the good, and preserve peace [Rom. 13:1-4; I Pet. 2: 13-14] is powerful and sufficient proof that war and killing along with all the .things that accompany wartime and martial law have been instituted by God. What else is war but the punishment of wrong and evil? Why does anyone go to war, except because he desires peace and obedience?" [10]

War is thus regarded as issuing from political order as such. It is implicit in the very existence of the state. "Consider for yourself. If we concede the one part, that war as such is unjust, then we shall have to concede all other parts and grant that they are unjust. For if the sword is an unjust thing in fighting, it is also unjust when it punishes evildoers or maintains peace." [11] The connection between war and the state is seen here in exactly the same way as Tolstoi was to see it later, except that Tolstoi drew the very opposite conclusions. Rejecting war,

---

[9] We have already discussed the significance of the state in salvation history at *ThE* 1, 361, 374-376, 417-418, so there is no further need to pursue this aspect here.

[10] *LW* 46, 95.

[11] The Luther quotation is cited without source by Emanuel Hirsch, *Deutschlands Schicksal. Staat, Volk und Menschheit im Lichte einer ethischen Geschichtsansicht* (3rd ed.; 1925), pp. 93-94.

he also rejected compulsion by law, and ultimately the state itself.

Second, in addition to this logical connection between the state and war Luther advances an ethical consideration. Just as the state is grounded in the sustaining love of God, and we are thus drawn into loving service of the neighbor by way of the state, so the office of the sword, exercised in this sense, is given its content by love: "Now slaying and robbing do not seem to be works of love. A simple man therefore does not think it is a Christian thing to do. In truth, however, even this is a work of love. For example, a good doctor sometimes finds so serious and terrible a sickness that he must amputate or destroy a hand, foot, ear, eye, to save the body. Looking back at it from the point of view of the organ that he amputates he appears to be a cruel and merciless man; but looking at it from the point of view of the body, which the doctor wants to save, he is a fine and true man and does a good and Christian work, as far as the work itself is concerned. In the same way, when I think of a soldier fulfilling his office by punishing the wicked, killing the wicked, and creating so much misery, it seems an un-Christian work completely contrary to Christian love. But when I think of how it protects the good and keeps and preserves wife and child, house and farm, property, and honor and peace, then I see how precious and godly this work is. . . . For if the sword were not on guard to preserve peace, everything in the world would be ruined because of lack of peace. Therefore, such a war is only a very brief lack of peace that prevents an everlasting and immeasurable lack of peace." [12]

We would simply note here in passing the extraordinary simplification which marked Luther's age. In virtue of it he can conceive of war as an encounter between good and evil. Hence his analogy of the doctor versus the disease-ridden limbs, or law and order versus the criminals. The quotation once again helps us to realize how very difficult it is to integrate the complex problem of modern world wars into the framework of the police actions which Luther had in view. However simplified this conception of war, at least it shows clearly how Luther ascribes to the office of the sword – and to legal order – as controlling impulses love of neighbor and the desire to protect, help, and save. He does the same in his exposition of the command-

[12] *LW* 46, 96.

ment about killing in the Large Catechism, where he describes as "murderers" not only those who actively deprive of life, but also those who stand passively by when they see their neighbors in peril. The work of love demands active assistance, if necessary by force. In this connection Luther appeals to Matthew 25:42-43.[13]

New Problems of the Atomic Age

We pause to recall our initial question. Realizing the change in the very nature of war effected by the advent of nuclear weapons, we have nevertheless decided to attempt a general and formal definition of war, provisionally and for heuristic reasons. The very attempt to come up with such a definition has shown that war cannot be isolated as an independent phenomenon. It is connected with the nature of the state, even if it is not simply "given" along with the existence of the state.

In philosophies of war and of history, this connection is usually taken to mean either that war is an instrument of politics or that politics is an instrument of war. In theological tradition the connection finds reflection in the fact that, with many variations, war is understood as a borderline task in the self-preservation of the state.

Interpretation of the connection has vacillated between the thesis that war can be justified in extreme cases as the emergency measure of a divinely willed order which is under threat, and the thesis that war is "given" naturally and normally along with the state. We believe that the second thesis betrays a decidedly heretical tendency, and we must be on guard against the dangerous conclusion that to have a (the state) is also to have b (war).

If the connection between war and the state is asserted on the basis of weighty philosophical and theological arguments and is apparently accepted by all, and if previous discussion has been essentially limited to the question of how this connection is to be understood, the age of nuclear weapons calls the connection itself in question. This may not be immediately apparent on the philosophical plane. From the standpoint of the philosophy of history one might still argue that states are the agents (or victims) of warlike encounters, though in the atomic age it has obviously to be added that it is in the interests of the self-preservation of states to avoid atomic war altogether,

---

[13] See Martin Luther, The Large Catechism, I, 189-193; BC 390-391.

regardless of its ostensible purpose.[14] Theologically, however, the objection to atomic war takes another form.

The state is an order of divine preservation in the fallen world. In prenuclear epochs war could still be regarded as an emergency instrument of this order. But in the atomic age war has ceased to serve any purpose of preservation and has become an exclusively destructive process. If what is to be defended is itself threatened by the act of defense, then the concept of a just war becomes highly dubious, if not completely invalid. Then the previously assumed connection between the state and war is broken in the sense that, in principle, war is no longer a possibility within but a threat to the order of preservation.

The question thus arises whether war can be a legitimate theme anymore in Christian ethics. To take an extreme example, no one would suggest that killing for the fun of it should be the subject of ethical consideration, because such killing is to be condemned unequivocally and without reservation, whereas tyrannicide is at least ethically debatable. In the statements already made about war in the atomic age, have we not really said all that theological ethics is called upon to say? Will not any further discussion be unrealistic, proceeding on the basis of outmoded questions and a superseded military situation?

There are two main arguments for not summarily dismissing war from ethical discussion in this way. The first is that it is doubtful whether atomic war is to be so unequivocally rejected as killing for the fun of it. Surely there is more to it than mere sadism and masochistic world destruction. There are two questions which the moment they are raised immediately suggest that an unequivocal rejection of atomic war as a theme of ethics involves an illegitimate oversimplification.

The first question is this: Does such rejection necessarily imply a renunciation of atomic self-defense, a renunciation based on the argument that defense will necessarily destroy what is being defended, and hence makes no sense? In this form the question may at first seem to be purely rhetorical, but closer reflection will show how difficult it really is. For would not the unwillingness to defend by means of atomic weapons give unconditional sway to the caprice of any op-

[14] Cf. Karl Jaspers, *The Future of Mankind*, trans. E. B. Ashton (Chicago: University of Chicago Press, 1961).

ponent armed with atomic weapons, and thus make the right of the stronger the fundamental principle of the constitution of the world? Would it not imply capitulation before the means of mass destruction, and before whoever is cynically prepared to use them? For the moment we are simply putting the question. Our answer will come later. But the question itself shows that we have to surmount higher obstacles than are usually set if we are to gain the right either to endorse or to repudiate atomic conflicts.

The second question runs as follows: In what *form* are we to put the ethical question regarding atomic war? Certainly not in the oversimplified and undifferentiated form of whether we can endorse it or must repudiate it. In this form the question can be answered only in the negative. But this negative does not have the advantage of clear resolution. It has the disadvantage of banal imprecision. It reminds us of the question whether we are for or against sin; no one can say that the self-evident reply rules out all further ethical reflection. Many discussions of the atomic problem remind us of this kind of playing with snap questions and answers.

To guard against such short cuts, it is necessary to revise the question. Hence the prior question as to the *form* in which we are even to pose the question of atomic war is the one which has methodological significance. With respect to this prior question there are two possibilities.

The question may be put in such a way as to require the individual state, or the individual citizen within it, to decide. In this case the question runs: Am I, or are we, in view of the radically destructive character of atomic war, bound to oppose it in principle, to renounce in principle all atomic defense, even though we know the other side has atomic weapons and will use them?

Or the question may be posed in such a way as to make the potential opponents in any atomic war decide the question together. In this case the question runs: What can we do toward (controlled) disarmament on both sides?

Even in this second form the question of one's willingness to defend by means of atomic weapons is still an urgent one. For, like all actions in the kingdom on the left hand, treaties and agreements between sovereign states are not usually made under such ethical norms as justice or equity, but under pragmatic norms like interest, balance of power, etc. But this makes it politically necessary for one partner — if it is to be duly regarded by the other — to *make* itself an interest to be reckoned with. It does this by attaining equality, or even superiority. Hence the question returns in a new form: To what degree may one strive for equality on the atomic level?

We thus see that even though atomic war has obviously to be repudiated by reason of its total destructive power, and even though it runs counter to the order of preservation, there are still a host of very difficult ethical problems to be faced. And even if atomic war should arise — a borderline case hitherto unknown in history — and demand a clear and realistic Christian witness in the kingdom on the left hand, i.e., a radical negation of all measures having to do with the preparation and waging of the war, this negation can be legitimate only if it is based on the kind of deliberations we have been undertaking.

The point of our ethical discussion of this question, then, is not to marshal reasons for or against the justification of atomic war. (This would be contrary to the thrust of our entire ethics, as has been repeatedly stressed, and would be a surrender to the kind of casuistry we have so firmly rejected.) On the contrary, our concern is to engage in the deliberations which must necessarily underlie any such decision.

This, then, is the first argument against the thesis that because it is to be repudiated from the very outset, atomic war cannot be a theme of Christian ethics. We believe we have shown that the question is a bit more complicated than this.

The second argument is that even reflections on the older, prenuclear form of war are not irrelevant in theological ethics. For this form is a classic model for showing how Christian insight, which rests on an awareness of creation, the fall, and redemption, has regarded theologically and handled existentially the borderline situation of the fallen world. Only as we utilize this model do we receive the pertinent information about man's involvement in the general situation of conflict.

For even if war in the older sense should come to be abolished because of the overwhelming power of modern weapons (not because man has gotten any better), warlike man, the power which impels to war, would still be there. But if man remains the same while humanity progresses (Goethe), this means that in principle the warlike element cannot be abolished. It is simply transferred into other arenas, into such spheres as civil war, economic and social struggles, or ideological conflicts.[15] This means, however, that the anthropological problems of war remain even though war in the strict sense should come to an end. War thus retains its significance as an ethical paradigm.

For us, this means first of all that we must investigate the phenomenology of war further if, under the guidance of theological perspectives, we are to attain a deeper understanding of the nature of war and of warlike man. We must carry further the inquiry we initiated into the relation between the state and history — this was already a bit of theologically directed phenomenology — and try to get at the anthropological background of war. We shall do this by examining the origins of war, and by seeking them both in the man who has fallen away from the God who created him, and in the world order through which man objectifies himself.[16]

[15] This is why the New Testament, which finds the causes of war in man's nature (Jas. 4:1 ff.; cf. Matt. 15:11), does not expect war to cease in this aeon; war is an essential mark of the aeon until the eschaton (Matt. 24:6; Mark 13:7; Rev. 9:16 ff., etc.).

[16] We have already discussed how man the creature and sinner objectifies himself in the orders of this world in *ThE* 1, 434 ff.

24.

The Origins of War

In the last sentences of the previous chapter we have already shown what we do *not* mean when we speak of the origins of war. We do not mean the many concrete causes which might be advanced in a historical review. Nor do we have in view the many substantive contributory factors — the economic or geopolitical considerations such as the quest for oil fields or the extension of geographical frontiers — which might be adduced for the sake of systematic completeness. For neither of these aspects is of specifically theological concern. Our concern is rather to see these and all other factors in terms of what we have called the anthropological background.

The Problem of Sovereignty in International Affairs

The first cause of war to which we would make reference might hardly seem on first glance to be of theological significance at all. It has been rightly pointed out that when disputes arise between nations the possibilities of settling them by international adjudication (international courts, leagues of nations, and other institutions) are very limited.[1] For, apart from the fact that such international bodies — for reasons yet to be delineated — have only limited executive power to enforce their will, decisive questions of historical destiny cannot be subjected to judicial arbitration. Thus the particular right which a people has historically claimed and confessed may often conflict with international law, which generally sanctions the *status quo* and cannot regard any change as justifiable.

Furthermore, these international bodies usually come into being, not in the name of law or for the preservation of law, but as unions to preserve and promote certain overriding interests. As such, they

---

[1] See Paul Althaus' article, "Krieg und Christentum," in *Die Religion in Geschichte und Gegenwart. Handwörterbuch für Theologie und Religionswissenschaft* (5 vols.; 2nd ed.; Tübingen: Mohr, 1927-1931), III, 310.

certainly serve the goal of peace, but are usually opposed to any alteration of the *status quo* or to the recognition of any new developments or explosive realities in international life. Hence the individual member state, not only because of the way it views its rights but also because of the conflict between its own interests and those of the group, may find itself at odds with the international body, which because it is not a superstate cannot, except in rare cases, bring sanctions to bear upon the member state to compel obedience.

As history shows, the bigger the recalcitrant member is, the harder it is for a league of nations to decide in favor of effective sanctions. Its restraining effect is thus most severely curtailed precisely where the threat to world peace is greatest. Moreover, sanctions usually consist in an economic or diplomatic boycott and thus do not pose any fundamental peril to the state being disciplined. Thus the basic decisions concerning war and peace are made not by an international body, but by the individual states themselves. This is because the modern state is by nature sovereign.

The Nature of Sovereignty

The concept of sovereignty is very broad. It can imply both external and (in the case of absolute rulers of totalitarian states) internal independence. It can mean the exercise of authority either directly or (in the case of "the people" in a democracy) indirectly. Finally, it can refer either to a single, personal, absolute ruler, or to the rights of constitutionally determined institutions.[2]

But these distinctions need not detain us here, since our concern is with the role of state sovereignty, not in domestic politics but only in the international sphere. Hence we may be content with the following generally accepted definition: Sovereignty is that power which belongs exclusively to the state to make its own will legally binding on all, and the impossibility of its being legally restricted against its will by any other power. He who is independent of any other equal or superior power is sovereign.[3]

---

[2] See F. W. Jerusalem, *Der Staat* (1935), pp. 213 ff. The "sovereign" in a constitutional monarchy represents but does not exercise real sovereignty; his actions make manifest but do not determine the will of the state.

[3] Our definition is taken from Oswald von Nell-Bruening and H. Sacher, "Zur christlichen Staatslehre," in *Beiträge zu einem Wörterbuch der Politik* (1948), p. 45.

So long as sovereignty is one of the constitutive qualities of a state, no state can surrender its independence in favor of another sovereignty, e.g., that of an international body, without renouncing its own character as a state. This means concretely that the sovereign state has no judge over it. It is itself the final earthly authority. It makes its own decisions, and, so long as it is sovereign, nobody else decides for it. This fact has been recognized, so far as war is concerned, by both statesmen and military men. Thus Frederick the Great says in the last chapter of his *Antimachiavel:* "No less justified [than defensive wars] are those wars by which a ruler maintains rights which others seek to contest. Kings are subject to no court of law and so their rights . . . [and the validity of the means used to establish them] . . . must be decided by the sword." [4]

We have said that the sovereign state has no judge over it, and yet is responsible for its decisions, i.e., must make decisions on the basis of commitment rather than caprice. This is true, however, only to the extent that the statesman is responsible to God (or the moral law), not in the sense that, as the representative of his state, he is responsible to some worldly authority outside his own state. Thus the war crimes trials at Nuremberg after the Second World War, however questionable in detail, assumed a new and legitimate task. They embodied more than just the illegitimate element of an earthly court, inappropriate in politics because it involves a denial of sovereignty. They also stood up against a denial of the moral law and of humanity hitherto unparalleled in its flagrancy. The statesman's responsibility for himself, i.e., his responsibility to God (or the moral law) and to no earthly court, means that the sovereign state has a power of decision even where its rights and interests conflict with those of the international authority, and that this power of decision takes precedence of the power of decision enjoyed by the larger body.

That it is in principle possible and even desirable for the several states to delegate specific functions of sovereignty to international authorities is not to be contested. To a modest degree this is going on already in the Western world. But the problem of sovereignty is not thereby overcome. In the first place, for the foreseeable future one can envisage only the delegation, not the surrender, of sovereign

---

[4] Ludwig Reiners, *Frederick the Great,* trans. Lawrence P. R. Wilson (London: Wolff, 1960), p. 79.

rights, and even this only in limited spheres (namely, in some military and economic areas). Then too what is involved here is not a true restriction or abolition of sovereign rights in principle but only a transfer of certain functions of sovereignty, which pass — but again only as functions — from the state to an association of states.

Thus the decisive point, which is so important precisely in the question of war, namely, the plurality of different sovereignties, is not met. This delegation of functions can at best produce only a reduction in the number of sovereignties from an unwieldy host to at most just two, one in each hemisphere, and whether such a development is really "best" remains, of course, an open question.

Thus, however we may turn or twist it, implied in the concept of sovereignty is the independent and — in decisive matters — unshackled coexistence of sovereignties. This pluralism is the unceasing source of wars. For where in the absence of any superior sovereignty disputes cannot be settled by law, self-help is the only way out. But self-help in the case of international disputes means force, or war.

Herein is expressed the ambivalence of the state as an institution between the fall and the judgment, an emergency order of the Noachic covenant. On the one hand the state prevents the war of all against all, discharging its function as an order set up against chaos. On the other hand, however, it is itself a potential element of chaos, because its sovereign authority to bind citizens within implies its own freedom from bondage without, and because the individual egoism which is restrained by the state recurs in the so-called sacred egoism of the state itself.

This is only one of the many illustrations of the Christian doctrine of sin. The earthly order cannot do away with sin; it can only render it relatively — very relatively — innocuous. The radical chaos which would be entailed in a war of all against all, the conflict of individual egoisms, is changed into the relative chaos of constantly threatening wars, of cold and hot conflicts between state egoisms.

Hence the assertion that a leading cause of war is to be found in the lack of any supranational judicial authority— a lack which is itself to be attributed to the sovereignty of states — brings us up against the theological mystery of the state. (We thus note that, even if from a completely different angle, we are still dealing with the traditional theme of the state and sin.)

433

The Theological Significance of Sovereignty

We must now ask concerning the theological significance of the concept of sovereignty in this connection. The state, as we have said, is a gift and blessing of God "in the as yet unredeemed world . . . [it] has by divine appointment the task of providing for justice and peace by means of the threat and exercise of force." [5] It can fulfill this task only if it is aware of its limits as well as its authority, and regards them too as obviously willed by God.

Now, so far as we can see, theological writings on the state generally contain only such statements on the limits of state authority as will restrict it internally vis-à-vis its own citizens. [6] Well-known examples of this kind of limitation are statements which attack the totalitarian state, whether in the modern form in which the state takes all spheres of life (education, law, the economy, welfare, etc.) under its direction and control, [7] or in the older form known to Luther in which the state disregards the distinction between the two kingdoms and the difference between Law and gospel, thus presuming itself to be lord over the souls of men, and attempting to be not only state but church as well.

There is another way of formulating the limits of the state, however, which appears never to have been the object of theological consideration. We are brought to it here by way of the concept of sovereignty. If we attempt to exploit our analysis of this concept theologically — and since this is a brand new undertaking it cannot be regarded as anything more than an attempt — the first point to be made is that the term sovereignty implies not merely an inward but also an outward restriction of the state, and that this outward restriction is constitutive of the state in the same sense as sovereignty is integral to its nature.

If the character of sovereignty as an outward limitation has been

[5] See the fifth thesis of the Barmen Declaration of 1934 in Arthur C. Cochrane, *The Church's Confession under Hitler* (Philadelphia: Westminster, 1962), p. 241; and the commentary on the thesis by Ernst Wolf in *Barmen. Kirche zwischen Versuchung und Gnade* (Munich: Kaiser, 1957), pp. 137 ff.

[6] Suggestions of the older ethicists that the state must respect its external limits as well — e.g., must avoid aggressive imperialism — may be ignored here since they refer less to the state as an institution than to the individual imperialistically inclined statesman.

[7] Cf. the whole of the Barmen Declaration in Cochrane, *op. cit.*, pp. 238-242; also Otto Dibelius, *Die Grenzen des Staates* (1949); and our discussion of ideologies above at pp. 23 ff.

largely disregarded, this is probably due to the fact that the heart of the concept has been taken to be the matter of power or authority over citizens. This aspect generally obscures the observation that the concept of sovereignty is indissolubly bound up with a pluralistic co-existence of sovereignties which mutually limit one another. Herein lies the outward limit of sovereignty.

Sovereignty, then, is characterized not merely by power or authority but also by fragmentariness, by the fact that it is not complete. This partial character or "particularity" finds negative expression in the fact that there is no universal authority, no world state; there are only individual states.

Nor is this a mere phenomenological fact established only a posteriori by historical observation. On the contrary, it is the very nature of the state which here comes to expression in an a priori sense. Hence we may legitimately conjecture that this fact of state pluralism has a theological affinity. The conjecture is supported by the observation that theology has always seen a connection between the state and war, and — though this has been given less attention — that this connection derives from the fact that there are these many states or sovereignties.

What, then, is the theological significance of the fact that the state by nature is not a world state but an institutional expression of the divided world?

In the Antichrist tradition the world state is not conceived as a kingdom of peace and fulfillment, an adumbration of the eschatological kingdom of God; it is instead a pseudomessianic imitation of this kingdom, a demonic revolt.[8] If we ask why the world state, thus mythically viewed, bears the marks of rebellion and of Antichrist, we are referred to theological considerations already presented in connection with the doctrine of the orders and the state.

As we have seen, the state is an emergency institution between the fall and the judgment. As such it is ambivalent in the sense that God here fights the chaotic tendency of the fallen world with the weapons of this world, opposing force with force in the sense of Genesis 9:2-6,[9] and giving these weapons institutional form in the state. The state, as we have put it, is an objectification not only of the divine will of preser-

[8] See above pp. 53-62.
[9] See *ThE* 1, 147-148, 570-571.

vation but also of the human desire for autonomy. It is a transformation of man's individual egoism into that collective form which since Machiavelli has been called sacred egoism.

Because a world state would have no immanent limits in other sovereignties and state egoisms, because it would not be subject to the necessity of self-restriction known in state pluralism, it would have a tendency towards unbridled upward expansion. The arrogant tendency of man and his institutions to want everything would take a vertical turn once it was satisfied on the horizontal level. It would become rebellion against God, and thus be led to play the role of Antichrist.

A world state would thus be, as it were, a posthumous repetition of the situation before the building of the tower of Babel. At one in the building of a world state, humanity would direct all its rebellious powers into a vertical upward movement, were it not yet – or in the last days no longer – limited on the horizontal plane (Gen. 11:1-9). God judges and defeats this revolt by confusing the tongues and dividing the rebellious powers. He lets the divided world come into being.

This seems to express the significance of what we said above about sovereignty and the pluralism of sovereignties. In the existence of states which are each sovereign and which thereby limit one another, there is expressed not merely an imparted power and authority but also the judgment of a divided world, confused languages, conflicting interests, and mutually exclusive rights. The world which no longer finds its unity under God is forced into a relative unity by the relative equilibrium which consists in the mutual self-restriction of sovereign powers as they rise and wane through history. The Noachic covenant includes both judgment as punishment and judgment as preservation. It includes both the division which renders innocuous and the division which is a remedy against inordinate and destructive pride. These are but two different sides of the same divine action.[10]

Hence it is not enough to say that wars arise because there is no supranational judicial authority, and because in the historical interplay

---

[10] Gerhard von Rad finds this two-sidedness – the richness of creation and the division because of sin – in the Old Testament's understanding of the multiplicity of the nations; *Old Testament Theology*, trans. D. M. G. Stalker (New York: Harper, 1962), I, 162-163.

of sovereign powers decisions have to be made by individual states on their own responsibility. This is true up to a point. But it refers only to a symptom of the world's condition, a symptom which for its part demands theological interpretation. The condition itself consists in the fact that before God the world has lost its unity, and consequently cannot bring forth a world state, unless it be a rebellious world state such as would necessarily precipitate a repetition of what happened at the Tower of Babel. And because there can be no world state, no ruler of the universe, there are also no universal courts or ruling bodies. This is the world's condition, and in it is to be seen the judgment of Babel.

The Tragic-Naturalistic Interpretation of Conflicting Sovereignties

It is thus nonsensical to interpret wars tragically, to regard them as the result of a world situation in which, for want of a superior forum, there are incessant conflicts of values and interests. Here, as elsewhere, the tragic interpretation of life is impossible for the simple reason that the world structure which constitutes the tragic is itself obviously not a matter of tragedy but of incurred guilt. Thus war too, as the result of this structure, is likewise a matter of guilt and not of fate. It is but another expression of human arrogance to regard war as a kind of natural necessity, in itself neither good nor evil. The laws of conflict in this aeon are to be regarded neither as a virtue nor as an ethically neutral necessity.

Now obviously this tragic-naturalistic interpretation of the world is tempting. Does not the antagonism between states and individuals, and hence also between sovereignties, rest on the "dynamic" character of history, on the incongruence between a people and the territory in which they live, on the tension between intellectual (or biological) superiority and inferiority, in short, on the pressures of history and the law of coercion to which they give rise? Does all this really derive from the original sin of greed and pride? Is it not rather, as Althaus contends, "grounded pre-ethically in the living movement of history itself"? [11] Is not the state really "a part of the struggle for existence,

---

[11] Paul Althaus, *Grundriss der Ethik* (2nd ed.; Gütersloh: Bertelsmann, 1953), p. 150.

a piece of armor . . . which for all its hardness is the precondition of culture?" [12]

To think here in terms of earlier or later, pre-ethical or post-ethical, however, is to pose the question wrongly from the very outset. If we derive the laws of human conflict from the prehuman animal stage of man's development, then death and sex must also be understood in the same way. While war, sex, and death occur in the human world as in the animal world, however, they are experienced not as biological forces which have the character of fate or destiny, but in such a way as to involve responsibility.

Thus warlike action is not just a dynamic process. It is a matter of ethics. The fact that I can maintain my right to live only at the expense of somebody else, is something I experience not just in terms of validation, but as a matter of guilt. Similarly, the biological medium of sex, which man shares with other mammals, is for him the vessel of responsible I-Thou relations. Finally, death is not just a biological withering; it is a judgment, a sign that the one who in the fall aspires to immortality is thrust back behind the barrier of his temporality, a demonstration that "the wages of sin is death." [13]

Thus, even though the natural laws of conflict, whose existence no one denies, operate also in the human sphere, they are changed in their very nature. Within the framework of human existence there is no part of nature which is not humanized, and consequently ethicized.

If we speak, as Althaus does, of "pre-ethical" facts such as "the living movement of history," we should not for a single moment overlook the fact that in so doing we are representing a scientific or prehistorical view, and that the moment man experiences and lives this "living movement of history" it becomes a matter of ethics and is no longer "pre-ethical." If we think otherwise, we have already allowed the partisans of naturalism to slip in behind the walls of Troy, where they will then carry the day.

The Theological Understanding of Associations of States

In relation to our present problem this means that the law of conflict

[12] Friedrich Naumann, "Briefe über Religion," No. 21, in Walter Uhsadel (ed.), *Friedrich Naumann Werke* (5 vols.; Cologne: Westdeutscher Verlag, 1964), I, 615. Friedrich Nietzsche, Oswald Spengler, and the earlier Ernst Jünger are typical representatives of the naturalistic view of the struggle for existence.

[13] Rom. 6:23; cf. Gen. 2:16-17; 3:2-3, 19. This thought is more fully developed in my book *Tod und Leben* (3rd. ed.; Tübingen, 1949).

and coercion in history, though it originates prior to and outside of man, can only be understood, so far as our human involvement in it is concerned, in terms of the judgment of Babel. We must regard the division into sovereign and mutually exclusive centers of power, centers which are outwardly limited but do not stand under any common judicial authority, as a symptom of what we have called the "divided world," the world divided in judgment.

The world state, which is an attempt to overcome the particularism of sovereignty, is thus a utopia which (retrospectively) seeks to undo part of God's history with man and (prospectively) seeks to anticipate part of this history. It seeks to overcome the sin of arrogance with a new kind of arrogance.

That this is wrong in principle is shown by the negative theses of the Reformation doctrine of justification. If we try to overcome sin by good works, i.e., by some human initiative, we end up intensifying it instead of mastering it. We drive out demons by Beelzebul (Matt. 9:34; 12:24, 27), namely, by the self-glory of boasting (Rom. 2:23; I Cor. 4:7; Eph. 2:9) and the false security of self-confidence.[14]

That the judgment which stands behind the divided world cannot be overcome by "good works" in the institutional field, e.g., by setting up international bodies or trying to achieve a world state, is a corollary of these observations. Even international associations in the form of leagues of nations cannot overcome the sovereignty principle of the divided world. They are thus unable to set up those judicial authorities which could bridge the gap between the mutually exclusive sovereignties and thus set aside in principle the pluralism that leads to war. For all such associations, of whatever kind, are simply special arrangements within a world of sovereign states. Each association of sovereign powers is itself a power complex within the world as a whole. Indeed, it may even be fractured itself by divisions of interest. Precisely because they do not transcend party interests, but themselves represent both a superparty and a conglomeration of parties, such associations can never attain the status of a supranational judicial authority but are always merely combatants, along with other individual sovereignties, in the conflict of interests.

When an individual sovereign power believes that its destiny is at

---

[14] *Securitas* and *superbia* were frequently cited by Luther as the chief effects of the curse of works of the law. See *ThE* 1, 25, 95-96, 313, 330, 492, 504-505, 615.

stake, it will always set its own sacred egoism above the decisions of international bodies. And, as history teaches, it will always do so with the same arguments, namely, that these decisions do not have the moral weight which would attach to those of an impartial higher authority, but derive from a counterinterest against which one's own interest must be maintained. And because each sovereign nation calculates from the very first that these international bodies might turn against it, not in legitimate judgment but in pursuit of alien interests and egoisms, it will always see to it when such bodies are set up that their executive power is kept to a minimum. (Recent history too bears this out.)

One might almost say that even as, in the state, individual egoism is transformed into the higher egoism of a political unity — but not thereby destroyed — so the sacred egoism of states is transformed into the higher egoism of an association of states. It is important to point out in connection with this formulation of the matter that we do not thereby intend any general leveling down. The statement cannot mean that the whole world is one vast night in which all cats are gray, that in spite of the various transformations egoism is still egoism, that it is self-deception to think that killing and coercion are wrong in individual life but permitted at the state level and even dignified with a moral sanctity when performed by an association of states.

It goes without saying that distinctions must be made. As a divine institution, state government does in fact change egoism from one form into another. Nor is the change merely formal. For one thing, individual egoism which is totally unrestricted, as in the war of all against all, is radically destructive and chaotic, whereas the collective egoism of states always implies a taming of that chaotic tendency, and can effect an admittedly relative but nonetheless real equilibrium in the world. Then too, state egoism is further distinguished from individual egoism by the fact that it is based on the sacrifice of the individual for the whole, and is thus linked with the ethical surrender of some part of individual egoism. The same is true to an even greater degree at the level where the sacred egoism of the individual state is transformed into the higher egoism of international associations designed to foster peace and promote common interests.

It would thus be false to regard our analysis of the transitions in egoism as an attempt to discredit the idea of a league of states or a union of nations. On the contrary, such a development seems to be desirable. Our only concern is to see to it that the expectations attached to such international bodies are kept within proper and realistic bounds and guarded against fanatical excesses. It would be inadmissible fanaticism to cherish the hope that the guilt which lies behind the division of the world can be overcome by the "good work" of creating such institutions or attempting to set up a world state. This would simply be a kind of righteousness by the Law worked out on the institutional plane and in the universal sphere. The world between the fall and the judgment is not only *empowered* to set up states; it is also *condemned* to do so. And states for their part are not just empowered to exercise sovereignty; they are likewise also condemned to do so. To ignore this situation is theologically most unrealistic. It is just as unrealistic as to think that there can be righteousness by the Law and its works.

If war is thus grounded — as undoubtedly it is — in the fact that sovereignty exists only in pluralistic form, restricted from above and from without and hence deprived of the support of a judicial authority, then war derives ultimately from that guilt which lies behind the division of the world, so that in any case, even at best, it can be regarded only as an alien work of God, an extreme borderline situation within the emergency orders of the Noachic covenant. The attempt to understand war as an ethically neutral symptom of the natural laws of conflict, or to elucidate it idealistically in the name of these laws ("the god of iron"), simply expresses an arrogance which in its rebellious quality is even more unholy than war itself.

We have been trying to show from ultimately theological perspectives why it is that the absence of a judicial authority over the sovereign nations constitutes a major factor in the origins of war. We have also shown that this constitutes not an excuse but an accusation, since it points to the background of guilt. This is an insight, however, which is hardly to be found in what the theologians have been saying on this theme. Paul Althaus in his various utterances on the ethical problem of war, and Emanuel Hirsch too, have impressively described the relevant phenomenology, but they have not evaluated it theologically.

"Significant in the historical claim [the claim which can perhaps be validated only by war] are such irrational factors as the feeling for life, the sense of power, bodeful self-confidence, the genial vision of a leader. In such cases decision . . . can hardly be reached by the judgment of a human court. . . . For the true historical vocation of those struggling for leadership simply cannot be ascertained by third parties seeking 'justice,' not even if they seek with the best will in the world. Even the peoples involved know the call of history only by way of free decision, as they venture to act. . . . We can never create any safeguard [against its misuse]; nor should we try, for in striking at irresponsible caprice and brutality we should at the same time strike also the serious sense of responsibility toward God which, because it involves obedience to God, cannot finally bow to any human judgment." [15]

Is not all this true – and yet at the same time tragically false? Though Althaus surely did not mean this, cannot these "irrational factors" justify literally everything, including every war? Is this really a theological assessment of the phenomenology of war, to speak of the "responsibility toward God" which cannot bow to any human judgment, and to which is also entrusted the duty of preventing a relapse into caprice and brutality?

What protection is afforded here against justifying the "irrational factors" religiously, or against supporting every conceivable sense of mission and every "genial vision of a leader" by appeal to a divine commission? And is not the possibility of this appeal made all the easier by the fact that this God has obviously instituted "pre-ethical" laws of conflict in this world, so that one can allege obedience to the unrefracted form of creation as he wages war in the name of these laws? Does not this mean that one places himself all too easily on God's side, foregoing that trembling which must accompany obedience wherever the alien works of God are involved?

As noted, what Althaus says is correct phenomenologically. No one can take from a sovereign state the responsibility to venture decisions. It has no recourse to a judicial authority. Historically there can be no doubt that in every age the sense of mission, sacred egoism, and all forms of imperialism, have been concerned to establish a moral alibi by appealing to the will of God or the laws of history. There can be no doubt that they will continue to do this.

But can this be the last word on the subject for a theologian? Does

[15] Paul Althaus, *Staatsgedanke und Reich Gottes* (1926), p. 73.

not everything depend rather upon our marshalling every resource of thought to combat and overthrow in the name of the church of Jesus Christ this self-assured and uncontrolled form of appeal, and therewith the logical consequence that others will draw, namely, the religious glorification of war?

Yet how can we do this unless we cease to make that dreadful appeal to the pre-ethical laws of the historical struggle for existence, and describe this whole sphere where the disputes between sovereign powers take place, and where there can be no judge, as the sphere of the world divided by the fall? As one can prevent the transfiguration, idolization, and totalization of the state only by seeing in it, not an order of creation, but merely a very relative and far from ideal emergency order, so the idealizing and idolizing of war can be prevented only by making it plain that war is a phenomenon of the fallen world, and that its major source — sovereign exclusiveness and the absence of any higher judicial authority — is connected with the judgment imposed on the world after the fall.

An injustice has often been done to Althaus by accusing him of a nationalistic theology. His integrity would not allow for such a thing. On the other hand, there is no doubt that in his theology there are elements which do not sufficiently restrain a theological nationalist, or a champion of the transfiguration and idealizing of war, from using its waters to turn his own unholy mills. These fateful elements consist in the fact that Althaus derives the laws of conflict, coercion, and war from the way history was created, so that they may appear intact rather than as refracted through the medium of the fallen world.[16]

The Idolizing of the Laws of Conflict

This leads at once to the second of the sources of war disclosed in the theological understanding of man, namely, the idolizing of the laws of conflict. We have already pointed to the root of this idolizing tendency in several different connections. There is, first, the justification of war by the laws of conflict in history and by the productive effects attributed to it, e.g., in bringing states into being.

In the second place there is the one-sided interpretation of these laws of conflict as laws instituted at creation which can never be chal-

---

[16] See Paul Althaus, *Theologie der Ordnungen* (2nd ed.; Gütersloh: Bertelsmann, 1935), pp. 11, 13, 16-25.

lenged, but which can be misused in "caprice and brutality," so that only their abuse can be called in uestion. The idea here is that a statement about the nature of the world – e.g., its structure as conflict – is first made into a kind of justification, and ethical consideration is then restricted to the question of whether there are deviations from the norm, either in the sense of being too belligerent and engaging in "caprice and brutality," or in the sense of not being belligerent enough and falling into unrealistic pacifism. In terms of our thesis that the laws of conflict are to be seen against the background of fallen creation, and therewith in the half-light between creation and the fall, one might say that on this view the world's necessity is turned into a virtue, and this is to embark upon a dangerous course.

This fateful transmutation of a necessity into a virtue can take place on the philosophical as well as on the theological level, as is well illustrated in Kant, who describes the basic structure of human existence in terms of conflict, namely, man's conflict with himself. In the light of Romans 7:7 ff. one would have to say that the cleavage in man, the antagonism between will and impulse, spirit and flesh, duty and inclination, is due to the loss of man's original unity, and can be overcome only by the total movement of the ego in love.[17] In Kant, however, this cleavage is itself the dignity of man's personal being. Indeed, the degree of human dignity is to be measured by the intensity of this conflict with self. The conflict is positive only because it discloses the ascendancy of human conscience and volition over against the animal's unilateral bondage to instinct.

For Kant, then, cleavage, polarity, and conflict stand under the patronage of human destiny; to put it theologically, they are in keeping with creation. The nature of man, insofar as it relates to this basic structure of his existence, cannot be questioned. The only challenge that can be brought is against the abuse of the structure, an abuse that must involve not a too radical waging of this war (for here there obviously cannot be "caprice or brutality") but a too great laxity, or pacifism, in waging it. Kant protects himself against any challenge to the basic polar structure by saying that the "dispositions" of man which come with it, and in whose possession he finds himself, are not a matter of ethics inasmuch as they are instituted at creation

---

[17] See *ThE* 1, 282, 64-65, 346.

and hence are "good" from the very outset. Here, then, is a fundamental constituent of being; Althaus, as we have seen, would call it a "pre-ethical datum of history."

As Kant turns the necessity of cleavage and the resulting laws of conflict into the virtue of ethical personality, the theological arguments follow a rather similar course. Since we have already touched on these in various contexts, we shall now sum them up systematically and give a few illustrations. The theological presentations, of course, try to guard against idolizing the laws of conflict or making a virtue of them.[18] But they leave themselves open to serious misuse in this direction by beginning with the apparently innocuous statement that when Luther says in explaining the First Article of the Creed, "I believe that God has created me," this means: "The life which I have by way of certain historical preconditions I have really from God."[19]

Althaus adds at this point that by "preconditions" he means especially parents, i.e., the biological sequence of the generations. But our earlier quotations and those yet to be adduced show conclusively that Althaus draws the circle of preconditions much more broadly to embrace also the people, the nation, and the vitality of history with its laws of conflict.[20] To be sure, he distinguishes between creation and sin in respect of the orders,[21] but it is hard to see wherein his distinction lies unless it be that the orders are understood as creation and their misuse as sin.[22]

It is incontestable that for Althaus, "the people" ranks as one of those unequivocal factors of creation through which we receive our life. It is thus to be reckoned among the "secondary causes" of creation, to which the idea of a confusion of tongues and a Babylonian judgment is not applicable.[23] This is clear from the way he is approvingly cited by Gerhard May[24] and Max Hildebert Böhm.[25] "What was once a fight for faith is today the rightly understood fight for the people as a divine creation"; "the totalitarian claim of the state finds its limit at the point

---

[18] This is certainly true of Althaus, though not of Hirsch.
[19] Althaus, *Theologie der Ordnungen,* p. 11.
[20] *Ibid.,* pp. 13 ff., 26 ff.
[21] *Ibid.,* p. 54.
[22] *Ibid.,* pp. 55 ff.
[23] *Ibid.,* pp. 65 ff.
[24] Gerhard May, *Die volksdeutsche Sendung der Kirche* (1934).
[25] Max Hildebert Böhm, *Das eigenständige Volk* (Göttingen: Vandenhoeck & Ruprecht, 1932).

of the people as a divine order." [26] To be sure, Althaus would not agree with the conclusion which the author quoted draws from these statements, namely, that "in disputes with the people of other nations the individual acts not as a private Christian [!] but as an official of his own people. My people and its future is at stake. This requires that there be no forgiveness." [27] But why does Althaus not draw this conclusion? Is he afraid to do so? [28] Thus it is that the historical particularities, the exclusive sovereignties, and the races, peoples, and nations marked by sacred egoism, are all in principle numbered among the "preconditions" of human existence and thereby protected with the sanctity of creation.

Typical of the second step in the theological argument is what Georg Wünsch says about hostile relations. While drawing the conclusion which Althaus omits, he holds that these foe relationships are given along with the historical particularities, and hence are among the created preconditions of human existence. Indeed, he goes so far as to maintain that the command to love our enemies (Matt. 5:44) is not directed against the structure of this aeon, which includes hostile relations. On the contrary, God has created the foe relationships of this world in order to provide the possibilities and presuppositions for displaying love for our enemies. For such love "could not be demanded if the hostile relation did not exist as a part of creation." [29] Hence war too is one of the spheres of creation, since it creates the most obvious presuppositions for the possibility of loving one's enemies, and since in addition – to go on in the spirit of Hirsch – it has productive or creative functions, e.g., in bringing states into being.

The third and most extreme step in this theological argument finds illustration in the so-called Ansbach Ratschlag of 1934, which is a classic example because it contains all the mistakes which could possibly be committed within the framework of a theology of an intact and unrefracted creation. It too begins, not literally but in substance, with the idea of preconditions of human existence in which we have to see the will of God as creator: "The Law, namely, the unalterable

---

[26] *Obrigkeit und Führertum* (1936), p. 42.
[27] *Ibid.*, p. 39.
[28] Cf. the dialectically forced discussion in Emanuel Hirsch, *Schöpfung und Sünde in der natürlich geschichtlichen Wirklichkeit des einzelnen Menschen* (1931).
[29] Georg Wünsch, *Evangelische Ethik des Politischen* (Tübingen, 1936), p. 63.

will of God . . . encounters us in the total reality of our life . . . it binds each to the estate in which he is called by God, and obligates us to the natural orders to which we are subject, such as family, nation, and race (blood)" These are "the means by which God creates and sustains our earthly life."

Thus far the thesis championed is that which we have ourselves been probing, namely, that the orders enumerated have about them the quality of creation. But there is no safeguard whatever, not even the remotest suggestion that these orders are also qualified by the fallen world. The argument runs wholly along the lines of natural theology. First the structure with its web of orders is delineated, and then on the basis of this conclusions are drawn concerning the will of God the creator which presumably comes to expression in these preconditions of our existence.

The consistency with which this thought is then pursued makes the Ansbach Ratschlag a model for this particular theological approach, and ensures that it will not be forgotten. For it is next stated that this kind of general analysis of the structure of history is not enough. God has not simply established the orders as such. He has also laid down their positive form. The preconditions of our existence must therefore be interpreted more specifically. We are not just set into "the nation" as such (e.g., as a kind of general Platonic idea). We are actually "incorporated into a specific people at a specific moment." Hence our duty to our nation is always determined concretely by the present state of affairs in that nation."

If this is the "authentic voice of Lutheranism," as the document claims, then it is only logical that the voice go on, and must go on, to speak as follows: "In this knowledge we as believing Christians thank the Lord God that in its hour of need he has given our people the *Führer* as a 'good and faithful sovereign,' and that in the National Socialist state He is endeavoring to provide us with disciplined and honorable 'good government.'"

Here then, after the manner of natural theology, the historical situation in which I find myself is described as a precondition of my existence, and hence an expression of God's creation. This leads to the same result as that which we developed from the starting point of this whole line of thought. As the laws of conflict, if they are orders of creation, justify war, so no theological objection can be brought against any particular war initiated presumably in defense of these orders by any particular government (e.g., that mentioned in the Ansbach Ratschlag). Such a war will be, if not a war of the cross, at least a war of creation, i.e., a war which preserves the benefits of creation by the instruments of creation – *quod erat demonstrandum.*

The Tempting Combination of Egoism and Altruism

We now press on to another factor in the origins of war within the framework of anthropology. War continually disguises its guilty character. It gives the appearance of consisting in something more than merely destructive acts committed for purposes of self-preservation. In all its forms, even those which are imperialistic and brutally egoistic, it appears also to foster the virtues of sacrifice and love of neighbor. War can thus present itself as the sum of many ethical positives and negatives which is itself neither a clear plus nor minus.

Man cannot bear the blessings of peace – any more than he can stand many other blessings – without some risk: he runs the risk of growing soft and lazy. This is why war sometimes seems like an elemental and fascinating remedy which will keep him from degenerating and cause him to grow beyond what he presently is. It is thus a mistake to ascribe war too directly to an excess of egoism, intoxication with power, and the lust for blood. Not the least part of its fascination consists in an appeal to the greatness of man.

Antoine de Saint-Exupéry is certainly right when in referring to man's "irrational susceptibility to war" he says, "The familiar explanations of [war in terms of man's] savage instincts, greed, bloodlust also seem inadequate keys to the dilemma. They overlook what may be truly essential. They ignore the asceticism that surrounds war. They ignore the sacrifice of life, the discipline, the brotherhood in the face of danger. They fail to take into account everything we find remarkable in men – in all men – who go to war and who, in so doing, tacitly accept privation and death." [30]

We can take very seriously this appeal of war to the greatness of man, to that which "we find remarkable in men who go to war." It would be self-deception to deny the respect which belongs to those

[30] Antoine de Saint-Exupéry, "Needed: A Language for Speaking the Truth," in *A Sense of Life,* trans. Adrienne Foulke (New York: Funk & Wagnalls, 1965), p. 134.

who have borne the burden of battle. Nevertheless, this appeal can be tragically misunderstood if it is thought that peace — with its sacrifice of the elemental and its attendant risk of softening — deprives man of the destiny which is his by creation, in other words, that peace is perverse and that man has to regenerate himself, become what he was originally intended to be, by undergoing a baptism of steel and fire in war, as laid down by creation.

Here too we can detect a tendency towards illegitimate mythologizing. As we are inclined to interpret power mythologically, regarding it as the agent of evil whereas in truth it is man himself who implements his own evil by way of the loftier instruments of power, so we have an inclination to mythologize peace, to make it the cause of softness and of alienation from the elemental whereas here again it is man himself who cannot bear the blessing of peace and hence turns it into a curse.

If war, besides being a terrible power of destruction and an antithesis to creation, also contains forces of regeneration, it does so, not as an institution of creation, but at best as a visitation to bring men to their senses. Hence it can be understood only as a judgment which is necessary because people are not mature enough for the blessings of peace but have become lazy, sated, and crazed with materialism.

Even in relation to wars which are felt to be just wars of defense, Christians have usually not forgotten this aspect of merited judgment; they have prayed for the aversion of well-deserved punishments. Judgment is both crisis and salvation. There can be restorations or regenerations as judgments are borne and their justice acknowledged. If we understand man's "growth" through war in these terms, if we regard the readiness for sacrifice and asceticism, not as the purpose of war intended by creation, but as a confirmation in the midst of judgment and a response in the midst of divine testing, we are saved from sanctioning and fostering war in the name of ethics. He who regards war as a phenomenon of creation by which man is to be brought to his destiny will necessarily want war and may even pray for it, so far as this concept of God allows. But one cannot pray for judgments, only that we may ourselves be turned so that they are no longer needed. And in judgments which have already fallen upon us, one can only pray for endurance, for their end, and for true conversion ($\mu\epsilon\tau\acute{a}\nu o\iota\alpha$). Hence it is a fatal error to think that, because we prize the virtues of altruism, asceticism, and bravery, we must regard war as a positive vital force which is productive to them.

The Psychological Fascination of War

This brings us to a fourth factor in the origins of war, which we may speak of as its psychological fascination. This is something that goes much further than what we have called the appeal to the greatness of man, which is related to the magic of "monumental history." [31] It is connected with a romantic attitude toward primitive tradition and with a longing for such contact with the elemental as no longer obtains in our comfortable middle class existence.

The fascination of war is thus rooted in a longing for "that collective action which provides an escape for the lost individual," [32] a longing for the adventure which disrupts the mechanical routine of normal living, for the intensification of life which comes with the frontier situation and the proximity of death, for an ultimate searing test in which the limits of our physical and moral powers are made manifest, for an acid whose action will distill the genuine from the false, the meaningful from the empty.

All these values, both the genuine and the more dubious romantic ones, can perpetrate the same deception as the appeal to greatness. They can put a halo around the abyss. They can make the unredeemed kingdom of action look like a worthwhile kingdom of logos and ethos. They can give real fascination to that which in fact is a powerful judgment.

The Concealment of Brutal Motives

All these factors in the origins of war have involved a mistaken idealizing of war. At this point we need only refer briefly to those factors which are obviously negative in character. They center on the naked drive for power in the political, and not least in the economic, sense.[33]

To be sure, these causes of war may sometimes not be as obvious

[31] Friedrich Nietzsche, *Thoughts out of Season, Part II: The Use and Abuse of History,* sec. 2, trans. Adrian Collins ("The Complete Works of Friedrich Nietzsche," ed. Oscar Levy [New York: Russell & Russell, 1964], V), 16-23.

[32] John C. Bennett, *Social Salvation: A Religious Approach to the Problems of Social Change* (New York: Scribner's, 1948), p. 17.

[33] *Ibid.,* pp. 14 ff.

as one might suppose, though for a reason different from that previously discussed. In the case of the earlier factors there was genuine self-deception in that the ethical by-products of war, the appeal to greatness, etc., were taken to be its essence and war was thus idealized. In the case of the brutal motives of power, however, deception is used as a strategic pyschological device. Since those who wage war have to mobilize the total war potential of the nation, they will try by all possible means to arouse enthusiasm and fanaticism. This cannot be done, however, unless ethical scruples are overcome and replaced by a conviction that the cause is good. Civilians as well as soldiers have to be stirred by the illusion that they are engaged in an ethically legitimate war of defense.

The need to awaken such illusions has brought into being in our time a new strategic weapon called the moral offensive, which abroad aims to destroy the offensive power of the enemy by overthrowing illusions as to the justice and prospects of his cause, and at home has the goal of evoking the corresponding positive illusions in one's own people. The chief means for waging this offensive is propaganda. Often the task of propaganda is to obscure the real, the cynical causes of war, so that people caught up in the war — men called into service, e.g., — will not have access to the information which is essential to any responsible ethical and Christian decision in the matter.

The ethical quality of this concealment may be defined in terms of the concept of ideology. As we have seen, ideology is characterized by the fact that appeals and statements concerning the actual war situation are not made on the basis of authoritative norms such as responsibility to God, or to what is right, or to historical truth, but are purely pragmatic in nature, and aim at producing certain psychological effects.[34]

[34] See above pp. 37, 40, and *ThE* 1, 413-414.

25.

The Relative Justification of War

The Problem in Tradition

The Bible

The Bible does not take an explicit position on the right and wrong of war and military service[1] except insofar as one may say that the Noachic covenant is a sign of the fallen world, and war bears this sign.

The Old Testament is full of wars and rumors of wars. Nevertheless, "there is in the Old Testament no general or fundamental statement on the religious understanding of the phenomenon of war."[2] War is accepted without question as something frequently initiated by God himself. As "holy war" it is justified,[3] and only rarely is war anything but that.[4] Yahweh raises up charismatic personalities (Judg. 4:14-16; 5:11-12) who wage defensive wars. Sometimes Yahweh does the fighting himself (Deut. 1:30; Josh. 10:14; 23:10); sometimes he gives the victory to those commissioned by him (Josh. 2:24; Judg. 3:28; I Sam. 23:4; I Kings 20:28). For those who thus fight in the name of God equipment, numbers, and strength are no longer decisive (I Sam. 14:6; 17:40-51; Exod. 30:12; II Sam. 24:1 ff.); God works miracles (cf. Exod. 15; Josh. 6).

But God can wage a holy war not only with and for Israel but also against Israel in execution of judgment, and with the help of foreign nations (Amos 2:14-16). This is true at least in the later periods.

---

[1] See Niels Hanson Søe, *Kristelig Etik* (2nd ed.; Copenhagen: Gads, 1946), pp. 403 ff.

[2] *Theologisches Wörterbuch zum Neuen Testament*, ed. Gerhard Friedrich (Stuttgart: Kohlhammer, 1933–), VI, 509.

[3] Gerhard von Rad, *Der Heilige Krieg im alten Israel* (Zurich: Zwingli, 1951).

[4] E.g., I Sam. 21:5-6; Judg. 17-18. Von Rad (*op. cit.*, pp. 24, 29) speaks of the "primitive pan-sacralism" whereby all of life was seen to be holy, the term being derived from Martin Buber, *Moses* (Oxford: East & West, 1946), p. 120.

At the end, namely, in the Messianic kingdom, the prophets expect a period of peace when swords will be turned into ploughshares and the earth will be filled with righteousness and peace (Isa. 2:2-4; 9:1 ff.; 11:1 ff.; 65:17 ff.; Jer. 23:5-6; Joel 3:15; 4:10; Zech. 9:9-10). But in the present, this aeon is still the time of war, and there can even be a "Book of the Wars of Yahweh" (Num. 21:14).

There is in the Old Testament nothing which can help to fix a theological position with respect to war as such, for the question of war as such does not arise there as it does for us. The wars of the Old Testament people are not war as such. They constitute a special category, that of the holy war. The existence of this special category is related to the special nature of the situation in Israel. Israel is not just a nation politically; it is also a chosen people, it is the church. This privileged position in salvation history whereby Israel is both nation and church, executing as such the will of Yahweh and acting as his earthly arm, precludes the possibility of any analogy between Israel and other nations with their historical functions. This is the one instance of a legitimate theocracy, for Israel is not a state in the ordinary sense.

For this reason, the Old Testament accounts cannot serve as a model for war as such. If we try to use them thus, we shall end up with a fateful crusades doctrine — which would demonstrate indirectly that the situation in Israel is without analogy.

War as such is not a theme in the New Testament either. As compared with the accounts and interpretations of war in the Old Testament, war is hardly mentioned in the New Testament. Unlike many other Old Testament themes, this theme is not taken up again or pursued in the New, except perhaps for mere hints, such as the destruction of Jerusalem (Luke 19:43-44; 21:6; 13:34-35) which is regarded as a kind of holy war, a judgment. The terms war and soldier occur only incidentally, by way of illustration or in a purely neutral recognition of the fact that they exist.[5]

When there are dialogues with military men, e.g., in Jesus' meeting with the Roman officer, it is striking that the soldiers are never advised to give up their job (Matt. 8:5-10). To the soldiers who ask for counsel, John the Baptist is content simply to give advice which can

[5] See, e.g., Luke 11:21-22; 14:31-32; Matt. 12:25; 22:1 ff.; Luke 14:31; 22:35; etc.

be implemented *within* the context of military life, namely, that they rob no one by violence and that they be content with their wages (Luke 3:14).[6]

None of the other passages which deal with the use of force, love of enemies, and patient endurance ("Do not resist evil") has anything to do with the theme of war. They all relate to the disciple's dealings with his neighbors, and in an eschatologically radicalized sense.[7]

Again, when Jesus commands his disciples not to use force, this is not even an indirect contribution to the understanding of war. For the command is not given in a political situation – which is constitutive for the problem of war – but in the context of the question whether they should use force to protect Jesus from pursuing his path of suffering. If there is any analogy here, it is to be found in the situation of the church, for it is the church which is forbidden to use force or revolution to protect itself against injustices.[8]

In the New Testament, war is simply presupposed as a phenomenon of this age: "This must take place" (Mark 13:7). Indeed, the situation will get even worse at the end, when the nature of this aeon becomes more intensively crystallized (Matt. 24:6 ff.).

The epistles have no more guidance to offer than the Gospels. Paul uses military pictures for our spiritual warfare (II Cor. 6:7; 10:3 ff.; Eph. 6:11 ff.; I Thess. 5:8), but these are mere illustrations. They no more relate to the problem of war than do some of the eschatological figures of speech in which the returning Christ is depicted as victor over the hosts of Antichrist (Rev. 19:11 ff.). The dealings of Jesus and John the Baptist with military men find their parallels, by the way, among the apostles. Neither Paul nor Peter demands that soldiers change occupation in connection with their conversion (Acts 10 and 13).

---

[6] Hans von Campenhausen points out, however, that "the text is not speaking of Christian soldiers," and that "Luke (who alone records the incident) may well have had an apologetic interest: to allay governmental suspicion of the infant movement." "Der Kriegsdienst der Christen in der Kirche des Altertums," in *Tradition und Leben. Kräfte der Kirchengeschichte* (Tübingen: Mohr, 1960), p. 206, n. 9.

[7] Matt. 5:9, 39, 44. On the interpretation of these passages see our discussion of the Sermon on the Mount in *ThE* 1, 332-382.

[8] Matt. 26:52; John 18:11. The sayings in Luke 22:36-38 are much debated, and it is highly unlikely that they can be applied to the matter of defense by force, especially in war; hence we leave them out of account.

The Old Testament line is followed up only in Hebrews where the holy war is adduced merely as a figure of faith, which the believer struggles to maintain against all temptations and assaults (Heb. 11:32 ff.).

The New Testament diverges from the Old Testament line in not glorifying war; it exalts peace (Rom. 12:18 ff.; I Tim. 2:2; I Pet. 2:20 ff.). But obviously again this does not bear on the problem of war, since peace is more and other than simply the antithesis to war.

The Church Fathers

Concerning the approach of the early church to the problem of war, and how it viewed military service by its members, we know comparatively little.[9] Tertullian condemns military service most sharply on the ground that "there is no agreement between the divine and the human sacrament, the standard of Christ and the standard of the devil, the camp of light and the camp of darkness. One soul cannot be due to two *masters* — God and Caesar."[10] Origen takes the same view when he claims that we have become "children of peace" through Jesus Christ, and that He alone has now become "our leader" instead of early territorial rulers. Christians will certainly fight for the emperor — not with weapons, however, but as an "army of piety" and of prayer.[11] It is to be noted, however, that even Tertullian does not so much attack war itself as the idolatrous customs and sins of sorcery which go hand in hand with military service.[12]

Nor should it be overlooked — von Campenhausen has rightly drawn attention to this — that the historical situation of the early church was such that it could hardly define a fundamental position with respect to the problem of war. There were at least three reasons for this.

[9] See von Campenhausen, *op. cit.*; Adolf von Harnack, *Militia Christi. Die christliche Religion und der Soldatenstand in den ersten drei Jahrhunderten* (1905); Roland H. Bainton, "The Early Church and War," *Harvard Theological Review*, XXXIX (1946), 189-212; H. Karpp, "Die Stellung der Alten Kirche zu Kriegsdienst und Krieg," *Evangelische Theologie* (1957), pp. 496 ff.

[10] Tertullian *On Idolatry* xix; S. Thelwall (trans.), *The Ante-Nicene Fathers*, ed. Alexander Roberts and James Donaldson (8 vols.; Buffalo: Christian Literature Publishing Co., 1885-1886), III, 73 (hereinafter cited as *ANF*). "Sacrament" in the original Latin means, among other things, a military oath.

[11] Origen *Against Celsus* v. 33 and vii. 73; *ANF*, IV, 558 and 668.

[12] This is particularly evident in Tertullian's *The Chaplet (de corona militis)* xi; *ANF*, III, 99-100.

First, the early church did not reflect on what should or should not take place in the world outside the believing community. The fathers had no doubt that wars had to occur, but they simply wanted nothing at all to do with military service.[13]

Again, war was a problem initially only in respect of the individual, the question being whether soldiers converted to Christianity should stay on in the army. Different answers were given. Tertullian thought not.[14] Clement of Alexandria, however, thought that they should; he quoted Paul's directive that Christians should remain in the calling wherein they were called, but he demanded that they pay heed to the voice of their commander, Christ, who calls his people to peace.[15]

Finally, there is the question — which is not identical with the question concerning war itself — as to how early Christianity understands military life in general. For the pastoral question of whether an individual Christian is to render military service to the emperor cannot finally be separated from this fundamental question concerning the military as such.

It was the pagan philosopher Celsus who compelled the Christians to face up to this question. He argued that from the political standpoint Christians are parasites because they will not render service and due honor to rulers who safeguard the empire and peace. At the critical point they will not bear the burdens which in principle all citizens should bear.[16] If all Romans were Christians, chaos would inevitably triumph, since no one would be prepared to establish law and order by force.

In answer to this sharp and basic question of Celsus, Origen admits that Christians should indeed be obedient and should bear the burdens laid upon them. With reference to the general obligation of military service, however — which is not just a Christian obligation — he makes the restriction that wars must also be just.[17] But if they are, Origen still thinks it impossible that Christians should themselves render military service, even at the emperor's express command, since

[13] Von Campenhausen, *op. cit.*, pp. 203-204.

[14] Tertullian *The Chaplet* xi; *ANF*, III, 100.

[15] Von Campenhausen (*op. cit.*, pp. 207-208) refers in this connection to Clement of Alexandria *The Instructor* i. 12.

[16] Von Campenhausen, *op. cit.*, p. 208.

[17] Origen *Against Celsus* iv. 82; *ANF*, IV, 535.

Christians have a different task and are called to a different kind of warfare.[18]

Faced by the difficulty of conceding the basic legitimacy of war on the one hand while rejecting Christian participation on the other, Origen seeks a way out by demanding that Christians, like the priests of the Old Testament, be accorded a privileged position in respect of military service. Von Campenhausen rightly points out, however, that the indispensable presupposition of such a postulate is that Christians in fact constitute a small numerical minority which does not amount to much as a historical factor and hence can afford to abstain from public life.

This presupposition, however, does not meet the incisive question of Celsus, which has reference to a state made up exclusively of Christians. Origen can think of no other answer to the question in this extreme form than that which Celsus — sarcastically — describes as the only possible logic of the Christian position, namely, that if all Romans were to become Christians they would conquer their enemies by prayer and supplication; indeed, they would have no enemies to conquer, since the power of God would protect them.[19]

It will be seen that the question had not yet been put with the final sharpness which would lead later to solutions in terms of natural law, or — in the case of Luther — to the doctrine of the two kingdoms. In the first stage of the church's encounter with the world and the responsibilities it brings, the radical question raised by Celsus produces a utopian construction whose vulnerability is obvious.

This line was pursued by many later fathers who tried to meet the challenge of Celsus with an even more radical utopia. They assumed the Christianization of *all* nations, and believed that this would solve the political dilemma of a *single* state consisting exclusively of Christians, since if all states were Christian, and all their subjects refused military service, peace would automatically ensue and the problem of Celsus would be solved.

In the age of Constantine when the tension between church and state relaxed, and to an even greater extent later when the Germanic tribes were incorporated into the church, opposition to war was increasingly silenced. Indeed, war could even be regarded as holy

---

[18] Von Campenhausen, *op. cit.*, pp. 209-210.
[19] Origen *Against Celsus* viii. 70; *ANF*, IV, 666.

war on behalf of the emperor as the representative of Christ (Harnack). Thus Augustine, who had dealings with statesmen, regarded military service as the divinely pleasing use of a divine gift:[20] "Do not think that it is impossible for anyone to please God while engaged in active military service. Among such persons was the holy David, to whom God gave so great a testimony; among them also were many righteous men of that time." [21] Augustine refers explicitly to the pagan centurion at Capernaum (Matt. 8:8-9), Cornelius (Acts 10:4), and the soldiers who came to John the Baptist (Matt. 11:11; Luke 3:14), pointing out that the only objections raised in these instances are to abuses, not to military service as such.[22]

Though Augustine holds that war is fundamentally legitimate and defends soldiering as a service which may be pleasing to God, he specifically guards against the perversion of this thesis into a glorification of war. Peace is not sought in order that war may come; on the contrary, war serves the one purpose of making peace possible. Hence peace is always the goal that we must seek. War is never the true goal of the will but only a "necessity" with which the will finds itself unwillingly associated.[23]

Roman Catholic Moral Theology

The position of Augustine is essentially that which Thomas Aquinas adopts, refines, and defends. The theses of Thomas shape to the present day the teaching of Roman Catholic moral theology,[24] which accepts the fundamental legitimacy of war, using arguments from natural law, tradition, and Scripture in support. It regards peace as "the ideal norm, the goal of war," [25] and seeks to fix the limits of legi-

[20] Augustine, Letter No. 189, To Boniface (4); Letter No. 138, To Marcellinus (12); *Reply to Faustus the Manichaean* xxii. 74-75.
[21] Augustine, Letter No. 189, To Boniface (4); trans. J. G. Cunningham in *NPF*, I, 553.
[22] *Ibid.;* cf. Harald Fuchs, *Augustinus und der antike Friedensgedanke* (Berlin: Weidmann, 1926) and Johannes Stelzenberger, *Lehrbuch der Moraltheologie* (1953), p. 341.
[23] Augustine, Letter No. 189, To Boniface (6); *NPF*, I, 554.
[24] Thomas Aquinas, *Summa Theologica*, part 2^{II}, ques. 40, art. 1; cf. Werner Schöllgen, *Ohne mich! . . . Ohne uns? Recht und Grenzen des Pazifismus* (Graz, 1951), esp. pp. 89 ff., and the thorough survey in Eberhard Welty (ed.), *A Handbook of Christian Social Ethics*, trans. Gregor Kirstein and John Fitzsimons (New York: Herder and Herder, 1963), II, 377 ff.
[25] Stelzenberger, *op. cit.,* p. 339; cf. Victor von Cathrein, *Moralphilosophie* (Leipzig, 1924), II, 768 ff.

timacy, the criteria being just cause and right intention.

Just cause is present when under vital threat a state exhausts all peaceful and diplomatic means of avoiding war. Hence just cause means the same as last resort. It is not merely a formal legal criterion resting on formal loyalty to a treaty, for it is conceivable that such treaties may be unjust, imposed by force, or outdated, in which case a just cause could not be linked with them. Pius XII probably had this in mind when in his Christmas message of 1941 he said: "History teaches that treaties of peace stipulated in a spirit and with conditions opposed both to the dictates of morality and to genuine political wisdom have had but a wretched and shortlived existence, and so have revealed and testified to an error of calculation. Human, indeed, but fatal nonetheless." [26] Just cause is thus a moral rather than a legal criterion; it raises the specific question whether in the given conditions everything possible has been done to maintain peace.

Right intention has basically in view a purpose similar to that assigned to the sword in Romans 13, and again by the Reformers: the suppression of disorder and evil, and the ensuring of peaceful conditions in which that which is good and righteous may flourish. This leads Roman Catholic moral theology to a vigorous and emphatic repudiation of wars of aggression and conquest.

One might perhaps reduce the Roman Catholic position to the simple formula that the criterion for the legitimacy of war lies in the question whether there is an armed threat to peace, and whether it can be deterred by any means other than force of arms.

It seems that, as of this writing, official statements have not yet tackled the question whether nuclear weapons have in principle created a new situation, so that the existing criteria for defensive war stand in need of revision. There has been lively theological discussion,[27] but papal utterances have thus far remained within the

---

[26] Pope Pius XII, Christmas Message of 1941; Vincent A. Yzermans (ed.), *The Major Addresses of Pope Pius XII* (St. Paul: North Central, 1961), II, 44.

[27] G. Stratenwerth, "Kann der bisherige Krieg seine bisherige politische Funktion noch ausüben," *Evangelische Theologie*, 1957, 5, p. 200; A. Hartmann, *Die sittliche Ordnung der Völkergemeinschaft* (Augsburg, 1950). Among Roman Catholics who hold that modern A.B.C. weapons can never be used under any circumstances are Pierre Lorson, *Wehrpflicht und christliches Gewissen* (1952); E. van Loen, "Kriegstheologie und Massenmord," *Neue Politik*, XIII (April 20, 1957); F. H. Drinkwater, "Zur Moral des Atomkrieges," *Dokumente* (June, 1955).

framework of tradition.[28] But the effect of the new situation may be seen in the fact that in view of the much depicted horror of new weapons [29] the emphasis has shifted from the legitimacy of war to warnings against war and to recommendations that it be averted.[30]

Some hint of future thinking may perhaps be discerned in the Christmas message of 1944, where the Pope says that he has "long upheld the principle that the idea of war as an apt and proportionate means of solving international conflicts is now out of date." [31] He makes a similar statement in 1954: "Should the use of this method [A.B.C. warfare] entail such an extension of the existing evil as would render man wholly incapable of controlling it, its use should be rejected as immoral. In such an instance it would no longer be a question of 'defense' against injustice, and of the necessary 'safeguarding' of legitimate possessions, but of the pure and simple annihilation of all human life within the radius of action. Under no circumstances is this to be permitted." [32]

Evangelical Theology

In order to fix the position of Evangelical theology, we shall now proceed to lay down some of the basic theses of Luther on the question of war. In so doing we shall be further elaborating on some of the things already mentioned in our chapters on resistance to state authority.

For Luther the problem of war arises within the doctrine of the two kingdoms. And this doctrine is to be understood only in terms

[28] See, e.g., the October 19, 1953, address of Pope Pius XII to participants in the Sixteenth Congress of the International Office of Documentation for Military Medicine, in which he says concerning the question whether defense against an A.B.C. war may ever be a necessity that "the answer can be deduced from the same general principles which are decisive to-day for the permitting of war in general." Yzermans, *op. cit.*, I, 262.

[29] See, e.g., the encyclical epistle *Mirabile Illud* of Pope Pius XII dated December 6, 1950; authorized English text in *The Catholic Mind*, XLIX, No. 1058 (February, 1951), 135.

[30] See, e.g., the 1946 Christmas message of Pope Pius XII in Yzermans, *op. cit.*, II, 100-108.

[31] Pope Pius XII, Christmas Message of 1944, in Yzermans, *op. cit.*, II, 86.

[32] Address of Pope Pius XII to participants in the Eighth Congress of the World Medical Association, September 30, 1954. See the text in *The Pope Speaks*, I, No. 4 (Fourth Quarter, 1954), 349; also in *The Catholic Mind*, LIII, No. 1108 (April, 1955), 244.

of the consideration that the love which we are charged to display undergoes profound modification of form according to the dimension of life in which it is to be practiced.[33] Thus in education love is combined with punishment. In politics love has to be armed. If the world is unjust, if there is thieving aggression in it, I exercise love for my neighbor by protecting him. If I let him fall among thieves, I am a murderer. Indeed, by laissez faire at this point I encourage the rabble, and plunge the world into the very chaos which God intended to hold at bay by the state's restraint of evil.[34] The dimension of life, then, in which it is to be practiced is highly important for the particular form love will take.

In politics there is thus a kind of warping of the shape of love. Love no longer consists in a direct and unbroken doing and desiring of good. It takes on a kind of dark reverse side[35] to the degree that I can practice it only if at the same time I involve myself in actual conflict, in some cases even violent conflict, with the forces which threaten my neighbor. As concerns himself, the Christian may be obliged to suffer. But he cannot let his neighbor and his people suffer; he has to resist those who inflict the suffering. "According to your own person you are a Christian; but in relation to your servant you are a different person, and you are obliged to protect him."[36]

To be sure, Luther can also speak of the right of an individual Christian to defend himself where necessary. The individual can assume vicariously the functions of government, and as a power of order oppose the chaos which lurks in robbery. In such cases it must be clear that what is in view is the Christian as citizen, as political man, and not as the bearer of spiritual office. If he is attacked as a representative of the church, then in that capacity he must accept suffering. The boundary between the two kingdoms thus cuts right through the individual Christian.

When asked whether he would exercise the right of self-defense

---

[33] See *ThE* 1, 412 ff.

[34] Cf. Luther's explanation of the commandment not to kill in The Large Catechism, I, 189-192; *BC*, 390-391.

[35] As we have repeatedly pointed out, Luther takes note of this dark side but does not relate it to fallen creation, which is why difficulties crop up in his doctrine of the orders, allowing orthodox Lutheranism and neo-Lutheranism to construct a massive doctrine of the orders of creation in his name, an extreme example being the Ansbach Ratschlag.

[36] *LW* 21, 109; cf. *LW* 45, 96.

if attacked by robbers, Luther answered in the Table Talk: "Yes, of course. I should then act the prince and wield the sword, since there would be no one else around who could protect me; I should strike out for all I was worth, and then go to Communion feeling I had done a good work. But if I were attacked as a preacher and on account of the gospel, with folded hands I should say: 'Well, my Lord Christ, here I am; it is you whom I have preached; if it is now time, I commit myself into thy hands,' and then I would die." [37]

If one carries this interpretation of love over into the impersonal sphere of the orders, even the waging of war can take on the aspect of love. For it has to be remembered that it is by the loving decree of God that the sword has been entrusted to the authorities; God wishes to protect the righteous and peaceful and to avert unjust violence.[38] He who discharges this office fulfills this decree of God and does a work of love in protecting his own. It is thus "a work of Christian love to protect and defend a whole community with the sword and not to let the people be abused." [39]

In this world of strife the right has to be defended; when necessary, love must prove itself by using the sword. Against a raving opponent committed to all sorts of violence it would be grotesque to remain passive or to restrict oneself to innocuous exhortation and diplomatic initiatives. Such a foe will understand the determination and resolve of love only if love is resolved and determined to protect and defend by force what is entrusted to it.[40]

Because of this understanding of love and how it is altered in the kingdom on the left hand, war for Luther can in principle never be called seriously in question. In principle it belongs among those governmental tasks performed by the judge, the policeman, and the executioner. War is a legitimate expression of the government's duty to protect its citizens. Military service too is governmental protection discharged by soldiers. As such it has a twofold significance. First, it is oriented to the preservation of the suprapersonal order which finds supreme representation in the divinely willed institution of the

---

[37] WA, TR 2, No. 1815; cf. WA, TR 1, No. 1023; WA, TR 2, No. 2666.
[38] LW 46, 95 ff.; WA 14, 232, lines 16 ff.
[39] LW 30, 76.
[40] Hence the sarcasm in Luther's voice when he speaks of diplomatic negotiations with the Turks. LW 32, 149.

state.[41] Second, it acquires the directly personal and human character of an exercise of love, since it involves sacrificial intervention on behalf of the neighbor.

On this level Luther cannot conceive of war being fundamentally called in question. He can conceive only of a restriction of war and the right to wage it. We have dealt with this elsewhere, and will simply sum up the limitation in two theses. First, there can be no right to wage war if the motivation consists, not in discharge of the protective office of secular government, but in egoism, e.g., the desire for honor, renown, or aggrandizement. Second, there can be no right to wage war if the war is for allegedly spiritual ends, if it takes on the character of a crusade, whether it be a case of Christianity defending itself (as Christianity!) — and thus being prepared to protect itself but not to suffer — or of Christianity seeking to crush the Turks by force rather than with the word and prayer.

The Right of Defense

Peaceful Order Through Power and the Dangers Involved in Breaking the Peace

One thought of Luther's will always be of significance in the theological discussion of war. Luther held that the dimension of life in which love is to be practiced makes all the difference in the world. In the kingdom on the left hand there is only the broken form of love, the love which has been altered by the orders and has become, as it were, indirect. The fact that executioners and soldiers can exercise love only at a distance and by force, shows that the world after the fall no longer rests in the peace of God but has disintegrated.

This is why within the sphere of the orders peace has to be defended by non-peaceful means as well as peaceful. Love can involve a moving apart from others as well as a drawing close to them. The order is to be protected not merely by the means of order but also by means of relative disorder, namely, by force.

---

[41] See Luther's *Temporal Authority: To What Extent it Should Be Obeyed* (*LW* 45, 81-129); *Whether Soldiers, Too, Can Be Saved* (*LW* 46, 93-137); and particularly *On War Against The Turk* (*LW* 46, 161-205). Luther's observation that the work of the authorities, including war, is a matter of resistance to the devil as the agent of chaos and disruption reminds us that action in the kingdom on the left hand is not controlled by an immanent autonomy, as Troeltsch and — along other lines — Deutelmoser supposed (see *ThE* 1, 362, 370), but has a spiritual affinity.

All of this serves to remind us that we are not living in the sphere of unbroken orders of creation, but under the burden of the emergency orders of the Noachic covenant in which the structure of the fallen world is objectified, though as we have seen, this latter thought is not prominent in Luther. Johannes Heckel has tried to show that the kingdom on the left hand *(regnum mundi)* is for Luther a "realm of Satan" which is always in opposition to the world of Christ.[42] In view of the evidence Heckel has assembled, it cannot be denied that in some of his statements Luther occasionally suggests this. If Heckel's thesis is correct one could even say that there is massive support in Luther for the idea that the kingdom on the left hand is a phenomenon of the fallen world, and consequently that the orders of this kingdom are emergency orders.

In view of our own doctrine of the orders, we would be most happy to find this thought in Luther, and to find that it is given a prominent place. Nevertheless, we are not convinced that this interpretation of Luther is correct. For one thing, these references are relatively infrequent compared to the mass of quotations bearing the other way. Furthermore, the main connection between sin and the orders for Luther seems to be that man misuses the orders,[43] not that the fall has helped to determine their very structure. The orders are connected with sin only to the degree that they are given because of sin and are directed against it, not to the degree that they too are qualified in part by the fallen world.[44]

We believe that Althaus has the better of the argument with Heckel when he contends that Luther's intention is to deduce the orders in their positive content from the original state of innocence, and to explain their intrinsic resistance to sin and chaos as a subsequent function in the fallen world.[45] What we have had to criticize in

[42] See Johannes Heckel, *Lex charitatis. Eine Juristische Untersuchung über das Recht in der Theologie Martin Luthers* (Munich: Bayrische Akademie der Wissenschaften, 1953), and especially *idem, Im Irrgarten der Zwei-Reiche-Lehre* (Munich, 1957), pp. 6 ff.

[43] Heckel, *Irrgarten,* pp. 30-31.

[44] Cf. also Franz Lau, *"Aeusserliche Ordnung" und "Weltlich Ding" in Luthers Theologie* (Göttingen: Vandenhoeck & Ruprecht, 1933), pp. 83 ff.

[45] See Paul Althaus, "Die beiden Regimente bei Luther. Bemerkungen zu Johannes Heckels 'Lex charitatis,'" *Theologische Literaturzeitung,* LXXXI, No. 3 (March, 1956), 129-136; *idem,* "Luthers Lehre von den beiden Reichen im Feuer der Kritik," *Luther-Jahrbuch,* XXIV (1957), 40-68.

Althaus is his attempt at systematic development of this doubtful aspect of Luther's doctrine of the orders.

To go back to what we were saying, the fallen world knows peace only under the threat of violence. The peace of this world is an anxious peace. This is why the political safeguarding of peace involves by its very nature the search for a balance of political, economic, and military forces which will set over against the smoldering lust for aggression and expansion the threat that the indulgence of such lust will carry with it a grave risk; it will not go unpunished. For in this world we cannot count on it that a general allegiance to law or even specific treaty pledges will be a sufficient barrier to the libido of power and to national and ideological egoisms. It has also to be added that in the very concept of sovereignty, as we have seen, there is a certain reservation concerning international law and a certain subscription to the thesis of individual standards of right.

The fallen world, which is controlled by these tendencies towards mistrust, no longer has any values or norms which can carry the weight or authority both to be in order and also to create order on their own; it has only values and norms which are in principle disputed, and thus must potentially be defended. Hence the espousal of values and norms carries with it the determination to defend them.

This leads, first, to the ethos of the state in general, since the state is called to reward good and resist evil, in the sense of Romans 13, by means of the power appropriate to it. And it leads, second, to the need for the state to assert outwardly the power entrusted to it. For the state is not instituted merely as a barrier against the chaos of individual egoisms. As we have seen, it is also the champion of a collective egoism. Because of the pluralism of sovereignties, it thus sets in motion certain elements of chaos at a higher level, elements however whose sharpness is somewhat blunted by a relative equilibrium.

Thus we see that the structure of the state in the present aeon is such that the dynamic balance of powers makes strife, or breach of the peace, dangerous. That is to say, peace is an object of interest, and its breach an object of dread. The peace of this aeon is an armed peace.

One may certainly ask whether this power compromise deserves the name of peace. Is it not rather a mere truce or cease-fire? There can certainly be no doubt that the peace which this aeon gives (John 14:27) is qualitatively different from the peace of Eden and the peace of the kingdom of God (Luke 2:14). Idealistic pacifism not only ascribes to this aeon the power to produce real peace; it also fails to differentiate between these two kinds of peace.

When we said that the peace of this aeon is an object of interest, and its breach an object of dread, we were again alluding to the point of the Noachic covenant, which is that God uses the instrumentalities of the fallen world in order to preserve this world; he takes up a position, as it were, on the ground of the facts created by man. But these "facts" include man's use of egoistic force — which is why man is held under restraint by legitimate and authorized force (Gen. 9:2, 6). They also include man's living not simply for what is right but for what serves his own best interests — which is why man is always found to have interests, in this case an interest in peace. And finally they include man's living presumptuously — which is why man is "cooled off" and held in check by means of dread.

The Radical Question of What May Actually Be Defended

These statements, however, do not solve the theological problem of war. Indeed, it is only now that we really come to grips with that problem. For thus far our concern has been with the question of armed peace and the prevention of war. Armed peace has of course a prophylactic value. It involves an appeal to man's stake and interest in peace. It is a potential defense.

But when it comes to actual defense, to the specific grounds of war, that is a very different question. Potential defense has to do with the totality of values and goods. It has to do not with the physical security of one's neighbors against aggression by force, but with an undisturbed economic and social development, in short with the free world's "way of life." Its object is a vast complex of life and possessions whose dimensions can hardly be assessed. The question of actual defense, however, is the question of sacrificing one's blood and property and possibly even risking the life of the nation, the hemisphere, or indeed the whole of civilization. The moment this question arises, therefore, a new problem is posed as to which elements in this vast complex are to be regarded as so important that they must actually be defended. Even on the assumption — which is a *sine qua non* — that one has the

466

power to defend them successfully, not every contested value or good will justify the effort and sacrifice of an active military defense.

Hence questions like the following arise. Can the disruption of commercial relations or business monopolies, i.e., can economic considerations justify defense by force? If so, what degree of disruption? Can the oppression of kindred minorities in other states, or — irrespective of how they are treated — can the incorporation of such minorities into one's own state, be a possible cause of war?

All these questions and others like them have in fact been raised at one time or another in concrete situations. And irrespective of how they have been answered, or how justifiable the answers may have been, they all have one feature in common, namely, that within the complex of goods to be defended distinctions as to relative importance have had to be made. Not all things, but only some things, are worth defending to the last.

Along with the question of "what" is to be defended, there is also the question of "when" it is to be defended. Has defense to wait for attack, or may there be a preventive defense against imminent attack? In the atomic age, when only a few minutes may decide between survival and obliteration, this question is posed differently from what it was in earlier epochs of the Christian ethical tradition, and an a priori answer can hardly be given.[46]

Finally, there is the question as to "how" the defense is to be made. If war is accepted as a borderline situation, this obviously involves acceptance of whatever means are appropriate to this formal end of "compulsory submission of the enemy to our will." [47] Hence an ethical recommendation to wage war with mercy would be out of place, since such a procedure would either fail to accomplish the purpose intended or prolong the operation and thus be the very opposite of merciful.

Once the basic decision concerning war is made, ethical questions are relevant only to the degree that there is need to guard against allowing violence to get out of hand and go beyond its specifically military purposes. For the use of force which is appropriate to war carries with it the danger of obliterating the boundary between mili-

---

[46] See *ThE* 1, 413-414 and Walter Künneth, *Politik zwischen Dämon und Gott. Eine christliche Ethik des Politischen* (Berlin: Lutherisches Verlagshaus, 1954), pp. 333-334.

[47] Carl von Clausewitz, *On War*, trans. J. J. Graham (London: Kegan Paul, Trench, Trübner, 1940), I, 2.

tary force and that which goes much further. Thus terror, robbery, capricious acts, and crimes tend to flourish more in time of war than in normal times. It is to this supplementary violence that the Baptist is probably alluding when he tells the soldiers to "rob no one by violence, and be content with your wages" (Luke 3:14). Among such acts one may include also the ruthlessness of the war machine itself, which in modern forms of total war engulfs the civilian population in its strategy of destruction to a measure far beyond what is unavoidable (terror bombing, etc.). Finally, included among these ethically required limits of war is respect for the status of prisoners and defenseless enemies (e.g., the wounded). The nature of force can easily lead to a denial of the distinction between combatants and noncombatants, or combatants and those who are no longer combatants. The limits are defined in the various international conventions on war.

These problems, of course, are on the margin of theological ethics, whose proper task is to provide a basic interpretation of the phenomenon of war itself. Certainly the task of ethics cannot be, after acknowledging the necessity of war in this aeon, to disapprove the instrumentalities for waging it and to offer suggestions for ameliorating the violence or even restricting the need to kill. This could only lead to naive, unrealistic, and pseudo-Christian sentimentality which would not be taken seriously by any statesman or military leader. For, contrary to Schleiermacher,[48] killing is not accidental but integral to war; it is of the very essence, the means by which war is waged.

From these necessary but secondary remarks on the relation between the what, the when, and the how of defense, we return to the cardinal ethical question which results from the basic decision concerning the right and wrong of war as such: What values and goods are worth actively defending? In other words, what kind of threat to what or to whom can be a cause of war?

It is obvious that not all the individual elements in the complex of goods to be defended can justify the unleashing of cataclysmic destruction by war, even though the attack on them may indeed lead to a perceptible loss in prestige. In attempting to decide whether a certain balance can be attained between the thing to be defended and the military force to be expended, the following consideration

---

[48] See Friedrich Schleiermacher, *Die christliche Sitte* (2nd ed.; Berlin: Reimer, 1884), p. 281.

seems to us to be of great importance. The clear prospect of certain victory because of one's own overwhelming military superiority distorts one's view of the ethical problem involved in determining whether the cause of war is just and adequate. For where no real risk obtains one might be tempted to go to war for the sake of secondary goods, e.g., to gain economic advantages, or to correct an undesirable political situation in a neighboring state, or to round off one's territory by a kind of geophysical clearing of the ground around it. In such cases the sacrifices demanded seem relatively small when measured against the assured gains. The instinct of self-preservation and readiness for personal sacrifice are only minimally involved inasmuch as a war which is sure to be a speedy success is not very likely to engulf me and mine in its operations. In such a case it is easy to commit the ethical misdeed of sacrificing people for the sake of lesser values, of using persons as merely means to an end. This has indeed happened so often that the history of war is overrun with a bloodguiltiness that cannot be excused by appealing to any aeonic necessity of war.

The true criterion for the rightness of war can be arrived at only where it is a question of life and death — which it is not in the case of such safe little wars — only where the very life of the nation and even international life itself is at stake. This is the criterion which has to be applied in respect of little wars as well. It is established by simply raising the question: Would I really be ready to wage this relatively harmless war if it could in fact lead to the complete extinction of my nation and of civilization itself?

When is there this readiness to perish utterly for the sake of something which is to be defended? Obviously it arises only when there is an elemental and radical threat, not only to my nation but also to our existence as a people, to our whole culture based as it is on freedom as a prized possession, indeed to the very possibility of meaningful human existence. For in goods such as these lie the "pounds" which are entrusted to us (Luke 19:11 ff.), which are not our own and which we therefore cannot surrender as we please, as we might surrender the fruits of our own achievements, e.g., in the economic sphere (though it must be granted that the boundaries are fluid in this respect).

It is true that these elemental values may all be misused or changed. But such as they are they constitute the presupposition of all human historical existence — which is why we cannot allow them to be threatened. Thus my nation or people may become an idol, but as the composite of those who by blood and history have been made my neighbors it represents an entrusted pound. To surrender it is to transgress against the one who entrusted it to me. (We have noted already that such a pound is not simply identical with a created good or an order of creation.) Freedom too may be misused by being regarded as a power in its own right. It may be debased to the point where it is nothing more than the freedom to achieve a certain material standard of living. Men can forget that freedom rests on authorization and that it may be truly experienced only in responsibility to the one who authorizes it. For all that, however, it is the precondition for achieving meaningful human life, for even where it is most debased and empty it still carries with it the opportunity of making decisions, i.e., of laying hold or failing to lay hold of human existence. Thus it always remains the antithesis to the wilfull degeneration of man into an insect or a purely collective being. This is why it is an entrusted pound which is not mine to surrender as I will.

These various values are not just interests which I am necessarily concerned to protect but which I may also subordinate to other values. On the contrary, in them I have to do with God himself. I have to do with God not merely in the sense that he demands *my* pound back but also in the sense that I must render an account to him of the way in which I have helped my neighbors and my people to protect these pounds, and of the sacrifices which I was ready to make to this end.[49]

In these deliberations it has become clear that we have posed the question of what is to be defended, and of the defensive war, in a very radical sense. We have pushed it to its extreme limit by asking whether a thing is to be defended if the very act of defense calls the thing itself in question, i.e., if by defending it we can destroy it completely, so that the saying of Pidder Lüng, "better dead than a slave," takes on a meaning quite different from that intended by Liliencron.[50]

[49] Cf. Karl Barth, *Church Dogmatics*, ed. G. W. Bromiley and T. F. Torrance (Edinburgh: T. & T. Clark, 1936 –), III⁴, 462.
[50] The perspective here is genuinely new, for we are thinking of total ideological enslavement, whereas the poet had in view only the relatively harmless state of slavery with which Pidder Lüng was threatened. See "Pidder Lüng" in Detlev von Liliencron, *Ausgewählte Werke*, ed. Hans Stern (Hamburg: Holsten, 1964), pp. 216-218.

It seems to be worth pointing out that this question first arose apart from the problem of atomic weapons. It has been given an enhanced relevance by these weapons, but it arose earlier. It has been radical-ized by the threat of ideological imperialism and its totalitarian tyr-anny. It is thus the special question of our age in respect of the prob-lem of war. It is much more radical than it was in the age of national wars. It would be an anachronism for ethics to go on considering merely the right and wrong of such wars.

Now certainly theological ethics can give no definitive direction con-cerning this radical question. It cannot answer with a universally binding Yes or No. In this extreme borderline situation, if anywhere, ethical reflection can only lay bare the ultimate issue to be decided and press men to face up to it. Ethics is in no position to make the de-cision itself, for this requires the making of certain prior judgments of facts which go beyond the competence of radical ethical evaluation. There are several such questions of fact to be resolved before a de-cision can be taken, even in the case where ideological tyranny lays hands upon the entrusted pound of nationhood or freedom: What are the chances of the tyrannical system changing from within? What pos-sibilities are there for infiltrating and undermining it by way of mis-sionary and other constructive activity? Is it possible to preserve at least relative forms of freedom, and therewith the entrusted pounds?

We thus stand before a complicated host of questions involving de-cisions of principle and judgments of facts, not all of which have the same claim to universality or can be answered with the same finality. This complexity is characteristic of the structure of the ethical situa-tion in general. Whoever decides purely in terms of principle becomes a doctrinaire utopian, blind to reality. And whoever decides purely in terms of factual judgments becomes an opportunistic tactician, de-void of conviction.

When we take both aspects into account we come to see that every decision we make in this aeon has the character of a compromise. The emergency Noachic orders of this aeon are themselves the best example of this compromise. For they speak of what God's command-ments require, not per se but in the situation as it actually is, i.e., under the pressure of the structure of this world.

At the same time, we have here confirmation of our thesis that we must see an ethical problem in terms of its fundamental structure if we are to avoid slipping into the spirit of compromise. There can be no side glances in the direction of whether a particular solution is indeed practicable and can actually be implemented. The question of principle must be strictly differentiated from that of factual judgment as to what the situation is and what the chances are. Only thus is it possible to keep normative principles clearly in mind without losing sight of them through compromise with the factualities of the situation.

26.

War in the Atomic Age

The Question of an Atomic Peace

The New Quality of War

We would return now to the point we made at the beginning of our discussion of war.[1] We said that atomic weapons[2] have brought about a qualitative change in the character of war. Following up a thought which occurs in Hegel and Marx, we may say that the enhanced effectiveness of modern weapons has involved such a change in quantity as to amount to a change in quality, a change in the nature of war.

The difference is so radical, we said, that in the strict sense one can no longer speak of "war" as such, since the general term "war" cannot embrace the use of military force in both the prenuclear and the nuclear age. The decisive difference between the two ages becomes clear once we realize that a future war between atomic powers of even approximately equal strength will involve not only destruction of the enemy but also self-destruction, not just killing but suicide.

Antoine de Saint-Exupéry says of the weapons technology of World War II: "War today is a kind of surgery; like insects, we locate the adversary's ganglia and administer the paralyzing sting." [3] In respect of nuclear weapons one might say that the insect dies of its own sting like the bee which inflicts a mortal wound on itself when it loses its sting. As early as 1932 in *Das Gebot und die Ordnungen* Emil Brunner could say of modern war that "all analogies drawn from the past break down," [4] that "war has begun to outlive its purpose," [5] that

[1] See Chapter 23.
[2] See above p. 420, n. 2.
[3] Antoine de Saint-Exupéry, "We Must Give Meaning to Men's Lives," in *A Sense of Life*, trans. Adrienne Foulke (New York: Funk & Wagnalls, 1965), p. 149.
[4] Emil Brunner, *The Divine Imperative*, trans. Olive Wyon (Philadelphia: Westminster, 1947), p. 471.
[5] *Ibid.*, p. 472.

it is now "suicidal," [6] and that "the meaning which it once had is lost." [7]

There are obviously only two possible conclusions to be drawn from this insight: first, that there must be no nuclear war, and second, that the old question of Christian ethics as to whether a just war is permissible is now outdated and cannot be asked with reference to an atomic war. For the concept of a just war, i.e., a war of defense, is meaningful only so long as defense is possible. This means that there has to be some chance of survival, and some reasonable relation between the destruction to be inflicted and the good to be defended. But if in the case of atomic powers of approximately equal strength both attack and defense come increasingly to be identical with self-annihilation, then these distinctions fall to the ground, and the whole concept of a just war becomes absurd.

In any case, the traditional concepts are no longer adequate to describe the problems of our day. It is difficult to see how a particular good or value can be worth defending if its defense involves not only the risk but the probability of total destruction. The war of independence, which could once arouse such emotion, has in our time become an empty phrase.

Now it would appear to be obvious that if atomic war is absurd then there ought not to be any atomic weapons either. If a goal is acknowledged to be impossible, then logically the means to attain it must also be regarded as impossible. If atomic war is to be abolished, then that which makes it possible should also be abolished. Or should it?

The step from these premises to this conclusion involves a peculiar difficulty. Both those who have and those who do not have atomic weapons all agree in the diagnosis that atomic war is absurd. But one group shrinks from the apparently logical conclusion that it should therefore destroy its atomic weapons. Why this logical self-contradiction? Why this negating of the goal while accepting, or at least appearing to accept, the means to attain it?

The Mistrust Which Leads to Retaining Atomic Weapons While Rejecting Atomic War

Perhaps one of the statements we have just made will help us at

[6] *Ibid.*, p. 697.
[7] *Ibid.*; cf. also Brunner's *Justice and the Social Order*, trans. Mary Hottinger (New York: Harper, 1945), pp. 231-232.

this point. We said that "if atomic war is to be abolished, then that which makes it possible should also be abolished." The very formulation raises the question whether atomic weapons are the only presupposition of atomic war, the only thing that makes it possible.

We have to answer this question in the negative. For apart from the weapons there is another presupposition that makes war possible, namely, the man who possesses and might be resolved to use them. If one cannot trust the possessor of atomic weapons, then the formula ought rather to run: "If atomic war is to be abolished, then that which makes it possible, namely, the questionable and dubious possessor of these weapons, should also be abolished." For *he*, after all, is the one who is capable of anything. He is the real basis of the possibility of atomic war. And for this reason he is the one who may well force me to try to keep pace in any armaments race.

Now "abolishing" him need not mean destroying him. It can mean simply doing away with the qualities which make him an object of mistrust. It is a question of changing him in order to remove the presuppositions which make atomic war possible. He must be made worthy of confidence. But how is this to be done?

One might object that this is a completely unrealistic question. If the presupposition of atomic war is man himself, then such war is unavoidable because man cannot be changed. It is impossible to transform someone who is an object of mistrust into a trustworthy partner. Our life is lived against the background of the post-Babel world.

But a different answer might also be given. For obviously, when there is mistrust, we have to remember that it is mutual. Each believes the other is a potential aggressor, capable of anything. And when he behaves accordingly, there is a progressive enhancement of the reciprocal mistrust.

But if this is so, there seems to be only one way out of the deadly circle. At some point, a point under my own control, I must demonstrate my own trust and confidence. The point in question is the point where I find that I am one of the two parties concerned. If the other came to trust that I really pose no threat to him, he might be softened by the resultant relaxation of tension. He might become a rival with whom I could speak, who would win my confidence too, and hence be changed.

It is true at other points in life too that I must change myself if another person's relation to me – and therewith he himself – is to be changed. Individuals and nations are bound together in the bundle of life. They are by nature in relation. There can be no change unless it involves both parties, and no desire for change except as I change myself, the one portion of the relationship which is under my control.

Can this insight be transferred to such suprapersonal powers as states and nations? The impossibility of assuming that the same laws obtain both in the personal I-Thou relation and also on the suprapersonal level of the orders brings us to the heart of the problem with which the doctrine of the two kingdoms is concerned. In the present case the impossibility seems to be as follows. The crisis of confidence between atomic powers can be overcome only if one of them takes the initiative of disarming unilaterally in order to break the vicious circle. In the personal sphere we are undoubtedly required to make the venture of offering such prior proofs of confidence and thereby giving the other person a chance to change. For in the personal sphere my confidence does not rest merely on his proven trustworthiness. My venture of confidence has constructive power. It makes the other person trustworthy.

The venture is possible and obligatory in the personal sphere because I can undertake it on my own responsibility, at my own expense, and on my own risk. In the suprapersonal sphere of the orders, however, the situation is different. Here I involve whole peoples and cultures in the venture. Again, I cannot bring to light the disposition behind the venture, as in the personal sphere. Indeed, where such complex entities as nations and states are involved such unequivocal disposition cannot even exist.[8]

However we twist and turn, there seem to be insuperable difficulties in the way of all such efforts to alter the world of mistrust in the post-Babel situation. This world can be overcome only symbolically and momentarily, namely, when the miracle of the gospel and its love is enacted in human encounters, i.e., with respect to one's neighbor.

The situation is all the more complex in the case of two opponents who do not have anything even remotely resembling a common philosophical platform. In the conflict of East and West the opposing

[8] Carl Friedrich von Weizsäcker admits that the great powers cannot and are not likely to engage in unilateral disarmament. At best only a small nation would be in a position to do that. *Die Welt*, No. 100 (1957).

powers have completely different norms. Each understands itself quite differently from the way its opponent conceives of it. Consequently neither knows what to expect of the other. The result is that they are involved in a fundamental mutual mistrust. Because of this confusion of tongues, norms, and concepts, there is reason to fear that the other will construe any proofs of confidence — such as our own unilateral disarmament — in a sense very different from that intended, perhaps as a tactical move on our part, as an indication of our confidence in the continuing superiority of our undisclosed stocks of hidden weapons, or as an admission of defeat in the arms race, or as a symptom of confused idealism.

These considerations at any rate strongly suggest that the peace of the world is very different from the peace of the kingdom of God. It is an anxious peace of servile fear. Indeed, this is why power is essential in the kingdom on the left hand. This is why the state and justice must be armed in order to restrain and to defend.

Hence the fact that all desire the abolition of atomic war, but not the abolition of the presuppositions on which it rests, is not grounded — despite all appearances to the contrary — in a logical self-contradiction on the part of those concerned. This would be so only if these presuppositions consisted in atomic weapons alone. But they also consist in men, in the very structure of the fallen world which cannot be done away.

If it is thus clear — more intuitively than consciously — that one cannot alter the one decisive factor among these presuppositions, then the abolishing of all of them together is an almost hopeless undertaking. There are thus theological grounds for the disarmament dilemma, namely, man in his situation before God, and therewith also the world in its situation before God.

In relation to the atomic question this situation before God works itself out as follows. Anxiety that the other might secretly produce atomic weapons, or in spite of disarmament treaties might fail to destroy existing bombs and instead hide them underground, or that he might unleash an atomic war moments before I could — this anxiety makes both partners unwilling to renounce the relative security of a balance of power. The nub of the problem is not primarily a matter of political and strategic considerations. It is grounded rather in something which underlies all such considerations, namely, the fact that human existence is given up to mistrust. What this means can perhaps be clarified by the use of a simple illustration. Two mortal enemies suddenly meet in a room with cocked pistols in hand. Because the situation is equally dangerous to both, they agree that at the count of "three" they will both throw their pistols out the window. The count begins but the word "three" finds both pistols still in hand. For each believes that the other, in spite of the agreement, will not throw away his pistol and will thus be in a position of superiority.

Treaties and agreements are of doubtful value if mistrust is not purged from the human condition. Otherwise we have to assume that the other will either break or evade the treaty, depending only on whether he has the power to back up such a unilateral liquidation of the treaty.

The Problem of the Physical Balance of Atomic Powers

To grasp the political ramifications of this mistrust, we may recall an idea which we advanced earlier in relation to the problem of power in general, and which receives fresh confirmation from our example of the two pistols. Mistrust intensifies to the degree that the other is armed and to the degree that the dangers implicit in his unpredictability are enhanced. Moreover, since power carries with it additional temptations, even a relatively harmless soul — not to speak of an unscrupulous and cynical enemy — can, if he possesses power, become a highway robber.

Democracy is built on this mistrust of the powerful, and hence on a thoroughly critical view of man. For it is an axiom of every democratic constitution that the concentration of power at one point, the monopolizing of power, must be prevented. Instead, power has to be distributed and controlled. The principle of the distribution of powers is founded on this insight. What is now taking place in the wider world of our own day is in fact nothing other than the attempt, based on the mistrust of those who have atomic power, to effect a kind of distribution of atomic powers, a balance of forces, and therewith a kind of neutralizing of atomic power, in short, an atomic peace.

At first glance — an even then only very relatively — this idea of an atomic peace seems rather intriguing. On further reflection, however, there at once arise serious objections which also call in question the legitimacy of the analogy drawn from the legal structure of democracy.

Atomic peace is illusory in the first place because, although it can make possible a temporary state of relative security, it can do so only by carrying with it a serious threat, and hence also the possibility of atomic conflict. For if the resolve to use the atomic weapons even at the risk of one's own destruction is lacking, the weapons seem to lose their psychological effect and hence can no longer impose an atomic peace. The result would be the same as if there were no such weapons, as if they had become an absurd specter.[9]

But if an atomic peace necessarily includes the resolve to enter into an atomic conflict and if need be to perish along with one's opponent, this would seem to mean not only that the possibility of defense and the whole idea of a just war are absurd but also, as a further consequence, that to support, approve, or actively participate in atomic armament is wholly incompatible with any kind of ethical and Christian sense of responsibility. For if the mistrust in the world, of which the Christian is particularly aware, can only be remedied by a balance of power, then such a remedy, grounded in the Noachic covenant, can be taken seriously by Christians only if it offers genuine possibilities of punishment, resistance, deterrence, and defense. The moment the readiness to exercise these particular functions of earthly order is not only coupled with inhuman atrocity towards countless hosts of combatants and noncombatants alike but also involves at the same time a readiness for collective suicide, the assumed remedy would seem to be not just logically absurd but also religiously blasphemous. For these functions are meaningful and right only in terms of a divinely willed preservation of the world. Here, however, they become a matter of the world's destruction.

The Choice between Communism and World Destruction

Is the conclusion correct, then, that Christians must have nothing to do with atomic weapons?[10] We must test it by a whole series of deliberations. In the first place, it would be well not to consider the matter abstractly, but in terms of present historical reality. From this

---

[9] Cf. von Weizsäcker, loc. cit.: "A threat which involves self-destruction is no threat. If everyone knows the bombs will not fall they are as good as non-existent. The danger for all of us lies in the fact that, if they are to serve as any kind of a threat at all, those who have them must be ready to drop them."

[10] This is essentially the position of Helmut Gollwitzer, Die Christen und die Atomwaffen (1957).

angle such a conclusion would carry with it two clear implications.

First, one of the present opponents, namely the West, is to disarm unilaterally and completely, because it must be unilaterally and completely resolved never to use atomic weapons even in the event an enemy should use them in an unprovoked attack. This unilateral and complete disarmament would logically be demanded of the West even if the East were not resolved upon a similar measure, i.e., even if all the atomic military power were to be concentrated on only one side, and this side were to use it in order actually to achieve the world dominion its doctrine has always postulated.

Second, the acceptance of such unilateral imperialism implies a readiness to allow the whole world to go Communist. This implication results not only from the theologically grounded consideration that where power becomes unlimited all limits go by the board, but also from the knowledge that in its ideological theory Marxism-Leninism has always unmistakably espoused world dominion. Much is to be gained by facing up to these consequences realistically, and by not letting "Christian" emotions blur the actual contours of the problem.

To state the consequences, however, is not yet to refute the position. Although neither the theologians nor the concerned atomic physicists seem thus far to have pressed the question to the point where, in the choice between destruction and Communism, one had to opt in favor of Communism, this alternative itself has in fact to be examined. In examining it we must certainly be on guard against aiming at a purely emotional response, e.g., that, given the alternative, we will not elect Communism at any price. For it is conceivable that, even though Communism be radically rejected in principle, capitulation to it may be necessary and permissible if the only alternative is devastation of the whole earth. One might then argue that survival at least offers some chance of outlasting Communism. For only on its own view is Communism the ultimate goal of history. We for our part may believe that it is an earthly power which can be overcome and perish. The total destruction of friend and foe alike, however, removes all chance of survival and victory. This line of argument cannot be rejected out of hand. Even those who see in Communism an unimaginable horror which must be removed no matter how high the cost can hardly refuse to consider the argument when they remember the alternative.

Yet the plane on which this argument moves is falsely chosen. We can thus meet the argument only if we call in question this plane of thought. The question is not whether we will choose between Communism and world destruction, but whether we mean in principle to acknowledge that in this world might is right. It is not a question whether in the last resort we should capitulate to Communism but whether we should in the last resort, and in principle, allow might to have everything its own way, unchecked by right.

This question is linked only to a limited degree with the fact that today might occurs in the concrete form of Communism. It could conceivably take a very different form. That Communism is its present form sharpens the question only to the degree that this power which represents the right of might has within it from the very outset — in terms of its ideology — a concept of right which as a corollary supports the primacy of might and of ends.

If we decide for the victory of unrestricted might we must realize what the decision implies. It is a decision against the Noachic order of the world in which arbitrary and unlimited power is to be restrained by further power, and within which the preservation of the world depends in principle on limits being set, limits which where necessary are imposed by force. If, then, we decide that might is right, we decide against that principle of order from which the state derives and on which all authority and law depend. We thus decide against the very foundation of the world, and we must realize that, once this decision is taken, the legitimacy of all other orders is mortally affected, e.g., that of the obedience of children to their parents, the fairness of economic and other forms of competition, the hierarchy of superiors and subordinates, the freedom of the individual within all order, etc.

It is useless to protest that the world has always known such triumphs of might and such capitulations of the weak and of their right, and that these actually confirm rather than refute the Noachic order of the world. The objection misses the whole point, for the decision in question does not relate to an isolated event off in a corner somewhere, an event which can still be embedded in a history in which the order of the world is preserved (at least in intention), where the principle of right before might is still in force. On the contrary, what is involved here is a global decision, a decision with respect to the whole earth.

While that may have an emotional ring about it, it is in fact the naked truth. For we have to grasp the following point. As surely as atomic weapons affect the whole earth, and are thus qualitatively different from all earlier weapons having only local significance, so decisions regarding these weapons affect the whole earth, and are thus qualitatively different from all earlier decisions, which had significance only for a particular locality and not for the whole course of human history. Our generation will be long in accustoming itself to this changed perspective, and in grasping the accompanying shift in the thrust and scope of every question having even remotely to do with atomic weapons.

If in the choice between Communism and destruction the decision is taken in favor of Communism, this affects incomparably more elemental fields than would appear at a first glance when the only question perceived is that of survival and the chances this offers against Communism. The question takes on an essentially different aspect when we see that the decision is between two *forms* of total destruction, namely, "physical" destruction and the "moral" destruction of a world in which it has been basically and universally decided that might is right, in which the ultimate principles of all order are denied, and in which physical deliverance can consequently be had only at the cost of "dead souls."

No one in our generation can measure the full implications of this decision. He can only decide the question for himself in an act of personal venture. No one is in a position or has the authority to make either the one answer or the other a matter of binding confession for Christianity as a whole. For no other generation has ever had to face this question — which may be why it is not even raised in the pertinent literature.

Now in a theological ethics which seeks to be more than a personal witness and lays some claim to general validity we obviously cannot base all our further deliberations on a decision of this gravity and admitted difficulty. Hence in terms of methodology the only course open to us is to pursue two different lines and to think through the two possible solutions.

First, if in face of this mortal trauma of world order I decide the question by ultimately choosing destruction, the implication is that I assent to a balance of power in the atomic field with a view to preventing an unrestricted development of atomic power at any one point. Also implied is my acceptance of the risk that the atomic peace might one day be ended by a world conflagration. Since I do not and cannot desire this, but only regard it as the lesser of the two evils in this anguishing dilemma, I shall do all I can to the best of my knowledge and ability to bring about controlled disarmament and to overcome the mistrust, and I shall be prepared to take considerable risks and make great sacrifices to this end.

Second, if I decide the question differently, if I refuse to consider accepting destruction as an ultimate possibility, then the new question arises whether I ought to accept the implication of Gollwitzer that I should have nothing to do with atomic weapons but should disarm unilaterally since to tamper at all with atomic weapons means the beginning of the end, *or* whether this implication can be circumvented by still thinking in terms of atomic peace through a balance of atomic powers. In order to proceed here it is necessary to point out at once that this solution involves the avoidance of open atomic war at *any* price, even though this should mean that the entire world capitulates to Communism, and that a cynical foe to whom humanitarian and Christian considerations may be quite alien is thereby allowed to march on unchecked to expansion and triumph. What this decision means is that I will necessarily prefer to forego all atomic defense *if* the possession of atomic weapons will automatically lead to atomic war, and this condition seems to be present when both sides are genuinely resolved not merely to restrict the effect of their atomic weapons to that of a psychological deterrent but to use them actively in case of need.

We are thus brought back again to the thesis of von Weizsäcker that if atomic weapons are to serve as a deterrent at all we must also be prepared actively to use them. For if the other side knows that even in an emergency we will not use them, they lose their deterrent value, and it is as though they did not exist. And if only one of the two sides is not prepared to use them, the other can act unhindered as though he had an atomic monopoly. Thus both sides must be seriously resolved to drop atomic bombs in case of need.

If this is so, or ought to be so, then on this level of thought, i.e., in terms of the second answer, one is driven to the conclusion that, if there can be no disarmament on both sides, then I must disarm alone and unilaterally.[11] Thus it all boils down to the one question of the relation between deterrence and the resolution to use atomic weapons, between the psychological and the more elemental effects. But is this thesis correct, that the two are indissolubly linked so that we cannot have the one without the other?

The Concept of the Psychological Deterrent

In our view, the thesis depends on a wrong way of putting the question. But how you frame the question is basic for all the theses which follow; indeed, it is in a real sense the key or basic question. Hence the false approach obscures the real issue.

As we see it, whether or not one is resolved to use atomic bombs in actual conflict has no decisive bearing on the deterrent effect and therefore on the warding off of nuclear war. If the goal of deterring aggression rests on a psychological consideration, that consideration must be thought through psychologically. Then the point is seen to be, not whether I am resolved to use nuclear weapons if needed, but whether my opponent *thinks* I am. These are two different things.

The question whether he thinks I am cannot be answered merely in terms of the obvious thesis that he will think so to the degree that I succeed in giving him this impression, whether by demonstrating my resolution convincingly or by using bombastic speeches to deceive him concerning my lack of resolution. This answer is only partially correct. It is true that the deterrent effect depends *in part* on how well I succeed in giving my opponent a specific impression of my resolution, so that he has to take it into account. But whether he will really take it into account depends far more on whether he himself is similarly resolved. He too knows the destructive potential of nuclear weapons. If he rates it so highly that in the interest of self-preservation he regards their use as out of the question, then he will not lightly assume that I am resolved to use them either. He will instead believe that I am *un*prepared to use them in an emergency, but he will believe this only to the degree that he himself feels constrained to prevent any such emergency from arising.

Hence the unreadiness which he ascribes to his opponent can do no harm because it simply corresponds to his own unreadiness, and thus

---

[11] Von Weizsäcker does not draw this conclusion because his attention is focused particularly on the question of German armaments.

the psychological balance is restored — unless he has such a preponderance of non-nuclear weapons that he believes that under the cover of atomic fear he can enforce his will militarily within the framework of conventional warfare and without nuclear intervention. (We shall return to this point later.)

This stage, in which the one side counts on the unreadiness of the other, seems likely to last for an indefinite period. The phase might be ended by further development in weapons technology or atomic strategy which, in distinction from all previous military history, would consist paradoxically in *reducing* the excessive power of nuclear weapons to manageable proportions, so that a strategy of local or at least limited encounters would again be possible.[12] But speculation of this kind is beyond the competence of theological ethics. There is a question, however, that does come within its terms of reference: If the deterrent effect of atomic weapons depends, not on my actual resolution to use them, but only on my opponent's assumption that I am so resolved; and if his assumption is based on his own resolution in this respect; and if at the present stage of weapons development a "balance of unreadiness" necessarily prevails, the question inevitably arises as to why the two sides plunge themselves into the appalling costs and risks of making and keeping nuclear bombs.

The answer might well be that they do this because the unreadiness would disappear at once if only one of the two possessed atomic weapons. For in such a case the one who had them could precipitate a conflict without running the risk of self-destruction (because there would be no atomic response and because he would not even be endangered by his own explosions). Unilateral possession of atomic weapons would permit invasion of a vacuum by means of nuclear power, without any necessity for this power to go beyond the incubation stage and become active. (The ending of the war against Japan following the two atomic "tests" is a good example.) Mutual atomic armament thus serves the purpose of preventing dangerous unilateral possession of nuclear weapons. The resolve behind the stockpiling of such weapons is primarily to prevent war by building an adequate defense, not to use them in actual conflict. A serious conflict is not likely to arise where both sides have atomic weapons, because of

[12] See Henry A. Kissinger, *Nuclear Weapons and Foreign Policy* (New York: Harper, 1957).

the mutual unreadiness of which we have just spoken. But where only one side has them it is certain that the resultant vacuum will be imperialistically filled, at least if the atomic power champions a doctrine of world salvation by militant expansion.

We thus arrive at a conclusion which is perhaps unexpected in the light of our earlier discussion: The false thesis that the deterrent effect of atomic weapons necessarily implies the resolution to use them in actual conflict, taken together with the thesis that even the threat of a world takeover by the Communists must not be met by an atomic defense which could mean total destruction, leads to the conclusion that a radical and unilateral renunciation of atomic weapons is indicated, and that for Christians at any rate there is no other choice. We cannot overthrow the second of these two theses by arguments, since it rests on an ultimate ethical decision which we must respect for the reasons indicated, and which we granted was legitimate. What we have tried to do is to undermine the first thesis.

If we have succeeded in this, the conclusion itself falls too. We cannot say, as Gollwitzer seems to contend between the lines (but clearly all the same), that unilateral disarmament is so self-evident that it can be made an integral part of the Christian confession, a necessary article of faith. There are obviously good reasons for believing that the basic law of the Noachic world — whereby in the kingdom on the left hand force is limited by force and servile fear has its place in the political use of the law — is not wholly invalidated when it comes to the matter of atomic force.

We have intentionally said "not wholly," for there can be no contesting the fact that this law is here seen in a borderline situation, indeed at its own extreme limit. The atomic peace which it establishes is more dangerous than any other peace based on fear. For in spite of the described balance and neutralizing effect, it is conceivable that unexpected sparks will set fire to the powder, and that the necessary balance of atomic powers will then give place to a sudden worldwide catastrophe. To envisage this possibility one has only to conjure up the apocalyptic vision of a Hitler having nuclear power at his disposal and dragging the whole world down with him. This is why atomic peace can never be a settled and reassuring peace. On the contrary, it will demand that we use all our powers to achieve an atomic disarmament on both sides.

Our opposition to the thesis of unilateral disarmament should not be allowed to leave the impression that we regard atomic peace as "not so bad," or that we complacently think we have safely incorporated and integrated the atomic age into the relatively solid emergency orders of the Noachic covenant, which are at least solid enough to endure to the day of judgment.

It is simply a question of choosing between two evils, and this is a matter of judgment, not of faith. We must judge which alternative poses the greater danger: having an atomic power on one side and a vacuum on the other, or having a balance of atomic potential which, while it involves a mutual unreadiness to precipitate a conflict, will always be precarious and uncertain so long as it is controlled by fallible men — and may even fall into the hands of criminals. Either way, it is the duty of the Christian, especially the Christian politician, to press for bilateral disarmament, and therewith for a diminution of the risk which is always inherent where supradimensional powers reciprocally limit one another.

The Church and Atomic War

The things we have just been saying yield two results. First, the peace grounded in a distribution of atomic power, and in the consequent neutralizing of forces, is an anxious peace. The world outside the gospel does not know the redeemed peace of the divine good-pleasure (Luke 2:14). It knows only the unredeemed peace of the world (John 14:27), namely, the quietude of anxiety, and an order of the world which pursues the neutralizing of disorder along the lines of the Noachic covenant. Servile fear takes the place of filial love.

Second, the mark of this peace is that it is very relative, for what it involves is not true calm and composure but only an uncertain quietude. The uncertainty — which has always been present in principle in the warlike situation of the present aeon — contains here an incomparably greater threat than that which obtained in earlier times, because this anxious peace is but a smoldering fire whose sparks can always lead to explosions, and man has to live always on the brink of disaster.

Christianity is thus summoned to bear here a witness of judgment, admonition, and comfort, because this situation of anxious peace is grounded in the situation of man himself and of his world. If it is man who is addressed by Law and gospel, then the world situation which corresponds to his nature must also be included in that message.

Realism in Church Pronouncements

Before we can define this Christian witness more precisely, we need first to discuss the dangers which confront such a witness and the wrong paths which it might take. We have only to consider the extraordinary host of utterances — pastoral messages, synodical resolutions, pulpit pronouncements, and individual statements — and note their confusing diversity to be convinced that fundamental reflection is sorely needed on the limits and reservations which must be observed if the church is to speak at all on this theme. Two considerations are particularly important in respect of the church's effort to help avert atomic war.

First, since the church does not have to act politically, and hence does not have at its disposal the information which is available to the statesmen when they make their decisions, and since the church does not stand under the burden of actually having to make the decisions, it is exposed to the very real temptation of making very general and absolute demands. Among responsible politicians, whether in government or out, these demands are felt to be unrealistic; they are therefore either regarded as an imposition or exploited tactically. Among the public they lead to certain misconceptions and to oversimplifications of the situation. Under cover of these radical and spiritually intended — or ostensibly spiritual — demands what actually takes place is vigorous political activity, but of the kind that lacks the necessary presuppositions to make it legitimate. The conscience which is not compelled by the facts at hand, is not burdened with making the decision, does not have to assume active responsibility for what happens, and is not exposed to the (relative) autonomy of such spheres as politics and economics, is all too inclined to be radical in the abstract — even to become Pharisaical or fanatical — because its ethical or Christian position apparently allows it to remain aloof.[13]

It was this consideration which led us to adopt in our theological ethics a methodology involving the use of models. For in this way

[13] We are reminded of Bismarck's words to his pietistic Pomeranian friends quoted above on pp. 104 and 105: they should put themselves in his shoes!

we are forced to analyze a concrete part of reality, and thus to respect the indissoluble interweaving of questions of principle with questions of judgment as well as to take into account the distinction between espousing a position of principle independently of the situation on the one hand and being forced to judge and decide *within* a situation on the other.

An illustration of the change in ethical approach which accompanies the transition from the one situation to the other is to be found in the case of atomic scientists, who to some extent can make this transition in person, changing suddenly from aloof scholars into active participants with political responsibility. This transition is usually accompanied by a change in the situation of the conscience. Thus up to around 1949 leading atomic scientists in America could seriously consider not helping to construct a super-bomb for reasons of conscience. In other words, they threatened a kind of strike of atomic scientists. They believed that they had an inviolable freedom of conscience in this sphere, and that they ought to guard it. The situation changed at a stroke, however, when they learned that the Soviet Union had fissionable material at its disposal. Their resolve under these changed circumstances to co-operate after all in the building of a super-bomb provides an excellent illustration of the thing we are talking about.

They were suddenly confronted with the shocking fact that every ethical decision with respect to atomic weapons comes under the political law of move and countermove. The decision is no longer whether one can take responsibility for bringing into existence such an elemental force of destruction as this bomb. Stated in this abstract form the question can only receive a negative answer. But now the question is different: Given the situation as it actually is, i.e., with a potential enemy already in possession of the atom bomb, can one take the responsibility of *not* constructing supernuclear bombs? Or, even more sharply, can one, by his refusal, take the responsibility of handing atomic superiority over to this foe? Is it not now an inescapable duty to contribute to an atomic balance, and to prevent one's own land from becoming a defenseless object of hostile caprice? Does not one need the surety of his own weapons, even if the proximate goal is that of establishing international control and of launching negotiations for disarmament?

It is easy to imagine the shock which this change in the framing of the ethical question — for that is what it is — caused to the scientists. Here the problem of political ethics emerged with all the clarity one could desire. Ethical decisions are not made in empty space. They are made under the pressure of specific conditions and within the framework of specific ineluctabilities.

One should not forget that Einstein, in his famous letter to Roosevelt, underwent and suffered the same experiences when he begged the American government to take up seriously the problem of uranium. He was a pacifist and a champion of humanitarian thought. Yet when he learned that the Germans had apparently begun work on atomic weapons, his decision moved out of the realm of abstract principle into that of facts. The question which the facts put to him was this: Dare the world just stand defenseless before the terror of the Nazis' atomic initiative?

The change in the framing of the ethical question which takes place with this transition from a position outside politics to a position inside is thus characterized by the fact that the new ethical decision must take into account the conditions under which and with reference to which it must be taken. Pre-eminent among these conditions is the fact that politics involves a conflict of forces, a seeking of power in order to achieve ends, and that any increase in the power of the opponent, whether in the sphere of economics or weapons, or by improvement of geophysical position or alliances, must be met by a corresponding increase on one's own side.

There is thus an inevitable interplay of move and countermove in the suprapersonal spheres of life. If there is important technological advance in any sphere of the economy, e.g., automation, entrepreneurs in the same line have to follow suit if they are to remain competitive. As we have seen, the same law obtains in the area of military potential, even where the desired balance of forces, or the desired superiority of one's own forces, is intended only to avert war.

It may be admitted that the armaments race inspired by this law is madness. Both sides may resolve to disarm. But disarmament too is subject to the same law of move and countermove. For the several stages of disarmament must involve a carefully synchronized reciprocity, since even during the reduction of military potential the balance has to be maintained for the sake of relative security in a world of mistrust. This is why the problems of stages and control are always central in all disarmament negotiations.

The law of reciprocity permeates all spheres of life, even the personal relation between neighbors. Only when we see this can we appreciate the radically new thing brought in by the gospel. For the gospel sets aside this law of retribution in respect of the I-Thou relation. It breaks the vicious circle. In the golden rule it lays on me the duty of making a new beginning, of daring freely to take the initiative. The creative breath which blows into my relation with others and can make all things new applies only with reservations, however, to the suprapersonal spheres of technology, economics, and politics, since here it has to take into account the conditions imposed by the structural laws of this aeon to which we have already referred.

The attempt to understand this distinction between these two areas of life, to differentiate them without separating them, finds its most important theological reflection so far as Reformation theology is concerned in the doctrine of the two kingdoms.[14] In Roman Catholic moral theology it may be seen in the distinctions made in natural law between nature, condition, and circumstances, and again between primary natural law and secondary natural law.[15]

The church itself is constantly tempted to confuse the two kingdoms. By reason of its aloofness, it is inclined — more in respect of military than of social questions — to overlook the sphere of conditions, be they those imposed by the concrete situation or by the structure of the various areas of life. All who would address the political world from without as ethical or religious advisers should be aware of this danger and of the need for exact factual analysis.

Not that they should cease to give advice! Legitimate themes and forms of Christian admonition can indeed be found. But the advice and criticism should not be as cheap as it often is, especially in relation to the atomic problem. Those who stand under the burden of a political mandate and are confronted by concrete conditions cannot be offered up as victims to absolutist fanatics and utopians, even those of Christian provenance.

Our second point is that in Christian utterances of this kind regard must be had to a circumstance with which we have already been

[14] See *ThE* 1, Chapter 18.
[15] See *ThE* 1, Chapter 20.

confronted in our earlier analysis of the atomic problem.[16] Faced by a specific choice, we must admit that as we stand just now on the threshhold of the atomic age we cannot see the full implications of many decisions, and that this restriction of outlook also affects theological reflection and the right of the church to make pronouncements on the situation. (Perhaps the hesitancy of the Roman Catholic teaching office on these questions, which contrasts favorably with the thematic breadth and vehemence of many Protestant utterances, is due in part to this insight.)

We think it important, and in view of manifold abuses even obligatory, to bring to light the difficulties and limitations inherent in any Christian message to the atomic age. The call for caution is especially important when it comes to the matter of speaking theologically about the averting of atomic war. For here we come dangerously close to stepping over into the area of incompetent counsels and empty generalities and platitudes.

All that the church has to say in respect of the atomic age, and especially with reference to atomic war, can be divided into two main categories. There is, first, the matter of the church's preaching, and second, that of its counsel. We shall begin with the question of what the church is to preach.

The Church's Preaching with Reference to the Atom

If the origins of war both cold and hot are to be sought in the most inward areas of fallen man, the church for one thing must warn against all false hopes, e.g., the hope that war can be overcome by institutional and organizational measures such as treaty systems, disarmament conferences, the achievement of an atomic peace, unilateral renunciation of defense, etc. For as man cannot justify or change himself by good works, so he cannot alter the world – which is the objectification of man – by organizational and institutional works. And even as he cannot set his hopes on such works, so he cannot point with despair to specific conditions (e.g., power groupings or even the discovery of atomic fission) and blame them for making nuclear war a possibility. Here too it is man himself who bears the ultimate responsibility, since it is he who calls into being a world of mistrust and of centrifugal tendencies. Hence the first theme in preaching

[16] See above p. 482.

to the atomic world and its anxiety must be that of the greatness, the misery, and the calling of man.

But the message of the church has also to convey the comfort of the gospel even across this landscape. This comfort is directed above all to the anxiety which thrives on the atomic threat. It is grounded not merely in a promise of the grace which gives peace to individuals and lifts them out of this world of anxiety, but also in an awareness that the rainbow of God's reconciliation (Gen. 9:13-14) stands over the fallen world as a sign that even *this* world will not perish by reason of its own destructive forces, but that "while the earth remains, seed-time and harvest, cold and heat, summer and winter, day and night, shall not cease" if and so long as there are within this world those who keep the covenant (Gen. 8:22; cf. Gen. 18:32 and Jer. 33:20, 25).

The preaching of the church has thus to resist the temptation to exploit men's fear of imminent destruction. It must not use the atom bomb as a homiletical device for evoking feelings of repentance and longings for a place of refuge. On the contrary, it must strive against emotional confusion and seek to establish the truth that redemption is a redemption to objectivity, that it bestows sobriety, that freedom from prejudice and a concern for the facts are among its fruits.

Finally, the preaching of the church will oppose false absolutizings and doctrinaire alternatives. In the present case this means that Christian realism can never will the absolute (since to will this is a utopian form of idolatry). It refuses to accept an absolute of fantasy and an absolute of terror as the only alternatives. It will not choose between the illusion of world peace and the illusion of a balance of atomic giants. Instead, it tackles the most immediate and practicable parts of the tasks confronting us.

The Lord's Prayer does not teach us to ask for the full ration of bread which will last us the rest of our days. It asks only for the piece I need "this day." The gospel sanctifies the next stretches, not the distant goals. This is what distinguishes it from utopias. The Word of God is a lamp to our feet (Ps. 119:105) which illumines only the next step and makes us trust for what lies beyond. It is not a searchlight illuminating the whole path at once. And just as faith sees that it must proceed into the darkness in trust, letting itself be led, so its task is simply the next installment of the thing to be done, not the whole program of all further action.

Proper, then, to faith, and to the love which stems from it, is the manner of improvisation, of addressing oneself to the immediate task (Luke 10:30-37). The church should not issue appeals for such absolutes as world peace or the complete abandonment of all atomic weapons. Such appeals will be ineffective. Indeed, they will be scorned, and without having even justified themselves in terms of occasioning an authentic offense. For they overlook the sphere of conditions. Instead it is fitting that the church call men to accept humbly the little tasks, encouraging them to care for the obligations of today, not despising them or mixing them with others in the name of some utopia.

Lest we ourselves remain in the sphere of generalities in this regard, we shall illustrate what we have in view by means of two models which will still be good examples even if the historical facts they presuppose should happen soon to be significantly altered. The first involves one of those lesser tasks which do not depend on emotional absolutes, namely, the readiness for a limited cessation of atomic testing and bomb production. Such a readiness is a good illustration of the way in which Christian ethics has to speak in politics. For it is a first and very modest step but an initiative nonetheless, one which does not simply follow the law of action and counteraction, move and countermove, but seeks to grope its way out of the armaments spiral. Here one no longer expects the opponent to take the first step in showing good faith. One does it himself, and if it fails he tries again. This is plainly an effort to do what the gospel demands, namely, to set aside the law of retribution and transfer the task of making a new beginning, so far as this is possible, from the plane of personal I-Thou relations to the field of political encounters.

Such an initiative is the only remedy which can to some small degree lift the burden of mistrust and thereby lighten the load of the world's suffering. For the first step in this direction is a proof of seriousness of purpose, and it thus helps to remove suspicion. Such a step can only be conditional and limited. It lays on the other party responsibility for what follows, whether there can be a further step. This is the most that can be done in the sphere of politics with its play of forces and its distinctive factual requirements. But the first step must indeed be taken if we mean business with respect to the greater goal of bilateral and controlled disarmament.

Our second model has to do with one of those illusory absolutisms which the church must rigorously oppose, namely, the thesis that the next war when and if it comes will necessarily be an atomic war. Now obviously the church cannot dispute this thesis on the basis of a different strategic prognosis. Such a prognosis would exceed its competence. The church can contest the statement only theologically or ethically. For it should see that the statement contains more than merely a strategic insight (if it even contains that). It embodies a specific understanding of man and of his world. We can in fact assume that behind the statement there stands a very different freight of meaning.

Possibly it is determined by the conviction that wars are always provoked and made possible by the weapons available for waging them. On this view the manufacture of armaments necessarily leads to war, and atomic weapons to atomic war. But if this is what the statement intends, one must reply that wars do not come upon man from without, from the world of things. They come from within man himself (cf. Matt. 15:11, 17-18). No matter what the form, the field, or the weapons of war, therefore, war is always an expression of this Babylonian heart and its Babylonian world.

But the thesis may also rest on the purely economic consideration that atomic armaments, and consequently atomic war, are much cheaper than war with conventional weapons. According to Gollwitzer,[17] Edward Teller is supposed to have said that a pound of fissionable material at that time cost seven thousand dollars, so that an atomic explosion was considerably cheaper than an equivalent explosion of conventional type. Similarly, the cost of delivering such a bomb to its target was much cheaper than the cost of the bomber squadrons needed for conventional bombs.

Against this argument the church must appeal to pastoral rather than theological considerations. Its appeal should be twofold. First, it has to ask whether we can assume responsibility for massacring millions of people and their posterity on economic grounds, and whether it is not part of the folly of the ungodly (Ps. 14:1; Luke 12:20) to engage in a clever calculation which, while it may be economically sound, hurls the calculator himself into the abyss and earns only the

---

[17] See Gollwitzer, *op. cit.*, p. 45.

divine derision (Ps. 2:4). Second, the church should not be afraid at this point to ask very concrete questions, since being concrete in such a case does not exceed the bounds of its competence. Realizing that war in this aeon has an indelible character and will persist in some form, in local acts of violence, revolts, guerilla activity, etc., the church must raise the issue whether these relatively small occasions afford a sufficient excuse for using ultimate weapons, the conventional means of waging war having been neglected. In a period when there is vacillation between relying on conventional weapons and relying on atomic weapons it is necessary, even in the nuclear age, to maintain conventional weapons in order to be able to control local conflagrations. To rely exclusively on atomic armament would be to reduce the flexibility of response. One would have to suffer passively the enemy's limited attacks by conventional weapons, since it would hardly be worth while to unleash a mortal conflict of titans simply on account of a local flare-up; in such a case atomic weapons would be useless to prevent such minor affrays. Again, to rely exclusively on atomic armament would carry with it the temptation to strike back once the limited attacks had passed a certain point, if for no other reason than that it was getting on one's nerves till he could no longer stand it.

It is part of the office of the church as watchman and pastor to keep alive the sharp and continuing question whether this consideration can or should be set aside, e.g., on the economic grounds we have adduced, whether we can refuse to face up to the terrible human, economic, and political demands that are involved in maintaining a capability in conventional weapons, whether we can thus hazard everything on the fateful card of atomic armament. One need only ask what would have happened had chemical and biological weapons been the only instruments of warfare available during the Second World War to realize what a demonic reckoning is involved in this kind of calculation of costs.

This is one of the cases in which the message of the church must go into political and strategic considerations in detail if the right pastoral and admonitory word is to be found. It also shows how the message of the church of Jesus Christ loses its force if, instead of tackling the partial and lesser tasks, it withdraws into the fanatical proclamation of absolutes. For if the church simply condemns war as such, demanding the total destruction of all atomic weapons, it is no longer in a position to put to the political and military leaders these highly refined questions of conscience, and the distinction between atomic and conventional weapons no longer poses a theological or ethical problem because both fall under the same condemnation. If the church merely pronounces this general condemnation, it makes it easy for politicians to say that its message is unrealistic, and to dismiss it quietly with a wave of the hand. Then they no longer have to wrestle with the critical questions mentioned above, since these are no longer even being asked. Thus we see how readiness to tackle the practicable partial tasks works out, and what it implies for the preaching of the church.

The Church's Counsel with Reference to the Atom

Having considered the preaching task of the church with reference to atomic weapons and atomic war, we must now turn to the second duty of which we spoke, that of considering what advice and counsel the church should give. This second task devolves upon the church because Christianity's awareness of the ultimate origin of disorder is significant also for society, a society which is made up of both Christians and non-Christians and which — as every view of the church admits — is never wholly identical with the congregation which listens to the preaching. The church's counsel, if it is to be anything other than a concretization of its preaching intended only for the listening congregation, if it is to stand in lieu of preaching and move beyond the walls of the church, must be concerned with just one question. This is the question as to how the bellicose spirit in man, if it cannot be rooted out by the means of law, can at least be kept in the incubation stage and prevented from becoming active.

In distinction from preaching, the counsel of the church can thus aim to deal, as it were, only with symptoms. But it will be a therapy of second degree, since it does not try — as politics does — merely to check the expansion of power by way of a distribution of powers and a balance of forces. It seeks rather to restrain the bellicose spirit itself, thus going to the very source in the heart of man.

The measures to be taken in this matter of the church's counsel are essentially as follows. First, the church must combat the ideological glorification of collectives. It must struggle against all idolizing of classes, races, nations, and unions based on mutual interests.

Second, the church must inculcate tolerance and a readiness for understanding in every possible sphere of everyday life. In this respect it will teach men to value compromise [18] in all matters involving interests and judgments. Only on this basis can the inclination to settle matters by violence be eradicated to some degree.

Third, the church must nurture the ability to distinguish between persons and causes, not to think statically in terms of fronts and antithetical ideologies, but to see the living man who is not identical with the position he espouses. (The New Testament command to love our enemies rests on the ability to make this distinction.) In practice this ability may be fostered by bringing opponents together and even making them live together. Institutional possibilities must be created for arranging such encounters and for seeking the relaxation of tension connected with them.

Fourth, Kierkegaard once defined sin as relating oneself absolutely to the relative. One form of this absolutizing is the ideological exaltation of positions which ought to rest on purely factual arguments. Even widely divergent arguments do not disrupt communication because they are still linked together by their appeal to the same third party, the factual criteria. Grounded in thesis and antithesis, the very structure of argumentation is such that each partner seeks the opposite partner. But the ideological exaltation of positions makes them mutually exclusive and plunges those who champion them into doctrinaire irreconcilability. This is why in matters of everyday life men try to reduce the sharpness of opposition. Ideological prejudices are contested even in children, and it is regarded as ethically praiseworthy to be sober and rationally objective.

The definition of sin as the inclination to relate oneself absolutely to the relative brings the macrocosmic situation of war once again into closest connection with the structure of disordered man. For it shows that disruption in the vertical dimension, the relation to God, brings disorder on the horizontal (Rom. 1:18 ff.); it leads to the contra-existence of what should be coexistent. It also shows that real peace between men and powers can be only the peace of God, the peace

[18] See *ThE* 1, Chapter 25.

which alone heals all disorder. Everything else, including what the church counsels apart from its preaching, is only emergency protection against strife. It is not peace. It derives from the awareness that in this aeon war can undergo many changes in form — world wars can become local wars, international wars civil wars, atomic wars guerilla wars, hot wars cold, military wars economic, etc. — but that wars themselves do not cease, because the greatness and misery of man never cease in this aeon.

The peace of the world is at best coexistence, not peace. Hence while the goal of preaching can never be too high, since it is the eschatological kingdom of God, the goal of counsel can never be too modest. If we confuse these — and this often seems to happen in Christian pronouncements — we rob the Christian message of all plausibility and harden men's hearts. We preach plans of reform instead of preaching the Word, and we counsel goals which are alien to the world, goals which belong to the sphere where there is no more suffering or crying and where the tumult of war ceases and the last enemy is overcome.

27.

Pacifism

In our deliberations thus far we have taken issue with many of the positions of pacifism, though not all. We shall now present systematically its main forms of expression, and pursue some of them futher as may seem necessary. Our primary purpose in doing so is not to impart information, but to engage in theological appraisal. Our wrestling with the various forms of pacifism will serve not only to test our approach to political ethics but also to broaden the scope of our inquiry. In particular, it will throw fresh light on questions relating to the doctrine of the two kingdoms. We shall speak of three different kinds of pacifism: the idealistic, the rationalistic, and the pragmatic.

Idealistic Pacifism

Idealistic pacifism needs only brief mention, since we have touched on it already wherever the doctrine of the two kingdoms was under discussion. We encountered it in both a Christian form and an ideological form.

In its Christian form idealistic pacifism is marked by five characteristic features. First, it makes the laws of the kingdom of God, especially those of the Sermon on the Mount, the principles of the constitution of the world. Second, it thereby transfers the Christian understanding of the direct I-Thou relation (love, long-suffering, forgiveness, etc.) to the indirect sphere of the orders, so that there is a critical attitude toward all forms of self-preservation, not merely toward war but also toward such institutions as the state and law. Third, it represents a violently anticipated eschatology which leaps over the Noachic interim between the fall and the judgment. Fourth, it thereby wrests control of God's kingdom from the hands of the Lord of history, not letting the kingdom "come" (Matt. 6:10) but making it the product of a human operation, a work of man.[1] Finally, the attempt to wrest the kingdom from the eschaton and bring it into the actuality of the present world involves an encroachment upon faith not merely in terms of works, but also in terms of sight (II Cor. 5:7).

In spite of this theological criticism it is surely more than a matter of illegitimate historical speculation to suggest that the Christian form of idealistic pacifism may have played a creative role in church history. Actually it has served as a corrective in two respects.

First, it has signaled the fact that the peace intended in the gospel cannot be reduced to the sphere of purely individual ethical demands, to the personal relation of God and man, or to mere inwardness, but includes within it a promise and a command for the social order. A divine power (I Cor. 4:20) cannot be restricted in its operation and range — any such restriction is inconceivable — but must relate to the condition of the world and seek to effect a life of peace (I Tim. 2:2).

The very word used in John 16:33 as the opposite of $\epsilon i \rho \dot{\eta} \nu \eta$ and translated as "tribulation," namely, $\theta \lambda \hat{\iota} \psi \iota s$, shows that peace means well-being, security, and hence a certain condition within the world.[2] "The 'healthy' or normal state which corresponds to the will of God is not to be limited to the soul or even to man. It extends basically to the structure of the world in its entirety." [3]

This idea of peace permeating the very structure of the world is suggested also in the New Testament idea of growth, which refers not only to the growth of faith (I Cor. 1:5; Eph. 4:13, 15) but also to the growth of the church (Acts 2:41) and finally to the call extended to the whole world in the great commission (Matt. 28:19; Mark 16:15). Though the presence of the kingdom is hidden in faith (Col. 3:3), it seeks to emerge from inwardness and presses for manifestation in the fruits of the Spirit (Gal. 5:22).

Only very artificial exposition can dispute that this outward movement ought to affect the outward order of life and the peace of this

---

[1] The legalistic ethics of Anabaptists like Thomas Münzer afford a negative indication that the Reformation doctrines of justification and grace are in their very nature bound up with a doctrine of the two kingdoms and a distinction of the two aeons.

[2] Werner Foerster, " $\epsilon i \rho \dot{\eta} \nu \eta$," *Theological Dictionary of the New Testament*, ed. and trans. Geoffrey W. Bromiley (Grand Rapids, Michigan: Eerdmans, 1964 –), II, 413.

[3] *Ibid.*, p. 412.

order. What is said about the hiddenness of faith and the dawn of the kingdom of God within it does not mean that there is no outward movement, no pressure toward manifestation. It simply means that no palpable form, no visibility transcending faith, will be achieved in this way. Ontically the kingdom of God is at work without. Noetically, however, it is accessible, not in this form, but only by the Word and faith. In form it is interchangeable.[4]

In any case, the idea that the kingdom of God leavens the form of this world (Matt. 13:33; 5:15) corresponds to the New Testament and is basically sound in spite of idealistic and utopian aberrations. This is why the program of the Pilgrim Fathers and the holy experiment of William Penn have the dignity of a sign and summons, of an admonition on the margin of church history. This is also what Karl Barth has in view when he says that there must be a modicum of millennialism in every ethics: "Ethics can no more exist without millenarianism, without at least some minute degree of it, than without the idea of a moral personality."[5]

Christian pacifism has also had corrective significance in a second way. By its very existence it has pointed to the fact that in the kingdom on the left hand the principle of self-preservation, and consequently the principle of force or power, is to be understood not as an order of creation, an expression of the true will of God, but as an emergency order of this aeon after the fall. It thus counters the inclination to ensconce oneself in this aeon, be satisfied with it, and to extol its laws of conflict as if they were right and necessary, given by creation.

In addition to the Christian form of idealistic pacifism there is also the ideological form, which we have come to know in the eschatology of Marxism-Leninism. Here, as in every consistent pacifist doctrine, pacifism is bound up with the abolition of the state. In distinction from all other forms, however, ideological pacificism is not a program for the present but is radically restricted to an eschaton within history. The dialectic of the materialist view of history brings the utopia of final peace into connection not with preliminary forms of relative peace but with an intensification of social conflict and a

[4] See *ThE* 1, 17 ff.
[5] Karl Barth, "The Problem of Ethics Today," *The Word of God and the Word of Man*, trans. Douglas Horton (Boston: Pilgrim, 1928), p. 158.

totalization of the state: the ultimate goal of international peace is to be achieved only by way of its antithesis. Our theological judgment of this view is implied in our diagnosis of it as an expression of ideology. It thus belongs in some sense to the sphere of pragmatic pacifism, which we shall be discussing a little later.

Rationalistic Pacifism

Rationalistic pacifism is to be characterized partly in terms of its diagnosis of the world situation and partly in terms of the therapy it proposes for solving the world's troubles. As concerns the diagnosis, rationalistic pacifism believes that war can be explained simply by the fact that men have not sufficiently perceived its horrors. They have not been adequately instructed in the possibilities of preventing it, and are therefore inclined to think that the extreme situation calling for use of the last resort has arisen whereas men of greater insight know that this is not so. "Insight" clearly shows that the international law of force is stupid, and this diagnosis suggests the main lines of therapy. The rational insight that war is avoidable necessarily leads to the assumption that it can be organized out of existence by such rational measures as leagues of nations, international courts, and similar bodies; faith in the effectiveness of such institutional rationality then leads to the view that the instrumental precondition of war — armies, weapons, and above all conscription — should be abolished. In its diagnosis and therapy rationalistic pacifism is thus guilty of at least four non-rational assumptions whose questionable nature is obvious from the standpoint of theological anthropology.

First, it assumes that war is due to a blindness — whether on the part of the public or on that of politicians — which one can dispel by means of rational insight. But, as Carl Friedrich von Weizsäcker rightly said in a radio address of March 3, 1957, war is in fact a "visible crystallization of the fuels of conflict which smoulder constantly in the irrational depths of man's being." What we have been attempting is to understand these fuels of conflict theologically.

But if these fuels — if warlike man himself, possibly in conjunction with the absence of authorized courts [6] — are the ultimate cause of war, then they cannot be overcome simply by means of rational in-

---

[6] We dealt with this question in our discussion of sovereignty; see above pp. 430 ff.

sight. As the insight that evil is purposeless does not avail to move man to do good, so war cannot be abolished by showing how senseless it is. For, as evil is located below the level of the rational and can even use man's reason in its service, so the motivation of war lies below this level, and it too can impress rational arguments into its service. Those who think that rational insight is an adequate answer to war are themselves guilty of highly irrational thinking. Because they do not take into account the irrational factors which help to cause wars, they miscalculate.

Second, this type of pacifism also overestimates the possible degree of rationality in the institutional field. We have shown already, and will simply point out again, that international leagues and courts themselves bear all the marks of interested parties though on a higher level. Hence they do not have the quality of genuine judicial (or rational) normativity. They too belong to the sphere of the emergency orders, and are thus grounded in the same irrational spheres from which the spirit of conflict derives.

Third, we can thus see how illusory is the assumption that war can be prevented by the abolition of armies and weapons. If for the reasons mentioned under our first point it is not possible compellingly to convince opponents of the senselessness of war, and especially of any particular war, then the possibility becomes purely hypothetical that I can convince myself of the wisdom of unilateral disarmament. This would again be to fly in the face of all rational calculation, for to create a vacuum is to arouse an abhorrence of the vacuum and thus to provoke aggression.

It is indeed "shortsighted" to believe that conscription leads to war.[7] For conscription spreads the burden of war over the widest possible segments of the population and thus, quite apart from any questions of justice, makes them all wholesomely aware of the problem of war, and of the question as to the legitimacy of any particular war. The burden of responsibility is in danger of being illegitimately eased if war can be delegated, if the people are not made to feel that they are themselves the acting subject, if they do not have to make personal sacrifices for the sake of the war. There is at least a relative delegation of such responsibility whenever the only par-

[7] Karl Barth, *Church Dogmatics,* ed. G. W. Bromiley and T. F. Torrance (Edinburgh: T. & T. Clark, 1936 –), III⁴, 466.

ticipants in a war are the volunteers, units made up of men who like to fight, contingents from other countries impressed into serving in a war which is not essentially their own, or — as in former times — foreign mercenaries. In such cases there may well arise that dangerous complacency of the citizen in Faust which moves men to "drain our glasses and see how each gay vessel down the river passes" while "off in Turkey, far away, the people clash and fight with one another." [8] When one's own life, and the life of one's neighbor, is at stake, war is existential, not just a matter of historical curiosity. It has to be pondered deeply. There can be no possibility of rendering it innocuous as rational pacifism is guilty of doing.

This leads us to the fourth and final questionable feature of rationalistic pacifism, which has to do with its concept of reason. Quite apart from the fact that rational insight does not determine the action of individuals or nations, reason, to put it bluntly, is not a means of international agreement because it does not operate as some kind of a timeless and universal human capacity.

Kant's doctrine of the categories, which proceeds on the assumption that reason is a timeless a priori capacity of this kind, is consciously working with an abstraction. It constructs an artificial model of a reason which stands alone and is not linked to concrete existence. As a working hypothesis it begins with the question as to how man can be rational, and thus defines him as a rational being. It does not raise the opposite question of how far (theological) reason is determined by man's existence.[9]

Along the lines of this second question one has to say that it is at the behest of existence that reason decides upon supreme philosophical maxims, postulates which are not themselves subject to the criteria of reason and which reason itself serves in the name of the existence which commissions it. In politics this means that reason is not that which autonomously posits the final goals. It sets them but only by commission. Reason is simply that which thinks out for itself the most serviceable means of attaining these goals. The goals

---

[8] Goethe, *Faust*, Part I, scene 2; in *Goethe*, trans. George Madison Priest ("Great Books," Vol. 47), p. 22.

[9] This second question stands at the very center of existential philosophy. It is most clearly articulated in Karl Jaspers' concept of the Encompassing; see *Reason and Existence*, trans. William Earle (London: Routledge & Kegan Paul, 1956), pp. 51 ff.

themselves, e.g., the object of a sense of mission, a specific national order, the historical role of one's nation or class, world revolution, etc., are posited on the basis of the same irrational background of existence from which the positing of supreme values and world views derives.

With this is linked the fact that reason is not just an international organ and consequently cannot be a means of international agreement. For what we actually have are different forms of reason (indeed reasons in the plural) which can be employed in the service of very different maxims.

If we are to understand the ultimate intentions of another political power, be it a state, a social class, or a philosophical group, it is not enough to understand only their rational arguments. It is necessary first to understand that these arguments are rationalizations of certain maxims, and then to understand what these particular maxims are which are here present in rational form. Thus the Communist idea of world revolution is not the result of a rational argument; on the contrary, it is a philosophical maxim. Nor is it referred to in Soviet diplomatic notes; on the contrary, Soviet arguments are all adapted to specific political or diplomatic needs. Similarly, all proofs, explanations, and justifications of specific measures and goals are ultimately no more than the rationalized form of this particular maxim of world revolution, a maxim which, though decked out in arguments, is of very different provenance from that of reason.

Hence I can understand a rational argument on the political level only if I look through it and see the ultimate intentions, which are determined by non-rational maxims, by passions, fears, and hopes. (This is true also as regards the ostensible grounds of conflict cited, e.g., in a declaration of war.) But more than rational insight is needed to do this, for rational insight cannot get beyond the arguments presented. What is needed rather is an instinct and a scent for the controlling interests.

Only the instrumental side of reason, i.e., reason as the tool of maxims and intentions, is international and universal. What this means is that in and of themselves the arguments may be quite logical; any rational man can follow them, or even construct them if he has seen through to the maxims, interests, and intentions behind them. Hence it is a good hermeneutical rule in studying diplomatic notes not merely to consider the stated arguments in such notes but to put oneself in the place of the other and see the interest which is here presented in rationalized form, indeed in rationalizing concealment.

This excursus on the role of reason in politics was needed in order to show up the inner weakness of rationalistic pacifism. This particular form of pacifism holds that war can be argued out of existence with rational arguments, that it can be organized out of existence with rational institutions. It thus assumes that reason is a universal means of agreement even at the international level. For to contest war by insight is possible only if all may have this insight. This assumption, however, overlooks the fact that reason stands in the service of maxims which transcend it, and is thus implicated in the dispersion which obtains in the post-Babel world. There are as many kinds of reason as there are human existences, as many arguments as there are interests.

To take an example, how can there ever be a rational discussion between East and West on the nature of war and its abolition, when on the two sides reason argues in the name of very different sets of values? The humanitarian arguments of the West for the abolition of war cannot be fitted into the system of co-ordinates espoused by Communist reason, whose dialectic allows the extreme inhumanity of war to be brought into harmony with the ultra-humanitarian goal of world revolution which such a war presumably helps to achieve. For the same reason, it is not even possible to agree on the meaning of peace. For the West peace is perhaps the co-existence of all nations within the framework of a peaceful balancing of interests, whereas in Marxist-Leninist thought peace is to be understood again only in connection with the world revolution achieved by conflict, i.e., by its temporary opposite. Where reason is an organ of the party rather than a timeless a priori capacity — and this is what it is in a world of conflicting interests, i.e., in the dimension of politics — there is a confusion of the concepts of reason as well as a confusion of languages.

We thus come up against a fact which can only be understood theologically, namely, the fact that reason is not a relic of creation surviving in the Babel world of conflict; it is itself involved in this world, in the historicity of man. Even as regards his rational nature man is a fallen creature. Roman Catholic theology expresses this in its distinction between the true *natura* of reason and the fallen *conditio* of man. Man's condition derives from the fact that in the fall there was a loss of *rectitudo;* reason no longer ruled over impulse but came into subjection to man's impulses, desires, and hopes.[10] Luther brings out the same idea by comparing reason to a harlot: It prostitutes itself for interests and supports all kinds of idolatry with arguments. "Reason mocks and affronts God . . . and has in it more hideous harlotry than any harlot. Here we have an idolater running after an idol . . . as a whorechaser runs after a harlot." [11] Thus the illusion of rationalistic pacifism is not just that it overestimates rational argument in politics but also that it rests on a profound, theologically based misunderstanding of reason itself.

This also shows how far a theological understanding of creation and the fall, and its attendant cosmology, make possible a realism which is unattainable in all forms of idolatry, including that of the deification of reason with the help of illusions. Political ethics, if theologically based, knows something of the reality of war as an expression of man's very existence. This is why one expression of existence, namely reason, cannot effectively be set over against another, namely war. In the Noachic world the forceful expansion of interests can be met only by counterforce.

The only rational argument against war when at least one of the contestants is a cynic is that such a war runs counter to one's own interest. This argument might be brought against atomic disputes, since these involve not only the interest of destroying the opponent but also that of self-preservation, and it would be illogical to combine the destruction of the other with one's own destruction. But this is again an argument of utilitarian reason, not pure reason. It is paradoxical that the general threat which the atomic bomb poses for all effects a co-ordination of interests and thus seems to produce momentarily a kind of universal reason.

Pragmatic Pacifism

In addition to idealistic and rationalistic pacifism there is yet a third type of which we would speak. Pragmatic pacifism may best be illustrated in terms of the political ethics of Leo Tolstoi and Mahatma Gandhi.

[10] See Jacques Maritain, *An Essay on Christian Philosophy,* trans. Edward H. Flannery (New York: Philosophical Library, 1955).
[11] *LW* 51, 374. See above p. 109, n. 45, and cf. Herbert Vossberg, *Luthers Kritik aller Religion* (Leipzig: Deichert, 1922), esp. pp. 31 ff.

Tolstoi

It might perhaps seem strange that we have not categorized the pacifism of Tolstoi, as so often happens, with that of the Christian idealists. It is true that Tolstoi rejected the use of force — whether military or that of the state — partly on religious grounds. It is also true that, following the idealist line of argument, he sought to make the radical commands of the Sermon on the Mount the principle of world order. Nevertheless, it would be a mistake to regard his ultimate motives as specifically Christian.

Perhaps we even miss the mark if we say that his motives were basically humanitarian. Though his thinking admittedly developed under the experience of a profound sympathy with human suffering, he is less moved by humanitarian emotion than by the rules of practical wisdom towards which he was impelled by what he strongly felt to be the relevance of the Sermon on the Mount. For him the radical demand of the Sermon on the Mount that we should endure violence — "Do not resist evil" (Matt. 5:39) — and practice non-violence was not alien to the world. He did not feel it to be too unrealistic, too uncompromising. On the contrary, he thought he detected in it a rule for mastering the world at a higher level.

In the diary of his later years he champions the idea that purely economic considerations confirm the correctness of the rules in the Sermon on the Mount: Resistance is too expensive, not merely as regards the gigantic miscalculation of war, but also in everyday disputes. For when we react to aggression and violence by force according to the law of retribution, there is a reciprocal expansion of the encounter, an intensification of the deployment and use of force on both sides, whereas if we were to let the hostile attack roll on, it would run itself to death, and the forces needed to resist it would not have to be expended. The use of force is such that by its very nature it seeks to elicit resistance. The drive toward an increase in power which is present in all power works itself out not merely in a tendency towards expansion but also in the joy at overcoming resistance, because power flourishes precisely where it is resisted. Thus power seeks both quantitative expansion and qualitative intensification. If we withhold the resistance on which it depends, it simply plays itself out and is quickly spent.

Perhaps it is too bold a conjecture to see in these thoughts of Tolstoi less the influence of the Sermon on the Mount and more the influence of the Russian landscape, whose endless extent suggests the strategic device of offering only light, token resistance to invaders in order that they may be allowed to run themselves to death in the vast expanses of the country. From this standpoint the non-resistance of Tolstoi is not primarily ethical. It is dictated by a "metaphysics of moral economy." [12]

These economical, energy-conserving tactics are designed first to cause the opponent either to perish through his own deployment and expenditure of force or to come to his senses by perceiving its futility. They are also designed to cause the disputes and antitheses of life to play themselves out and neutralize one another in this way, so that a state of happiness and peace will emerge. As we read in the diary of his later years, "Active Christianity is not a matter of doing something, creating something; it is a matter of absorbing evil." [13] There is thus a note of irony in the word "active": I become active by passively accepting evil; this is how the great processes of evil's self-destruction are set in motion.

Behind this theory there is thus a eudaemonistic urge not to apply moral effort or other activity to hopeless beginnings or to enterprises which can be accomplished — and bring happiness — by more economical means. There is here more of Epicureanism than of the Christian obedience which dares to act in faith, without counting the cost and without calculating the chances and possible gains.

Linked with this — and here is the most revealing point — is the fact that this energy-conserving technique for living does not spring from the motive of love, at least in the New Testament sense. For the love intended in the gospel is love which gets involved, which consumes itself and is ready for sacrifice. Such involvement is directly opposed to the goal of Tolstoi's economy of life, which is more in the nature of a basic self-preservation, or, if you will, a new and much sublimer form of sacred egoism.

Thus in Plato Karataiev Tolstoi depicts a man who exudes love for men, for all men in an impersonal way, but who does not thereby es-

---

[12] Karl Holl, *Gesammelte Aufsätze zur Kirchengeschichte,* II (Tübingen: Siebeck, 1928), 446.

[13] See the June 12, 1898, entry in *The Journal of Leo Tolstoi,* trans. Rose Strunsky (New York: Knopf, 1917), p. 234.

tablish real communication with any particular man.[14] He thus protects himself from the kind of involvement in the lives of other individuals which might be dangerous to him in terms of the sympathy it elicits or the personal demands it makes upon him. The possibility of communication is here so attenuated that even greetings and farewells, while they are tender and imply unending (if impassive) good will, do not carry with them any true vibrations of the soul.

Having spoken of the Epicurean element in this theory of life, we thus find also a Stoic ingredient, namely, the attempt to keep one's distance, to remain aloof, in order to avoid disappointments and arrive at a state of energy-conserving impassivity.

One sees here how impossible it is to interpret Tolstoi in the psychological categories suggested by his autobiography. The original experience of sympathy may well have been the initial motive which set him on this line of thought. It may well have been due to the intensity of this sympathy that his theory of life attempted to overcome the consuming element, and the self-destructive force of this sympathy, by discovering the technique of aloofness, of passive withdrawal from the battle of life. Nevertheless, sympathy is only an incidental attribute of this attitude to life. The substance itself has long since broken free from the residual husk of sympathy and moved off into other areas.

What is involved here is neither a pacifism of humanitarian love nor a pacifism which in idealistic fanaticism seeks to do away with the orders of this aeon and bring in the kingdom of God by force (Matt. 11:12). Involved is rather the pragmatic judgment that sees in pacifism the best, most energy-conserving technique for living. It is not a matter of overcoming or transcending the world order but of attempting to implement and establish its true intention which has been distorted by the exercise of force, namely, the intention to master life by bringing order and peace to the world with a minimum of effort and expense.

Gandhi

The same pragmatism is found in Gandhi, though here it is much more complex and difficult, being set against a religious background which involves far less severe tensions between non-teleological love

---

[14] See Holl, *loc. cit.*

(lived out in faith) and pragmatic political intentions. Max Weber distinguishes between an ethics of disposition and an ethics of responsibility,[15] and it is fruitful to consider Gandhi in the light of these alternatives.

By ethic of disposition or of ultimate ends Weber means commitment to unconditional norms which in their Christian form might be characterized by the imperative: "Do what is right, and leave the result to God." If God has commanded it, I dare not ask about the consequences of doing it, for they are then no longer my responsibility. But the man who bears political responsibility cannot achieve this disposition which is committed to unconditional norms, for he *is* responsible for the results of his actions and hence must consider the conditions under which he will act. In other words, he and his action are caught up in the nexus of means and ends.

This does not mean for Weber that political action is ethically neutral. On the contrary, the politician must ask responsibly whether an end is worthful and important enough to "justify" questionable but necessary means. Nevertheless, unconditional demands, whose results he may leave to God, are exorbitant and unrealistic. For the sake of his ends he must be ready to do evil to others, risk the use of morally dangerous means, accept guilt, and thus "endanger the salvation of his own soul." [16] In the ethics of political responsibility, therefore, the command not to resist evil becomes instead the very reverse: "Thou *shalt* resist evil, and by force — otherwise you are responsible for evil's winning out." [17] To turn the other cheek, unconditionally and without asking what right the other has to smite, is "an ethic of indignity, except for a saint." [18] In this distinction between an ethics of disposition and an ethics of responsibility one can see traces, though not all and not the most decisive traces, of Luther's doctrine of the two kingdoms.

How does Gandhi fit into this scheme? Can he escape the alternative with his non-violent methods? Is it possible to follow an ethics of disposition and yet also to achieve political results, to keep clean hands and yet be strong?

[15] See Max Weber, *Politics as a Vocation*, trans. H. H. Gerth and C. Wright Mills (Philadelphia: Fortress, 1965), pp. 46 ff., and esp. p. iii.
[16] *Ibid.*, p. 53.
[17] *Ibid.*, p. 46.
[18] *Ibid.*, p. 45.

In innumerable cases Gandhi is understood in terms of such a synthesis, and consequently as a living refutation of the principle of force, of means to an end, in politics. Since solutions by force seem to become more and more questionable in an atomic age, his program appears to offer a way out of the historical dilemma which has arisen with the advent of super-weapons and the consequent self-contradiction of war.

If Gandhi does represent this synthesis, he may seem at a first glance to be the very opposite of Weber's ideal politician. We find in him statements which derive from a clear-cut ethics of disposition. E.g., he will not accept the thesis that the end justifies the means. Accordingly, he preaches the readiness to suffer in the face of injustice. He espouses with rigid consistency the principle that the methods of conflict are more important than the end. "Our movement," he can say, "is essentially religious. It is the business of every God-fearing man to avoid evil irrespective of the consequences. He must have faith that a good act will bring only good results." [19] As a result his acts are often illogical from a political point of view because they accord with categories whose sphere is not that of politics. As he himself says, he often refuses to prophesy or even to consider what may be the outcome of certain measures because it is enough for him to know that the proper disposition requires them.

Nevertheless, it would be a mistake to see in this practice of a pure disposition the attempt to pursue politics in aloofness from all pragmatic or tactical considerations. On the contrary, for Gandhi the two things go together. He holds that in a specific *situation* — this is very important and we will deal with it in a moment — the consistent maintenance of a disposition which is pure, committed to non-violence and ready to suffer, is the best strategy for attaining the end in view. This synthesis is grounded in the philosophical axiom that honesty is the best policy, to act according to the truth is to act wisely, and the means that are pure are the means best adapted to the end in view. Thus Gandhi's preaching of disposition involves at one and the same time — not as a mere addition or accompaniment — the pragmatic

---

[19] The quotation from Gandhi is cited without reference in Wilhelm E. Mühlmann, *Mahatma Gandhi. Der Mann, sein Werk und seine Wirkung* (Tübingen: Mohr, 1950), p. 213; cf. Jawaharlal Nehru, *Toward Freedom: The Autobiography of Jawaharlal Nehru* (New York: Day, 1941), pp. 72, 83.

conception of moral warfare; the preaching of pacifism implies also the mobilization of forces which, though secret, are nonetheless effective in attaining the intended goal.

Similarly, it is a matter of both tactical cleverness and faithfulness to the proper disposition when one does not give way to emotion and acts of violence, not merely because these would morally discredit the resistance movement, but also because they would transfer the moral initiative to the opponent and enhance his fighting power. Consistent non-reaction on the contrary has a deadly effect on the enemy. If he sees himself compelled by the passivity of his opponent to be only an inflicter of suffering, unable to establish the validity of his own cause by doing some suffering himself, this drains from him the passion for his cause. It tears him apart morally, and also pulls out from under him the launching platform which is basic to the exercise of his physical superiority.

The idea behind this laissez faire principle is thus very like the pragmatic approach of Tolstoi's pacifism. When the enemy is forced into the position where he can only act, and is never involved in the tension of action and reaction, his unilateral action simply runs itself to death. "If we carry out this doctrine in practice," says Gandhi, "the [British] government will be forced to succumb. The suppression will lose its edge because there is no reaction, just as an arm outstretched to strike is dislocated if it finds nothing there to hit." [20] This statement, which could have been made by Tolstoi, has a different nuance only to the degree that in Tolstoi there is not the same balance between religiously grounded morality and pragmatic considerations, but the pragmatic consideration seems to stand on its own feet. If we are right, this may be seen especially in the fact that Gandhi deliberately seeks the kind of involvement which Tolstoi pushes into the background. Gandhi's call for non-violent methods is made in such a way that he demands the investment of the whole person and a readiness for any sacrifice.

Against Gandhi the theological objection has been repeatedly urged that his theory of political encounter, if carried over into the system of co-ordinates of Reformation ethics, would involve a confusion of the two kingdoms. The patient suffering of evil belongs to the kingdom on the right hand, while it is one of the laws of the temporal kingdom

[20] Mühlmann, *op. cit.*, p. 174.

that it cannot escape from the Noachic laws of force. Although we ourselves accept this definition of the relation of the two kingdoms, we are forced to state that the theological objection which sees in Gandhi such a confusion of the two kingdoms is mistaken in its facts. For Gandhi's campaign is set within the sphere of a historical situation which by its special structure seemed to commend the attitude of forbearance, patience, and non-violence also from a *tactical* standpoint, as being quite realistic and consonant with the conditions of the temporal kingdom.

To this degree there is here no illegitimate transferral from the one kingdom to the other. We are rather confronted by an exceptional situation in which the intentions of both kingdoms — at least as concerns the action demanded — point in the same direction, so that the two ethics distinguished by Max Weber are for a moment congruent. In certain circumstances, then, Gandhi's mode of fighting may be a legitimate form of conflict in the kingdom on the left hand. It is thus wrong to number Gandhi among the idealists.

On the other hand, those who make Gandhi's principles the guiding principles of a general pacifism, thereby uprooting them from the solid soil of a concrete situation, are undoubtedly idealists. By this act they indeed achieve a confusion of the two kingdoms such as (*mutatis mutandis*) is not present in Gandhi.

The Relevance of Non-Violence to Atomic Disputes

We have repeatedly called attention to the specific situation within which Gandhi's pragmatic pacifism [21] is legitimate. In conclusion we must describe this situation more precisely. This is necessary for two reasons: first, because this is the only way in which to show how precisely Gandhi's non-violent method fits the situation, i.e., is within it an appropriate political means to specific ends, pragmatically oriented; and second, because only thus can it be demonstrated that this type of pacifism is not applicable in every situation — quite apart from the fact that it is so intimately connected with a charismatic (not just a talented) politician like Gandhi.

Three conditions set this particular situation apart from others.

[21] It is surely clear by now that this designation does not have reference to a pure pragmatism, but simply denotes a pacifism which rests on a particular coincidence of the ethics of disposition and the ethics of responsibility.

The first is that it is historically unique in form and scale. Its unprecedented character is what makes possible a surprise victory: it runs counter to the whole tradition as regards treatment of an opponent in matters involving colonial rule, conquest, war, and police action. This is why the historic rules of military strategy could not be applied, and because they could not the result had to be uncertainty and confusion, and the consequent loss of resolution and of ability to fight. There can be no doubt, however, that as this method of passive resistance becomes a general, acknowledged, and customary mode of conflict it will lose the strategic advantage it had in Gandhi's case and be met by appropriate counterstrategy.

Second, Gandhi himself is clear that the ethics of disposition can bring political pressure to bear, and overcome an opponent, only under specific conditions; it cannot be applied unconditionally and in blindly doctrinaire fashion. The non-violent method functions, according to Gandhi, only when it is practiced by not too small a minority,[22] and it functions best when practiced by a numerically overwhelming majority. Thus the Indians were the vast majority compared with the numerically small forces of the British government. Forceful action of this kind demands great numerical strength.

The method of passivity thus aims at success. The numerical proportion between friend and foe is nicely calculated. Passive resistance is not purely an act of confession, in which the resister is prepared to stand or fall unconditionally and without regard to success. This might be true in the case of individuals, but it does not apply to the resistance as a whole. The aim is kept clearly in view. There is clear understanding of what one is after, and of whether it can be accomplished.

Gandhi's allusion to the not too small a minority reminds us of the idea we noted in Tolstoi, namely, that the tactics of non-reaction, of yielding, demand a large space, vast quantities of land and of men, in order that acts of violence may trickle away in infinity. This causes us to reflect on the differences in size and population between the lands of Tolstoi and Gandhi on the one side and the tiny lands of western Europe on the other. This contrast alone shows how difficult it is to carry over this kind of pacifism into radically different parts of the world.

[22] Mühlmann, *op. cit.*, p. 214.

The third and final distinctive feature of Gandhi's situation is perhaps the most important of the conditions which allowed his non-violent method to succeed. It calls sharply into question the hope that passive yielding might be a suitable means of conflict where atomic weapons seem to have reduced the use of force to an absurdity. It shows that one cannot assert the applicability of the method to the conflict between East and West simply because it proved successful in the experience of Gandhi. Such an assertion contains a fatal error, and overlooks the close tie between a fundamental decision — even at the ethical level — and the given situation in which that decision is made.

This essential feature of the situation was that Gandhi had as his opponent a constitutional democracy. In spite of the questionable nature of British policies, the men in charge could not act as if ethical norms were non-existent. It is true that they could wink at what was going on, as happens in politics. It is true that they could even use ethical principles as a pretext for very different and highly egoistic manipulations. They could thus be guilty of hypocrisy, or else make no secret whatever of their sacred egoism ("my country, right or wrong"). All this was quite possible. What was not possible was that Gandhi's effort should make no impression on a political power which at bottom acknowledges ethical principles. Such a government is bound to be embarrassed and stymied when its opponent sets it so continually and publicly in the wrong, simply by acting according to distinctly ethical maxims — and suffering.

Along with the strategic aim of having the opponent's physical power trickle away by being spread too thin there was the plan to cripple him morally, to which we referred earlier. Neither the officials on the scene nor public opinion back home (which was never left in the dark, as happens in totalitarian regimes) could in the long run endure being pictured as murderers and terrorists. Yet this was the picture that inevitably emerged as they continually had to seize "innocent" men, men of peace who put up no resistance, who when they are reviled — or dispersed or even shot down — do not revile in return. The penetrating demonstration of the Indians' good conscience while the British were forced to be the sole perpetrators of violence, unable to break the powerful resistance of the enemy at some personal cost (and therefore with some moral justification) much less to act in self-defense – all this has a paralyzing effect on people who have even the remotest ideal of chivalry and pay at least some modest heed to conscience. For a humanitarian conscience it is quite intolerable that it should rampage like a beast of prey in a herd of sacred cows. This capitulation before what was intolerable is the goal towards which Gandhi's psychological strategy maneuvered his opponents. He used their own virtues to render them helpless.

It is for this very reason, however, that the transfer of Gandhi's principles to the East-West conflict seems highly questionable. For the question arises at once whether the opponent who fights in the name of Marxism-Leninism would react in the same way, whether the psychological calculation would not be completely erroneous in his case. Quite apart from the way the lives of men are so largely manipulated in the ideological world, in Communist ethics unilateral acts of extreme violence can still stand under the moral shelter of the ideal goal, namely, world revolution and a just social order.

The observation that Gandhi's form of pacifism, both in respect of its aims and in respect of its ends, is linked with a historical situation that is highly distinctive and in no way typical, shows us how little one can speak here of the triumph of an ethics of disposition over an ethics of responsibility, and also how little we can overlook the pragmatic features of this pacifism. The success of the experiment, therefore, is not a refutation of the doctrine of the two kingdoms but only a special application of it in a very special case. The attempt to hold up to Western Christianity a critical mirror in the person of the "heathen" Gandhi can be legitimate and meaningful only insofar as we are supposed to see in him a person of humbling purity of disposition and integrity of action. The mirror is quite unable to provide a model for Christian action in a very different situation. The attempt to achieve a Christian solution of the atomic problem by following Gandhi, and to impress a Christian seal on the self-defeat of violence through the renunciation of the use of violence, is an attempt to attain an impracticable object by impracticable means.

28.

Conscientious Objection

The Basic Question and its Modern Variants

When we come to speak of conscientious objection it is imperative that we first understand the problem and the way to approach it. It is important to point out that we are no longer dealing with the basic question of war itself and how it is to be understood, whether war is legitimate or illegitimate and what place it has in the world order. Of this we have already spoken at length. As we take up this new theme it is important to note that we face instead a twofold problem of political ethics.

First, there is the question as to what ethical right the individual has to decide against war, and on this basis to refuse military service. This is a problem of conscience. It thus is and remains an ethical problem, even in cases where the factual and theological grounds on which a particular decision rests may be regarded as dubious. There can be no circumventing the question as to whether conscience is to be respected — and also defended — even when it is in error, or is thought to be in error. If this question is not broached, if it is dismissed without a hearing as illegitimate, the implication is that the conscience is, or ought to be, under tutelage. The conscience as such is regarded as immature, or as the monopoly of a chosen few, or as the prerogative of a particular institution which helps to make the decision on behalf of the ethically immature.

Thus a strict differentiation has to be made in theological ethics between discussion of two questions which are not the same: first the basic problem of war, and second the question as to what dignity is to be accorded an individual decision of conscience regarding war in general or a particular war. This is why it is a fatal error when, as so often happens in theological ethics, the fundamental rejection of pacifism appears to be tantamount to a denial of the right of consci-

519

entious objection.[1] Where this is so, these two questions are not distinguished but confused.

Second, there is the task of establishing the ethical duties devolving upon the state in consequence of this respect for the individual conscience. Does such respect mean that the state must make the question of its own defense a matter of completely free decision on the part of each of its citizens, or that it must allow the officially declared duty of military service to be avoided at least in specific cases? Would not respect for the ethical dignity of the individual conscience lead to an undermining of the ethical authority of the state by preventing it from discharging one of its essential functions, that of protection and defense?

But even assuming that the state is ready to make this dangerous concession to conscience, what possibilities does it have of distinguishing a conscientious decision against military service from a purely political opposition to, and even sabotage of, its considered measures? Questions multiply at this point, and we can allude only to some of them.

Here too the directives of the Reformers and of the Reformation confessional writings offer little help, and least of all when Luther, e.g., speaks directly of the right of refusing military service. For subsequent developments in politics, and especially in war itself, have basically changed the problems and put them in a completely new

---

[1] In Roman Catholic moral theology the question of conscientious objection crops up for the most part only indirectly, in relation to the question of the just war waged by a legitimate ruler. Although conscientious objection is then a theoretical possibility — insofar as the individual may judge the legitimacy of a particular ruler (though not the justice of his war) — in practice the possibility hardly exists. Cf. the statement of Pope Pius XII: "If, therefore, a body representative of the people and a government — both having been chosen by free elections — in a moment of extreme danger decides, by legitimate instruments of internal and external policy, on defensive precautions, and carries out the plans which they consider necessary, it does not act immorally. Therefore a Catholic citizen cannot invoke his own conscience in order to refuse to serve and fulfill those duties the law imposes." (Pope Pius XII, Christmas Message of 1956; Vincent A. Yzermans [ed.], *The Major Addresses of Pope Pius XII* [St. Paul: North Central, 1961], II, 225). Thus Roman Catholic theology does not draw the distinction we draw between a general theological position on the problem of war and the decision of the individual conscience. Individual decision plays a lesser role because the individual lacks the maturity and competence to judge the necessity and admissibility of a particular war — responsibility for such a judgment having been taken from him by a duly authorized institution — and because he cannot object to war in principle inasmuch as the teaching office of the church affirms, on his behalf too, the legitimacy of a just war.

light. There are three points in particular at which this change is apparent.

First, the sixteenth century had no constitutions laying down the rights of the state and the rights of the individual, and protecting each against violations by the other. For this reason the refusal of military service as a constitutional problem within a complicated complex of legal, political, and ethical concerns could not even arise in the sixteenth century. But today the problem is characterized by precisely this complex of interrelated questions. At the time of the Reformation it cropped up only in the form of pastoral admonitions: subjects should not support unjust wars, and princes should not wage unjust wars.

Second, the corresponding problem of conscience was incomparably less complicated at the time of the Reformation because the average citizen could more easily distinguish the rights and wrongs of the little wars of the time (and even the bigger Turkish war) than is possible for the average man today, confronted as he is by great wars which he cannot properly comprehend and by modern techniques for beclouding the issues and concealing the facts.[2]

This is why the directives of Luther in this matter, clear though they are in principle, are hardly practicable today. For as he puts it the question of legitimacy or illegitimacy of a war is answered in terms of whether that war is just or not, and to know the answer to that question presupposes a knowledge not only of the goal of the war but also of its origins, especially of whether it is a war of aggression or of defense. To expect such knowledge of the modern citizen is to demand more than was demanded of citizens in Luther's time.[3]

Third, the difficulty of the problem is increased by the fact that

---

[2] See *ThE* 1, 412-414.

[3] Luther asks, "What if a prince is in the wrong? Are his people bound to follow him then too?" (*LW* 45, 125). He answers, "If you know for sure that he is wrong, then you should fear God rather than men (Acts 5:29), and you should neither fight nor serve, for you cannot have a good conscience before God. 'Oh, no,' you say, 'my lord would force me to do it; he would take away my fief and would not give me my money, pay, and wages. Besides, I would be despised and put to shame as a coward, even worse, as a man who did not keep his word and deserted his lord in need.' I answer: You must take that risk and, with God's help, let whatever happens, happen. . . . since God will have us leave even father and mother for his sake (Matt. 19:29), we must certainly leave lords for his sake. . . . If they put you to shame or call you disloyal, it is better for God to call you loyal and honorable than for the world to call you loyal and honorable" (*LW* 46, 130-131).

the Reformation message on its ethical side could count on hearers whose world of values was somewhat homogeneous. Apart from the left-wing fanatics, no one disputed such concepts as authority, military service, obedience, etc.; at most only their application to concrete cases aroused discussion. Thus the state could count on a relative uniformity of will on the part of its subjects so long as it observed the underlying criteria whereby that will was formed, i.e., did not cause too great offense to the Christian conscience. The state could thus assume – and Reformation ethics only served to strengthen the assumption – that the question of refusing military service would constitute no great handicap so long as the war did not conflict too blatantly with Christian ideas of a just war.

But this condition of relative homogeneity has undergone a drastic change in the modern period. This is true not only in respect of the greater philosophical and religious differences, which in part bear on the questions of war, pacifism, etc., but especially in respect of the range of factual judgments which necessarily broadens with the trend toward political maturity.

A final factor of significant difference between then and now is the fact that in a democratic state people can, and in large measure have, organized themselves into groups which powerfully influence and even limit the will of the government. In the matter of refusing military service such groups can play a role whose significance is not to be underestimated. This change in the structure of state and society complicates the problem considerably and, where there is unrestricted freedom of conscience, involves the state in frictions which necessarily pose a serious threat to its security and to its fulfilling its tasks.

To the decrease of inner homogeneity, whether philosophical and religious on the one side or political and social on the other, there necessarily corresponds an increase in the homogeneity of the will established by the state. There may even be a temptation to totalitarianism, a development which can in fact be avoided only if the problem is clearly grasped. In any case, the state is compelled to enforce its will and thereby to establish the binding nature of its laws and sovereign acts. Otherwise it runs the risk of becoming merely an umbrella organization embracing a confused complex of warring individual and group tendencies, in which case it would cease to be a state in the sense of a divinely willed order.

The result is that in this matter of refusing military service the conscience cannot be allowed an unconditionally free decision. If it is argued that the decision of conscience is an obligation before God, then appeal can be made to the fact that the state too, and the exercise of political power, is likewise an obligation before God.

Two points, therefore, are important in this connection. First, the right of refusing military service on grounds of conscience cannot be simply affirmed or denied; it involves a whole host of ethical problems. Second, the complexity of the question is closely connected with the changed conditions resulting from modern forms of state and society. Unless in our ethical treatment of the problem we keep constantly in view the concrete situation, the specific historical background, we shall never really see the problem aright but only lose ourselves in abstract declamations.

The Reasons for Refusing Military Service and the Appeal to Conscience

Fundamentally, there are two very different types of reasons for refusing military service.[4] The first type derives from the religious or philosophical sphere and leads to a rejection of war as such, i.e., to pacifism of whatever variety. Groups representative of this type are, e.g., the Quakers, Mennonites, and Jehovah's Witnesses, though we include here all those who oppose war as a matter of disposition or confession, whether Christian or humanitarian in the secular sense. In these circles there is no need for the individual to decide whether a particular war is just and justifiable, since every war is regarded as unjust and unjustifiable.

The second type derives from the sphere of factual judgment and undergirds the objections raised against a particular war or particular methods of waging a war. Here there is a wide range of possibilities in detail. Thus it is conceivable that a war may be regarded as ethically unjustifiable because it is thought to be a war of prevention or aggression, or because one is not persuaded that it is truly unavoidable. Again, it is conceivable that a war may be regarded as

---

[4] For the sake of simplicity we shall use the term in a broad sense to cover both peacetime military service and active participation in war, though there are admittedly cases in which the repudiation of the latter need not mean a repudiation of the former.

hopeless and to that extent politically insane. Again, it may be that in a given situation it will seem that for the forseeable future there cannot possibly occur a war which would be ethically, or politically, or ethically *and* politically justifiable; hence all preparations for such an eventuality are rejected.[5] Again, and finally, it may be that war is regarded as outmoded in the atomic age. Not that one is a pacifist in principle and by confession; he may even accept the Reformation understanding of war as justifiable or at least theoretically possible in the historical situation of that time. But he recognizes that in the atomic age war is no longer an action which, as in the earlier thinking, can fulfill political functions. Pacifism is thus adopted, not as a matter of principle, but in the light of the circumstances of the age, and on the basis of a factual evaluation of modern weapons technology.

In all these and similar cases the declaration of opposition to war, whether in general or in face of a specific conflict, rests on a casuistical appraisal of the given situation. The number and diversity of such attitudes, whether for or against war, will increase as the sense of individual responsibility and political maturity becomes the more widespread.

Now it would be quite false to attempt to distinguish between these two types of reasons in terms of their presumably different ethical dignity, as though the first type were radically ethical and the second only relatively and conditionally ethical, or as though ethical reasons and factual reasons, reasons of disposition and reasons of judgment, were mutually exclusive alternatives.

The second reasons too, those based on factual judgment, can represent ethical positions of the first order. Indeed, ethical positions as a rule (a rule which, as we have seen, is only confirmed by the exception to it) are intimately bound up with assessments of the situation, and with judgmental decisions. This is obvious in the present instance. He who regards a war as completely hopeless and therefore politically insane may, e.g., be expressing responsibility for his nation and for humanity when he refuses to participate. The same ethical responsibility may find expression in the demand that no Christian should take part in the construction, testing, or use of atomic weapons;

[5] Thus West German rearmament following World War II was opposed by many on the ground that in a divided Germany it could only help to promote an unacceptable civil war.

or in the conviction that an atomic war, whether offensive or defensive, can only be blasphemous massacre.

One cannot discount the ethical character of these positions on the grounds that they rest "only" on a subjective evaluation, and that they involve a twofold pretension: first, by claiming that such evaluation is at all possible and that one's own subjective opinion is a serious objective appraisal, and second, by claiming that this opinion, inflated to the status of an objective appraisal, is to be accorded the rank of an ethical conviction and a confessional stand. On the contrary, an evaluative judgment in a vital question can unquestionably be binding on the conscience. This is true at least on two presuppositions.

The first is the particular judgment that relates to a truly vital question. One hardly need prove that the question of war and peace is indeed vital in this sense. Evaluative judgments in questions of utility, e.g., tariff or traffic regulations, do not usually have any affinity to the disposition, and consequently cannot be determinative of a confessional stance.

The second presupposition, if an evaluative judgment is to bind the conscience and have ethical dignity, is that the one who judges should not have come to his conviction lightly and should still be open in principle to better instruction. To be more precise, his judgment should be grounded in a true effort at objectivity, and should not derive from an unobjective fondness for, or obstinacy in, his own opinion. In other words, it should be more than merely a pseudo-objective presentation of one's own foregone conclusions or prejudices. Where these two conditions are met, the ethical dignity of an evaluative judgment is not affected in the least by whether it is right or wrong, or whether the reasons for it are regarded as valid or invalid.

Two further questions arise at once. The first is the question as to what rank is to be accorded to ethically responsible judgments in the proclamation of the church. The second is the question as to how such judgments are to be put into effect, or what role they are to play, in politics.

The first question was particularly acute in the German churches after the Second World War, and the way in which it was presented and handled affords a good illustration. Prominent Protestant officials and church groups repeatedly made positional statements on questions of political judgment, e.g., the East-West conflict, the right of labor to share in the decisions of management, the flexible work week, and particularly the problem of war and conscientious objection.[6]

These utterances were not meant to be taken as the convictions of individual Christians, to whom the right of decisions of conscience in matters of fact would be conceded at once. Instead they raised the claim to be the voice of the believing community, declarations of the church itself in its office as watchman. They thus claimed the rank of potential synodical decisions and pulpit declarations.

The basis of the claim was seen again and again in the fact that those doing the speaking felt that the binding of their conscience by God's Word forced them into specific judgments, e.g., as to the madness and illegitimacy of atomic war or of West German rearmament, and that a decision of such provenance carries with it the postulate that it is binding on the church as such.

Now there can be no doubting the right and the ethical dignity of decisions in these and similar areas. Where doubt arises is with respect to the asserted conclusion that the decision is consequently binding on the church, and is to be proclaimed officially rather than as just a personal conviction. For it is conceivable – and experience bears this out – that other members of the church may reach different judgments, and that for their appraisal they can claim the same right of conscience, and possibly even greater technical competence.

If, then, an evaluative judgment is officially and even prophetically inflated on the grounds of its ethical rank, this means not merely that differences of opinion exist in the church, which is quite legitimate, but that the judgments behind these differences are articles of faith by which the church either stands or falls. They thus divide the body of Christ. Differences of political conviction are made to entail a choice between orthodoxy and heresy. It is thus evident that in questions of judgment the unconditional nature of a conviction of conscience cannot form the basis for the universal validity of church teaching. Within the framework of such universal validity there must still be room for a wide range of convictions on these matters of judgment.

In the final analysis what is involved at this point is a failure to give due regard to the doctrine of the two kingdoms. For here differences in the one kingdom are changed into differences in the other;

[6] We have in view especially the Niemöller-Heinemann group and the paper *Die Stimme der Gemeinde.*

divisions on substantive issues become divisive of the church. The very thing which links the two kingdoms and will not let them drift apart, namely, the fact that in both I am bound by the commandments of God and am responsible to him, can give rise to the misconception that in both kingdoms my responsibility to God is structured in identically the same way.

This misunderstanding carries with it two possible consequences. The first is that I claim for factual judgments in the kingdom on the left hand an authority which goes beyond the merely factual, thereby arrogating to myself the kind of prophetic authority which is connected with the spiritual kingdom. The second is that I carry over factual judgments into the kingdom on the right hand, thereby disrupting the unity of faith by the party distinctions of this aeon.

Judgments of conscience may indeed be unconditional. But the quality of unconditionalness is not the same in the two kingdoms. In the kingdom on the left hand it is an unconditionalness "for me," in the kingdom on the right hand an unconditionalness "for all." In both cases there is a need to impart the unconditionalness to others. But in the first case I can meet this need only by arguing the point and convincing others through factual discussion, whereas in the second case I do it by preaching (Acts 4:20; I Cor. 9:16; Jer. 20:9). To preach when one should argue, or to argue when one should preach, is to confuse the two kingdoms. This means that it is illegitimate for Christians to demand that the church make the refusal of military service an obligation of conscience, for to do this would be to change unconditionalness "for me" into unconditionalness "for all."

The second of the two questions of which we spoke has to do with how ethically responsible judgments are to be put into effect, or what role they are to play, in politics. This question goes far beyond the specific problem of refusing military service. As will be recalled, we faced it already in connection with the right of resisting state authority.

We pointed out that in the modern constitutional state there are certain legal ways in which effect can be given to convictions of conscience based on factual judgment, even though these convictions conflict with measures prescribed by the governmental authority. Thus an official may resign his office, and in a parliamentary democracy conscientious objection may be expressed indirectly by ballot.

Conscience may also impel one to resist directly and on the spur of the moment when governmental regulations would involve me in procedures forbidden by my conscience. This may happen, e.g., when by conscription I am compelled to join in making ready for a war which I repudiate for reasons of conscience, whether it be that I reject all war, or that I reject war in a particular situation or epoch, or that I am not convinced of the prophylactic or deterrent value of armaments. In such cases conscience may force me to refuse military service, whether or not my right to do so is protected by statute, i.e., whether or not I can do so legally.

The question which here arises is whether and how far the state can yield to these demands of conscience, offering legal possibilities for exceptional decisions of conscience. It is a question whether and how far the state can mitigate or even remove the possible illegality of such decisions.

The Situation of the State

The ethical problem thus arises for the state as well as for the citizen. It is one of the fundamental principles of every constitutional democracy that the citizens are not the objects, but also the responsible subjects, of political actions. This means that the individual must be respected and treated as mature. This can happen, however, only where there is respect for conscience. But such respect is impossible if the conscience is granted no freedom. Again, freedom cannot be granted to conscience without conceding that it is fundamentally possible for conscience to set its own ethical legitimacy over against that of the state.

The problem is an old one, and has played a part in the dialectic of law and morality – written vs. unwritten law [7] – for a very long time. To this degree the state is indeed ethically involved. The problem of refusing military service affords an excellent illustration of such involvement. For here the possible antagonism between the demands of the state and the demands of the individual becomes acute and

[7] See Immanuel Kant, *General Introduction to the Metaphysics of Morals,* in *Kant* ("Great Books," Vol. 42), p. 387; also *idem, Die Metaphysik der Sitten, Teil II: Metaphysische Anfangsgründe der Tugendlehre* ("Immanuel Kants Werke," ed. Ernst Cassirer [Berlin: Cassirer, 1922], VII), 234, 240; cf. Sophocles' *Antigone;* and Rudolf Bultmann, "Polis und Hades in der Antigone des Sophokles," in *Theologische Aufsätze. Karl Barth zum 50. Geburtstag* (Munich: Kaiser, 1936), pp. 78 ff.

looms larger in importance, at least just now at the dawn of the atomic age, than any other comparable concrete problem.

We have already seen from our introductory deliberations that there are here no easy solutions. It is not easy to mark off the respective spheres of competence. The complications which arise in respect of this problem affect the very character and existence of the state and produce a situation of authentic conflict.

To mention some of the main difficulties and considerations, we may recall first what we said at the beginning, namely, that the state can maintain and exercise its legitimate power only by fashioning a solidarity of will. It creates solidarity within by enforcing a uniform and general will through its laws and administrative measures, and it creates a solidarity toward the world outside by protecting its people from attack through its readiness and ability to defend itself. Both these tasks devolve upon the state by virtue of its position as a divinely authorized order of this world.

This order can function effectively only so long as conscientious objection to the measures it takes for its own protection — e.g., military service — remains the exception.[8] If through propaganda or the multiplication and activity of organized groups such objection were to become a mass phenomenon, or if the willingness to serve and the refusal to serve were to become equally legitimate and competing options, the situation of the state would be radically altered. Its function as an order would be radically affected. It is thus forced on grounds of the ethics relating to the state to set limits to the sphere in which the ethical decisions of conscience can have free play.

A second difficulty for the state lies in the fact that reasons of conscience may be mere pretexts. It is possible for groups which are political enemies of the state to make a hypocritical appeal to conscience purely for the sake of its political effect, in order that they may enjoy the protection of a constitutional state whose ethical foundations they perhaps reject. Just as opposition groups after the First World War formed semimilitary organizations under the guise of athletic societies, so it is conceivable that similar groups may practice a similar deception as conscientious objectors.

[8] Cf. the situation in Britain, where between 1939 and 1948 — including the years of World War II — only 2937 persons (including women) registered as conscientious objectors.

Third, it has also to be considered that conscience is not subject to any control. Courts have been set up in many lands to examine conscientious objectors, and psychological tests have been used. But these make sense only so long as the refusal of military service is exceptional. The moment it is practiced by organized groups there is the possibility of coaching in the right answers. Then governmental and military examinations become wholly illusory.

Fourth, the state cannot use other organs, such as the church, in its attempt to find out whether there is a genuine decision of conscience. If the church and its ministers had to play the role of inquisitors of conscience, this would not only open the door to hypocrisy. It would also discredit the message and the pastoral ministry of the church, and put the church in the wholly intolerable position of being an officer of the state — precisely at the point where it seeks to be the very opposite!

It is thus dangerous for ministers, even on subjectively honorable pastoral grounds, to offer to guarantee the integrity of conscientious objectors known to them in their parishes. In time of crisis this might lead to a mass movement in the direction of the pastor's study, and to corresponding orgies of hypocrisy. True conscientious objectors would thereby not be protected; they would be discredited.

Consequently it cannot be the task of the church to protect the conscience of individuals against the state. Its task is rather to work basically and generally for statutory regulations which will allow as much room as possible for conscience. It has also to resist any forceful violation of conscience. It does this in its office as watchman by holding up before the state the evil which the state may be doing or threatening to do, and, e.g., by publicly declaring when an oath has become invalid, thus freeing the consciences which were bound by it.[9]

Fifth, for the sake of conscience itself the state dare not be too generous in protecting those who refuse military service. For those who escape military service are also escaping burdens and dangers. This carries with it the dangerous possibility that the way of conscience may be easier rather than harder than that of those who do not have these ethical scruples, and that the decision of conscience

[9] See above pp. 397-405.

may consequently be dictated by the law of least resistance. A realistic view of man — and the Christian view is precisely that — forces us for this reason to distrust mass decisions of conscience. This is true at least when conscience chooses the outwardly easier way. But whether the way is really easier or not ultimately depends not least of all on whether the state makes the way of the conscientious objector easier or harder, on whether it punishes or patronizes the objector.

An analogous case may serve as an illustration. Whether or not in certain circumstances there may be an obligation of conscience to dissolve a marriage, it seems advisable that the state should make legal divorce difficult. If it does not, if the state makes the contracting and ending of marriage simply a matter for individual decision, it can certainly expect a rapid rise in the number of divorces, a decrease in the public estimation of marriage, and an accompanying appeal to "the voice of conscience," whether in conscious hypocrisy or unconscious self-deception. Here again the way of conscience would be the way of least resistance, and the question would arise as to whether it is a way of conscience at all. Even at the risk of making its legislation appear unjust and oppressive in individual cases, the state must make divorce difficult in order not to make too great demands on the weaker conscience of the great majority, and thereby bring conscience itself into disrepute.

When the conscience which claims to be exceptional suffers under the law and its rules, the temptation of opportunism is removed. Instead it is summoned to self-criticism: Am I really speaking only in the name of conscience? Is this something I really must do unconditionally? Or am I conditioned by considerations of utility or fear?

Sixth, from all this it follows that the state must insist on its right to pass conscription laws and to have them respected. If this involves the punishment of those who refuse military service on ethical grounds, this need not be out of any disregard for conscience. On the contrary, it may express a high regard for conscience. For if there were no punishment, conscientious objectors and draft dodgers would be put on the same level. It is difficult for the naked eye to distinguish between reasons of conscience and reasons of cowardice when it comes to the refusal of military service.

An honest objector will see this, and fear. For the sake of his ethi-

531

cal concern and the integrity of his action he will not wish it otherwise. He will therefore claim no exceptional ease for the way of conscience, and he will readily recognize in principle the right of the state to demand conscription. For only by this recognition can he make three things clear. First, he is not expecting the state to spare him personal sacrifices by sacrificing its own legislative rights and therewith calling in question its very being as a state. Second, he acknowledges the basic tension between legality and morality, and does not desire that it be resolved just for his benefit. Third, by his refusal he does not wish to call the state itself in question or come under the suspicion of espousing anarchy.[10]

The honest objector can thus claim no protection. He must be ready to suffer. He will take his stand, not as a stateless individual, but as a responsible citizen, one engaged in that conflict which is inherent in the state and in the human existence which is bound to it. "This readiness to suffer, which proves that the rejection of military service does not spring from fear of the sufferings of war, is the true touchstone of the genuineness of the refusal – a genuineness which demands respect."[11]

We referred just now to a conflict resulting from the fact that man has both a moral and a political existence, a conflict which is reflected in the dialectic of legality and morality. It may also be seen in a conflict of the state with itself. At least, this is to be expected when the state is prepared constitutionally to respect the moral responsibility of the individual. For then the state can no longer see itself merely as an autonomous institution standing in unequivocal tension with the moral responsibility of the individual. Instead, it then shares in this responsibility. The state itself is composed of these very individuals! In a parliamentary democracy such moral individuals are the ultimate bearers of the state. As voters, they *are* potentially the government. Hence the conflict between legality and morality is necessarily a conflict between the state and itself.

The orders of the fallen world – including the order of the state – do not possess the unequivocal status of creation. The values and

---

[10] Karl Barth, *Church Dogmatics*, ed. G. W. Bromiley and T. F. Torrance (Edinburgh; T. & T. Clark, 1936 –), III⁴, 467.

[11] Walter Künneth, *Politik zwischen Dämon und Gott. Eine christliche Ethik des Politischen* (Berlin: Lutherisches Verlagshaus, 1954), p. 391.

norms which they embody do not meet at some ultimate point. On the contrary, they are in conflict. The orders of this aeon are such that they cannot be harmonized or brought under a common denominator. Tragic drama speaks of this conflict of values even, indeed precisely, when its theological significance lies beyond the dramatist's field of vision.

In theory, i.e., in constitutional principle, this conflict often remains hidden. It is lost in the peaceful coexistence of articles which set forth generally approved ideals and seem not to clash. But the moment they are put into practice, the moment a question arises like that of how to handle conscientious objection, the conflict of values is evident. In the narrow quarters of the specific case the values clash, e.g., equality before the law and freedom of individual conscience. So too do those who represent the values, e.g., the state and the individual.

Since the matter has to be faced and action taken, the conflict must be resolved in some way. But there is no easy solution. There thus arises the ethical problem of compromise. In theological terms, and in the sense which we have in view, compromise is therefore the form of action within the emergency orders of this aeon.

This statement commits us to realistic sobriety. For it certainly teaches that any radical solution will rest on a misunderstanding of what the orders of this aeon can achieve. This is particularly true when the radical solutions are ideologically inflated, and either the universal duty of service or the full freedom of individual decision is lauded as the ideal. Christian ethics might well make a vital contribution simply by showing how fanatically unrealistic these absolutizations are, and by bringing to light the theological background of such lack of realism.

Possibilities of Regulation

If the conflict is inherent in democracy, and if in principle there can be no easy solution, this does not mean that the state is therefore justified in deciding on one of two radical alternatives: either an uncompromising insistence on universal military service and a complete suspension of the constitutional principle of freedom of conscience in this particular sphere, or the concession of unlimited play to the individual conscience and the practical introduction of completely voluntary military service. For in the case of the first alternative the state would be fanatically overlooking or violently setting aside the tension of values in which it is implicated. And in the second case it would in part be doing the same thing – challenging equality before the law and making the distribution of the burdens of state dependent on the whim of the individual – and in part impairing its own capacity to function effectively as a state.[12]

This means concretely that the state must be ready to compromise in order to do justice to both principles. In consequence, it cannot avoid distinguishing between conscientious objectors. The difficult problem, which defies any wholly satisfactory solution, is that of the criteria to be applied in making such distinction.

Two criteria which suggest themselves in theory cannot in fact be used, as we have seen. First, the state cannot distinguish between objectors whose refusal rests on a philosophical pacifism that repudiates all war, and those who as a matter of conscience reject a specific war, or a specific mode of war, e.g., atomic war, on the basis of a factual judgment; for both these decisions of conscience can have the same ethical rank. Second, the state cannot distinguish between true objectors on the one hand and opportunists, cowards, and habitual dissenters on the other, for conscience is invisible. This fundamental inability to read the motive necessarily leads to incalculable consequences, both political and otherwise, if the state regards any arbitrary appeal to conscience as sufficient ground for granting an exemption from its legislative requirements.

Thus the state can accept only those distinctions which (a) offer some guarantee that the motives underlying the objection are truly those of conscience, (b) are based upon a certain tangibility attaching to the decision of conscience, and (c) are so structured that they can apply only to a limited number of cases, thus offering safeguards against an incalculable quantitative extension and intolerable political and military complications. These three limitations in respect of the manner of distinguishing among objectors are themselves only very indirectly ethical. They rest rather on the pragmatic consideration of how under certain conditions, especially where the very existence of the state is threatened, the state can do some kind of justice to the

---

[12] One need only imagine the extension of the principle of voluntarism to the area of taxation in order to see its political consequences.

ethical question of freedom of conscience. Since the state itself has by nature a pragmatic side, the ethical aspect, while it is not obliterated by such considerations, can come into play only indirectly at this point in virtue of the fact that the pragmatism of the state — e.g., its desire for power and for the capacity to use it effectively — is itself ethically justified and must submit to ethical criteria in its application.

The three conditions mentioned seem to be met, if not very fully, in the case of certain religious or philosophical groups such as the Quakers,[13] Mennonites, and Jehovah's Witnesses. For here we have, first, clearly defined societies, so that for the state a measure of visibility attaches to the circle in which the decision is made — as distinct from other equally serious decisions which are not visible. And second, the recognition of conscientious scruple is limited to a specific group of citizens, so that the state is protected against any threat to its own existence.

Reference should also be made to another quality of these societies and groups which may suggest how it is possible for the state to dispense from military service in limited number other persons who are not at all connected with these societies. The convictions of these groups are not determined solely by the thesis of non-violence and the repudiation of war. On the contrary, this thesis is itself an easily checked deduction from the totality of the basic teachings concerned.

The fact that the rejection of war is grounded in the totality of beliefs enables the state in two respects to deal generously with the objectors involved. First, it can be sure that conscientious objection does not rest on an *ad hoc* decision but has behind it a long preparation and derives from quite other than political considerations. If it were simply an *ad hoc* decision, as in the case of many other objectors, it might be equally serious, but externally it might well seem that

---

[13] As regards the Quakers, their rejection of military service is very interesting and not at all doctrinaire. For although they reject war and are prepared only for alternative service (particularly as medics), and although their rights are recognized in Anglo-Saxon countries, many of them voluntarily enlisted as combatants in 1914 under the influence of the crusading propaganda. Here freedom of conscience in respect of military service is doubly compounded. First there is the general freedom of the whole company of Friends as it stands solidly over against the state, appealing to conscience (the "inner light") and claiming dispensation from military service. And second there is the freedom of each individual as he stands over against his "friends," appealing to the "inner light" and claiming the freedom in extreme cases to go ahead and render military service — "voluntarily" to be sure.

the appeal to conscience is merely a pretense. Second, there is some measure of assurance that in times when the problem becomes acute there will be no mass movement into these societies to swell their numbers with those who simply wish to exploit their privilege of conscientious objection.

There are two reasons for such assurance. First, since these societies have a comprehensive legacy of beliefs, and since these beliefs are bound up with a specific manner of spiritual life and conduct, it is usually easy to detect the outsiders who come in for ulterior motives.[14] And second, whereas a league of radical opponents of war would have to seek political power to achieve its aims, and would thus have to seek the greatest possible number of adherents, the societies mentioned (and others too) are not interested in achieving their goals by pressure, and are thus clearly protected against any large and sudden influx of members.

Although legislative provision for exceptions is thus conceivable in this matter of military service, the state cannot wholly suspend equality before the law. Hence it cannot grant unconditional relief. That is to say, it must demand equivalent service which, so far as possible, will be of such a kind that it comes very close to normal military service in terms of sacrifice for the common good and also in terms of danger.[15]

It may also be noted that in practice the only groups to which such legislation may be applied without suspicion are those which practice their freedom of conscience even when this is not conceded to them by the state. Their readiness to suffer is a sign that their decision is truly one of conscience.

This discussion of the ways in which the state can distinguish between objectors and do practical justice to conscientious scruples is naturally not to be construed as an attempt to formulate binding casuistical directives for Evangelical ethics. In the course of this work we have often enough pointed out that theologically qualified directives of this kind are impossible, since there is no such casuistry.

---

[14] Think of the difficulty an outsider would have in meeting the demands for Bible study and personal sacrifice of the Jehovah's Witnesses without being unmasked.

[15] In their readiness for alternative service the Quakers are a model. At great risk they gave medical help to friend and foe alike in two world wars. See Rufus M. Jones, *The Faith and Practice of the Quakers* (London: Methuen, 1927).

Our discussion is intended simply as an experiment in thought, a model, to show what considerations must be borne in mind in arriving at a concrete political decision in respect of conscientious objection.

The specific conclusions to which such a discussion might lead, e.g., in a representative assembly, could be quite different. Indeed, if I were a practicing politician, I might myself reach very different specific conclusions in specific situations. But the considerations to be taken into account would be the same.

This, then, is our decisive and basic conclusion: The state can never achieve all-around and wholly satisfying justice in dealing with exceptional cases like that of conscientious objection. If it treats all alike with radical equality, it does wrong to those who cannot be treated according to the common rule — the rule of Lord Omnes (Luther) — because in one way or another they do not fit the pattern.[16] But if it treats each one differently, it does wrong to itself, and hence indirectly to all, since it robs itself of its power to establish order. In face of an exceptional right, the state can seek to be only minimally and not maximally just. This is evident from the fact that out of all the objectors to war it can accept wholly and unequivocally only an infinitesimally small contingent, and that the criteria according to which it can fix this contingent depend upon judgments that are certainly subject both to debate and to change.

In the last resort, the inability of the state to do justice to each and all is grounded in the fact that it is in no position to achieve a satisfying balance among the basic maxims of its own constitution. These have, and will continue to have, contradictory features, for the rift in the world affects the state too. The state stands in the half-light between what it ought to be in virtue of its origin, namely, a divinely willed institution to guard against chaos and to help bring the world through to the last day, and what it actually is, namely, an objectification of man himself, and consequently a reflection of the cleavage in man between creation and sin, blessing and judgment, destiny and present condition.

The state is an emergency order between the fall and the judgment. Herein is its dignity and its limitation. Herein is the ultimate defense

---

[16] Rationing, e.g., would be unjust if it were to allot the same portion to the old woman with an appetite like a sparrow and to the young man who eats like a horse.

against its being ideologically overinflated. And herein too is a call to sobriety, a warning against either demanding or expecting too much of it. The virtue of sobriety, which is to be numbered among the political virtues, is a fruit of faith. For faith knows the background of the state. It therefore sees its limitation. But faith also perceives in the state a sign of hope set up by the Lord of history himself. Thus faith does two things for the man with a political mandate: it enables him to act with sovereign freedom and assurance, and it enables him to strive for — and live with — solutions which are admittedly only partial and limited.

Part Four

THE THEOLOGICAL DEBATE ON CHURCH AND STATE

29.

The Roman Catholic View of Church and State

It cannot be our task in this fourth part to survey the whole range of questions relating to church and state. Actually, the political ethics we have been developing in this volume is itself one long explication of this overall theme. By its very nature, a theological ethics of politics has implicit within it an interpretation of the state and its functions which derives from the message preached by the church, and this interpretation implicitly includes the church-state relation.

Naturally, the subject of church and state can also be understood in a narrower sense. One may think, e.g., of the legal and institutional connection between the two, in which case treatment of the theme belongs properly to the study of law, and we cannot deal here with the particular problems — including ethical problems — which are involved. Again, one may think in terms of the fundamental distinction and connection between the two spheres of competence. This approach involves a whole host of subsidiary problems, among which we might mention the question as to how church and state are related as representatives of the two kingdoms; the question as to how the church in its office as watchman is to speak on concrete questions of the state, politics, and public affairs in general, i.e., what kind of political preaching is incumbent upon it;[1] or again, the question as to how far the church may resist an unjust state and what assistance it can give to those who resist on grounds of conscience.

These special problems, however, are not to be dealt with as a question apart, under the rubric "church and state." They actually arise within the larger framework of systematic ethics in general. For good methodological reasons, therefore, we have discussed them in the relevant contexts, e.g., in our treatment of the two kingdoms, the orders, the constitutional state and the totalitarian state, the right of resistance, the refusal of military service, etc.

[1] See below pp. 617 ff.; cf. also *ThE* 1, 586 ff.

Since in every case we developed these themes in terms of a theological conception controlled by Lutheran thinking, however, there is need — despite our continuing deliberate self-criticism — for a concluding orientation with respect to non-Lutheran approaches to the problem. We have of course touched on these already more than once. But they have cropped up so sporadically in the course of our presentation that it was hardly possible for a well-rounded picture to emerge. To supplement what we have already said, therefore, we shall now sketch briefly first the Roman Catholic and then the Reformed views of the state. Our concern will not be to paint a full portrait, but only to focus on possible points of comparison in respect of specific questions which have arisen during the course of our basic presentation.

The Theocratic Tendency in the Interrelating of Spiritual and Temporal Power

According to Roman Catholic teaching, at least in its modern form, the state is grounded in natural law. Thomas Aquinas held that even if there had been no fall society would still have been constituted in the state.[2] It is the very nature of man which "commands all to contribute to the public peace and prosperity."[3] What all must do, however, and how they must do it, is not learned from nature. It is left to the wisdom of "competent authority."[4] But as thus qualified, this authority, even as regards its statutes, will keep within the limits of nature and its laws.

In this light the state is not under the theocratic tutelage of the church. On the contrary, church and state are both autonomous powers, each supreme in its own sphere: "The Almighty, therefore, has given the charge of the human race to two powers, the ecclesiastical and the civil, the one being set over divine, the other over human, things. Each in its kind is supreme, each has fixed limits within which it is contained, limits which are defined by the nature and special object of the province of each, so that there is, we may say, an orbit

---

[2] See Thomas Aquinas, *Summa Theologica*, part 1, ques. 96, art. 4.

[3] *Libertas Praestantissimum*, 9, encyclical letter of Pope Leo XIII, June 20, 1888; in Etienne Gilson (ed.), *The Church Speaks to the Modern World: The Social Teachings of Leo XIII* (Garden City, New York: Doubleday Image Books, 1954), p. 63.

[4] *Ibid.*

traced out within which the action of each is brought into play by its own native right." [5]

If such formulations were taken alone, it would seem that what we have here are two completely separate and empirically independent spheres. But this is by no means the case. The areas of competence actually overlap, so that there is a belt of tension on the boundaries where they intersect. We would mention three aspects of this matter of intersection.

Christians as Members of Both Spheres

In the first place, both powers have to do with the same men. In personal union these men are at one and the same time citizens of the state and members of the church. Hence "it might come to pass that one and the same thing — related differently but still one and the same thing — might belong to the jurisdiction and determination of both." [6] Among such mixed matters may be mentioned marriage, schools, education, etc. These things come under the dominion of the state on the one hand, insofar as they must be ordered by its laws. But on the other hand they are also connected with the salvation of souls and with the order willed by God.

Since it has to watch over both of these, the church for its part is also interested in the regulations imposed by the state. It is for this reason that the two spheres of competence have to be demarcated by way of concordats involving both political and ecclesiastical law. "There must, accordingly, exist between these two powers a certain orderly connection, which may be compared to the union of the soul and body in man. . . . One of the two has for its proximate and chief object the well-being of this mortal life; the other, the everlasting joys of heaven." [7] The conclusion of concordats which will safeguard and institutionalize this relation between the two raises a host of legal problems, since a concordat is not possible in every state. It is possible only where a state is able in terms of its constitution to accord recognition to the church. [8]

---

[5] *Immortale Dei*, 13, encyclical letter of Pope Leo XIII, November 1, 1885; Gilson, *op. cit.*, p. 167. Quoted by permission of Catholic Truth Society, London (see "The Pope and the People," p. 51).

[6] *Ibid.*

[7] *Ibid.*, 14; Gilson, *op. cit.*, p. 168 ("The Pope and the People," p. 52).

[8] Cf. Ernst Deuerlein, *Das Reichskonkordat* (1956), p. 217.

The fact that such legal regulation of the relation between church and state is necessary shows that the relation is potentially loaded with conflict. This is particularly true in the case of the modern secular state, partly because it is not aware that its power is derived from God — and it accordingly deduces no duties from this fact — and partly because it construes its relation to God differently from the way Roman Catholic teaching understands it (think for example of the denominationally, or religiously, or philosophically pluralistic state). From the Roman Catholic standpoint the basic rule for such arrangements is that "whatever in things human is of a sacred character, whatever belongs either of its own nature or by reason of the end to which it is referred, to the salvation of souls, or to the worship of God, is subject to the power and judgment of the Church. Whatever is to be ranged under the civil and political order is rightly subject to the civil authority." [9]

The State Defined by Natural Law, Which Is in Turn Defined by the Church

A second aspect of the intersection of the two spheres arises from the fact that the secular state cannot know of itself "what is according to its nature." For "the present condition of the human race" [10] leaves nature in disorder — the *rectitudo* lost [11] — and hence unknowable. What nature is can be perceived only when its orientation to the "supernatural end" [12] is discovered.

If we do not have this insight — and this is true in the case of the secular state — we shall be confused as to the immanent state of nature and hence also as to the true nature of the state. [13] We may think, e.g., that a totalitarian state answers to human nature. The natural limits of the state will inevitably be hidden from him whose eyes are closed to the upper section of nature because of the loss of the supernatural end.

[9] *Immortale Dei,* 14; Gilson, *op. cit.,* p. 168.
[10] See Chapter 2 on "Revelation" of the Constitution on the Catholic Faith promulgated by the Vatican Council of 1869-1870 in *The Church Teaches: Documents of the Church in English Translation,* trans. John F. Clarkson, John H. Edwards, William J. Kelly, and John J. Welch (St. Louis: Herder, 1955), No. 59.
[11] On the loss of the *rectitudo* see ThE 1, 204 ff.
[12] *The Church Teaches, loc. cit.*
[13] On this relation of nature and supernature see ThE 1, 203 ff.

Thus the nature of the state, and also its apparent autonomy — as defined and sustained by the concept of nature — are brought under the superior authority of the church. For, after all, it is the church to whose knowledge and control the supernatural end is entrusted. The church is thus the normative court which passes legitimate judgments on the qualities of nature, e.g., the nature of the state. Logically, then, this is why its teaching office has defined in terms of natural law a specific order of state and society [14] — while leaving room, of course, for significant variations in concrete actualization.

Yet we would be doing Roman Catholic moral theology an injustice if we were to suggest that in terms of its own self-understanding it thereby rides roughshod over the state and with a theocratic claim prescribes the latter's task. For in principle the Roman Catholic church always has to accept the fact that the orders of state and society are not authoritatively stipulated by its teaching office but are disclosed to all men by natural law. The only question, though, is whether man in the present condition of his existence is open to the message of nature, or whether he is not obstinately closed against it.

For the Roman Catholic church, then, a "Christian" state is not one which is ruled or regulated by the church. It is not a church state, a theocracy. In principle the state "never is a *super*natural community or in itself Christian." [15] It is Christian (in an admittedly figurative sense) only when it is "according to nature."

This seems at a first glance to be a contradiction, but the contradiction is easy to resolve for those who think in terms of natural law. For "only Christianity can proclaim the principles and order of the natural law with that reliability and rightness which the State needs as a firm foundation." [16] Only Christianity knows of the correlation of creation and redemption, nature and supernature, and hence also of the true character of man within this correlation.

Thus the state is a true and valid state in the sense of natural law only when it is "conscious of this relationship and draws from it the

[14] See, e.g., *Quadragesimo Anno*, the encyclical letter of Pope Pius XI dated May 15, 1931; text in William J. Gibbons (ed.), *Seven Great Encyclicals* (Glen Rock, New Jersey: Paulist Press, 1963), pp. 125-168.
[15] Eberhard Welty (ed.), *A Handbook of Christian Social Ethics,* trans. Gregor Kirstein and John Fitzsimons (New York: Herder and Herder, 1963), II, 214.
[16] Welty, *op. cit.*, pp. 214-215.

necessary conclusions for its conduct." [17] It is conscious of this relationship, however, only when it allows itself to be told what nature is by the only authority competent to do the telling. In this sense a state which is according to nature is also a Christian state.[18] The one is impossible without the other.

If the state would know what it is by nature, and what it therefore ought to be *de facto*, it must come to see its nature – like nature generally – within the context of the hierarchy of nature and supernature. It can do this, however, only as it secures the relevant information from the church, which alone has knowledge of supernature and is thus able to embrace within a single perspective the total order of creation and redemption. I.e., it has to be Christian.

Conversely, if the state seeks to be Christian, it cannot attain this end simply by asking Rome what it should do, and thus trying to integrate itself into a theocracy. Rome would disclaim any competence in this sphere and refer it back to the obligations imposed on it by natural law. The state would thus be referred back to its own authority.

But it would have to admit that as a secular state it does not know its own proper nature, or what it really ought to be, with the requisite "clarity" and "assurance." It would then have to be taught by the authority which knows both "the basis and the goal of all things" – and hence also the way in which nature is embedded between the two.

Thus is the circle closed. On entering it, we find ourselves in a system in which natural law has its own authority and is not just under tutelage to the supernatural law of the church. Nonetheless by a roundabout way it is still brought back under the authority of the church, i.e., by the argument that fallen man has a corrupt nature, that he therefore neither knows nature nor has access to it but must be led back to it by the uncorrupted guardian of the blessing of salvation. Indeed, one might formulate the intentions of Roman Catholic thinking on the state as follows: By right of natural law the state is autonomous to be sure, but it cannot get back to the nature intended by natural law except by way of supernature.

---

[17] *Ibid.*, p. 215.

[18] This is why Leo XIII can speak of a "Christian order of the State" and a "Christian state" even while emphasizing the natural origin of the state and its norm in natural law. See Welty, *op. cit.*, pp. 215-216.

Whoever does not understand the theological context, might regard this ambivalence as hypocrisy, and charge that Roman Catholicism is only pretending to recognize the independent authority of the state — or even of philosophy — while in fact it is constantly interposing the authority of the church. If this charge is to have any validity, however, one must at least be aware that the interposition is theologically based, that it is a logical development from this base involving no immanent contradiction in the system itself. Charges of hypocrisy must not be raised gratuitously.

All the same, one may discern here a tendency toward indirect theocracy. For the church's claim to be the normative authority in articulating natural law necessarily implies that its teaching office is able to sketch the basic models of an order conceived in terms of natural law (as has in fact happened in the truly grandiose encyclicals of recent popes).

This claim means in addition that the state must not be allowed to let its concrete orders go beyond these basic models. To make its weight felt to this end it is necessary for the church to operate from positions of strength. These may be attained in many different ways, e.g., by way of political parties and social groups, through concordats, and through the position of the pope as an earthly sovereign who even conducts foreign affairs.

He who establishes the basic models will also have a tendency to want to see to their actualization, even their detailed execution, especially if he cannot trust the state to know and discharge — and observe the limits of — the authority which accrues to it by natural law. This is what gives rise to the tendency which is usually referred to, disparagingly, as political Catholicism.

In the present context it is not our purpose to refute this charge but only to define it more precisely (precision sharpens the true tensions and relaxes the false). We do an injustice to the political tendencies of Roman Catholicism if we see in them an arbitrary lust for power that is merely tacked onto faith, as though what is involved here is nothing but the human, all too human, libido of the will to power. We have to realize instead that the tendency to seek political power is given in and with the theological point of departure. First, it is the church which is the custodian of natural law; the secular state has lost all access to it. Second, the church thus has the task of safeguarding and applying it. And finally, the question whether this task should have reference only to the general outlines of the basic models or should include the matter of their detailed execution, is a question of judgment, and hence depends on the particular circumstances involved.

In an address delivered at Rome on November 2, 1954, Pius XII makes a definite claim in favor of the church's authority even in matters of detail. Here he speaks out against movements which "presume to check and set limits to the power of Bishops (the Roman Pontiff not excepted), as being strictly the shepherds of the flock entrusted to them. They fix their authority, office and watchfulness within certain bounds, which concern strictly religious matters, the statement of the truths of the faith, . . ." Over against them the Pope argues: "The power of the Church is not bound by the limits of 'matters strictly religious,' as they say, but the whole matter of the natural law, its *foundation*, its *interpretation*, its *application*, so far as their moral aspects extend, are within the Church's power. For the keeping of the natural law, by God's appointment, has reference to the road by which man has to approach his supernatural end. But, on this road, the Church is man's guide and guardian in what concerns his supreme end. . . . Many and serious are the problems in the social field. Whether they be merely social or socio-political, they pertain to the moral order, are of concern to conscience and the salvation of men; thus they cannot be declared outside the authority and care of the Church." [19]

Reformation ethics does not commit to the church such a political task. In fact, it reacts quite strongly against all direct or indirect theocracies, for reasons we have already discussed.[20] Among the weightier reasons we would here mention only this one, that in the strict sense the different doctrine of sin in Reformation theology does not recognize natural law. For natural law presupposes that in spite of the fall a component of existence known as "nature" has remained in some sense intact from creation. The only result of the fall is that nature is "impaired." [21]

[19] Pope Pius XII, Address of November 2, 1954, to 250 cardinals, archbishops, and bishops assembled at Rome. *The Catholic Mind,* LIII, No. 1109 (May, 1955), 315-316.
[20] See *ThE* 1, 388 ff., 434 ff.
[21] See *ThE* 1, 207-210.

It is not true that for Reformation thinking the world is totally corrupt and has thus become more or less the domain of the devil. For the ontological categories of Roman Catholic thought it is natural to interpret the Reformation doctrine of sin in this way, since they necessarily regard every negative statement as a statement about qualities of being, whereas in Luther such statements refer only to man's "existence before God," i.e., not to his being as such but to a relationship in which he stands.

The Reformation, whether in Lutheran or Calvinist form, understands the fall then, not as something which destroys creation in the ontic sense, but as something which totally permeates it, so that it is necessarily illegitimate to divide creation into intact relics on the one side and elements of corruption on the other. If creation is a relational concept, i.e., if the term refers to creation "by" God and "before" God, then though the disruption of this relation is total it cannot wholly annul created existence. At any rate, one can no longer try to distinguish areas outside the relation which have remained ontically unaffected.

To take an example, let us suppose that mutual trust has disappeared from a marriage, which is a relation between two persons. The ontic qualities of the persons remain relatively intact. But now they all stand under the sign of this breakdown in communication, so that neither partner can see them clearly in the other. All the qualities, whether good or bad, stand under the verdict that they have contributed to the growing mistrust. They have all had a share in the disruption of the relation.

The misunderstanding of each church by the other rests to some degree on the basic difference in approach. Roman Catholic thinking tends to be ontologically structured whereas Reformation thought is more personalistically structured.[22] The difference leads to misunderstanding on both sides.

Now if Protestantism does not recognize a component of existence — a nature — which has remained relatively intact in spite of the fall, then logically it does not recognize or acknowledge natural law either. This fact has a further implication: Wherever natural law is accepted, it is necessarily credited with being able to set up in the positive

[22] See *ThE* 1, Chapter 12.

sense an order which corresponds to this intact component of existence, i.e., to creation, with the result that there arise those claims of the teaching and pastoral office of the Catholic church to which we have already alluded, claims which contain within them indirectly theocratic tendencies.

Reformation theology takes a different path. Perceiving the total permeation of creation by sin, it recognizes neither an intact component of existence nor — it goes without saying! — an ideal order of nature and creation in which this component of existence might be objectified and over whose "foundation, interpretation, and application" the church should exercise "watchfulness." Reformation theology thus finds in the Law of God for the fallen world, not directives for a positive order, but primarily a negative protest against disorder: "You shall not kill — because you *are* a murderer." [23]

In accord with this, the church in its office as a watchman has, on the Reformation view, a clearly defined function which leaves no place for theocratic tendencies. The world orders themselves are not matters of natural law. They cannot therefore be regulated by the church but are to be fashioned according to the rules of reason. Secular authorities are independently competent to do this regulating.

Because reason is fallen, however, chaos and disorder threaten. Thus the church, on the Lutheran view at least, discharges its office as watchman by being on guard against these negative factors, by issuing warnings, and preaching judgment. It does not preach natural law but is on guard against natural law-lessness.[24] It marks a path which is guttered on both sides by the depths of all that is contrary to God's will, but within which there are broad possibilities for reason to steer a political, economic, and social course in keeping with either its own basic conceptions (i.e., according to the particular political and economic systems) or the concrete circumstances involved.

It is for this reason that the church is here denied any voice. Here the two kingdoms must be differentiated. The church takes a position on questions in the kingdom on the left hand only insofar as they touch upon the kingdom on the right, i.e., only insofar as the commandments of God — not the interests of the ecclesiastical institution — are institutionally or actually transgressed (though violations of the

[23] On the negative structure of the Decalogue see *ThE* 1, 440 ff.
[24] See *ThE* 1, 444 ff.

church's interests, if they take place within the kingdom on the left hand, may also be protested). This happens when the institutions of the kingdom on the left hand, e.g., the state, seek to be more than merely secular constructs, when they try to be an anti-church, when they inflate themselves ideologically and in totalitarianism lay arrogant claim to the souls of men. We thus see that the pointed opposition of Reformation theology to theocracy and its respect for the secular sphere [25] root in its doctrine of the two kingdoms.

It might be profitable to compare the Roman Catholic form of this doctrine, e.g., in the extracts quoted from the *Immortale Dei* of Leo XII, with the corresponding Lutheran teaching. As we have seen, the Roman Catholic form of the doctrine implies that the church has an indirect but active influence on the shaping of the worldly kingdom by way of its knowledge and guardianship of natural law. By contrast, on the Lutheran view, the worldly kingdom is independent of the church. It is on its own. To be sure, on the Lutheran view too the church is not wholly excluded from the secular realm, as is clear from the very notion of the church having an office as watchman. But there is here no theocratic involvement. If the church stands in a continuing relationship to the secular sphere, this is simply because the two kingdoms are not only separated but also interconnected.[26]

In the present context we may mention especially two of these interconnections as seen in Lutheran theology. First, both kingdoms are grounded in the divine governance. They are simply two modes of the divine rule;[27] they thus come together in God.

Second, they are related by the fact that the Christian stands in both at one and the same time, and is summoned in both to obedience. Since love is the fulfilling of the Law, this means that even within the orders the Christian acts in love.[28] His action is not oriented primarily to the institutional side of the orders, but is conceived as service to his neighbor; the orders are understood as media through which he is related to this neighbor.

[25] On Friedrich Gogarten's distinction between secularization and secularism — which must be recalled here — see his works listed above at p. 152, n. 12 and p. 108, n. 41.
[26] See *ThE* 1, 373 ff.
[27] See Gustaf Törnvall, *Geistliches und weltliches Regiment bei Luther* (Munich, 1947). This first point is to be found also in the encyclical *Immortale Dei*.
[28] See *ThE* 1, 376 ff.

Luther in particular thinks at this point of the person rather than the institution, of the human side rather than the material and mechanical. In this respect he is different from Melanchthon, whose ethics is expressly defined in terms of natural law. This may be seen already in Melanchthon's concept of *societas*. He is dominated by "regard for an ideal state of human society which is to be sought after in all concrete action, and which thereby also provides the norm by which all such action is to be measured both as a whole and in detail." [29] Whereas for Roman Catholic theology, and to some extent for Melanchthon, the commandments of God in their givenness as natural law demand certain orders, and even specific ways of putting them into effect,[30] for Luther the commandments of God demand a specific attitude towards God and neighbor.

It goes without saying that for Luther these commandments do indeed influence the orders, yet not because they contain basic models (as in natural law), but because the relation to neighbor which they demand of the Christian, his concern for his neighbors' well-being both inwardly and outwardly, his love for them, already carries within it the question of orders which may be able to do justice to this task. Thus all the proffered possibilities of political, economic, and social order are set under the criterion of this one question; and how they are realized is left to the judgment of reason in the light of concrete circumstances.

The preaching of Law and gospel which is enjoined upon the church accompanies man as it were only to this point, where he sees that he is obligated to his neighbor in secular matters too. Then, according to his own insight and judgment, he goes on to seize opportunities to set up appropriate orders, or within existing orders to take appropriate action. The one thing which the church still does when

[29] Werner Elert, *Morphologie des Luthertums* (Munich: Beck, 1932), II, 29.
[30] This is true of Calvin only insofar as he thinks the orders of the church and the world should be fashioned according to the revealed commandments of the Bible. That there is natural law in Calvin is asserted by Günter Gloede, Theologia naturalis *bei Calvin* (Stuttgart, 1935), esp. pp. 178 ff., but denied — at least in the sense asserted by Gloede — by Karl Barth, "No! Answer to Emil Brunner," in Emil Brunner and Karl Barth, *Natural Theology,* trans. Peter Fraenkel (London: Centenary, 1946); cf. also Peter Barth, "Allgemeine und besondere Offenbarung in Calvin's *Institutio,*" *Evangelische Theologie* (1934), pp. 189 ff.; *idem, Das Problem der natürlichen Theologie bei Calvin* (Munich: Kaiser, 1935); and Wilhelm Niesel, *The Theology of Calvin,* trans. Harold Knight (Philadelphia: Westminster, 1956), pp. 39 ff., 92 ff., 229 ff

it leaves him go on alone at this point is to refer him to the limiting possibilities of public *dis*order, which would in any case be detrimental to his neighbor.

In political preaching this fixing of the frontiers — the guttered path — might consist in a positive advocacy of the authority of the state and hence a warning against letting the state degenerate into a mere nightwatchman, for a state bereft of authority simply abandons the neighbor to chaos and renders him none of the service of order which it owes. At the same time, the church can also issue warnings against allowing this authority to be extended unduly, to the point of totalitarianism. As it thus fixes the limits, the Evangelical church, acting in its office as watchman, is discharging a pastoral office, and that in two senses. For one thing, the church encourages man to accept personal responsibility, and within these limits to make active use of his reason. Second, the criteria for drawing these limits arise out of the question as to where the orders cease to serve man and begin instead to dominate him, and hence to impair his existence.

In contrast, the Roman Catholic church carries its office as watchman beyond this point. It does not merely indicate the frontiers between just order and unjust order, but by way of its control of natural law it also sketches the outlines, and possibly fills in the details of both.

The Implications of Christology and Ecclesiology

We have cited two aspects of the intersection between the church's sphere of competence and that of the state: Christians are members of both spheres, and the state is under the natural law of which the church is the custodian. We would mention now a third and final aspect of this dialectical intersection between nature and grace, secular order and church authority, an aspect which comes clearly into view at the point of Roman Catholic Christology and the Roman Catholic view of the church.

If God has resolved to give man supernatural grace, and to prepare him for this grace in the sphere of nature, this can only mean that the preparation relates to the whole range of nature, to the social being of man as well as to his individual existence. But this means further that the order of his existence in society is also referred to the order of redemption.

If in the person of the Mediator there is a hypostatic union between the godhead and human nature, then the social dimension of human existence is also encompassed within this union. It is this christological relevance of the social factor which gives the church a direct responsibility for the social order within the sphere of human nature. According to the Roman Catholic understanding, as the church itself is an extension of Christ, so the shaping of life in society is also determined at least in part by the incarnation. For what is taken up into the hypostatic union is human nature in all its modes of being, including the social.

What we have called the dialectical relation between nature and supernature in Roman Catholic thinking is what apparently comes to visible expression in the peculiar half-light which seems to lie over the relation of the church to the world and its political orders. On the one hand Roman Catholic moral theology emphasizes the independence of the secular authorities and acknowledges the state as the supreme power within the sphere of its particular functions; from this standpoint it can explicitly banish from the modern scene the theocratic system of the Middle Ages.[31] On the other hand, however, it asserts control over the worldly kingdom by regarding itself as the guardian of that normative realm wherein the independence of the worldly kingdom is grounded, namely, natural law – which definitely swings the pendulum in the direction of theocracy.

The Background in the History of Dogma

It is obvious that this carefully worked out system of relations must have come to its provisional final form only over the course of a long tradition, during which it would frequently have oscillated between the two poles indicated. The fact is that in all the various stages of development this dialectic has indeed taken concrete historical form. The one extreme may be seen in Boniface VIII (1294-1303), who regards himself as also the highest temporal authority, and who delegates [32] this authority directly to princes in the form of a *potestas directa*. But we overlook the theological background of the development if we try to explain the two-powers theory of Leo XIII in purely

---

[31] See Johannes Stelzenberger, *Lehrbuch der Moraltheologie* (1953), p. 348.
[32] Though the word "delegate" apparently was not used, it seems to convey what was really intended.

secular terms as a progressive clipping of the papal wings by a world awakening to a new sense of its own maturity. Such an exogenous explanation of the development completely misses the mark, or is at least only very partially on target.

The development of the traditional Roman Catholic teaching on politics is rather to be explained endogenously, in terms of the two polar forces inherent within the system — nature and natural law on the one hand and the church as the authoritative court of supernature and of Christ's worldly dominion on the other — necessarily coming to terms with one another and striking a balance. The modern dialectical form of the doctrine simply formulates and embodies the tensions expressed in all the various historical phases. The fundamental motif throughout is that political power goes back to God (is not of human origin), and that the church has thus to supervise the application and uphold the limits of this power.

The first stage in the development, namely, the *potestas directa* of the pope — and hence his unmistakeably theocratic position — is to be found in the two bulls of Boniface VIII, *Apostolica sedes* (May 13, 1300) and *Unam sanctam* (November 18, 1302): [33] According to the former, the principate by which heads of state rule and administer justice belongs intrinsically to the papal throne. The papacy has "conceded" to certain ecclesiastical and temporal princes the right to elect the Holy Roman emperors. It has thus merely *delegated* its supreme authority. All the honor, dignity, and rank which the empire enjoys — including even the power of the sword — has simply "flowed" into it as a grace, favor, and concession from this throne. Accordingly, in the further development of these ideas in the *Unam sanctam*, there are two swords, the spiritual and the temporal, and both are under the control of the church. To be sure, the relation to the church is different in each case: the spiritual sword is wielded by the church *(ab ecclesia)*, the temporal on its behalf *(pro ecclesia);* the one is in the hands of the priest, the other in the hands of kings and soldiers. But both are administered in the name of the church and at its behest.

Along similar lines Augustinus Triumphus (d. 1328) in his *Summa de potestate ecclesiastica* [34] advances the thesis that the papacy has

---

[33] See the texts in Carl Mirbt, *Quellen zur Geschichte des Papsttums und des römischen Katholizismus* (5th ed.; Tübingen: Mohr, 1934), pp. 209-210.
[34] Mirbt, *op. cit.*, p. 216.

power over all temporal and physical goods, and that worldly matters are to be given to emperors and kings only as their "hire." Here the delegated nature of earthly power finds pregnant expression.

In Bellarmine (d. 1621) we find at least the beginnings of a separation between the spiritual and the temporal power, though here the argument from natural law does not yet play any essential part. The relative independence of the temporal power finds expression in the fact that the pope is now assigned only a *potestas indirecta* in political matters.

Adopting an image of Gregory of Nazianzus, Bellarmine describes this power as similar to that of the soul over the body. Though "the pope has no temporal power in the pure sense," nevertheless, "with a view to what is spiritually best he has the supreme power to control the temporal affairs of all Christians," since otherwise evil princes might violate religion unchecked.[35]

In Leo XIII and succeeding popes this *potestas indirecta* is combined with the doctrine of natural law and thus integrated into the schema of nature and grace. But the use of this schema in the theological definition of temporal power is in no sense a discovery of modern Catholicism. It goes back to ideas present already in Thomas Aquinas.[36]

As thus developed, the doctrine of indirect or directive power *[potestas directiva]* allows for quite a variety of kinds of government. Thomas Aquinas regarded monarchy as the best form,[37] but Leo XIII in his encyclical *Diuturnum illud* of June 29, 1881,[38] favors the possibility of democratic states, and says that the custom of choosing rulers by election of the people is in full accord with Roman Catholic teaching. But even this seeming concession to what one might call a world come of age takes place within the framework of natural law, through the mediation of which the church again interposes itself as authority. For it should be remembered, says the encyclical, that the people as such is in no way authorized "to delegate or convey the rights of power," since it does not possess this power in the first

[35] *Ibid.*, pp. 359-360.

[36] See Thomas Aquinas, *De regimine principum,* in F. Schreyvogel, *Ausgewählte Schriften zur Staats- und Wirtschaftslehre des Thomas von Aquin* (1923), pp. 7 ff.

[37] See Walter von Loewenich, *Modern Catholicism,* trans. Reginald H. Fuller (New York: St. Martins, 1959), p. 323.

[38] Mirbt, *op. cit.*, p. 477.

place. The rights of power are conveyed by God. In democracy all that the people does is to designate by its election those who are to hold and wield the power. Power is not established by the people. Their decision has to do only with its exercise. Thus the power of rulers does not derive from the people but is a "share in the divine power." This is what gives it its more than human dignity.

Taken alone, these theses on the divine origin of political power simply say what we ourselves have been saying from the standpoint of Reformation theology. For we too had to take steps to avoid the misconception that the dominion of the people means the end of the state as a divine institution (in the sense of Romans 13) and its replacement by an institution of the people's own making. Our contention was that the state, even in its democratic form, exercises authority in virtue of its quality as a divine order. But this is unthinkable if the people undertakes to do the authorizing instead of seeing that it is itself set within the framework of a state which is already authorized in advance. The people can only decide to whom it should commit the exercise of this given power, this prior authority which is not of its own making.

Thus the theological statements of both confessions meet in respect of state authority. Nevertheless, one cannot ignore the fact that the Roman Catholic understanding of natural law as the source of this authority enables it to bring the concept, the forms, and the limits of the exercise of political power under the control of the *potestas indirecta* of the church's teaching and watching office. Thus even in the modern understanding of papal power, the frontiers are never radically sealed against theocracy. The debate between Reformation and Roman Catholic positions on this score is not yet at an end.

We should, however, pay heed to the important nuances of the controversy. With the help of the schema of nature and grace, and the related concept of the indirect or directive power of the papacy, theocratic ideas have been very highly sublimated in modern Roman Catholicism. Yet they are still there in principle. They have an indelible character in the Roman Catholic system. This is reflected in the fact that even the widest divergences in the interrelating of state and church, empire and papacy, have by no means been superseded and corrected. On the contrary, the whole tension of the tradition has been taken up into this newer sublimation (in the sense of Hegel).

The Implications for Catholic-Protestant Co-operation

This difference in theory between the Protestant and Roman Catholic views of church and state should not be exaggerated in respect of its practical effect, at least as regards the modern situation of the secularized state. For here, in face of the given historical factors, the theocratic drift of Roman Catholicism remains indirect in the extreme. To the readiness for self-limitation inherent in its theology, as expressed in the theory of the two powers, there is added the historical constraint that derives from the very structure of the modern state.

It is this structure too which causes the political ethics of the two confessions to come together despite their fundamental differences. For though the theocratic tendency of Roman Catholicism and the two kingdoms doctrine of the Reformation are very differently constructed, both lead in the end to a common front against secularism, i.e., against a world which seeks to transcend its worldliness by self-exaltation through ideologies, utopias, and philosophies.

Here again, as we have done before,[39] we would underscore Gogarten's distinction between secularism and secularization: The former promotes the self-exaltation of the world, whereas the latter implies merely its coming of age.[40] As a form in which the kingdom on the left hand exercises responsibility, secularization is theologically justifiable. Roman Catholic theology, of course, can concede this only in part, because the concept of "secularization," while it can include the maturity of a world which knows that it is under God, can in no case be understood theocratically. One might perhaps put it this way: Secularization implies emancipation from all theocracy in the name of one's own maturity, but it does not carry with it — at any rate does not necessarily carry with it in principle — any protest against the understanding of the world set forth in the doctrine of the two kingdoms (indeed, it can even express this understanding) whereas secularism connotes a protest against both positions. It is the fact of this common adversary, especially as it takes shape in the various forms of ideological tyranny, which makes it possible for the two confessions to go a long way as brothers in arms.

---

[39] See above p. 551, n. 25.
[40] On the concept of maturity and the world come of age see Dietrich Bonhoeffer, *Letters and Papers from Prison* (New York: Macmillan, 1962), pp. 194 ff., 208 ff., 224.

Even apart from this common front, however, the fundamental theological differences — as we have repeatedly suggested — do not imply any difference in concrete programs of social and political action. Here too the concrete implications of an ecclesiastically controlled natural law, and those of a conscience which though oriented to the kingdom on the left hand is also aware of its responsibility before God, may be very much the same. Thus the wisdom of papal encyclicals with respect to matters of political, social, and international affairs may often be admired on the Protestant side even though the underlying idea of natural law cannot be accepted.

This far-reaching parallelism in concrete programs is possible, for one thing, because of the fact that in the ethical sphere differences at the level of motives are not identical with differences at the level of acts.[41] This is why even where two do the very same thing it is in fact not the same. Behind a common action there may be a very different understanding of the action, and hence a very different motivation. This feature of ethics we have already described in terms of "interchangeability." [42] Parallelism at the level of concrete programs is possible, in the second place, because of the fact that between Evangelicals and Roman Catholics there is a broad common zone in the understanding of reason. Each in its own way knows something of the threat to reason, and of its redemption.

Nevertheless, in spite of this possibility of common decision and action in political ethics, there will be not a few borderline cases where the difference between the Roman Catholic and Protestant approaches is brought to light. This will be particularly true in areas in which the confessions are affected politically, culturally, and socially as institutions, e.g., in attempts to influence politics through persons, in educational questions, in the problem of mixed marriages, and in the constitutional and legal regulation of these (and not a few other) questions. Yet these borderline cases remain the exceptions which confirm the rule of possible co-operation.

The Problem of the Christian Party

This brings us to the final problem on which we need to comment, the problem of a "Christian party" embracing both Protestants and

[41] See *ThE* 1, 20 ff.
[42] See *ThE* 1, 17 ff.

Roman Catholics. If common action is accepted in principle, this would seem to imply the possibility of building a common political will by way of a common political party. Nevertheless, there are reasons for rejecting this implication, of which we shall mention only two.

First, the program of a political party – at least in principle – does not have the same significance for Protestants as for Roman Catholics. For Roman Catholics such a program has its basis in natural law. This natural law basis is such that it must necessarily find expression in a particular party because – for all the variety and elasticity it allows in respect of diverse concrete situations – it carries within it the general outlines of a political program, and hence also an impetus toward the building of a political will in keeping with that program. To this degree the idea of a Christian party flows naturally from the Roman Catholic understanding of natural law and of the relation between church and state.

For Christians in the Reformation tradition, on the other hand, the situation is radically different. Their theological ethics does not contain in principle any such program but is content, as we have seen, simply to indicate the concrete forms of natural law-lessness. This means that the idea of constituting a party of its own is in principle inconsistent with Protestant ethics. For such an idea would require not simply that the guidelines of political action be tested in terms of their encroachment upon the frontiers of natural lawlessness but also that positive programs be developed which could qualify as specifically "Christian" in distinction from all other programs.

What is more in accord with Protestant ethics is not to declare a specific institution (in this case a party) particularly Christian, but to have Evangelical Christians in all the various parties. According to the Protestant way of thinking, the adjective "Christian" applies, not to institutions, but to men. On the basis of their own maturity, and in responsibility to the commandments of God in the kingdom on the left hand, these men have to act independently and on the basis of the facts, deciding in favor of a specific program of action, whether by ballot, by active membership in a party, by helping to draw up party programs, or by representing the parties in government.

Thus the situation regarding political parties is different in principle for Protestants and Roman Catholics. This must be said, even though common political action — and consequently common action within one political party — is possible in principle. What should not be overlooked is that the basis of such a party is very different in the two cases, since on the Protestant view the party cannot be based on fundamental axioms. This question of the basis is obviously not a matter of indifference, as we shall see when we come now to our other objection to the idea of a Christian party.

Second, Evangelical Christians who belong to such a party or are active in it expose themselves to the misconception that the term "Christian" in the party title contains normative controls not merely for the theoretical program of the party but also for its concrete political measures. This suspicion is not damaging to Roman Catholics, since in part at least it correctly describes their fundamental position: the guide-lines do in fact have their norm in Christian natural law; they simply find specific embodiment in politics.

But the same is not true for Evangelical Christians. In principle, i.e., in terms of their faith, they can belong equally well to Socialist, Liberal, or other parties. It is thus possible that by belonging to a "Christian" party they open the door to the misunderstanding of which we have just spoken: as if matters of political judgment were to be decided in principle by specifically Christian criteria, as if there were, e.g., a distinctively Christian attitude toward armaments and atomic war (as indeed there is for Roman Catholicism, but in principle cannot be for Protestant ethics). This might conceivably carry with it — the possibility has to be taken very seriously — the further implication that Christians in other parties, by rejecting the "Christian" solution, are guilty not merely of political error but also of heresy.

To be sure, the word "Christian" occasions at least some hesitation and discomfort on the part of the Roman Catholic as well. In the sphere of principles and theoretical programs he regards the term as perfectly legitimate, but even he would not claim that every concrete implementation of the principles and programs, i.e., the whole gamut of tactical, pragmatic, technical, and opportunistic affairs from treaties to tariffs, can be similarly regarded as "Christian," specific embodiments of natural law. It is impossible to say precisely how far natural law extends to details, i.e., how far specific actions may be deduced from it. It can be said, however, that certain areas of action, e.g., tariffs, can certainly not lay claim to having been established under the criteria and authority of natural law. Hence even from the Roman Catholic standpoint there is always a certain risk involved in calling a particular party "Christian." Thus for both sides — and certainly for Christians in other parties — it would undoubtedly make things easier if a party consciously committed to the heritage and ethics of both confessions would avoid the term.

We thus have these two objections. First, the confessions have a different understanding of institution and person which is bound to have implications for their respective attachments to the idea of a Christian party. Second, the name Christian, which is a radical stumbling-block to Protestants, is equally dubious for Roman Catholics in the matter of day-to-day decisions, however legitimate it may be in the sphere of basic principles.

Nevertheless, even though the authentic Reformation solution is to allow Christians to co-operate with various parties and to join various parties, there are certain circumstances which seem to make it conceivable and even advisable to found a party which is specifically "committed to the heritage and ethics of both confessions." Without wishing to break up associations of long standing we would mention the following possibilities for consideration in terms of principle.

First, it is possible that there should be a specifically Roman Catholic party which is based on the principles of natural law and which elaborates a very detailed political program in the course of putting these principles into practice. Since the Protestant Christian can in principle join any party which does not fall under the verdict of natural lawlessness (like the totalitarian parties), and since it is possible for him to co-operate in practical matters with groups whose action rests on very different theological — or other — motivation than his own, it is altogether conceivable that Protestants should join with their Catholic fellow Christians in a party of this kind, and thus bring into being a common Christian party. Two critical questions would remain with respect to this possibility. First, might not a Roman Catholic party contain some theocratic or confessionally egoistic features which would make co-operation impossible? And second, even if this were not so, would the combination of circumstances indicating such union be enough both to outweigh the increased burden imposed on the Christians in other parties and to offset the misconception of a supposedly "Christian" norm in politics?

The second theoretical possibility is that, for all its ambivalence, a Christian party may seem to be indicated when there is a kind of political emergency in Christian affairs. Such an emergency might be of two kinds.

First, it might be that Christians in the other parties are in no position to implement certain Christian concerns, perhaps because they are too few or too weak in quality, or perhaps because the dogma and organization of the parties are so fixed and rigid that an alternative voice is not even granted a hearing. In such a case it might serve a useful purpose if Christians get together for the sake of the Christian cause in order to work in democratic fashion as a party endeavoring to shape the political will. One has to realize, however, that the built-in tendency of every political party to operate as a law unto itself means that this shaping of the will cannot be restricted to "Christian concerns" in the narrower sense (e.g., education, the church-state relation, the understanding of law) but will necessarily embrace the whole spectrum of factual judgments as well, the *adiaphora*. Agreement will have to be reached not merely in matters of moral theology and social ethics but also in areas in which there cannot be any common Christian norm. Thus it is obvious that there will be a certain imprecision about the designation "Christian."

Again, an emergency situation might obtain in the event of a historical catastrophe, when the very foundations of life are so radically threatened that a return to Christian substance must be ventured and politically effected in a direct way such as would hardly have been possible in normal times. If all other authorities break down — as happened in Germany in 1945 — the church itself may feel called, vicariously as it were, to spring into the breach on behalf of the kingdom on the left hand which has become totally ineffective. It may feel impelled to undertake such a venture because the emergency situation demands it.[43] The Christian party which might emerge in

[43] This is why it is wrong to criticize the gigantic assistance program undertaken by the Evangelical church in Germany after the war in 1945 on the ground that it wiped out the boundary between the two kingdoms by undertaking large-scale commercial operations (factories, transport, currency exchange, exports, imports, etc.) and by making its chief a director of operations extraordinary. Eugen Gerstenmaier, who guided *Hilfswerk*, has rightly pointed out in reply that the church had an emergency right to act in this way when there was a direct threat of death by cold and hunger.

such a situation will naturally undergo a structural change as circumstances return to normal. It will be faced increasingly by the question how it can achieve a common policy in areas where there is no Christian norm, especially after the situation which demanded its emergency diaconal help has come to an end. It can hardly be expected, however, that it should immediately dissolve once the emergency ends. For it is in accord with all psychological and historical probability that the common fight will have resulted not merely in a measure of communication among the personalities and groups involved but also in some new-found consensus as regards goals and methods, a consensus which will itself press for continuing nurture and expression.

The historical emergency, however, may not involve any breakdown in the effective operation of the kingdom on the left hand such as would call for direct Christian action. It may instead take a different form, e.g., when the threat is not political but philosophical, when the critical problem has to do not with order in the narrower sense but with the ultimate foundations of all form and order. Such is the threat, e.g., when one is exposed to the attack of an ideological tyranny such as Communism. If one is compelled to admit that in face of this threat all purely political or military considerations of strategy and tactics, indeed all merely humanistic and ethical stances, are inadequate, then implicit in such admission may be the demand that the forces of Christianity, as the only remaining power of resistance, should be mobilized with a political directness which does not accord with the indirectness demanded in normal times. Such mobilization can again be justified only on the grounds of the emergency situation.

One last ethical question arises in respect of such a Christian party once it actually exists. Then it is no longer a question whether it is desirable or not. The only question then is with respect to the policies it is actually pursuing, and whether one can accept them or not. Here the decision depends on two things: first, whether one can accept the foreign, social, and other policies of such a party from the standpoint of their political utility, and second, whether the implications of the term "Christian" in its title are obviously intended to remain an open question, so that there will be no doctrinaire appropriation of the word and so that justice will be done to Christians in other parties, and the body of Christ will not be rent by the claims of one party that it alone is Christian.

30.

The Reformed View of Church and State

Calvinist "Activism" and Lutheran "Quietism"

That there are discrepancies between the Protestant confessions in respect of the relation between church and state is acknowledged even by those who have little awareness of the underlying theological differences. Something of the extent of these discrepancies is indicated by the very fact that at least in this sphere they have become widely apparent. The oversimplified formula normally used to express the distinction is that, while Lutheranism is politically passive, allowing the state a wide measure of autonomous rule as an authority, Calvinism shows an incomparably greater and more active interest in politics, being concerned to bring it under a religious norm and control.

This common understanding of the political ethics of the two confessions is often thought to have found confirmation in a significant recent actualization of the distinction. In the struggle of the Confessing Church with the Hitler state — and with the "German Christians" who were its champions — it was unquestionably Reformed theology which took the lead, both as regards the theological and strategic undergirding of the conflict and the energetic waging of it. Even where Lutheranism put up notable resistance, as in Bavaria under Bishop Hans Meiser, its style of fighting was largely defensive as compared with the offensive strategy and tactics of the Reformed groups. There are, of course, exceptions to this rule. But on the whole the characterization is correct. Nor should one conceal its fundamental significance by advancing the empirical pretext that the Reformed side had an outstanding spiritual leader in the person of Karl Barth.

If we ask concerning the theological backgrounds of these manifestly different positions on the relation of the church to the state and to politics, we come up with a variety of answers. The task of our present inquiry is to test these answers, but also to undertake an independent analysis of this theologically determined distinction.

Two answers in particular immediately suggest themselves. The first is that in Reformed theology church and state are two distinct but equally direct expressions of the divine dominion. They should, therefore, not conflict but must be seen as standing together in some kind of analogous relationship, however that may be defined. To the church has been entrusted the Word of God, that Word in which God declares his will to be sovereign over both kingdoms and his purpose that both should serve his glory. For this reason it is the office of the church to watch over this matter of how the state is defined, and whether it remains in this analogy.

Thus does there arise what has been called a "political service of God" *[politischer Gottesdienst].*[1] The question whether a given state is Christian or not, whether its orders correspond to the commandments or not, whether it acts in keeping with the commandments or not – all this is not an additional concern of the church over and above that of its proclamation of the Word and its pastoral ministry. On the contrary, it is a direct part of the church's spiritual responsibility, an area which calls for a forthright Christian stance. This is why the church can consider itself called to active resistance – even to the point of initiating or at least supporting violent revolution – if the state becomes tyrannical, if it hinders the preaching of the Word or in other ways resists the divine commandments.

In his October, 1898, Stone Lectures at Princeton [2] Abraham Kuyper brings this out by pointing to the Calvinistic character of several revolutions which, on his view, were directed against the prevailing tyrannies in the name of God and of the divinely willed goods of personal freedom and the freedom of the gospel. To be sure, he endorses the French Revolution of 1789 because it was directed against abuses, against despotism by the crown, and because it stood up for the rights and freedoms of the people, but he distinguishes this revolution from others which were directly inspired by Calvinism. Among the latter he reckons the Glorious Revolution of 1688 when William of Orange re-

[1] Karl Barth, *Eine Schweizer Stimme 1938-1945* (2nd ed.; Zurich: Evangelischer Verlag, 1948), p. 6.

[2] See Abraham Kuyper, *Calvinism: Six Stone Foundation Lectures* (Grand Rapids, Michigan: Eerdmans, 1943), esp. pp. 78 ff.

placed James II of England, and the Dutch revolt against the Spaniards under William the Silent. Here he also mentions the American Revolution: "It is expressed in so many words in the *Declaration of Independence,* by John Hancock, that the Americans asserted themselves by virtue — 'of the law of nature and of nature's God'; that they acted — 'as endowed by the Creator with certain inalienable rights'; that they appealed to — 'the Supreme Judge of the world for the rectitude of their intention'; and that they sent forth their 'declaration of Independence' — 'With a firm reliance on the protection of Divine Providence.' In the 'Articles of Confederation' it is confessed in the preamble, — 'that it hath pleased the great Governor of the world to incline the hearts of the legislators.' . . . In one of the meetings of the Convention, Franklin proposed, in a moment of supreme anxiety, that they should ask wisdom from God in prayer." [3] Kuyper finds the religious and Reformed character of the American Revolution confirmed in a statement of Alexander Hamilton: "The French Revolution [is] no more akin to the American Revolution than the faithless wife in a French novel is like the Puritan matron in New England." [4]

In this endorsement of active revolution not merely by Reformed Christians but by the Reformed church we find indeed an essentially different attitude towards revolution from that of Lutheran political ethics — even of that explicitly critical reconstruction which we have developed in the light of our experience with modern totalitarian states. On this Reformed view it is the church itself which is summoned to direct political intervention of a kind which is in fact alien to Lutheranism.

The second answer to the question of the theological distinction between the two views of church and state usually is to the effect that the Reformed thesis of direct church involvement in politics implies an antithesis to the Lutheran doctrine of the two kingdoms. For the Lutheran doctrine, it is said, leads to the church's being aloof from and disinterested in the political sphere. It assumes that the state has a sphere of its own which is beyond the competence of the church, and in respect of which the church becomes alarmed only when the state does damage in matters of "direct ecclesiastical concern," e.g., when it hampers the preaching of the gospel, when it seeks a voice in

[3] *Ibid.,* pp. 86-87.
[4] *Ibid.,* p. 87.

biblical and confessional matters, or when it tries to interfere in church order. So long as the damage is inflicted outside the sphere of the church, so long as the state does nothing but persecute the Jews, or eliminate the mentally unfit, or commit similar crimes against humanity, the church which takes its bearings from the two kingdoms doctrine will issue admonitions and warnings all right but will not feel constrained to offer radical resistance. Through this very aloofness the church, it is argued, creates within the secular kingdom a spiritual vacuum which will be inclined to fill itself with ideologies and world views. There thus arises a hopeless rift between ecclesiastical and political, or spiritual and secular, responsibility. Through the false — the Lutheran — distinction of Law and gospel both are torn away from their relationship to the one God who is sovereign in both dimensions. Thus the church is guilty, not only in respect of its own nature and task, but also in respect of the state. By abandoning the state to its own devices, the church delivers it up to demonism and error. Thus even Hitler's state does not bear sole responsibility for its corruption. The church shares this guilt. For it is the church that, by failing to intervene actively through its office as watchman, helped to make the state what it was.

Now it is true that historically the church did bear a measure of guilt in this matter. The church itself — and not just the Lutheran — solemnly acknowledged this fact in the famous Stuttgart Declaration of guilt of October 18, 1945. It is open to question however, whether this guilt derives from the two kingdoms doctrine, or whether that doctrine was not rather twisted beyond recognition by those making this charge, whether the neo-Lutheran misunderstanding of it was not substituted for the doctrine itself. In this theological ethics we have tried to show that the two kingdoms doctrine does not issue in a separation of church from world. That is neither its purpose nor its effect. The doctrine aims only at maintaining a distinction, a distinction which Reformed theology — as we shall see — also makes in its own way. However, it is not our purpose to undertake at this point a defense of the doctrine of the two kingdoms. We have already said what needs to be said concerning it.[5] It is important here only insofar as we regard it as a foil for understanding the Reformed teaching.

[5] See *ThE* 1, Chapter 18.

This is what Karl Barth does when he complains that the German Evangelical church — he means so far as it is determined by Lutheranism — has not yet learned to see gospel and Law, or church and state, in their interconnection, and consequently to bring political responsibility within the framework of Christian responsibility. By isolating political responsibility it has created a vacuum in which demonism, or more soberly, a human misconception of the state, has been able to flourish. Even in the Confessing Church, National Socialism, though rejected philosophically, was often approved politically. What is needed in the future, says Barth, is that this uncontrolled vacuum should be filled by the gospel, which would make such an accursed political endorsement impossible.[6]

What this means is that the church cannot have certain minor Christian quarrels with the state while otherwise acknowledging its overall authority. It cannot reject a particular authority in some respects and approve it in others. It must utter either a total Yes or a total No. Logically, a total No has to imply that which was already apparent in Kuyper's view of revolution, namely, unconditional resistance by every political means, and hence the overthrow of the government if possible. (We should add again that it is the church which is supposed to initiate all this, not the individual Christian or group of Christians, for it is the church as such which knows that it bears or is summoned to bear responsibility in the worldly kingdom.)

"The knowledge that the power of Jesus Christ extends over all powers strongly suggests the corollary that the state too, as the legal order of society, belongs to his kingdom and not to any other."[7] By way of interpretation it may be said that, as here formulated, Barth's statement could well stand within the framework of the Lutheran doctrine of the two kingdoms, for according to this doctrine too the kingdom on the left hand clearly falls within the sovereignty of God. However, one should not miss the important nuance that according to the two kingdoms doctrine church and state are *both* subjected — if not in identical at least in similar fashion — to the power of Christ. What the two kingdoms doctrine is concerned to show is that, while God has power over both kingdoms, since both are his "governments"

---

[6] Karl Barth, *Die Evangelische Kirche in Deutschland nach dem Zusammenbruch des Dritten Reiches* (Stuttgart, 1946), pp. 26 ff.

[7] *Ibid.*, p. 27.

[Regimente], the mode or manner in which he exercises his power is altogether different in the two cases. This is where the difference really lies. Barth attempts to locate it elsewhere, which is why he suggests that the church has every reason to adopt a critical attitude towards Luther and his division of the two kingdoms, or, if possible, to press on to a different and better understanding of the Reformer's teaching.[8]

Barth's point is variously expressed, and with a polemical thrust enhanced by the urgent matters which occasioned his writing, in a book called *Eine Schweizer Stimme*, a collection of lectures, statements, and letters which he sent to Christians in the various resistance groups in German occupied countries during the politically critical years from 1938 to 1945. The book is intended as a witness to the *"political* service of God."[9] The vacuum in the worldly kingdom, which Barth believes is caused by the two kingdoms doctrine, is given a much fuller interpretation in a letter to Holland in 1940. Here, after expressing certain qualifications and reservations, Barth argues that "Lutheranism in a sense has left the door wide open for German paganism. By isolating creation and the Law from the gospel, it has allotted to it a sacral sphere of its own. The German pagan can use the Lutheran doctrine of the authority of the state as a Christian justification of National Socialism, and the Christian German can feel that through the same doctrine he is invited to recognize National Socialism. Both these things have actually taken place."[10]

Similarly Hermann Diem can find two fatal flaws in the doctrine of the two kingdoms. The first is that it distinguishes between "person" and "office,"[11] thus in fact abandoning the latter to the autonomy of all secular occurrence. (Here Troeltsch's well-known criticism is adopted,[12] though Diem does not quote him.) The second is that it completely separates the kingdoms, and runs the dividing line between them right through the individual Christian.[13]

---

[8] *Ibid.*, p. 29.
[9] See above p. 566, n. 1.
[10] Karl Barth, "Brief an Pfarrer Kooiman," *Eine Schweizer Stimme*, p. 122; cf. also p. 328.
[11] Hermann Diem, *Karl Barths Kritik am deutschen Luthertum* (Zurich: Evangelischer Verlag, 1947), p. 40.
[12] See Ernst Troeltsch, *The Social Teaching of the Christian Churches*, trans. Olive Wyon (New York: Macmillan, 1931), II, 506 ff.
[13] Diem, *op. cit.*, p. 44.

We maintain that behind these criticisms of the doctrine of the two kingdoms there stands a co-ordinating of church and state in the name of a principle of unity which allows no division of responsibility whatever but insists on indissoluble mutual interpenetration. It is necessary at this point to define this principle of unity more precisely. We have already had some indications as to the direction such a definition should take. The relation between Law and gospel, e.g., will have to play a significant role, for only when this relation is more fully expounded can one see that this principle of unity is something very different from what we meant by the "linking" of the two kingdoms in Lutheran teaching.[14] Contrary to what might appear from Barth's interpretation, the antithesis between the divergent confessions is not between unity and separation, but between two different views of unity.

We might provisionally sum up our deliberations thus far as follows. Reformed theology recognizes a direct interrelation of church and state, Lutheran theology an indirect; and even as the historical outworkings of these definitions of the relationship are concrete and dramatic, so the dogmatic ideas from which they proceed appear to be lofty and esoteric.

The Underlying Theological Differences

Two themes in particular are at work here: first, the relation between providence and predestination, and second, the relation between Law and gospel. We turn now to the first of these themes.

Monistic Thinking in Terms of the Decree

Reformed Orthodoxy departs from Calvin — and from Luther[15] — in fixing the systematic locus of the doctrine of predestination. In the 1536 edition of his *Institutes* Calvin treated predestination as the first part of his doctrine of the church. The definitive 1559 edition placed it just after the doctrine of justification and prayer. In sub-

---

[14] See *ThE* 1, 373-378.

[15] Luther regards the doctrine of predestination as a kind of delayed continuation of the doctrine of justification, and hence as a theologoumenon, something secondary. In his Preface to Romans he calls attention to the fact that predestination does not come under discussion until chapters 9-11, *after* the doctrine of justification, and that it cannot take effect until *after* the Christian has experienced justification: "Beware that you do not drink wine while you are still a suckling." *LW* 35, 378.

THEOLOGICAL ETHICS – POLITICS

stance, of course, the doctrine has an overriding significance for Calvin, inasmuch as it is predestination which determines salvation and damnation; the grace given in Christ is only an instrument and vehicle for effecting the gracious resolve. At the same time it is a fact that the doctrine of predestination comes not at the beginning of Calvin's system but only later. This fact has theological significance. It means, first, that the decree takes effect only in Christ, and second, that assurance of election is enjoyed only in faith.[16]

Reformed Orthodoxy, on the contrary, sets the doctrine at the very apex of its system. Thus Polanus says that in a pretemporal resolve God elected those whom he has given to Christ for the attainment of everlasting life. The rest he has passed over and rejected according to his "free, most holy, most righteous, and unsearchable will." [17] Among the Supralapsarians this principle was elaborated in such a way that the fall itself was determined by this pretemporal decree, whereas the Infralapsarians of Dort spoke only of God's permitting the fall, following which God resolved to deliver up one portion to merited damnation and to address his grace to the other portion in Christ.

In keeping with this pretemporal character of predestination all the other loci follow systematically upon that doctrine, including even the article on providence. Creation is treated between the doctrines of predestination and providence, thus underscoring the leading role of the decree of election.[18]

The plurality of decrees, however – on predestination, creation, the fall, providence, etc. – does not imply an unrelated coexistence of individual resolves. On the contrary, these can all be comprehended in a single primal decree of God which – in post-Kantian terms – is divided up into this plurality simply for the sake of our discursive, temporally conditioned way of thinking. This original

---

[16] See John Calvin *Institutes of the Christian Religion* 3. 24. 3 ff. (*LCC* 21, 967 ff.); cf. Peter Barth, "Die Erwählungslehre in Calvins *Institutio* von 1536," in *Theologische Aufsätze. Karl Barth zum 50. Geburtstag* (Munich: Kaiser, 1936), pp. 432 ff.

[17] See Ernst Staehelin, *Amandus Polanus von Polansdorf* (1955); cf. Otto Ritschl, *Dogmengeschichte des Protestantismus* (Göttingen: Vandenhoeck & Ruprecht, 1926), III, 291 ff.

[18] This is the sequence of topics, e.g., in the source book of Heinrich Heppe, *Reformed Dogmatics*, ed. Ernst Bizer, trans. G. T. Thompson (London: Allen & Unwin, 1950).

decree is called the absolute decree.[19] (In this connection the Reformed dogmaticians are not afraid to speak of God, in his quality as the decreeing God [Deus decernens], as the "first cause."[20]) This means that what takes place sequentially in salvation history is to be presupposed as taking place in God at a single moment, a moment which comprehends in a single unity all the polarities of salvation history: providence and election, the civil community and the Christian community, world history and salvation history, Law and gospel.[21]

This unification in the absolute decree has extraordinary theological and ethical consequences. Theologically, Old and New Testaments are brought into very close proximity. In the strict sense the gospel is no longer the actual changeover of the aeons which breaks the dominion of the Law. It is not an overcoming of God's wrath by his love, but only a continuation of the "explication" of the pretemporal decree which was begun in the Old Testament. Christ is not new in the sense that he is the cause and foundation of election. He is simply — and this thought occurs already in Calvin — the "means" of election, an executor of the decree.[22] Christ does not initiate a new covenant. He simply executes an eternal pact.[23]

The ethical consequences attributable to the idea of the absolute decree, so far as economics is concerned, have been pointed out by Max Weber in his famous study The Protestant Ethic and the Spirit of Capitalism.[24] Weber's thesis is that the decree of predestination raises the question of "how the individual can be certain of his own election,"[25] and answers that such assurance is possible only when a man sees God's blessing on his life. This possibility of deducing faith on the basis of fruits, election on the basis of success and blessing, releases in daily work an intense amount of activity

[19] "The decrees are plural by reason of the things decreed [meaning they take place in temporal succession in salvation history] but the decreeing action is a single whole." Leonardus Riissenius, Summa theologiae (1703), I, 125.
[20] Daniel Wyttenbach, Testamen Theol. Dogmat. (1741), I, 334.
[21] Felix Flückiger, "Vorsehung und Erwählung in der reformierten und in der lutherischen Theologie," in Antwort. Karl Barth zum ziebzigsten Geburtstag (Zurich: Evangelischer Verlag, 1956), pp. 509-526.
[22] Franciscus Turretinus, Institutio Theologiae elencticae (1701), I, 387.
[23] Franciscus Turretinus, Compendium Theologiae didactico-elencticae (1702), p. 205; Ritschl, op. cit., p. 457; Heppe, op. cit., pp. 404-409.
[24] See Max Weber, The Protestant Ethic and the Spirit of Capitalism, trans. Talcott Parsons (New York: Scribner's, 1930), esp. pp. 108 ff.
[25] Ibid., p. 110.

which is aimed at achieving the successes needed as premises for drawing the appropriate conclusion.[26] "The belief that the Christian proved his state of grace by action *in majorem Dei gloriam* [to God's greater glory]"[27] acts as a stimulant to efficiency. "Intense worldly activity is recommended as the most suitable means . . . to attain that self-confidence."[28] Thus a dogma dealing with a pretemporal decree and marked by a high degree of theoretical abstraction leads to highly temporal and concrete results (a remarkable conjunction of dogmatics with ethics).

An ethical consequence of more immediate significance for our present context is that involving the relation of church and state. Like world history and salvation history, or providence and predestination, both church and state have their common origin in the absolute decree. For this reason, they do not stand in dualistic tension but are connected by a monistic bond.

According to the Lutheran view, the state, as we have seen, was elicited by the fall, and is intended to avert the ensuing chaos by use of the methods of the fallen world itself. On the Reformed view, the state is grounded in the decree and hence is not a subsequent emergency institution but a providential a priori institution. For Luther there is necessarily a tension between state and church because the state is a strange work *[opus alienum]* of God, whereas the church, deriving from his proper will *[voluntas propria]*, has his heart "directly" in the forgiving and consoling Word of God. But this antithesis is expunged the moment the world and the kingdom of God are grounded in the one act of the pretemporal decree.

For the decree is, as it were, a "proper" decree only. Here there is no more place for the duality of *proprium* and *alienum*. Such a duality makes sense, and then of course becomes necessary, only when God's action is understood as historical action, and hence is presented in the way the Old Testament paradigmatically portrays it, as action and reaction, resolving and repenting, judging and bringing the judgment to an end, action according to the Law and the wondrous disruption of this action in the grace of the gospel. On the Lutheran view the institution of the state rests indeed on such an

[26] *Ibid.*, pp. 114 ff.
[27] *Ibid.*, p. 108, n. 30 (which is printed on p. 224).
[28] *Ibid.*, p. 112.

action and reaction of God in face of man's prior rebellion, and also on an action and reaction of God in face of his own wrath, whereby man is snatched from judgment and granted a καιρός, a season of order in which he is enabled to live.

Behind the Lutheran dualism and the Reformed monism in the relating of church and state there thus stands a prior theological decision whose ethical significance only comes out later. According to the view of Reformed Orthodoxy, the common basis of both church and state in the original decree of God means their close interrelationship, since the will of God cannot be in self-contradiction. In contrast, it is of the heart of the Lutheran view that God does contradict himself, that he sets his grace in opposition to his judgment and his love in opposition to his holiness; indeed, the gospel itself can be traced to this fundamental contradiction within God himself.

It is thus typical that in his doctrine of Law and gospel Luther should lay great stress on the rejection of any teleological connection between them. For to seek a point where the difference between them is dissolved in an overarching unity is to rob the gospel of its character as miracle. This is why the tension between them must be maintained. "Only the Holy Spirit can do it [distinguish between Law and gospel]. Even the man Christ could not do it";[29] otherwise he would not have been a man like us.

Reformed theologians have understood the interrelationship of church and state in many different ways, but these are all variations on the theme of an original unity in the decree. For Bucer, e.g., the state is integrated into the kingdom of Christ, from whence it derives the (ecclesiastically supervised) norms for all its functions, for its financial operations, its constitution, its organizational structure, and its social ordinances in general. Or again, for Wolfgang Musculus[30] the state, i.e., the Christian state, regards the church as a kind of agency of cultic administration, and hence shelters it and provides for its needs; if on this view the church does not even govern itself, this does not mean that it is being deprived of its rights, but only that these rights are being cared for by the state on its behalf.

Thus for both men church and state constitute a single whole, a unity in multiplicity which is ultimately grounded in the one divine

[29] LW 54, 127, No. 1234; cf. WA 39I, 445, lines 11 ff. and ThE 1, 117 ff.
[30] See Ritschl, op. cit., p. 249, and Flückiger, op. cit., p. 520.

decree and marked for inclusion in the one reign of Christ. The parts of this unity are closely interrelated in both origin and goal. Hence it makes very little difference theologically whether the whole is seen and developed in terms of the one part or the other; the guaranteed unity allows for great variation in this respect. If this underlying unity is not perceived, the political theology of the Reformed world might seem to be full of contradictions. Once it is perceived, however, the apparent contradictions prove to be variations on the one basic theme.

A typical elaboration of this idea of unity in recent theology is to be found in Karl Barth. For him church and state constitute two concentric circles with a common center in Christ. The "inner circle" is the kingdom of Christ, which is represented on earth by the church. The "outer circle," in which Christians therefore "automatically" participate, is the state, which embraces both Christians and non-Christians.[31]

Barth emphasizes, to be sure, that church and state have different tasks. He explicitly rejects the view of Richard Rothe that the state can take over the tasks of the church and finally absorb it.[32] According to Rothe, "the state when it has become perfect will completely exclude the church," making it superfluous.[33] For "the point of Christianity is to make itself increasingly more secular, i.e., to divest itself of the ecclesiastical form which it had to don on its entry into the world, and to put on the generally human and intrinsically moral form of life."[34] In an analogy to Lessing's *The Education of the Human Race*, Rothe thinks that the specifically religious aspect, God's special covenant with Israel and its institutional successor, the church, serves only a temporary purpose. By fulfilling its task of propagation and christianizing the world, the church makes itself superfluous. It secularizes itself, and thus is ultimately absorbed in the state as the representative of the worldly kingdom.

[31] See Karl Barth, "The Christian Community and the Civil Community," in *Community, State, and Church: Three Essays* (Garden City, New York: Doubleday, 1960), p. 158; cf. also my critique of Barth's position in *Kirche und Öffentlichkeit* (Tübingen, 1947), pp. 37 ff., *Christliche Verantwortung im Atomzeitalter* (3rd ed.; 1957), pp. 60 ff., and *ThE* 1, 275.

[32] Barth, "The Christian Community and the Civil Community," *op. cit.*, p. 157.

[33] Richard Rothe, *Die Anfänge der christlichen Kirche und ihrer Verfassung* (Wittenberg: Zimmerman, 1837), p. 47.

[34] Richard Rothe, *Theologische Ethik* (2nd ed.; Wittenberg: Koelling, 1869-1871), V, 397.

In opposition to this view Barth points out that in the state "Christians are no longer gathered together as such but are associated with non-Christians (or doubtful Christians)." Citizens of the state "share no common awareness of their relationship to God. . . . No appeal can be made to the Word or Spirit of God in the running of its affairs. . . . For this reason the civil community [in distinction from the Christian community] can only have external, relative, and provisional tasks and aims." [35]

The word "only" in this sentence expresses conceptually what the image of concentric circles expresses graphically, namely, that church and state stand toward one another in a quantitative relation rather than a dialectical polar relation. They have a closer or more distant, a more direct or indirect, relation to the common center, Christ. But they are related to him in fundamentally the same way.

Here we see the influence of that common foundation in God's original decree which has repeatedly been so determinative in the Reformed tradition. Both church and state have a common "origin" and a common "center," the origin being the decree, and the center its actualization, i.e., the instruments and vehicles with which God executes it: Christ, the Word, and the Spirit.

"However much error and human tyranny may be involved in it, the State is not a product of sin but one of the constants of the divine Providence and government of the world in its action against human sin: it is therefore an instrument of divine grace. The civil community shares both a common origin and a common centre with the Christian community. It is an order of divine grace inasmuch as in relation to sinful man as such, in relation to the world that still needs redeeming, the grace of God is always the patience of God." [36]

It is typical that here, where there is a supralapsarian tie-in with the original decree that preceded creation and the fall (though this is not expressly mentioned), there are also linguistic echoes of the Scholastic doctrine of nature and grace. For according to Roman Catholic teaching, in the nature which survives the fall relatively intact, there are something like Barth's "constants of the divine providence and government." Indeed, it is only the uncomfortable proximity to elements in Protestantism which he elsewhere vigorously re-

[35] Barth, "The Christian Community and the Civil Community," *op. cit.*, p. 151.
[36] *Ibid.*, p. 156.

jects that keeps Barth from using the term which is otherwise normal at this point: "order of creation."

To be sure, Barth erects a barrier against this concept by constructing his massive analogy, not at the point of the common "origin" in the pretemporal decree — as he might well have done, and as seems to be plainly intimated — but at the point of the other pole in the church-state relation, namely, what he calls the "center." In other words, he makes the Second Article, the christological criterion, his norm. The state's "analogical capacities and needs"[37] are accordingly worked out — even in a detailed way — within the framework of the christological analogy.[38]

Hence "the real Church must be the model and prototype of the real State. The Church must set an example so that by its very existence it may be a source of renewal for the State and the power by which the State is preserved."[39] Indeed, "its constitution, order, government, and administration" must be, says Barth, "a practical demonstration of the thinking and acting from the gospel which takes place in this inner circle."[40]

The analogy is thus so complete that even the secular form of the church, its legal and organizational structure, is of its very essence. There is not even the smattering of an alien presence in it. Church law is in a direct sense christologically shaped, and for this reason — for this reason alone! — it can have paradigmatic significance for the orders of the state.

Legal order does not stand over against the church as the form of the fallen world in which the church must participate on account of the incarnation of the Word. On the contrary, the legal order is to

---

[37] *Ibid.*, p. 168.

[38] Behind this conception is that of the analogy of faith (or of relation), a conception which Barth sets over against the analogy of being, and which dominates his whole dogmatic system (think, e.g., of his definition of evil as "nothingness" [*das Nichtige*]). His own development of the concept may be seen in his *Church Dogmatics*, ed. G. W. Bromiley and T. F. Torrance (Edinburgh: T. & T. Clark, 1936 –), I², 144; II¹, 74 ff; III¹, 185; III², 220 ff.; III³, 352; IV¹, 149, etc.; cf. also Hans Urs von Balthasar, *Karl Barth. Darstellung und Deutung seiner Theologie* (Cologne: Hegner, 1951), pp. 116 ff. and 124 ff., and Gustaf Wingren, *Theology in Conflict: Nygren, Barth, Bultmann* (Philadelphia: Muhlenberg, 1958), pp. 32-33, 36.

[39] Barth, "The Christian Community and the Civil Community," *op. cit.*, p. 186.
[40] *Ibid.*

be derived from the church, i.e., from its christological center.[41] As the legal order of the church it conforms directly to the Word — even as Reformed church constitutions are biblically determined, and thus are a matter of confessional definition. It is for this reason that the constitution of the church can serve as an example for that of the state.

The analogy between church and state goes so far that even individual structures within the state are derived from it, i.e., christologically. Thus the fact that members of the church are linked to one another through their relationship to a single head, Christ, finds a political parallel in the fact that the freedom of the citizen must always be understood within the framework of reciprocal responsibility,[42] and "the Christian line that follows from the gospel betrays a striking tendency to the side of what is generally called the 'democratic' State." [43] This christological deduction can be worked out in such detail that secret diplomacy is shown to stand in contradiction to the light which has shone forth in Christ. The church "lives in the dawning of the day of the Lord and its task in relation to the world is to rouse it and tell it that this day has dawned. The inevitable political corollary of this is that the Church is the sworn enemy of all secret policies and secret diplomacy. It is just as true of the political sphere as of any other that only evil can want to be kept secret. . . . Where freedom and responsibility in the service of the State are one, whatever is said and done must be said and done before the ears and eyes of all." [44]

While we for our part have sought to restrict the autonomy of politics and to reduce its significance to a minimum, it is characteristic of Barth's view that for him this question of autonomy falls by the board. In theory the christological principle must control even the legal procedures of political life, so that the duty or at least the admissibility of, e.g., secrecy, cannot be deduced from the way things

---

[41] Sohm's thesis that church law stands in contradiction to the essence of the church — and is alien to the very nature of the church — although it is in theological contradiction to the incarnation nonetheless represents a notable challenge for it draws attention to the tension between the kingdom of God and the orders of this aeon. Barth's understanding of church order might be described as the diametrical opposite of this dubious view. See Rudolph Sohm, *Kirchenrecht*, Vol. 1 (Leipzig: Duncker, 1892); II, 1922.

[42] Barth, "The Christian Community and the Civil Community," *op. cit.*, p. 174.

[43] *Ibid.*, p. 181.

[44] *Ibid.*, p. 176.

are actually done in the political sphere. Even the modes of action must be dictated, not by their appropriateness to a given field – at any rate not out of regard for such appropriateness – but altogether "christocratically."

Now one might say that one of the results of our political ethics has been to show that politics cannot be set under the norm of orders of creation, or the First Article of the Creed. It must be conceded, however, that at least certain guiding principles may be deduced from this quarter, as the various views of natural law all demonstrate. In contrast, one can only say that a "super-natural law" deduced from the Second Article will lead to very strained and artificial analogies. Barth's rejection of secret diplomacy is simply an extreme example of this, from the standpoint of the basis on which it is argued and the impossibility of implementing it.

But we have drawn attention to this doubtful and unrealistic aspect only in passing. For our present purposes the important thing is to see how completely antithetical this view is to a doctrine of the state worked out within the framework of Lutheran theology, however broadly construed. For Lutheran theology, the state is not just an outer circle quantitatively distinguished from the inner circle of the church. On the contrary, in respect of their relationship to the kingdom of Christ church and state stand over against one another in dialectical opposition and connection. This means that the state is not to be deduced along with the church in supralapsarian fashion from the original decree of God. Like the Law, it is an emergency measure "interposed" [45] by God in the fallen world.

Whereas there lies behind Barth's conception the pretemporal decree, in which all things are foreseen together and in which everything is grounded as in a "first cause" (though Barth would certainly reject this phrase), Luther understands the state as a miracle of God whereby he intercepts the blow of man's primal sin and reacts against it, in *history*. In our treatment of Law and gospel [46] we have already shown that the very historicity of God's dealings with men is rooted in this divine reaction, in the changeover of aeons which it effects, in the breaking of the nexus of sin and punishment by the intervention of the

---

[45] παρεισῆλθεν, Rom. 5:20.
[46] See *ThE* 1, 94 ff.

gospel. We have also shown that there is plainly an element of non-historicity in Barth's monistic interrelating of Law and gospel.[47]

As the tension of Law and gospel is relaxed in Barth, so also is the antithesis of church and state. It is true that for Barth too the state has the task of resisting chaos in the fallen world and of arresting the destructive power of sin;[48] it even uses the instruments of force to that end, and hence acts within the framework of the Noachic world. But in none of these Barthian statements do we find expressed the distinguishing feature of this divine action which Luther brings out so well when he speaks of God's "alien work," namely, the fact that in instituting the state as a dam against the fallen world God uses the very instruments of this world, so that the state — as we have had to understand it — stands at the point of intersection of two conflicting analogies. On the one hand, it stands in broken analogy to the kingdom of Christ; for using the instruments of force it builds a peace which is distorted almost beyond recognition, a peace which is adequately fashioned only in the kingdom of Christ (John 14:27). On the other hand, it stands in broken analogy to the kingdom of the devil. For it is a self-objectification of the fallen world and the Babylonian heart. In it there is legitimate power. But in it there lurks also the rebellious will to power. Thus it is "also" the domain of the ruler of this world.[49]

This way of looking at the matter produces a unique "qualitative" distinction between church and state, between God's proper works and his strange works. It is true enough that this distinction can be abused. In connection with a misunderstanding of the two kingdoms doctrine, it can lead to a complete dualism of powers, to a radical separation between private morality and official morality, to the political aloofness of Christians, to the establishment of politics as a law unto itself, and thus concretely to schizophrenia in the Christian life. But all this is no argument against Luther's basic principle as such, which with its manifold bracketing of Law and gospel, worldly king-

---

[47] Cf. Wingren, op. cit.; Regin Prenter, "Glauben und Erkennen bei Karl Barth," Kerygma und Dogma, II (1956), 176-192; Gerhard Gloege, "Zur Praedestinationslehre Karl Barths," Kerygma und Dogma, II (1956), 193 ff.

[48] The civil community "serves to protect man from the invasion of chaos and therefore to give him time: time for the preaching of the gospel; time for repentance; time for faith" (Barth, "The Christian Community and the Civil Community," op. cit., p. 156).

[49] ἄρχων τοῦ κόσμου, John 12:31; 14:30; 16:11.

dom and kingdom of God, in reciprocal relationship affords fundamental safeguards against such disintegration.

It is of great significance that Barth's idea of the two concentric circles developed, not merely under the influence of such elements in the Reformed tradition as the doctrine of the divine decrees,[50] but also in conscious opposition to undeniably flagrant perversions of Lutheranism. At least it found confirmation in its angry rejection of these perversions.

One may see in Wilhelm Stapel how drawing this kind of analogy between church and state can lead to political abuse of a very different sort. For Stapel draws anti-Barthian conclusions on the basis of this same analogical relationship. He speaks of the "great correspondence between earthly and heavenly life" which he thinks justifies "a paternal form of government" [51] — which ultimately brings us suspiciously close to the *Führer* principle and totalitarianism. It would be interesting in this connection to see how frequently Barth's analogies could be pressed to diametrically opposed conclusions. Rather naughtily one might suggest that where Barth concludes against secret diplomacy because in Jesus Christ the light of God has come into the world, one might conclude that secret government is justified by the fact of the Messianic secret. Similarly, the lordship of Christ the head over his body might be adduced in favor of a paternal or *Führer* state rather than a democratic state — if one is to operate at the level of such devious conclusions. In many cases the formal analogies thus erected are apparently so inappropriate that they are intrinsically ambiguous

[50] This point needs careful consideration. Barth has changed the traditional doctrine of the decrees by interpreting the original decree christologically and relating it to Christ's pre-existence. "There is no such thing as a *decretum absolutum*. There is no such thing as a will of God apart from Jesus Christ" (*Church Dogmatics*, II², 115). In his original decree God is already the God who elects in Christ. In the name of Jesus Christ the (pretemporally) electing God and (pretemporally) elect man meet (*ibid.*, p. 59). But this only makes it the plainer that the decree contains *in nuce* all salvation history (*ibid.*, p. 14), and that there is no genuine history of God involving divine resolves, changes of mind, and even "repenting." The focus of events is the pre-existent Christ, not the incarnation. The incarnation is merely the form of execution in which the decree-event is actualized, an epilogue and nothing more. The dehistoricizing tendency may thus be seen in the relation between the pre-existent and the incarnate Christ as well as in the relation between Law and gospel. Cf. *ThE* 1, 110 ff.

[51] See Walter Künneth, *Politik zwischen Dämon und Gott. Eine christliche Ethik des Politischen* (Berlin: Lutherisches Verlagshaus, 1954), p. 536.

and hence say either everything or nothing. One may interpret them as he pleases, even from such diametrically opposed angles as those of Barth and Stapel. If I had to choose I would prefer the analogies underlying Roman Catholic natural law; for if the premises are dubious and even unacceptable from the Reformation standpoint, the conclusions are less subject to individual caprice and hence can produce a far larger measure of agreement than can the arbitrary maneuvers in Barth's analogical thinking.

The two points thus far considered, that for Barth the state stands in unbroken analogy to the kingdom of Christ instead of being at the same time an objectification of the fallen world and hence an alien work of God, and that the concrete conclusions to be drawn from this analogy can be many and varied, take on real significance in relation to the conflict with totalitarian states. Because of the ambiguity of the analogies it is possible to deduce diametrically opposed attitudes toward the totalitarian state and to arrive at very different theological evaluations. The arbitrariness with which the analogy is interpreted carries with it the possibility of highly subjective political evaluations ranging from sympathy to complete antipathy.

This may be seen in the puzzling difference in Barth's own attitude to the National Socialist form of totalitarianism on the one hand and to the Communist form on the other.[52] The question arises as to how Barth can be a passionate opponent of the one, even to the point of speaking of the beast from the abyss and of spearheading the church's theological opposition, while he advises patience and a relative recognition in the case of the other, and certainly does not speak of it in terms of the beast. With reference to the Communist state Barth says that there will never be either a perfect Christian state or a wholly demonic state, and that if the state begins to show traces of the beast, Christians must not fly to extremes and pose the alternative of either subjection or martyrdom. In virtue of their Christian freedom they can simply wait and see how things develop: Why should they not, even in a state which emerges as a threat, cling to "what remains of the Word," or to "what has perhaps been re-established of the Word"?[53]

[52] See Karl Barth, *Die Kirche zwischen Ost und West* (Munich: Kaiser, 1949), esp. pp. 14 ff.
[53] See *News Bulletin, Official Organ of the Lutheran World Federation*, Vol. III, No. 9, Sept. 15, 1949; cf. also Thielicke, *Christliche Verantwortung im Atomzeitalter*, p. 61.

Whoever reads the collection *Eine Schweizer Stimme* will readily see that in respect of the two forms of totalitarianism Barth finds himself in a completely different human situation. National Socialism affected his own life. It posed a military threat to his own land. It was an immediate and dangerous neighbor. The anti-Communist propaganda of the Hitler regime was well adapted to instill in its enemy certain sympathies for what was being vilified, for after all Barth was allied with the Communist state insofar as both were engaged in common resistance to German Fascism. It is easy to see, and ought not to be a reason for reproach at the human level, that in this light he could not view with the same anger or attention the much more monstrous form of inhumanity found in the dictatorship of Stalin.

At first, this purely human estimation was not buttressed or controlled by theological categories. But later it came to take on theological significance, because the concept of analogy permits arbitrary judgment on the basis of very different standards, even on the basis of human prejudices. And this is precisely what seems to have happened. In face of National Socialism the idea of concentric circles, i.e., of analogy, seems to have been applied by Barth as follows: This state is so corrupt that it bears no analogy to the church. It is the antichurch, the beast from the abyss. Hence one cannot cling to "what remains of the Word," for nothing whatever remains. Regard is no longer had to those governmental functions of external order which the state still performs no matter how depraved its form. Once the state is seen to offer no further analogy, it can only be regarded as a demonic opponent, as "organized chaos." [54] Consequently, total resistance is demanded, and it is logically absurd to divide the resistance as though one could reject the state philosophically but approve some of its political functions.

The same concept of analogy, however, can be applied in exactly the opposite way. It can be viewed from the standpoint that in bad states as well as good "constants of the divine providence and government" remain, however perverted they may be in form. In relation to Stalin's state, which is the one Barth has in view, the implication is that its social action, e.g., bears witness to these constants of order. And in spite of the "bloody hands," Barth finds here a supralapsarian

[54] This is how Barth once referred to it in a conversation we once had together back in 1935.

feature which bears witness to the fact that something of the Word does in fact remain, or has even been re-established. The supralapsarian element in this interpretation of Stalin's state comes out even more clearly in the fact that Barth can say of this state that it is not anti-Christian but just "impudently a-Christian." [55] Here Barth pushes the idea of the constants so far that he no longer asks in whose name, by what power, or under what sign (Matt. 21:23-27) Stalin's state undertakes what Barth construes as social achievement. Instead Barth is prepared to accept social values as if in respect of any Christian content they were perfectly neutral. In a puzzling way, he fails to inquire concerning the system of co-ordinates in which these values are inscribed, whether it be that of dialectical materialism, or general humanitarian concern, or Christian love. He thus does away with the basic category of all Christian evaluation, namely, the question as to the sign or mark under which a thing is done. He introduces instead the alpha-privative (a-Christian) which is diametrically and uncompromisingly opposed to the biblical way of speaking about individual or political action. This is possible only because Barth thinks in terms of the decree, for in supralapsarian fashion this type of thinking leads to a leveling down of all secular things: whatever their different motives and goals, in the final analysis they are all related to a common source.

Thus one can interpret the state, indeed all secular phenomena, in two ways after the manner of the Delphic oracle. On the one hand, one may see them in terms of the one pole of Barth's thought, namely, their "origin," in which case they fit into the series of supralapsarian "constants." If a state is doubtful in respect of its sign, then one may look for remnants of the analogy within the bracket following, e.g., a genuine or ostensible social concern for man, secular and a-Christian approximations to the Christian *diaconia* of love of neighbor. This is in fact how Barth views the Stalin state. On the other hand, one may use the other of Barth's two poles as the standard of judgment, namely, the "center" of the two concentric circles. Here the question is whether the particular state is directly for Christ or against him. In principle, it is still possible even in this case to establish analogies such as the secular, a-Christian *diaconia*. But the task

[55] Barth, *Die Kirche zwischen Ost und West*, p. 15.

of differentiating is obviously the more pressing one. And this is how Barth views National Socialism.

To ask Barth whether his divergent evaluations in the two cases is politically "or" theologically based is to put the question imprecisely. Both aspects count, because the analogical relation between church and state is applied so broadly, ambiguously, and arbitrarily that theological cover may be found for evaluations of a very different provenance.

Calvin's View of Law and Gospel

Again and again it has been intimated that the analogy between church and state corresponds to a similar analogy between Law and gospel which is of decisive significance in the Reformed tradition and has exerted a continuing influence from Calvin to Karl Barth.[56] There is no need to work out extensively here the connections between Law and gospel in Calvin.[57] It may simply be recalled that they do not stand in dialectical tension in Calvin as in Luther. The Law does not stand for the nexus of sin and punishment, and the gospel is not the miraculous breaking of this nexus. On the contrary, the Law is the Word of the same God who also enacts the gospel, and hence is already full of promise and comfort, for it stands within the framework of the old covenant, in which God gives himself into fellowship with his people, and which thus bears evangelical features. Again, just as the Law already preaches the God of grace, and thus carries gospel within it, so the gospel has some of the features of Law insofar as it makes demands upon me. This is why Barth can say that the Law is the "form" of the gospel and the gospel is the "content" of the Law.[58] This interrelation of Law and gospel, which is at first only a sublime construct on the theological drawing board, has widespread effects on theological and ethical thinking.

In the first place, it defines the relation between the Old Testament and the New. If the thrust of the gospel is not to overcome the Law, but only to bring to light its secret evangelical point and to open the sealed letter of grace, then the Old Testament as the Book of the Law

---

[56] See Karl Barth's essay on "Gospel and Law," *Three Essays*, pp. 71-100; also Hans Iwand, "Jenseits von Gesetz und Evangelium," *Theologische Blätter*, 1935, 3/4, pp. 75 ff.

[57] We have already done this to some extent at *ThE* 1, 120 ff.

[58] Barth, "Gospel and Law," *op. cit.*, pp. 80-81.

is not superseded, but only fulfilled, clarified, and explained by the New Testament. Law and gospel, Old Testament and New, do not stand in a relation of dialectical antithesis but are "complementary," in "mutual accord." [59]

Thus the Old Testament is not, as in Luther, the background against which the light of the gospel shines. It is not partly the dark foil and partly the reflector of the gospel light.[60] On the contrary, it is a present light in its own right. It shares in the *monon* of the one Word of God and thus affords a textual basis for preaching the gospel directly, not just by way of counterpart and prophecy. Since the Old Testament is the covenant book of a theocratically ruled people, it is full of legal directives for the concrete shaping of individual, social, economic, and political life.

To the degree that the Law is thus a present Word, to the degree that its tension with the gospel *(usus elenchticus)* is supplanted by its normative significance for order *(usus politicus)*, the tables of the Law necessarily come to apply to the political sphere, indeed to public life in general. The Old Testament thus becomes a depository of divine statutes for the ordering of life in general, not just within the church, but also in the state. It thus comes to play an important role in political ethics.

Since Lutheranism relativizes the Law it has the freedom to adapt church constitutions and political orders to existing conditions. Love is its only criterion.[61] For the sake of love there has to be order all right, but no spiritual pre-eminence is attached to any particular order.

Reformed Christianity, on the other hand, with its different understanding of Scripture and the Law, believes that the form of the orders,

[59] Commenting on Matthew 5:17 Calvin writes that the gospel "is nothing else than a fulfillment *[complementum]* of the law: so that both, with one consent *[mutua concordia]*, declare God to be their Author." *Commentary on a Harmony of the Evangelists Matthew, Mark, and Luke,* trans. William Pringle (3 vols.; Grand Rapids, Michigan: Eerdmanns, 1949), I, 275; see *ThE* 1, 121.

[60] Both ideas occur in Luther. The Old Testament as Law is the antithetical counterpart of the gospel, but as prophecy it also "inculcates Christ" *[treibt es Christum;* cf. *LW* 35, 396 and 236]. Luther's dialectic thus avoids both the abstract antithesis of Emmanuel Hirsch *(Das Alte Testament und die Predigt des Evangeliums* [Tübingen, 1936] and the simple equation of, e.g., Wilhelm Vischer *(The Witness of the Old Testament to Christ,* trans. A. B. Crabtree [London: Lutterworth, 1949]).

[61] See Articles XIV and XV of the Augsburg Confession and the Apology to the Augsburg Confession.

and especially the constitution of the church, is biblically prescribed.[62] This is why — whether one accepts the basic principle or not — it achieves a great measure of stability and solidity. For it manages to avoid a host of questions and hence also the necessity of arriving at corresponding judgments — and hence also the dangers involved in accommodating church structures to the prevailing political situation.

This may be seen in the church conflict with the Third Reich. Lutheranism (at least part of it) had to feel its way slowly in its relation to the totalitarian state. At times it was uncertain how far it could or should go in adopting certain principles of the political order (e.g., the *Führer* concept, the Aryan principle, etc.) into its ecclesiastical constitutions. Lutheran theologians and faculties made the most astonishing pronouncements on these matters, and quite obviously did not know (or only thought they knew) how to apply their freedom from the Law. There were times when the demands of freedom seemed to be too much for them. Crises were more easily dealt with on the basis of either Roman Catholic canon law or the Reformed view of the Law.

This helps to explain the Reformed leadership in the conflict, of which we have already spoken. But this observation is certainly no judgment on the Lutheran doctrine of Law and gospel and its attendant concept of freedom. It is a judgment on the Lutherans themselves, or better, on that portion of them who succumbed to the temptation not to be obedient in freedom (i.e., without the crutches of the Law), but to use their freedom as a pretext for evil (I Pet. 2:16), and to establish a new law in the church, namely, the law of least resistance.

We do injustice to the Reformed view of the Law and of the Old Testament's normative significance for order, if we expect it to lead to an attempt simply to copy the orders of ancient Israel, to make the church as keeper of the Scripture a lawgiver for the state — or at least the guardian of its laws — to provide "sacred" orders for the state, and thus to rule the world theocratically. The Scripture principle and the primacy of the inner circle over the outer need not lead to legal rigidity. They can in fact be accompanied by a large measure of that elasticity which in Lutheranism is called the freedom of accommodation. This may be seen clearly in Calvin.[63]

[62] See the citations in Salnar's *Harmonia confessionum fidei*, ed. August Ebrard (1887), pp. 137 ff.
[63] See, e.g., John Calvin *Institutes of the Christian Religion* 4. 20 on "Civil Government" (*LCC* 21, 1485 ff.).

When Calvin adduces the kings and judges of Israel as examples,[64] and again when he discusses the magistracy's concern for both tables of the law,[65] he does not suggest the theocratic "constitution" of Israel as a model either in detail or even in general. Instead he simply points out that those who bore office (e.g., Solomon) received their office "by divine providence and holy ordinance," [66] so that they had to fulfill it — especially as regards the administration of justice — responsibly before God. The example here is not the institution but the attitude brought to its administration, an attitude that must be one of obedience to the divine commission. It is also obvious that the commission itself may vary and hence may be different from the particular mandates given to the kings and judges of Israel.

Only very occasionally are the divinely sanctioned orders of Israel taken over directly, e.g., in the case of taxation. Thus "David, Hezekiah, Josiah, Jehoshaphat, and other holy kings . . . were, without offending piety, lavish at public expense." And as they received "a very large portion of the land," so also do these belong to the secular princes today, not as "private chests," but as "treasuries of the entire people." [67]

Apart from these special instances of a direct model, Calvin makes a very precise, rigorous, and sometimes even polemical distinction between the demands of the Old Testament in the special situation of Israel and their relevance for our own very different situation. The "perpetual duties" of the Old Testament which still apply to us relate not to the form of the Law but to the motive behind it. Thus, behind the "ceremonial law" is the purpose of a "tutelage" in piety by means of an adumbration in "figures" of things whose reality was yet to be revealed.[68] Again, behind the "judicial law" is the purpose of guiding "the very love which is enjoined by God's eternal law" into the right channels, and of finding "how best to preserve" it in specific ordinances.[69]

We thus have to say that involved in the commandments there is an element other than ("something distinctive from") the motive of piety

[64] *Ibid.* 4. 20. 4; *LCC* 21, 1489.
[65] *Ibid.* 4. 20. 9; *LCC* 21, 1495-1497.
[66] *Ibid.* 4. 20. 4; *LCC* 21, 1489.
[67] *Ibid.* 4. 20. 13; *LCC* 21, 1501.
[68] *Ibid.* 4. 20. 15; *LCC* 21, 1503.
[69] *Ibid.*

and love.[70] They are the medium, conditioned by time and circumstances, within which the piety and love of Israel are fulfilled. For us only the motives count, not the media. The motives alone are "perpetual duties." In particular – and this is connected with the distinction between motive and medium – the sacrifices and ceremonies which remained in force only until Christ came, have been terminated.[71] To adopt or revive them would be to obscure again with shadows the clarity which has been given by Christ.[72]

There thus arises that elasticity in application of the Law to which we referred, which is often overlooked by Lutheran expositors of Calvin. Calvin repeatedly expressed and concretely illustrated this elasticity in the matter of adjusting to different situations. Thus he shows from the example of penal law that in Israel certain offenses (e.g., stealing, murder, adultery) were punished in certain ways, while the same offenses are rightly punished in different ways among other peoples. For "there are countries which, unless they deal cruelly with murderers by way of horrible examples, must immediately perish from slaughters and robberies." [73] Again, in times of war, drought, and pestilence – i.e., in borderline situations – punishments have to be inflicted with draconic severity. Hence we do no "dishonor" to the Mosaic Law if we prefer new and different laws suited to the situation. Here regard has to be had to "the condition of times, place, and nation." [74] This can hardly mean "abrogation" of the Mosaic Law, since it "was never enacted for us." [75]

One has to take into account, therefore, the special privileged position of Israel, which is different from our own situation. We do not live in a theocracy such as was established in Israel by the fact that God "willed to be a lawgiver especially to it." [76] If we understand Calvin correctly, to take over the Mosaic Law would thus be not only to turn back from the manifested reality to the mere shadows, but also to arrogate to ourselves the special theocratic privileges of Israel which are not ours.

[70] *Ibid.*
[71] *Ibid.* 2. 7. 16; *LCC* 20, 364.
[72] *Ibid.*
[73] *Ibid.* 4. 20. 16; *LCC* 21, 1505.
[74] *Ibid.*
[75] *Ibid.*
[76] *Ibid.*

Almost everything that Calvin says about this change in the form of the Law, and about the distinction between its motive and its form, might equally well have been said by Luther. If, in spite of this, one thinks he can insist that there are certain theocratic features in Calvin's thought, he will have to bypass these statements. We must not caricature Calvin's legalism;[77] it is a complex, multistoried edifice.

Despite the agreement in detail, however, there is nevertheless, an essential difference from Luther. The elasticity which we have noted does not consist for Calvin in a freedom which the gospel gives us *over against* the Law, but in a freedom *within* the Law which is itself gospel. Christian freedom does not mean freedom *from* the Law. It means freedom in the use of the Law, because the Christian has from Christ criteria which enable him to distinguish between the motive and the form of the Law, between an eternal precept and a precept valid in Israel prior to Christ's coming.

In our view this is a decisive distinction. Calvin's view that freedom is freedom in the use of the Law, not freedom from it, comes very close to Luther and his totally different concept of the relation between Law and gospel so long as the question at issue is how far the ceremonial and civil law of Moses is still binding on Christians. This partial overlapping, however, should not blind us to the deeper differences between the two. For the significant consequence of Calvin's view is that strictly speaking Christ does not liberate *from* the Law but himself comes *within* it as a new Legislator, giving universal extension to the divine legislatorship which formerly applied to Israel alone.

This helps us to understand both the legalism of Calvin and also his elasticity in the handling of the Law. The legalism arises because a kind of Christocracy is now possible, for which the way is already prepared by that other strand of thought which we followed in our discussion of the two concentric circles. The freedom in the use of the Law of Christ arises because Christ is in direct relation to all peoples and situations, and obedience to him in principle may vary far more than in the case of the Law of the old convenant which was applicable to the one theocratic people. We thus maintain that the different relation between Law and gospel in Calvin — and in Reformed theology generally — the greater prominence given to the *usus politicus*, the

---

[77] Even Troeltsch did this to some degree. See Troeltsch, *op. cit.*, II, 615 ff.

political function of the Law, as compared with the *usus elenchticus*, the accusing role of the Law, means that Christ – as the content of the gospel – takes on some of the features of Law.

But this is not all. The redemption effected in Christ is regarded as one of the "means" by which the primal decree is fulfilled, and since this decree spans universal history as well as salvation history, it follows that Christ himself has a direct relation to universal history, to all its orders and factors. The monistic thrust in Reformed theology, which derives from the original decree and works itself out politically in the doctrine of the two concentric circles, is thus strengthened by the equally monistic relating of Law and gospel. Christ is both in one, and in virtue of this he acquires his immediacy to the world as its Legislator. Thus Christ is both Head of his body, the church, and at the same time Head of the world as well. He embraces both.

Now Luther too could say the very same thing. For him too Christ is the cosmocrator. But Luther would define the lordship differently. He regards it as a hidden lordship, and that in two senses. From the standpoint of the gospel, Christ's universal lordship is hidden under the cover of the cross, i.e., under its opposite.[78] From the standpoint of the Law,[79] it is hidden because the God revealed in Christ performs only an "alien work" in establishing the postlapsarian orders; he preserves the world by using only its available Noachic possibilities, and thus makes concessions out of his preserving love.[80] For this aeon, then, the divine lordship in Christ is present only under the aspect of self-alienation – a self-alienation in love. Thus the theme of the two kingdoms may be seen again at this point.

Things are very different in Calvin. Here the relation between Christ and the world is fully as direct as the relation between Christ and the church. In both relations what is at stake is the one universal lordship. In view of what we have already said about the elasticity of the Law in Calvin this obviously cannot mean that for him the Gospels are a treasury of legal directives for ruling the world christocratically. But it does mean that the directness of Christ's lordship finds expression in what is in principle a very close connection between state and church.

---

[78] *Sub tecto crucis, sub contrario absconditus.* See *LW* 31, 52-53; cf. Walter von Loewenich, *Luthers Theologia crucis* (2nd ed.; Munich, 1933), pp. 151 ff.
[79] In this case what is meant is the political use of the Law.
[80] See *ThE* 1, 567 ff.

We thus arrive from the christological standpoint at the same church-state relation as was reached from the standpoint of the absolute decree in the image of the two circles. The fact that from two such very different approaches the theological system arrives at the same point is an indication of its imposing logical consistency.

The fact is that Christology does lead us to the same view of the relation between church and state. A theoretical separation between them is impossible. The relation is such that the normative impulses flow from within outwards, from the narrower circle to the wider, from church to state. For it is the people of God in the narrower circle who know God's declared will; they know the Legislator. In order that this will may be known, however, and then further proclaimed, this people must be able to live. They must be afforded protection in a secular order. This is why the state is necessary for the church. Indeed, it is this necessary political *diaconia* in relation to the church which really gives the state its theological meaning and purpose.[81]

For Calvin, therefore, every government must necessarily be a Christian government, aware of its task: "If the government does not decide for Christ, then it decides against Him." [82] For the task of the government is not only to guarantee the external conditions of life ("that men breathe, eat, drink, and are kept warm" [83]) and to secure "public peace" and constitutional order. These are simply the physical presuppositions of its true ministry, namely, to see to it "that a public manifestation of religion may exist among Christians [not just within the church!], and that humanity be maintained among men." [84]

Here, then, there is an intensive mutual interpenetration of church and state. In the face of chaos the state provides the possibility of an ordered life, and hence of life itself; but this is only the presupposition of spiritual life, i.e., of life in the kingdom of Christ. On the other hand, the state can fulfill this task only when it knows its goal to be the *diaconia* of order, i.e., only when it is composed of Christians ("among

---

[81] In the first edition of the *Institutes* (1536) Calvin entitled his section on civil government: "The civil order is necessary for the well-being of the church." Wilhelm Niesel, *The Theology of Calvin,* trans. Harold Knight (Philadelphia: Westminster, 1956), p. 230.

[82] Niesel, *op. cit.,* p. 235.

[83] Calvin *Institutes* 4. 20. 3; *LCC* 21, 1488.

[84] *Ibid.* It would seem that the idea of "public manifestation" *[publica facies]* underscores even terminologically the antithesis to the Lutheran view of hiddenness.

Christians"). Hence the church with its Word – this is the formal dialectic – constitutes in turn the presupposition on which alone the state can fulfill its task of providing physical order. For only as the church streams into the political sphere and establishes the "public manifestation of religion," only as it affords the civil community an "analogical capacity" in Barth's sense, does it create the presupposition of humanity which is the foundation of all order.

It is on account of this mutual dialectical interpenetration of church and state that Calvinism presses for a Christian form of the state, for a "public manifestation [*publica facies*] of religion." This is why the Christian element attaches, to the institution. There really can be a Christian state, not just Christian statesmen.[85] At any rate, there can be no question here of the alien character of the political order vis-à-vis Christ's kingdom. The two kingdoms do not stand over against one another. What God does in the worldly kingdom is not an alien work. What we have here is instead an analogy, a reflection (*facies*) of Christ's kingdom.

This is worked out in the detailed mutual obligations which church and state owe to one another. The state has not only to prevent political rebellion. It has also to regard as rebellion, and to punish accordingly, any public contempt of God, any malicious offense against his Word.[86] For this reason the state must prevent "idolatry, sacrilege against God's name, blasphemies against his truth."[87] But on the positive side it has also to see to the ascendancy of the true doctrine taught by the church, promote its work, and – in keeping with Isaiah 49:23 – make kings "foster fathers of the church."[88] If the church-state relation is seen in this way, then the church also has the right to help bring about the overthrow of an unchristian state, and this opens the way in principle to the idea of a crusade which Luther so passionately repudiated.

In spite of this close connection between church and state in Calvin, one should not overlook the fact that there is also a separating factor.

[85] There are clear reminiscences of this in Barth's "The Christian Community and the Civil Community" – though with variations which are to be expected in an age of secular states so very different from Calvin's Geneva – especially where the analogy works itself out in political order and practice.

[86] *Corpus Reformatorum*, ed. C. G. Bretschneider and H. E. Bindseil (Halle/Saale, 1834-1860), XXVII, 246 and 688.

[87] Calvin *Institutes* 4. 20. 3; *LCC* 21, 1488.

[88] *Ibid.* 4. 20. 5; *LCC* 21, 1490; see Niesel, *op. cit.*, p. 234.

This separating factor, however, is different in kind from that which Luther has in view when he speaks of the separation of the kingdoms. For Calvin the separation arises, not from the fact that the church stands in a direct relation to Christ's kingdom whereas the state stands only in an indirect relation, but merely from the pragmatic observation that the effectiveness of each — which is in the interest of both — can be maintained only if limits of competence and distinctions of jurisdiction are observed.

Thus the church is restricted vis-à-vis the state to the degree that the gospel which it preaches makes all men (without hierarchical distinction) equal in respect of grace, but this freedom and equality cannot be transferred into the political sphere. It is fanaticism to argue in the name of our Christian liberty that no power should be set up over us. And "it is Jewish vanity to seek and enclose Christ's kingdom within the elements of this world." [89] In this respect civil order and the kingdom of Christ are completely different in structure.

But the state too is limited vis-à-vis the church. Its laws and ordinances cannot claim power over the inward man. Such power belongs only to God, who as the "spiritual lawgiver" disposes of body and soul, whereas the "mortal lawgiver" has jurisdiction only over the "outward political order." [90]

Today one might see in this limitation of the state a barrier against totalitarianism and ideologizing. Calvin, however, has concretely in view a Christian state. For him the restriction means that the state should not itself preach the gospel but leave that task to the church. The state should be content, first, to place the presuppositions for such proclamation at the church's disposal, and second, to desire such preaching of the gospel, i.e., to desire as an institution to stand under the commandments, and thus to present a Christian image or "manifestation" (facies).[91] The state is thus put under the Word of God. It is regarded as a Christian state, not a secular state.

Even though one might thus find christocratic features in the political thought and practice of Calvin, however, one cannot speak of his espousing ecclesiocracy. Richard Niebuhr rightly points out that "it is an error to regard Calvinism as hierocratic; the state was

---

[89] *Ibid.* 4. 20. 1; *LCC* 21, 1486.
[90] *Ibid.* 2. 8. 6; *LCC* 20, 372.
[91] *Corpus Reformatorum*, XXIV, 357; XLIII, 135; cf. Niesel, *op. cit.*, p. 236.

no more subordinate to the church in its theory and practice than the church was to the state. They were both subject to a common constitution, the will of God declared in Scripture and nature." [92]

As the sphere of God's rule church and state thus constitute an indivisible whole even though they have different functions. They are equal members within a commonly binding theocratic or christocratic constitution. Since Calvin has in view only the Christian state, not the secular state, it is even questionable whether Barth's image of the concentric circles is directly applicable to Calvin. Is it not rather an extension of Calvin's concept to the situation of secularization and secularism? A more apt illustration of Calvin's own view would perhaps be that of two congruent circles imposed one upon the other.

In conclusion we may emphasize again some of the main points of difference from Luther. Luther's separation of church and state, of world and kingdom of God, which in principle is something more than merely a distinction of functions within an indivisible whole, is determined by his concept of the "two kingdoms." This concept, for its part, is based on the assertion that the unconditional will expressed in the Sermon on the Mount can be fulfilled only in part within the orders of the fallen world, that it suffers refraction in the Noachic covenant. There thus arises the distinction between God's "proper works" in the kingdom on the right hand and his "alien works" in the kingdom on the left.

In distinction from the theologies of Melanchthon and Lutheran orthodoxy, which become increasingly satisfied with this coexistence of the two spheres of authority and which finally press towards the idea of a more or less autonomous worldly kingdom, Luther himself gives evidence of continuing unrest over the fact that the worldly kingdom lives in institutional and structural apostasy as well. The stronger the impact of this observation, and of the consequent unrest, the more emphatic is the distinction between the "two governments" of God, because only thus can there be adequate emphasis on the proper and unconditional will of God in the kingdom on the right hand.

It would almost seem like a tragedy of thought — if the word tragedy were appropriate in theology — that this distinction, which was intended to do honor to the "proper" will of God, should subsequently

---

[92] H. Richard Niebuhr, *The Kingdom of God in America* (Chicago: Willett, Clark, 1937), p. 39.

lead precisely to a growing dissociation between this proper will and the "alien" zone of the secular kingdom, so that in the name of Lutheranism there could arise a kind of autarchy of this world, with a corresponding impulse towards secularism.

Luther's unrest at any rate had its roots in the observation that within the orders of the worldly kingdom God's will can be realized only in compromise, that the state is not a direct expression of the will of God but has been permitted because of the hardness of our hearts and is an emergency order, an order of patience, appointed by God to keep the world from destroying itself. The idea of a Christian state for Luther is impossible in principle. His very concept of order precludes the possibility of the Christian element ever finding institutional expression. Its operation is rather personal, in the sense that Christians, who know God's proper will and who are enabled to live in the penultimate sphere under God's grace, do their work as a "vocation."

By contrast, Reformed theology integrates, within one and the same theocratic constitution the kingdom of Christ and the worldly kingdom, church and state, on the monistic basis of the doctrine of the decrees and the corresponding Christology. Even where secularization no longer leaves room for the kind of Christian state which this conception originally had in view, the unity remains, at least in the form of the two concentric circles.

In purely pragmatic terms, we should have to say that this Reformed view of the relation between church and state avoids the temptation of lending theological sanction to a secularized independence of the state by way of the two kingdoms doctrine. It also prevents Christians from a quietistic and laissez faire withdrawal from political life. The Reformed Christian is unable to find a theological excuse if he tries to reduce to a minimum, or to abolish altogether, the church's office as watchman.

When the Lutheran Christian looks about for such an alibi, he does manage to find one that seems to serve. The fact is though that at this point Lutheran theology is beset (or blessed) by greater temptations. It is in a more dangerous and exposed position. Nor can one say that it has always honorably resisted these temptations. On the contrary, it has frequently succumbed to them. We need only mention such rubrics as "throne and altar," "Lutheran quietism," or "the handicap of being a Lutheran in a totalitarian state" in order to put our fingers on some of the faults, not of Lutheranism as such, but of certain circles within it.

At the same time, "danger" is not a theological concept. And to state which theologians have in practice shown greater immunity to such dangers is not yet to say anything about the question of truth. To think and to live dangerously can even be a sign of worth. Thoughtful persons will not regard it as flirting with danger if they feel summoned by the dangerous nature of this thinking to examine its basic concept, and to determine whether the fateful developments which actually took place in Lutheranism derive from the defective structure of its two kingdoms doctrine or are due rather to the abuse of a structure which is fundamentally sound. Since no harm can be done by such examination, the attacks and sharp questions of Reformed theologians like Barth and Diem, as well as the questions which are put to them in reply, are a two-way ministry, a reciprocal admonition on the part of brothers within the same church.

The Intermediate Position of Abraham Kuyper

In the present context it is not our purpose to give a complete picture of Abraham Kuyper's views of church and state. We shall simply try to see how far a flexible handling of the Calvinistic principle can lead to a definition of the church-state relation which approximates that of a synthesis with the corresponding Lutheran heritage. We think Kuyper can be regarded as representative of such a synthesis, though we know of course that he is not usually interpreted in this way.

That there is more to Kuyper than merely a repristination of Calvin may be seen in the way in which he criticizes the burning of Servetus.[93] He regards this criticism, however, as an imminent criticism. That is to say, he thinks that what he is criticizing is an alien element, which has illegitimately intruded upon or survived in Calvinism but is not characteristic of it. To this degree it may be said that he thinks to do justice to the Calvinistic principle not by simply taking over its

---

[93] See Kuyper, *op. cit.*, pp. 99-100. "I not only deplore that one stake, but I unconditionally disapprove of it; yet not as if it were the expression of a special characteristic of Calvinism, but on the contrary as the fatal after-effect of a system, grey with age, which Calvinism found in existence, under which it had grown up, and from which it had not yet been entirely able to liberate itself." *Ibid.*, p. 100.

sixteenth-century form, but by applying it in a critical way so that Reformed Christianity can be further reformed.[94]

In this sense Kuyper largely rejects, e.g., the theocratic ideas of Calvin, but here again in such a way that he bases his criticism on Calvin's own fundamental concepts to which he simply gives different emphasis. As we have seen, Calvin had himself pointed out the distinction between the theocratic situation of Israel and his own contemporary situation, even though his close "christocratic" integration of church and state constantly suggested analogies to the situation of Israel.

Kuyper makes an even sharper distinction between the present situation and that of Israel — one has to speak here in comparatives — and thus arrives at a more marked separation between church and state. In so doing he still believes he is in the unique position of criticizing Calvin in the name of Calvin, of understanding Calvin better than Calvin had understood himself. Kuyper thus reinterprets the theocratic tendencies of Calvin in terms of their own starting point. He finds their root in two theses: first, "God only — and never any creature — is possessed of sovereign rights, in the destiny of nations, . . ." and second, "In whatever form this authority may reveal itself, man never possesses power over his fellow-man in any other way than by an authority which descends upon him from the majesty of God." [95] This starting point leads to very different results in the privileged situation of the chosen people of Israel and in our own situation. In our new situation the task is to establish what "confession of the Sovereignty of God" means with reference to the whole wide world of nations. Theocracy in the strict sense could arise "only . . . in Israel, because in Israel God intervened immediately . . . He held in His own hand the jurisdiction and the leadership of His people." [96] This distinction from the theocracy of Israel leads, as it were automatically, to an emphasis on the separation of church and state which outweighs the emphasis on that which unites them, and here Kuyper undoubtedly deviates from Calvin to

---

[94] Thus Kuyper can say that "he who is reformed must always reform. The confession on which we have been working for centuries must be developed, and related to the thinking of our time" (Wilhelm Kolfhaus, *Dr. Abraham Kuyper* [2nd ed.; Elberfeld], pp. 195-196). For Calvin "did not fully see or develop what was implicit in his basic motivating principle" (*ibid.*, p. 196 n.).

[95] Kuyper, *op. cit.*, p. 85.

[96] *Ibid.*

whom he appeals. Calvinists were always "aware of the non-ecclesiastical origin of government, and therewith of its independent task and special sphere. They also had too high an estimation of the church of Christ to permit it to spend itself in political dealing or power-seeking. Finally, it was their clear confession that the Holy Spirit not only dispenses spiritual grace to those who are called, but also gives to governments their own gift and sufficient light to understand God's Word. . . . In both spheres it is God who rules, not man. In both spheres too, however, the sovereign God gave institutions of their own, and persons with responsibilities of their own, all so interrelated once again that his church owes honor and obedience to the earthly fatherland, while the earthly fatherland serves the heavenly fatherland by giving free course to the gospel." [97]

The true and theologically most profound reason for this sharper differentiation between the state and the church is certainly not to be found in the argument that our situation is basically different from that of Israel, for Calvin too was aware of that fact. It is rather a case of Kuyper — in a way which is astonishingly similar to that of Luther and very different from that of Calvin — setting the state in a relation to sin which completely shatters the monism of the genuine Reformed view of the church-state relation as derived from the doctrine of the decrees. Indeed Kuyper can make statements reminiscent of the two kingdoms doctrine of Luther: "Sin has, in the realm of politics, broken down the direct government of God, and therefore the exercise of authority, for the purpose of government, has subsequently been invested in men, as a mechanical remedy," [98] i. e., as something "unnatural" and contrary to "the deeper aspirations of our nature."[99] Given the situation as it actually is, the establishment of the state is a merciful act of divine care and preservation. Indeed, it can no longer be said that the state stands on the same level as the church so far as its origin is concerned. The church stands too much under a direct election, calling, and blessing, whereas the state has the features of an indirect emergency order.

Here, then, there crops up in Reformed thinking a line which clearly departs from the monistic tendencies of the doctrine of the decrees. It

[97] Kolfhaus, op. cit., p. 181.
[98] Kuyper, op. cit., p. 85.
[99] Ibid., p. 80.

may be that these correctives, which remind us of the antithesis of the two kingdoms in Luther, are induced by Kuyper's situation. Here is a case of an active politician whose entire thinking is deeply affected by secularism. Indeed his theological *and* political passions are decidedly influenced by the struggle against secularism.

Though Kuyper's thinking cannot be described as disguised Lutheranism — for at essential points it is very definitely Calvinistic — one may suspect that the relation between the state and sin to which he pointed would be bound to have concrete implications for the position of the church in political life. And this is in fact the case. If one ignores this relation between the state and sin, if one interprets Kuyper as a simple Calvinist, one can easily get the impression that his thought is marked by explicitly theocratic features.[100] For Kuyper strove for a Christian permeation of the state which to all appearances is reminiscent of the similar attempts of Calvin in Geneva, and which one would expect to find supported by the same theological justification.

It is characteristic of Kuyper's relating of church and state, however, that in distinction from Calvin he thinks in personal rather than institutional terms. As "institution"[101] the church is unique, and strictly separate from the state. But as "organism," i.e., from the standpoint of the people comprised in it, it is most intimately connected with the state, since its members are at the same time citizens and perhaps even rulers. Here again, then, Kuyper approximates Luther's idea of Christian persons making up the state. Accordingly, Kuyper does not speak of a Christian state in the institutional sense. The demand he makes on the state is rather the negative one that it not exceed its divinely ordained functions, and that it vouchsafe freedom to the individual and to the church's proclamation. The very notion of a "Christian state" would run counter to his usage. He speaks instead of the "people of God" or a "Christian people," thus giving preference at this point also to personal categories. In the age of sociology we might say that he speaks of a Christian society rather than a Christian state. Since the state is a form of social organization, a Christian permeation of society will affect it too.

[100] Künneth has not quite avoided this trap. See Künneth, *op. cit.*, pp. 530 ff.
[101] See K. H. Miskotte, "Naturrecht und Theokratie," in *Die Freiheit des Evangeliums und die Ordnung der Gesellschaft. Vorträge von K. E. Løgstrup, K. H. Miskotte, et al.* ("Beiträge zur evangelischen Theologie," XV, ed. Ernst Wolf [Munich: Kaiser, 1952]), 29 ff.

If Kuyper thus speaks of a Christian shaping of the state (and in this connection can even refer occasionally to the "Christian state"), he does so in a very different sense from that of the Reformed fathers when they defined church and state as two congruent or concentric circles. Their way of looking as it presupposes that the church helps to shape the institution of the state. But this is precisely what Kuyper in an age of secularization could no longer presuppose. For him, Christianity streams into the sphere of the state only insofar as it permeates society and mounts, as it were, an invasion by Christian persons.

It may be noted that the cultural policy which Kuyper pursued also derives its strategic laws from this principle. He could never have fought for the legislative establishment of exclusively Christian universities and schools, or for a press law which would permit only Christian newspapers. Kuyper knew that in an age of secularization such a policy would lead to nothing but Christian facades, since the state with its institutions cannot be anything other than the society in which it exists. Thus he himself, according to the measure of possible Christian permeation, established such Christian institutions as the Free University,[102] schools in which the Bible was taught,[103] and a Christian newspaper *(De Heraut).*[104] For faith can claim only so much public and national space as it is able to occupy. And by "occupy" we mean be in a position not only to furnish with personnel, but also to master theologically the various fields of secular life and culture, supplanting their non-biblical and secularistic interpretation by a Christian understanding.[105]

Thus the Christian shaping of the state is not accomplished from above by way of determining the character of its order. It is accomplished from below through the influence of Christian persons (the "people of God") and impulse centers in the form of specific Christian institutions (university, school, press, etc.) which will bring it to pass.

In this connection, one may perhaps distinguish in Kuyper between zones of primary and secondary Christian influence and character. Pri-

[102] Kolfhaus, *op. cit.,* pp. 152 ff.
[103] *Ibid.,* pp. 50 ff., 119-120.
[104] *Ibid.,* pp. 54-55.
[105] Thus in the successive chapters of his Stone Lectures, Kuyper specifically undertakes to provide a Calvinistic interpretation of history, religion, politics, science, and art.

mary Christian zones are those where the people of God have a direct influence (e.g., in specifically Christian institutions). Secondary Christian zones are areas of wider influence such as those provided by even a secular culture in which Christians participate. "A city set on a hill cannot be hid" (Matt. 5:14). In this sense the thing to do is to fill society with a genuine sense of authority, with a feeling for definite forms which will resist undisciplined individualism, with good morals, etc.[106]

Consequently one can hardly speak here of a theocracy which is always interested primarily in the institutional aspect. From the standpoint of this personal and social idea of the "people of God" the institutional aspect is decidedly secondary. It arises only later, after the "people of God" has won solid positions, first in the primary Christian spheres which it fills directly, and then in the areas of its wider influence.

The end result might be — though this is a purely theoretical construction — a Christian state comparable to that which Calvin had in view. However, it would not arise in the same way, or be justified along the same lines, as the state which for Calvin is congruent with the church (in the sense of the two congruent circles). On the contrary, Kuyper here takes a path which is to a great extent parallel to the way of Lutheran political and social ethics, which envisages a Christian influence on the worldly kingdom — and hence also on the state — by way of the person, whether he be a member of the "Christian people" [107] active in the kingdom on the left hand, or a Christian ruler who, as "the chief member of the church," [108] again maintains his Christian stance in the kingdom on the left hand as well (by his concern for justice and by the way he uses the power of his office).[109]

One can only conjecture how this astonishing parallelism arose. In explanation the following line of thought is worth considering. For Luther the decisive impulse toward the idea of the two kingdoms doctrine comes from the fact that the divine commandments are refracted when they enter into the medium of this world. This world with its orders is not "according to" the kingdom of God. This is

---

[106] Kolfhaus, *op. cit.,* pp. 68 ff.
[107] WA 32, 161, line 7.
[108] See above p. 10, n. 8.
[109] See LW 45, 118 ff.

why the unconditional requirements of the kingdom of God, e.g., in the Sermon on the Mount, do not fit smoothly into this world but instead call it in question. Thus the two kingdoms doctrine originates in a horror at the otherness of the world, a horror which persists as disquiet of conscience through all Luther's teaching on the orders.

Whereas for the reasons already indicated Calvin does not feel this disquiet, but regards the state as a piece of world to be sure, but a Christian piece, one that bears a certain analogy to the kingdom of God, in Kuyper there is operative once again that horror at the otherness of the world, at its remoteness from the kingdom of God. For what Kuyper is confronted with is the secular state whose a-Christianity underscores that otherness and does not project the optical illusions easily created by Calvin's "Christian state." This horror may also be a factor in the theological consideration that the state is an emergency measure taken in light of the fall, and that it is thus "unnatural" when measured by the original nature of man.

There is thus constituted a qualitative distinction between church and state, from which certain consequences naturally follow, consequences which are implicit also in the Lutheran doctrine of the two kingdoms. The most important of these is that the church does not press for an institutional Christianizing of the state. Instead it sees individual Christians at work in the secular kingdom. The church thus seeks to influence this kingdom through persons. Hence the problem of society takes precedence of that of the state.

At any rate, we see here what a broad range of thinking can proceed from the same Reformed starting point. We also see that the idea of the decrees does not always have to be determinative. In the case of Kuyper at any rate the "central doctrine of Reformed orthodoxy" [110] certainly plays a very subsidiary role.

The Extreme Theocracy of Arnold van Ruler

The breadth of Calvinistic possibilities is also manifested in the opposite direction. It can provide the occasion for proclaiming the establishment of a theocratically controlled worldly kingdom as the goal of salvation history, and for understanding the church as merely a temporary means to the realization of this goal. We use the word

[110] Flückiger, *op. cit.*, p. 515.

"occasion" advisedly in order to show critical appreciation of the fact that the Calvinistic principle does not necessarily provide a "basis" for this theocratic construction. It simply contains certain possibilities which may be used — or misused — to that end, just as Luther's doctrine of the two kingdoms can provide the occasion for a radical separation between personal morality and official morality, or for the consolidation of an autonomous secular kingdom severed completely from the will of God.

Of course, a doctrine or confession is in some sense characterized by the possibilities of perversion inherent within it. In this respect the idea of an autarchical worldliness seems to be the specifically Lutheran perversion, while the idea of a theocratically controlled worldliness seems to be the specifically Reformed perversion.[111]

Van Ruler represents an extreme example of the theocratic kind of thinking. In keeping with the Reformed tradition, he bases his conception especially on the Old Testament, whose theocratic features he regards not as restricted to Israel alone — in the manner of Calvin and particularly Kuyper — but as applicable to the whole world. In this van Ruler is influenced partly by a Jewish interpretation which finds depicted in the Old Testament "a visionary belief in the possibility of the sanctification of the earth," [112] and partly by a particular doctrine of salvation history which he claims to have found in some New Testament scholars and which he arbitrarily interprets to suit his own purpose. Thus, he speaks of a double movement in salvation history, not just in the direction of reduction (peoples — the people — the remnant — the One) but also in the direction of expansion (Messiah — Spirit — conscience — the state — the whole universe).[113]

---

[111] We say this of course only with reservations, for, even as there are points of contact between the Reformed Karl Barth and the Lutheran Wilhelm Stapel on the analogy between church and state, so too there are theocratic features in Lutheranism. These are classically delineated by Ernst Ludwig von Gerlach in letters to his friend August von Bethmann-Hollweg. (Selections from these previously unknown letters have been printed by Friedrich W. Kantzenbach in *Zeitschrift für Religions- und Geistesgeschichte,* 1957, 3, pp. 257 ff.).

[112] The reference is to Martin Buber, *At the Turning: Three Addresses on Judaism* (New York: Farrar, Straus, and Cudahy, 1952).

[113] Van Ruler's view, set forth in his *Die Christliche Kirche und das Alte Testament* (Munich: Kaiser, 1955), p. 65, represents a divergent application of the idea of a double movement as set forth in Ethelbert Stauffer, *New Testament Theology,* trans. John Marsh (New York: Macmillan, 1955), pp. 72 ff., 153 ff., and in Oscar Cullmann, *Christ and Time,* trans. Floyd V. Filson (rev. ed.; Philadelphia: Westminster, 1964), pp. 115 ff.

The theological center of van Ruler's thought is indicated by the question which he puts with reference to the Old Testament: What is the significance of Christ for salvation history in the Old Testament? His answer is that Christ cannot be understood either typologically [114] or directly [115] as the goal and content of this salvation history; he is only an interposition or an interim means [116] to bring about the desired dominion of God over the earth. This means-to-end schema is the point of the whole system and leads to an inversion of all customary perspectives which is at least very clever, original, and challenging. We can illustrate this by a few examples.

To scholars like Friedrich Baumgärtel, Leonhard Goppelt, and Gerhard von Rad who espouse the correspondence between prophecy and fulfillment van Ruler puts the question whether God is really concerned "about Israel for the sake of Jesus Christ," or "about Jesus Christ for the sake of Israel." [117] Is not Christ just a means to make of holy Israel such and such a people and state?

But this schema raises a chain reaction of further questions. "Is God concerned about the peoples of the earth for the sake of Israel, or is he not concerned rather about Israel for the sake of the peoples of the earth? And then one must pursue the question to the bitter end: Is God concerned about creation for the sake of grace, the covenant, and salvation, or is he not concerned rather about salvation for the sake of created reality, that it may stand before his face?" [118]

The goal of all the intervening and instrumental stages of salvation history is the sanctification of the earth, and in a comprehensively theocratic sense which involves not merely the sacral exaltation of the orders of the world, but also the saving and sanctifying of man. Hence the focal point and goal of history is not Christ but the new world, the new humanity, brought into being through him. "God's concern is not for the One who saves us, but for us who are saved through him. We are not men in order that we might be Christians, but we are Christians in order that we might be men." [119] Hence

---

[114] See Leonhard Goppelt, *Typos. Die typologische Deutung des Alten Testaments im Neuen* (Darmstadt: Wissenschaftliche Buchgesellschaft, 1966).

[115] Cf. the views of Wilhelm Vischer and Hans Hellbardt set forth in *ThE* 1, 100 ff.

[116] Van Ruler, *Religie en Politiek* (Nijkerk: Callenbach, 1945), p. 172.

[117] Van Ruler, *Die christliche Kirche*, pp. 63-64.

[118] *Ibid.*, p. 64.

[119] *Ibid.*, pp. 64-65.

reconciliation with God is not the goal but only the means to the greater end of sanctification. Hence also the purpose of the church cannot be to preach "Christ," for Christ has come "for the sake of the kingdom." [120] Christ is thus a mere interim. Indeed, he is "an emergency measure which God kept in abeyance as long as possible. Hence one must not try to force this matter of finding Christ in the Old Testament." [121]

In view of these christological theses one need not be surprised that the state too occupies for van Ruler a very different position from that assigned to it in both Lutheranism and Calvinism. The state is the order of a world which God had in view already in the decree of creation and for whose sanctification salvation history is ordained. Hence the state is not only an order of creation but also an eschatological order, for "it is an earthly, or better a Messianic, form of divine sonship." [122] To this degree the state takes decisive precedence of the church. For the church as the body of Christ shares with Christ an interim character. It is interposed, whereas the state extends from the beginning of creation to its eschatological consummation.

The consequence is thus unavoidable — and van Ruler draws it — that the state, as an institutional expression of the earth which is to be sanctified and actually has been sanctified, bears a direct spiritual commission. Hence it can no longer be said that the functions of the state are restricted to the second table of the commandments, the political use of the Law. On the contrary the state is also concerned with the first table, relating to acknowledgment of the name of God. Indeed, it is concerned with the gospel itself. For this reason the fundamental law of the state must be "a confession, a confession which can only be ecumenical in the Reformed sense."

Here is the diametrical opposite of the doctrine of the two kingdoms. Indeed, Calvin's teaching that church and state are two congruent circles is also set aside. From the standpoint of both time and space, of both history and salvation history, the state is now the more inclusive concept. It is an encompassing construct within which the church renders interim assistance as an "emergency measure."

---

[120] *Ibid.*, pp. 85-86.
[121] Van Ruler, *Religie en Politiek*, p. 172.
[122] Van Ruler, *Die christliche Kirche*, p. 65.

In van Ruler Barth's image of the two concentric circles is thus inverted. The state is still the outer circle and the church the inner, but the relation between them has been fundamentally altered. For Barth the inner circle of the Christian community must control and permeate the outer circle. It is the more durable of the two inasmuch as it is grounded in the pretemporal decree of election and oriented to the eschaton. For van Ruler, on the contrary, the outer circle of the state is the more durable, lasting from creation to the end. Within it the inner circle is drawn only for an interim period. For van Ruler all ways thus lead to the theocratically ruled world, the "sanctification of the earth."

At least five points of criticism may be brought against van Ruler, of which the first is that the eschatology which permeates the whole of the New Testament is here set aside and the Messianism of the Old Testament revived. Debate with Jewish exegesis of the Old Testament, then, no longer centers on the question whether Christ and the New Testament are the legitimate fulfillment of the Old, but on the question whether they have a legitimate place within the Old Testament line, whether they are a legitimate stage on the Old Testament way of salvation. For at root the New Testament says nothing more than that God's goal, the sanctification of the earth, cannot be attained without a temporary concentration on the problem of guilt and atonement which crops up along this way. This "one-sided," "enormous, and structurally forced concentration" [123] implies a reduction of the fullness of the Old Testament, and once this necessary reduction has been accomplished salvation history must again take up the original theme of the Old Testament and pursue the goal of the divine rule over all peoples, indeed over the whole universe. The New Testament thus ceases to be the canon within the biblical canon, the hermeneutical criterion for "Moses and the prophets." Instead, it becomes an "accident," and van Ruler can sometimes denote its incidental nature by saying that it is only a supplementary commentary on the Old Testament, an explanatory appendix to it. [124] It is thus with good reason that van Ruler sees the need for a fundamental

---

[123] *Ibid.*, p. 48.

[124] He once put it that way to me personally in a seminar discussion. Cf. also W. J. de Wilde, "Die holländische Diskussion über die Bedeutung des Alten Testaments in sozialen und politischen Fragen," *Quellenmaterial der Studenten-Abteilung des Oekumenischen Rates,* 51/G/125 (July, 1951), pp. 9-10.

revision of our concept of the canon,[125] nor does it matter whether one has in view the Lutheran or the Calvinist nuance in the Reformation concept of Scripture.

A second criticism has to do with the way van Ruler's inversion of New Testament eschatology shows itself precisely in his assumed church-state relation. According to the New Testament, it is the law which "comes in" (Rom. 5:20) or is "added" (Gal. 3:19). This means that the state too is an interposition having only interim significance.[126] The eschatological abolition of the state, of the principalities and powers, is only a logical consequence (I Cor. 15:24). But what the New Testament says about the state, van Ruler now says about the church. His contention that the church, like Christ, is a temporary emergency measure makes unavoidable the demand that what "began late"[127] should come to a speedy end as soon as it has discharged its emergency function. Although van Ruler does not explicitly draw this logical conclusion, it is implicit in his christological and ecclesiological premises. It is also suggested by the fact that the function assigned to the state in the end means a practical takeover of the tasks of the church: the state represents both tables of the Law as well as Law and gospel in one.

Here may be seen a strong formal similarity to Lessing's understanding of history. Lessing advances the thesis that the revelation of God (and hence also the church which preaches it) will ultimately make itself superfluous by bringing about a sanctification of the earth, naturally in Enlightenment terms as the age of the gospel of reason.[128] Even more strongly does van Ruler's eschatology remind us of the way in which Richard Rothe causes the church to be absorbed into the state once it has poured its Christian powers into the state and thus "sanctified" it for its eschatological function.[129]

Third, whereas the New Testament sees history ending with the *parousia* of Christ, so that Christ is the goal of history and this

---

[125] Van Ruler, *Die christliche Kirche*, pp. 87 ff.

[126] Cf. Wolfgang Schweitzer, *Die Herrschaft Christi und der Staat im Neuen Testament* (Munich: Kaiser, 1949), pp. 23 ff.; and Oscar Cullmann, *The State in the New Testament* (New York: Scribner's, 1956), pp. 54-55, 59 ff.

[127] Van Ruler, *Die christliche Kirche*, p. 65.

[128] See Helmut Thielicke, *Offenbarung, Vernunft und Existenz. Studien zur Religionsphilosophie Lessings* (3rd ed.; 1957).

[129] See above p. 576.

aeon gives way to a new heaven and a new earth (Rev. 21:1),[130] van Ruler draws upon the line of teaching in the Old Testament which has in view the perfecting of this present world. Now it is evident that New Testament eschatology cannot be fitted into this line, but represents a departure from it. The Evangelists and apostles know something which the patriarchs and prophets did not know – and could not know, for it was in Jesus Christ that God effected the miraculous changeover of aeons, thus breaking up every consequential nexus: not merely the nexus of guilt and punishment (through the tension of gospel and Law) but also the consequences which presumably derive from prophetically extrapolating the apparently solid premises of salvation history. This new thing known only to the Evangelists and apostles is that the old aeon cannot of itself produce the perfecting of the earth, that its orders can only remain emergency orders between the fall and judgment, that the peace of the world is and will always be deceptive (John 14:27; 16:38), that wars and rumors of wars will not cease (Matt. 24:6), that death, the last enemy, will be destroyed only at the resurrection of the dead (I Cor. 15:26), and only then will the tears be wiped away from all eyes (Rev. 7:17).

This overthrow of the world at the last day implies a different eschatology from that of the prophets. It is not that they are necessarily contradicted. It is rather that their prophecy has to be interpreted in the light of the correctives found in its fulfillment – if Old and New Testaments are really to remain united as the one book of the Word of God. These correctives make it clear that what the New Testament understands by fulfillment is in the Old projected on the plane of this world, and with this projection undergoes the distortions which are necessarily bound up with the idea of a perfect world in which there is fullness of peace and the lion lies down with the lamb (Isa. 11:6-7).

Hence one can speak of an analogy between the eschatology of the Old Testament and that of the New only if the new covenant fulfillment is regarded as the dominant element in the analogy, the criterion of interpretation. Where this is not done, Jewish and Christian readers can never arrive at a common exegesis in the reading

[130] See Helmut Thielicke, *Geschichte und Existenz* (1935), pp. 323-337.

of the Old Testament. For there is no abstractly demonstrable analogy. Only he who knows Christmas as the fulfillment, and hence waits for the second advent, knows him for whom the patriarchs and prophets were waiting. Only he stands in analogy to them, and understands too the analogy between the testaments, one of which "inculcates" Christ, the other of which "brings" him.[131]

Thus the debate between Christians and Jews can be conducted only by way of confessing one's faith, not by way of disputation or marshalling "proofs" from Scripture. For such debate must hinge on a criterion of Scripture which is non-demonstrable because it is the Lord himself in whom we believe.

In contrast, when van Ruler takes up the debate he has to stand on the same ground as the Jewish partner, namely, on the soil of the Old Testament. He has to show in terms of the logic of Old Testament salvation history that there must be that temporary and forced reduction to the problem of justification and reconciliation, a reduction which takes place in the New Testament but only in order that the salvation history of the Old Testament may pursue its course to the consummation of all things. This idea of a divine theocracy over the sanctified earth thus knocks New Testament eschatology right off its hinges and fundamentally alters the relation between the Testaments.

Fourth, the conception of van Ruler may well derive its decisive impulses from observation of the fact that the supraworldliness of the kingdom of God and the overthrow of this aeon, as these are proclaimed in· New Testament eschatology, carry with them the temptation to be indifferent to this earth and interested only in the hereafter.[132] Though he does not mention it, van Ruler was probably conscious here of the Marxist reproach against Christian eschatology. We believe that we have already shown that the relation between eschatology and ethics is fundamentally very different: [133] Realization

---

[131] *[Treibt* (see p. 587, n. 60) and *bringt.]*

[132] Van Ruler can say: "On the basis of the New Testament the church was certain that the cross of Christ was necessary. It therefore drew the false conclusion that this earth is beyond help: nothing can be done with it" *(Die christliche Kirche,* p. 85). Thus the church despairs of attempting to shape this world, because — as Baumgärtel puts it, "the demand of God simply cannot be empirically realized." Friedrich Baumgärtel, *Verheissung. Zur Frage des evangelischen Verständnisses des Alten Testaments* (Gütersloh: Bertelsmann, 1952), p. 58.

[133] Cf. also *ThE* 1, 44-47, 379-380, 572-577.

of the fact that the eschatological demand of God cannot be fulfilled provides the strongest impulse for ethics and for the shaping of the world. For this demand not only impels us in the direction of what it has in view. By calling in question the orders of this aeon, it also constitutes a barrier against the absolutizing of these orders. It is precisely the eschatological content of the demand which finds expression, as we have said, in the attitude of the Christian to the totalitarian state.

Furthermore, justification and reconciliation are not, as van Ruler suggests, a reduction of the event of salvation to the personal relation of God and man irrespective of the world. On the contrary, they are the content of an indicative with which the imperative of action, of bringing forth fruit, of shaping the world, is constitutively linked. The idea that Christians are dispensed from acting in the world, which has sometimes been advanced in the name of justification and reconciliation (e.g., in some Pietist groups), rests on a wholly heretical thesis. This thesis of Christian separation from the world is what van Ruler obviously has in view; and he reacts against it, not by pointing out the true New Testament and Reformation connections between the indicative of reconciliation and the imperative of action in the world, between faith and works, eschatology and ethics, but by making the shaping of the world the theme of faith instead of a consequence and by-product of faith. Thus reconciliation, and faith in reconciliation, are integrated into the greater theme of shaping the world; they become mere means to this end. One might say that here the New Testament becomes merely the handmaiden of the Old. Indicative and imperative, Law and gospel, Old Testament and New, are thus exchanged the one for the other.

Fifth and finally, van Ruler says that one of the ultimate goals of salvation history is the perfecting of humanity, for "we are not men in order that we might be Christians, but we are Christians in order that we might be men." [134] This thesis carries with it a radical challenge to theological anthropology. The question runs as follows: What is this "manhood" which our Christianity is intended to serve? What does it mean to become a "man"? Is it a matter of developing to full perfection the manhood which came into existence at creation?

---

[134] Van Ruler, *Die christliche Kirche,* p. 65.

And what precisely is this "created man"? Is it a matter of the ontically given form, the entelechy? Does perfection mean, then, the full and complete development of all the potentialities present by creation?

Simply to raise all these questions is necessarily to answer them in the negative. For in both the Old Testament and the New man does not exist as an ontically autonomous being, but only in his relation to God. Any statement about man's being must therefore always have the structure which such statements have in the Bible: Man occurs only as a predicate of the substantive "relation to God." To be a man is thus to be created by God and to be fallen from him, to be judged and visited by him, and finally, in Jesus Christ to be found, redeemed, reconciled, and brought to perfection by him. All other ontological statements about man — about his sexuality, his attributes, etc. — can be regarded only as secondary definitions within this ultimately determinative framework. To be a man is thus to be "from God" and "to God," and responsibly to lay hold of one's existence on these terms.

But if our relation to God is determined by Jesus Christ, if he is our peace with God (Eph. 2:14, 15; Col. 1:20), this means that one has not yet fully become man until this peace and fellowship are realized. By its very nature this communication with Christ cannot be a temporary thing which, once it is dissolved, leaves me capable of perfecting my humanity apart from him. It can be only an end in itself.

Indeed, the very image of man — we can even say the very concept of humanity — is not plain to me outside of Christ. If I seek it apart from him, what I come up with is simply the ideal of man in conflict with himself, or the ideal of the beautiful soul,[135] or a labor factor, or a vital potency, or one of the many other variants. What these all have in common is that they construct their image not from what man was at creation and what he is intended to be but from what he presently is; they take fallen man as their model and idealize him.

The image which God has of us men [136] has taken form in the humanity of Jesus Christ. Any doctrine of the divine image is thus christologically determined. What man is, I know only in face of the

---

[135] See above p. 146, n. 7.
[136] See ThE 1, 165 ff.

humanity of Jesus Christ. To become a man is to share in this humanity of Jesus Christ. It is to grow into the union with the Father which Jesus Christ "is" in virtue of his being the God-man. To grow into humanity is to grow into Jesus Christ.

Thus being a Christian cannot be regarded as a means to the end of becoming a man. If, on the other hand, to be a Christian means to be a member of the body of Christ, then there is implicit here also that *telos* to which our humanity is oriented, just as the theological purpose of the emergency orders of this aeon is to provide the ontic conditions and presuppositions of existence which enable us to lay hold of our salvation, and without sinking into chaos before the coming of the last day.

So much for our five points of criticism. We have taken the theses of van Ruler quite seriously, treating them along with the great expressions of Lutheran and Reformed theology and engaging in extensive debate with them, because we felt we could not simply ignore them on the grounds of their eccentricity. Because van Ruler's theology is an exact and consistent inversion of previous Christian tradition it helps to illumine this tradition by way of contrast.

It also fittingly illustrates in a concentrated way our repeated contention that every ethical problem has a theological background. Thus the dialogue with van Ruler is not merely a dialogue about the relation of church and state or the problem of theocracy. It also takes us into the sphere of theological axioms. Fundamentally, all the theological loci come into play as we deal with this single problem: the doctrine of creation and eschatology, the doctrine of Law and gospel, the problem of the canon, anthropology and Christology. All the problems of theological ethics have this theological reference. And this is true not merely as regards political ethics but as regards politics itself. For "no political scheme has ever become dominant which was not founded in a specific religious . . . conception."[137]

[137] Kuyper, *op. cit.*, p. 78.

Part Five

THE MESSAGE OF THE CHURCH TO THE WORLD

31.

The Church and Politics

Before concluding this portion of the Theological Ethics I should like to deal more specifically with one of the special problems referred to at the beginning of Part Four, namely, the church as it acts and speaks in the political sphere. We shall first undertake certain basic considerations concerning church and world, and then examine the church's political preaching in specific situations.

Church and World in Connection and Separation

We have already pointed out that Christianity is both related to the world and separated from the world.[1] It is related to it insofar as the world is loved and visited, and insofar as in all of this the world is the sphere of faith (not yet of sight). But Christianity is also separated from the world insofar as it does not take its standards from the world but recognizes that in pressing for autonomy the world is setting itself against God, and thus is doomed. It is in terms of this dialectic of freedom from and orientation to the world, of distance from it and belonging to it, that we have attempted to work out the basic Christian attitudes to life. This dialectic is the background of all that we have said about compromise as the *res* form of all action (including Christian action) and about the situation of conflict. All these discussions had reference to the man who as a Christian lives in the zone of intersection between this aeon and the coming aeon, who stands under both the judgment and the grace of the divine Word, and who as sinful in fact and righteous in hope *[peccator in re, justus in spe]* lives through the καιρός allotted to him.

The Word that Comes and the Word that Goes Forth

When we speak in this way of "the judgment and the grace of the divine Word," what we have in view is the Word which becomes

[1] See *ThE* 1, 478 ff. and 39 ff.

concrete for the man of a specific place, calling, time, and situation, the Word which both judges him and raises him up, binds him and makes him free. But this is not the only aspect of this Word to come under consideration in theological ethics. If we have thus far investigated the Word from the standpoint of the way in which it "comes" [ankommt], becoming real as indicative and imperative with reference to a specific worldly action, we must now consider it also from the standpoint of the way in which it "goes forth" [ergeht], becoming audible in the proclamation of the church.

We have already seen at various points in our investigation that the Word undergoes a transformation as it passes from the lips of the church to the ears of the hearer. We may recall only one example. The imperatives and directives mediated by the divine Word are not to be construed legalistically and casuistically; for casuistry, as we have seen [2] prefabricates the required decisions and thus does away with decision altogether. When the Word proclaims to me that I am loved, and that love is demanded of me, what it says to me – in this context – is this: "Do what you will" [fac quod vis].[3] Thus it leaves to me the decision as to how I will relate the law of love to the concrete case at hand. At every point in my life I am bound to the commandment that I should "fear, love, and trust God." [4] But the specific way in which I understand and actualize this obligation is the content of my own free decision, my filial obedience. It is not prefabricated in casuistic fashion, as a matter of servile obedience.[5]

The process which we have called the transformation of the Word on its way from the lips of the church to the ears of the hearer is thus a process of specialization. It involves the application to a concrete situation of a Word which is valid in every time and for all times.

A word of caution, of course, is immediately in order here. The Word of the church – the church's preaching – is not valid "in every time and for all times" in the sense that it is timeless, i.e., indifferent

---

[2] See ThE 1, 455 ff., 494 ff.

[3] See Augustine Ten Homilies on the First Epistle General of St. John vii. 8, trans. John Burnaby; LCC 8, 316.

[4] See Martin Luther's explanation of the First Commandment in The Small Catechism, I, 2; BC 342.

[5] A good illustration of this indeterminate situation, in which the decision is mine to make all right but I must make it within the context of a theological obligation, is to be found in the episode of the coin in Mark 12:13-17: "Render to Caesar the things that are Caesar's and to God the things that are God's."

to temporal distinctions. The fact that it cannot be so construed is demonstrated both by fundamental theological considerations and also by the history of preaching. There is such a history only because preaching has had to deal with men, the men to whom it goes forth and the men by whom it is proclaimed. And there could and can be this history with men only because these men are always "in a situation," and hence must allow the Word to apply to each of them in a different way. The history of preaching is thus the history of actualizations of the Word with reference to specific situations in which men find themselves.

From the standpoint of preaching there thus seems to be a vacillation in the meaning of the term "situation." On the one hand, preaching is wholly addressed "to the situation," not to man in the abstract, apart from his situation (in which case it would be bad preaching, not likely to "come" to the man it intended to reach). Preaching that is really true to the substance of its own proper message [Wort zur Sache] will for that very reason also be addressed to the particular situation [Wort zur Lage].[6] On the other hand, however, the church's speech in the situation is not to be interpreted casuistically, as if the church were able to master the situation ethically in advance by way of legal directives.

How is this apparent contradiction to be resolved? Well, the fact is that no real contradiction exists. It is simply that the general situation and the special situation are not the same thing. The fact that preaching is always done in a specific situation means that there are in the first place certain general situations which confront the preacher in his congregation, or the synod in its deliberations. Included among these general situations are such things as the structure of society — and hence also the social situation of the congregation — the state of peace and war at that particular historical juncture, political circumstances (e.g., a forthcoming election), encounters with nature and all

<hr/>

[6] In saying this I mean to take issue to some extent with the famous 1933 theses of Karl Barth, in which he plays off against one another as mutually exclusive "the chanting of the hours by the Benedictines near by in the *Maria Laach,* which goes on undoubtedly without break or interruption, pursuing the even tenor of its way even in the Third Reich" and that speaking "to the situation" which at the time was an admittedly urgent and theologically impossible undertaking. See his *Theological Existence To-day!,* trans. R. Birch Hoyle (Lexington, Kentucky: American Theological Library Association, 1962), pp. 9-10.

sorts of terrestrial and infernal powers (from harvest festivals to Mardi Gras). It is in relating its message to these general situations that the church introduces the themes which are to be handled specifically in the decisions to be made and in the words of command and consolation to be received.

But in spite of these common factors in the general situation, the special situation of the individual is always unique. Nor is it unique merely in the sense of the historical individuation which, contrary to what happens in the sphere of nature generally, forbids a complete subsuming of the individual under the universal. It is unique above all in the theological sense that, notwithstanding the hypothetical similarity of external circumstances, the summons to each is different, the freedom of each is different, and each has a different measure of freedom,[7] so that even where two do the very same thing it is in fact not the same. We would also recall in this connection the ethical concept of the "exception," that which cannot be subsumed, and the significance which it has had for us.[8]

This means, then, that while the preaching of the church may speak to general situations, it can only sketch the themes of the special situations and of the decisions which they demand. It cannot be specific in the sense of making the decisions for the individual and in his stead.

We can illustrate what we mean by the example of voting. The church can speak about an election as such. It can show how the duty of voting derives from the character of the state as a theological fact. It can even discuss particular Christian concerns (social, educational, and others) in relation to a particular election. But normally it cannot tell the individual how to vote. Indeed the different dimensions of the Word of which we have just spoken, the Word that "goes forth" and the Word that "comes," and the process of transformation which takes place in the transition from the one to the other are both to be seen — in this context — in the fact that the church stands *above* the political parties, providing pastoral care to all members irrespective of their various party affiliations, whereas the individual Christian stands *in* the parties, if only by the way he casts or fails to cast his vote.

We thus understand that theological ethics is dealing with two different aspects when it speaks of the Word that comes and of the Word

[7] We recall as a case in point the eating of meat sacrificed to idols.
[8] See *ThE* 1, 631 ff.

that goes forth. Thus far we have been speaking only of the former. Now we must turn to the latter. In so doing, we naturally limit ourselves strictly to that sphere of the latter which is relevant for theological ethics, which in a special way is commissioned to give direction in the matter of deciding and acting in specific situations.

We may expect to find the clearest differentiation between these two dimensions of the Word at the very point where there is the most obvious divergence between the general situation and the special situation. As the example of voting shows, this divergence is clearest where the church speaks to a political situation. Here the question arises as to how the church is to fulfill its task of political preaching, how it is to discharge its office as watchman in political affairs, without itself making political decisions, without prejudicing the decision of the individual in his special situation, without taking away his right to make his own decision or — if he will not allow the decision to be taken out of his hand — without dividing the body of Christ by endorsing the decisions of some and discrediting the decisions of others. In other words, how is the church to speak without on the one hand falling victim to timeless abstractions wholly divorced from the situation, whereby it does nothing but issue very general and for the most part very trivial appeals to conscience, and without on the other hand actually meddling in the situation, falsely construing it as one that directly involves a man's stance before God?

Thus "the situation" is not the same for the church as it is for the individual Christian in his secular office. The church lives, speaks, and acts in a different dimension from that of the individual Christian. For the church is not just the sum of all individual Christians. The *communio sanctorum* is qualitatively different from the individual Christian.[9]

With these questions we come once again — this time no longer from the standpoint of the individual Christian but from that of the church — to this whole matter of connection with the world and separation from it. We come up against the church as at once "above" the times and situations and also "in" them.

[9] This is why it is better to construe the genitive *sanctorum* as neuter, denoting fellowship in holy things, as the early church did. Cf. Theodosius Harnack, *Die Kirche, ihr Amt, ihr Regiment* (Nuremberg, 1862), § 69 ff., esp. § 76; Georg Wehrung, *Kirche nach evangelischem Verständnis* (1945), p. 32.

The Church above the Times

In a very provisional orientation, we would here mention three points expressive of the fact that the church is above the times. First, the church is not founded by men. The New Testament indicates repeatedly that God elected his believing community "before the foundation of the world." The church lives, as it were, in the thoughts of God even when there was no world, and certainly no man. And if the church is older than the world, it will also live when the world perishes and comes to an end. It will survive the last day in the eternal communion of saints. For the Word on which it is founded is eternal, whereas "the world passes away, and the lust of it" (I John 2:17). The principalities and tyrannies, the glories of culture and civilization, will sink into the great grave of the world, and over the abyss there will be only the One who is with us always, even unto the end of the world (Matt. 28:20). Thus the existence of the church arches like a rainbow over the times, since it is itself not founded in time.

One can readily understand that the breadth of the church's lifespan, and the measure of eternity from which it takes its orientation, bring with them the temptation to overlook the things of time, to despise that which passes away, to yield to world negation, asceticism, fanaticism, and "Christian Stoicism." But the moment we are tempted even briefly to despise the temporal and penultimate in the name of ultimate reality,[10] we must ask ourselves whether we do not thereby succumb to an abstract and all too human antithesis between time and eternity, an antithesis which has nothing more to do with the way these two dimensions are related in the Bible. For after all, the mystery of the gospel consists in the fact that the "time" of this world is not just self-contained finitude, and conversely that the "space" of the eternal is not just self-enclosed transcendence, but that the barrier between the two has been shattered in the event of Jesus Christ, in the act of the incarnation. If we have understood the miracle of Christmas we know that such human and earthly things as guilt, pain, and death, tears and laughter, hunger and satiety, fear and hope, seedtime and harvest, are so important to God that he has given himself to be in these things. He has carried the burdens of life and death, and he

---

[10] Cf. Bonhoeffer's ideas on the relation of ultimate and penultimate things in his *Ethics*, ed. Eberhard Bethge, trans. Neville Horton Smith (New York: Macmillan, 1955), pp. 79 ff.

has found a place for flowers and birds, for seedtime and harvest, in the parables of our Lord. Let no one' despise this earth, whose worth derives from the fact that Jesus Christ was born in it. Let no one despise human history and each present moment, for it was in this history, in one present moment, that Jesus Christ died. Let no one despise the world in which the cross of our Lord was raised. Let no one despise the daily bread for which the Son of God taught us to pray.

It is obviously impermissible to get so enamored of an abstract eternity that we relativize what God has taken seriously. We must not allow ourselves to hold aloof from that to which God himself, through the incarnation, has drawn near. To despise the world is to despise the sphere for which and in which the Son of God died. Hence despising the world is not an act of piety but of blasphemy, since it involves the attempt to be more divine than God himself, and to serve God in ways of one's own arbitrary choosing. This is why piety and pride are often so close. To despise the world is no less idolatrous than to deify it.

Thus the church stands above the times, since it does not have a temporal origin. But it is also ordained to serve time, and consequently to do service with respect to the pressing questions of the day.

Connected with the fact that the church exists both before and after the time of this world — and for this very reason, as we have seen, exists also *in* the world — there is a second fact, namely, that the church can never originate in the same way as a club or association whose founding rests on human resolves.[11] Clubs and associations usually come into being when people group together for a common purpose, e.g., when tenants decide to resist the inordinate demands of landlords. Or they may arise when people feel united by common interests, pursuits, or talents, as in a literary society or bridge club. One might at first be tempted to see in the church a parallel to such associations, in the sense that people having a common religious feeling or people inclined to a certain type of piety come together, perhaps also with the common goal of seeking salvation. But this is a false parallel.

The church does not arise because believers get together with other

---

[11] Cf. Dietrich Bonhoeffer, *The Communion of Saints: A Dogmatic Inquiry into the Sociology of the Church,* trans. R. Gregor Smith (New York: Harper, 1963), pp. 175 ff.

believers to form a society. On the contrary, strange as it may seem, the church is present even before our faith. It is not the sociological product of faith but its indispensable prerequisite.

The founding of the church may thus be divided into the following phases (though we must be on guard here against thinking in terms of a chronological succession): There must be someone who has been reached by the Word of God, i.e., the Holy Spirit must have disclosed the Word to him and brought him into living contact with it. Only from someone thus "illuminated" can the Word which calls with authority be transmitted to me, even as it was once transmitted to him.

The moment we have to do with the dimension of the church, we are thus involved in a whole web of relations, a web which goes back ultimately to what we call the Word of God, or more precisely, God's resolve to have fellowship with us and to make us his beloved children. In the present context the point that really matters is that the church is not the product of human initiative. On the contrary, it is something into which we are called. This call is a wholly one-sided affair. To be sure, use is made of the human causal nexus. We come into contact with Christians only on the basis of specific historical and other connections. But there is more to it than just this causal nexus. The one-sidedness of the call is underscored in the Bible where we are told that the divine resolve was taken "before the foundation of the world."

The third fact, which was conditioned by this fact of the church's extra-earthly, extra-human origin, is that the church is and always will be a foreign body. The world senses that here is something out of this world (John 15:19). It comes to see that the church cannot be subjugated and made to serve temporal goals, not when it remains faithful to its Head, and hence also to itself. This is why the world usually reacts against the church as an organism reacts against a foreign body which has invaded it. It mobilizes against it all the forces of resistance at its command. It tries to expel it. This is what Jesus has in view when he says in his high-priestly prayer that the world "hates them" — the disciples — because they are not "of" the world (John 17:14). History is full of illustrations of this constantly recurring defensive operation. They range from the trial of Jesus before Pilate, through the Neronian persecutions, to more recent and modern forms of political anti-Christianity.

The Church in Time

The affirmation that the church spans the times and thus lives in some aloofness from them cannot imply, of course, that it stands timeless and unmoved like a fixed star above the flux of things, impervious to change and to decay. On the contrary, the church bears on its countenance the marks and traces of the impelling forces of its time. Of the many examples which might be given, we will choose only two because they have the stamp of actuality.

We think first, e.g., of the church's involvement in the existing social situation. The territorial church structure of Luther's day works itself out in a specific attitude of the church toward governmental authority and in a particular church doctrine of governmental authority, indeed in a specific relation of church and state. The famous, or infamous, combination of throne and altar is one end result of this partly unconscious involvement of the church in the social situation. We might also think of the alliance which the state churches of Europe concluded, after the fall of Napoleon, with antirevolutionary — and in this sense conservative — forces and ideas, an alliance which blinded most of the church and its theology to the problems of labor and to the fateful rise of the fourth estate. Many positions adopted by the church in the political sphere or in relation to the social question have been more or less unconsciously determined by categories and evaluations to which the church was driven by this involvement in the social situation, or better, to which it has succumbed in consequence of this involvement.

A further sign of this involvement in time is the complex of questions now referred to under the rubric of demythologizing. Rudolph Bultmann has drawn our attention to the fact — nor is he the first to do so, the Enlightenment theologian Semler being his greatest and earliest precursor — that the Christian message, the kerygma, is inscribed in forms of expression which are conditioned by their age, e.g., those of late Jewish apocalyptic and the Hellenistic redeemer myths. Since it is the preacher's task to actualize the message for his own time, he must make the temporally conditioned shell transparent, and adapt the kerygma to our ears, so that it can be absorbed into the categories of our understanding. But this means that our present understanding of the message takes place within the framework of temporally conditioned, i.e., modern concepts, questions, and views, and that later generations will have to repeat the process in their own way. Not only that which is to be understood, but also he who is to do the understanding and the act of understanding itself are historical. Here is a true involvement in time, a true coming of the divine Word into this aeon, a true incarnation. There can be no doubt of that, even though the resurrection of the Word in each new time points to the fact that it does not originate in time and thus cannot be fixed at a specific point in the time line. Bultmann has thus raised a legitimate and inescapable question. His answer to this question, i.e., his definition of the relation between the temporally conditioned form and the eternal content, obviously calls for critical scrutiny, but this need not concern us in the present context.[12]

All this, i.e., the political and theological involvement of the church in the present situation, makes it clear that the church cannot refuse to take a stand on the questions of the day. It is of course called to do so as a part of its pastoral ministry. Think, e.g., of the highly political decisions the Christian has constantly to make in the totalitarian state, of the crises of conscience these decisions entail, and the pastoral obligation they impose upon the church. Yet quite apart from this pastoral kind of concern, the church is summoned to take a stand on the current political, economic, social, and cultural situation in order that it may not succumb to the present state of affairs unconsciously, uncritically, and under the bewitchment of alien ἐξουσίαι, in order that it may not become the unwitting agent of the spirit of the age – in whatever form – instead of being impelled by the Holy Spirit. How much that was once proclaimed as the commandment of God with respect to governing authorities (Rom. 13:1) was in reality determined by the contemporary ideology of throne and altar! How much that is now preached concerning a social kingdom of God on earth has its origin in Marxist ideology rather than in the Spirit of God!

The two truths, that the church spans the times and is thus above them, and that the church is involved in the world situation and is thus in the times, if isolated from one another can lead to false absolutizations. The supratemporal dimension of the church – if we may speak of it in such pointed terms – inclines towards a false conserva-

[12] See Helmut Thielicke, "The Restatement of New Testament Theology," in *Kerygma and Myth: A Theological Debate*, ed. Hans Werner Bartsch, trans. Reginald H. Fuller (London: S.P.C.K., 1953), pp. 138-174.

tism, whereas the temporal involvement of the church inclines towards an equally false revolutionism.

False Conservatism

False conservatism expresses itself in the inclination to accept world conditions as they are.[13] Under this pseudoconservative banner a corrupt social order, which keeps part of humanity living at substandard economic levels while allowing another class to exploit and profiteer, is regarded as a matter of divine providence — or visitation — calling for simple acceptance and submission. Along the lines of the synthesis of Calvinism and capitalism to which Max Weber has drawn attention,[14] the profiteering class can even see in its dubious profits a divine confirmation of its labors and consequently a form of blessing, whereas the exploited class is asked to see in its misery a test or visitation by the God who desires to elicit in the vale of proletarian woe a longing for the heavenly Jerusalem.

To be sure, this is a caricature, but exaggeration may perhaps serve to bring out the point at issue. To refer the existing social and political situation directly to divine providence, and to ignore the secondary human causes — the guilt and error of individuals and of organized groups — is to create among Christians a condition which we might describe as political apathy. If everything that takes place is regarded as God's doing, then it is obviously sanctioned by what is assumed to be the will of God. Logically, then, it can never be opposed. Even

[13] Reinhold Niebuhr has significantly commented on this false conservatism: "Another root of the social conservatism of religion, which tempts it to practice charity within the limitations of a social system without raising ultimate questions about the justice of the system itself, is the natural determination of religion. To the religious imagination, God is at one moment the ideal toward which all things must strive and by comparison with which all contemporary social standards are convicted of inadequacy; and in the next moment he is the omnipotent creator of all things, whose power and wisdom guarantees the goodness of existing social organizations. Paul put the logic of this determinism clearly in Romans 13:1-2. . . . The idea that social and political arrangements must be virtuous because they exist under an omnipotent God who could change them if he would, grows out of a natural inclination in the very heart of religion, the inclination to aggrandize the object of worship, God, until it becomes coextensive with the whole of reality." Reinhold Niebuhr, *The Contribution of Religion to Social Work* (New York: Columbia University Press, 1932), pp. 22, 23. Cf. here what Gerhard Ebeling has to say about "the traditionalism that forgets itself" in *The Problem of Historicity in the Church and its Proclamation*, trans. Grover Foley (Philadelphia: Fortress, 1967), pp. 42 ff.

[14] See above p. 573.

though child labor, malnutrition, and the oppression and humiliation of millions cry out to heaven, they must simply be accepted.

It is a terrible judgment on Christianity and on false theology that the decisive social movements of the last hundred years have not originated in any will on the part of the church to play the good Samaritan. The church has not taken the Lord's command to "love thy neighbor" as a concrete commission to change a blatantly unjust social situation. No, the decisive impulses for change have come from within the ranks of the oppressed and humiliated themselves. There has thus been nourished a kind of revolutionary instinct, the terrible symptoms of which may now be seen throughout the world, in their extreme form in Communism.

Small wonder, then, that the fourth estate distrusts the message of the church, and laughs at the argument that the church's task is not to oppose social injustice but to comfort its victims with the hope of a better hereafter. The church is itself at fault. Between a rationalization of the *diaconia* such as is pursued in the modern welfare state, and a purely individualized love of neighbor which cannot cope with the collective misery, there is a middle zone of Christian social obligation which the church has fatally ignored. To be sure, Christians have helped the needy. Think of the church's many works of mercy and of the countless acts of private charity. But these were bound to be regarded as alms, and hence as humiliating to the recipients, a cover-up for the unjust situation, so long as the proletariat was given the impression that the church actually tolerated the unjust situation as a whole — and did so in the name of that evil conservatism which even dared to claim sanction for itself in the will of God. This distorted view of the church, which has been given to countless numbers of men, has necessarily had further consequences.

To the fourth estate it seemed a necessary conclusion from this theologically grounded conservatism that the church was allied with the middle class, and that it had given a privileged position to one class at the expense of others. For the middle class naturally had an interest in maintaining the social conditions from which it profited.

A false theology was thus understood — and who can criticize such an interpretation? — as the expression of social egoism and economic ruthlessness. Perhaps this interpretation is not mistaken at all but is an accurate diagnosis. For this false theology of conservatism did in fact drive the church into the arms of the middle class and it was only the fateful experience of the Third Reich, in which social reformers and churchmen suffered and died together in the concentration camps, that compelled Christians very largely to revise their position.

The sin of the church against the fourth estate is in the final analysis the result of a false theology. Where the supratemporal character of the church is absolutized the church is no longer seen in terms of its historical involvement and responsibility. Love of neighbor is made a private affair. Existing social conditions are perpetuated as divinely ordained. And Christianity is delivered up to the kind of political apathy which drives the forlorn victims of social injustice to resort to revolution.

False Revolutionism

Illegitimate revolutionism commits the opposite error, again under the Christian banner. Here the attempt is made, as by fanatics in every age, to transfer the kingdom of God and its radical laws directly into this aeon. The circumstances of the kingdom are transferred to our present world in such a simple and unrefracted way as to overlook the fact that the kingdom of God and this fallen world are altogether different.

The outstanding recent example of this attempt is Leo Tolstoi. He took the kingdom law of radical love of neighbor as a law of political action. By making the command to turn the other cheek a principle of political action, he not only came to repudiate the use of all personal force, even in self-defense, but he also had to reject national defense by military means, and the maintenance of domestic order by the police and judiciary. For the unconditional prohibition of self-preservation which is implied, or thought to be implied, in the command to love necessarily becomes on this view the structural law of human society in general. The inevitable result is a hopeless confusion between the kingdom of God — not the church really — and the world.

For the world thus imagined is one which no longer tries to protect itself against crime and violence through the duly constituted authorities, if necessary by force. Indeed, by banning force in the name of the command to love, does not such a world actually provoke the forces of chaos? This is why Bismarck holds that one cannot rule the world by the Sermon on the Mount.[15] He does not mean thereby to discredit the Sermon on the Mount as if it were something altogether remote from the world. Rather, he is arguing that in the very nature of the case it is illegitimate to take what applies to the direct personal relation of man to God and make it the structural law of the world, thus confounding the dimensions in which the laws apply. It is not that the Sermon on the Mount is so remote from this world that it cannot be practiced here. On the contrary, it is the world which is so remote from the kingdom of God that it cannot simply take over the Sermon on the Mount and adopt it as its constitution.

The theological problem involved here was worked out by Luther in terms of his doctrine of the two kingdoms.[16] The form love is to take as we practice it in relation to our neighbor according to God's will depends on the sphere of life in which we concretely exercise it. In the personal sphere it takes a different shape from that which it has on the level of service, calling, and office. And again even in the personal sphere there is a difference between the love of husband and wife, parents and children, friends and comrades. Love undergoes a kind of refraction according to the medium in which it is practiced. Similarly, in the kingdom of God love has a different shape from what it has in this aeon of ours between the fall and the judgment. For in the kingdom of God authorities and governments are done away. If we may put it thus, the plane of earthly order is abolished, and therewith the medium which gives earthly love its distinctive shape. In the kingdom of God they neither marry nor are given in marriage (Matt. 22:30).

One might express it thus. This world of ours, with its orders, possesses a certain autonomy [Eigengesetzlichkeit]. Economic life cannot be regulated by an abstract law of love. On the contrary there are definite laws of supply and demand. There is the principle of productivity, and the law of competition. If a business man were

---

[15] See above p. 97.

[16] See Helmut Gollwitzer, Die christliche Gemeinde in der politischen Welt (Tübingen, 1954) for a treatment of the two kingdoms which differs considerably from that presented here.

to ignore the medium in which he operates and were to act solely on the basis of an abstract law of love, never undercutting his competitors in price or surpassing them in productivity lest he do them harm, he would destroy the very ground rules of economic life. He would in fact be fostering the same kind of chaos as the disciple of Tolstoi who confronts the criminal with the same abstract law of love by refusing to resist him by force.

With this relative autonomy of the different spheres of life is linked the fact that the church cannot just address the various secular spheres of politics, economics, and social organization in the name of the command to love. Indeed it cannot speak to them directly and casuistically in the name of the divine commandments at all. Or, to put it in a different and better way, the church must of necessity speak to them again and again, and that for two reasons which we may briefly specify.

First, there is no area of life beyond the pole of God's sovereignty, no area to which the commandments of God do not apply. To admit the existence of such a sphere would be to restrict the validity of the commandments to the area of one's private life, and perhaps even to the purely inward circle of the disposition.

Second, the very destiny of men is constantly being decided in these spheres of life, e.g., in politics and social organization. How many lives are lost in a war! How deeply it affects the family! What testing and temptation goes with it in the moral sphere, and even in the most intimate circles of faith! This is why Christians must be deeply concerned with this question of war and peace, a cardinal political question, precisely for the sake of man. For the question involves life and death, love and hate, the building up and tearing down of the souls of men for whom Christ died. Obviously the church must deal with these questions. Obviously it must speak out and make its confession in respect of them. Here the church is called upon in a profound way to fulfill its office of watchman and shepherd.

But the church cannot just do this in any way it sees fit. It cannot itself engage in politics. It must rather consider very carefully the nature of its intervention, both in terms of principle and in respect of actual cases. We can best show how the church should speak to its time by considering two cases in point.

Political Preaching in Specific Situations

The East-West Conflict

We intentionally choose a specific historical situation in order to illustrate the matter of the church's proper stance on a decisive political question. In face of the cold war between East and West, and the closely related question of how a divided Germany can be re-united, two fundamentally different conceptions are hotly debated both within the parties and among churchmen.

The first is that West Germany must be integrated into the West. It must add its own military might to that of the West in such a way that Russia will not dare attack. Russia will thus drop its plans for a showdown with the West. And because such a conflict no longer portends Russia will finally give up its East Zone hostage. The goal of a bloodless reunification of Germany will thus have been achieved.

The opposite view is that such a course is bound to provoke a war. For the rearming of West Germany will force Russia to create equivalent armed forces in East Germany, and these will neutralize the West German contribution to the military might of the Atlantic powers, thus rendering it futile. West German rearmament may also tempt Russia to go to war because Russia would necessarily feel itself threatened. Instead of rearming West Germany, therefore, one should rather seek reunification by way of bilateral negotiation. A reunited Germany might then form a kind of neutral buffer state between the enemy camps. Only thus can a new world war – involving a German civil war – be averted.

Against this second thesis the counterthesis is at once advanced that a neutralized Germany would form a kind of vacuum which both power blocs would necessarily seek to fill and dominate. Instead of pacifying the opposing fronts, a buffer state would actually incite them further, and thus constitute a source of unrest.

Here in any case it becomes clear how the church ought and ought not to speak on worldly matters. It speaks appropriately and in keeping with its commission if it helps to avert war, and in this most fateful of all questions sharpens the conscience against the lust for power, the love of adventure, and nationalistic passions. It also speaks appropriately and in keeping with its commission if it warns against laying a burden of Western egoism on the backs of brothers and sisters beyond the Iron Curtain, e.g., by holding up before them our higher standard of living.

With such questions and admonitions the church has constantly to attack the champions of both political conceptions and summon them to responsibility. But to decide in substance between the two conceptions is not within the competence of the church. Both groups are seeking the peace and reunification of their country, albeit in different ways. It is not the church's task to say which of these ways is right, and thus to decide a matter of political judgment. It can only lay upon the consciences of the Christians entrusted to its care the fact that they must make this decision as Christians, i.e., before God and on the basis of all the facts they can muster. It cannot give ecclesiastical sanction to any particular solution, thereby discrediting as heretics those who decide otherwise.

Let it not be said that the church thus keeps aloof from fateful decisions of conscience, putting all responsibility entirely on the individual conscience which it has deliberately failed to instruct. Obviously the individual pastor, when he is consulted on these questions, will allow the questioner to know his own decision. He will share with him not only his thinking in the matter but also the concrete result to which it has led his conscience. Still, it is impossible for the church as a whole to adopt a position in matters of political judgment, e.g., as to what methods are to be recommended in reaching such specific goals as the peaceful reunification of Germany. The reasons for this conclusion are as follows.

First, and supremely, it cannot be contested that the church is in a very different position from that of the individual Christian when it comes to taking a stand on a political question. The individual citizen, whether charged with the responsibility of office or simply as a voter, has to help decide concrete political questions. To take a specific example which is basically on the same level as the East-West conflict, how would the church answer the question as to what role if any labor should have in the management of industry? Is there such a thing as *the* Christian answer to this question? Let no one say that these are purely technical questions unrelated to the humanity of man, that they are not directly a matter of conscience and hence that there is no need of pastoral direction here. In the last resort it is a question as to how the effective operation of the economy, which requires (at least in the Western system) a measure of individual responsibility and free initiative on the part of the owner, can be harmonized with the need of the employees to share in the responsibility. The humanity of man is very much at stake in this question.

For we know — and do not need Marxism to tell us — that the technological age has put the prerogatives of power into the hands of those who control the means of production, so that those who are dependent upon them are in danger of being reduced to the inhuman status of being mere means to an end, of being valued solely in terms of the worth of their productivity. We also know that this threat becomes all the greater as business concerns become more impersonal, directed by managers rather than personally responsible owners. In face of these developments, who would dare to say that the church is not involved in this question? Is it not a matter of protecting the members of a particular social class lest they be reduced to mere functioning objects and be treated as things rather than persons?

Nevertheless, it cannot be the church's task to advance *the* Christian solution to the problem, and to recommend or even make obligatory a specific system in which responsibility is divided between owners and employees according to some "Christian" formula. For a host of factual considerations also enter into this human question. The apparently simple and Christian recommendation that for the sake of the human dignity of the worker employees must share full responsibility with the employer is not only technically naive. By its oversimplification it also constitutes a threat to true humanity from the opposite side. For the question at once arises: How can this co-responsibility be actualized, and who will represent the employees? Might it not be that in all but the larger firms and plants there would be a shortage of workers fitted for this task? And might it not be that in such instances representation would be taken over by union people who may know little or nothing of the local operation at first hand? And would not this perhaps mean — we are simply raising the question — the introduction of all sorts of ideological involvements and new political entanglements? Would the worker then be any less an object, any less a mere means to an end, than he was before as a pawn in the hands of the impersonal corporations?

We would only raise the question, and in this admittedly sketchy way. Merely to raise it, however, merely to mention even a small fraction of the problems involved, is to show clearly that in terms of its vocation the church has no substantive solution to this problem. The individual Christian, however, whether as an indirect participant through the ballot or as a direct representative of one of the two social groups concerned, has to struggle to arrive at a concrete solution, a *modus convivendi* which at the same time is in accord with the postulate of an effectively operating economy. This cannot mean, of course, that the church may pander to quietistic reserve in respect of this question. Indeed, the church has three main tasks.

First, it can help men to gain a more precise knowledge of the real issues. It can clarify the interests, ethical intentions, and proposed solutions on both sides, thus assisting the individual in the decision of conscience which is his to make. It can free him from dependence on demagogic slogans by laying bare the substantive and human concerns which are really at stake. Conscience cannot be sharpened simply by making more or less abstract and general appeals. Conscience grows by the decisions — indeed the substantive decisions — it has to make. This means above all that the pastor must orient himself to the issues and be able to state them clearly.

Thus, to guide the conscience in the matter of taxes one must know the actual problems, including the institutional friction in which the conscience lives today. He must know the considerations that must be involved in the levying of taxes. The depressing failure of the church's pastoral ministry is due not least of all to the fact that the church is suspiciously bound by the fetters of an individualistic theology and ethics. It has not yet begun to see and to consider the extent to which individual decision of conscience is all mixed up with problems which derive from the institutions of society and from the various social and political systems. In a theological examination it can still happen that students will be able to spout endlessly about the duty of honesty, without having the faintest inkling of the real theological and ethical problems which can arise for the person who is trying to be honest in a dishonest system, e.g., a dubious tax system or a bad economic system. It is said that "even the best of us cannot live in peace unless the bad neighbor allows it." Can I be righteous if I live in the midst of organized injustice? Can

I be honest if I live in the sphere of institutional deception? One has only to consider the situation in a totalitarian state to see extremes of both. Thus it is that even the orders within which we live are a matter of ethics. This is why it is essential that the church and its pastors know the facts and understand the situation.

Second, the church has the duty of speaking to both sides — e.g., to both labor and management — and of showing them what is ultimately at stake. It can point out, e.g., that human dignity is the real issue, that human dignity derives from the fact that man has been "bought with a price" [I Cor. 6:20; 7:23], that there is consequently more to man than just his capacity to produce. The aim will be, not to surprise both sides by coming up with an unexpected solution, but to address both sides with respect to the ultimate object of their decision. Once this is known, they can be left to argue the matter out. The fact is that there are questions which can be handled only by those directly concerned, or by the arbiter who has listened to both sides.

Third, the church must see to it that the parties to the dispute meet face to face, and in an atmosphere charged with the influence of the living voice of the gospel, so that they confront one another as "neighbors." For it is profoundly Christian to see in the other person not just the champion of an interest, ideology, or front, but the man who is of value to God, who has cost God something. (This is the foundation of, e.g., the command to love our enemies.) It is an eminently pastoral act, where a conflict of principles is involved, to relax the rigidity of the lines of opposition by transforming a confrontation of abstract positions into an encounter of living persons. One need not have lived very much to know that real results always follow from this kind of assistance, which is itself a product of the realism of the gospel.

The Church in the Totalitarian State

If we have said that the church as such is not competent to take a position regarding a particular political conception, and if we have strictly distinguished between the substantive questions involved in political action and the pastoral concerns which the church must have in view, we must now consider whether this is still true in respect of modern totalitarian states. The answer must be negative.

In the totalitarian state things are radically different, because the totalitarian state is always an ideological state. A large proportion of its political acts have an ideological significance. Social measures, e.g., are taken and demanded in the name of ideological goals. The same is true with respect to educational policy, the organization of the sciences, and foreign policy (one has only to think of modern Russia). It is also true with respect to the campaign against undesirables (e.g., the campaign to exterminate the Jews and the mentally unfit in the Third Reich).

This is why every time the church confesses its faith over against the ideological confession of the totalitarian state it is logically construed by the state as a protest against its political measures, from which the ideological content cannot be separated. As a matter of fact, the totalitarian state's diagnosis in such cases is quite accurate. This is why in the ideological state the church is repeatedly forced to take a direct stand on political measures.

Here the doctrine of the two kingdoms is hopelessly confused by the state itself. For the state no longer understands itself as the kingdom on the left hand, the secular kingdom. On the contrary, it sacralizes itself. It effects a transfiguration by metaphysically inflating itself. As a result, in the totalitarian state the two kingdoms doctrine is largely irrelevant so far as direct applicability is concerned. That being true, two corollaries necessarily follow.

The negative consequence is that the church is in no case permitted to say — incidentally this is true even in "normal" circumstances — that the so-called political sphere is entirely a matter for the secular kingdom, from which the church can hold piously aloof, refusing to assume any direct share of responsibility. For if the state is untrue to its function as secular kingdom, if in the strict sense the worldly kingdom no longer exists but has been supplanted by a pseudo church, then it is logically impossible to ascribe to the secular kingdom a sphere of competence which would be distinct from that of the church. How impossible this is may be seen from the observation that the ideological tyranny is quite willing to ascribe to the church — at least for an interim period pending the complete liquidation of the church — the sphere of the hereafter, while it claims this world exclusively for itself. This very partition shows how nonsensical is the idea of a secular kingdom in these circumstances. And the further fact that for secular ideologies there is no such thing as a hereafter makes the division a matter of the purest cynicism.

The positive consequence to be drawn from the destruction of the secular kingdom and the proclamation in its place of the antichurch is that the church must ask the question as to when the hour for confession has struck in the totalitarian state. When and in what form will the church have to stand up for its faith by publicly declaring opposition to the antichurch?

In terms of the two kingdoms doctrine, the idea of the church acting as opposition makes no sense, since such action would presuppose a contest on the same level (in this case the political), whereas the two kingdoms doctrine emphasizes the fact that church and state exist on two different levels. Where the two are on different levels the church's resistance can relate only to specific measures in which the state at most oversteps its limits. In principle, such specific resistance cannot lead to the point where the church would establish a kind of antistate and regard itself as an opposition group.

But the situation is quite different in the totalitarian state. By abandoning its character as secular kingdom, the totalitarian state denies that it is on a different level. Church and state are illegitimately forced onto the same level. From the church's standpoint there is thus a confrontation between church and pseudo church. From the state's standpoint the apparently legitimate state is contested by a sacral and theocratic antistate. Common to both perspectives is the fact that the two parties are seen to stand on the same level, the one contending for a legitimate claim, the other for an illegitimate.

The question then becomes acute as to the obligation of confession thereby imposed on the church. More precisely: Is it not the church's duty from the very outset, i.e., from the very inception of the ideological tyranny, to confess its faith by dissociating itself from the antichurch, refusing to acknowledge it as state and secular kingdom, and abstaining from every kind of collaboration? Or, in virtue of certain functions of state which even the most perverted state still discharges (e.g., the regulation of traffic, the provision of a monetary system, etc.), should not even the most dubious state still be respected as a kind of emergency state, and accorded at least some measure of co-operation? Can this limited co-operation be justified on the ground that even the pathological state is still to some extent a bulwark against chaos so that, however corrupt, one cannot do without it? Or should one withhold even limited collaboration on the ground that the seeming order of the totalitarian state is really "organized chaos," [17] and that the church's only option is to speak out against its sabotaging of the divinely willed functions of order?

One certainly has to respect a church which answers that its obligation is to bear witness against the ideological dictatorship from the moment of its inception, and to make no secret of the fact that it fundamentally rejects the totalitarian state as being anti-Christian in its very structure. Nonetheless there would seem to be certain objections to this approach, the chief of which may be expressed in the form of a question: Will the totalitarian state be able to recognize this kind of initial confession for what it really is, namely, a *Christian* confession?

Now the question whether a confession can be heard is obviously not the final criterion of its legitimacy or necessity. On the other hand, it should not be overlooked that the time and situation in which confession is made cannot be matters of indifference. If the totalitarian state is dismissed summarily and totally, if it is rejected absolutely as an ideological and political factor, will it not be formally forced into the misunderstanding that what is here confronting it is simply another world view? Will it not assume that the forces of tradition – the Western ideologies – are here conspiring against it under the Christian banner? This misunderstanding is made almost inevitable by the fact that Communism regards religion, and consequently Christianity too, as an ideology, i.e., as the reflection and spiritual weapon of a specific social situation which seeks to perpetuate itself. Obviously, then, this kind of confession is not rooted in a real καιρός, an authentic kerygmatic situation.

But for what moment should the church wait? To answer this question we must recall that in consequence of its ideology – its unexpressed thesis that man is simply a creature to be used – the totalitarian state is forced into certain modes of action. Its policy is such as to make its citizens mere functionaries within an antlike society, creatures having no wills or choices of their own. This very quickly becomes clear in its educational theory and practice. Its thesis about

---

[17] On this term from Karl Barth, and his whole treatment of this complex of questions vis-à-vis National Socialism and Communism, see above pp. 583-585.

the utility or non-utility of human life as being either useful or not useful necessarily leads to concentration camps, torture, and executions, and to propaganda by way of loudspeakers and books of sayings which make their appeal, not to conscience and conviction, but to the nerves, thereby betraying the covert estimate of man which underlies it.

It is against these excesses, this ideologically conditioned contempt for man, that the church is summoned to make confession. Here too it will naturally be accused of championing a world view, a rival ideology. But at this point the charge does not have the same significance as when it is brought against what we have called the church's initial confession. For now it is a polemical formula, a routine discrediting in the stock phrases which are always employed when the totalitarian state detects opposition. It is also an attempt to salve the state's own conscience by self-persuasion. For its conscience is not dead. This is something we know, not simply as a matter of theological principle, but also because it is so obviously betrayed in the constant concern of every dictatorship to erect a human facade. The constitutions of totalitarianism all exude oily affirmations of human dignity, freedom, and other ethical values. In order to escape the condemnation of hypocritical self-contradiction, the totalitarian state when it is accused of orgies of terror is forced to protest – as it has always done without exception – that these accusations against it are not a real indictment of its offenses. They simply express the revolt of a hostile ideology and are not to be taken seriously, but are to be regarded as a crafty pretext which must be avenged by annihilating the accuser.

The crucial thing, of course, is that in its preaching of judgment and in its condemnation of actual injustice the church should not be a mere moralist or defender of culture and civilization (though it may have to play this role as well, perhaps as the only authority qualified to do so). For this would give rise to an even worse misunderstanding than that in which the church appears as merely a rival ideological power. The church has to preach real judgment, not morality.

How can it do this? It has to attack the crimes of the state in its preaching, confession, and pastoral work in such a way that they are seen to be not merely actions contrary to the moral law but the necessary result of a decision with respect to God. In terms of our present discussion, this means that when God is done away, and a deliberately atheistic state arises with the corresponding ideology, man too can no longer be esteemed. For the dignity of man, as we have seen, consists exclusively in his alien dignity, i.e., in the fact that he is related to God as child, as image, as one who is bought with a price. He thus stands under the patronage of an eternal goodness. He cannot be touched, for he is "the apple of God's eye" [Zech. 2:8; Deut. 32:10; Ps. 17:8]. If, however, he is dissevered from this sustaining relationship, then he can only be evaluated —and must necessarily be valued — in terms of his immanent worth, which means in practice his utility.

This utility will be judged according to the criteria provided by the various ideologies. In dialectical materialism the values are exclusively social and economic. If man is no longer socially and economically useful, he is hopelessly exposed to liquidation in all its forms, from the most refined to the crudest.

This is why anxiety is the rule in ideological circles. Everybody is an object of suspicion to everybody else. When a man no longer stands under eternal norms, he becomes unpredictable; one can only fear him. Where God is no longer feared, anything is permitted.[18] And where anything is permitted, anything is possible. One might reverse the saying of Bismarck: He who no longer fears God fears everything in the world. For the world is then a sinister place.

Crimes against humanity are no longer a matter of a man's character, or not primarily so. Even the noblest of men, even the scion of the best families, is compelled to commit excesses when under the dominion of these philosophical first principles. Only a lack of consistency, of hardness — and in this sense of character — could cause him to shrink before the ultimate consequences of his ideological axioms. These phenomena simply cannot be understood in moral categories. They are accessible only to theological criteria.

This is the context of thought in which the church in the totalitarian state has to make its confession. This is the context of thought in which it has to attack injustice and crime. Indeed, in its best moments

---

[18] See our discussion of Raskolnikov and the concept of "the exception" in Dostoevski's *Crime and Punishment* at *ThE* 1, 631 ff.

and utterances during the Third Reich this is exactly what the church did. Thus we see in this connection once again that totalitarian dictatorship means a radically new situation in which every act of confession on the part of the church involves it in direct political activity, and in which the church has to deal concretely with the concrete decisions of party and state.

We also see once again what this means for the doctrine of the two kingdoms. Even where in comparison with Luther's presentation that doctrine has been refined and safeguarded, it still cannot be applied directly to this new situation, because the totalitarian state refuses to be identified with the secular kingdom which Luther had in view. Nevertheless, even in such instances the doctrine is not abrogated. For in the totalitarian state too the church can speak only on the basis of this doctrine, whereby it summons the state at every moment to become again what it was intended to be, namely, a secular kingdom rather than a demonically perverted and mythically inflated theocracy.

The Law of Infiltration and Subversion

At this point one final thought may be briefly advanced, and its main aspects delineated. We are referring to what may be called the law of infiltration and subversion which has been operative again and again in the course of history. The Hellenistic world, e.g., may be said to have infiltrated Christianity at certain stages in its history by way of Gnosticism. What this means is that Gnostic Hellenism did not set itself up as a hostile front over against Christianity. It did not enter into dispute with Christian dogmatics on individual points of theory. On the contrary, it adopted the Christian vocabulary. It spoke of the processes of salvation history and redemption, and thus surreptitiously substituted for Christian revelation a mystery religion of Hellenistic origin. By way of underground infiltration, by the insinuation of Hellenistic influences, mystery religion suddenly made its appearance on Christian territory and filled the vacuum.

This fact would seem to suggest the propriety of asking whether a similar law of infiltration and subversion might not apply in respect of the Christian church's influence upon the world, not as a matter of deliberate tactics or as an operative factor in Christianity's attempt to master the world, but as a law of action which is grounded in the nature of the Christian message itself. For the task of the church is not to take over the orders of this aeon and change them, but to address in a responsible way the men to whom these orders are entrusted by virtue of the offices they fill.

Herein too lies, e.g., the answer to the question why the New Testament has nothing to say against a social order which tolerates slavery. The way in which Paul deals with this particular social and political problem may be seen, e.g., in the Epistle to Philemon. The slave Onesimus had run away from his master Philemon, and by chance had come to be an attendant on Paul. After Onesimus had become a convinced Christian under Paul's influence, the Apostle sent him back to his former master and owner, with the accompanying letter which we find in the New Testament. In this letter there is not the slightest suggestion that Paul disavowed slavery, which was the prevailing order of society. Had he been opposed to it, he would certainly not have sent the man back into slavery. Yet this is precisely what he does: he sends Onesimus back. It is hard to believe that Paul would not face up to the problem, that he would simply subscribe to whatever the people of his age took for granted. It seems much more reasonable to assume that it was some basic consideration which caused Paul to keep silent, to hold in abeyance this matter of the social problem itself and thus to relativize it.

What Paul does is to tell Philemon that he, Philemon, and his slave Onesimus are now brothers in Christ. This means that in the relationship between them from henceforth two levels of order intersect: first, the order of society involving the master-slave relation, and second, the order of the kingdom of God involving the brother-brother relation. This line of intersection will always be exposed to a good deal of friction. The social order of Paul's day, e.g., could justify slavery only with the help of a particular doctrine of man whereby the slave is not really a "man" at all. The slave has no soul. He is not a person. The privileged status of manhood belongs only to the citizen.[19] Hence the slave — in antithesis to Kantian ethics — must be

---

[19] Thus for Aristotle "the sole and exclusive moral fulfillment of the idea of man was held to lie in citizenship. Whence too the acceptance of slavery. The slave, it was maintained, is by nature unfitted for citizenship; he is incapable, in the Aristotelian sense, of being educated to virtue." Heinrich A. Rommen, *The Natural Law: A Study in Legal and Social History,* trans. Thomas R. Hanley (St. Louis: Herder, 1947), p. 32.

regarded as a means to an end. He cannot be regarded as an end in himself.

On the Christian level, however, man is an end in himself. He is a child of God, bought with a price. He is a brother. In referring to Onesimus Paul uses terms which forcefully express an evaluation diametrically opposed to that of the prevailing social order. He thus addresses the social level with the urgency of an indirect, Socratic kind of approach. For Paul tells Philemon to receive the slave as "my very heart" (v. 12), as a "beloved brother" (v. 16), "as you would receive me" (v. 17). Paul sends him back in order that Philemon may "have him for ever" (v. 15); they are to enter into a relation which will no longer be determined by questions of temporal utility. Each word is thus an indirect protest against the idea of Onesimus being merely a slave. When anyone is bought with an infinite price there is more to him than merely his functional contribution to society.

The remarkable thing is that Paul does not expressly speak to this question of the line of intersection between the two levels. He actually sends Onesimus back into slavery. Indeed, he even tells Philemon that "formerly he was useless to you" (v. 11) because he rebelled against being a slave and ran away. Now he is returning voluntarily, as a brother, and this personal commitment in Christian freedom will hold him more firmly than the legal relation which makes the slave a possession.

All this is very paradoxical. For what binds him now to his function as a slave is the exact opposite of what the social institution of slavery has in view. It is freedom which binds him now. Only in this freedom can Onesimus actually achieve the usefulness and loyalty which the social order vainly seeks to provide through slavery. For trustworthy service is possible only when one is treated as a person and a brother rather than a thing.

Has Paul really said nothing then against slavery, the social order which embraces it, and the view of man which accords with it? No one can argue thus who has perceived what is so forcefully said between the lines. Whether Paul thought it all through in detail, or whether he simply assumed it and spoke and acted on the basis of it, what he had in mind was as follows. If I deliver Philemon a lecture on the fact that the social order of slavery is incompatible with the

Christian understanding of the person, I shall involve myself in an endless discussion. For it will be asked in reply whether any "Christian" social orders whatsoever actually exist, and whether I can mention one social order anywhere worthy of the name Christian. Instead of appealing directly to the Thou of Philemon in terms of his personal commitment, I should then be shifting the burden of my preaching from the person to the thing, i.e., the social order. (It is very likely that Paul did not actually take this point into consideration at all, because his address *ad hominem* is so explicit and unequivocal that this shifting of the question into the realm of things would presumably not even have entered his head.) If, on the other hand, I send Onesimus back as a Christian brother, if I put him back among the ranks of his master's servants, but in a way that is diametrically opposed to that of slavery morality, then at this one point at least the order of slavery will have been shattered from within, then at this one point at least this particular structure of society will have been undermined. The changing of persons will necessarily mean the changing of the order — if we ever get that far in these last days. Knowing this, I can keep to my theme. I need not engage in sociological debate. I can simply continue to speak *ad hominem*. This does not mean that I will merely proclaim the doctrine of justification in the form of a general dogma. Oh no; I have in view a very concrete aspect of the doctrine. I have in view what men of the twentieth century will call its sociological aspect. I shall proclaim the doctrine of Philemon in such a way that he will be bound to hear what it has to say in respect of his slave, that all of us, without social distinction, are sinners, and that all of us are similarly justified sinners. This is exactly what I have always been saying. But I will apply it now to this specific situation. You may call my approach Socratic. That is all right with me. But I am not just "teaching" here, anymore than did the Greek sage, or anymore than Kierkegaard will do in time to come. On the contrary, I am unleashing through my preaching something which will continue to have effect, and which, without legal imperatives, will impel men to do that which the Law intends but cannot achieve. I thus set processes in motion, yet make it impossible for the church to be the instigator of revolution. The changing of orders is only an incidental by-product of the changing of lives, a necessary result not dependent upon any deliberate effort in that direction. Something of this sort is what we might expect Paul to say if we were to talk with him today.

This law of infiltration and subversion has also been grasped in modern missions. In times past monogamy was made a prerequisite for baptism. Candidates for baptism were forced to dissolve their polygamous unions. But this policy has largely been abandoned today. For reasons which we need not go into at this point it is plainly realized today that, while monogamy is the Christian form of marriage, monogamy is not made mandatory as a law, since the Law kills. Instead we reason today as follows. If the chief with the great harem really becomes a Christian, he will one day inevitably come to the point where he sees that the social order of polygamy contradicts his baptism, and then step by step he will draw the logical conclusions, conclusions which might well vary in nuance from case to case. His turning to monogamy will be genuine only when he grows into it in Christian freedom. It will certainly not be genuine if it is imposed upon him by a coercive law which stifles such growth.

Thus here too the church acts, if you will, Socratically, or indirectly. It does not debate *things;* it aims at the conversion of *persons.* Those who "seek first the kingdom of God" will find not only that certain new things will "be added" [Matt. 6:33] but also that certain old things will drop away. Direct political action is not for the church. Indirect influence by way of infiltration and subversion is more appropriate.

In this connection it is perhaps not without significance that the church is constantly referred to symbolically as a wife. It is the "bride" of Christ, the "mother" of all believers. In Paul's repeated analogy between the relation of husband and wife on the one hand and that of Christ and the church on the other the church is also represented as a woman. By nature the woman influences the world indirectly, through her husband. A man's standing in life, and the influence he then exerts in the orders, depends essentially on whether he has a wife and on what kind of a wife she is. For this reason the emancipation of woman, her penetration into public life, her insistence on the equality of the sexes – all of this may involve an admission that she is no longer able to exercise this influence through the man, in which case it may well represent, not a victory, but a capitulation in which woman is untrue to herself.[20] A gifted woman, when asked her opinion about the newfound equality with men, answered with wry humor: "It used to be that we had more say."

The same is true of the church, when understood symbolically as a wife. Its loud claim to public status, its direct intervention in secular politics, betrays an admission that it no longer exercises an influence through men. To a large degree the church no longer has men under the pulpit, and when it does, it is often unable to come up with the right word. It puts them off with a private and purely personal kind of pastoral care which all too often does not get at what is really troubling them in conscience, namely, the duties and dubieties of their workaday world.

Many statements of the church and its appointed representatives as reported today in the newspapers do not necessarily signify a triumphal entry into the world, a newfound openness to the world, or the fact that the church is speaking in the name of the Lord to whom all power is given in heaven and on earth, and hence also in politics, economics, and culture. They may instead be a sign that the church has abdicated its proclamation of the Word, its speaking *ad hominem*, its cure of souls, and that it is now crying aloud to people outside the house what it ought to be saying quietly and with different words to the people within, even if it has to seek them out when they do not come in of their own accord.

Only when the church has learned again to speak in this way will it show itself to be a divine institution standing above the times, knowing that to it have been entrusted the men who wander here in time on their journey toward the last day. In the name of the incarnate Son of God the church is called into the vales of woe, to the streets of men, to be a companion and fellow traveler of those who stand either to lose their souls or to save them. The church has been promised that the powers of death shall not prevail against it [Matt. 16:18]. This is why it must see to it that the concerns and problems of time do not prevail against it and rend its body.

We may now sum up four main results of our discussion as follows. First, in the political sphere the church has the task of liberating the commands and promises of God so that they are not falsely restricted

---

[20] One has to speak with caution here, for there are many sociological reasons for female emancipation. But this motif should not be overlooked.

to the purely personal and private arena but are seen to involve a claim upon public life as well.

Second, the church cannot do this by advancing political and social programs. What it must do is to show men whose consciences are bound by the Word of God that the divine commands have particular relevance also to the substantive decisions they make. In so doing the church will be countering the political apathy of Christians. It will be demonstrating that to make faith a purely personal and private matter is to manifest lack of faith. It will be proclaiming the royal dominion of God over every sphere of life. Third, two errors are to be avoided in this connection. In the first place, the church must be careful not to let its political preaching consist only in abstract and empty appeals to conscience. For conscience grows and develops – indeed first comes into being – precisely in the making of decisions, including the substantive decisions. The church must be informed on the facts that are pertinent to these decisions, e.g., labor-management relations, sex equality, defensive alliances, etc., and it must elaborate the pastoral concerns involved in these controversial issues.

Then too, the church must be careful not to reject categorically specific judgments and programs, just as it must be careful not to endorse categorically certain others – or set up its own – on the ground that these alone are Christian and in keeping with God's commandments. The church has all Christians under its pastoral care, whatever it may think of their particular social or political convictions.

Fourth, theology and theologians, pastors included, must give up their age-long reserve in matters of political ethics. They must strive to answer from the standpoint of the theological center of the Christian faith – the doctrine of justification – the question as to what a conscience which is taught by God and lives in the peace of God has to say and signify for the way of the Christian in the world, even the world of work, politics, and society.

32.

Review of Methodology

This volume on political ethics is intended as the first of several in which we seek to apply the foundational principles and methods of our theological ethics generally to the several suprapersonal spheres of life. We have intentionally given the theme extended treatment here because we are taking politics as a model for such other spheres as law, economics, and society. Having once sketched the basic outline of the I-Thou relations mediated through the orders, we should now be able to deal with the other spheres much more briefly.

But precisely because we have taken politics as a case in point, the question of methodology arises with particular urgency. We have already introduced methodological discussions into the presentation from time to time, and will do so here once again. In this respect our political ethics must again play a vicarious role in relation to the themes yet to be treated. Therefore in conclusion, and with a view to the treatment of other areas yet to come, we may briefly summarize the main points in our methodology.

A theological doctrine of reality, such as underlies or is implicit in every Evangelical ethics, because it is imbedded in the context of Reformation doctrine cannot commence its reflection deductively by setting up basic principles or establishing axioms of natural law. It will have theology and tradition "behind it," to be sure, but it must begin inductively with the details of historical reality. Then it can go on to ask concerning the basic principles, and in the asking work them out afresh. It is for this reason that we cannot regard the doctrine of the Reformation and its tradition as a fixed system of norms into which we then try to integrate our present concrete reality.

The intellectual processes involved here can be grasped only if it is seen that this form of inquiry is not analogous to that of the judge in a trial. The judge has to subsume the concrete case under the pertinent law. His verdict is the result of this process of subsumption. The theological quest for the relevant principles, however, is something quite different, since the principles in question do not exist as laws in a codified form but have to be discovered in the very process of inquiry. A theological ethics that operates in the context of Reformation thought thus involves an essentially greater venture of decision than is involved in the act of mere subsumption. For the act of subsuming rests more on a technique of understanding than on reason's making a choice (even the reason which is bound by faith).

Because the venture is greater there is also an essentially broader range of possible casuistic solutions, and of possible decisions as to which authorities are normative. The technique of formal subsumption, which will often follow traditional rules and become almost automatic, leaves incomparably less room for individual decisions. This may be seen not merely in judicial practice but also in the methods of Roman Catholic moral theology, which on the basis of natural law and codified decisions of the church's teaching office has at its disposal clearly fixed rules under which the concrete cases are to be subsumed.

The results are obvious to those who compare Roman Catholic and Protestant ethics on specific issues, such as war, military service, and conscientious objection. Roman Catholic literature manifests a much greater consensus than does Protestant literature; indeed, it takes a highly trained theological sensitivity even to detect the slight differences of emphasis which may derive from the various traditions, schools, and individual thinkers in Roman Catholic ethics. One is reminded of the unison of the Gregorian chant on that side, and on the other of the polyphony which has a melodic theme to be sure (otherwise the general term "Protestant" would be absurd) but a theme which cannot easily be detected because of the rich and lively counterpoint.

The resultant quest for the pertinent norm is thus a characteristic concern of Protestant ethics. The decisions to be made in this regard are not restricted to the narrow sphere of "how" to subsume or "whether" one is ready to obey in practice the directives thus arrived at. On the contrary, decision takes place already in the sphere of thought where consideration of the question actually proceeds. It relates to the question of whether there is a norm that applies here, and if so what it is. Indeed, it is in reflection on concrete cases such as the question of war that the doctrine of creation and sin is first developed.

To be sure, the understanding of creation and of sin is to a large degree given already in church doctrine and theological tradition, but only in outline. In many cases we could not make this understanding our point of departure, because it simply did not anticipate modern problems and often seems to be shattered by them. (One need only think of war in the atomic age, or of resistance within the totalitarian state.) Only to a limited degree can we count on that which is simply given by tradition.

In no case, however, is this tradition susceptible to a direct, i.e., a casuistical appropriation by ethics. What creation and sin really mean in detail becomes clear for the theological thinker as a result of the individual decisions he has to make in the course of interpreting specific problems. Thus Luther did not develop his basic doctrine of Law and gospel theoretically, possibly by deduction from the master concept "Word of God." On the contrary, it became increasingly clear to him as he reflected on the particular question which so greatly concerned him, namely, how to find a gracious God. And after he had elaborated his doctrine of Law and gospel, he did not deduce from it his ethically normative doctrine of the two kingdoms. On the contrary, that came into being as he refined and developed his doctrine of Law and gospel by asking a host of concrete questions relating to the kingdom on the right hand and the kingdom on the left, e.g., questions of calling and office, of war and institutions. Luther did not solve these problems by subsumption under the existing normativity of Law and gospel. Instead he worked out the doctrine of Law and gospel by constantly raising questions concerning its content and the range of its applicability.

On might regard the risk therein entailed (and of course also the corresponding uncertainty) as both the greatness and the misery of Protestant theology. It certainly involves greatness, for it represents freedom, not the freedom of caprice, but the freedom of those who are bound. When we dare to say not only that Protestant ethics is unable to subsume under firm principles the factors and problems demanding ethical interpretation, but that these principles can only be found in the course of inquiry, we are certainly making a very dangerous statement. Does this not cut away all solid ground from under the feet of Protestant ethics? Does it not remove the boundary between venture and non-commitment? Two answers may be given to this obvious and justifiable question.

In the first place, the ultimate issue is not whether there is such solid ground. There obviously is, otherwise faith would not be faith "in" but a wild orgy of subjectivity. The real question is rather how to find this ground. I do not have it before me. I have to seek it. Nor do I have the object of faith before me in the form of objective assurance or intellectual demonstration (e.g., a proof of God), so that all I have to do is resolve to believe. On the contrary, I find the object of faith only in the act of faith itself. I do not first find outside of faith some solid ground which, after testing, I can declare as worthy to bear the weight of my faith. I find this solid ground only as I move out onto it — in faith. To be sure, I "know" in what I believe. I know it, however, only as a believer, not before I believe.

Second, in this believing I acquire an inventory of specific norms such as is given to Reformation Christians through Holy Scripture. For in Scripture I encounter the message in which I believe, or better, the message which wins me to faith. This has two further implications.

First, in the act of inquiry I do not invent norms and principles, as a metaphysican might establish them in the fullness of his own authority and responsibility; I have to find them here in this given sphere. Thus, as regards the choice between creation and the fall in my interpretation of war, it is to be found among the materials of the biblical message and not in just any spheres of the human spirit.

Second, this finding of norms in the context of Holy Scripture is not a matter of using the Bible as a code of law, for then I would be treating it as a store of fixed laws, and ethical thinking would again be reduced to the act of subsumption under these laws. This act of subsumption would differ in only one respect from similar acts on the part of those who think primarily in terms of natural law. It would differ only insofar as the latter relate to basic axioms which are universally known, whereas the champion of the Bible as a law code would be a kind of positivist. He could appeal only to biblical directives which have their origin in historic fact but whose axiomatic character is by no means obvious. In fact it is impossible, and according to the Bible's own self-understanding illegitimate, to treat the Bible casuistically and try to draw from it direct guidance for the actualities of the present day. He who, ignoring the true intention of the biblical message, nonetheless makes this desperate attempt — and it has often been done — will be betrayed into hopeless dead ends by the contradiction between specific directives literally understood (e.g., the Mosaic Law on the one side and the Sermon on the Mount on the other), and also by the gap in time between the biblical situation and the problems of today.

It is thus evident that I cannot use the Bible as a storehouse of available norms. On the contrary, I must go through a hermeneutical operation in order to find the biblical direction relevant to the given problem. To be more precise, I cannot find this direction by way of a theoretical confrontation between the Bible and myself which will produce the biblical norms that are binding for me today. I can find the biblical direction only if I begin with the special problems which weigh upon me today (e.g., what man is, how he can be protected against modern threats, what guilt means in particular contexts, or what the commandment and conscience have to say concretely), and then consult the message of the Bible, allowing myself at the same time to be questioned by it with respect to these problems.

The biblical message is not concerned with the nurture of individual souls (for what is an isolated soul anyway?). It is not concerned with purely subjective edification (for what is pure subjectivity detached from all environmental factors?). Finally, it is not concerned with mere preparation for the hereafter (for where is this hereafter really attested in the Bible?). The message is addressed to us rather as promise and claim, as consolation and direction, as indicative and imperative. It meets us at the point where we actually have our being, i.e., at the intersection of the various spheres of life wherein we are citizens, members of a profession and a social class, married or single, old or young. Our existence is always at this point of intersection and concretion. This is why the message does not speak to some kind of a personal core at a level beneath these various levels of existence, a core which can be located only by way of rather frantic theorizing. Instead it addresses us precisely in these various spheres in which we have our being. Thus the gospel is relevant to our work and to our leisure, to our relations with others, and hence also to such concrete questions as the welfare state, political opposition, social and industrial partnership, the rearing of children, and marriage.

The commandments of God thus have a function rather like that of the compass. They indicate direction. We ourselves, however, operating in the most varied spheres of life within our specific historical situation, and hence taking into account all sorts of given concrete factors, must seek out the particular way which leads in this direction. The simile of the compass makes clear once again how impossible it is to derive from the Bible ready-made norms which can be directly applied casuistically. I simply cannot "deduce" from the direction of the compass needle which route to follow. In plain terms, it is nonsense to suppose that when the Bible points the direction it thereby solves all substantive and technical questions. Such an assumption not only misunderstands the Bible; it actually leads to an indescribable dilettantism in the matter of the concrete orientation one gives to his life. To possess a compass and to keep an eye on its needle does not excuse us from knowing the territory, but such knowledge can be gleaned only from the specialized geographical science of cartography, or the information supplied by the people who live there.

In sum, the Protestant ethicist cannot appeal to a fixed and given system of normative principles which would enable him to subsume every concrete case and to deduce concrete directives from guiding principles. Instead, he must find these directives by proceeding from the object of his faith to the concrete facts and then working back from there. The measure of decision involved in the act of seeking leads, as we have seen, to an incomparably broader range of possible solutions than any mere process of deduction and subsumption. Hence it is inappropriate to assess the great diversity in Protestant ethics as regards political matters in merely negative terms, as an expression of uncertainty. It is more relevant to ask concerning the validity of the principles which lead to these results. This is the cardinal question, for here is where the decision is made. It is certainly not made by arguing on practical or aesthetic grounds which type of ethics is easier to live up to and best reduces the burden of decision imposed on those who practice it, or even which type (the closed and homogeneous ethics of Roman Catholicism or the polyphonous and sometimes seemingly atonal and unregulated ethics of Protestantism) makes the better and stronger impression.

Our thesis concerning this matter of the true locus of decision may even serve to link us more closely to our Roman Catholic partner in the discussion. Certainly it is a good sign of the togetherness of the two confessions that the feeling of community grows, not as differences are suppressed or concealed, but as we do away with the false fronts which have been established and pursue the question of truth at the points of real difference.

INDEXES

\

Authors

Scripture References

Names and Subjects

Abortion, 40, 312
Absoluteness, 38, 39
Absolutes, 42
Absolutization(s), 52, 54, 72, 128, 129, 154
  of authority, 184
  of autonomies, 120, 122, 134
  of ideological dogma, 114
  of the trend of history, 118
Abstraction(s), 86, 90, 91, 153 n. 14
"Abysmal phenomenon," 55
Accountability before God, 92
Action, 132, 617
  capricious, 68, 112
  Christian, 69, 518, 564
  concrete, 89, 107, 110, 121, 148
  divine, 436
  ethical, 76, 101, 144
  historical, 107, 111, 153
  of God, 574, 580
  military (see Military action)
  political (see Political action)
  and principles, 118
  secular, 20, 99, 100, 113
Acton, Lord J. E. E. D., 173
Actualization process, 69
Adjudication, international, 430-431, 433, 436
Adultery, 393
Advertizing, 78 n. 9, 79
Aeon, this, 242, 324, 382, 384, 385, 388, 414, 419, 429 n. 15, 446, 453, 454, 532, 579 n. 41, 592, 610, 617
Aestheticism, 121, 125 n. 4
Affluence, 310
Agape, 307
Agencies, 509
Alexandrov, Georgi, 31 n. 14
  History of Western European Philosophy, 34
Allvater, 289 n. 1
Althaus, Paul, 388, 437, 438, 441, 445, 464-465

Altruism, 448-449
Ambrose, St., 297 n. 6
American Revolution (see Revolution)
Americans, 567
Amorality
  of the beast, 115
  dynamic, 115
Anabaptists, 501 n. 1
Analogy, concept of, 578, 578 n. 38, 579, 581, 582, 583, 585
  between Law and gospel, 586
  between the testaments, 611
ἀνάμνησις, 149
Anarchists, 25
Anarchy, 340
Animals, symbolism of, 56, 58
ἄνομος (lawless one), 371, 375
Anonymity of government, 11
Anselm, 193
Antagonism
  creative, 30
  social, 31
  (see also Class antagonism)
Anthropology, 55, 118, 129, 134, 136, 138, 163, 232
  and power (see Power)
Antichrist, 55, 59, 61, 372, 435, 436, 454
Anti-Christianity, 62, 63
Anti-church, 55, 60, 551, 638
Anxiety, 493
Apostles' Creed
  First article, 580
  Second article, 578, 580
Aquinas, Thomas, 325, 458, 542, 556
Arbitration, 127
Arcere malum, 156
Arcere peccatum, 17
ἀρετή (virtue), 147, 149
Aristocracy, 95 (see also Nobility)
Aristotle, 146, 643 n. 19
Armament, 495
  mutual, 485
Armaments industry, 81, 82

INDEX

defined, 23
self-absolutization of, 254, 277
trend toward, 12, 216-219, 228, 251, 262-264, 290
Tradition, 118, 184, 192, 363, 368, 458, 639
Christian, 63
ethical, 10, 325-332, 419, 429, 651
Greco-Christian, 67
weight of, 3
Western legal, 42
Tragic drama, 87, 533
Transition, 11
from authoritarianism to democracy, 6, 71
forms of, 6, 6 n. 7
Treaty, 117, 131, 459, 478
Trent, Council of, 182 n. 8
Trials, ideological, 42-46
Tribute, exacting of, 106
Troeltsch, Ernst, 111, 244 n. 17, 463 n. 41, 570
Trotsky, 43
True, the, 36, 42
Truth, the, 36, 37, 38, 39, 46, 48, 62, 148, 151, 154, 382, 403
as authority, 117
norm of, 29, 86
objective, 33
Turk(s), 61, 370, 371, 461, 462 n. 40, 463
Turkish War, 371-372, 521
Two Kingdoms, doctrine of, 11, 15, 20, 22, 26, 60-61, 73, 74, 98, 99, 100, 108, 144, 152, 244 n. 17, 248, 249, 269, 270, 273, 278, 290, 307, 322, 323, 354, 357, 361, 367, 373, 374, 385, 400, 427, 434, 457, 461, 462, 463, 491, 501 n. 1, 502, 512, 514, 518, 526-527, 541, 550-551, 558, 561, 563, 567-571, 594, 596, 603, 604, 605, 630, 638, 642, 651
applicability of, 326, 344, 368-369, 374, 420, 486
misunderstanding of, 581, 597-598, 637
the separation of, 595, 601

Tyche, 208
Tyrannicide, 235-239, 426
Tyrant, 55, 115, 168, 335, 336
ideological, 38, 50, 247
universal, 370-371, 372
Tyrannus — quoad titulum/quoad executionem, 335
Tyranny, 59, 126, 168, 186, 189, 202, 325, 335, 370, 471, 566
ideological, 4, 6, 22, 25, 26, 45, 53-61, 62, 108, 117-120, 125, 144, 213, 263, 330, 334, 344, 348, 349, 365, 369, 370, 398, 399, 419, 558, 564, 637
open, 43
secular state, 62

Unbelievers, 62
Union(s), labor, 216-218, 350, 352
United Nations, 133
Universal Declaration of Human Rights (*see* Human rights)
"Universal Father," 289
Uno moto digito, 17 n. 15, 143 n. 2
Unreason, 27
Usus elenchticus, 587, 592
Usus normativus, 19
Usus organicus, 19
Usus politicus, 587, 591
Utility, concept of, 41, 101, 121, 159
Utopia(s), 108, 134, 136-137, 292, 311, 439, 457, 493
Utopian, 130 n. 6, 135

Values, 19, 31, 63, 65, 66, 69, 76, 85, 115, 125, 128-129, 134, 135, 139, 465, 470, 506, 532
conflict of, 87-89, 121, 437, 533
as goal of faith, 64
and law, 159, 160
sense of, 66
sphere of, 66, 84
spiritual, 129
universal, 67-68
Van Ruler, Arnold, 604-614
Vatican Council I, 182 n. 8
Vietnam, viii
Violence, 24, 468, 509, 518
Virtue, 64, 116, 118, 123, 128, 132,